Microsoft SharePoint 2013 Inside Out

Darvish Shadravan
Penelope Coventry
Thomas Resing
Christina Wheeler

Published with the authorization of Microsoft Corporation by:
O'Reilly Media, Inc.
1005 Gravenstein Highway North
Sebastopol, California 95472

ISBN: 978-0-7356-6699-3

Second Printing: April 2014

Printed and bound in the United States of America.

Microsoft Press books are available through booksellers and distributors worldwide. If you need support related to this book, email Microsoft Press Book Support at *mspinput@microsoft.com*. Please tell us what you think of this book at *http://www.microsoft.com/learning/booksurvey*.

Microsoft and the trademarks listed at *http://www.microsoft.com/about/legal/en/us/ IntellectualProperty/Trademarks/EN-US.aspx* are trademarks of the Microsoft group of companies. All other marks are property of their respective owners.

The example companies, organizations, products, domain names, email addresses, logos, people, places, and events depicted herein are fictitious. No association with any real company, organization, product, domain name, email address, logo, person, place, or event is intended or should be inferred.

This book expresses the author's views and opinions. The information contained in this book is provided without any express, statutory, or implied warranties. Neither the authors, O'Reilly Media, Inc., Microsoft Corporation, nor its resellers, or distributors will be held liable for any damages caused or alleged to be caused either directly or indirectly by this book.

Acquisitions and Development Editor: Kenyon Brown
Production Editor: Rachel Steely
Editorial Production: S4Carlisle, Inc.
Technical Reviewer: Neil Hodgkinson
Copyeditor: S4Carlisle, Inc.
Indexer: BIM Publishing Services, Inc.
Cover Design: Twist Creative • Seattle
Cover Composition: Karen Montgomery
Illustrator: S4Carlisle, Inc.

This book is dedicated to my four amazing children: Hannah, Sydney, Devin, and Zoe. Being your daddy is the most magnificent opportunity life has presented to me.

—Darvish Shadravan

I dedicate this book to my lifelong friend and sister, Paula, together with her husband, Bruce. They may be far away, but they are close to my heart.

—Penny Coventry

To the love of my life, Kerri, and my daughter, Elise. I love you and couldn't have done this without your support.

—Tom Resing

I dedicate this book to my wonderful and amazing daughter, Kiana. She is such a blessing in my life and I couldn't imagine my life without her.

—Christina Wheeler

Contents at a glance

Table of contents

What do you think of this book? We want to hear from you!

Microsoft is interested in hearing your feedback so we can continually improve our books and learning resources for you. To participate in a brief online survey, please visit:

microsoft.com/learning/booksurvey

What do you think of this book? We want to hear from you!

Microsoft is interested in hearing your feedback so we can continually improve our books and learning
resources for you. To participate in a brief online survey, please visit:

microsoft.com/learning/booksurvey

Introduction

Welcome to *Microsoft SharePoint 2013 Inside Out,* the definitive guide to working with Microsoft SharePoint 2013. SharePoint has been helping teams stay connected and work smarter for over a decade—and the 2013 version builds on that legacy with a plethora of new capabilities and improvements to many of the existing features. With SharePoint 2013, you have at your fingertips the most powerful web-based platform on the market. The capabilities SharePoint 2013 provides are numerous; some of the areas of functionality you will learn about in this book are:

- Document and web content management

- Designing SharePoint websites

- Enterprise search

- Business intelligence (BI) and reporting

- Workflow

- Business forms

- Enterprise social networking

Who this book is for

This book offers a comprehensive look at most of the major features contained within SharePoint 2013. The most likely readers of this book go by many names—power user, site owner, business analyst, web designer, and so forth. The book is intended for both business and technical people who need to accomplish meaningful tasks with SharePoint. It will be most useful for readers who have some experience with prior versions of SharePoint, but that is certainly not a prerequisite. Although there is some administration and development content within various chapters, this book is not aimed specifically toward SharePoint farm administration or heavy custom development; Microsoft Press has other SharePoint books that cover those areas in depth.

This book serves both as an introduction to each subject and as a comprehensive reference. It will help you use the features of SharePoint to accomplish business and technical goals. In addition, this book goes a step or two further, providing useful information to advanced users who need to understand technical strategies that work in the real world. In this book, distinctions are not made for different versions of SharePoint; most of what is covered applies to all versions: Foundation, Standard, Enterprise, and SharePoint Online.

> **Note**
> To get the most out of this book, you will need access to an installation of SharePoint 2013, either in your data center or in the cloud with Microsoft Office 365.

How this book is organized

This book is designed to provide a comprehensive and practical guide to a majority of the out-of-the-box features in SharePoint 2013. The early chapters in the book are applicable to nearly everyone who is going to use SharePoint 2013 in their organizations. As the book continues, some of the topics become more specialized. However, the book is not structured in a sequential or linear way; in other words, each chapter stands on its own as a general reference when you need to learn about a particular topic. Feel free to read the book cover to cover if that suits your needs, or head straight to a relevant chapter when you need to dive into a particular capability.

Chapter 1, "Introducing SharePoint 2013," provides a high-level overview of the six major workloads of SharePoint: Sites, Communities, Content, Search, Insights, and Composites. It discusses what is new in SharePoint 2013 and how the features and capabilities map to particular business scenarios such as Sharing, Organizing, and Discovering. This chapter also introduces the concept of SharePoint as a cloud-based service.

Chapter 2, "Administration for business users," breaks down the administration of SharePoint into two categories: Business User Administration and Information Technology Professional Administration. The chapter covers a variety of administrative tasks that advanced users or site owners would typically perform. Topics covered include security, the physical and logical architecture of SharePoint, storage, and more.

Chapter 3, "Working with list and library apps," is an entire chapter dedicated to using lists and libraries, which are the primary repositories for documents, tasks, and most other SharePoint artifacts. The chapter covers creating, modifying, securing, and designing List and Library apps so that you can put them to work storing and presenting your content in the most effective manner possible.

Chapter 4, "Working with collaboration sites," delves into the most popular type of site in SharePoint: team sites. In this chapter, you will learn all about the team collaboration capabilities in SharePoint 2013 team sites, including task management, shared Microsoft OneNote notebooks, and SkyDrive Pro.

Chapter 5, "Using Office applications with SharePoint," explores the myriad of ways that the Microsoft Office client products integrate with SharePoint. In this chapter, you will learn about saving documents to libraries from Office applications, coauthoring, Office Web Apps, Access Services, integrating Microsoft Excel data with SharePoint lists, and much more.

Chapter 6, "Sharing information with SharePoint social networking," tackles the new enterprise social features available in SharePoint 2013. The primary focus of this chapter is on understanding how to create, customize, use, and moderate the new community sites. In addition, this chapter provides an in-depth look at the personal Newsfeed, which provides aggregation of each user's view of enterprise social data.

Chapter 7, "Using and creating workflows," delivers a thorough look at many aspects of SharePoint 2013 workflows. You will learn about methods for designing workflows and the primary products for creating workflows, such as SharePoint Designer and Microsoft Visio. The differences between reusable, site, and list workflows are explained so that you will be fully equipped to add workflow automation to your sites.

Chapter 8, "Planning site content," looks at the important topic of information architecture and the management of all types of SharePoint content. This chapter dives deeply into how to best design your sites for effectively governing and managing large amounts of content. Special attention is given to ensuring that you understand the differences between managing content on Internet-facing sites versus internal sites.

Chapter 9, "Creating and formatting content pages," helps you understand how to use the various types of content pages in SharePoint: wiki, publishing, web part, and so forth. After working through this comprehensive look into SharePoint content pages, you will be ready to begin designing and building your own content pages with SharePoint Designer.

Chapter 10, "Adding, editing, connecting, and maintaining web parts," is all about web parts. SharePoint pages are generally comprised of a number of web parts; therefore, it helps to have a solid understanding of the primary web parts you will use. In this chapter, you will learn what each web part does and how to manage it.

Chapter 11, "Managing documents," provides a thorough reference to one of the most popular SharePoint capabilities: managing documents. Document management is common in almost every business and organization; therefore, an entire chapter is dedicated to understanding all SharePoint has to offer around this workload. Some of the features covered in this chapter are document sets, record centers, document centers, and document metadata.

Chapter 12, "Designing web content management sites," is the chapter for those who need to build rich websites in SharePoint with highly customized themes and layouts. As SharePoint has become an increasingly popular platform for hosting intranet, extranet, and Internet sites, the capabilities of SharePoint have had to keep up in order to match customer demand for robust websites. Capabilities covered in this chapter include Design Manager, page layouts, the Content Search web part, and managed metadata navigation.

Chapter 13, "Implementing compliance, records management, and eDiscovery," covers SharePoint features that help with compliance and the legal requirements for storing, maintaining, and discovering content. Among other things, in this chapter you will learn about defining retention schedules, the new eDiscovery center, and implementing a records management strategy.

Chapter 14, "Planning for business intelligence and key performance indicators," is the first of three chapters related to BI and reporting. In this chapter, you will learn the basics about how Excel Services, Visio Services, and PerformancePoint all play a role in creating BI and key performance indicators within SharePoint sites. As the chapter continues, thorough coverage is given to installing, configuring, and administration for each of these services.

Chapter 15, "Implementing better business intelligence with Excel Services and SQL Server 2012," picks up where the previous chapter left off. This chapter focuses on the actual process of using BI features to build sophisticated analytics solutions with PowerPivot, Power View, and Excel Services.

Chapter 16, "Building powerful dashboards with PerformancePoint Services," again complements the previous two chapters. While Chapter 15 focused on Excel-based technologies, this chapter is all about PerformancePoint. PerformancePoint is the premier set of enterprise BI tools and web parts in SharePoint. The chapter covers how to use the PerformancePoint Dashboard Designer, how to create PerformancePoint items, and building out dashboards for business users to perform deep data analysis.

Chapter 17, "Working with Visio Services," focuses exclusively on Visio integration with SharePoint. Visio Services allows you to share drawings with users who do not have Visio installed on their computers. The chapter covers Visio web parts, security considerations, connecting shapes to external data, and nearly everything else that a SharePoint power user would ever need to know about Visio Services.

Chapter 18, "Discovering information with SharePoint 2013 Search," introduces the reader to the enterprise search capabilities in SharePoint 2013. You will learn about the new search interface, how search is tightly integrated with different types of content, and the new unified search architecture. In this chapter, you will learn the building blocks of search applications: query rules, result sources, and result types.

Chapter 19, "Creating a customized SharePoint 2013 search experience," takes off where the previous chapter ends: building upon your knowledge of Search. In this chapter, you will be exposed to more advanced topics for building customized search experiences. Display templates, web parts, search verticals, search navigation, and many more topics are covered. A full walkthrough of building a search customization is also included.

Chapter 20, "Creating, managing, and designing sites," takes you on a tour of creating and designing SharePoint sites that go beyond the out-of-the-box templates. In this chapter, you will learn about using SharePoint Designer to create and customize sites. Changing the look of your sites is covered, as are CSS and the creation of custom site templates.

Chapter 21, "Creating enterprise forms," covers the common business requirement of inputting data into forms and having that information stored in SharePoint. This chapter will help you understand the options for creating forms in SharePoint, such as Access Services, Microsoft InfoPath, and HTML5. You will learn about best practices for designing the forms. The chapter includes guided form design walkthroughs, and sample forms are available on the book's accompanying website.

Chapter 22, "Working with external content," delivers a comprehensive look at connecting SharePoint to external data and business systems. Primarily working with Business Connectivity Services (BCS), you will learn how to create secure connections to external data so that you can build powerful composite applications. The tools for building the external connections covered in this chapter include SharePoint Designer and Microsoft Visual Studio.

Chapter 23, "Introduction to custom development," closes out the book with a look at custom development for SharePoint 2013. The chapter will help you understand the major aspects of custom development at a high level. Topics covered include the new cloud app model, client and server application programming interfaces (APIs), and custom workflow development.

Features and conventions used in this book

This book uses special text and design conventions to make it easier for you to find the information that you need.

Text conventions

Convention	Meaning
Abbreviated commands for navigating the ribbon	For your convenience, this book uses abbreviated commands. For example, "Click Home | Insert | Insert Cells" means that you should click the Home tab on the ribbon, click the Insert button, and then finally click the Insert Cells command.
Boldface type	**Boldface** indicates text that you type.
Initial Capital Letters	The first letters of the names of tabs, dialog boxes, dialog box elements, and commands are capitalized. Example: the Save As dialog box.
Italicized type	*Italicized* type indicates new terms.
Plus sign (+) in text	Keyboard shortcuts are indicated by a plus sign (+) separating key names. For example, Ctrl+Alt+Delete means that you press the Ctrl, Alt, and Delete keys at the same time.

Design conventions

INSIDE OUT   This statement illustrates an example of an "Inside Out" heading

These are the book's signature tips. In these tips, you get the straight scoop on what's going on with the software—inside information about why a feature works the way it does. You'll also find handy workarounds to deal with software problems.

Sidebars

Sidebars provide helpful hints, timesaving tricks, or alternative procedures related to the task being discussed.

TROUBLESHOOTING

This statement illustrates an example of a "Troubleshooting" problem statement.

Look for these sidebars to find solutions to common problems that you might encounter. Troubleshooting sidebars appear next to related information in the chapters. You can also use "Index to Troubleshooting Topics" at the back of the book to look up problems by topic.

Cross-references point you to locations in the book that offer additional information about the topic being discussed.

Note

Notes offer additional information related to the task being discussed.

Your companion ebook

With the ebook edition of this book, you can do the following:

- Search the full text

- Print

- Copy and paste

To download your ebook, please see the instruction page at the back of the book.

About the companion content

We have included companion content to enrich your learning experience. The companion content for this book can be downloaded from the following page:

http://aka.ms/SP2013InsideOut/files

The companion content includes the following: completed examples of the InfoPath, Microsoft Access, and HTML forms generated in Chapter 21.

System requirements

To build the sample forms in Chapter 21, you will need a copy of Office 2013 on your system. You must have InfoPath 2013 and Access 2013 installed.

Acknowledgments

When embarking down the path of creating a large, complex project such as this book, many people necessarily play supporting roles. With their patience and support, we, the four authors, were able to overcome the multitude of challenges along the way. While we can never thank all of them individually in this small space, you know who you are, and this group of authors thanks you sincerely.

The authors were fortunate to have an exceptionally talented extended team on this project, including editors Katharine Dvorak and Ken Brown, our brilliant technical reviewer Dr. Neil Hodgkinson, and our contributors Javier Barrera and Sam Larko. We have also received assistance from Steve Peschka (PDF previews), Matt Bremer (HTML sample form), and Andrew Connell (WCM). In addition, thank you to our copy editor, production team, and all the other people at O'Reilly who helped with the creation of this book behind the scenes.

Thanks to you, our readers, for without you, this book would have no purpose. We are pleased to be able to share our combined decades of SharePoint experience with you.

Finally, yet most important, our deepest gratitude to our friends and families for their continued support while working on this book; we love all of you.

The Authors
June 2013

Support and feedback

The following sections provide information on errata, book support, feedback, and contact information.

Errata

We've made every effort to ensure the accuracy of this book and its companion content. Any errors that have been reported since this book was published are listed on our Microsoft Press site:

http://aka.ms/SP2013InsideOut/errata

If you find an error that is not already listed, you can report it to us through the same page.

If you need additional support, email Microsoft Press Book Support at:

mspinput@microsoft.com

Please note that product support for Microsoft software is not offered through the addresses above.

We want to hear from you

At Microsoft Press, your satisfaction is our top priority, and your feedback our most valuable asset. Please tell us what you think of this book at:

http://www.microsoft.com/learning/booksurvey

The survey is short, and we read every one of your comments and ideas. Thanks in advance for your input!

Stay in touch

Let's keep the conversation going! We're on Twitter at:

http://twitter.com/MicrosoftPress

Introducing SharePoint 2013

Microsoft SharePoint 2013 is a software application. In fact, it is just one out of a sea of millions of software applications. However, those of us who know and love SharePoint recognize that it is more than that—something more profound than just another business application. It has a unique appeal to information workers that makes it much more than merely software. SharePoint transforms the way people work. It makes their jobs, and therefore their lives, easier and more productive. It helps people collaborate on tasks and documents, it assists people in finding the information they need to do their jobs, and it enables people to connect with colleagues and share their work. SharePoint is an enormously powerful piece of technology that has a myriad of potential means by which you can improve the way you work every day.

The SharePoint platform has been on the market for more than a decade. Microsoft SharePoint Portal Server 2001 was the first version to use the SharePoint brand name. Now, after more than a decade of investment in research and development, SharePoint 2013 represents the fifth major version of the product. It truly sets the standard for a modern, web-based collaboration tool.

SharePoint's humble beginnings were in web-based document management and collaboration sites. Those popular capabilities certainly have continued to grow and flourish, but the Microsoft SharePoint Server product has now matured into an enterprise-ready, cloud-capable platform that provides many types of capabilities and services.

The SharePoint wheel

Given the breadth and depth of the SharePoint platform, it can be a challenging task to grasp all of the functionality it is capable of delivering. Therefore, in previous versions, the SharePoint marketing team developed the idea of the SharePoint "wheel" (also known as the "SharePoint pie"). As shown in Figure 1-1, the wheel did an effective job of helping people understand the six primary categories (or "workloads") of functionality that SharePoint offers: sites, communities, content, search, insights, and composites. Within each of these six areas, there is a massive amount of functional and technical details, but the wheel makes the challenge of understanding the product's capability at a high level more manageable. So for those of you who may not have experience with prior versions, let's start by taking a look at the SharePoint wheel to ensure that we are all on the same page before we dig in to what's new with SharePoint 2013.

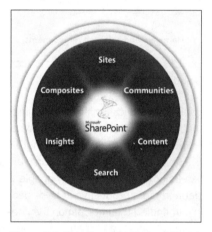

Figure 1-1 The SharePoint wheel illustrates the six primary categories of functionality offered in SharePoint.

Sites

SharePoint sites provide a common platform for all your business websites. SharePoint allows a user to easily and quickly provision a new site using the SharePoint browser-based interface to rapidly meet business needs. There are many types of site templates available with SharePoint depending upon the requirements: team sites, document management sites, search sites, wiki sites, and so forth. On these sites, you can accomplish many important tasks, including sharing documents with colleagues, working on team projects, publishing information to customers, and dozens more. Sites are the basic technology engine in SharePoint; they are the place where users go to get things done.

Communities

SharePoint communities enable social networking and collaboration in the enterprise. SharePoint assists in the process of working with a team of people through blogs, wikis, newsfeeds, tagging, personal sites called My Sites, and many other features. Sharing of ideas, finding and collaborating with the right people, and connecting with subject matter experts are experiences that SharePoint can help with.

Content

Document management, web content management, records management—these content-related capabilities are required at nearly every business and government organization. SharePoint provides site templates and features for each of these areas of content management. SharePoint has evolved over the years to include support not only for traditional document types such as Microsoft Office, but also for rich media files, photographs, Adobe PDF files, and many more. Close integration of the content management features with desktop productivity products ensures that much of users' interaction with the content can still be performed naturally in the tool that they are already working in every day—Microsoft Office.

Search

SharePoint has contained search capabilities since the beginnings of the product. In the most recent versions of the product, SharePoint Search has matured into a fully functional enterprise search engine. SharePoint Search helps users discover content, people, and a wide variety of business data. The relevance and accuracy of the information returned to a user when a search query is performed is on par with any of the major Internet search engines; thus, this feature provides a compelling and valuable experience that empowers employees to perform their jobs more efficiently.

Insights

Insights (also known as *business intelligence*) make it possible to easily access and present data stored in databases, SharePoint lists, and Microsoft Excel spreadsheets. Utilizing features such as Excel Services, PerformancePoint, and SQL Server Reporting integration, SharePoint enables the creation and sharing of dashboards and reports that help workers identify business trends, work together toward shared goals and metrics, and pinpoint exactly the information they need to make better decisions.

Composites

Composites are SharePoint applications that combine business data with a variety of out-of-the-box tools, web parts, and methods to assemble do-it-yourself solutions. Access Services, Visio Services, workflows, and digital forms are among the abundant features SharePoint delivers for building composite applications. Applications that fit into the SharePoint composite model are often built in days rather than weeks or months, often with no code required. This agility is part of the business value of SharePoint—rapidly designing, building, and deploying business solutions that provide a near-instant return on investment.

What's new in SharePoint 2013

The evolution of the SharePoint platform continues in bold and exciting new ways in SharePoint 2013. SharePoint 2013 builds and extends upon the SharePoint 2010 product line—the core capabilities of the previous versions continue to evolve with many profound improvements.

In addition to across-the-board improvements in most of the previous version's capabilities, SharePoint 2013 functionality is designed with the notion of ensuring that people are in the center of the SharePoint experience. Putting the user experience first was foremost in the planning and development process. In order to provide an improved user experience, SharePoint 2013 focuses on five key principles:

- Share

- Discover

- Organize

- Build

- Manage

In the remainder of this chapter, you'll be introduced to SharePoint 2013 at a high level. Then, throughout the rest of the book, you will come to understand the improvements to the core capabilities of the SharePoint platform, new concepts, and the innovative new capabilities of SharePoint 2013 in depth.

Share

When you boil it down, much of what we define as "collaboration" is really just sharing— sharing ideas, sharing documents, sharing our expertise. Much like previous versions of SharePoint, SharePoint 2013 is a place where people can go to share and collaborate on documents, tasks, projects, and many other types of content. The prolific content creators in your organization will find that their opportunity to share their work has never been easier or faster. This type of collaboration around content is squarely in the traditional core competency of SharePoint sites.

Sharing content

SharePoint 2013 firmly establishes itself as a platform for document sharing with both internal *and* external users, partners, and customers. You can publish content to SharePoint from Office 2013 desktop applications, as shown in Figure 1-2. You can also share the content with colleagues inside your organization or external partners and customers in a few simple clicks, as shown in Figure 1-3.

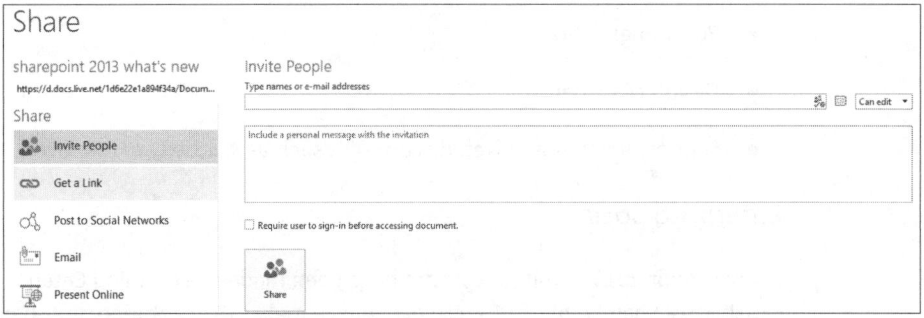

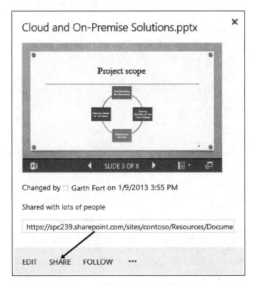

Figure 1-2 The Share menu, as seen in Microsoft PowerPoint 2013, enables users to select people with whom they want to share content.

Figure 1-3 From a SharePoint 2013 document library, a user may choose to edit, share, or follow a PowerPoint file.

If your idea of sharing content extends to people outside of your organization, SharePoint 2013 has many incremental improvements in the area of web content management (WCM) that will help you share your sites with the world. SharePoint 2013 has matured into a fully capable, cross-browser WCM platform. A few of the improvements are listed here:

- Search-driven sites with the Content Search Web Part (CSWP)

- Search engine optimization (SEO) site maps

- Device channels

- Managed navigation

- Recommendations

- Design Manager

- Support for standard web design tools such as Adobe Dreamweaver

Enterprise Social

In SharePoint 2013, significant strides have been made in extending Enterprise Social capabilities. SharePoint 2013 social experience makes the capturing and sharing of ideas and tacit knowledge possible through microblogging and community sites, such as the one shown in Figure 1-4. In a community site, discussions are fundamental, participation is simple and inviting, and expertise may be acknowledged and rewarded.

Figure 1-4 A SharePoint 2013 social experience is delivered via a SharePoint 2013 community site.

SharePoint 2013 contains a number of new social features that can assist the users in your organization as they share ideas. Some of the most significant features include:

- Microblogs

- Hash tags and @mentions

- Company, site, and personal newsfeeds

- Yammer integration

- Hash-tag trending and other social analytics via the new search engine

- Community sites

- Richer SharePoint user profiles populated with useful social information

Yammer integration in SharePoint

Yammer integration in SharePoint 2013 has been set to become a critical piece of the story since Microsoft purchased the social networking software in 2012. Yammer's strength has traditionally been in stand-alone, cloud-based social networking. Now, under the Microsoft umbrella, Yammer is becoming not only a solid choice for stand-alone social, but also an aggregator of all social touch points a user might have in your organization. For example, Yammer has connections to SharePoint and Microsoft Dynamics, and will soon have deep integration into other Microsoft properties, such as Office 365 and Skype. In addition, Yammer excels at integrating feeds of external cloud-based activity along with information from existing business applications, such as enterprise resource planning (ERP), customer relationship management (CRM), and so forth, thereby creating a truly comprehensive social experience in the enterprise.

Mobile

Increasingly, a major component of sharing and collaborating involves mobile access. SharePoint 2013 has several key improvements and architectural changes that improve sharing capabilities for the mobile user. The user interface of SharePoint 2013 was rewritten using HTML5. This inherently means that modern mobile devices that support the HTML5 standard will have a dramatically better SharePoint browsing experience—even if you do nothing else to optimize your site for mobile access.

In addition, there is a new feature called *Channels* that enables a site to serve up the same set of content to mobile devices, but in a mobile-optimized fashion. For example, you may want your site to autodetect when a user is currently browsing with her smartphone so that you can dynamically tailor your site's visual design appropriately. You can choose to have your mobile device channel deliver alternate *renditions* of images and videos to reduce page size for limited-bandwidth consumption.

Among many other mobile-enabled capabilities, you can share documents, update your activity feed, and participate in community discussions from your mobile phone or tablet. Figure 1-5 shows a team site where a mobile tablet user is searching for marketing documents shared by his colleagues.

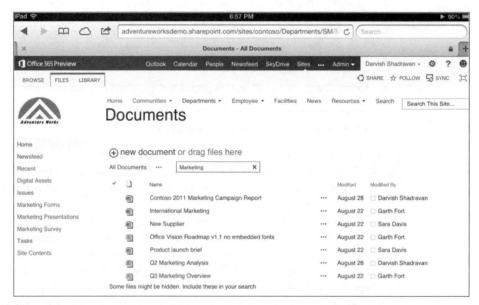

Figure 1-5 A user on a tablet device may access shared documents in a SharePoint document library.

Discover

The new unified search platform in SharePoint 2013 takes information discovery to another level. The improvements in the search platform help users find more relevant results—and go beyond that by also surfacing knowledge and then sharing relevant insights. The search engine of SharePoint goes further by actually understanding the meaning of a query. It can be integrated with your line-of-business (LoB) applications to help you discover answers from all of the sources of information that are important to you.

Information

As information, documents, videos, reports, and other types of content continue to proliferate on private networks and in the cloud, having a robust enterprise search platform is more critical than ever. To assist users to search and discover the data they need to perform their jobs, the SharePoint 2013 search engine has received a significant overhaul of features and architecture, including:

- A new and improved HTML5-based search interface

- The addition of *result types,* which are a set of rules that can be used to identify certain items in the search results that match a specific set of predefined criteria

- The addition of a custom *display template* that highlights and promotes items identified by result types in the interface

- Consolidated search architecture that no longer requires a separate install of FAST Search

- Continuous crawling to ensure up-to-the-minute search index freshness

- Re-architected the relevance engine and ranking model

Insights

Every business has requirements to share analytical information. That information is often lurking in reports and spreadsheets that users may not be aware of or have access to. Business users are clamoring for better ways to visually discover and share insights so that collaborative decision making can be more effective across the organization.

SharePoint 2013 takes its business intelligence capabilities to an entirely new level by offering very close integration with Excel 2013, Power View, PowerPivot, and Microsoft SQL Server 2012. With built-in tools such as Excel Services, Visio Services, and PerformancePoint, building interactive dashboards in a SharePoint site is quick and powerful. Following is a partial list of the types of solutions you can build in SharePoint 2013:

- Connect to data from nearly any source to create fully interactive reports and insights on your site.

- Publish and share reports with your colleagues.

- Combine and analyze large sets of business data with PowerPivot.

- Integrate with SharePoint Search and create a custom "Reports" search vertical, as shown in Figure 1-6.

- Perform interactive data exploration to find answers and make well-informed business decisions.

- Ensure spreadsheet integrity and compliance, and apply information management policies as business requirements dictate.

- Consolidate and simplify the management of data that has traditionally resided in unmanaged Excel spreadsheets and Microsoft Access databases.

Figure 1-6 Here is an example of using a custom "Reports" search vertical to discover analytical information.

Experts

SharePoint 2013 provides many intuitive ways to discover, connect, and collaborate with people across your business. You can still search for people in the same way as in previous versions of SharePoint, but now you can also easily discover common interests, projects, and documents they have worked on. Then, as shown in Figure 1-7, you can take actions based on what you find.

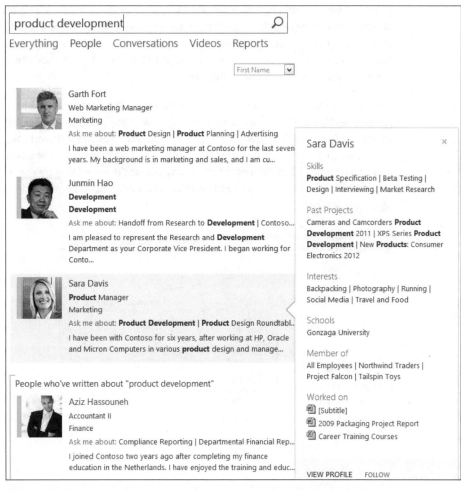

Figure 1-7 Discovering a product development expert in a SharePoint 2013 people search.

Organize

SharePoint 2013 excels at organizing information and teams, running the gamut from personal tasks to team projects to enterprise data. Organizing information and applying a governance strategy to manage enterprise content and records is a core part of the SharePoint platform.

Team sites

Team sites have long been at the heart of what most people experience when they use SharePoint. In 2013, team sites receive a refreshing update that orients them more toward groups of people working together on tasks and projects. People working together on projects tend to require the same basic types of tools—document sharing, task sharing, shared note taking, a team newsfeed, and so on. SharePoint 2013 team sites allow a site owner to easily add these common apps, customize the theme of their site, and invite people to participate and follow the site.

One of the most interesting new team site features is the team mailbox. Because most projects involve a lot of email, team sites now have the option to host a team mailbox, as shown in Figure 1-8. The team mailbox is an app that provides a shared Microsoft Exchange inbox that all the members of your site can access. For those users, the site mailbox serves as a central email filing cabinet, which is only accessible for editing by site members. It also enables members of the site to work with files from document libraries directly within Microsoft Outlook 2013.

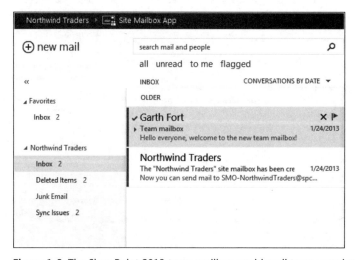

Figure 1-8 The SharePoint 2013 team mailbox enables all team members access to team email.

Store and synchronize your documents

Document collaboration has always been at the heart of what SharePoint provides. Now in 2013, the personal document storage capability of previous SharePoint versions has morphed into an updated feature for document storage and synchronization entitled SkyDrive Pro. This new capability of SharePoint enables organizations to easily provision a personal, secure document space for their users. It is available in the cloud or on-premises.

In addition to providing a place to store and share documents, SkyDrive Pro offers easy synchronization to a user's device with a single click. SkyDrive Pro replaces the Microsoft SharePoint Workspace 2010 product as the new offline client for SharePoint documents. The figures that follow show a 2013 SharePoint SkyDrive Pro site (Figure 1-9), and the synchronized files on the client system (Figure 1-10).

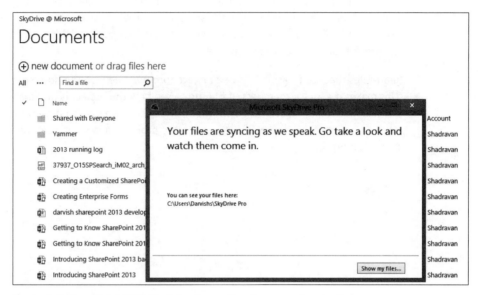

Figure 1-9 SharePoint 2013 SkyDrive Pro performing a synchronization.

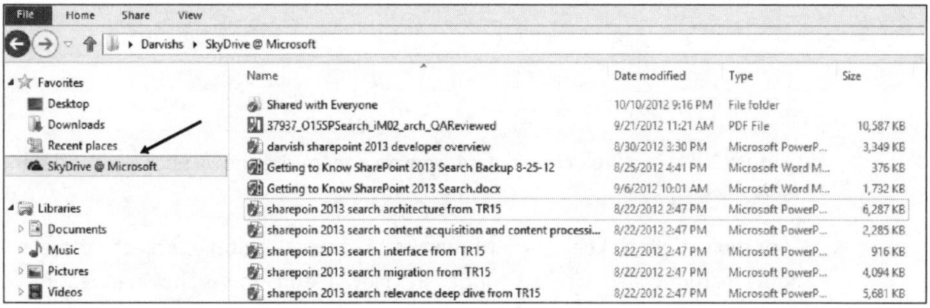

Figure 1-10 The SkyDrive Pro client in Windows Explorer.

Managing tasks and projects

Keeping in line with the idea that a SharePoint site is an ideal place for a team to manage a project, SharePoint 2013 has a new lightweight task management feature to help coordinate tasks across the entire team. Task management capabilities can be added as a supplemental feature to any team site so that the group can track tasks, stay organized, and communicate deadlines; all in the same site where you store files, team mail, and notes. In addition, the tasks you work with in SharePoint are available to synchronize with Microsoft Project and Exchange as well.

Team sites that use tasks now have a *Project Summary* view on the home page of the site. This makes it easy for members of the site to see how the project is going and easily see the next upcoming milestone. As shown in Figure 1-11, anyone who goes to the site will have a good high-level view of progress on the project—and what items people should be completing next.

Figure 1-11 The Project Summary view on a team site shows upcoming tasks and project documents.

For individuals to keep track of many tasks across multiple projects, there is now a new feature called *My Tasks* under the Newsfeed Hub. As shown in Figure 1-12, this enables users to see at a glance all of the things they need to accomplish across projects aggregated in one place.

My Tasks can pull together all tasks assigned to you in SharePoint, Project, and Exchange into one interface. Therefore, a user is empowered to organize and manage both personal and assigned tasks from projects from a single location.

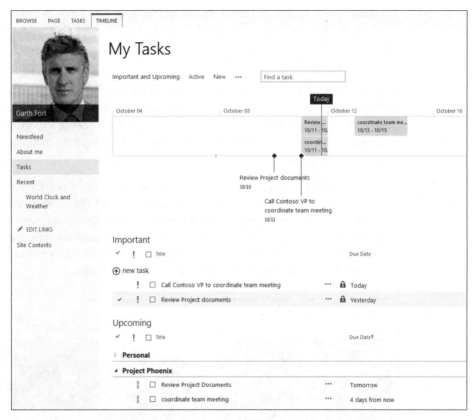

Figure 1-12 My Tasks shows all personal and project tasks in your Newsfeed.

Build

SharePoint 2013 has more opportunity than ever for building solutions—building sites,
building apps, building cloud solutions, and more. The SharePoint UI is updated to HTML5
and JavaScript, and this allows more rapid and more standards-based solution creation.
There has never been a greater opportunity for people tasked with building SharePoint-
based solutions to create solutions that address business challenges.

Build apps

SharePoint 2013 introduces an architectural change to support a new *Cloud App Model* that
enables you to build a new class of SharePoint apps that extend and personalize the way
users interact with SharePoint. The Cloud App Model enables you to create and consume
information based on standard web technologies such as JavaScript, REST web services,
and HTML5. In the past, SharePoint made the distinction between "lists" and "libraries."

But now lists and libraries are just a type of app. In fact, most things in SharePoint are now consolidated under the term "app." There are technical differences between task list and picture libraries and a third-party app built by your developers. However, from an experience perspective, they are all apps.

Apps for SharePoint provide users with a dependable way to discover, obtain, and implement new capabilities. Inherent in this new app model is the capability for SharePoint site owners to easily add an app to their site that provides a specific capability they may need. Apps cover a broad range of functionalities—everything from mapping apps to world clocks to sales reporting.

SharePoint customers can build their own apps using a variety of developer tools and then easily publish them to a special type of new SharePoint site called an *app catalog*. Alternatively, there is also a public SharePoint app catalog (shown in Figure 1-13) that resides on Microsoft's website. It provides many types of SharePoint apps, many of which are available at no extra cost. Because apps can be hosted in the cloud, they are independent from SharePoint and Office version upgrade cycles.

Figure 1-13 The public SharePoint app store provides many types of SharePoint apps.

Build great-looking sites

SharePoint 2013 sites have an updated architecture that enables a web designer to build a rich, interactive SharePoint site without the requirement of SharePoint-specific development skills. Tools such as Adobe Dreamweaver and Microsoft Expression Blend are now fully supported for creating SharePoint pages and layouts.

SharePoint 2013 introduces a new tool called *Design Manager* that enables site designers to easily customize SharePoint sites in the browser. The need to edit ASP.NET files to create SharePoint items such as master pages and page layouts goes away. Now designers can edit in HTML and SharePoint Design Manager will convert these files automatically. As shown in Figure 1-14, a site designer is able to edit a master page in Design Manager. Notice that HTML *snippets* can easily be added to a site to quickly provide a modern web experience.

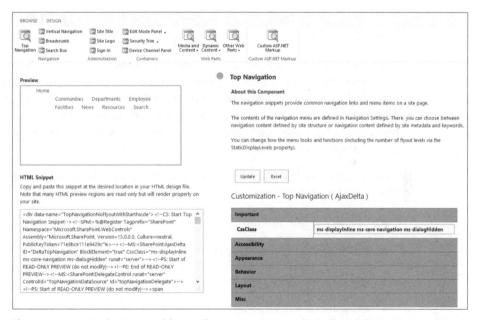

Figure 1-14 A site designer is able to edit a master page easily in SharePoint Design Manager.

Manage

From a management perspective, SharePoint 2013 is designed to work equally well in the cloud or on-premises. In either case, you can still take advantage of the performance and scalability benefits in the product. Infrastructure and management costs can be reduced across the board. Significant investments in records management and e-discovery have been made in order to help meet the demands of compliance and risk management.

Manage risk

For organizations that are concerned with managing risks associated with their digital assets, SharePoint 2013 supports several scenarios including e-discovery, disposition, and retention policies for SharePoint, Microsoft Lync, and Exchange data. Along with that, SharePoint 2013 can help you with the challenge of controlling access to company- and customer-sensitive data. Thus, SharePoint 2013 is a robust platform for the storage, management, and consumption of sensitive information.

One key new feature is that it is now possible to define retention policies for sites *and* mailboxes using the SharePoint data protection tools. An administrator can ensure content is preserved in real time, which will ensure the data integrity of the information stored not only in SharePoint, but also in Lync and Exchange. In addition, SharePoint 2013 makes authorization and audit management more centralized and adaptable to customer-specific policies.

Manage costs

SharePoint 2013 is constructed in such a manner that administrators will find the process of upgrading and managing their infrastructures significantly easier than in past versions. With the new cloud delivery model, adding new features is far more streamlined. In addition, the option now exists for reducing infrastructure costs by hosting SharePoint farms (or a portion of them) in the cloud. This effectively reduces the cost of administration, storage, server hardware, and so on.

SharePoint 2013 has several new tools for administrators to keep things running smoothly. Some of the most notable include:

- Self-service site creation

- Schema vs. site collection upgrade

- Site collection health checks

- Evaluation site collections

- System status notifications

- Usage and health data collection

- App management service

- Request management

- Shredded storage

Perhaps one of the most useful tools is the new *Site Collection Health Check,* shown in Figure 1-15. It allows an administrator to identify common issues such as missing features or templates, and points out any issues with a site collection that might pose a problem if an upgrade is performed.

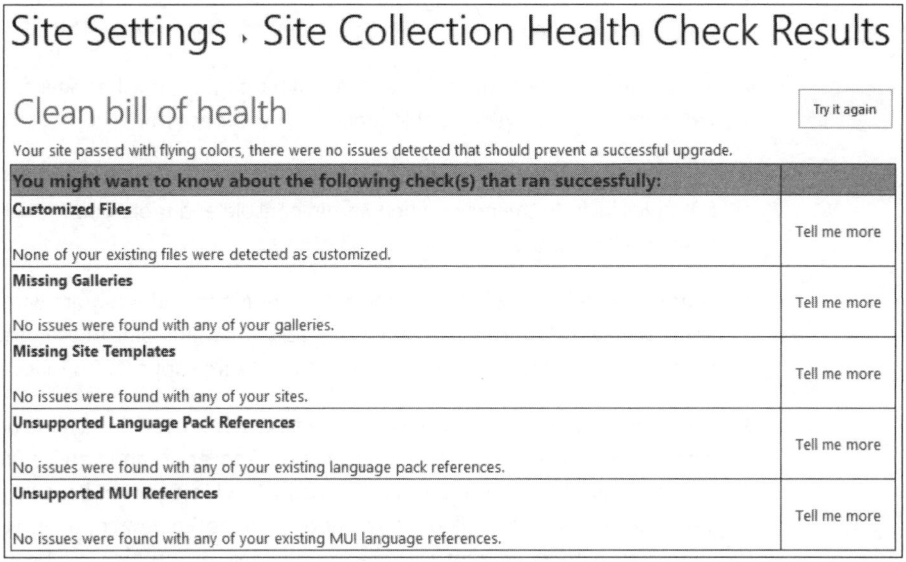

Figure 1-15 The new Site Collection Health Check tool allows an administrator to easily identify common issues within a site collection.

Built for the cloud

SharePoint 2013 is the first version of SharePoint developed from the ground up to be fully "cloud ready." As the development process unfolded, priority was given to ensuring that SharePoint Online features were very near parity with the traditional on-premise versions of SharePoint. It is effectively the first release of SharePoint that is available simultaneously as a service or as a server. Part of making a product like SharePoint cloud enabled is to not only port features to support the cloud, but also to re-architect core aspects of the product in order to better suit the more agile, cloud-based application world in which we live.

As part of the Office 365 offering from Microsoft, SharePoint Online inherently has the same cloud benefits for customers who wish to push a portion (or all) of their SharePoint infrastructure requirements online. Office 365 has a simplified administration and deployment model that enables customers to get their SharePoint 2013 projects up and running quickly. In addition, because SharePoint Online is part of Office 365, it is protected by Microsoft's geo-redundant data center environments around the world.

Some of the specific features that make SharePoint 2013 more cloud ready than ever before are listed here:

- The Cloud App Model allows for easy publishing and updating of apps in the cloud.

- Common web standards for applications, security, and data access are now supported. Examples include JavaScript, OAuth, OData, and HTML5.

- SharePoint includes a unified search architecture that now has near feature-parity regardless of which version of SharePoint you choose to utilize.

- SharePoint uses common administration tools across the cloud and on-premises. Examples include the new unified admin console and more comprehensive Windows PowerShell support.

- SharePoint Online now has the ability to connect to and integrate with the Windows Azure data and services. This opens the door for SharePoint to use other application models beyond .NET. For example, Windows Azure supports PHP, Node.js, and Java.

- Deep Windows Azure integration also means that SharePoint Online now gets access to Microsoft SQL Azure, Blobs, Tables, AppFabric, and Service Bus. Therefore, the possibilities for cloud-based data hosting and integration have increased geometrically, and this will open the door to an entire new set of applications. Customers with SharePoint sites that require geo-distribution will be able to leverage Windows Azure as a content distribution network (CDN) in order to deploy and globally replicate their SharePoint assets such as videos, images, and documents.

- SharePoint Online updates come on a very regular basis, with new features and capabilities, so your organization will receive the latest technology without the need to upgrade servers.

Hardware and software requirements

SharePoint Server 2013 requires that a number of specific software components be in place prior to installation. For a complete reference on hardware and software requirements, browser support, and so on, please refer to the Microsoft TechNet site at *technet.microsoft .com/en-us/library/cc262749(v=office.15)*. On this webpage, you will find several categories of comprehensive information that can assist you in planning an installation of SharePoint 2013.

Summary

This introductory chapter gives you a small glimpse of the new capabilities in SharePoint 2013. Whether you are already a SharePoint virtuoso, a business user, an IT professional, or just a budding SharePoint prodigy, in the remainder of this book, you will learn about all the major areas of functionality that were introduced in this chapter—and much more.

Along the way, you will learn the "Inside Out" story about these capabilities and best practices for how to use them. This will enable you to harness the power of this new platform for *sharing, discovering, organizing, building, and managing* with SharePoint 2013.

Chapter 1

Administration for business users

T HE first chapter of this book gave you a quick review of Microsoft SharePoint 2013. This second chapter begins the introduction to more advanced SharePoint terms and concepts that will help you through the remaining chapters of the book. SharePoint is a server product. As an advanced information worker, you might mostly interact with the front end of the product by adding documents and list items, but you are also a key part of the SharePoint team at your organization. This chapter introduces you to some parts of SharePoint that you may not usually come across in your day-to-day job. However, by getting an overview of how SharePoint is structured and secured, you will gain a better understanding of the product as a whole. In addition to helping you discuss SharePoint on a more level playing field with developers and IT professionals, the administration basics that you learn here will help you with planning and using SharePoint.

Two categories of administration

Administration of SharePoint 2013 can be broken down into two categories: business user administration and IT professional administration.

Business user administration

If you are a typical person who works in the business user administration category:

- Your main job is not technical computer work.

- You create and modify sites, libraries, and lists.

- You might also be responsible for the site content. For example, you might upload documents to libraries for others to download.

The majority of this book includes information targeted to the advanced business user who might perform some of this type of administration. This chapter will give you the tools to set up your SharePoint sites that are serviced on the back end, either by your organization's IT group, an external hosting company, or both.

IT professional administration

If you are a typical person who works in the IT professional administration category:

- You work in a room surrounded by the server's network hardware.

- You install and configure SharePoint on a server.

- You create web applications and site collections for business users to administer.

The IT professional at an organization with SharePoint is often an advanced user of SharePoint as well. Although this chapter is not intended to describe the step-by-step processes to implement back-end changes for Microsoft SharePoint Server 2013, an IT professional can benefit from this chapter by learning the business perspective of the same changes.

Why administration matters: One search example

Have you ever searched a website and been disappointed by the results? Maybe your search for "coffee" on your favorite shop's website returned no results, as in the following image. What would you do next? With the amount of websites available to choose from today, you're probably heading over to your second favorite shop's website or a search of the Internet. You're less likely to continue on that website when your search comes up with no results. Not only that, but you are less likely to return to it in the future.

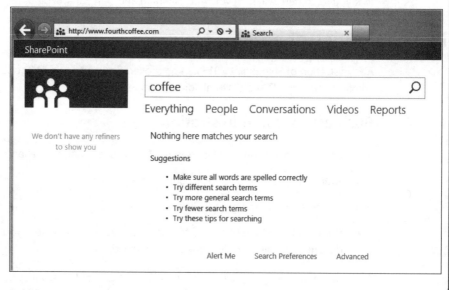

Now, think about the sites for which you have some responsibility in your organization's world of SharePoint. Do you want visitors to your sites staying for more and returning the next time they want to find something you've got there? Of course you do, or you wouldn't have created the site or accepted some responsibility for it in the first place. With your name on the site, you want to make every visit to it rewarding and enjoyable. Understanding administration will help avoid bad experiences like this search example. Ownership of a site in SharePoint doesn't make you an IT professional. You might not be the one pushing the buttons on the computers that host the site, but what that person does affects how your site is perceived. You need every visitor to come away with the information they came for (especially if that visitor is you).

Installation and configuration decisions

You might not be the one installing and configuring SharePoint. However, if you expect SharePoint to become an important tool in your work life, you will want to be a part of the planning process that should come before the installation and configuration.

During installation and configuration of SharePoint, important choices are being made that, in part, determine your user experience. For the health and performance of your SharePoint sites, it's always better that the installation and configuration follows a preset plan that takes into account the needs of you and others in the business community at your organization. Depending on who is responsible for the back-end administrative tasks, you might have the opportunity to tailor the installation and configuration to your exact needs or choose a hosting provider whose terms match your needs.

To get the most out of your effort—both for you and for those with whom you plan to share web content via SharePoint—read this chapter and perform the planning steps before installation. If SharePoint is already installed and configured, many of the decisions have been made. Understanding the effect of this configuration on the pieces you care about will help you decide if you need to make a change.

INSIDE OUT I've successfully installed Microsoft Word before, and even installed Windows, so why wouldn't I install SharePoint?

SharePoint is a different kind of software from traditional titles that you might be used to. Unlike Word or Windows, which are installed once per computer, one SharePoint install provides services to many computers. SharePoint is installed in one place and then accessed from web browsers like Windows Internet Explorer, Safari, or Firefox by many people.

For very active installations used by hundreds of people at the same time, SharePoint is installed on more than one server, and it might be supported by other servers, such as directory servers that handle all the logons and database servers to hold all the content. When deployed on multiple servers, there will likely be a dedicated IT support staff with specialized skills to maintain this environment.

A list of all supported web browsers

The Microsoft TechNet article, "Plan browser support in SharePoint 2013," located at *technet.microsoft.com/en-us/library/cc263526(v=office.15).aspx,* contains the latest support information for all browsers. Currently 32-bit versions of Internet Explorer 8 and Internet Explorer 9 have full support for all collaboration actions in SharePoint 2013. Versions of Google Chrome, Apple Safari, and Mozilla Firefox (and 64-bit versions of Internet Explorer) have limited support; these limitations are listed in the TechNet article.

Internet Explorer 6 and Internet Explorer 7 are explicitly not supported, with the following caveat: SharePoint 2013 publishing sites can be designed to support any browser for readers, at the discretion of the site's designer, and the HTML markup used to lay out the publishing site. Creating a publishing site does require a supported browser.

Hosted SharePoint or on-premises SharePoint?

Knowing who is responsible for your installation is important so that you know whom to go to when you need a change. This responsible party is called your *service provider.* The location of your installation is called your *host.* Because your host might not be physically close to you, you depend on your service provider to keep the installation running and make changes.

SharePoint installations normally fall into one of two models: on-premises or hosted.

On-premises

If IT staff in your company is comfortable installing, configuring, and maintaining a computer server, you might decide on an on-premises installation. In such a situation, the computers running SharePoint 2013 are located within your business or maintained at an off-site data center.

On-premises installs are typically how the majority of SharePoint sites have been implemented. When set up with great in-house IT support and dedicated resources, Share-Point has proven to be a reliable and worthwhile addition to the server rooms of many organizations.

The "Under-the-Desk" effect

Watch out for the "Under-the-Desk" effect. SharePoint is so easy to download and install that an entire subset of on-premises installations can sometimes be found on desktop workstations. The term "Under-the-Desk" refers to the fact that a careless kick of a foot can turn the power off on the computer hosting the SharePoint site.

These types of installations can quickly prove the value of SharePoint within your organization; watch out for the negative feelings that can quickly occur when a kick of the foot disrupts the work of many others. You might find that one extended outage can quickly cause the loss of a lot of user goodwill. A site that regularly experiences outages will not be used by nearly as many people as a reliable site.

If you are using an on-premises installation, Active Directory can be configured to block SharePoint installations on the corporate network. This type of configuration is appropriate when there is a strong desire for centralization of resources or to prevent loss of data without IT professional support.

Hosted

A hosted SharePoint server is an opportunity to both get started quickly and have a website that is highly available for those who depend on it. If SharePoint isn't running on computers at your business location, you can take advantage of a growing number of online service offerings.

Microsoft introduced the Microsoft Office 365 service with SharePoint Online powered by SharePoint 2010, and Office 365 has recently been updated to SharePoint 2013. For a low fee per user per month, you can use servers at a Microsoft data center to host your collaboration site on a SharePoint installation that Microsoft engineers will maintain for you. SharePoint's ability to support many different organizations on one SharePoint farm is supported by a feature set added in SharePoint 2010 called *multi-tenancy.* Multi-tenancy features have been improved in SharePoint 2013 and benefit from what was learned by deploying and maintaining SharePoint Online.

To learn more about Office 365, go to *office365.microsoft.com.*

The designers of SharePoint 2013 specifically had this "hosted SharePoint" design in mind to allow more people access to SharePoint without the need for dedicated in-house IT support staff and the specialized skills required to install and configure SharePoint.

Offshore hosting

If you know that some of your organization's data cannot be stored outside your company facilities or at the physical location of the hosting provider, hosted SharePoint might not be a good fit. At the very least, you and others at your organization are responsible for the information that you post to sites on the Internet, and you must keep this in mind when selecting a provider and deciding what kind of projects to host with the provider. For example, you might come across laws or regulations that prevent you from hosting your data in another country.

Note

SharePoint 2013 introduces new, distributed development options referred to as the *app model*. The app model helps remove some of the bottlenecks that may have prevented SharePoint enhancements on shared servers in past versions of the product.

Chapter 23, "Introduction to custom development," covers extending SharePoint. You can also read more about the new cloud app model and programming with web standards on Microsoft's MSDN website at *msdn.microsoft.com/en-us/library/jj163091(v=office.15).aspx*.

Figure 2-1 summarizes the key strategic considerations when choosing on-premises versus hosted SharePoint.

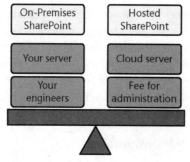

Figure 2-1 SharePoint installation models: on-premises versus hosted installations.

INSIDE OUT   SharePoint moves into the cloud

What the cloud really refers to depends on who's saying it, but it can be described as a metaphor for the Internet; simply put, SharePoint in the cloud means running SharePoint as an Internet-based service. If you've ever used web-based email, you understand the benefit of using software running on a server in the cloud.

Cloud-based SharePoint is just another step in the direction away from relying on in-house IT for installation and configuration of every server-based application you use. Sometimes moving toward a service provider allows a business to benefit from huge economies of scale that most businesses can't achieve with their own in-house IT staff.

The SharePoint structure

Have you ever thought about the way a SharePoint site is built? In this section, key structural pieces of a SharePoint installation will be explained. SharePoint sites often grow organically—the "Comparing a SharePoint web application to a tree" section will introduce you to the basic building blocks of a SharePoint installation's structure. Table 2-1 lists the nine main SharePoint structural elements of interest.

TABLE 2-1 The nine main SharePoint structural elements

Structure element	Definition
Farm	The term *farm* is used in two main ways. The farm can be considered to be the physical computers and the software required to be running on them to host SharePoint. In addition, each farm's settings are held in a unique configuration database stored on a Microsoft SQL Server instance.
Service application	A service application runs within a farm to provide capability to the sites hosted on it or another farm.
Content database	The majority of the information added to a SharePoint site is stored in a content database.
Web application	A SharePoint site is accessed through a web application that provides the address and authentication settings, among other configuration properties. A web application must have a corresponding website in Internet Information Services (IIS).

Structure element	Definition
Site collection	One or more sites are grouped together into a site collection. Sites are organized hierarchically in site collections, and some configuration settings and administrative actions applied to site collections affect every site in the group.
Site	A site is a logical grouping of content within SharePoint. Each site collection has a root site, which is the main point of entry.
Document library	Document libraries are historically the most used element of a SharePoint site. Library settings control visibility and content types among other critical configurations.
List	The majority of all content in a SharePoint site is held in a list. Sites have many lists of many types. Even a document library is a list, but a specialized kind of list with tools designed to work best with documents.
Webpage	Since SharePoint 2010, webpages have taken on new importance for SharePoint sites. Every webpage in SharePoint 2013 has rich-text editing capability. Each webpage that you create from the browser is stored in a document library.

Comparing a SharePoint web application to a tree

Think of a web application as a tree. Each trunk is a site collection, with the first site collection in the web application coming from the same set of roots as the other trunks. The branches are like sites branching off the site collections and the leaves are list items and documents.

Some web applications are like a pomegranate tree, which can have more than one trunk in the same tree. SharePoint Server 2013 has a good example of this type of tree in the web application configured to be the My Site Host. Each individual's My Site is itself a site collection; in an organization with 80,000 users, you may end up with 80,000 site collections sprouting out of the same web application root base.

The base address of the My Site Host, my.litware.com, for example, redirects to the current authenticated user's personal site collection, which is located at an address relative the base address—for example, *my.litware.com/personal/*<username>. In this example, you could browse to any other My Site public profile by entering **my.litware.com/personal/** followed by the other user's name (if you know it).

As another example of a SharePoint implementation, consider a public website for a multinational organization. Such a website might have separate site collections for each of the many regional groups within the organization. There may be one main web address, and a corresponding SharePoint web application, associated with multiple site collections. Picture the SharePoint components of such a public website as a tree with many trunks and even more main branches. Figure 2-2 illustrates how the web addresses of such a site might map to the tree picture.

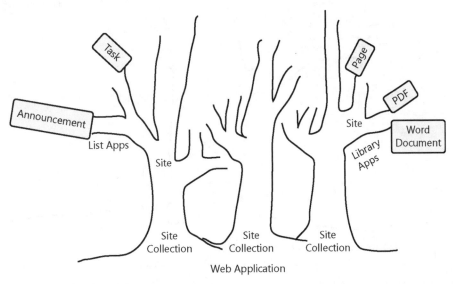

Figure 2-2 The SharePoint pomegranate tree.

On the other hand, many web applications look more like a pecan tree. One trunk, the site collection, has a few thick, strong branches off it, supporting other branches and lots of leaves (not to mention tasty nuts in the fall). Figure 2-3 illustrates how the web addresses of this type of site might map to a single-trunk tree.

A classic intranet publishing portal matches this version of the metaphor: *portal.contoso.com* is the address of the web application and the first site of the site collection. The entry page for this web application is at the address *portal.contoso.com/pages/welcome.aspx*. Human Resources might have a main trunk site at *portal.contoso.com/hr/*. Benefits information might be stored in a leaf document library at *portal.contoso.com/Locations/Lists/Benefits/*. The webpage about medical benefits might be at *portal.contoso.com/Locations/Lists/Benefits/Medical.aspx*, with a link to the provider's benefit statement at *portal.contoso.com/Locations/Lists/Benefits/Provider-Statement.pdf*.

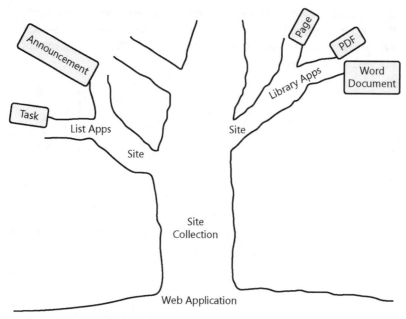

Figure 2-3 The SharePoint pecan tree.

INSIDE OUT   Host-named site collections

An improved feature of SharePoint 2013 allows more flexibility in SharePoint site address choices. A host-named site collection can use a shorter URL for its address. It's different from a path-based site collection, which appends the site collection part of the address after the domain name in the URL. For example, in *www.contoso.com/partners*, "partners" is the site collection identifier. A host-named site collection includes the site collection identifier before the host name, such as *partners.contoso.com*. Shorter addresses are easier to type and remember.

The details of the changes that allow this new flexibility may not interest you, but the impact of the changes may affect your site architecture. For example, Microsoft's recommended design for an Enterprise Corporate Portal has been updated to reflect the suggested use of host-named rather than path-based site collections.

For example, the part of the Corporate Portal design for the fictional organization Fabrikam shown in the next graphic represents the intranet site collection. Using path-based site collections, the address might be *portal.fabrikam.com/intranet*. The address would become even longer for other sites in the collection (such as *portal.fabrikam.com/intranet/purchasing*).

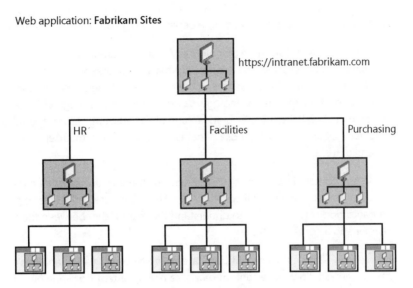

Web application: **Fabrikam Sites**

https://intranet.fabrikam.com

HR   Facilities   Purchasing

An alternative to host-named site collections is moving toward more web-based applications. For example, a separate web application for the intranet part of the portal could retain the *intranet.fabrikam.com* address. The downside to this approach is the requirement for extra resources in the farm, and ultimately a higher cost of equipment.

Farm scalability, service applications, and databases

The SharePoint farm is the set of servers hosting all of the sites and support they need. A farm can have as few as one server, which would host the entire infrastructure needed for a small organization.

SharePoint is very scalable. A farm supporting higher user demand benefits from a larger amount of server resources. To carry on the tree metaphor, a high-demand farm can be pictured like a nut orchard providing benefits of its fruit to large amounts of people.

Some service applications provided to the SharePoint farm are similar to the water and fertilizer that are applied to a literal orchard. Other service applications are applied with more discretion, similar to spraying insecticide at the site of an infestation. Business Data Connectivity (BDC) is an example of a SharePoint service that can be applied across all the web applications and the content in their site collections. A SharePoint user can configure a connection to a business data source, such as Microsoft customer relationship management (CRM) software, once and provide that data to all the web applications in a farm. In the preceding examples, a workflow that begins when a new client is added in CRM might add a task list item to an external list. Because BDC is a shared service, you can use the data that it provides on a user's My Site or in a department's team site from the same BDC source.

The database is important in planning any implementation of SharePoint. You might or might not know about the relationship between SharePoint and the database. The designers of SharePoint chose to employ the power of the entire Microsoft platform stack. One place where mature technology was exploited is the storage of items added to or created in SharePoint. By taking advantage of the efficient, secure, and reliable platform provided by SQL Server, all those benefits are passed on to the users and administrators of SharePoint sites.

All of the content in a SharePoint 2013 farm is stored in one or more databases on one or more servers running SQL Server. When SharePoint use really takes off in a large organization, it is important to understand the relationship between the items discussed earlier and a content database.

The relationship of the content database to the web application and site collection is explained as follows: one content database holds content from one or more site collections of one web application. In the example web applications presented earlier, at least two content databases would be required to hold the two web applications for the My Sites and the intranet. Further, the contents of a single site collection must be stored together in the same database; however, one content database can hold the content of multiple site collections. A web application can spread out the storage of multiple site collections across multiple content databases.

The tree metaphor is helpful in picturing administrative concepts of SharePoint. Visualizing the structure of your SharePoint environment can be helpful in decisions about content upload, creation of webpages, and new site creation. You will be well on your way toward understanding the structure if you can keep in mind the relationship between the first five main structural elements described previously. The farm, web application, service application, content database, and site collection are critical concepts for the intermediate to advanced user of SharePoint who wants to speak to IT professionals about the supporting structures of her SharePoint site or sites.

The content database as a unit of storage

Of all the SharePoint structural concepts introduced so far, the content database might be the most important one to understand toward achieving a successful SharePoint implementation. If the users in your organization begin to depend on SharePoint for hosting all of their critical files, lists, and webpages, the amount of storage used can grow dramatically. You can take your understanding of the tree metaphor, add your understanding of content databases, and apply it to an example where quick storage growth becomes a challenge for performance and stability of the SharePoint implementation. You will also be able to see how the same elements can explain the solution.

Let's go back to the intranet portal example and assume that the entire organizational structure was represented in the site structure, such as the Human Resources department. A common business structure might have sites for Sales, Marketing, and Operations. Teams under those groups might also receive sites below their parent group site. As more and more sites are created, with more and more members of the organization creating and uploading documents, pictures, list items, and webpages, the one content database for this one tree in the orchard is storing all the content.

This implementation is a classic example of three issues common in unsuccessful SharePoint implementations: 1) disorganization of information, 2) delays backing up and restoring the content, and 3) deteriorating performance of the entire web application. All these issues occur gradually over time, so a great approach is to be aware and monitor growth and change in order to plan for reorganization or new hardware purchases ahead of time.

Using a content database as a unit of backup and restoration

Let us first consider the case of backing up and restoring the content of your intranet in this example. A successful SharePoint implementation with a SharePoint structure like this can result in a database measured in terabytes of storage space. If you've ever tried to back up a 200-GB hard disk, you understand the amount of time required to save your important information.

The amount of time it takes to back up data is affected by two critical restore parameters. The first is how often data can be backed up; if it takes eight hours to back up the content database and you run only one backup at a time, your SharePoint content will be safely backed up only once during a business day. For certain tasks at some organizations, it is acceptable to lose a day's worth of information; for others, losing even a minute of information could be trouble.

The second restore parameter affected by large content databases is the amount of time it takes to restore. Again, it is up to the task and the organization to determine how long is too long. However, in some situations, waiting a day for SharePoint to be restored after a disaster or an unexpected failure is just too long.

Chapter 2

INSIDE OUT Backups use a lot of resources

You might not care for the full detail of the backup operation, but as a site user and business influencer, you must pay attention to at least some backup details. Backups are resource intensive and might cause competition with user operations. This issue can be mitigated by scheduling backup tasks during off hours (if you do not run a 24-hour operation). Awareness of how and when your backups are running can help you to understand the performance implications for your users.

Organizing for content database growth

Next, let's consider the case of disorganization of information. This one is probably not hard to imagine if you've been using a computer for many years and you've ever lost a file on your hard disk or a file share. Over time, file storage tends to become filled with documents that are rarely accessed and out of date. The same can happen to any kind of content in a SharePoint site. Remember that a SharePoint site is intended to be dynamic; therefore, you need to plan accordingly. Identify the areas that are important to the users of your site. Plan to repeatedly highlight timely, relevant information. Collect feedback from your users on organization and usefulness to ensure that your growing site meets not just your needs, but the needs of your collaborators as well.

The best-case scenario for your organization is to plan ahead of time and accommodate growth where anticipated. SharePoint sites intended for team collaboration and document sharing tend to grow in database size over time. Document sharing sites are popular, but they can often be isolated into site collections by audience. Site collections are natural security and audience boundaries. Interaction within a legal team, for example, deserves this type of isolation for the sensitivity of the information alone. However, other teams can also follow the model, whereby internally important information is contributed to one site collection and more generally interesting information is uploaded to a shared portal. Again, if we look to the SharePoint Product Team's example of building out My Sites in SharePoint Server, we see this model in its extreme. A My Site gives a user a place to upload content and control access in his own site collection. If the team designing SharePoint puts that architecture forward as a model, you can feel safe in assigning small- to medium-sized project teams similar workspaces that they can control.

Creating site collections for unique audiences reduces the amount of content in each site collection. The added benefit beyond security is added mobility of the content within the content database. Individual site collections can be moved between content databases with more flexibility than sites or lists. Also, storage size quotas can be placed on site collections, but not sites or lists. If the size of a content database becomes an operational issue, the ability to move content to reduce the size of existing databases becomes a big benefit.

If you find yourself in the situation where too much content has been added too quickly, there is good news. Others have been through this before, and strategies have been developed to overcome all three of these issues related to the inevitable growth in a successful SharePoint implementation. For example, if you find that you want to reduce your backup or restore period time, there are two possible paths. Starting with IT professional analysis, identify if the current read or write speed for your content database storage, your backup storage, or the network in between can be increased by purchase of new hardware or optimization of the current hardware.

At the same time, use your understanding of the SharePoint structure to look at how you might reorganize your sites to meet your goals. If all your sites are currently held in one site collection and subsequently one content database, you have an opportunity to create a new site collection, in a new content database where existing sites can be moved. However, moving is always stressful and sometimes items become lost in the move. Professional tools and consultants will help you move more quickly with less loss, but there is always a cost associated with that kind of help. The best strategy is to be proactive and move early. If you identify the level of service you need from SharePoint and you can estimate when potential support milestones will be hit, you can build a roadmap for potential changes ahead.

The amount of time that a backup or restore takes to complete is a common service-level requirement for electronic information. When you use the site collection as a mobile unit of SharePoint content, you can arrange your content databases to accomplish your service-level requirements. In a common method of backup, the content database is the container that is backed up or restored. Moving your most critical site collections to a new content database will allow your IT professionals to back up and restore those sites more quickly. If you consider this type of reorganization, keep in mind that you can host multiple site collections under one web application. In that way, you can maintain one base web address for multiple site collections and reduce the backup and restore time of your most critical information.

Search administration

Search is one of the most powerful pieces of functionality that Microsoft has provided with the SharePoint product. Think about how often you use search on the Internet. Is a web search engine one of the most frequently accessed websites in your browser? If you are taking advantage of the large amount of information available on the web through search, you probably don't have to stretch your imagination too much to see how search can benefit you in SharePoint as well. A great SharePoint search experience can help you tap into the information you and your colleagues create on computers about and for your organization.

Using a well-configured SharePoint Search against your own webpages and files, your results will be more refined and specific to the needs of your organization. If the material is there, you should expect to find customer service guidelines, training materials, or experiences that relate specifically to your product and customer. Understanding SharePoint Search better will help you maximize the benefit of Search against the information that your organization has captured electronically.

Search improvements in SharePoint Server 2013

Search is so important to SharePoint that Microsoft has continued to make improvements to the capabilities in every release of SharePoint. SharePoint Server 2013 is no exception. Microsoft has finally created a new enterprise search experience that builds on the software acquired with the FAST Search server. The results include fresher search results, new publishing options for content, and better refinement of search results.

Chapter 18, "Discovering information with SharePoint 2013 Search," and Chapter 19, "Creating a customized SharePoint 2013 search experience," cover search in depth and offer suggestions for the best use of this improved tool.

Security

SharePoint offers secure, web-based collaboration that is easy to set up. Security options are pervasive throughout the product. You'll find information about security's role in different contexts in various chapters of this book. The focus of this section, as well as the rest of the chapter, is on security options in the product that are often hidden from you as an advanced business user. Whether you are preparing for a new SharePoint installation, making configuration changes, or you just want to learn more about security, pay close attention to the rest of this section.

Note

Microsoft SharePoint Foundation 2013 is a separate product that also serves as the infrastructure for SharePoint Server 2013. This book focuses on SharePoint Server 2013, and the differences between the two products are not normally described. However, security is a fairly stable feature set across the two products. Most of what applies to security as described here for SharePoint Server 2013 also applies to SharePoint Foundation 2013.

Authentication and authorization

Regardless of the secure application, two important security principles to understand are authentication and authorization. *Authentication* is the method of identifying the current user of the application. *Authorization* is the access the user has within the application. Together, these two concepts provide a means for securing your SharePoint sites.

Most important authentication settings are configured by IT at the web-application level. An example of the effect of these settings is when and how you are prompted for logon information to a SharePoint site. Your business needs determine how the web application should be configured for authentication.

On the other hand, authorization settings are pervasive throughout the product. In fact, the number of places and ways that SharePoint can be configured for access has increased over previous versions of the product. For example, Microsoft responded to customers' needs to limit the access IT professionals have to content and settings that only business users need to see or set. User policy for web application zones can override the permissions that a site collection owner will set, and this can cause confusion. If you question this level of security for your site or site collection, be sure to discuss this with your site host to guarantee that the proper safeguards are in place. Another similar change that can be made is in auditing. SharePoint provides auditing of item and page views, updates, and deletes, but it is not configured by default.

INSIDE OUT   Authentication isn't just for the Internet browser

Authentication settings configured by IT can be critical to your SharePoint solution's ultimate level of success or failure. Also, these settings often determine your ease of use. For example, the Office integration features depend on the proper authentication settings for the web application and your client environment.

The Connect To Outlook button, visible on a SharePoint Calendar, is one place that an incorrect configuration for your environment can have an effect. If your web application is set to use Forms-Based Authentication and your Microsoft Outlook client does not have the latest update that works with this setting, clicking the button will have no effect. This type of error is one of the quickest ways to lose the trust of your visitors because it gives no indication of what is wrong. If you were the visitor who clicked a button that doesn't do what you expected, would you think the site is not working? Some visitors might lose confidence in the entire solution after a few experiences like that because they are not sure what will work and what is broken or why.

Types of authentication

The five most common authentication types are outlined in this section. Each of these authentication types play a part in the secure web scenarios presented in the next section. Of the five, the classic Windows authentication has been most common in past SharePoint deployments, and it is the type that SharePoint has supported most completely over the course of the product's history. In contrast, claims-based authentication was newly introduced in the 2010 versions of the product to broaden the scope of authentication approaches used for SharePoint sites. For example, you can use claims-based authentication to allow Windows Live ID accounts to authenticate against your SharePoint site. In SharePoint Server 2013, claims-based authentication has been improved on the back end and promoted to the default choice for administrators creating new sites.

Classic Windows integrated

Classic Windows integrated authentication is no longer the default option when your IT administrator is creating a new web application. It won't be commonly in use for new web applications, but it is an important consideration for migrations from older versions of SharePoint. (Upgrades and migrations are covered in the "Upgrades and migrations" section later in this chapter.)

Claims-based Windows integrated

Claims-based authentication was new for SharePoint 2010, but it takes a more important role in SharePoint 2013. All web applications created in SharePoint 2013 through Central Administration will use claims authentication. Upgrades from SharePoint 2010 can also use this setting, but if customizations are being upgraded, they might need code changes to work with the new security model.

Forms-based

Forms-based authentication can only be enabled with claims in SharePoint 2013. This type of authentication is popular in extranet scenarios because it doesn't require an Active Directory account for each authenticated user. However, you might find that certain features don't work as well with this setup. Particularly challenging is Office integration without the latest versions of the Office clients.

Claims-based without Windows

Claims-based without Windows authentication was also introduced with SharePoint 2010. This new authentication method was much different than anything available in the previous version of the product. For SharePoint 2013, claims-based without Windows authentication remains an important part of many deployments. This authentication method allows some advanced scenarios but also requires more complexity on the back end. If you require claims-based authentication without Windows integration, keep in mind that this is a new technology, and it might take some time for the administration best practices to be established. If you need to integrate with some external types of identification systems, like Windows Live authentication, claims-based authentication is the answer.

Anonymous access

Anonymous access is most commonly used with publishing sites that are public facing, but might also make sense within a large organization where many readers access the site, but only a few content authors publish information. Anonymous access can be used in combination with the previous four authentication types on one web application. Be sure to provide your content publishers with a way to log on through a link published on your intranet or on the page in the public site. In addition to the IT settings for the web application, ensure that you enable your site for anonymous access in the permissions settings of your site collection settings.

You can read more about authentication methods and modes on the TechNet website at *technet.microsoft.com/en-us/library/cc262350(v=office.15).aspx.*

Securing web applications

There are three common scenarios for web application security needs:

- Public websites available for anyone on the Internet to read

- Secured intranets for use only by users of one organization

- Secured extranets for access by visitors across more than one organization

Public websites

In the first scenario, your web application might be configured by IT for both anonymous access, for readers, and authenticated access of any type, for content authors. If your business needs demand extra security through separation of authoring from reading environments, you would need two separate web applications—possibly in different SharePoint farms—and you would need a method to copy the content between the two.

Secured intranets

Secured intranets are probably the most common use of SharePoint technologies over all versions of the product. Windows integrated authentication is a great choice for this scenario because it provides a great user experience. When all the users of a SharePoint installation are members of the Active Directory domain, you can avoid logon prompts in many scenarios. Also, a secured intranet environment is most likely to benefit from the maturity of the Office client integration with SharePoint when combined with Windows integrated authentication. The other types of authentication will also work in this scenario, but they do increase the complexity of the configuration for the SharePoint farm's host IT staff.

Secured extranets

Secured extranets are a special case because they often involve collaboration between members of more than one organization. This scenario, in particular, is a great example for the use of claims-based authentication and how it might be of the most use to you.

The implementation of claims in SharePoint uses open standards. The use of open standards for authentication allows integration with a wide and growing amount of identification systems. So, when you use claims to authenticate your SharePoint web application, you might be able to allow more users from outside organizations with greater ease.

As mentioned earlier, forms-based authentication has historically been a popular option for extranets because it provides the option to use an account database to store user account information (instead of Active Directory). Whether you use forms-based authentication with Active Directory or another user directory, you might want to invest in a firewall such as Microsoft Unified Access Gateway (UAG) 2010. UAG integrates well with SharePoint and provides an extra layer of protection beyond the security provided through SharePoint and Windows Server.

More security settings at the web-application level

SharePoint Server 2013 includes other security features that are configured outside the site collection that you might want to take advantage of. Each of the following features has settings that must be configured by the farm administrator at the web-application level. Configuring each can have a significant effect on all the site collections in a web application.

Extended web applications for your site collection

In some cases, you might need more than one method of authentication for your SharePoint sites. The previous section described the authentication options that are available for your web application. Public websites can allow anonymous authentication and another method, but other combinations require some additional changes.

For example, you might want multiple forms of authentication for an extranet. You might use forms-based authentication for extranet users outside your organization so that you don't need to add them to your internal directory. You also might use your existing Active Directory to provide identification for your internal users so that they don't have to learn a new password.

In this case, you would like your IT staff to extend the web application to include an additional authentication method at a new web address. In this way, you effectively have two doors into your SharePoint house. One is locked with Active Directory, the other with a database of external user names and passwords.

User policy on a web application

In the previous section, authentication is described as the way of identifying the person who has logged on to your SharePoint site; authorization defines what SharePoint resources the identified person is allowed to access. You can read about controlling permissions for site collections, sites, lists, libraries, and individual content items later in this book.

The User Policy setting is an important authorization setting that affects authorization on your sites; configuration of this setting is left up to the IT staff supporting your SharePoint web application. The User Policy setting defines global authorization rights to a user for all the site collections in a web application.

> **Note**
> Ask for your IT staff to communicate changes made to this setting. Changes aren't visible to site or site-collection administrators, and the user policy changes override the authorization set by sites and site-collection administrators. There are some valid reasons for user policy changes, but understanding SharePoint security is crucial to getting the best value out of your SharePoint sites. You can put yourself in the driver's seat of your site collection by requesting information such as this from your operational staff, if it is not already clearly documented in the support policy or service level agreements.

Self-Service Site Collection Creation

An IT professional can enable Self-Service Site Creation on each web application individually. This will give the specified users permission to create new site collections in a web application. Did you notice the disconnect between the last two sentences? The former uses the word *site* and the latter the words *site collection*. The former is the wording used in Central Administration, but it would be clearer if it used the words *site collection* in the place of the word site.

There is a big difference between creating a site collection and a site. Acting as a site administrator, you control the permission of users to create new sites as child sites or subsites to yours; however, those sites are all contained within one collection of sites. On the other hand, allowing creation of site collections can be useful as well. Each site collection provides a unique security boundary, a storage quota, and a context boundary. Often, Self-Service Site Collection Creation is extended with customizations. For example, it might be useful to track the reasons that the site collection is needed and the length of time it will be needed for. My Sites can serve as an example of this type of customization. To start, each My Site is provisioned through Self-Service Site Creation when first accessed by the owner of the site. SharePoint Server includes a workflow for decommissioning the site when the user is deactivated in Active Directory. By automating site-collection creation and removal, the My Site model both enables users and conserves resources.

Enabling client integration

Forms-based authentication can be useful, as described in the "Types of authentication" section earlier in this chapter. However, it doesn't work well in some situations, such as SharePoint integration with older versions of Office. If your site uses forms-based authentication and the visitors to your site encounter problems with older versions of Office, you can ask to have this setting disabled at the web-application level. Disabling client integration can prevent errors that otherwise are confusing. However, some features, such as the Edit-In-Datasheet option for lists in the browser will also be disabled for all users when client integration is disabled.

Encryption

You're probably familiar with encryption for purposes such as securing online banking accounts. Banks add this layer of security because without it, all information passed over the Internet is sent in clear text that can be captured and read by anyone between you and your bank. If your SharePoint site contains information that is sensitive, you will want encryption configured for your web application. Ask your IT staff to purchase and install a Secure Sockets Layer (SSL) certificate on the web servers and configure your web application for encryption. You will know when you are accessing an encrypted site when the web address begins with https:// instead of the normal https:// prefix.

Another situation for which encryption is important is when your site's authentication doesn't encrypt user names and passwords. For example, forms-based authentication should always be used in combination with encryption to ensure the security of your SharePoint sites. You are using forms-based authentication when you type your user name and password directly into a webpage rather than a Windows Security dialog box.

> **Note**
>
> In some cases, for example with Windows integrated authentication, user names and passwords are sent securely without SSL encryption. However, it is still a good practice to encrypt your site if other personal or sensitive information might be sent to or from your website besides user names and passwords.

Upgrades and migration

If you've been managing a website previously and would like to move it to a SharePoint Server 2013 environment, you have two choices for bringing over the content: upgrade and migration. Upgrade and migration are often confused because they both cover moving content into SharePoint; however, there are distinct differences between the two. Understanding the choices available to you will help make the decision easier when you do choose to plan and execute a move.

For more details, view the TechNet article, "Overview of the upgrade process to SharePoint 2013." Though TechNet is tailored to administrators and IT professionals, this article answers questions for advanced business users whose organizations are upgrading to SharePoint 2013. You can view the article at *technet.microsoft.com/en-us/library/cc262483(v=office.15)*.

Upgrading from SharePoint 2010

Microsoft supports upgrades from SharePoint 2010 to SharePoint 2013.

Content database upgrade

If you've read the section "The SharePoint structure" earlier in this chapter, you've seen one explanation of the connection between the content database and SharePoint sites.

All the information you see when you use your SharePoint site is held in a content database as follows:

- Each content database can hold more than one collection of sites.

- Each site collection is stored in one, and only one, content database.

The one upgrade approach in SharePoint 2013 is called a *content database upgrade* because each content database can be upgraded individually.

When IT executes an upgrade from SharePoint 2010, you can choose not to upgrade every content database in a farm at the same time. If you have more than one content database, this offers some flexibility for a phased upgrade.

For example, you might choose to move the database containing your most important sites first. Alternatively, you might choose a less important database as a first upgrade to refine your process and become more familiar with the steps involved.

A benefit of the content database upgrade approach is the option to leave the existing content available for viewing only while the upgrade is being performed. Because the content database can be copied to the new server, the original copy is still available for read-only use while the new copy is being converted to the SharePoint 2013 format. This is especially helpful for large content databases that require a long time to upgrade.

This approach requires that the customizations applied to your SharePoint 2013 installation are well documented and ready to move to the new environment. It also requires a strong understanding of the configuration settings on the farm and web-application level. In many organizations, this might not be a problem because configuration and customization documentation are also both required for disaster recovery.

The content database upgrade occurs on a new SharePoint 2013 farm. This means that additional hardware is required besides the hardware currently running your SharePoint 2010 farm. Besides being a requirement, it is also a benefit to have two environments available because the upgrade can be tested and repeated on the new hardware before committing to the final move from the old hardware.

Deferred Site Collection Upgrade

Deferred Site Collection Upgrade is a new feature of the SharePoint 2013 products that can keep your upgraded site looking a lot like your old site.

When a content database is upgraded to 2013, site collections can be left running in SharePoint 2010 mode on the new SharePoint 2013 farm. The reason for this mode in your new upgrade is to allow time to update your old sites to the new features of SharePoint 2013.

SharePoint 2013 makes some important and wide-ranging changes to the pages on a site. It may take some work to transition from your old site. You can test your upgraded sites in SharePoint 2013 with a copy of the site collection before making the permanent move to SharePoint 2013 mode.

INSIDE OUT   **Deferred Site Collection Upgrade allows new upgrade flexibility**

Don't discount the amount of flexibility this new upgrade feature allows in your upgrade planning. One of the benefits of this approach is that you can now plan to upgrade all your content databases in a farm from SharePoint 2010 to SharePoint 2013 with less risk. Highly customized SharePoint 2010 sites can remain in SharePoint 2010 mode while not blocking the upgrade of other sites.

Migrating content to SharePoint Server 2013

If you have content on websites that are not running SharePoint 2010, you have two options for moving that content to SharePoint Server 2013. You can migrate the content manually to a SharePoint 2013 farm or you can do it with a third-party tool.

Note

For the purposes of this chapter, an upgrade is moving from SharePoint 2010 to SharePoint 2013. Any other move is considered a migration. In either case, customizations, including installed third-party add-ons and branding, must be considered separately from the content. The migration steps that follow discuss moving content.

You can find more help for branding and enhancing SharePoint in Chapter 12, "Designing web content management sites," which covers branding with respect to master pages and CSS. Refer to Chapter 20, "Creating, managing, and designing sites," and Chapter 23 for more information on authoring customizations.

Manual migration

For sites that have a small amount of content, manual migration can be a good option. You might choose to replicate the previous sites as closely as possible through the creation of lists and libraries first and the addition of content second. Alternatively, you can take the chance to redesign the information architecture of your site. If you take the time to review the site to be upgraded, you might find that you only need to move over a small amount of information that is still relevant and useful to you and your users now.

Manual migration is often a team effort. You might want to involve site designers to work on a new look that matches or builds on the previous look. You want to plan for some testing, even if it's just to get a second set of eyes on the work you do yourself. Breaking up the repetitive parts, like copying and pasting documents or text from old to new, can help make this go faster.

INSIDE OUT Manual migration might sound hard, but it can be a great option

It could be easy to dismiss manual migration as an unacceptable option for moving your content. After all, it can be hard enough to motivate yourself to do repetitive manual work for any period of time—motivating a team can be harder still.

If your team is excited about the new capabilities of the platform, as many are, this one-time division of labor can pay off with big dividends. Often, the time saved in the future with modern tools provided by SharePoint 2013 can be a great reward when you've become frustrated with the technology that you've been using for a long time to update your old site. Keep in mind that even with automated migration tools, you will want to do extensive testing to ensure that your content has moved over correctly. When you move over content manually, you can be confident that everything you've moved over went to the right place.

Migration tools

Many migration tools are specifically built to move content into new SharePoint 2013 sites. The basic premise of migration is no different than that of the manual migration. You can still choose to try to replicate the site that you are migrating from or you can take the opportunity to reassess your site and build into a new design that fits SharePoint 2013 better.

The big difference is that migration tools help do some of the repetitive, manual work that is involved in migrating to SharePoint. In fact, you might find yourself appreciating one of these tools so much that you keep it around to help you reorganize your content in SharePoint long after the initial migration is complete.

There are two kinds of third-party migration tools available. The simplest kind treats the source website as a collection of HTML webpages. Using this kind of tool, you move each page over, one by one, into a document library in SharePoint. That method really works only if all you have is content in pages, as opposed to items in lists or documents in libraries.

On the other hand, many of the third-party tools have specific features that target particular sources of information from which to migrate. You can find tools that help you pull data from older versions of SharePoint, competing products like Lotus Notes, and other technologies used to share information like Networked File Shares and Exchange Public Folders.

Each tool available works a little differently, so it's best to go to the vendor for information on how to use the tool you choose. They are all happy to provide product demonstrations, and many provide trial versions of their products so that you can test them out on your actual content.

The websites *www.EndUserSharePoint.com* and *www.SharePointReviews.com* both have great collections of information on third-party migration tools. Look in both the "Migration" and "Content Organization" categories.

Summary

A successful SharePoint environment is the result of a close interaction between the site users, site owners, and supporting technical staff. This chapter introduced you to some of the concepts that you need to understand before considering some more advanced business uses of SharePoint.

The SharePoint list items that you add and the documents that you upload all reside in a SharePoint site. Every SharePoint site is part of a site collection, which is a hierarchy that starts with one top-level site at the root of a tree, and sites which can grow from it. Site collections are accessed through web applications and contained in content databases. Web applications and content databases run on the servers that make up the SharePoint farm that hosts it all. Service applications provide supporting resources to the farm.

Your day-to-day work is done on the site and at the site-collection level. Understanding the full structure can inform your design decisions when you would like to improve your SharePoint installation.

Search is a very powerful tool provided by SharePoint technologies. With the incorporation of technology from the FAST Search Engine into the main SharePoint 2013 product line, SharePoint is now the top-of-the-line enterprise search product from Microsoft.

Regardless of the search product that you choose, it is important to pay attention to how well your searches perform and follow up on issues such as stale results.

It's also important that SharePoint identify your site's users and you understand the options for securing your site content. SharePoint 2013 includes a few authentication changes for your web applications. Choosing authentication methods for your web applications requires identifying who your users are and what level of access they need. The authentication methods you may choose from include classic Windows integrated, claims-based with Windows or without, and anonymous authentication. Authorizing the users to perform actions in SharePoint is mostly controlled in the site collection. However, user policies can affect permissions across many site collections and are not visible outside the web-application settings. Working closely with IT, you can ensure a secure experience for the visitors to your site and the content you host in SharePoint.

You probably have been using some tool to share files and other information with others before moving to SharePoint 2013. Any sites that you have running in SharePoint 2010 can be upgraded by copying the content databases to SharePoint 2013. If you'd like to migrate data from other sources, you might choose to move the most important pieces over yourself manually. If you have a lot of data, you might consider purchasing a third-party tool to help you move into SharePoint 2013.

This chapter has been an introduction to administration settings made beyond the site collection. In the chapters that follow, you will find other ways with which you will interact with SharePoint Administration outside site settings available to an advanced business user. For example, you will find information on importing BDC models in Chapter 22, "Working with external content." Chapter 12 and Chapter 23 both cover creating solutions for SharePoint that can be added to the farm by an administrator. Chapter 20 focuses on SharePoint Designer and covers some settings exposed only to technical staff.

U SING the list and libraries functionality in Microsoft SharePoint determines how you leverage or don't leverage the true power of SharePoint. Whether that means you are using SharePoint as a glorified file-sharing tool or a true collaborative platform, lists and libraries play a key role.

Lists and libraries are at the core of SharePoint functionality in a collaborative environment. You can leverage SharePoint to house, organize, and track files. For example, a law firm could have thousands of Microsoft Word documents and a need to track any aspect of an ongoing or a past case. With SharePoint, there are several options on how to organize the information. There is not a single right way or wrong way. The best option is to use a workflow routine that matches your existing work process. It is better to let SharePoint augment the real-world business process rather than trying to mold your work around it. Using a combination of document libraries and lists allows us to organize and track the life cycle of documents in our law firm. Lists such as issue tracking can follow a case, like an issue, from the start to the end of a case. A Contact list app can store the associated law firm employee and clients in a single convenient location. The calendar list app can coordinate important dates for everyone to note. A customized document library can store all of the case's documents organized into document sets.

In our law firm example, we're able to use three individual predefined lists and one document library—all without having to open any custom-developed tools for any of the libraries and lists used. They are out-of-the-box solutions directly from SharePoint.

This chapter takes a look at the various list and library apps that are available in SharePoint 2013. This includes the most basic lists and libraries that require little to no customizations, as well as the more complex, custom-created lists and libraries. Once the lists and libraries are created, you'll then take a look at how to modify specific settings, helping you to create the perfect list to suit your needs. Additionally, we take a close look at permissions and the pivotal role they play in lists and libraries. Next, we look into how views can be tailored to help navigate and leverage lists and libraries. After that, we explore how to manipulate list and library item data to create calculated columns and validations. Finally, the most common problems and limitations are detailed and addressed with workarounds.

What's new with list and library apps

In this section, we examine some of the key components that are new to SharePoint 2013. We take a look at SharePoint's new drag-and-drop functionality, preview capabilities, and ellipsis feature. If you are migrating from a SharePoint 2010 environment, then this chapter covers many general topics that may already be familiar to you.

We also take a deeper look into each aspect of SharePoint 2013 list and library concepts. If you are migrating from SharePoint 2007, then this chapter is geared to help you with a thorough and deep understanding of all the possibilities when working with SharePoint 2013 list and libraries.

Drag-and-drop functionality

A fantastic feature added to SharePoint 2013 is the drag-and-drop functionality in libraries. This simply allows a SharePoint user to select a file on a local computer and visually drop the file into a SharePoint library—all without having to open Windows Explorer View, as was necessary in SharePoint 2010. As you might expect, there are some browsers that will not be supported. Most commonly used modern browsers that support HTML5 will support SharePoint 2013. Table 3-1 lists the browsers that SharePoint 2013 supports.

TABLE 3-1 SharePoint 2013–supported browsers

Browser	Supported	Not supported
Internet Explorer 10	X	
Internet Explorer 9	X	
Internet Explorer 8	X	
Internet Explorer 7		X
Internet Explorer 6		X
Google Chrome (latest released version)	X	
Mozilla Firefox (latest released version)	X	
Apple Safari (latest released version)	X	

For more information about browser support in SharePoint 2013, go to *http://technet .microsoft.com/en-us/library/cc263526.aspx.*

> **Note**
>
> While not all current or future browsers are listed, most are supported to some degree if they can leverage HTML5 functionality.

In SharePoint 2010, the easiest way to transfer documents from one library to another involved using two Explorer Views and dragging and dropping. While this process works, it is incredibly inefficient and slow. The files must literally first be transferred to the user's workstation from the server, then moved back the server and onto the final destination library.

You can now select single or multiple files and drag them into a folder, or document set, located in the same library, all within the browser. You no longer have to open up separate Explorer Views; the move is handled at the server level. Additionally, you can drop a single document, or several documents, right from the library into another library by simply selecting files and dragging them over the target document library on the Quick Launch bar.

There are some limitations, however. The primary limitation is that you cannot drag files directly into folders on a second level or lower. You will need to drag and drop the file into the first-level folder and repeat the same action with the next-level folder until you have reached the folder you are targeting as the destination. You cannot drag and drop between site collections. This is true even if the same account is granted rights to the separate site collections. You cannot move individual videos or list items in any fashion. Finally, you cannot move entire folders or document sets from one location to another location.

Live preview thumbnails

Live preview thumbnails is an idea that was born when FAST search was integrated with SharePoint 2010 and brought the ability to quickly get thumbnail document previews. While it was never intended to be a complete viewing experience, it did provide a peek into the document that let users identify documents beyond file names. You could even turn pages in a Word document. In SharePoint 2013, the live preview thumbnails functionally moved into the Office Web Apps 2013 program. Once Office Web Apps Server 2013 is connected to the SharePoint 2013 farm, this functionality is automatically available in SharePoint, as shown in Figure 3-1.

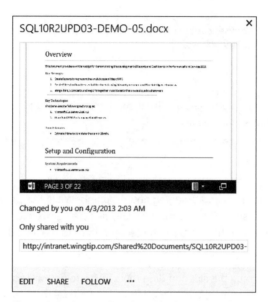

Figure 3-1 Live preview thumbnails are available in SharePoint once Office Web Apps Server 2013 is connected to the SharePoint 2013 farm.

Note

Without Office Web Apps 2013, you will still get relevant contextual information but be missing the live thumbnail preview.

INSIDE OUT   The missing thumbnail preview

Office Web Apps (OWA) 2013 is an add-on server product to SharePoint 2013 that has taken radical steps in its maturity and capabilities. Using OWA, a user can preview, open, and edit Microsoft Word, Excel, PowerPoint, and OneNote files. Among the new features in OWA 2013 are:

- Revision tracking

- Comments

- Coauthoring

- Embedding

- Ink-support

- Quick preview

- Share by link

OWA 2013 has even moved beyond the confines of SharePoint and now offers the same services to Microsoft Lync 2013, Exchange 2013, and standard files shares. Since the actual installation and full configuration of this great product now relies on a separate product, it is therefore beyond the scope of this book. However, we did want to help out with some troubleshooting techniques you can use.

Your first clue that OWA 2013 is either missing or broken will be when your thumbnail preview either disappears or displays the now-standard error message, "Sorry, something went wrong."

> **Note**
>
> You will need direct administrative-level access to run the following steps from the SharePoint web front end.

Your first step will be to verify that the SharePoint web front end can reach the OWA 2013 server. On the SharePoint web front end, start Internet Explorer and navigate to the OWA 2013 discovery URL. This URL will be the fully qualified domain name (FQDN) of the OWA 2013 server followed by '/hosting/discovery': *http://FQDN/hosting/ discovery.*

If you receive a response displaying an XML-formatted page, then you can assume that at the very minimum, the OWA 2013 server is installed and running as expected.

As a second step, you can ask your SharePoint administrator to verify that your SharePoint web application is using claims authentication. If you wish, you can verify this yourself by using the following Windows PowerShell command on the SharePoint web front end. The following Windows PowerShell command URL will be the full URL of the top-level SharePoint site:

```
Get-SPWebApplication | Select URL, UseClaimsAuthentication
```

If the command returns the UseClaimsAuthentication value as TRUE, then your SharePoint web application is using claims authentication. If a FALSE value is returned, the web application must be converted from classic, or NTML, authentication into claims-based authentication. Check with your SharePoint administrator, as this can have some unintended consequences.

Finally, you can verify how SharePoint is trying to communicate with OWA 2013. Run the following Windows PowerShell commands on the SharePoint web front end:

```
Get-SPWopiZone
```

```
Get-SPWopiBinding
```

If the returned results from Get-SPWopiZone and the WopiZone results from Get-SPWopiBinding are not identical, alert your SharePoint administrator that SharePoint is not forwarding OWA service requests to the correct server.

While these are some of the basic troubleshooting steps you can take, you should still make sure that you are communicating with your SharePoint administrator before making any changes to your farm.

The ellipsis

An easily overlooked and fantastic feature is the new ellipsis functionality that has been implemented into lists and libraries.

> **Note**
>
> The ellipsis is officially termed the Edit Control Block (ECB) and now plays an important role in how we use the contextual menu in SharePoint 2013.

As you can see in Figure 3-2, when the ellipsis is selected in File View, you receive the three most common commands used when dealing with files in a document library:

- **Edit** Selecting this option allows you to open the file in the locally associated program or if you have implemented Office Web Apps 2013, open and view them in the browser.

- **Share** This option lets you add sharing permissions to additional users. You can set the level of access whether read-only or edit levels.

- **Follow** The Follow selection sets the new social My Site features in action by following the file in your Newsfeed.

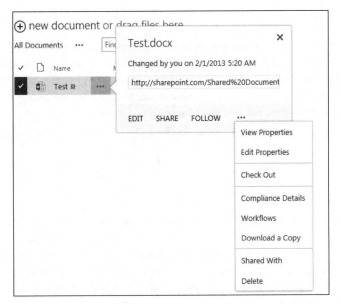

Figure 3-2 When the ellipsis is selected in File View, you may choose from three additional options: Edit, Share, and Follow.

The second set of ellipses contains actions that are less commonly used, but still important to have easily available. The available actions are:

- **View Properties** This opens a read-only display of that file's properties.

- **Edit Properties** This opens an editable properties page for that file.

- **Check Out** This allows you to check out a document by protecting it while it is being edited.

- **Compliance Details** This displays any specific information if compliance has been set for this site or library.

- **Workflows** This shows any associated workflow with that specific file.

- **Download A Copy** This allows you to download a copy of the file to your local system.

- **Shared With** This displays a report of who has access to this specific file.

- **Delete** This deletes the file either permanently or into the site recycle bin, depending on how the site collection is configured.

> **Note**
>
> It is important to keep in mind that all of these commands and more can be easily accessed from the ribbon controls. The ellipsis adds an extra layer of convenience not found in previous versions of SharePoint, and the commands found in the ellipsis are relevant to the list or library purpose. As an example, a task list will display the same ellipsis but contain different first-level common commands.

Creating lists

To start creating a list in SharePoint, make sure that you are at a SharePoint location where you will want the list to reside. As noted in Chapter 1, "Introducing SharePoint 2013," the apps model is a concept that encompasses simple lists to the more complex apps with cloud-driven functionality. If you are in the SharePoint 2013 standard team template, then you will see a central picture icon specifically stating, "Add lists, libraries, and other apps." If you are using another site template design, then you can select the settings cog in the upper-right corner and choose "add an app." Once there, you will see the apps page, as shown in Figure 3-3.

Figure 3-3 This is the default view when adding a new app.

If SharePoint Server 2013 is fully enabled, then there will be 12 built-in apps. These predefined apps are listed in Table 3-2.

TABLE 3-2 Apps available in SharePoint Server 2013

List app type	Description
Custom list	A list that lets you add customizations to suit your needs. If you find that a predefined app does not meet your needs, then building a custom list with your specific goals might be a better approach.
Tasks	A list specifically designed to store and track individual tasks using a classic to-do style.
Links	A list specifically designed to show a set of URL links which might be handy for site users.
Announcements	This list is your common company announcement board showing news and short bits of information with greater functionality, like expiring content controls.
Contacts	The Contacts list holds and displays all the common items you can find in a Rolodex. You can choose to store employees, partners, customers, or all of the above.
Calendar	As you might expect, this is a list of calendar items commonly used to track appointments and events.
Discussion board	The discussion board is the new modernized version of bulletin boards. It allows detailed electronic conversations that might be relevant to your users. Subjects can vary as needed, and discussion boards have email capability.
Survey	This survey list can be as simple as a yes or no response or offer more complex multiquestion formats. The feedback is stored and can be compiled for use at a later time.
External list	The external list is an app designed to leverage information from external resources. The external resources can vary from Business Connectivity Service (BCS), SQL databases, or custom web services. Once the information is pulled and stored into this list, it will be available to other parts of SharePoint to allow even greater capabilities.
Promoted links	These are external links that are designed to draw attention to a specific URL resource. Much like a URL list, this takes it even further by using tiles and customized animated launch controls.
Issue tracking	This list tracks and stores issues that are parts of a project or item. Expanding on the task list concept, this allows for assignments, prioritization, and status.
Custom list in datasheet view	A list that lets you add customizations to suit your needs. Building the list app follows the same steps as using a standard custom list. The difference lies in how the information is displayed. By using a datasheet view, much like an Excel or Microsoft Access table, you can quickly display and edit information.

Chapter 3

> **Note**
>
> Do not implement any version of the once-popular Fab 40 templates. SharePoint 2013 does not provide the necessary mechanism for the Fab 40 templates to work properly and will cause unintended results.

Each list carries a set type of characteristics that differentiate each in function and form. Most of these characteristics can be changed or removed, but some of those characteristics cannot be altered. As an example, the last name, modified, created, created by, and modified by columns in a basic, predefined contacts list cannot be deleted. The remaining characteristics may be altered to suit your needs. This gives you a good start whether you decided to leverage a built-in app or build from the group up by using a custom list.

Creating a new list from the predefined lists

Follow these steps to create a new list from the predefined lists:

1. Click the Settings sprocket in the upper-right side. From the drop-down menu, select Add An App.

    You can scroll through the available options that extend to a second page. Additionally, you can filter available apps from the built-in search on the apps page.

2. Select the app you wish to create, such as the Tasks or Contacts List app.

3. After selecting the desired app, you will be asked to fill in the name of the app. Click Advanced Options if you desire additional options while creating the app.

    The options will all be available for use after the list is created.

4. Click Create once you have entered the desired initial settings.

Once the list is created, the view will switch to a Site Contents page that lists your new and existing apps. It will not automatically enter into the list the app that you have just created.

Note that your new app will have the new! icon, and it will also be added to your recent Quick Launch toolbar if you are using the standard team site template. You can see an example of this in the following graphic.

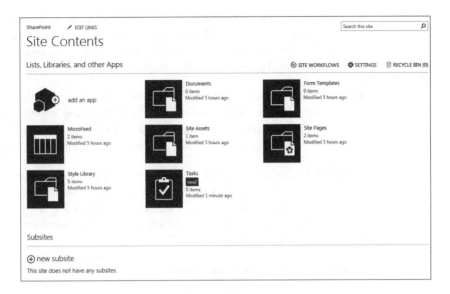

5. Select the new app to go in to the newly created list.

6. Now that the list is created, you have to further modify the data and settings to satisfy your needs. Examples of how to do this are presented in the "Modifying list and library settings" section later in this chapter.

Creating a custom list

If you need a list with design and requirements that are not met by the predefined list apps, you have the option of creating a new custom list. The process to create a custom list is much the same as for creating a predefined list app. If you choose to create a custom list, then your options are narrowed down to the following:

- **Custom list** This is a list that lets you add customizations to suit your needs. If you find that a predefined app does not meet your needs, building a custom list with your specific goals might be a better approach.

- **Custom list in datasheet view** This is a list that lets you add customizations to suit your needs. Building the list app follows the same steps as using a standard custom list. The difference lies in how the information is displayed. By using a datasheet view, much like an Excel or Access table, you can quickly display and edit information.

- **Import spreadsheet** This list is built from an Excel sheet page. As part of the import process, SharePoint will try and format the list to closely resemble the source Excel sheet. It is important to keep in mind that any customizations in Excel, such as calculations, formatting, or macros, will not carry over into the new SharePoint list.

An example of a common request is a custom list to track product inventory. There are several ways to fulfill this request in SharePoint. The easiest way to accomplish this task is to build a custom list. In most cases, we recommend using a predefined existing list, but one may not exist to suit your needs. In such cases, we can leverage the unique power and flexibility of SharePoint.

To create a custom list, follow these steps:

1. Click the Settings sprocket in the upper-right side. From the drop-down menu, select Add An App.

2. Select the Custom List app.

3. Enter an appropriate name that would make its purpose easily recognizable.

4. From the Site Contents page, select the new created Sales Inventory app.

5. Select the List ribbon section and then select the List Settings option.

   You will note that the custom list is already populated with mandatory columns that cannot be deleted.

6. Add a "Price" column by selecting Create Column and adding it as a Currency type. Add any additional settings for this column as shown in the next graphic.

7. Click OK when the price column options are complete.

Name and Type

Type a name for this column, and select the type of information you want to store in the column.

Column name:

Price

The type of information in this column is:

- ○ Single line of text
- ○ Multiple lines of text
- ○ Choice (menu to choose from)
- ○ Number (1, 1.0, 100)
- ◉ Currency ($, ¥, €)
- ○ Date and Time
- ○ Lookup (information already on this site)
- ○ Yes/No (check box)
- ○ Person or Group
- ○ Hyperlink or Picture
- ○ Calculated (calculation based on other columns)
- ○ Task Outcome
- ○ External Data
- ○ Managed Metadata

Additional Column Settings

Specify detailed options for the type of information you selected.

Description:

Require that this column contains information:

○ Yes   ◉ No

Enforce unique values:

○ Yes   ◉ No

You can specify a minimum and maximum allowed value:

Min: [＿＿＿]   Max: [＿＿＿]

Number of decimal places:

Automatic ▾

---

8. Add a Description column by clicking Create Column and naming it Description. Choose Multiple Lines Of Text as the column type and any other options as deemed appropriate.

9. Click OK when complete.

10. Click the Sales Inventory crumb trail.

As you can see in Figure 3-4, we now have a complete and functional Sales Inventory SharePoint app list.

Figure 3-4 The newly created custom list app with sample data.

Creating libraries and site columns

Often, one of the first apps used within SharePoint is the library. In SharePoint Server 2013, there are many kinds of library apps geared to meet specific needs, as listed in Table 3-3.

TABLE 3-3 Library apps available in SharePoint Server 2013

List app type	Description
Document library	Much like traditional file sharing, document libraries store and organize documents for sharing among other SharePoint users. The document library can specifically contain certain file types, allow the management of permissions, and leverage metadata.
Form library	Like a standard document library, a form library is specifically designed to house and leverage Microsoft InfoPath forms. Making this the central repository of InfoPath forms allows you to easily track and organize these forms as your site grows.
Wiki page library	Leveraging the concept of wikis is an important part of building SharePoint site pages. The wiki page library houses and organizes these wiki pages, which are created and customized by other SharePoint users.
Picture library	The picture library is designed to store and organize image files. The library has built-in controls for storing, organizing, and manipulating image files, making it an ideal place for pictures.
Data connection library	A data connection library stores Office Data Connection (ODC) files or Universal Data Connection (UDC) files. This library works hand in hand with InfoPath, forming a connectivity conduit to external resources.

List app type	Description
Report library	Generating reports is critical part of displaying business data. A report library is used to create and manage SharePoint reports. These reports will typically work hand in hand with the data connection library.
Asset library	The asset library is used to manage SharePoint media assets, such as image, audio, and video files. The intent behind an asset library is to create a central library of commonly used media. An example would be a company logo. To help facilitate this functionality, the asset library has specific controls that it uses for the media files and metadata capability.

Libraries are the core of SharePoint collaboration functionality. Unlike list apps, libraries allow you to store a wide variety of file types that might include standard documents like a Word document or various picture files.

Creating a library

When using the standard team site template, a default documents library is already configured. However, you can also create a new document library to service a specific purpose.

> **Note**
>
> It is important to remember that just like lists, libraries are considered apps within the SharePoint 2013 model. They serve very specific needs but are grouped together with other apps to minimize confusion.

To create a new document library, follow these steps:

1. From the SharePoint 2013 default team site home page, select Add Lists, Libraries, And Other Apps.

   If the default page has been modified or you are using another template, you can select the Settings sprocket on the upper-right side and click Add An App.

2. From here, the standard Document Library will normally be the first app available for consumption.

   If you don't see the Document Library app you desire, you can easily enter the library type into the Your Apps search bar.

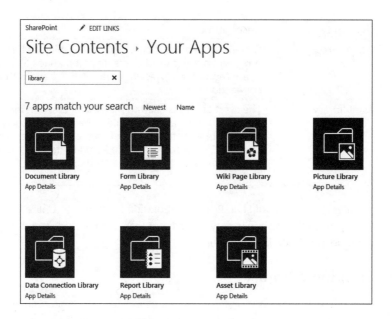

3. Select the desired library to best suit your needs. For our example, we will create a document library.

4. After selecting the Document Library app template, you are offered the chance to name the new library. We are interested in setting some additional initial settings for our library, so click Advanced Options.

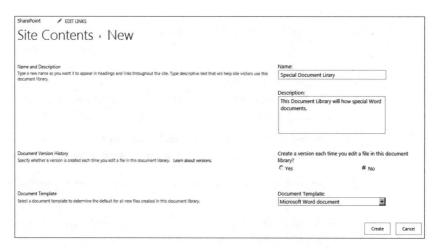

5. Now you have to opportunity to specify the name, description, versioning, and specific documents for this particular library. Once completed, click Create.

Unlike the previous list app example, this one is immediately placed into the newly created document library. From here, you can take further steps to modify, create, or delete the document library as needed for our purposes.

Creating a site column

As SharePoint has continued to evolve, site columns and their use have grown in importance and capability. While it is certainly possible to use SharePoint without leveraging site columns, using them brings SharePoint to a new level. At a site-collection level, site columns can be used to define information for sorting and filtering. They can also be leveraged to work with workflows.

To create a new site column, follow these steps:

1. Select the Settings sprocket on the upper-right side and click Site Settings.

2. Select Site Columns under the Web Designer Galleries.

3. Click the Create link at the top of the page.

4. Enter a name and select a column type.

    You can also add or create a new group for this new site column.

> **Note**
> As you select different column types, note that the additional column settings change to suit your needs. At the very minimum, you will need to enter a name, description, whether the column requires information, and whether the column must enforce unique values.

5. Click OK to create the new site column.

If you find that you need to modify an existing custom or default site column, follow these steps:

1. Select the Settings sprocket on the upper-right side and click Site Settings.

2. Select Site Columns under the Web Designer Galleries.

3. Select the site column that you wish to modify.

Take extra care when modifying system default site columns. In most cases, you will want to manually duplicate existing site columns and modify that to suit your needs.

Modifying list and library settings

Part of the power of SharePoint is to take what is already there and reuse it, saving time and effort. While we could create a brand new list or library every time we needed one, this would be reinventing the wheel over and over. If an existing list or library can be leveraged with just some minor changes, a lot of time and administration can be saved. Additionally, as functional requirements change over time, so do the settings for that resource. Here, we will take a look at how easy it is to make changes to list and library settings.

Modifying general settings

SharePoint Server 2013 has numerous options available in the General Settings section of the Settings page.

> **Note**
> When creating a new list or library, try to pilot each of these features ahead of time. Otherwise, changing an existing table after data is in use can cause a terrible migration headache. The general settings are specific in that they are options that are set when you first create the list. They are not intended to be changed at a later date.

Changing basic characteristics of a list, including the list name, description, and navigation, can be accomplished by clicking the List Name, Description, And Navigation link. This will display the General Settings page, as shown in Figure 3-5, where the following general settings may be changed:

- **Name** Enter a name that will quickly and accurately describe the list or library.

- **Description** This field allows a more detailed explanation of the purpose of the list or library.

- **Navigation** Selecting Yes allows this list or library to be displayed on the Quick Launch toolbar.

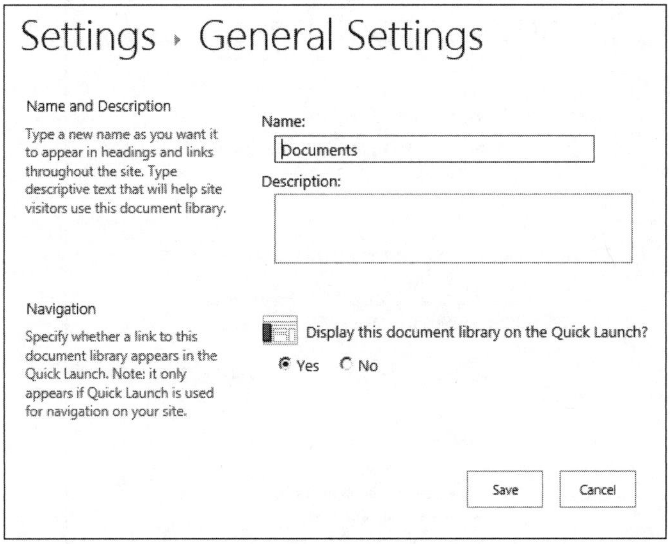

Figure 3-5 The general settings for a list app are changed here.

Modifying versioning settings

Enabling versioning settings will let you control every aspect of the powerful versioning tool set offered by SharePoint. While the concept will remain the same across a list or library, each brings different configurations to the table.

More information about document versioning can be found in Chapter 11, "Managing documents."

Modifying versioning settings for a list

Versioning settings for a list offer a restricted number of configuration options. This is due to the nature of lists and how they operate. To open the version settings in the list, first open the target list, select LIST from the ribbon menu, select List Settings, and finally select Version Settings. This will open the Versioning Settings page for that particular list, as shown in Figure 3-6.

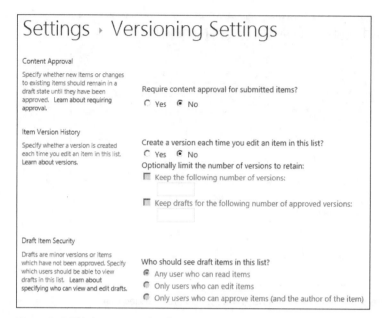

Figure 3-6 This is an example of version settings for a list app.

Once the Versioning Settings page is open, you can make any changes you deem necessary.

- **Content Approval** Selecting Yes will require approval of submitted items. Conversely, selecting No indicates that approval is not needed.

- **Item Version History** The default selection for this option is No. This indicates you will not be leveraging the versioning capacities for this list. Selecting Yes activates the versioning feature set for this list. When Yes is selected, you then have the ability to limit the number of versions that are kept. This is an important consideration due to sizing restrictions. While a reasonable limit of 5 may keep the space under control; an unlimited versioning history can quickly grow if the item is in constant flux. Each change saves a version. The option to limit the drafts for approved versions is available. Use these versioning options as appropriate to business requirements.

- **Draft Item Security** If content approval or versioning is enabled, a draft item is created by default for all new items and revisions of items. By default, all users have the ability to read these drafts via the option that allows any user to read items. This can be altered as needed to either only users who can edit items, or only users who can approve items (and the author of the item).

Modifying versioning settings for a library

If you are leveraging a library's versioning settings, you will be presented with a different set of options specifically geared for library functionality. To open a library's version settings, open the library, select LIBRARY on the ribbon control, select Library Settings, and finally select Versioning Settings under General Settings. The Versioning Settings window appears, as shown in Figure 3-7.

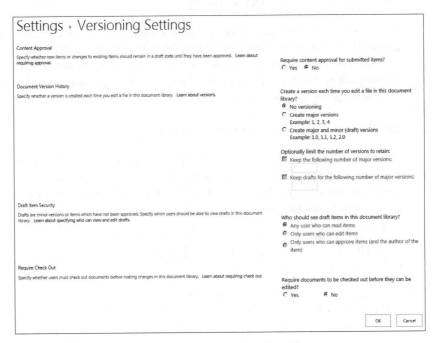

Figure 3-7 This is an example of the version setting for a library app.

With the Versioning Settings page open, you can make your desired changes:

- **Content Approval** Similar to the list version functionality, selecting Yes enables library items to use content approval functionality.

- **Document Version History** By default, the versioning is not enabled by evidence of the No Versioning option. Selecting Create Major Versions enables versioning but only tracking of large file changes, and also enables the ability to limit the number of major history versions. Selecting Create Major And Minor (Draft) Versions gives users the ability to store versions of documents. Typically, major document revisions should be indicated as major revisions and minor document editing should be noted as minor versions. Enabling this final option additionally gives users the ability to control the drafts stored without approval.

- **Draft Item Security** By default, any user who is able to read the library also has the ability to view draft items. This can be limited to edit level, designated approvers, and item authors.

- **Require Check Out** Enabling this option forces the user to check out a document before any other changes can be made.

Modifying advanced settings

As we take a closer look at all of the available settings for a SharePoint list or library, you can see that there will be even more settings that may not be easily categorized. While these settings may not be easily accessed or are too few in number to have a dedicated setting page of their own, this does not diminish their importance. We will take a look what these settings are and what impact they have.

Modifying advanced settings for a list

The Advanced Settings page for a list contains options that are not frequently accessed. To access the list of advanced settings, open the target list, select the LIST link on the ribbon control, select List Settings, and select Advanced Settings under the General Settings section. The Advanced Settings window will appear, as shown in Figure 3-8.

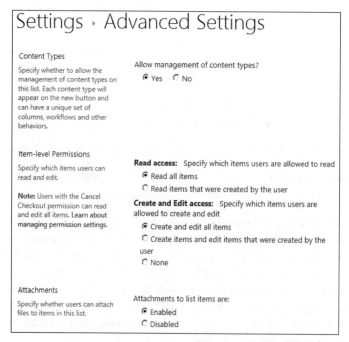

Figure 3-8 The Advanced Settings window lists the advanced settings for a list app.

With the Advanced Settings page open, you can make your desired changes:

- **Content Types** If you are leveraging the functions available to content types, then you will need to select yes. By default, management of content types is not enabled.

- **Item-Level Permissions** Specifying permission on final item-level objects can grant another level of control. The Item-Level Permissions are first broken by the read access. By default, all users of the list can read all items. You also can limit that so users can only read items that were created by them. The second Item-Level Permissions option Create And Edit Access allows administrators to again set specific permissions. All users can create and edit all items, only create and then edit items that were created by those users, and finally, users can have no permissions to create and edit list items.

- **Attachments** This option gives the list the ability to store attachments to individual items. By selecting Enabled, an attachment can be added to an item. Selecting Disabled does not allow attachments in this list.

- **Search** By default, all lists are returned in search results if that particular user has the appropriate access. If the Search setting is No, then the list will never be indexed by the search engine.

- **Reindex List** Reindexing a list gives the administrator the ability to reindex the entire list during the next search crawl.

- **Offline Client Availability** SharePoint has the ability to synchronize list data from the server to be stored locally by clients.

- **Quick Edit** The Quick Edit feature is used in specific circumstances where the list must be quickly updated in an inline fashion.

- **Dialogs** If forms are leveraged to help list functionality, you will need to enable dialog functionality. Selecting No opens full webpages as opposed to specific forms.

Modifying advanced settings for a library

Changing the advanced settings for a library is similar to changing the advanced settings for a list. In the target library, select the library control on the ribbon, select Library Settings, and select Advanced Settings under the General Settings column, as shown in Figure 3-9.

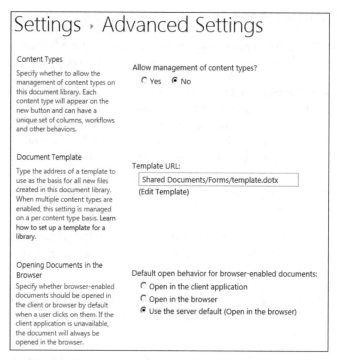

Figure 3-9 The advanced settings for a document library may be changed here.

With the document library's Advanced Settings page open, there are several changes that can be applied, including:

- **Content Types** If you want to add additional content types beyond the default library content types, you will need to select yes. By default, management of content types is not enabled.

- **Document Template** By default, the default document template will be a standard Word template. You may alter that to meet your needs for a file library.

- **Opening Documents In The Browser** You can override server settings and specify whether the library will open documents in the browser or the client application.

- **Custom Send To Destination** This allows you to specify a custom send to a destination that is associated with this particular library.

- **Folders** Selecting Yes allows a user to create a folder within the library. Conversely, selecting No does not present that option to the user.

- **Search** By default, all library items are returned in search results only if that particular user has the appropriate access. If the Search setting is No, then the library results will never be delivered as part of search results, regardless of permissions.

- **Reindex Document Library** Reindexing a document library gives the administrator the ability to force the reindexing of all items in the library at the next crawl.

- **Offline Client Availability** Selecting Yes allows this library to be down as part of an offline mechanism. This can be disabled by selecting No.

- **Quick Edit** The Quick Edit feature is used in specific circumstances where the document library must be quickly updated in an inline fashion.

- **Dialog** If forms are leveraged to help document library functionality, you will need to enable dialog functionality. Selecting No opens full webpages as opposed to specific forms.

Modifying validation settings

To change the validation settings for a library and not just the settings for a specific column, navigate to the library's Settings page and select Validation Settings under General Settings. The Validation Settings window appears, as shown in Figure 3-10.

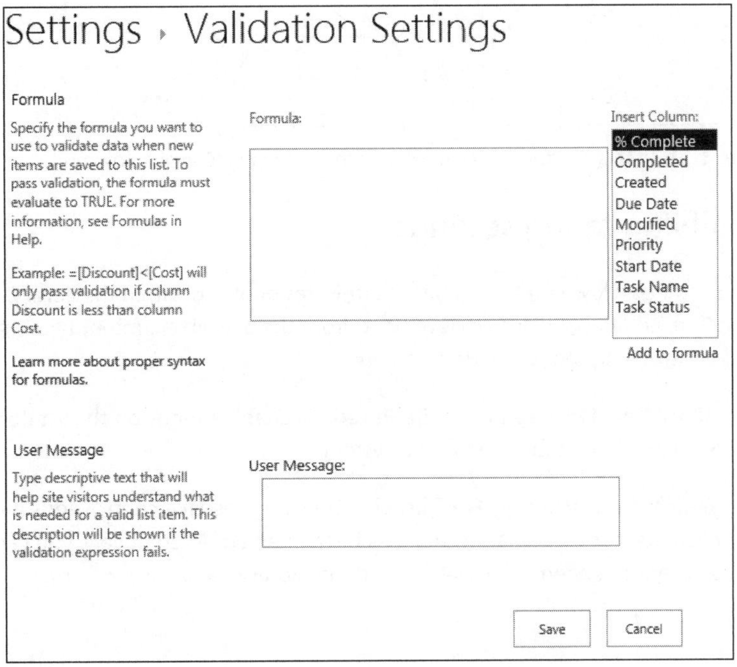

Figure 3-10 Validation settings are changed in this window.

You can make the following changes in the Validation Settings window:

- **Formula**   By using SharePoint built-in validation mechanisms, library administrators can use complex formulas to verify newly saved items to a library. A formula result must return a true value to pass validation. As an example, you can validate against is =[Revenue] > [Cost]. If the Revenue column is greater than the Cost column, then the validation will pass.

- **User Message**   If validation fails, then you can craft a custom message to be displayed.

Modifying column default value settings

If you need to add default values to a column, you can leverage this advanced option. The default option value is Do Not Specify A Default Value For This Location. If you require a specific default value, then you select Use This Default Value. An example is shown in Figure 3-11.

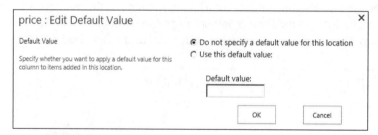

Figure 3-11   In this window, you can specify the default values of a column.

Modifying rating settings

Rating settings allow you to add rating attributes on items within the library. By enabling this option, additional fields are leveraged from the available content types. Additionally, a rating control is added to the default view.

- **Allow Items In This List To Be Rated**   To enable ratings on the list items, select Yes. Selecting No disables the rating system.

- **Which Voting/Rating For This List**   Selecting the Like control adds a simple Like characteristic to the rating that has been enabled. Alternatively, you can enable the star ratings system for the items with the library.

Modifying audience targeting settings

If this control is activated, an additional "targeting" column is added that will leverage the audience capability. From there, a web part can leverage that particular column to display appropriate information to the desired audience.

Modifying form settings

Enabling the InfoPath service in the SharePoint farm gives you the ability to customize existing forms within a list to suit your needs. This is not a supported control with a library app; it only applies to a list app.

Updating permissions and management

Permission and management controls have more of a direct effect on how a SharePoint list or library functions. These are settings that you will be using more often after the list or library is already created. While general settings are separate from permissions and management settings, great care should be taken when making changes.

Deleting lists or document libraries

Regardless of whether you are deleting a list or library, the steps you must take are similar. While each will delete their respective information, there are some things to keep in mind. For either a list or library, first open the app you want to delete. Once inside that particular app, select the list or library section on the ribbon panel. Once the desired ribbon is open, select the List Or Library Settings button. Under the Permissions And Management column you will note a link labeled Delete This List or Delete This Library. Once selected, sites that have the recycle bin enabled will present slightly different dialog text.

> **Note**
> Recycle bins provide a good first catch for accidental deletions, but they do consume space and will show up against the site storage quota.

If you are deleting a list, you will receive a dialog box asking you to confirm the deletion action. The text will indicate whether the list will be moved to the site recycle bin or permanently deleted.

The deletion of a library will present a dialog box indicating that you will not only be deleting the library but also deleting any files contained with the library at that time. The text will confirm whether the library is targeted to be moved to the site recycle bin or permanently deleted.

Saving a list or library as a template

As in previous versions of SharePoint, a great emphasis has been placed on usability and functional reuse. This allows SharePoint users and designers to minimize the amount of redundant work when creating an app list. After we have created our customized list, we would like it available to other site collections in order to thereby maximize the amount of effort expended while creating this new custom list.

When creating a custom app list, we can also include any content, views, and data that may be currently stored in the source list. Generally, we recommend excluding content data to minimize the size of the target template. This allows for the greatest amount of flexibility and portability.

Using the Sales Inventory list app we created earlier in this chapter, follow these steps to export it as a site template:

1. Open the Sales Inventory app, select List from the ribbon control, and click List Settings.

2. Under the Permissions And Management column on the Setting page, select Save List As Template.

3. In the Save As Template page, enter in the desired settings (similar to the settings shown here) and click OK.

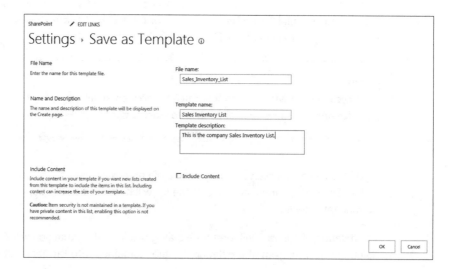

4. Once the operation is completed, the template will be available to reuse in this site collection from the list template gallery.

You may select the List Template Gallery from the successful page result. You may also return to the List Template Gallery from the Settings cog on the upper-right side by selecting Site Settings.

5. Once at the Site Settings page, select List Template under Web Designer Galleries.

Once inside the List Template Gallery, you will see the newly created Sales_Inventory_List template.

Optionally, you may wish to export this template to other site collections that have no access to this particular List Template Gallery.

6. Click on the Sales_Inventory_List link in the List Template Gallery and you will be given the option to export the customer list as an STP, as shown in the following graphic.

That STP file, in turn, can be imported into other site collections as needed for further reuse.

Once the template has been created, it is an easy process of selecting the new template from the Your Apps page under Site Contents. The new template will be located in the apps you can add section of the Your Apps page, ready for your use. As each new list is created from the template, it will use that existing structure and a new name. While at first glance this may not seem a worthwhile investment of time and energy, consider a SharePoint site with multiple subsites for each dedicated product line and reusing this template will quickly pay off in time and effort.

Editing permissions for a list or library

Editing permissions in SharePoint has not always been an easy matter. Management and control of different permissions that can exist with SharePoint has been a governance nightmare. If you will need to change permissions, make sure each change is well documented to help alleviate any future troubleshooting issues.

As with previous versions of SharePoint, SharePoint 2013 can apply permissions from the top of the site all the way down to a single item within a list. By default, when you create a list or library, they are automatically set to inherit permissions from the parent they were created under. As an example, if you create a new custom list app under a subsite that has different permissions than the parent site collection, the list will automatically inherit the permissions of the subsite rather than the parent site. If permissions are modified on the subsite, then they will cascade down the list app that has been created. This cascading permissions behavior will automatically happen unless you specifically break permission inheritance.

If a list or library permission's set has been customized, causing it to break inheritance, you can later reinstate the inheritance behavior. Reinstating the inheritance behavior removes all custom permission that may have been set earlier.

As a recommendation, we highly encourage the use of either Windows Active Directory groups or SharePoint groups to track and mange permissions. When deciding which to use, consider how your company is interacting with SharePoint and leveraging its functionality. If SharePoint is being used primarily as an intranet and there are already well-established Active Directory security groups, leveraging the established structure would make sense. If SharePoint is a partner portal where there is no other organization structure that can be leveraged, then using the internal SharePoint groups can offer this structure.

To edit permissions for a list or library, follow these steps:

1. Open the target list or library app.

2. Once inside the app, select the list or library section on the ribbon panel.

3. With the desired ribbon open, select the List Or Library Settings button.

4. Under the Permissions And Management column, select the Permissions For This Document Library or Permissions For This List.

    Once on the Permission Settings page, you will note that it lists all current permissions and whether that list or library is inheriting permissions from its parent.

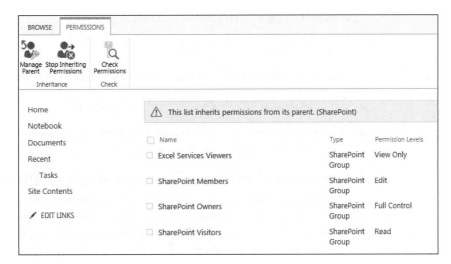

If the list or library is inheriting permissions from its parent, as you can see in the previous graphic, you will not be able to modify permissions here without either breaking that inheritance or managing the permissions of the parent.

5. If you choose to break inheritance, then click Stop Inheriting Permissions.

6. You will receive a warning regarding your choice to break permission inheritance. Select OK to continue the process.

    The permissions screen will refresh and the list or library now has unique permissions. The unique permissions that are initially set are a copy of the inherited permissions.

7. Check the target user or SharePoint group and select Edit User Permissions.

    Note that this will only change permissions on this particular library, thereby making it unique.

8. On the Edit Permissions page, you can modify the permissions as you see fit and select OK.

Adding a user to a list or library

Adding a user to a list or library is similar to editing permissions for a list or library. Keep in mind that you can only add a user to a specific list when permission inheritance has been broken. Otherwise, the user will need to be added to the parent.

To add a user to a list or library, follow these steps:

1. Open the target list or library app.

2. Once inside the app, select the list or library section on the ribbon panel.

3. With the desired ribbon open, click List Or Library Settings.

4. Under the Permissions And Management column, select the Permissions For This Document Library or Permissions For This List.

5. Check the desired SharePoint group permission level you would like to assign the user.

    This will specify what permissions are assigned to the new user. If multiple SharePoint groups are selected, the user will be added to all groups and gain the combination of permissions. If none of the groups are chosen, you will have the opportunity to specify permissions in the next step.

6. Click Grant Permissions on the Permissions page.

    A dialog box will appear asking to invite your requested user. Additionally, you can specify permissions for that user, as shown here.

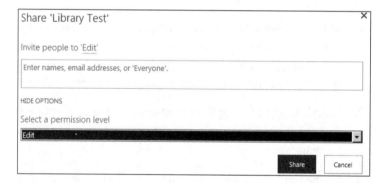

7. Select Share to complete adding a user.

Removing a user from a list or library

To remove a user from a list or library, follow these steps:

> **Note**
> You can only perform the following steps if you have the necessary permission level and you have already broken permission inheritance.

1. Open the target list or library app.

2. Once inside the app, select the list or library section on the ribbon panel.

3. With the desired ribbon open, click List Or Library Settings.

4. Under the Permissions And Management column, select the Permissions For This Document Library or Permissions For This List.

5. Check the box next to the user you wish to remove.

6. Click Delete Unique Permissions.

    These buttons will be available only if permission inheritance has been broken. If the Delete Unique Permissions button is not available, you can stop inheritance via the Stop Inheriting Permission button. Alternatively, you can remove the user at the parent level by editing the parent levels via the Manage Parent button.

7. Confirm your action by selecting OK.

It is important to keep in mind when removing a user from a list or library, any item level security details for that user are also removed. If they need to be reapplied, it will have to done manually via the Add User permissions to each item.

Checking permissions on a list or library

As with previous versions of SharePoint, it is highly recommended that permission inheritance be used whenever possible. At times, breaking inheritance will have to be done to meet business or security demands. Whenever these circumstances arise, it is important to document these changes properly. Another tool to validate security permissions for a user is the built-in check permissions with a list and library.

To check permissions on a list or library, follow these steps:

1. Open the target list or library app.

2. Once inside the app, select the list or library section on the ribbon panel.

3. With the desired ribbon open, click List or Library Settings button.

4. Under the Permissions And Management column, select the Permissions For This Document Library or Permissions For This List.

5. On the Permissions page, click Check Permissions.

6. Enter the name or email address of the account you wish to verify against the list or library and then select Check Now.

7. The Check Permission function will check that user's permission against the target list or library, as shown here.

Managing files that have no check-in version

As part of the great versatility of SharePoint 2013, one of many options is to require verification of newly uploaded files through a screening process. In most cases, SharePoint will allow you to upload a file that needs to be approved but in a checked-out state. This checked-out state can leave your files in an undetermined state where the file is unavailable. If the file is never checked in through the various SharePoint options, the file will remain in this undetermined state where only the original authors or site administrators can access the file. Unfortunately, if your site is large and you have multiple document libraries, the file might quickly get lost. To combat this problem, SharePoint has the option to manage those files that have never been checked in, and allows you to forcibly check them in.

> **Note**
> Forcibly checking in files is only available as an option for libraries, and it only applies to files that have never been checked in.

To manage files that do not have a checked-in version, follow these steps:

1. Open the target library app.

2. Once inside the app, select the library section on the ribbon panel.

3. With the desired ribbon open, click Library Settings.

4. Under the Permissions And Management column, select Manage Files Which Have No Checked In Version.

5. Click the box of a document and take ownership of selection. This essentially reassigns ownership to you so that you can then check in the documents.

Modifying workflow settings

Workflows are important tools within the SharePoint arsenal. Workflows allow the development of business-driven processes via an automated fashion. What in the past would have been a complicated approval process dependent on manual approval, now can be automated and tracked through SharePoint. As you might expect, SharePoint workflows can range from simplistic three-step workflows to custom-designed processes that can be triggered in an automated fashion.

To add, edit, or remove a workflow to a list or library, follow these steps:

1. Open the target list or library app.

2. Once inside the app, select the list or library section on the ribbon panel.

3. With the desired ribbon open, click List Or Library Settings.

4. Under the Permissions And Management column, select the Workflow Setting link.

   This will send you to the Workflow Settings page. In this page, you will now have the opportunity to first select to show the workflow associations of the following types: This List, Document, and Folder. From the context selection, you can edit the existing workflow or add a new workflow in that context. As shown here, we have the ability to either add or edit a workflow in the document association type.

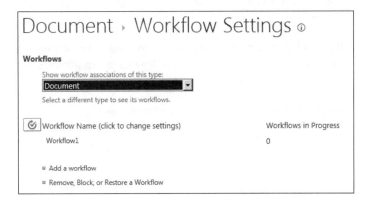

5. Selecting an existing workflow will open the Workflow Settings and allow you to modify them as needed.

6. Selecting Remove, Block, Or Restore a Workflow gives you the ability to delete a workflow via the remove option. You prevent a workflow from starting with the block option. You can also restore a previous deleted workflow.

7. If you are creating a new workflow, first select the workflow association and then select Add A Workflow.

   This opens the Add A Workflow page. From here, you can select the type of workflow you wish to create.

> **Note**
>
> In SharePoint 2013, you will only see a SharePoint 2010 template workflow if you do not have the new SharePoint 2013 workflow services properly installed and associated to the SharePoint 2013 Web Applications.

8. Enter a name for the workflow. This name must be unique.

9. To track the current state of a workflow, select an existing task list or select Create A New Task List.

10. To track the historical steps a workflow took during the process, select a history list or create a new history list.

11. Set the start options for the workflow.

    The default allows for the workflow to be manually started by an appropriate level user. You can change these settings to include automatic triggers during certain events.

12. If you selected to create a new three-state workflow, clicking Next will bring you to the Customize The Three-State Workflow page. From here, you can specifically track and modify the workflow as needed.

13. Finally, click OK to finish creating a new workflow.

Modifying information management policy settings

Information management policy settings allow administrators to apply a set of policies against a particular content type. Policy setting can include mandatory retention schedules, auditing trails, or disabling the printing functionality from SharePoint 2013. The primary binding of these policies is the usage of content type. This lets administrators create policies that will work if applied to multiple libraries across different subsites. You can also change the association from content type to specific library and folder. Be aware when this is changed from content type to library and folder, that this will override the normal behavior you might have set from a content type. Policies are created in the site collection policies in the site collection administration of the SharePoint site collection section. They are bound to SharePoint at a site-collection level, but they can be selectively applied as needed to lists and libraries. Once this has been completed, you can then edit a target list or library to enforce the policy.

To modify information management policy settings, follow these steps:

1. Open the target list or library app.

2. Once inside the app, select the list or library section on the ribbon panel.

3. With the desired ribbon open, click List Or Library Settings.

4. Under the Permissions And Management column, select Information Management Policy Settings.

5. In the Information Management Policy Settings page, your first option is to change the source retention from content type to files and folders.

    Each of the policies that had been bound to the site and appropriate for the list or library will be indicated under the content type policies section. If you wish to enable a specific policy, you can select the named link.

6. Once a policy has been set, click OK.

Modifying enterprise metadata and keywords settings

The use of standardized metadata in SharePoint has come into the spotlight as a way to govern information. Having a strict enterprise metadata policy helps to minimize confusion between departments and allow for smoother communications. As an example of global metadata, the term set group Human Resources would be created to contain terms such as job titles and executive level. This provides companywide term standardization. While the SharePoint managed metadata service goes a long way in providing standard-izations, enterprise keywords augment this functionality to provide better descriptive metadata when needed. While both the metadata and enterprise keywords can be used concurrently, it is highly encouraged to centralize that data in one structure. The usage of enterprise metadata and keywords is nearly identical for lists and libraries. First, selecting the target list or library and opening the Enterprise Metadata And Keyword Settings on the Settings page. In a list or library, you will see the check box to enable this functionality. If enabled, a column for the enterprise keywords will be added to the list or library to contain the metadata or keywords. In a library, you will have an additional check box to enable metadata publishing. If this is enabled, then the additional metadata and keywords can be leveraged in SharePoint 2013–expanded social tags on My Sites.

Generating a file plan report

A *file plan* is a tool for identifying what information is kept on a set of particular records. A file plan will outline the specific type of records, storage location of the records, retention periods, and disposal routines. Information that outlines a report plan can be generated from SharePoint for a specific list or library. To create a report, open the List Or Library Settings page and select the Generate File Plan report. Select a document library to eventually contain the report and click OK.

Once this is completed, you will receive a confirmation page confirming that the report has been created.

Creating and modifying list and library views

As business requirements and user working patterns change, there is often a demand to change what information is displayed in a list or library. These changes will lead to easing work practices and help facilitate adoption.

Creating a list or library view

As an example, a contact list is commonly kept in SharePoint so that a company has a centralized list of contacts. Often the default contacts list will not contain enough metadata or, conversely, contain unneeded metadata.

The default view will always display all the preconfigured columns for a standard app. To display the appropriate column, we can either create a new view or modify an existing view.

To create a new list or library view (or modify an existing view), follow these steps:

- Open the list or library for the view you wish to modify.

- Select the list's or library's ribbon section, and then select Create View, as shown here.

- In the View Type page that opens, select the particular view you wish to use, as shown here.

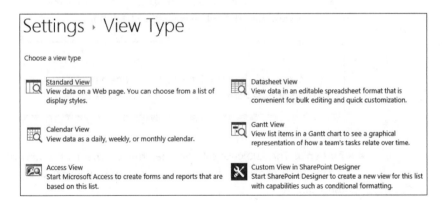

- As shown next, once you have chosen your desired view, the Create View page opens, and you are able to configure your settings:

```
┌─────────────────────────────────────────────────────────────────────────┐
│ Name                                                                      │
│                                                    View Name:             │
│ Type a name for this view of the list. Make the name descriptive, such as │
│ "Sorted by Author", so that site visitors will know what to expect when they │ ┌──────────────────┐
│ click this link.                                                          │ └──────────────────┘
│                                                                           │
│                                                    ☐ Make this the default view │
│                                                      (Applies to public views only) │
│                                                                           │
│ Audience                                                                  │
│                                                    View Audience:         │
│ Select the option that represents the intended audience for this view.    │
│                                                    ○ Create a Personal View │
│                                                      Personal views are intended for │
│                                                      your use only.       │
│                                                                           │
│                                                    ◉ Create a Public View │
│                                                      Public views can be visited by │
│                                                      anyone using the site. │
│                                                                           │
│ ⊞ Columns                                                                 │
│                                                                           │
│ ⊞ Sort                                                                    │
│                                                                           │
│ ⊞ Filter                                                                  │
│                                                                           │
│ ⊞ Tabular View                                                            │
│                                                                           │
│ ⊞ Group By                                                                │
│                                                                           │
│ ⊞ Totals                                                                  │
│                                                                           │
│ ⊞ Style                                                                   │
│                                                                           │
│ ⊞ Folders                                                                 │
└─────────────────────────────────────────────────────────────────────────┘
```

- **Name** The first option is to add a name for the new view. You then can decide to make this view your default view via the check box.

> **Note**
>
> **If a default view is desired, the view must be a public view, and you must have the appropriate permissions to change the default view.**

- **Audience** The Audience selection determines whether the view you are creating is either a personal view that can only be used by yourself, or a public view that all users can view.

- **Columns** Expanding the Columns view lets you specify the exact columns and order that will be displayed in the view.

- **Sort** The Sort section allows you to enable sorting of the view dynamically. Up to two columns may be sorted in the view. Once the first sort is completed, then the second sort is preformed to further refine how the data is presented. Sort By Specified Criteria determines how the folders, if any, will be used in the sort.

- **Filter** The Filter option allows a view to only show items that match specific criteria. Your options are to show all of the items or those that match specific criteria, resulting in a true rule set. The rule set can be leveraged into specific combinations by using the AND/OR operators.

- **Tabular** The Tabular view adds individual check boxes to each of the items that are being displayed. They give the user the ability to select a row and take needed actions on those items.

- **Group By** The Group By option lets you group items together to display information in a logical manner. The groups are then put together in a collapsible heading section. An example of this would be if we had a region column, then we could group regions together and then sort as we wish. By default, the groups are collapsed into the heading, but you may change that behavior and select Expanded. You also have the option of limiting the number of groups that appear on each returned page.

- **Totals** The Totals section allows the view to display a dynamic total, which can be either Count or Addition for enabled columns. If you select a column that is a text type, then you will get a count of the items in the view. If you select a currency type column, it will display a sum value for the column.

- **Style** The Style option lets you change how the views are displayed. There are several options, and each has a particular advantage when trying to display the information in a particular way.

- **Folders** If your list or library has a folder structure, you may choose to display or not display the information inside folders as items within the folder or items without a folder structure.

- **Item Limit** The Item Limit option controls how many items are displayed to the user per page. This is an important consideration if you are working with large tables, as the user will experience slow rendered pages while trying to display large data sets. You can control the number of items to display. Additionally, you can set whether a table will only display a set number regardless of the actual amount of items or number of items to be broken into pages.

It is not normal to have the default public view be the default mobile view. Here, you can choose to make this public view enabled for mobile consumption. This will also make this view the default view for mobile users. By default, SharePoint has a default mobile view, which you can override with this control. You may also select the number of items that display in a mobile view.

Modifying and deleting views

Many of the predefined lists have other views that provide additional formats to view the same data. As an example, the standard task list has seven built-in views. They range from All Tasks to My Tasks views. If you need to modify one of these existing views for your own purpose or delete a view, the steps are fairly easy and similar to creating a new view. All of the same options that are listed for a new view are available to you while modifying a view.

To modify an existing view, first open the list or library. Select the list ribbon control and click Modify View. This will open the Edit View Settings page. From here, you can modify the view as you desire. Additionally, you will have the option to delete the view if it is no longer needed, which you can access by using a Delete button. (The Delete button will not appear on the designated default view.) When you have completed your modifications, select OK.

Working with list content

SharePoint 2013 gives us the ability to work with list items and library documents in an extensible manner. Leveraging these tools doesn't require advanced programming skills or a large project implementation plan. Next, we'll take a look at calculated columns, validation processes, and folder structures.

Calculated columns

Calculated columns in SharePoint allow you to leverage dynamic information as it is needed. Leveraging Excel-like abilities, calculations can be used with system-specific functions or other lists. Calculations are executed at two specific times:

- When a new item is created in a list

- When the item is retrieved from the list

Calculations are refreshed each time the list is requested.

When gathering data from other columns within the list, it is a recommended practice to surround the column name with square brackets. Using square brackets specifies to the system that this is information from a column with this specific name. As an example, if we used a predefined task list app, but we wanted to leverage calculations to set a due date five days after the start date, the formula you would use will look like this:

```
= [Start Date] + 5
```

In addition to number calculations, text manipulations are available to SharePoint. In our predefined Contact app, we could define our calculation column as follows:

```
= [First Name] & " " & [Last Name]
```

As an example, using the concatenation Excel-like function allows us a great amount of flexibility.

List validations

List validations can perform the vital job of keeping bad information from becoming part of the SharePoint data. Validation tools are included at both the table level and the column level. The validation must pass True in order to enter any information. If the validation check fails, SharePoint will not submit the item to the table, and it will return the custom-specified message.

If we open the List Or Library Settings page, we can then navigate to the specific column on which we wish to enforce a specific validation test. Opening the Edit Column page allows us to use the column validation that can be enabled for this location. In our example, we want to ensure, when a user is inputting information into the Task list app, that the due date is greater than the start date. Navigating the Column Settings page, we can locate the column Validation section and enter the following information:

- **Formula** =[Due Date]>TODAY()

- **Message** Enter a date that is greater than today's date.

In the Column Validation section of the column Properties, there is a help link to provide more information on the proper formula and application for validations.

When to use folders

In many ways, using folders, represents a link to the more traditional file share. Previously, we had addressed the advantages of using metadata and keywords to help organize and track information and documents. While these are great tools, at times, we have very specific reasons to use a folder structure:

- **Ease of use** If you have a well-engrained user community with a deep understanding of an existing file structure, forcing metadata concepts will cause frustration to grow and slow the adaption of SharePoint within your organization.

- **Complex security** A folder structure does a great job of providing easy mechanisms to apply security settings. Each folder can contain an easily separate security policy.

- **Document sets** Document sets inherit content types via the folder system.

- **Default metadata** Each folder can implement its own set of default metadata. This allows your users to leverage and add metadata without any extra steps.

- **Windows Explorer** If you are a user of Windows Explorer functionality in SharePoint, a folder structure will provide a more organized approach than a metadata format, where all files appear in the root folder library.

Limitations and workarounds

While the theoretical maximum for a single list or library is 30 million items, you will see a performance degradation well before you come close to this limitation. There are several factors that play a role in SharePoint list general performance degradation. This makes setting any set-in-stone number difficult. When working with large lists, your first option should be to break up the list using a tool such as the content manager. Performance issues from a single list can prove to cause other widespread problems throughout your SharePoint site. For example, a content query web part may be fetching information from multiple SharePoint lists while implementing a complex rule set on the data retrieved. The pressure of such a large and complex job is handled by the machine running SQL server and therefore runs the risk of performance degradation.

Software boundaries, limits, and thresholds

Microsoft has broken down their recommendations into limits, boundaries, and thresholds categories. *Limits* are generally recommended values that can be exceeded but should be discouraged. *Boundaries* are those values that are hard limits that cannot be exceeded. A *threshold* is a value that has been set within SharePoint, but can be altered to accommodate larger values. As an example, a document's file size has a default threshold of 250 MB when SharePoint is first configured. This can be changed to accommodate larger sizes, but only to the boundary size of 2 GB. When approaching either the threshold or the boundary, special care should be taken to account for the added workload. If not, SharePoint will have a degraded performance. Table 3-4 lists the most common limits and boundaries when working in the context of list and libraries.

TABLE 3-4 Common software boundaries, limits, and thresholds

Object	Value	Limit
List row size	8,000 bytes per row	Boundary
File size	2 GB	Boundary
Documents	30,000,000 per library	Limit

Object	Value	Limit
Major versions	400,000	Limit
Minor versions	511	Boundary
Items	30,000,000 per list	Limit
Row size limit	6 table rows internal to the database	Limit
Bulk operations	100 items per bulk operation	Limit
List view lookup threshold	8 join operations per query	Threshold
List view threshold	5,000	Threshold
List view threshold for auditors and administrators	20,000	Threshold
Subsite	2,000 per site	Threshold
Coauthoring for Office files	10 concurrent editors	Threshold
Security scope	1,000 per list	Threshold
Unique permissions limit	50,000	Boundary
List view size for auditors and administrators	20,000	Threshold
URL length	256	Threshold

For more information about software boundaries and limits for SharePoint 2013, go to *http://technet.microsoft.com/en-us/library/cc262787.aspx.*

Throttling

List throttling is another important factor to consider when you are working with large lists in SharePoint. As noted in Table 3-4, the list view threshold is 5,000 items. This can be altered, but you run a high risk of generating SQL performance impact that may not only affect your particular site performance, but also the SharePoint farm in general. Therefore, as an added safety mechanism, list throttling was put into place. The throttle will control the number of rows in a list or library that can be returned at any one time from SQL. In SharePoint 2013, the list view throttle is set to 5,000 items. If you try to fetch more than 5,000 items, you are warned that not all potentially retrievable items were returned—only the first 5,000. The list view threshold for auditors and administrators is 20,000 items. If a request query hits the throttle point, then the machine running SQL server can potentially lock the table where it is pulling the information to ensure that all data is being properly correlated. Effectively, any other users in SharePoint who are trying to retrieve information from this same table will be locked out until that first query completes. If you are running into problems with list threshold and list throttling, it is not advisable to override these limitations. A better route is to alleviate the problem using alternative methods without modifying the established threshold or throttle.

Indexing columns

Indexing columns is a method used by site collection owners and administrators to help compensate for slow performance of large lists within SharePoint. Creating an index and leveraging that index appropriately via a view filter will greatly enhance the speed of returning large datasets.

In a SharePoint list or library, you can create an index of a specific column. Each list or library can contain up to 20 individual columns. As a new index is created, more resources are used to maintain that column. A lot of forethought should be used with indexing columns. Creating 20 indexes because you can, or because you might need them in the future, may cause larger problems. When creating an index, ensure that the index and associated filter will not return more than 5,000 results. The index is still subject to the list throttling limitation. When creating the view for a list filter and leveraging the index, ensure that the first filter is based on the index. There can be additional filters as needed, but only one index can be used in the filter. When using a filter with the OR operator, it cannot leverage the index properly. If imposed, even a manual item limit set in options will not have the same effectiveness as an index column.

In the following steps, we will create an index on a Contacts app. As an example, we have found that after years of entering in customer contact information into a SharePoint list app, the degradation in performance has become unacceptable. We needed a filtered view of all customers in the San Francisco area.

1.   Open the target list or library app.

2.   Once inside the app, select the list or library section on the ribbon panel.

3.   With the desired ribbon open, click List Or Library Settings.

4.   On the Setting page in the Columns section, select Indexed Columns.

5.   Once on the Indexed Columns page, as shown next, select Create A New Index.

Settings ▸ Indexed Columns

Use this page to view and change the indexing settings for this list. You can create a new index or remove an existing one. Learn more about column indices.

You have created 0 of maximum 20 indices on this list. These indices are:

Create a new index

6. From the Primary Column, select the column that will act as your primary index. Here, we will select the City column.

7. Click Create, and it will create the index before returning you to the Indexed Columns page. We will now have one index column to help sort through the large list.

Once the index is created, we now have the opportunity to leverage it in a list filter view. Creating or modifying a filter view will show that, the City (Indexed) option will have to be the first filter element, as shown in Figure 3-12.

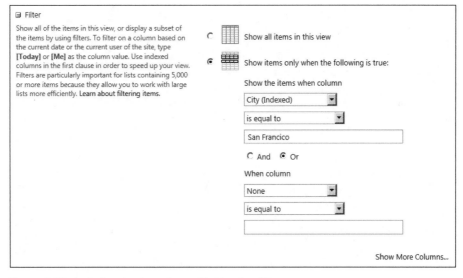

Figure 3-12 An indexed column is used in the view filter.

Summary

In this chapter, we discussed working with lists and library apps in SharePoint 2013 and leveraging the built-in apps to suit our needs. Taking stock of business requirements and making necessary modifications can be a powerful action for site collection users and administrators to harness the potential of SharePoint 2013. This can all be accomplished within a browser, using nothing more than SharePoint default tools. The next chapter takes a look at working with collaboration sites.

Working with collaboration sites

S INCE the launch of Microsoft SharePoint over a decade ago, team collaboration around documents, tasks, projects, and various other types of content has been the sweet spot of the software. SharePoint 2013 continues this tradition by maintaining the areas of collaboration that have been core to the product since the beginning—and building on that foundation with plenty of new collaborative features to help teams stay organized and share information. Specifically, SharePoint team sites provide a place where your team can communicate, share documents, and work together on a project. Much of this chapter focuses on understanding the team site (and its close cousin, the project site).

The other primary type of Collaboration Site template is the *community* site. Community sites are covered in depth in Chapter 6, "Sharing information with SharePoint social networking."

The ubiquitous SharePoint Team Site template provides the foundation for creating web-based team collaboration sites in a very quick and simple manner. Within seconds of clicking Create, you are presented with a team site that is ready to go. A site generated from the Team Site template is streamlined with only a few of the most important team components, such as a document library for sharing files and a newsfeed for social interaction. The 2013 team sites allow the site owner to add more collaboration apps easily as necessary, such as calendars, tasks, forms, and team mailboxes.

> **Note**
>
> The only significant difference between the Team Site and Project Site templates are that the Project Site template includes a calendar and task app by default and a Project Site template contains a Project Summary Web Part on the site home page.

Creating team sites

In this section, you will learn about the new interface for customizing team sites. In the past, a site owner needed to go into various site menus and dig around for options; as you will see, the new Getting Started tiles make it much easier for the novice site owner.

Customizing team sites

When you create a new team site, you are first presented with the Getting Started tiles shown in Figure 4-1. The tiles help explain some of the ways that you can adapt the site to meet your requirements.

Figure 4-1 The Getting Started tiles help you easily accomplish basic tasks necessary to customize your site.

The tiles and their purpose are enumerated as follows:

- **Share Your Site** This is a shortcut to the new sharing interface that helps you share your site with other people and groups.

- **Working On A Deadline** This is a shortcut to add a task list and calendar to your site if your site will be used for projects and task management.

- **Add Lists, Libraries, And Other Apps** This tile is a shortcut to add apps and additional functionality to your team site.

- **What's Your Style?** This takes you into the new gallery of style templates for team sites. The style templates are an easy way to give your site a unique and pleasing look.

- **Your Site. Your Brand.** This tile is a shortcut to the settings for the logo and site description.

- **Keep Email In Context** This tile helps you add a site mailbox for your team to share emails that are relevant to the entire team.

> **Note**
>
> After you have finished with the initial setup of your site, click Remove This, and the Getting Started tiles will be removed. If you want to use the tiles again later, you can use the Getting Started option on the Settings menu.

Working with document libraries

Document libraries have been an ever-present feature of team sites for several versions of the product, and that continues in SharePoint 2013. A *document library* is a SharePoint app that is used to save and store documents in a shared location. Document libraries are similar to network file shares, allowing team members to contribute, edit, and collaborate on documents. However, document libraries can go far beyond this basic functionality by using some of the other SharePoint features such as workflows, metadata, versioning, and content types.

For information on more advanced document management capabilities, see Chapter 11, "Managing documents."

When a new team site is created, a document library named Documents is created by default. The document library is placed front and center as a web part on the team site home page and as a left navigation link, as shown in Figure 4-2.

Figure 4-2 Navigation to a team site document library is possible from multiple points.

The most basic task that teams need to perform when collaborating on documents is getting the documents into SharePoint. Now that document libraries support dragging in SharePoint 2013, the process of getting documents into a library is easier. The interface for working with documents is streamlined and clean; some of the menu options remain hidden until you click the ellipsis icon (...) next to a document's title. You may also see the new ellipsis menu referred to as an Edit Control Block (ECB) menu in other areas of this book. When you click the ellipsis, you will see a preview of the document in a hover panel. Notice in Figure 4-3 that another ellipsis icon appears on the hover panel that will take you into even more options for the item you are working with.

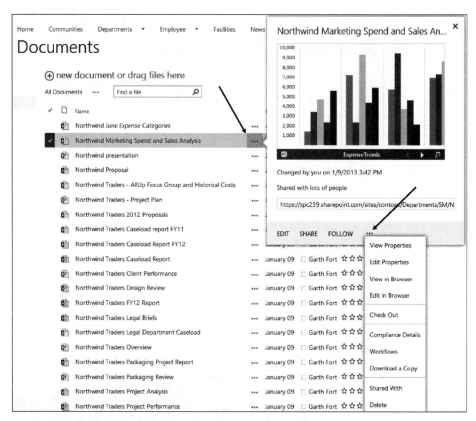

Figure 4-3 When the new ellipsis (Edit Control Block/ECB) menu is selected, a preview of the document appears in a hover panel.

Often, after a team member has put a file into a document library, one of the key tasks is to share the document. In SharePoint 2013, it is easier than ever to share an item in a document library with others. Sharing is covered in depth later in this section.

Using SkyDrive Pro

SkyDrive Pro is a SharePoint location to save and share the files that you work with every day. If you have used one of the consumer cloud-storage services such as SkyDrive, SkyDrive Pro in SharePoint should feel comfortable and familiar. SkyDrive Pro, however, is a

SharePoint-based service optimized for users within organizations to manage their business and work-related documents. Each SharePoint user has a SkyDrive Pro page and libraries to work with. It is available to you in the browser providing the normal SharePoint document library functionality. In addition, for the times when you are on the go, you have the option to synchronize your documents on to your client system with the SkyDrive Pro offline client. You can access and edit files across multiple devices, and have the files automatically synched up when you connect.

> **Note**
>
> **If you use SharePoint 2013 in the cloud, each user is allocated a maximum of 7 GB of storage for personal documents. If you use SharePoint 2013 on-premise, the maximum amount of storage each user receives is up to your SharePoint administrators to determine.**

Getting to your SkyDrive Pro is easy in SharePoint 2013; it has been added to the upper right of the main navigation bar. After you click the SkyDrive link, you are directed to your personal document library. Once in your library, creating new documents in SkyDrive Pro is also easy to do. Create a Word document, Microsoft Excel workbook, Microsoft PowerPoint slideshow, or Microsoft OneNote notebook directly from your browser by clicking the + New Document button, as shown in Figure 4-4.

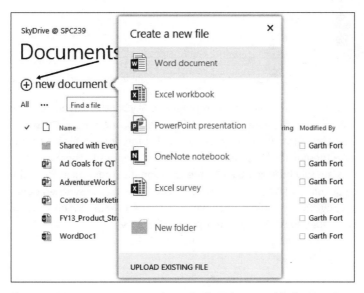

Figure 4-4 You can create new items in SkyDrive Pro with the New Document link.

> **Note**
>
> If you plan to use Office Web Apps to create new items, as shown in Figure 4-4, your SharePoint farm administrators will need to install and configure an Office Web Apps farm. Configuration details are available at *http://technet.microsoft.com/en-us/library/ ff431687.aspx.*

Alternatively, you can create the document in the Office 2013 client applications on your device and save them directly to SkyDrive Pro, as shown in Figure 4-5. Notice that Garth has the option to save to either his SkyDrive Pro (denoted by the "S" icon), or to his consumer version of SkyDrive if he is creating items that are not for work usage.

Figure 4-5 In Office 2013, users have the option of saving directly to SkyDrive Pro.

To synchronize your files to a local computer, the SkyDrive Pro Sync button is now ubiquitous in SharePoint libraries in the upper-right portion of the page. Clicking Sync will make a copy of the files from your personal library (or any team document library). You can take these files offline with you and make changes to them; when you reconnect, the changes are synchronized back to the appropriate library. Likewise, if there are new files in the document library, when you connect, those will be synched down to your local computer's SkyDrive Pro folder, as shown in Figure 4-6. Your SkyDrive Pro folder is created automatically for you within your user profile directory.

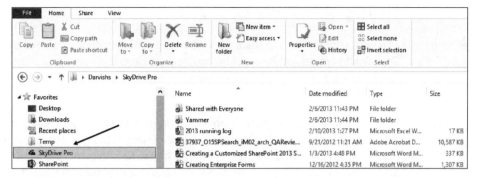

Figure 4-6 The SkyDrive Pro client application is displayed within a user's profile directory.

INSIDE OUT   What happened to SharePoint Workspace?

With the introduction of SkyDrive Pro, SharePoint Workspace is no longer being developed for the 2013 platform. SkyDrive Pro replaces the feature that SharePoint Workspace 2010 was most commonly used for: offline document synchronization. However, if you need to continue supporting it, the 2010 version of SharePoint Workspace still works just fine with SharePoint 2010, SharePoint 2013, and SharePoint Online.

In addition to your own documents, SkyDrive Pro lets you manage documents you care about across SharePoint by displaying a list of your followed documents. You can see in Figure 4-7 that SkyDrive Pro keeps track of documents that you have followed from other sites.

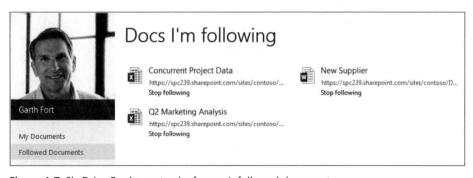

Figure 4-7 SkyDrive Pro keeps track of a user's followed documents.

Sharing sites, libraries, and files

Making it easy for users to share sites, libraries, and files (without the need to understand SharePoint permissions) is one of the key new concepts in SharePoint 2013. Sites and libraries are for sharing with people that you need to collaborate with, and sharing a site is simple in SharePoint 2013.

Sharing items with team members in a location such as a document library is easy—*if* everyone has access and is aware that you are putting in the files. However, if they are not *following* the library or a member of the site, it may be necessary to grant them permissions and let them know that you have files you would like to share with them. The tools and process for sharing and notifying them are significantly enhanced in SharePoint 2013.

As shown in Figure 4-8, the Share button is ubiquitous in SharePoint sites and libraries. You will find it in the upper-right part of the page. Just click Share, and then using the new people picker, type in the username of people with whom you want to share.

Figure 4-8 The Share button appears in many locations throughout SharePoint.

After you have shared a site, library, or document with someone, that person will be notified via email, as shown in Figure 4-9.

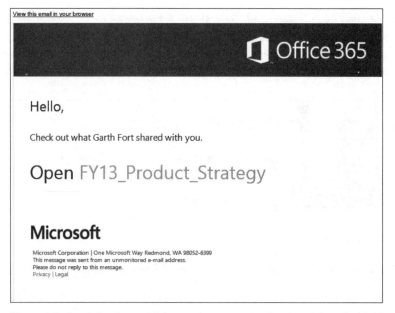

Figure 4-9 A recipient's email link to a document that has been shared with him or her.

External sharing

If you use Office 365 for your SharePoint environment (SharePoint Online), and if your administrators have configured the farm for external sharing, SharePoint 2013 provides the option of easily sharing items with external users as well. People who need to view or edit your content but do not have user accounts for your SharePoint Online farm are referred to as *external users.* This "extranet collaboration" scenario is one of the most popular motivations for business customers to use SharePoint Online. It is relatively quick and simple to get set up for external collaboration in a cloud-based instance of SharePoint relative to an on-premise environment.

The external sharing process is the same as sharing with internal team members, except that you enter the external person's email address. As before, you can send that person an invitation via email, and he or she will get a link to the document.

> **Note**
> Before external users can access the item you shared, they will need to link their email accounts to a Microsoft LiveID.

In some cases, you may want to share an item with external users without requiring any permissions at all (that is, anonymous access). An example might be a product brochure that you want to share with several of your customers for viewing, but you do not want to email it to them. Perhaps the document is in Word format.

> **Note**
> The ability to share anonymously with external users is dependent upon the SharePoint farm being configured to allow external sharing. The details to configure your SharePoint Online properly for external sharing may be found at *http://office.microsoft .com/en-us/office365-sharepoint-online-enterprise-help/share-a-site-with-external-users-HA102476183.aspx.*

To share an item externally without email notification, first put the item in your personal SkyDrive Pro library. Then using the ellipsis, click Share for the item you wish to extend to external parties. As shown in Figure 4-10, type in the email addresses (or Everyone if applicable). Change the permissions level to Can View, and clear the Require Sign-In check box.

Figure 4-10 A file is shared with the Everyone security group from SkyDrive Pro.

After you have made those selections, click Share. After you have done that, go back to the menu using the ellipsis, and an option to get a guest link appears, as shown in Figure 4-11.

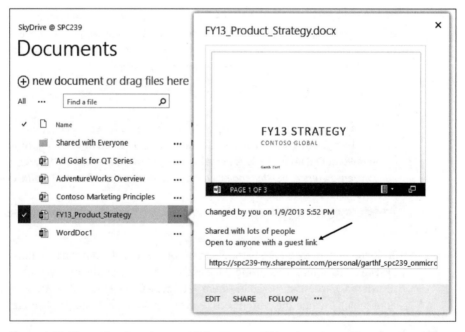

Figure 4-11 The option to get a guest link appears within a hover panel in a document library.

The guest link can then be used in whatever way you need (email, link on a webpage, and so on). As shown in Figure 4-12, when external users click the link, they will be taken to the Office Web App for whichever file type you are sharing (assuming that it is a Office file type). When they enter the web app, they will either be able to edit, or just view, depending on what level of permission you granted. The entire process from initially putting the file into SkyDrive Pro, to sharing it, and then external users consuming it in the Office Web Apps, is seamless and easy.

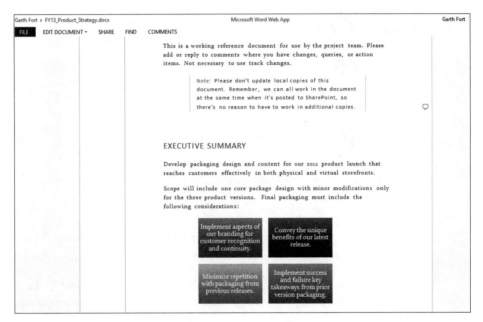

Figure 4-12 A Word document is opened in the Word Office Web Application.

Checking sharing permissions

Checking to see the people with whom something is shared is much easier in SharePoint 2013. You can choose the Shared With option in a document, library, or site. For a library, the Shared With button is on the ribbon in the browser, as shown in Figure 4-13.

Figure 4-13 The Shared With window indicates who has access to items within a document library.

To do the same check for an entire site, look under the Settings menu in the upper-right corner of the browser. Then click Shared With, and you will see the people who have access to the site.

Using a team notebook

OneNote 2013 received some significant improvements in the client version of the application. It also received a major overhaul in the web app version in order to bring the browser version closer to parity with the rich client. Based on usability studies of what many teams actually do with SharePoint team sites, three major new components are available to team sites: a shared OneNote team notebook, a team project summary with task timeline, and team mailboxes.

To access the team OneNote notebook, click Notebook in the navigation menu on the left side of the page, as shown in Figure 4-14. This will open the notebook in the OneNote web app by default. You can also choose to open the team notebook in OneNote on your PC, Mac, or mobile device. Opening it in a native OneNote client app provides the additional benefit of making it available offline and keeping it automatically synchronized.

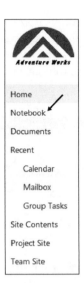

Figure 4-14 A team notebook appears on the left side of the page in the Quick Launch navigation of a site.

When using a team notebook, all team members who have membership permissions to the site will be able to take notes and share content in the notebook. Sometimes when multiple people are editing the same page, you may need to go back and review (and restore if necessary) a prior version of the page. To accomplish this, you can click the Page Versions button on the View tab of the ribbon.

In a team notebook, multiple people can edit the notebook at the same time—you will see their notes appear as they type them and vice versa. When you have multiple authors working on content in the browser-based version of OneNote, you can click the Show Authors button on the View tab on the ribbon, shown in Figure 4-15, to see what notes various team members are editing.

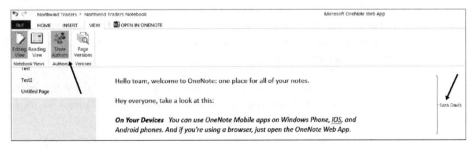

Figure 4-15 Click Show Authors to see what notes team members are editing.

As with the other Office Web Apps, you can access a team notebook from any computer or mobile device. Perhaps your primary work laptop has OneNote 2013 loaded on it, but you also want to read and edit notes from a tablet or other mobile device. As shown in Figure 4-16, even if you are accessing team notes from a device without a native OneNote app installed, you can still participate and collaborate.

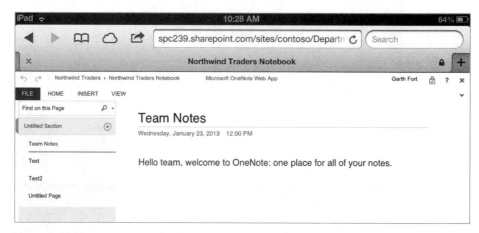

Figure 4-16 Here, a team notebook appears on a tablet from within the OneNote web application.

Using a site mailbox

SharePoint team sites have historically centered around shared documents, calendars, and tasks. However, many customers find that email is another major source of collaborative information when managing a project or team. Therefore, SharePoint 2013 introduces *site mailboxes* to team sites so that team members can have a shared repository of email related to their team and projects. The site mailbox is an innovative new feature in Microsoft Exchange 2013 that improves collaboration and productivity by allowing access to SharePoint 2013 documents and Exchange email via the same interface. With site mailboxes, you can view email in SharePoint, and likewise, you can view documents in Outlook. And just like sharing documents, when a team member puts email in the site mailbox, any member can then access the content.

To add a site mailbox to your team site, select the Site Mailbox tile by clicking Add An App on the Site Settings page. The Site Mailbox tile is shown in Figure 4-17.

Figure 4-17 Click the Site Mailbox tile to add a mailbox to a team site.

As shown in Figure 4-18, site mailboxes appear not only in SharePoint 2013, but also in Outlook. This gives users easy access to the email and documents for the teams and projects they work with, regardless of whether they are in email or in the SharePoint site. Also, team members can add new documents to a team site's document libraries directly from Outlook 2013.

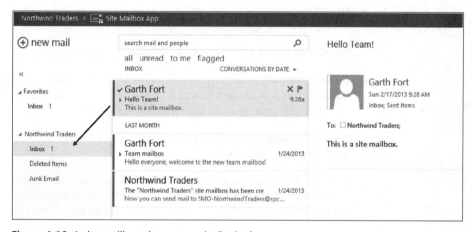

Figure 4-18 A site mailbox also appears in Outlook.

While site mailboxes appear to be in SharePoint, Exchange Server actually stores the email. By taking this approach, users are able to use the same interface for both their personal email and their team email. SharePoint still stores the documents in the mailbox, thus enabling standard document collaboration features, such as coauthoring. Exchange Server gathers the necessary data from SharePoint to create a document-centric view in Outlook for the user that includes items such as size, most recent author, document title, modified date, and so forth.

From an administrative point of view, SharePoint and Exchange share responsibility for site mailboxes. SharePoint is used to manage the lifecycle and retention of the site mailbox. SharePoint's eDiscovery console is also used for site mailboxes when you need to perform searches and legal holds. For backup and restore, however, Exchange 2013 is in control. Site mailboxes should be part of your regular Exchange disaster recovery program. Exchange also takes care of quotas for site mailboxes, thus allowing control over settings such as maximum mailbox size, maximum number of emails in a mailbox, and so forth. These quota settings are configured via an Exchange cmdlet called New-SiteMailboxProvisioningPolicy.

For more information about site mailboxes, go to *technet.microsoft.com/en-us/library/ jj150499.aspx*.

INSIDE OUT   Site mailbox requirements

To add site mailboxes to your team sites, several prerequisites must be in place. At a high level, the following items must be configured prior to using site mailboxes:

- Site mailboxes are only supported with Exchange 2013.

- The Exchange web services application programming interface (API) must be installed on all web front-end (WFE) servers in the SharePoint farm.

- OAuth trust must be configured on both SharePoint and Exchange.

- Because there will be server-to-server authentication between Exchange and SharePoint, SharePoint Server must have Secure Sockets Layer (SSL) configured for the zones containing web apps with site mailboxes.

- The app management service application must be added to the farm prior to initializing site mailboxes.

- Access to files in a document library from a site mailbox requires that users configure the document library as a trusted site in their browsers. If this is not done, they will repeatedly receive a warning that asks them if they trust the file.

For more details about configuring site mailboxes, go to *technet.microsoft.com/en-us/ library/jj552524.aspx*.

Understanding project sites

The Project Site template is new in SharePoint 2013. A *project site* is essentially a standard team site, but it adds the Project Summary Web Part to the home page of the site, and apps for managing projects (such as calendar, tasks, forms, and team mailboxes) are included by default. It is ideal for collaborative projects that have a team of people sharing tasks, documents, and other resources. The project site is one of the most powerful out-of-the-box project management tools ever to be in SharePoint. That said, however, it is certainly not intended to replace Microsoft Project Server for those who need all the features included with an enterprise project management system.

When you select the Project Site template, the description of the template says, "A site for managing and collaborating on a project. This site template brings all status, communication, and artifacts relevant to the project into one place." To add a new project site or subsite, choose Project Site within the Collaboration tab in the New SharePoint Site page, as shown in Figure 4-19.

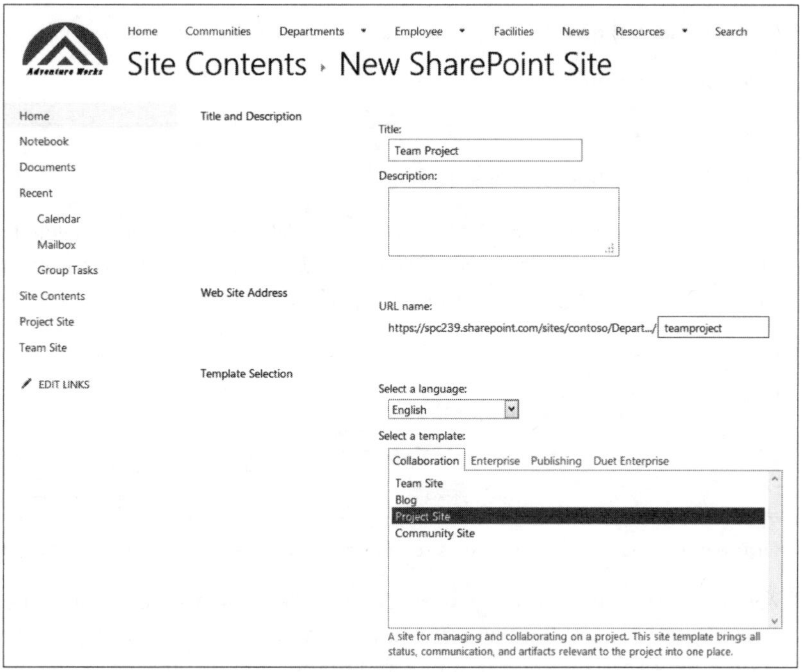

Figure 4-19 Select a Project Site template from within Site Contents.

After you have created a project site, you are likely to first notice that the Project Summary Web Part is displayed prominently at the top of the page, as shown in Figure 4-20.

Figure 4-20 A Project Summary Web Part is used to communicate project status visually within a project site.

The project summary easily communicates to team members and visitors of the site how the project is going. In addition, it calls out the next upcoming milestone on the left so that someone can see "what's next" at a glance. If you have appropriate permissions, you can add a new team task directly from the Project Summary Web Part by clicking Add Task. When you add a new task, SharePoint keeps the interface simple, so the only questions that you really need to answer are the following:

- Name of the task

- Start date

- End date

- Whom the task is assigned to

By clicking anywhere on the Project Summary Web Part itself, the Timeline tab on the ribbon becomes active, as shown in Figure 4-21. This allows you to customize the details of the manner in which you are viewing the project summary.

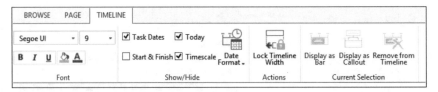

Figure 4-21 The Timeline ribbon as seen from within the Project Summary Web Part.

If you click an actual task list, you will be presented with a Timeline view. The timeline is a new way to represent the status of team tasks visually. Adding tasks to the timeline is easy: choose the ellipsis icon next to a task and choose Add To Timeline.

Once again, as with the Project Summary Web Part, clicking an item in the timeline activates the ribbon presenting you with multiple options, as shown in Figure 4-22.

Figure 4-22 The Timeline ribbon as it appears from the Timeline Web Part.

Managing tasks

Because most of us work on more than one project at a time, SharePoint 2013 now provides an aggregated view all your tasks called *My Tasks*. This includes tasks from team and project sites, Outlook tasks, and Microsoft Project tasks. This pulls all your tasks into one view and allows you to organize and manage both personal and assigned tasks from team and project sites. You will find your tasks by going to your Newsfeed and clicking Tasks in the navigation on the left side of the page. As shown in Figure 4-23, your tasks are grouped by source and by project so that you have context of where the tasks are coming from.

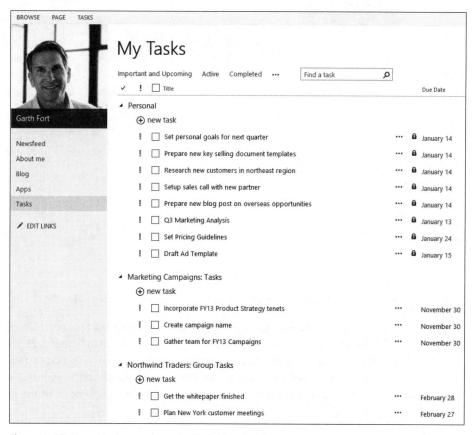

Figure 4-23 Users' tasks are shown in their Newsfeed.

On the My Tasks page, you can click the exclamation mark next to any task to mark it as important and add it to the Important And Upcoming view, which is a useful way to look at what is most urgent for you to get working on. This view provides a personal timeline to visualize all your tasks that are due in the upcoming weeks and any tasks that are marked as important. An example of this is shown in Figure 4-24.

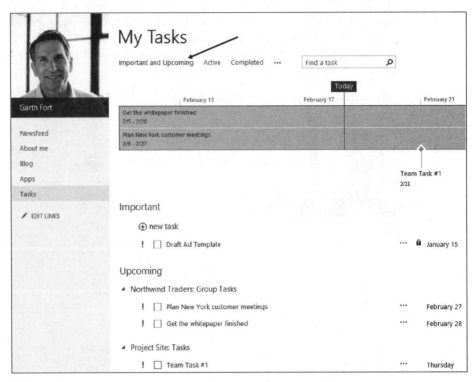

Figure 4-24 Important and upcoming tasks are shown in a user's Newsfeed.

If you need to work with a task in Project, you can select the task and then click the Open With Project button on the List tab of the ribbon, as shown in Figure 4-25. (Note that this is the same ribbon where you can opt to synchronize items to Outlook.) If you choose to synchronize your tasks to Outlook, they can also be displayed in your task app for mobile devices, such as the Outlook calendar hub on the Windows Phone or the Reminders app on iOS.

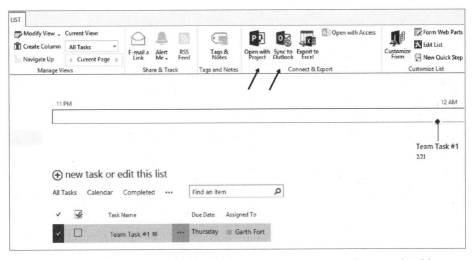

Figure 4-25 The options to open a task with Project and Sync To Outlook are on the ribbon.

Summary

Team and project sites in SharePoint 2013 are the most popular site templates for a reason: They provide a better way to perform many day-to-day business functions. Team and project sites help you do the following:

- Organize a team of people to collaborate on a project.

- Spend less time providing and receiving status updates.

- Get new team members on board rapidly.

- Retain all project documents, tasks, and email together in one master location.

- Communicate status and timelines to the team and other stakeholders efficiently and at the same time.

Now that you have a good grasp of team and project sites, you will turn your attention to understanding all the integration points between SharePoint and the Office 2013 client software in the next chapter. Gaining a full understanding of the myriad possibilities for how Office can be integrated with SharePoint will help you get even more value from your collaboration sites.

Using Office applications with SharePoint

C HAPTER 3, "Working with list and library apps," explained how Microsoft SharePoint 2013 enables you to use SharePoint lists and libraries to store data and files, including Microsoft Office files. Using the browser, users can easily edit documents and content. When the user clicks a file, if on the user's computer, there is a program associate with file extension that program opens. Therefore, from the browser, you can interact with client applications; however, Office 2013 client applications improve the user experience because the capabilities of SharePoint are directly accessible from within the Office applications.

Using SharePoint 2013 as a collaborative platform with Office 2013 client applications, you can improve an organization's overall content management strategy, which in turn improves search results from SharePoint and the user's information retrieval performance. By using the SharePoint capabilities and using the Office client application in place of the browser, users have a seamless user experience. Individual users can share files easily with their team and coauthor a document in almost real time.

However, the integration of Office applications with SharePoint goes beyond opening an Office application, modifying content, saving the content to SharePoint, and then closing the Office application. Users can now complete whole tasks or business processes within an Office application, especially with the use of apps for Office, which is new in Office 2013.

The new apps for Office enable users to run the same solutions across applications, platforms, and devices, and provide an enhanced experience within Office applications by integrating rich content and services from the web. These apps can be managed by using Group Policy settings and monitored using the new Telemetry Dashboard.

More information about the types of apps for Office and the applications that support them can be found at *technet.microsoft.com/en-us/library/jj219429.aspx.*

This chapter walks you through how Office 2013 applications can act as the client to SharePoint 2013. This chapter covers a wide array of the Office applications, including Microsoft Word 2013, Microsoft Excel 2013, Microsoft PowerPoint 2013, Microsoft Access 2013, Microsoft OneNote 2013, Microsoft Publisher 2013, Microsoft Outlook 2013, Microsoft InfoPath 2013, Microsoft Visio 2013, Microsoft Project 2013, SkyDrive Pro, and Office Web Apps (OWA). This chapter does not discuss the capabilities of SharePoint Server 2013 as a document management solution, which is covered in Chapter 11, "Managing documents."

> **Note**
> Organizations that have implemented SharePoint 2013 but are still using Office 2010, Office 2007, Office 2003, or Office XP should experience no loss of functionality within their environment. If they have upgraded their previous Office version to Office 2013 but are still using versions of SharePoint prior to SharePoint 2013, they will find some features and functionality that will not be as robust as they would be if they were using SharePoint 2013.

Editing documents in Office

The vast array of applications offered in the Office suite provides various ways of properly editing documents and content so that you can not only take advantage of the technology at your fingertips, but also allow SharePoint to interact and assist in editing and managing this content. Today's workers are highly mobile and often need to collaborate from different physical locations. When Office is used in concert with SharePoint 2013, users can create and collaborate on content simultaneously with other members of the organization.

When you edit documents with Office, you have the option of locking the editing to a single user at a time or opening the file to multiple users for real-time coauthoring. By using the collaborative functionality found in SharePoint, you can cross departmental, cultural, and organizational hurdles to receive feedback and additional ideas from a much larger audience quickly.

Office allows for similar editing of content in Word, Excel, PowerPoint, Visio, and OneNote files stored within SharePoint. Not only can users edit content in document libraries from within the Office application, they can also use SharePoint's collaborative editing features to enable users to work on content in an environment separated from the main SharePoint site. Office applications can initiate ad hoc knowledge management around a particular document or piece of content to gain insight from other users and take advantage of their best practices, lessons learned, or in-depth knowledge on a topic. Office applications have the Save To SharePoint functionality in the Backstage view under the Save As tab, as shown in Figure 5-1. The new look to the Save As tab lists SharePoint and SkyDrive before the Computer option. The position of Computer in this list reflects the trend that you may use many different devices, so it makes no sense to save files in folders on a specific computer.

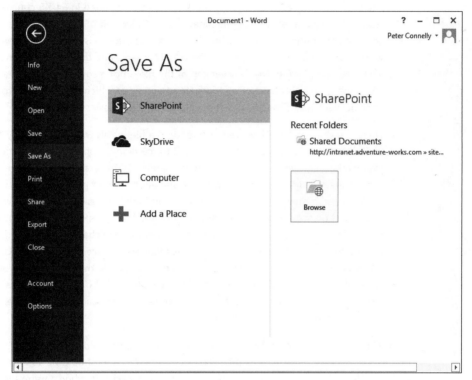

Figure 5-1 In Office client applications, you can save documents to SharePoint and SkyDrive using the Save As tab in the Backstage view.

> **Note**
>
> Publisher 2013 is a notable exception. This is because the tools' functionality makes the collaborative feature of no substantial value.

INSIDE OUT Shredded storage

SharePoint 2013 implements a new functionality called *shredded storage* that is used when storing files. When versioning is enabled on a document library, only the changes made while editing a version of a file are added to the content databases. The default size of a "shred" is 64 KB, meaning that files can be managed in 64-KB chunks and stored in the database, not as one Binary Large Object (BLOB) per file; instead, they are saved as multiple BLOBs per file, so long as the file size is greater than the default write chunk size. Therefore, in SharePoint 2013, there is no duplication when saving a new version of a file. The new version of the file is not a complete copy of a single file; rather, it is a construct of multiple shreds, some of which are obtained from the previous versions of the file and some are specific to this version of the file.

There is some overhead involved in shredding a file in this way, and typically 10 KB to 50 KB of extra storage per file is needed to manage the shreds. This additional overhead is negligible when versioning is enabled. With versioning the changes made to a file are managed on the client to the SharePoint server interface by the Cobalt protocol and between the SharePoint server and the SQL server as shreds. When a file is changed on the client, the changes are uploaded to SharePoint. SharePoint then processes the changes so just the shreds that contain the changes are uploaded as new BLOBs to the SQL server. The old BLOBs that are replaced by the new BLOBs are retained for version history management. Therefore, a file that has, say, 10 versions stored in SharePoint will no longer be represented by 10 different full copies of the file. Instead, the first version plus the shreds changed at each stage are stored, resulting in a significant reduction in required storage.

With the use of shredded storage, network utilization should be reduced, which will improve both performance and infrastructure costs. Users should be able to start working with a file before it is completely downloaded, and when a user saves a document to SharePoint, the document is uploaded to the server in the background; thus, it seems as if the save happens immediately and control of the application is returned to the user nearly instantaneously, providing a great user experience (UX).

With the use of shredded storage, you can expect the size of your content databases to be smaller relative to the equivalent SharePoint 2010 database. However, be aware that when you upgrade from SharePoint 2010 to SharePoint 2013, your stored files are not automatically shredded. Shredded storage will be used only the next time the user needs to modify a file, after the upgrade has been implemented.

So as a recap, the Cobalt protocol is used between client-side programs and SharePoint server to ensure only net changes are replicated across the network from the client computer to the SharePoint server. Between the SharePoint server and the SQL server, only shredded BLOBs that correspond to the change are written to the database, known as *partial file updates (PFU)*. When a user uploads and replaces a file using the browser, then a full file update (FFU) occurs, where the file is reshredded. Shredded storage is not limited to Office file format; therefore, shredding is applicable to all file types. Shredded storage is implemented by SharePoint 2013 and is supported by both Micro-soft SQL Server 2008 R2 Service Pack 1 and SQL Server 2012.

To learn more about shredded storage, read Bill Baer's blog posts at *blogs.technet.com/b/ wbaer/archive/2012/12/20/shredded-storage-and-the-evolution-of-sharepoint-s-storage-architecture.aspx* and at *blogs.technet.com/b/wbaer/archive/2012/11/12/introduction-to-shredded-storage-in-sharepoint-2013.aspx*.

Opening and saving files in SharePoint libraries

SharePoint and Windows offer several ways to save content directly into SharePoint. The File Open and File Save As dialog boxes are the most popular and well-known options for saving content, and they will continue to be the most popular methods to save content directly in SharePoint. To save content directly in SharePoint, use the following steps:

1. In any Office program, on the Backstage view, select the Open or Save As tab.

2. There are several options for locating the SharePoint site where you would like to save your file:

   - In the right pane, under Recent Folders, click the link to a document library. This list contains SharePoint libraries where you have recently opened documents.

   - When the Recent Folder list does not contain the required library, click Browse to open the Save As dialog box.

   - When the SharePoint option is not available on the Open or Save As tab, click Computer, and then click Browse to open the Save As dialog box.

   When using the Save As dialog box, you can do either of the following:

   - Under Favorites, click SharePoint, and then click one of the libraries that you synchronize between your computer and SharePoint, as shown in the following graphic.

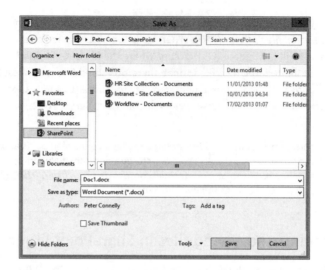

This option is available if you have SkyDrive Pro installed and you have clicked Sync on the global navigation bar of any SharePoint site. More information on SkyDrive Pro and the Sync option can be found later in this chapter.

- Alternatively, type or paste the site's URL into the File Name input box and press Enter. The Save As dialog box will switch into Web view, displaying the site's content. All the site's document libraries will be displayed in addition to all related sites and workspaces, as shown here.

Double-click the library that you would like to open and browse to the appropriate location within the library to save your file. In this example, the file is being saved at the top level of the document library. The user is able to view the other files that exist within the library, as shown here.

3. If you want to overwrite an existing file, double-click that file. Otherwise, type in the name of the file in the file name input box, and then click Save.

Saving documents directly from Office applications to a SharePoint is a best practice when a file is to be shared with other users, as it allows for one definitive copy of that file and users do not have to worry whether they are looking at the most up-to-date copy of that file.

More information on managing documents can be found in Chapter 11.

Checking in and checking out files

When editing files, a key feature of SharePoint and Office applications is the check-in and checkout capability. This feature enables a user to temporarily prevent other users from making simultaneous changes. The edits made while the document is checked out are not accessible or viewable by anyone until the document is checked back into the library. This feature works with the version control and tracking mechanism found in SharePoint so that a new version of the file is created only when the file is checked back in, not every time a file is simply opened, closed, or saved.

Using Word, PowerPoint, Excel, or Visio, you can check in files to a SharePoint library. SharePoint enables users of the Office applications to work with checked-out files on their local hard drive, regardless of whether they are connected to the local network. When a copy is checked out, it is stored by default in the Office Document Cache folder in the My Documents folder on your computer (%userprofile%\Documents\SharePoint Drafts). When traveling, or if you are unable to connect to the network, saving an offline copy of files allows you to work with a file on your local hard drive while SharePoint indicates to other users the document's status.

INSIDE OUT   Changing the offline location where SharePoint files are stored

The Office Document Cache is used by the Office Upload Center to give you a way to see the state of files that you're uploading to a server—keeping track of how uploads are progressing and whether any files need your attention. You can manage the Office Document Cache settings by customizing the settings in the Office Upload Center, and you can also change the location where offline files are stored from within Office applications by navigating to the Backstage view and then clicking Options to display the Word Options dialog box, shown here. In the left pane, click Save, and then, in the Offline Editing Options For Document Management Server Files area, select the required option and save location.

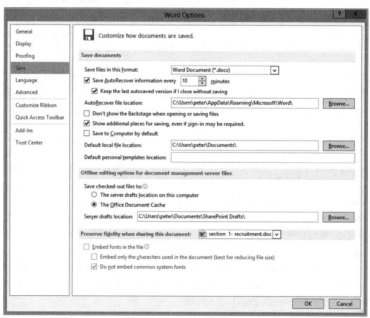

When you change the Office Document Cache location and click OK, the registry key, HKEY_CURRENT_USER\Software\Microsoft\Office\15.0\Internet\OfficeCacheLocation is modified.

The value of the Office Document Cache location must point to a valid location that exists on a local drive to which the user has write access. Changing this location to a location that is accessible to other users has security risks.

When a file is checked out, a green arrow icon appears on the icon to the left of the file; other users are able to open a read-only copy of the file, but they will not be able to make any changes or save the file that is checked out. Site administrators can configure libraries to require users to check out files before editing them. Most Office applications allow you to comment on the content of the file. These comments are stored within the document.

A user can check in a file and select the Retain Check Out option to allow other users to see the changes that were made but to continue to leave the document in a checked-out state.

> **Note**
>
> If checkout is required within a document library, a user who wants to work on the file will be notified that the file is being checked out prior to editing being enabled.

Checking out a file with the browser

When you check out a file from a library, you cannot use the coauthoring functionality. By checking out a file for your exclusive use, it is only editable by one person: you. While the file is checked out, you can edit and save the file, close it, and reopen it. Other users cannot change the file or see your changes until you check the file back into the library. To check out a document using the browser, use one of the following methods:

- Pause the cursor over the file you wish to check out, and then select the check box that appears to the left of the file. On the Files Ribbon tab, select Check Out in the Open & Check Out group. This method can be used to check out multiple files at the same time.

- Click the ellipsis to the right of the document and then, in the Open menu, click the ellipsis to open the List Item menu (LIM). Select Check Out, as shown in Figure 5-2.

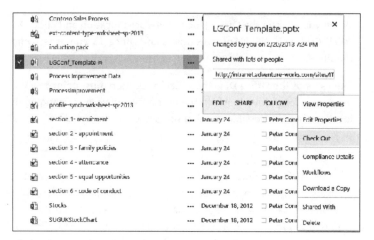

Figure 5-2 A user can select the Check Out option from the document, the Ribbon menu, or the drop-down list within a document library.

Checking out a file from within Word, PowerPoint, or Excel

When you have already opened a document from a library, you can use the following steps to check out that document within Word, PowerPoint, or Excel:

1. Navigate to the Info tab on the Backstage view.

2. Click Manage Versions, and then click Check Out, as shown here.

The content of the file is displayed. If you return to the Backstage view, you will see a new section, Checked Out Document, added above the Protect Document section on the Info tab, that allows you to check in the file or discard the check out to undo the previous checkout.

Checking out a file from within Visio

As with other Office files, you can save Visio files in SharePoint libraries, and also if you have purchased SharePoint Server Enterprise CALs, then you can use Visio Services to display Visio diagrams. Chapter 17, "Working with Visio Services," details Visio Services and the use of the Visio client application to facilitate the development of solutions using Visio Services. This section explores how to manage files from within the Visio client application.

When a user has used Visio to open a document that resides in a SharePoint library, the following steps can be used to check out that document:

1. Navigate to the Info tab on the Backstage view.

2. Click Check Out, as shown here.

A dialog box briefly displays, stating that the file is being checked out and then the Check Out button on the Info tab is replaced with a Check In split button that allows you to check in the file or discard the check out to undo the previous checkout.

Editing a file that is configured as Check Out Required

When you click a file in a library that is configured as Check Out Required, the relevant application opens and displays the contents of the file. In Word 2007, Excel 2007, or PowerPoint 2007 and later, you will see a warning message at the top of the document as shown in Figure 5-3, stating that you have to check out the file in order to edit it. You can close the warning message by clicking the X icon to the right of the message. In the title bar of the application, (Read Only) is appended to the name of the file.

Figure 5-3 A security message notifies you that you have to check out the file in order to edit it.

In Visio, there is no visual indication that the file must be checked out; however, as with other office applications, when you display the Backstage view, you are notified that checkout is required, as shown in Figure 5-4. Therefore, in Visio, unless you display the Backstage view, it is not obvious that checkout is required.

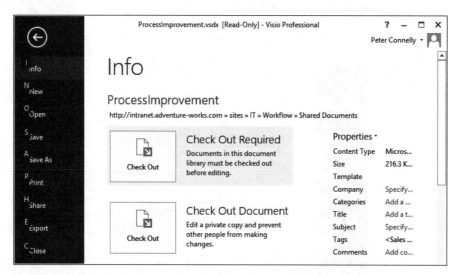

Figure 5-4 Only in the Backstage view of Visio are you notified that documents in this document library must be checked out before editing.

If you do not check out a Visio file when checkout is required, you can modify the draft copy of the file, then when you try to save the Visio file, a warning message is displayed at the top of the document, as shown in Figure 5-5.

Figure 5-5 An Upload Failed message is displayed when you try to save a Visio file if it is not checked out, and the library where it is stored is enabled for Check Out Required.

When an upload has failed, then a Resolve menu is displayed on the Info tab in the Backstage view in Visio, as shown in Figure 5-6. The Resolve menu provides the options: Check Out & Upload, Save A Copy, and Discard Changes.

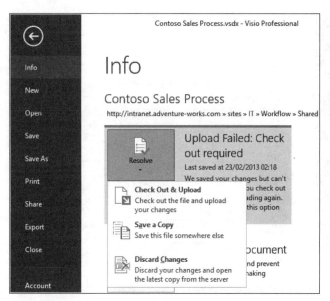

Figure 5-6 In Visio, you can use the Backstage view to resolve upload failures due to checkout-required configurations on a library.

Closing a checked out file

When you close a file that is checked out, a dialog box opens and asks whether the file should remain checked out to you or whether you would like to undo the checkout so others can edit the document, as shown in Figure 5-7.

Figure 5-7 When closing a checked-out file, you are prompted to decide what to do.

Checking in a file from within Word, PowerPoint, Excel, or Visio

When you use an Office application to open a document that is checked out in a library, from within the Office application, you can check the document in. Use the following procedure in Word, PowerPoint, or Excel to check in a document to SharePoint.

1. Within Word, PowerPoint, or Excel, navigate to the Info tab on the Backstage view and then click Check In, as shown here. In Visio, you will then need to click Check In again.

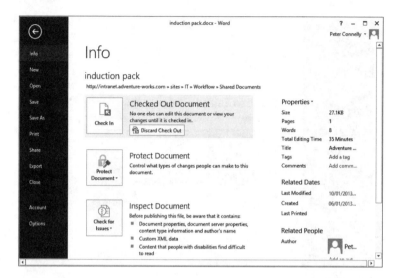

2. The Check In dialog box allows you to type a comment and provides the option to keep working on the file after checking in the document. When minor or major versioning is enabled for a library, you can also select if you want to check the file in as a minor or major version, as shown here.

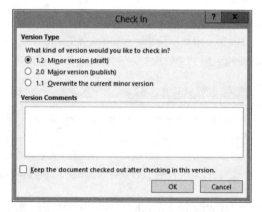

On the Info tab to the right of the Check In option, you can choose to discard checkout to undo the previous checkout. A dialog box opens and warns you that you have changes that haven't been checked in yet and whether you still want to undo the checkout.

> **Note**
>
> The Keep The Document Checked Out After Checking In This Version option is available when versioning is not enabled. When a library is enabled for versioning, then this option is not available if you are checking in a major version or publishing a file. It will be available when checking in a minor version of the file.

Coauthoring with SharePoint 2013

You can use the coauthoring feature in SharePoint 2010, SharePoint 2013, or Office 365 to enable multiple users to work on a document, at any time, without interfering with each other's changes. It can only be used in libraries where versioning is enabled and checkout is not used. Office 2010 users have the same set of coauthoring features when they open documents from SharePoint 2013 or Office 365 as they do when they open documents from a SharePoint 2010 document library.

> **Note**
>
> The coauthoring functionality is also available to Office 2013 users who have SkyDrive accounts, whether or not SharePoint 2013, SharePoint 2010, or Office 365 are used. This chapter only covers use of coauthoring in SharePoint.

Coauthoring removes barriers to server-based document collaboration and helps organizations to reduce the overhead associated with traditional methods of sharing documents, such as attaching files to emails, thus reducing the likelihood of someone editing an out-of-date version of the document. The coauthoring functionality requires no additional server setup. The functionality is available by default for documents stored in SharePoint 2013 and Office 365 when using the same tools and technologies that are already used by users to manage files in SharePoint. For example, you can coauthor Word 2010 and Word 2013, Excel 2010 and Excel 2013, PowerPoint 2010 and PowerPoint 2013, OneNote 2010 and OneNote 2013, and Visio 2013 files using one of the Office client applications or one of the Office Web Apps.

Coauthoring using Visio 2013 is detailed in Chapter 17.

Coauthoring is easy and seamless from a user's perspective. To edit a document, she only has to click the document in the document library and begin making her edits. If another user already has the document open at the same time, then access to the document is not blocked for either of them, nor will they have any errors appear.

If the users are using the Word or PowerPoint client applications or Word Web App and they save the documents, the other users in the files will receive a notification that there are new edits. By refreshing their view (pressing the F5 key), they can see the new edits immediately. Alternatively, they can continue making their changes and refresh at a later time in order to see the other edits. PowerPoint Web App and Excel Web App autosave so that users can view any changes automatically. Because of the powerful versioning and tracking tools included within the SharePoint platform, the document is protected so that it is possible to roll back to previous versions easily should there be any issues with the quality or integrity of the edits entered. As an added bonus, if Microsoft Lync Server is installed in the network, the online status of each of the users is viewable and instant messaging can be initiated so they can chat with each other concerning their changes.

When using OneNote, that is OneNote 2010, OneNote 2013, or OneNote Web App, users are able to share notes easily. If a user edits one page of a notebook, those edits are synchronized automatically with other users of that notebook. By doing so, each user is assured that they are working with a complete set of notes. Edits made by multiple people on the same page appear automatically, thus enabling near real-time collaboration. Versioning makes it possible for users to see what edits are new, who made a specific edit, and roll back to previous versions.

Excel 2010 and Excel 2013 do not support coauthoring of workbooks on SharePoint or Office 365. However, the Excel client application does support non-real-time coauthoring of workbooks stored locally or on network (UNC) paths through the use of the Shared Workbook feature. SharePoint does support coauthoring of notebooks through the use of the Excel Web App, which is included with OWA. More on OWA can be found later in this chapter.

INSIDE OUT   Improvements when coauthoring with Office 2013

Changes in coauthoring for Office 2013 include:

- Coauthoring is now supported in Visio Professional 2013, Word Web App, and PowerPoint Web App.

- Seeing other editors who join the document to coauthor is faster in Word 2013, Excel 2013, PowerPoint 2013, and Visio Professional 2013.

- Updates are faster when multiple users coauthor in the same OneNote page.

Users who coauthor also benefit from these changes in Office Web Apps, Office 2013, and SharePoint 2013:

- Users can view, add, and reply to comments in Word Web App and PowerPoint Web App.

- Users can open Word files that contain revision marks in Word Web App.

- Users can set document permissions and send sharing notifications easily by using the Share With People feature in Office 2013 and SharePoint 2013.

Important considerations

Coauthoring was designed to be easy to set up and require minimal management support. However, there are several issues that must be considered when you set up and manage coauthoring:

- **Permissions** In order to have multiple people edit the same document, the users will require edit permissions for the document.

- **Versioning** SharePoint will keep track of the changes to the document through versioning. By default, this feature is turned off. SharePoint supports two kinds of versioning: major and minor. If major versioning is enabled, set a reasonable maximum number of versions to store.

- **Number of versions** The number of versions that are saved will have an impact of server storage requirements. As such, you should monitor this number carefully. The number of versions saved can be controlled in the Document Library Settings. OneNote notebooks that are frequently updated may result in many versions being stored on the server. In order to avoid using space unnecessarily, it is recommended that an administrator set the maximum number of retained versions to a reasonable number on document libraries used to store OneNote notebooks.

- **Versioning period** The versioning period refers to how often SharePoint will create a new version of a Word or PowerPoint file that is being coauthored. By setting this to a low value, you will cause SharePoint to capture versions more often. This is useful for tracking more detailed information, but you will also incur a higher usage of space on the server. The versioning period does not affect OneNote notebooks. This value can be altered on the server by adjusting the coAuthoringVersionPeriod property.

- **Checking out** When you check out a file, you lock the file for editing so that only the person who has the document checked out can edit the file. As such, when a file is checked out, coauthoring is checked out. Therefore, Require Check Out should not be enabled on libraries where coauthoring will be used. Also, users should not check out a document manually when coauthoring is being used.

More information on planning and configuring versioning can be found in Chapter 11.

Coauthoring OneNote notebooks

OneNote notebooks store version information within the file itself. This is unlike Word or PowerPoint, which store version information within SharePoint. Due to this difference, content owners should not enable minor versioning when storing OneNote notebooks in a SharePoint library, as this will interfere with the synchronization and versioning capabilities that are built into OneNote.

Table 5-1 summarizes the Office application versions that are needed to take advantage of the coauthoring functionality that is available with SharePoint.

TABLE 5-1 Coauthoring in SharePoint 2010, SharePoint 2013, and Office 365

Office version	SharePoint 2013 configured to use Office Web Apps Server	Office 365	SharePoint 2010 with Office Web Apps enabled
Excel 2013	No	No	No
Excel Web App	Yes	Yes	Yes
Excel 2010	No	No	No
OneNote 2013	Yes	Yes	Yes
OneNote Web App	Yes	Yes	Yes
OneNote 2010	Yes	Yes	Yes
PowerPoint 2013	Yes	Yes	Yes
PowerPoint Web App	Yes	Yes	Yes
PowerPoint 2010	Yes	Yes	Yes
Word 2013	Yes	Yes	Yes
Word Web App	Yes	Yes	Yes
Word 2010	Yes	Yes	Yes
Visio 2013	Yes	Yes	Yes
Visio Web App	No	No	No
Visio 2010	No	No	No
Office 2007 client applications	No	No	No

Coauthoring in a mixed Office environment

You may have a scenario where you want to use coauthoring in an environment where users have different versions of Office available for use.

Mixed environment that has PowerPoint 2007 and Word 2007   Users of earlier versions of Word and PowerPoint can share and edit files stored in SharePoint 2013 or Office 365, exactly as with previous versions of SharePoint. They cannot, however, use coauthoring to work on the files simultaneously. It is highly recommended that Office 2013 be deployed in order to facilitate the best collaboration environment. Users of Office 2007 will not notice a significant difference between their current experience and Office 2013. For example, if a user opens a document stored in SharePoint 2013 that is currently being edited by another user, that person will receive a message informing them that the document is in use and he or she will not be able to edit the document. If no other user is editing the document, Office 2007 users will be able to open it as usual. When an Office 2007 user opens a document, a lock is created on the document, thus preventing Office 2013 users the ability to coauthor the document. This behavior matches earlier versions of SharePoint.

OneNote mixed environments   OneNote 2013 and OneNote 2010 is backward compatible with the OneNote 2007 file format and supports coauthoring. In a mixed environment, however, the OneNote file must be saved in the OneNote 2007 format in order to give OneNote 2010 or OneNote 2013 users coauthor capabilities with users who are using One-Note 2007. By upgrading to at least OneNote 2010 file format, however, users gain several key features, including compatibility with the OneNote Web App that allows users without any version of OneNote installed to edit and coauthor notebooks.

Information on upgrading to OneNote 2013 from a previous version can be found at *go.microsoft.com/FWLink/p/?LinkId=275818*.

Performance and scalability

SharePoint Server and Office applications have been designed to minimize performance and scalability issues associated with coauthoring documents. Office clients do not send or download coauthor information from the server until more than one author is editing the document.

When the server is under heavy load or when a user is not actively editing a document, Office clients are configured to reduce the frequency of synchronization actions related to coauthoring.

Managing versions of a file from within Word, PowerPoint, Excel, or Visio

On the Backstage view Info tab, to the right of Manage Versions, is a list of versions. The Manage Versions menu allows you to manage versions of a file. The options available on this menu are dependent on the Office application used. Figure 5-8 displays the Manage Versions menu in Word.

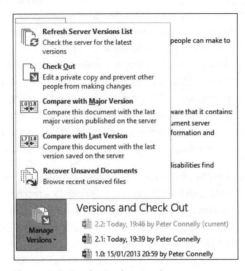

Figure 5-8 On the Backstage view, you can manage file versions that are saved in a SharePoint library.

Users of Word, Excel, and PowerPoint can refresh the list of versions from the server and recover unsaved files, which recovers a draft from the local draft folder in cases where the document author discarded their changes and now wants to recover them.

The following two options allow users within Word to compare versions without opening a separate application:

● **Compare With Major Version** This option opens a window that gives the document author a side-by-side view of every major versions of document.

● **Compare With Last Version** This option opens a window that gives the document author a side-by-side view of the current version and the last saved version.

To manage file versions within Visio, complete the following steps:

1. Navigate to the Info tab on the Backstage view, and then click View Version History, as shown in the following graphic. You may need to scroll to the bottom of the window to see the Versions section.

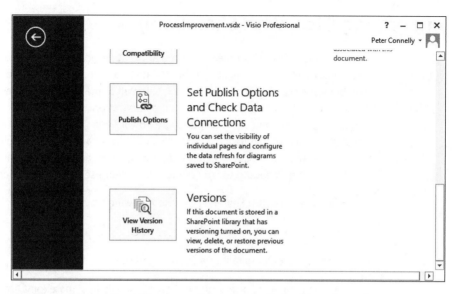

The Versions Saved For *<Filename>* dialog box is displayed, as shown here.

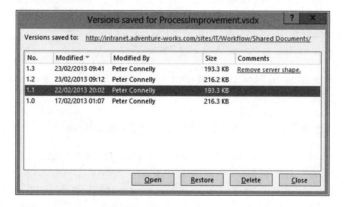

2. Use the dialog box to do one of the following:

   - Open a previous version.

   - Save a version as the current version by selecting a file and then clicking Restore.

   - Delete a previous version.

3. To view the comments of a previous version, click the link in the Comments column of the selected file to display the Check In dialog box.

Integrating Excel with SharePoint

Excel 2013 remains one of the most used applications in the Office suite, providing business users a flexible tool for collecting tabular data and performing day-to-day business analysis. The biggest enhancement in Excel 2013 is that all of the popular business intelligence (BI) features are embedded within the core application. This means that it is no longer necessary to download any add-ins to use PowerPivot, Power View, or the new features in Excel 2013, such as Inquire. Now, all Excel 2013 users have their own built-in set of BI tools. They can analyze and visually explore data of any size, and integrate and show interactive solutions without needing to connect to a SharePoint server or a SQL Server database.

Excel can integrate with SharePoint in the following ways:

- Sharing a workbook.

- Importing Excel data into a SharePoint list.

- Using data in an Excel workbook that is stored in a SharePoint list.

- Using Excel Services to view and interact with Excel workbooks that have been published to SharePoint sites. With SharePoint 2013, you can explore data and conduct analysis in a browser window just as you would by using the Excel 2013 client, including PowerPivot and Power View.

More information on Excel Services can be found in Chapter 15, "Implementing better business intelligence with Excel Services and SQL Server 2012."

Sharing a Excel workbook with SharePoint

Excel workbooks include the ability to merge changes from users, so that several users can access and edit an Excel workbook at the same time. This feature, when coupled with SharePoint, provides a secure collaborative environment for working with Excel files. To do this, you must first save the file to SharePoint, and then, on the Review tab, select Share Workbook in the Changes group, as shown in Figure 5-9.

Figure 5-9 Use the Share Workbook command to share an Excel workbook with SharePoint.

The Share Workbook dialog box is displayed, as shown in Figure 5-10, where you can select the check box to allow changes by more than one user at the same time.

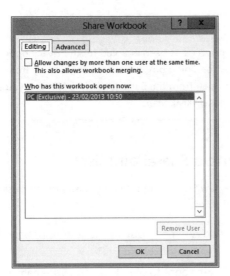

Figure 5-10 Use the Share Workbook dialog box to allow workbook merging and to see who has the workbook open.

When you have allowed workbook sharing, you can then use the Advanced tab in the Share Workbook dialog box to decide to track changes, when to update changes, how to manage conflicting changes, and what to include in personal views (see Figure 5-11).

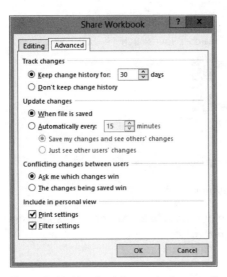

Figure 5-11 Use the Advanced tab to configure how you want to share the workbook.

> **Note**
>
> You cannot share a workbook if privacy has been enabled for it. Privacy options can be configured using the Trust Center dialog box, which you can display from the Excel Options dialog box that you can open from the Backstage view. Nor can you share it if the workbook contains Excel tables or XML maps.

Importing Excel data into a SharePoint list

SharePoint enables you to create a new SharePoint list easily based on an existing Excel spreadsheet by using the following steps:

1. From the Settings icon, click Add An App to display the Your Apps page. Then under Apps You Can Add, click Import Spreadsheet.

   You may need to page through the apps to see this section. Alternatively, type Import into the Find An App input box, as shown here, and press Enter.

2. Using the New page, do the following actions:

   - Type the name and description of the list.

   - Either type the location or browse to an existing Excel spreadsheet to be imported into a new custom list.

   - Click Import.

3. When Excel opens, do the following actions, as illustrated in the following graphic.

   - Select Range Type: Range Of Cells, Table Range, or Named Range.

- Select Range: Select a range within the spreadsheet based on the range type chosen.

- Click Import.

The SharePoint import functionality is powerful; however, you should check that all the columns and data within the new SharePoint list are imported as expected. Once the list is created, you can view or change the data types of the list. There is no connection between the data in the spreadsheet and the data in the SharePoint list.

Analyzing SharePoint list data in Excel

Excel makes it possible for users to create a one-way connection to data that resides in a SharePoint list, so that once changes are made to the list, they can be introduced to the Excel spreadsheet automatically. With this type of one-way connection, the Excel spreadsheet will always be current because the SharePoint site will overwrite any data in the worksheet with the latest SharePoint list data. This makes it easy for users to avoid the pitfalls of emailing Excel attachments to multiple users, managing the retrieval of those updated files, and performing the daunting task of updating the "master" copy in an efficient and accurate manner.

With these two options, you have a choice whether or not to have the data in the Excel spreadsheet updated after a change is made in a SharePoint list. If you want to keep it updated, a one-way connection can be created. If not, you can simply export the table data to a SharePoint site without creating this connection.

You can make the connection between list data and Excel in the browser by clicking Export To Excel on the List or Library tab in the Connect & Export group. Once the data has been copied into the Excel workbook, then, from within Excel, you can use the Refresh command on the Refresh split button on the Design tab in the External Table Data group, as shown in Figure 5-12.

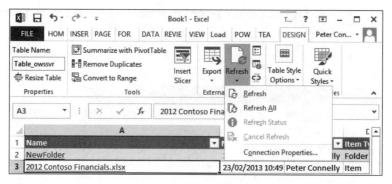

Figure 5-12 Use commands in the External Table Data group on the Design tab to unlink the data in the Excel workbook with the data held in the SharePoint list, open the connected list in the browser, and export table data to SharePoint and to a Visio PivotDiagram.

You can also configure the connection properties using the Connection Properties dialog box, as shown in Figure 5-13, which opens when you click Connection Properties on the Refresh split button.

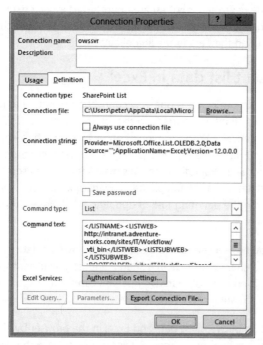

Figure 5-13 Use the Connection Properties dialog box to enable background refresh, authentication, and the connection string.

Integrating Access with SharePoint

Starting with Windows SharePoint Services 3.0, users were allowed to move away from storing their Access database files on file shares and storing the Access databases in SharePoint libraries, providing ways for users to collaborate with Access databases. You can also move data held in Access tables to SharePoint lists, replacing the lists in the Access database as linked tables that will allow updates in SharePoint lists to be reflected in the Access table and vice versa. The data in the linked tables is stored locally on the user's computers and enables users to work offline with data. By centralizing your organization's Access databases and content within SharePoint, you help manage corporate data and improve the ease of access over traditional unmanaged file shares.

However, there are some performance issues with this approach, and it did not allow users to model some of the more complex scenarios built using Access; therefore, new with the Enterprise edition of SharePoint Server 2010 was the ability to create a SharePoint site based on an Access database. This has been extended in SharePoint 2013 with a new, completely rewritten, Access Services service application.

Using Access Services

SharePoint Server 2013 now contains two Access Services service applications:

- **Access Services 2010** This mimics the Access service application on the Enterprise edition of SharePoint Server 2010, by which the tables in your Access database are stored as SharePoint lists on the site that was built from an Access web database site definition.

- **Access Services** When Access 2013 databases are published to SharePoint 2013, an Access web app site is created and your data is now stored in a full-fledged SQL Server database, which is automatically generated in an instance of SQL Server 2012 that was selected by a SharePoint administrator.

> **Note**
> To use either of these service applications, Enterprise Client Access Licenses (CALs) are required.

Using the Access service application, you can quickly build no-code, web-based form applications, known as *web apps*. These web apps are SharePoint apps that can be deployed to SharePoint App Stores. With SharePoint Designer 2013 being deemphasized as a no-code forms tool, Access web apps is a welcome addition.

A SharePoint 2013 Access web app will not have the same limitations that SharePoint 2010 Access web databases had in terms of numbers of fields and sizes of tables. This SQL-integrated approach improves the performance, manageability, and scalability of the web app. It also makes it possible for SQL Server developers to extend the solution by directly connecting to the tables in the database, including building reports with Desktop Access Reports, Excel, and Power View. However, as the data is not stored in SharePoint, some functionality is lost when compared to creating a forms-based application by using InfoPath. For example, you cannot create or initiate a SharePoint workflow on data in Access form applications, nor can you have unique permissions at the list or row level; however, they have far more capabilities for rich forms and reports than were provided in Access Services 2010.

More information on creating Access web apps can be found in Chapter 21, "Creating enterprise forms."

The databases created have a name, such as, db_<guid>, where <guid> is an automatically generated number. The tables, queries, macros, and forms are all stored in this database. Whenever a user visits the app, enters data, or modifies the design of the app by using the browser or Access 2013, she will be interacting with the database; however, the UI will give no indication of this. This does have implications for your database administrator, as well as the operational-level agreements your IT department might have with the business with regard to the maintenance of these Access 2013 web app databases.

The servers that run SQL Server 2012 where the Access web apps databases are to be created do not have to be the same SQL Server instance that SharePoint uses. In fact, it is recommended that the databases for the Access web apps use a different SQL Server instance than the one used for the SharePoint databases. It must be a SQL Server 2012 server configured in mixed security mode, though, because you cannot use previous version of SQL Server to host Access Services databases. Office 365 uses SQL Azure.

For more information on installing Access Services for an on-premises installation, go to *www.microsoft.com/en-us/download/details.aspx?id=30445*. **The setup of Access Services is complex and has many configuration dependencies on SQL Server; therefore, you should strongly encourage your SharePoint administrations to review this information if your organization plans to use Access Services.**

Moving Access data into SharePoint lists

If you do not want to use Access Services, you can link to data held within SharePoint sites. The Access client application allows users to import data, export data, and link to data in SharePoint lists and libraries. The Access file can be uploaded into a SharePoint library, thereby making it easy for users with the access client to share access databases. As the data is held in SharePoint, you can use many of the SharePoint features, such as the alert feature, to inform users when an update to the database content has occurred. You can also run workflows against the data and content managed within SharePoint can be restored like other files in SharePoint using the Recycle Bin, so SharePoint provides a backup benefit to Access users.

A user can move existing content from an Access database into SharePoint via the Move Data SharePoint wizard within Access. This feature exports all the current tables of the database into SharePoint lists. The lists will have all the standard features of SharePoint lists, including the ability to add, delete, and modify content. These links are stored within the Access database along with the other standard Access items such as reports, forms, and queries.

> **Note**
>
> The Export Tables To SharePoint wizard is a powerful and easy-to-use tool, but when moving an existing database into SharePoint, you need to consider the database's size in addition to the performance of your overall environment. An Access Services web-based solution may be more applicable.

To use the Export Tables To SharePoint wizard in Access, perform the following steps:

1. On the Database Tools tab, shown here, click SharePoint in the Move Data group.

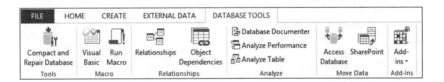

2. In the Export Tables To SharePoint wizard dialog box, specify the SharePoint site where the data should be moved. While the wizard is running, you can cancel the operation at any time by clicking Cancel.

3. Once the wizard has completed, select Show Details to display the details of the move.

   The move process takes a backup of your Access database, creates SharePoint lists for each table in your database, and then replaces the tables with linked tables. By default, the name of the table is used for the name of the new SharePoint lists if the list name already exists on the SharePoint site, a number will be appended to the name of the list.

> **Note**
>
> If you receive a warning message during this process, you should review the log table to confirm that all the data was properly moved and to determine if any actions are necessary on your part to allow for a successful data move.

Should you only want to export or import a single table to SharePoint, in the All Tables window, right-click the table that you want to export and then, from the context menu, select Export and then click SharePoint List, as shown in Figure 5-14, to display the Export – SharePoint Site dialog box. You can also find the SharePoint List option on the More split button on the External Data tab in the Export group.

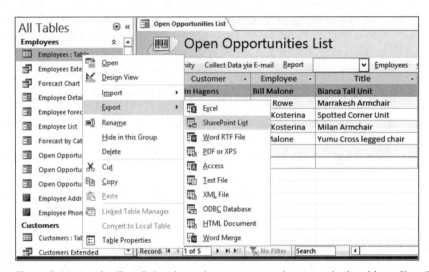

Figure 5-14 Use the SharePoint List option to export or import a single table to SharePoint.

In the Export – SharePoint Site dialog box, enter the site where you want to create a new list, provide a name for the new list, and then click OK. Any related tables will also be moved to SharePoint.

By default, the browser will open and display the list just created. You can save the export steps for later reuse, as shown in Figure 5-15.

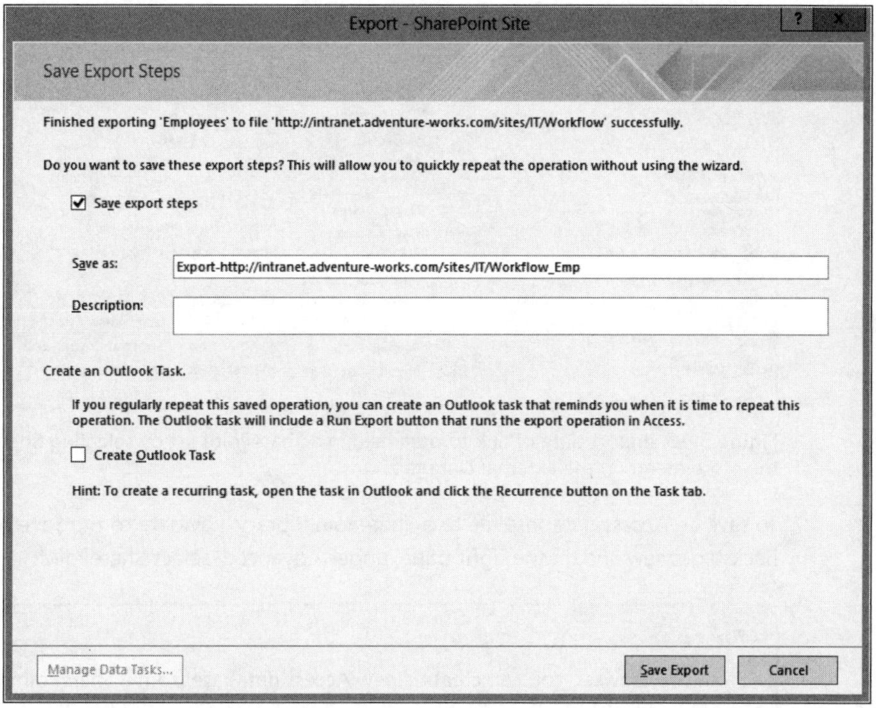

Figure 5-15 Once you have exported data to a SharePoint site, you can save the export steps, rename it, and create a recurring task in Outlook to act as a reminder when it must be done. The task will include a shortcut to repeat this export action.

> **Note**
>
> Users exporting Access tables to SharePoint will need to have the permissions to create lists in order to use the export to SharePoint lists commands.

If the data already resides in a SharePoint list and you want to use it within an Access database, you can either copy the data into a new Access table or create a linked table that points to the SharePoint list. You can open the Get External Data – SharePoint Site dialog box by right-clicking a table in the All Tables pane or by clicking SharePoint List on the More menu on the External Data tab in the Import & Link group, as shown in Figure 5-16.

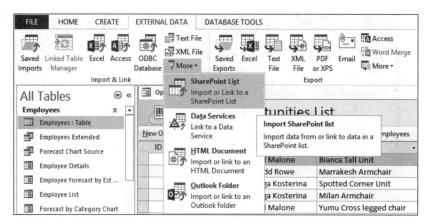

Figure 5-16 Import data or link to data held in a SharePoint list by selecting SharePoint List from the More menu on the External Data tab.

To save an Access database file to a SharePoint library, navigate to the Save As tab on the Backstage view and, in the right pane, under Advanced, select SharePoint.

> **Note**
>
> From the browser, you can create a new Access database from a SharePoint list. The list can become either a linked table in the new Access database or the data from the list can be copied to a new table in the database.

Integrating OneNote with SharePoint

OneNote and SharePoint enable users to share their notebooks with multiple users within SharePoint, where they can update a notebook's data in a secure and collaborative environment. From SharePoint, the OneNote notebook owner can specify the permission level for the notebook, allowing specific users to view the notebook and giving other users rights to contribute to the notes. Version history can also be enabled to track the changes that have occurred to the notebook's individual pages. Users can set up alerts and even receive Really Simple Syndication (RSS) feeds about the notebook.

When a notebook is shared, those with the appropriate permissions can contribute. Each coauthor selects whether his or her changes are manually or automatically synchronized in SharePoint. OneNote also places an offline copy of the notes on each user's computer to allow for offline editing. Changes can be synchronized when users go back online.

> **Note**
> A notebook's permission level is set through the SharePoint library security settings.

After integrating Office Web Apps Server with SharePoint Server, a OneNote shared notebook will be created automatically upon creation of a Team Site. We can use this notebook to collect and share information.

Users can create a shared notebook within a SharePoint library easily. When the notebook is shared within the library, it becomes a folder, and each of the sections of the notebook is stored as a file.

To create a new shared OneNote notebook for a SharePoint library, complete the following steps:

1. From the New tab on the Backstage view, select SharePoint and either select a recently visited site or click Browse and specify a SharePoint site.

   Once the notebook is created, a Microsoft OneNote dialog box opens that allows you to invite other people, as shown here.

2. Click Invite People to display the Share tab on the Backstage view, which allows you to send email to the users you want to notify about the new shared notebook, as shown here.

Users can upload an existing notebook to the SharePoint library by using the Share tab on the Backstage view.

OneNote allows users two synchronization options for notebooks maintained in SharePoint. The user can either automatically synchronize the file as changes are made or manually synchronize the file while working offline. Synchronization is set by each user for their local OneNote client; therefore, all open notebooks share the same synchronization settings. In a library where Check Out Required is enabled, automatic synchronization cannot be used because the notebook needs to be checked out before it can be synchronized.

To select a synchronization opinion for the OneNote client, perform the following steps:

1. Navigate to the Info tab on the Backstage view and then click View Sync Status to open the Shared Notebook Synchronization box, shown in the following graphic.

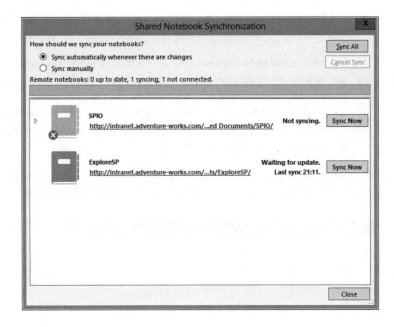

2. Complete one of the following actions:

    •   For automatic synchronization, select Sync Automatically Whenever There Are
        Changes.

    •   Select Sync Manually, if you plan to work offline and will manually synchronize
        by clicking Sync Now when you are connected to the network.

3. Click Close.

Integrating Outlook with SharePoint

The integration of Outlook with SharePoint enhances collaboration and information sharing
within your organization. Outlook enables users to access and update content, as well
as share information within SharePoint across multiple sites. Users can maintain shared
items from calendars, contacts, and tasks lists, in addition to searching, previewing, and
editing documents from within Outlook. Outlook also enables users to receive updates and
notifications about changes that occur within SharePoint in two ways:

- RSS feeds allow users to subscribe to a list, so that when changes occur in a SharePoint list or library, they receive periodic feeds right to Outlook.

- The alert notification features of SharePoint are another powerful way that users can be kept up to date on any content changes within SharePoint. Alerts are much more configurable, and you can receive them at specific times or intervals. You can choose to be notified of any changes that may have occurred within a specific area of SharePoint. The alerts can be modified to deliver a more granular layer of detail so that you are not inundated with alerts.

To connect calendar, contacts, tasks, or a library to Outlook, use the Connect To Outlook command on the List or Library tab, in the Connect & Export group, as shown in Figure 5-17.

Figure 5-17 Use Sync To Outlook to view the contents of tasks, calendar, contacts lists, or libraries with Outlook.

INSIDE OUT   Task synchronization in SharePoint Server 2013

To sync tasks between SharePoint and a user's inbox, and to work with them anywhere and have them also appear under Newsfeed in a user's My Site, their mailboxes must be on a server running Microsoft Exchange Server 2013. Information on configuring Exchange Server task synchronization with SharePoint Server can be found at *technet .microsoft.com/en-us/library/jj554516.aspx.*

Once connected to Outlook, users can share information throughout the organization from within Outlook or SharePoint. In Outlook, connected libraries can be found below SharePoint Lists, as shown in Figure 5-18. Calendar lists are displayed under Other Calendars in the calendar navigation pane, contact lists are displayed under Other Contacts, and task lists will be listed on the Tasks navigation pane under Other Tasks.

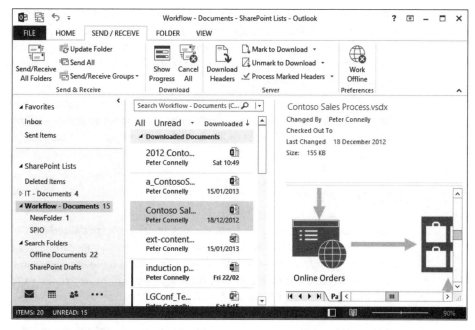

Figure 5-18 Within Outlook, you can see the files stored within a library and a preview of the contents of the file.

Outlook users can access connected lists and libraries, the contents of which can be taken offline and updated when the Send/Receive command is run. New files added to a SharePoint folder that is connected to your Outlook should download automatically. If they do not, you can download a file from a SharePoint library into Outlook by performing the following steps:

1. In Outlook, select the SharePoint list connected with Outlook that contains the file that you want to download.

2. In the SharePoint Library Folder message list, in the Available For Download group, right-click the file that you want to download.

    If you would like to download multiple files at once, you can also hold down the Ctrl key as you select the files you'd like to download.

3. Select Mark To Download on the Send/Receive tab in the Server group.

    If you have a connection to the server, the file will be downloaded. If file does not download, click Send/Receive.

With connected calendar lists, users can view an overlay of the calendars for an all-encompassing view of event information. Users can connect to and view multiple calendars simultaneously to check for possible event conflicts, allowing for greater control over their schedules. This feature also assists managers in proper resource scheduling and planning by avoiding overbooking people.

If you no longer want a SharePoint list or library connected to Outlook, navigate to where you can see the list or library in Outlook, right-click the list or library, and then select, for example, Delete Folder. The list or library will no longer appear in Outlook but will still exist within the SharePoint site.

Using form libraries

InfoPath forms are managed in form libraries, which are a specialized class of document libraries optimized to work with XML-based forms. A site owner can specify a particular InfoPath form as the form library's document template. They can then use its browser-enabled document option to display InfoPath forms within the webpage, using InfoPath Form Services (IFS), which requires SharePoint Server Enterprise CALs. This allows for seamless integration with SharePoint's web-based collaboration platform. Form libraries also have the option to allow for content type management and version control. They inherit all the other powerful features that a standard SharePoint library has to offer.

There are two InfoPath products:

- InfoPath Designer 2013, which is used to design and publish forms.

- InfoPath Filler 2013, which is used to enter data into a form. Many organizations do not use this product because forms are published as web forms and users use the browser to display the form and enter data.

A user can publish a form template directly from InfoPath Designer to a SharePoint form or document library in the same way that users can save Word documents directly from Word into a document library. Before an InfoPath user publishes a browser-compatible form template, they should run the Design Checker in InfoPath Designer to identify and fix any compatibility issues that the form's design might have prior to publishing. Design Checker can be found on the File tab and is a great tool for final testing and review.

More information on using InfoPath can be found in Chapter 21.

INSIDE OUT   InfoPath 2013 and SharePoint Server 2013

InfoPath 2013 has not changed much from InfoPath 2010, and that is also the same for IFS in SharePoint Server 2013. InfoPath 2013 has a new look, as do other Office 2013 client applications. The Microsoft Visual Studio Tools For Applications integrated development environment is removed from InfoPath Designer 2013. The developing environment is now Microsoft Visual Studio 2012 with the Visual Studio Tools For Applications 2012 add-on installed. However, no new functionality or scenarios have been introduced.

Integrating Project with SharePoint

Project can be used to share project plans with team members when integrated with SharePoint. Key features include the ability to create a project plan based on an existing SharePoint task list and dynamically produce task lists for new project plans. As with the other Office applications, Project can use SharePoint's version control and real-time coauthoring features.

Note

Project Server enables the user to create and publish SharePoint project sites for dedicated project plans. When My Sites are used, users can see an aggregation of their SharePoint, Project Server, and Outlook/Exchange Server tasks on their My Tasks page. For example, users can update their existing Project Server assignments on the My Tasks page, and the results are synchronized to Project Server 2013.

You can connect tasks lists with Project using the browser or from within Project. In the browser, on the List tab, click Open With Project in the Connect & Export group. Task items stored in the task list will be directly imported into the project plan. This feature saves the Project author tedious data entry work because values, such as start dates, task progress, and due dates, are carried over into the plan.

To create a new project plan based on an existing task list, use the following steps:

1. In Project, on the New tab of the Backstage view, click the New From SharePoint Task List to display the Import From SharePoint Tasks List dialog box.

2. Enter the URL of the SharePoint site that contains the task list that you want to use and click Check Address.

3.   In the Tasks List drop-down field, select the task list and then click OK.

A new project plan will be created using the imported task items and related metadata. The Info tab on the Backstage view allows you to sync your project plan, details the site and task list the project plan is connected to, and allows you to map Project fields with the columns in the task list.

If you already have a project plan, then you can save it and make your project tasks visible in a SharePoint task list. Once saved, team members can use SharePoint to add, modify, or delete tasks without having direct access to the project plan. You can then synchronize the updated tasks in Project.

To save and synchronize a Project file, perform the following steps:

1.   On the Save As tab on the Backstage view, click Sync With SharePoint.

2.   In the Sync With menu, select Existing SharePoint Site, type the URL of the SharePoint site that contains the tasks list, and then click Verify Site. A valid URL will populate the Tasks List drop-down box, as shown here.

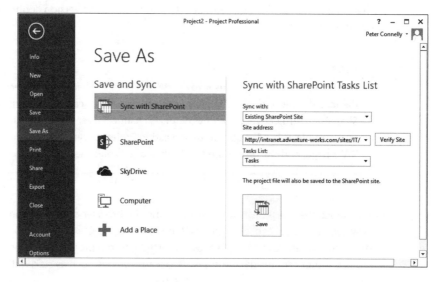

3.   Select a task list, and then click Save.

The Project file is now enabled for synchronization with the selected task list, which contains a task item for every project task.

> **Note**
>
> A project plan can be synchronized only to a single task list at a given time.

Using SkyDrive Pro with SharePoint

SkyDrive Pro is part of Office 2013 (Standard or Professional edition) or an Office 365 subscription that includes Office applications. SkyDrive Pro replaces SharePoint Workspace. SkyDrive Pro is used to create a synchronized copy of a SharePoint library in the SharePoint folder of your home directory (%userprofile%\SharePoint). The SharePoint folder is displayed under Favorites in the Windows Explorer and has the naming convention *<site name> - <library name>*, as shown in Figure 5-19.

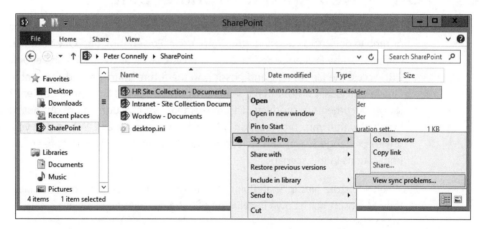

Figure 5-19 You can use SkyDrive Pro to take synchronized files between your computer and libraries on SharePoint sites.

To create a synchronized copy of a document library, in the browser, navigate to the document library, and then, on the global navigation bar, click Sync. After you sync a library, you can access all the files within it from Windows Explorer and Office, even if you don't have an Internet connection. A SkyDrive Pro icon is provided in the Windows system tray, with which you have easy access to the SkyDrive Pro menu, as shown in Figure 5-20.

Figure 5-20 The SkyDrive Pro menu in the Windows system tray can be used to start the Sync Library Wizard.

> More information on keeping teams and workgroups in sync can be found in Chapter 4, "Working with collaboration sites."

Using Office Web Apps with SharePoint

Office Web Apps enables you, when using a supported web browser on a computer or mobile device, to view and edit Word, Excel, PowerPoint, and OneNote files. OWA can be used by Exchange Server 2013 and Lync 2013, as well as by SharePoint 2013, URL-accessible file servers, and possibly in the future, third-party document stores, such as Oracle Universal Content Management (UCM) and EMC's Enterprise Content Management (ECM) Documentum products. This means that even though you might not have SharePoint installed within your organization, you might want to install OWA so that you can use it with Exchange Server and Lync to render documents. However, there are license implications in this scenario.

When you store files in SharePoint Online with Office 365, or if you store files in SkyDrive, then Microsoft has its own installation of OWA so that you can view, create, and modify those files.

INSIDE OUT Mobile browser-based Office viewers

OWA provides mobile browser-based viewers: Word Mobile Viewer, Excel Mobile Viewer, and PowerPoint Mobile Viewer. These are optimized to render documents on phones.

Unlike SharePoint 2010, OWA is no longer a service application. It is now packaged as a separate product and installed on its own set of servers (a farm). This allows you to scale, manage, and maintain Office Web Apps as a separate entity without affecting your installation of SharePoint. The separation of Office Web Apps from SharePoint 2013 also frees the Office Web Application team to enhance the product independent of SharePoint. It is also licensed separately from SharePoint licenses.

There is no licensing required for viewing documents in SharePoint 2013; however, if you want to use OWA to create or modify documents that are stored in SharePoint 2013, you will need to purchase licenses.

More information on about licensing OWA for editing Office files can be found at *technet.microsoft.com/en-us/library/ff431682.aspx#license.*

Some improvements that you will see if you use Office Web Apps in SharePoint 2013 include the following:

- Documents can be viewed in full-screen mode or by using web parts. However, Visio is not part of Office Web Apps, so you should use Visio Services to display Visio files.

- Not-so friendly URLs are removed.

- Multi-authoring is now available with PowerPoint and Word, in addition to OneNote and Excel.

- When a user pauses the mouse over the item on the search results page in SharePoint, OWA displays a preview of the item's content.

> ## Note
>
> If your SharePoint Server farm has been integrated with Office Web Apps Server and Excel Web App, the features available in Excel Services will depend on how Excel Web App has been configured. Excel Web App runs in one of two modes:
>
> - **SharePoint view mode.** In this mode, Excel Services is used to view workbooks in the browser.
>
> - **Office Web Apps Server view mode.** In this mode, Excel Web App is used to view workbooks in the browser.

To integrate Office Web Apps Server 2013 and SharePoint Server 2013, follow these steps:

1. Install and configure SharePoint Server 2013.

2. Install either Windows Server 2008 R2 or Server 2012 on the servers where you plan to deploy OWA.

These servers do not need access to a SQL server, because it does not create any databases. You cannot install Exchange Server, SharePoint, Lync, SQL, or any version of the desktop Office programs on the same servers on which Office Web Apps is installed. If other products that are installed on the same servers as Office Web Apps use web services, they cannot use port 80, 443, and 809.

3. Activate Web Server Role, Application Server Role, and Ink and Handwriting Services Feature on the OWA servers.

4. Deploy Office Web Apps Server 2013 using the guidance provided at *technet.microsoft.com/en-us/library/jj219455.aspx*.

5. Bind the SharePoint Server 2013 farm to the Office Web Apps Server 2013 farm by using the Windows PowerShell New-SPWOPIBinding cmdlet on one of the servers in your SharePoint farm, as documented at *technet.microsoft.com/en-us/library/ff431687.aspx*.

6. Now, you can view and edit Word, Excel, PowerPoint, and OneNote files using a web browser on computers and mobile devices.

Office Web Apps uses a shared XML configuration file called Farm-Settings.xml for the farm, and then each server in the farm has its own Machine_Name.xml file.

Once OWA is installed on a server, there are no visible signs on the Start menu that it is installed. Therefore, other administrators in your organization might incorrectly identify the OWA server as a candidate for a clean install of another product or business purpose that they can use the server for. To manage Office Web Apps, you use Windows PowerShell.

INSIDE OUT PowerPoint Broadcast site template is not supported in SharePoint 2013

In SharePoint 2010, you create the PowerPoint Broadcast site at a site-collection level by using the Central Administration website or Windows PowerShell. This site used OWA and the PowerPoint service application. As OWA is now a separate server product that can serve multiple SharePoint farms, in SharePoint 2013, sites created by using the PowerPoint Broadcast site template are not supported. Any content in such sites must be moved and the sites deleted prior to upgrading any SharePoint 2010 content databases that contain them.

Summary

This chapter explained how Office has powerful integration points with SharePoint. These two platforms together enhance an organization's ability to share content in a secure, efficient, and controlled manner.

Organizations do not need to deploy Office applications to take advantage of the integration of Office with SharePoint. They can instead use Office Web Apps. Office Web Apps Server 2013 is now a separate product that cannot be installed on the same servers as SharePoint 2013, but instead needs its own servers if you want to use it.

The next chapter will explain the principal social tools in SharePoint 2013, such as community sites and Newsfeeds.

Sharing information with SharePoint social networking

Microsoft SharePoint has included features that are "social" in nature for quite a long time now. User profiles, My Sites, blogs, ratings, and so forth all helped SharePoint evolve beyond team collaboration into a social networking tool designed for the enterprise. It was not until the introduction of the Noteboard and other related features in SharePoint 2010 that customers truly began to consider SharePoint a viable enterprise social platform. However, SharePoint 2010 still had many shortcomings, perhaps the most significant of which was that it did not have a true microblog and the threaded discussions were no longer sufficient. Customers that wanted something like an "internal Twitter" were left wanting because of this gap.

Fortunately, the improvements in SharePoint 2013 for social networking are significant. Not only were the features from SharePoint 2010 improved, SharePoint 2013 has upped the game, thanks in part to the following new features:

- Community sites

- The community portal

- Personal newsfeeds

- Ability to follow people, content, sites

- Ability to use @mentions, #tags, and "likes"

- Reputation scores for people and content

There are dozens of interaction points for a user's social experience in various parts of SharePoint 2013, but the center of gravity for the social experience centers around two primary places: the Newsfeed and community sites. Those two key areas of functionality and the details of their subcomponents are what this chapter will focus on.

The Newsfeed

When users sign into SharePoint, they get a Newsfeed link in the upper-right navigation pane that will take them to a personal view of their Newsfeed. Although the My Site infrastructure that was in prior versions of SharePoint still exists, the UI has been completely redesigned in SharePoint 2013 and is sometimes now referred to as a *personal site*. My Site functionality still exists, but the UI has been replaced with the Newsfeed and SkyDrive Pro.

The Newsfeed is robust and filled with socially driven information that is most relevant to the user. The Newsfeed truly becomes the Grand Central Station of the SharePoint 2013 social experience. It is a landing page that is personalized to each user with information that he or she cares about. The Newsfeed displays information from items that you follow, such as people, documents, sites, and tags. It shows several items in the feed, sorted in reverse chronological order. Each user will also see an Everyone feed that shows the last several posts or replies by all users, not limited to the people followed. As shown in Figure 6-1, the Activities feed shows all activity connected with a specific user. Other users can see your Activities feed while browsing your profile or About Me page.

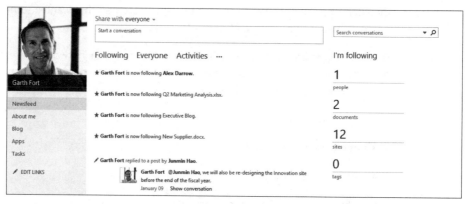

Figure 6-1 The Activities feed shows all activity connected with a specific user.

In addition to notifications about content, the Newsfeed is a place where users can go to view a list of notifications for their social activities within SharePoint communities. The Newsfeed displays items that are specific and relevant to each user. The following is a partial list of community activities that are posted to the Newsfeed:

- Joining a community

- Creating a new post or reply

- Achieving a new level

- Having your reply marked as the Best Reply on a discussion

- "Liking" or rating a post

Public information from each user's profile is displayed in the About Me page. It has a rich view of personal profile information regarding your interests and social connections. The About Me page also displays presence information for the user if he or she is logged onto Microsoft Lync. You can view a new People Card by pausing the mouse over someone's network presence icon. The People Card includes standard contact details, but it now also has a user's personal photo, status updates, activity feeds, and Facebook and LinkedIn account information. You can see an example of the About Me page in Figure 6-2.

Figure 6-2 The About Me page includes a user's personal profile information.

Community sites

The Community Site template is a new SharePoint 2013 site template designed for enterprise social networking. Fundamentally, community sites are a place where people can come to learn about specific topics and share information with a group of people with whom they have something in common. SharePoint communities are a place to ask and answer questions, share knowledge and interesting content, and engage with people who have similar interests.

The four major components of the new Community Sites feature built for SharePoint 2013 include:

- The Community Site template

- Reputation for people and content

- A redesigned discussion experience

- Membership, management, and moderation tools

Details about these four areas are provided throughout this chapter.

INSIDE OUT Community sites or email distribution lists?

In some cases, you may find yourself confused about why you would use a community site when email distribution lists have been in place at your organization for years. While email is still useful for some group collaboration scenarios, it falls far short of providing modern social networking capabilities. Following is a list of potential weaknesses with email distribution lists that might cause you to consider community sites with discussions instead of email:

- Experts are not acknowledged or easily discoverable.

- There is no reward or incentive to contribute.

- There is no easy way to "like" someone's contribution.

- Depending on your systems, email content may not be easily archived.

- New members cannot see the rich history of interaction.

- Frequently asked questions may be asked over and over.

- Email is not as easily searchable by the entire member community.

Community portal

SharePoint 2013 includes a Community Portal Site template so that users can see an aggregated list of all community sites. As shown in Figure 6-3, the portal uses Search to access all the community sites, although you have the option to exclude certain communities if you choose. In addition, security trimming is still in effect, so users will see only portals where they have access. The community portal will also display open communities where users can request to join if they are interested in the topic.

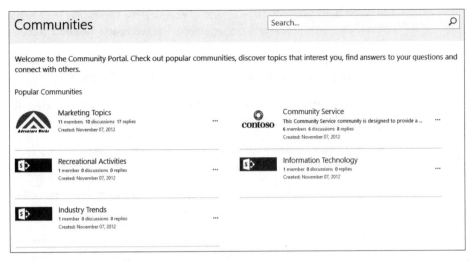

Figure 6-3 Users can see an aggregated list of all community sites in the new Community Portal Site template.

The most popular community sites, as determined by the system, will receive prime time spots on the Community Portal page. Popularity of a community is determined by activity, membership, and other factors. When you create a community portal on your farm/tenant, the portal is added to the promoted sites page. Your users will benefit by being able to quickly discover and navigate to communities they might care about.

Community Site template

The Community Site template provides the UI that members interact with when working in a community. In some ways, it is not much different from a standard team site in that it has the ability to host most of the other common app web parts (such as tasks). However, the site template has four core pages that help set it apart from other SharePoint templates:

- **Home** This is the main landing page for community members.

- **Categories** This page provides the user with a graphical view of the different categories of conversations that are going on within the community. The icons representing each category are definable by the community owner using Community tools. Every discussion post must be put into a category.

- **Members** This is the list of all community members.

- **About** This includes information about the community, such as established date, community guidelines, and so forth.

The community sites also have a handful of web parts specifically built to help with community participation and management. The web parts included in community sites are:

- **Activity Dashboard** ("What's Happening") This web part provides a summary on the community home page of discussions, replies, and members.

- **Community Tools** This web part is a management tool for moderators and owners to perform various community tasks.

- **Top Contributors** This is a web part on the home page that displays some of the most prolific contributors.

- **Discussion List** This web part provides the UI that displays discussions and allows users to interact with the items.

An example of a community site created with the Community Site template is shown in Figure 6-4. On this community home page, you can see most of the items mentioned in the previous lists.

Figure 6-4 A community site home page.

Visiting and joining communities

When you visit a community site that you are not a member of, you will notice a Join This Community button at the top of the page. If the community allows it, you can click this button to join. At that point, the site is also automatically added to your list of followed sites so that community activity will be pushed to your Newsfeed. Until you click Join, you are considered a visitor, which essentially means you can read content, but you cannot contribute anything.

When you join a community, you will be added to the Members list within that community site. Membership status is stored in a Members SharePoint list that exists in each community site; it is not in the site permissions.

INSIDE OUT   Visitors vs. members

Members of a community are entitled to several capabilities that visitors are not. When someone becomes a member, he or she is immediately granted access to the capabilities to not only read content, but also to start truly interacting with it. The following table illuminates the various privileges granted to visitors and members.

Capability	Visitor	Member
View and read discussions	X	X
Follow a community and its associated Really Simple Syndication (RSS) feed	X	X
Follow other community members	X	X
Set "Alert Me" notifications on discussions	X	X
"Like" and reply to other members' posts		X
Receive badges and reputation points		X
Create new discussions		X
Designate a reply as the Best Reply		X
Report items to the moderator		X

Discussions

Within SharePoint community sites, *discussions* provide the tools necessary for community members to create a vibrant, interactive social experience. Discussion capabilities have evolved dramatically in this version of SharePoint, adopting many popular features of consumer social networks (such as microblogging and hash tags).

Any member of a site can create a new discussion. When a new discussion is created, the user must select one of the predefined categories in which the post should be classified. Site owners and moderators define the categories for discussions (more on that later in the chapter).

When creating a new discussion, the member can choose to mark that thread as a question. This allows other community members an opportunity to answer the question, thus bolstering their reputation score in the community. Marking discussion posts as questions is also useful because other community members can filter on answered or unanswered questions, as shown in Figure 6-5.

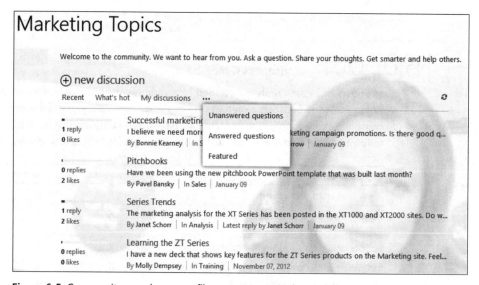

Figure 6-5 Community members may filter on unanswered questions.

Within the discussions, members have take several different actions. They can reply to a post, or to a reply. They can mark one response as the Best Reply for discussions that they created. Any member of the community can report an offensive or inappropriate post to the moderator.

Within a reply, members can use the @ sign to tag other users who will then be notified via email and on their Newsfeed. In addition, within a reply, they can use a hash tag (#) to add a tag. Users who are following that tag will receive a notification on their Newsfeed. Figure 6-6 illustrates an example of how to use @ and # in replies. Sara Davis is replying to Pavel; she has used the @ to include her colleague Alex, and she used the # to include a relevant tag.

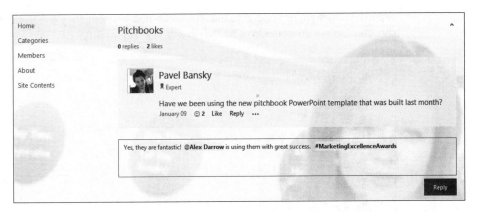

Figure 6-6 The @ sign and # tags are used in a discussion post.

Figure 6-7 shows the Newsfeed of a user who follows the tag that Sara used in her reply. Because he follows the #MarketingExcellenceAwards tag, anytime someone adds that tag to a community post, it will be displayed in his Newsfeed.

Figure 6-7 Tagged conversations are displayed in a user's Newsfeed.

Reputations

Community participation revolves largely around posting, replying, and "liking" discussions. These activities are the ones that determine a member's reputation. SharePoint 2013 provides a visual indicator of a user's reputation score within that community. Many types of SharePoint content can be part of a discussion (such as tasks and documents), but only interaction with the discussion is used to determine a reputation score. Community owners and moderators can determine the optimal point system for reputations—more on this later in the chapter.

Related to reputations are *Badges*. Badges are a way for community moderators to provide special recognition to a member who has a particular impact on the community (such as an expert). Badges are not tied in to the reputation point system; they are assigned by a person. You can see an example of Badges in action in Figure 6-8.

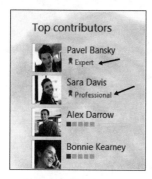

Figure 6-8 Community member Badges are assigned to two members of this community.

Performing community site management

Two primary roles perform community site management: owners and moderators. Site owners have administrative capabilities that allow them to perform many of the behind-the-scenes tasks required to establish and customize a community site. A partial list of these activities is as follows:

- Community site creation

- Modifying community settings, such as established date, reputation settings, and reporting

- Customizing the community by editing the Home and About pages and the site theme

- Creating categories for discussions

- Adding apps to the site (such as calendars)

- Defining permissions for the site and determining whether or not auto-approval will be enabled for people wishing to join the community

Creating communities

Thanks to the new Community Site template, it is relatively quick and easy to get a new community up and running. As shown in Figure 6-9, the Community Site template will be available when you create a new site or subsite.

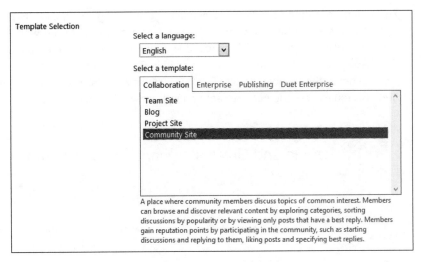

Figure 6-9 The Community Site template is available when you create a new site.

> **Note**
>
> For larger communities, it is recommended that you create the community as the root site in a site collection. This provides a number of benefits, including the ability to move the entire site collection if necessary.

Community-site functionality can also be added to existing team sites if you activate the community features, as shown in Figure 6-10. Enabling this capability will add the standard community functionality, underlying lists, and features to an existing site.

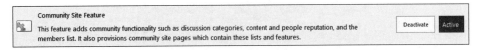

Figure 6-10 Activate the Community Site feature to add functionality to team sites.

Setting permissions

During (or after) the creation of a community, you will decide what type of community you need (such as public or private). Permissions need to be assigned to the groups that will have access to the community. This will determine what type of capabilities people will have when they visit the community.

Permissions for a community site are defined as usual using SharePoint site permissions and groups in Site Settings. One thing to note is that if you want users who click Join Community to be automatically approved as members, you need to ensure that the Auto-Accept Requests option is turned on within Group Settings for the group in question. You can get to this by going to Site Settings | People And Groups | Settings | Group Settings. You can see the Auto-Accept Requests setting in Figure 6-11.

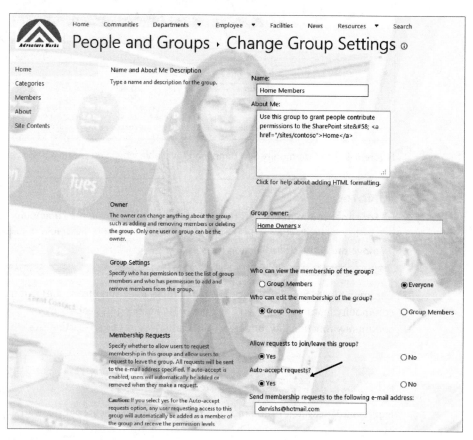

Figure 6-11 Turn the Auto-Accept Requests option on if you want users who click Join Community to be automatically approved as members.

INSIDE OUT   Site permissions for different types of communities

In order to join a community, the user must have a minimum of Visitor permissions to the site. This allows the user to view the site and then request access if desired. Site permissions and site settings can be used to determine what type of community experience you want visitors to have in terms of membership. See the following table for details on the four primary types of community permission strategies:

Community Type	Permission Level	Membership Approval
Private/secure	Permissions to be in the community are explicitly provided only to members. No one else can see the site.	None required
Closed community	Grant Visitor permissions to the Everyone group. This allows people to view the site and request to join.	In Site Settings, enable Access Requests.
Open community with an explicit join policy	Grant Visitor permissions to the Everyone group. This configuration allows people to view the site and join as members.	In Site Settings, enable Auto-Approval.
Open community	Grant Member permissions to the Everyone group. This particular configuration allows all users to participate without approval or requests.	There will be no Join button since everyone is a member.

Changing community settings

In Site Settings, each community has a Community Settings link that has some general settings for the community. The Established Date defaults to the date that the site was created, but the owner can change it if it is desired to convey the fact that the community has existed longer than the site itself. The Established Date is displayed on the community About page.

Also within Community Settings, you will find the option to enable Reporting Of Offensive Content. If you want community members to be able to report objectionable or offensive content to the moderator, enable this option.

Managing and creating categories

All discussion posts in a community must be in a category. The moderators and owners of a community are the people who define the categories. The category settings can be found by using the Community Tools Web Part or by choosing Manage Categories under Site Settings.

Each category has four basic properties, as shown in Figure 6-12:

- Category Name

- Description

- Category Picture

- Picture Description

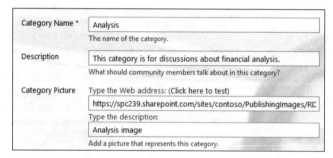

Figure 6-12 Category properties.

Because categories will be one of the primary methods that users have to navigate and filter discussions, it is important that you put thought and planning into what categories you create for a site. At the same time, it is important not to create an overabundance of categories or ones that overlap. If you make that mistake, your users will be confused on how to categorize new discussions.

Setting achievement and reputation settings

"Likes" and ratings are optional; owners can enable or disable ratings by choosing Community Reputation Settings under Site Settings. Ratings can be either "likes" or stars. Also, on that same administration page, the owner can enable and configure a member achievement points system. This includes defining the value of specific types of activities; posting a new discussion might be worth more than replying to an existing discussion post, for example.

In addition to enabling and defining the point structure, the owner decides whether to display a member's level in the community as a bar image or a text title. You can see this configuration option in Figure 6-13.

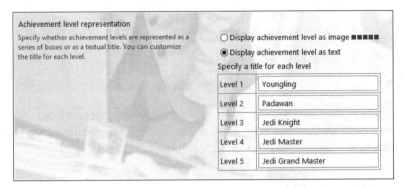

Figure 6-13 Achievement settings may be displayed as text or as images.

INSIDE OUT   Ratings data

Unlike SharePoint 2010, this version stores all the ratings data in the SharePoint list itself. One benefit of this approach is that if you switch between "likes" and star ratings sometime after a community has already been in use, there is no data loss. The ratings and "likes" data for a particular user is not aggregated across communities. This is by design, so that a user's rating and contribution within a particular community is not influenced by how much they contribute to other unrelated communities.

Moderating a community

Communities introduce the requirement for moderation, which therefore introduces the need for a moderator. SharePoint 2013 sites with the Communities feature enabled add a new permissions level called *Moderate*. When a user is assigned the Moderate permission, she is allowed to perform various community stewardship tasks, such as recategorizing discussions and addressing content that has been reported.

The job of community moderation primarily consists of two major areas:

- Managing and monitoring, which includes:
    - Ensuring that content retains desired quality levels
    - Dealing with inappropriate content or disputes

- Helping to make sure that posts get replies and questions get answered

- Ensuring proper categorization of discussions

- Promoting, which includes:

  - Assigning badges as appropriate

  - Marking replies as Best Reply

  - Designating important discussions as Featured

For a community to grow and thrive, moderation is often necessary, but unfortunately, this role is often overlooked. A best practice is to assign the Moderator role to someone who has a stake in the community's mission, purpose, and success.

Moderation tasks

Moderators will have access to the main community settings and the lists in the background that provide functionality for the community (such as members). The moderators will see the community settings displayed in two places:

- In the Community Tools Web Part, as shown in Figure 6-14

- In the Community Site Settings

Community Administration
Manage Discussions
Manage Categories
Manage Members
Community Settings
Reputation Settings
Manage Reported Posts

Figure 6-14 Community settings are displayed in the Community Tools Web Part.

When someone is assigned the moderator role in a community, the Community Tools Web Part will be displayed on his or her page. Because the Community Tools Web Part is security trimmed, only owners and moderators have access to it.

If your community has enabled Reporting Of Offensive Content in the Community Settings page, as shown in Figure 6-15, moderators will also have access to the Reported Posts Moderation tool.

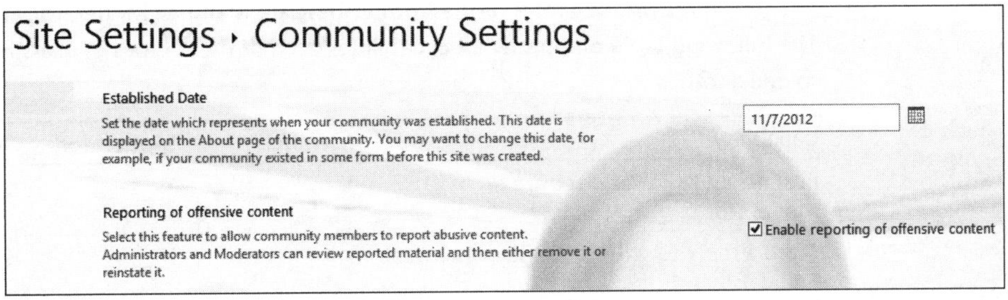

Site Settings › Community Settings

Established Date

Set the date which represents when your community was established. This date is displayed on the About page of the community. You may want to change this date, for example, if your community existed in some form before this site was created.

11/7/2012

Reporting of offensive content

Select this feature to allow community members to report abusive content. Administrators and Moderators can review reported material and then either remove it or reinstate it.

☑ Enable reporting of offensive content

Figure 6-15 Enable Reporting Of Offensive Content on the Community Settings page in Site Settings.

A moderator can navigate to reported posts easily by clicking Review Reported Posts on the Community Tools Web Part. This will take the moderator to a SharePoint list that stores reported post information. As shown in Figure 6-16, the moderator can edit or delete the post or dismiss the complaint.

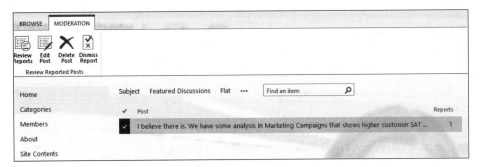

Figure 6-16 A moderator can easily edit a post, delete a post, or dismiss a complaint simply by selecting a post and then using the Moderation tab on the ribbon.

INSIDE OUT Members vs. moderators vs. owners

Your ability to manage content or make changes in a community site depends on your role. The three primary roles (aside from Visitor) are Member, Moderator, and Owner. The following table outlines what capabilities each of these types of users has relative to one another.

Capability	Member	Moderator	Owner
Post, reply, "like," and report to moderator	X	X	X
Mark a reply to your discussion as a Best Reply	X	X	X
Mark a reply to any discussion as a Best Reply		X	X
Mark a discussion as Featured		X	X
Generate and assign badges		X	X
Create categories		X	X
Edit/delete posts by other users		X	X
Change reputation settings		X	X
Edit the community site pages; add or remove apps		X	X
Edit community settings			X
Modify community permissions			X
Accept access requests			X

Promoting people and content

Promoting people and content is an important part of a thriving online social community. SharePoint 2013 provides a number of tools and methods for moderators to assist in this process.

Moderators can mark content as Featured within a given category. In Figure 6-17, a moderator has marked the "Successful marketing campaigns and SEO" discussion as featured. There are a variety of reasons that a moderator might want to do this. For example, perhaps a question or recurring theme is being repeated in the community. By featuring the discussion, hopefully users will notice it before they post a redundant discussion.

Moderators can also mark a reply as a Best Reply. This helps a particular discussion stand out, and it boosts the reputation of the person who posted the reply. If the post is a question, selecting a Best Reply also marks the question as "answered."

Moderators can assign badges to users who go above and beyond in their contributions to a community. The badge is simply a custom text title such as "expert"), but the impact is significant because it identifies the real champions of a community. This task is performed using the Community Tools Web Part. Once you have selected Assign Badges To Members, you can pick the user you want to give a badge, and then press the Give Badge button on the Moderation toolbar, as shown in Figure 6-18.

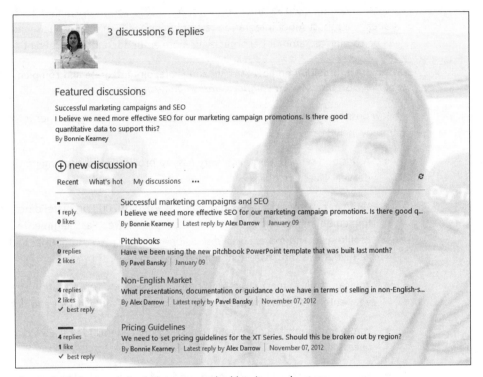

Figure 6-17 Featured discussions are marked by site moderators.

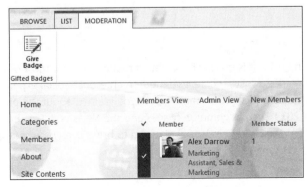

Figure 6-18 Moderators can assign a badge by pressing the Give Badge button on the toolbar.

Extending your community to the cloud with Yammer

With the recent acquisition of Yammer by Microsoft, customers now have a significant new option to augment their SharePoint social experience. Yammer is a cloud-based social tool that has seen a huge popularity surge in recent years, with well over a million active users. For SharePoint customers, there are many potential scenarios where you might have a business need for both Yammer and SharePoint 2013 social capabilities. Fortunately, there is already a robust set of integration technologies between the products—and much more will be coming as Yammer becomes even more embedded into SharePoint.

For more information on how Yammer and SharePoint integrate and complement one another, visit *https://www.yammer.com/company/sharepoint.*

A few possible reasons why you might want to consider adding Yammer to your social strategy include:

- As a cloud service, Yammer is very easy to provision and implement; therefore, it can deliver value very quickly.

- Yammer can integrate into an existing SharePoint 2007 or SharePoint 2010 implementation using tools such as the Yammer Web Part, Yammer federated search, profile sync, and more. Social discussions can take place in Yammer and integrate with your existing SharePoint implementation.

- You can easily extend Yammer to people outside your organization to participate in your enterprise social network with minimal effort and without additional cost.

- Yammer is highly scalable; your social network can include millions of users if necessary.

- Yammer has robust and advanced support for nearly every type of mobile client device and operating system.

Summary

Social networking in business is quickly becoming a requirement for most organizations. SharePoint 2013 provides a solid, secure, and modern enterprise social experience for your users to collaborate and share. In this chapter, you learned about the principal social tools in SharePoint 2013, such as community sites and the Newsfeed. For certain scenarios, Yammer can augment the SharePoint social platform to bring even more power to your users, partners, and customers.

Using and creating workflows

MICROSOFT SharePoint 2010 introduced a considerable array of new functionality concerning the creation, maintainability, reusability, and deployment of workflows. However, this new functionality often was difficult to scale in organizations that made heavy use of workflows, especially if their SharePoint farms were not properly architected, and the added workflow functionality often had a negative effect on the ability of the SharePoint servers to respond to users' requests for SharePoint webpages. Fortunately, SharePoint 2013 introduces new capabilities to help solve these challenges.

In Microsoft SharePoint Server 2013, you have the option of no longer running a workflow within a SharePoint process. SharePoint Server 2013 introduces a new, highly scalable workflow framework that is implemented by using the Workflow Manager, originally known as Windows Azure Workflow (WAW). Workflow Manager is not installed automatically; therefore, a default installation of SharePoint Server 2013 can only use the same workflows that can be used in SharePoint 2010. The new workflow framework is not designed to work with Microsoft SharePoint Foundation 2013, and therefore, with SharePoint Foundation, you can use and create only SharePoint 2010 workflows.

Once you install Workflow Manager, your SharePoint server administrator needs to register the Workflow Manager with the SharePoint Server 2013 installation. SharePoint Server does not contain any SharePoint 2013 workflow templates, only SharePoint 2010 workflow templates; therefore, even though Workflow Manager is installed, users will still only be able to use SharePoint 2010 workflows. SharePoint 2013 workflows and SharePoint 2013 workflow templates need to be created before you can take advantage of the Workflow Manager.

> **Note**
> You can create SharePoint 2013 workflows or SharePoint 2010 workflows by using Microsoft SharePoint Designer 2013 or by using Microsoft Visual Studio 2012. SharePoint 2013 also contains new Windows PowerShell cmdlets that allow you to manage workflows.

There are no enhancements to SharePoint 2010 workflows in SharePoint 2013. You have the same actions and conditions as in SharePoint 2010, and they are built on Microsoft .NET Framework 3.5. If you are upgrading from SharePoint 2010 to SharePoint 2013, all of your workflows that were built in SharePoint 2010 will continue to work in SharePoint 2013. You can modify SharePoint 2010 workflows in SharePoint 2013 using either SharePoint Designer 2010 or SharePoint Designer 2013.

INSIDE OUT   The use of SharePoint 2010 workflows

Microsoft has stated that the SharePoint 2010 workflows are deprecated in SharePoint 2013, which means that in future versions of SharePoint, they may not be available. To future-proof your SharePoint 2013 installation, you should, wherever possible, use SharePoint 2013 workflows. This may be difficult to achieve because some functionality is not supported in SharePoint 2013 workflows. With SharePoint 2013 workflows, only those activities built on .NET Framework 4.0 and Microsoft Windows Workflow Foundation (WF) 4 run time can be used. When a SharePoint 2013 workflow needs to use any WF 3.5 artifacts, control is passed back to the SharePoint 2010 workflow host in SharePoint 2013. When the WF 3 process is complete, control returns to the Workflow Manager using the "interop bridge."

The basic usage and manageability of workflows has not changed, whether they are SharePoint 2010 or SharePoint 2013 workflows. Users interact with workflows using the browser or Microsoft Office applications. You use the browser to add workflow templates to lists, libraries, content types, and sites.

You can use SharePoint Designer to create reusable workflows that can be associated with multiple lists or libraries, and you can then save the reusable workflow as a workflow template in the form of a Windows SharePoint solution file (.wsp). This workflow template can then be imported to another site to be used to create the same workflow on the new site or imported into Visual Studio 2012, where it can be further enhanced.

This chapter details how to use the out-of-the-box SharePoint 2010 workflows in the browser. It then looks at creating and extending SharePoint 2010 and SharePoint 2013 workflows using SharePoint Designer. Also in this chapter, you will use a holiday request business process to explore the use of the out-of-the-box workflows, Microsoft Visio 2013 Premium, and SharePoint Designer.

SharePoint workflow basics

For the past several years, there has been a push across both government and commercial sectors to do more work in less time, to minimize the number of files attached to email, and to reduce the amount of information that needs to be printed. Many large organizations, especially in the civilian government, finance, and healthcare industries, have been clogging their email systems with duplicate data and choking on paperwork and processes. Of course, forms and processes are required, and SharePoint can address many of these issues by using the WF components to provide user-driven process automation. WF offers all the functionality required for building enterprise-level workflows, such as built-in support for transactions, tracking, and notifications. WF does not act as a stand-alone application but always works with an application, which in this instance is either SharePoint for WF 3.5 or Workflow Manager for WF 4.0. And because SharePoint Server 2013 is built on top of WF 3.5 and can communicate with Workflow Manager, once installed, it too has workflow capabilities.

Process automation methods

SharePoint can help automate business processes by using one of the following methods:

- **Really Simple Syndication (RSS) feeds** Use RSS feeds for finding information from a variety of sources on an ad-hoc basis. Use this method when the information is not needed on a day-to-day basis. RSS feeds use a pull mechanism to find information; that is, you only find information exposed by RSS feeds when you open an RSS reader, such as Windows Internet Explorer or Microsoft Outlook.

- **Alerts** Use alerts for regular notifications of new, modified, or deleted content. Alerts can be configured to send email immediately when SharePoint finds information in which you have registered an interest, or a daily or weekly digest of that information.

- **Content approval** Along with versioning, you can use content approval to manage content and control who can see content that is classified as draft. When you enable content approval on a list or library, a column named Approved Status is added to the library, together with a number of views. In addition, enabling content approval activates the Approval/Reject command on the list item menu and on the ribbon. The Approval Status column can contain the choices Approved, Rejected, or Pending. Users who are assigned the Manage Lists permission can approve or reject items. No email is sent to users with the Manage List permission. They would need to visit the list to see if any items are in a pending state.

However, with none of these three methods can you automate business processes beyond a one-step method. You can combine these methods with other SharePoint functionality, such as using content approval with alerts to provide a lightweight workflow that sends you email when your team members publish documents as a major version so that you can approve documents according to a specific timescale. However, such a solution can help solve only a small number of your business processes. You might want to route a document or a webpage to a number of people before publishing it.

The Microsoft TechNet website contains an article on versioning, content approval, and check-out planning. You can view this article at *technet.microsoft.com/en-us/library/ff607917 .aspx*.

SharePoint provides two other methods to help automate processes:

- **Workflows** Workflows are used to automate and track processes that require human intervention, such as notifying users when their action is required to move the process forward. Such processes can take days, weeks, or months to complete and might need to wait for an event or another process to complete. Workflows can be created by using the browser, SharePoint Designer, and Visual Studio.

- **Event receivers** Event receivers are used to automate processes that require no human intervention, such as moving job applications from one document library to a series of other document libraries for some purpose. Event receivers can only be created by using Visual Studio.

Planning for process automation

Workflows and event receivers cannot automate a task unless time is taken to understand it at a very detailed level. A workflow cannot track the status of information stored on paper documents, nor can you force users to perform a particular task by using the workflow you created. You must have a clear understanding of how the business process operates. If you do not understand how to complete a business process manually, you will not be able to describe the business process in sufficient detail to automate it. You also need the reassurance of the business process owners that upon the introduction of this workflow, it will be used by the process users. Using workflows to automate parts of a business process really means that you are involved in business process re-engineering. Managing the change of the new process and understanding the people, their fears, and their worries are the most important parts of automating process into the business workspace.

Therefore, there is more to creating a successful workflow than using the browser or SharePoint Designer to configure one. You need to plan how you intend to automate a process, taking into account people, processes, and technology. You need to choose the process that you are going to automate carefully—do not attempt to automate every

Chapter 7

process in your organization. Look for processes that are predictable and for which the startup cost of creating a workflow and ensuring that your team is happy with the new process will be offset by the productivity improvement that the automated process will provide. Understand the technologies you are going to use to automate the processes, which in this case are SharePoint and WF.

The TechNet website contains a SharePoint 2013 Workflow Resource Center at *technet.microsoft.com/en-us/sharepoint/jj556245.*

Introducing workflow terminology

In the same way that you base a new site, list, or library on a template, you base a new workflow process on a workflow template. These templates are implemented as features that can be activated or deactivated at the site or site-collection level by using the browser or by using a custom program or Windows PowerShell. A workflow template is available only when a workflow feature is activated.

Workflow templates

SharePoint Foundation ships with only one SharePoint 2010 workflow template—the Three-State workflow—whereas SharePoint Server contains a number of document-centric SharePoint 2010 workflow templates:

- **Approval–SharePoint 2010** Provides an approval mechanism for documents.

- **Collect Feedback–SharePoint 2010** Provides a feedback mechanism for documents. The feedback is not stored within the document but in a list. Most users prefer to use the built-in review functionality of Microsoft Word to collect feedback, as such comments are stored within the document.

- **Collect Signatures–SharePoint 2010** Provides a mechanism for collecting digital signatures for completing a document. This workflow can be used only in conjunction with Office documents that contain one or more of the Office signature line controls.

- **Disposition Approval** Provides an expiration and retention mechanism that allows you to decide whether to retain or delete expired documents. This workflow can be started only by using the browser.

- **Publishing Approval** Similar to the approval workflow. Used on sites with the publishing feature, where you would associate it with the Pages library and allow publishing pages, also known as *web content management (WCM) pages,* to go through an approval process.

INSIDE OUT The Translation Management workflow template

SharePoint Server 2013 contains another SharePoint 2010 workflow template: Translation Management. This workflow routes documents that need to be translated into different languages between users who can do that task. The site feature that enables this workflow template is hidden from the Site Features page in the browser, and has to be enabled using a Windows PowerShell command similar to *Enable-SPFeature TransMgmtLib –URL http://intranet.adventure-works.com/divisions/financials/payroll*. You then create a list of translators, based on the Languages And Translators list template, and store documents that you want to be translated in a library based on the Translation Management library template. To use the TransMgmtLib site feature, the TransMgmtFunc feature must be enabled at the SharePoint Server farm level and the TransMgmtLib feature must be activated at the site collection level. By default, both of these features are activated. More information on the Translation Management library and the workflow can be found at *office.microsoft.com/en-us/sharepoint-server-help/use-a-translation-management-workflow-HA010154430.aspx*.

No version of SharePoint 2013 contains site workflow templates. SharePoint Server 2010 contained two site workflow templates that were associated with Web Analytics. In SharePoint 2013, Web Analytics is no longer a separate service application; it is now part of SharePoint's search engine. Search is a lot smarter in SharePoint 2013 and can be used to analyze individual actions by the user as well as click through rates of sessions. This information can then be used to provide relevance and suggestion information for users. You can find the analytic information for a site in a Microsoft Excel file named Usage.xlsx. To access this file, on the Site Settings page, under Site Administration, click Popularity Trends.

More information on search and usage analytics can be found in Chapter 19, "Creating a customized SharePoint 2013 search experience."

Workflows and workflow instances

Workflows are a series of tasks that produce an outcome. To create a workflow, you configure and add (also known as *associating*) the workflow template to a list, library, or site. An instance of the workflow can then be initiated by using the configured workflow template, which defines the conditions that should be tested to decide what tasks to complete to produce the outcome. You can also associate a workflow template with a content type, and then associate the content type with a list or library to define a workflow.

The workflow always has a start and an end. An instance of the workflow is created when a workflow event is triggered for a specific list item or file. The workflow instance then enters the workflow at its start point and progresses through the workflow process as defined by the configured workflow template until it reaches the end point, at which time the workflow instance is set to Completed, as shown in Figure 7-1. The workflow then does no other work until a new workflow instance is created. A workflow can contain one or more workflow instances. A list item or file can be related to more than one workflow instance, so long as each workflow instance is related to different workflows.

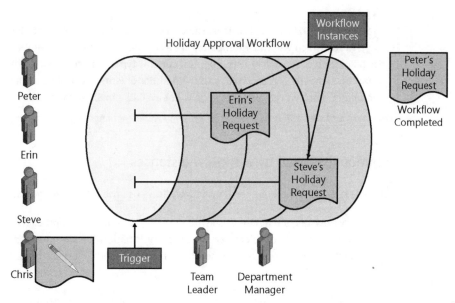

Figure 7-1 A holiday request workflow with workflow instances progressing through the workflow. One workflow instance is completed.

Association and initiation forms

To create a workflow, you must provide a workflow name, choose how you want workflow instances to start, and complete an association form to provide values that are needed by the workflow, especially if the workflow is configured to start automatically. When a workflow allows workflow instances to be started manually, then users may be provided with an initiation form that allows them to define values that the workflow requires. These might be similar to the values provided on the association form. When a workflow instance is automatically started, the initiation form is not displayed and the default values or the values provided on the association form are used. Once a workflow is created, users with modify permissions can start workflow instances within that workflow.

Using workflow templates and workflow instances

Using the browser, you can create a workflow by using a workflow template with lists, libraries, content types, and sites. Workflows are commonly created on lists and libraries. Users interact with workflow instances either via email or through task items in a task list.

> **Note**
>
> In SharePoint 2010, at the top-level site of a site collection, you can use the Workflows page to see which workflow templates are available and active, the number of SharePoint objects (such as lists, libraries, content types, and sites) with which the workflow template is associated, and the number of workflow instances that are running in those workflows. This page is not available in SharePoint 2013.

Common lists used by workflow instances

Although it is not strictly required, most workflows use the following two lists:

- **Workflow tasks list** Use this list to create task items to remind users of the work that needs to be completed or to collect information for the next step of the workflow. Workflows can also send email to users with a link to the task items that are assigned to them.

- **Workflow history list** This list keeps track of the workflow instances that are running or have been completed for a given list item or document. The workflow writes key information to this list, such as the date, status, participant, and description. The default workflow history list is a hidden library and is not shown on the Site Content webpage. The default workflow inherits permissions from the site; therefore, any user who is mapped to the contribute permission level can update items in this list. You can display this list in the browser by appending /lists/ workflow%20history/ to your site's URL (such as *http://hr.adventure-works.com/lists/ workflow%20history/*). By default, workflows cannot write to the description field of a workflow history item that is larger than 255 characters.

> **Note**
>
> SharePoint Server 2010 provides Activity Duration and Cancellation and Error reports that use the workflow history list to analyze the workflow instances and the activities within the workflow process. These are not available in SharePoint 2013.

If you use the same workflow tasks list and workflow history list for all workflows in a site, then these two lists can become large. This was more of a problem in SharePoint 2010, when it could cause performance problems. As a result, SharePoint 2013 includes a daily timer job to remove all history and task items that exist 60 days after the related workflow instance completes. Because of the default security settings on these lists and the 60-day purge of list items, you should not use these lists as an audit of what the workflow is doing.

You can use an existing task and workflow history list when you first create a workflow. If you believe that you will have many workflow instances, create a task and workflow history list for your specific workflow. There is a daily Workflow Auto Cleanup timer job for each web application that purges items in the task and workflow history list for workflow instances that have been marked complete or cancelled and removes the links to those workflow instances on the workflow status pages.

INSIDE OUT   Tracking workflow information for auditing purposes

When you create your own custom workflows—that is, those that are not provided by default with SharePoint—and you want to keep audit information concerning the workflow, then you should write such information to another list and apply appropriate permissions for the list to secure the items written to it, or use Visual Studio to create a custom audit report using the SPAuditEntry class. You can find more information at *msdn.microsoft.com/en-us/library/ms453817(v=office.15).aspx*.

Adding a workflow template to a list or library

The person who has Manage List permissions on a list or library can use the Workflow Settings page to associate a workflow template with that list or library, and thereby create a workflow for that list or library. List and library workflow templates can be specific to one content type, or they can be used for any content type. From the Workflow Settings page, you pick where the workflow tasks and history information are stored and set the conditions that trigger a workflow instance for a list item or file. You can also modify and remove an existing workflow process on this page.

Note

To use the Three-State workflow template, you need a choice column on the list or library with which you are associating it. The choice column is used to store the three statuses of the workflow (such as Holiday Request Submitted, Holiday Request Approved, and Holiday Taken). The default value for the column should be set as the first status in the workflow (in this case, Holiday Request Submitted).

Perform the following steps to add a workflow template to a list or library:

1. Use the Quick Launch or Site Contents page to navigate to the document library or list with which you want to associate a workflow template.

2. On the ribbon, click the List or Library tab. (This tab could also be named Calendar if the list was created from a calendar list template.)

3. In the Settings group, click the arrow to the right of Workflow Settings and then click Add A Workflow, as shown next.

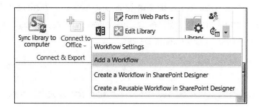

4. On the Add A Workflow page, in the Workflow section, select a workflow template.

> **Note**
>
> **The remaining steps in this procedure assume that you have selected the Approval–SharePoint 2010 workflow.**

5. In the Name section, type a new name for this workflow, such as **Holiday Request Approval.**

   This name will be used to create a column in the list or library, and therefore, it must be unique in the list or library. You must not use the name of an existing column or any of the reserved column names, such as Title, Created By, Modified By, Checked Out To, or Approval Status.

6. In the Task List section, select an existing tasks list or Task (new).

   If you select Task (new), the name of the new task list will take the format of *<workflow name>* Tasks, such as Holiday Request Approval Tasks.

7. In the History List section, select an existing workflow history list or Workflow History (new).

   The name of a new workflow history list will take the format of *<workflow name>* History. You can see these steps in the following screenshot.

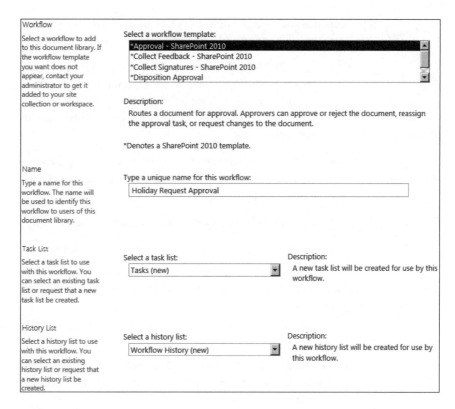

8. In the Start Options section, select one of the options that will initiate a workflow instance, as shown next.

Depending on the workflow template and its configuration, the start of a workflow instance can be triggered using one of the following options:

- Manually, when you want to test a newly added workflow or when the list or library to which you have added a workflow has a list item or document that needs to progress through the workflow. This option can be limited so that only users who have the Manage List permission can start a workflow instance manually.

- Automatically, when minor and major versioning is enabled and you want to approve publishing a draft version (minor version) of a list item or document to a major version.

- Automatically, when you create a list item or document.

- Automatically, when you change a list item or document.

When you first create a workflow to test the workflow quickly, select the Allow This Workflow To Be Manually Started By An Authenticated User With Edit Item Permissions option.

> **Note**
>
> When using SharePoint Server 2013, another option is available for initiating a workflow instance by using information management policies on content types at the site, list, or library level.

9. Click Next to go to the association page named Change A Workflow Holiday Request Approval.

    The association page for the Approval–SharePoint 2010 workflow template is a Microsoft InfoPath form that is rendered in a webpage in the browser by InfoPath Form Services (IFS). If you create InfoPath forms and you want them to render in the browser, then you need the Enterprise edition of SharePoint Server; however, if the form is used as a workflow association form, then only the Standard edition of SharePoint Server is needed.

10. In the Approvers section, type the name of one or more users that you want to approve the document, as shown next.

Approvers	Assign To		Order	
	Peter Connelly; Erin M. Hagens	🔍 📖	One at a time (serial)	▾
	Jack Creasey; Jane Dow	🔍 📖	All at once (parallel)	▾

☑ Add a new stage
Enter the names of the people to whom the workflow will assign tasks, and choose the order in which those tasks are assigned. Separate them with semicolons. You can also add stages to assign tasks to more people in different orders.

Expand Groups	☑ For each group entered, assign a task to every individual member and to each group that it contains.
Request	Please process the expense form document. This message will be sent to the people assigned tasks.
Due Date for All Tasks	[ ] 📅 The date by which all tasks are due.
Duration Per Task	3 The amount of time until a task is due. Choose the units by using the Duration Units.
Duration Units	Day(s) ▾ Define the units of time used by the Duration Per Task.
CC	[ ] 🔍 📖 Notify these people when the workflow starts and ends without assigning tasks to them.
End on First Rejection	☐ Automatically reject the document if it is rejected by any participant.
End on Document Change	☐ Automatically reject the document if it is changed before the workflow is completed.
Enable Content Approval	☐ Update the approval status after the workflow is completed (use this workflow to control content approval).

11. Make any other changes as needed and then click Save to be returned to the Workflow Settings page.

This page displays all workflows that were added to the list or library, together with the number of workflow instances that are progressing through each workflow, as the following graphic shows.

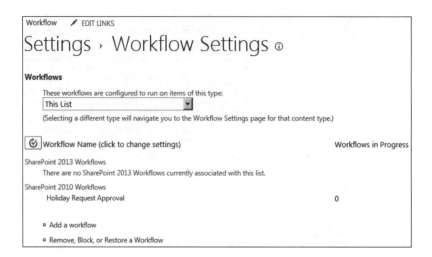

Modifying a workflow

Once a workflow template is added to a list or library, you might need to make changes to its configuration. To modify a workflow, follow these steps:

1. Navigate to the library or list to which you added the workflow template and then on the ribbon, click the List or Library tab, on the ribbon. In the Settings group, click the Workflow Settings command to display the Workflow Settings page.

2. Under Workflow Name, click the workflow that you want to modify (such as Holiday Request Approval) to display the Change A Workflow page. If you cannot see the workflow that you want to monitor, under Workflows, click Show All Workflows.

Note

The Change A Workflow page may not always be displayed. If the workflow template was developed by using Visual Studio, you might be able to change association parameters by clicking the workflow name. If the site workflow was created by using SharePoint Designer, you can change the site workflow only via SharePoint Designer, and therefore, clicking the workflow name displays a message box, stating that you need to use a SharePoint-compatible workflow editing tool, as shown next:

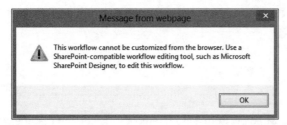

Use the Change A Workflow page to change the task list, the workflow history list with which this workflow is associated, the name of the workflow, and the start options.

3. Click Next to open the association page and modify what you want to happen when a workflow instance is initiated.

4. Click Save to confirm your changes.

Removing a workflow

When a workflow is no longer needed, you should remove it from the list or library to prevent confusing users who use that list or library. To remove a workflow from a list or library, follow these steps:

1. Navigate to the Workflow Settings page for the library or list to which you added the workflow template.

2. Click Remove, Block, Or Restore A Workflow to display the Remove Workflows page.

   This page displays each workflow that was added to this list or library, together with the number of workflow instances that are currently progressing through the workflow. The three options allow workflow instances to start in the workflow, prevent any workflow instances from starting, or remove the workflow from the list or library. If you feel that you might need the workflow in the future, select the No New Instances option, as seen in the following graphic.

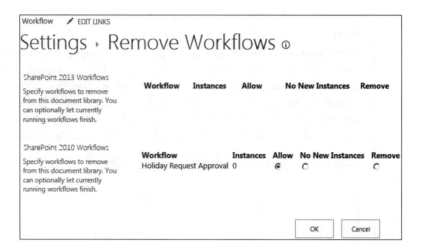

When you remove a workflow from a list, it removes the column that the workflow uses to indicate the status of a workflow instance in the workflow process. This column was created when a workflow template is associated with a list or library and contains such values as In Progress, Cancelled, and Completed. Removing columns on lists and libraries causes a database operation proportional to the number of items or files in the list or library. When the list or library contains more than a million items, do not remove the workflow from the list or library; instead, set the workflow to No New Instances.

> **Note**
>
> When you remove a workflow, all the task items and workflow history items that were created for that workflow are also removed.

Using a workflow

Once a workflow is added to a list or library, a list item or file can progress through that workflow. The trigger that SharePoint uses to initiate a workflow instance for a list item or file is dependent on the following:

- The Content type with which the workflow is linked and whether the list item or file is of the same type.

- The Start options that you configured on the association forms. You can start a workflow instance by manually starting the workflow, uploading or creating a new file, or modifying an existing list item or file.

To start a workflow instance for a list item of a file manually, perform the following procedure:

1. Pause your mouse over the list item or file for which you want to start a workflow, and then select the check that appears to the left of the list item or file.

2. On the Items tab (if this is a list) or the Files tab (if this is a library), click Workflows in the Workflows group.

   The *<list or library name>*: Workflows: *<file or item name>* page is displayed, as shown next.

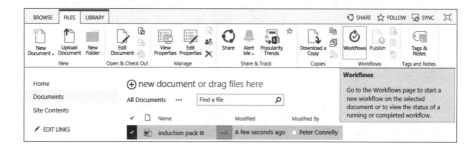

3. Under Start A New Workflow, click the name of the workflow that you want to start, such as, Holiday Request Approval, as displayed next.

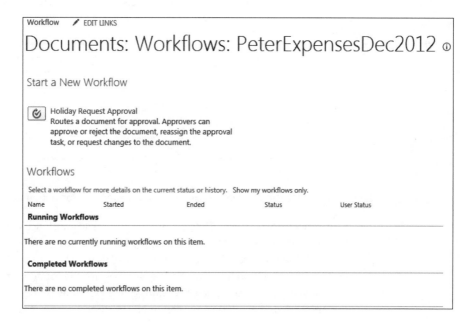

If the workflow has an initiation form, it is displayed. Click Start. The Working On It message appears, stating, "Please wait while your workflow is started." Once SharePoint has started your workflow instance, you are returned to the default view of the list and library, where a new column might appear. This new column is named with the workflow name, with a status of In Progress. This new column is not added to the default view when the default view is a calendar view.

To review the workflow progress of the list item or file, follow these steps:

1. Browse to the list or library where the item or file is stored.

2. In the workflow column, click In Progress. If the workflow column is not shown, select the check to the left of the item, and then on the Items tab, click Workflows. Under Running Workflows, click In Progress for the workflow that you want to review. The Workflow Status page displays, as shown next.

Workflow Information

Initiator: Peter Connelly	**Document:** PeterExpensesDec2012
Started: 10/12/2012 6:46 PM	**Status:** In Progress
Last run: 10/12/2012 6:47 PM	

- Add or update approvers of Approval
- Cancel all Approval tasks
- Update active tasks of Approval

If an error occurs or this workflow stops responding, it can be terminated. Terminating the workflow will set its status to Canceled and will delete all tasks created by the workflow.
- Terminate this workflow now.

Tasks

The following tasks have been assigned to the participants in this workflow. Click a task to edit it. You can also view these tasks in the list Tasks.

	Assigned To	Title		Due Date	Status	Related Content	Outcome
☐	Peter Connelly	Please approve PeterExpensesDec2012 ☐ NEW		10/15/2012	Not Started	PeterExpensesDec2012	

Workflow History

The following events have occurred in this workflow.

	Date Occurred	Event Type	User ID	Description	Outcome
☐	10/12/2012 6:47 PM	Workflow Initiated	Peter Connelly	Approval was started. Participants: Peter Connelly;Erin M. Hagens;Jack Creasey;Jane Dow	
	10/12/2012 6:47 PM	Task Created	Peter Connelly	Task created for Peter Connelly. Due by: None	

The Workflow Status page summarizes workflow instance information in three sections:

- **Workflow information** This section details workflow instance information, such as who initiated the workflow instance, the start time, the name of the item that the workflow instance is linked to, and the status. You can also use the line at the bottom of this section to terminate the workflow for the list item or file. When you terminate a workflow instance, the status of the workflow changes from In Progress to Cancelled, and any task items created by the workflow are deleted.

- **Tasks** This section displays task items that are associated with this workflow instance. It provides a link to the list item or file and a link to the task list associated with the workflow. When you click the title of a task item, if you have Microsoft Silverlight installed, a modal dialog box opens and displays the details of the task item.

- **Workflow history** This section details messages that the workflow instance wrote to the workflow history list.

To complete tasks assigned to you as a list item or file progresses through a workflow, complete the following procedure:

1. Browse to the Workflow Status page, as described in the previous procedure, or alternatively, display the workflow task list by using the Site Contents page if a link to the workflow task list is not displayed on the Quick Launch toolbar.

2. Click the title of the task item assigned to you to display the task input form.

   The layout of the task input form is dependent on the workflow template used to create the workflow. For the Approval–SharePoint 2010 workflow template, the task input form is an InfoPath form.

3. Select Approve, Reject, Cancel, Request Change, or Reassign Task.

   If the workflow instance has completed all tasks, then the status of the workflow will change from In Progress to Completed.

TROUBLESHOOTING

If the tasks do not appear in the Tasks section and in the Workflow Information section, a message in red text states that due to heavy loads, the latest workflow operation has been queued. Refresh the page, and then click OK in the message box that appears.

Using site workflow templates

Site workflows are not associated with a list or library. However, site workflows can work with any SharePoint object within the site. By default, SharePoint 2013 does not provide any site templates to use with any sites; therefore, you would need to develop a site workflow template by using Visual Studio, or you can publish a workflow to a site by using SharePoint Designer.

To manually start a site workflow instance or to monitor a site workflow by using the browser, follow these steps:

1. On the Quick Launch toolbar, click Site Contents, or on the Settings menu, click View Site Contents to display the Site Contents page, and then, on the right, click Site Workflows.

2. Under Start a New Workflow, click the site workflow that you want to start, or under My Running Workflows or under My Completed Workflows, click the workflow that you want to monitor.

To manage the site workflows associated with a site, follow these steps:

1. Browse to the Site Settings page and then, under Site Administration, click Workflow Settings.

2. Click Remove A Workflow to display the Remove Workflow page.

   This page displays each workflow that was added to the site, together with the number of workflow instances that are currently progressing through the workflow. You can use this page to prevent the start of any new workflow instances or to remove site workflows.

To create a site workflow by using SharePoint Designer, follow these steps:

1. Open the site in SharePoint Designer, and then in the Navigation pane, click Workflows.

2. On the Workflows ribbon tab, in the New group, click Site Workflow to display the Create Site Workflow dialog box, shown next.

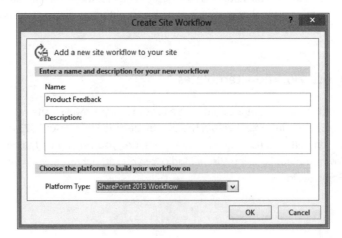

3. Type the name and description, and then click OK to open the Workflow Editor.

You can then create an initiation form, use actions and conditions, and publish the workflow, as described later in this chapter.

INSIDE OUT   Site workflow templates and SharePoint Designer

You cannot create a site workflow template by using SharePoint Designer; therefore, within SharePoint Designer, you cannot create association forms or association form variables for site workflows.

Gathering requirements using Visio diagrams

The ability of a business analyst to communicate effectively with developers is greatly improved by using Visio process diagrams. This capability was first introduced in SharePoint 2010, and you can use this same method in SharePoint 2013. You can create your SharePoint process diagram in Visio 2013 using either the SharePoint 2013 Workflow template or the SharePoint 2010 Workflow template. You no longer need the Premium edition of Visio to create a SharePoint Visio Workflow diagram.

However, SharePoint Designer does provide a new way of creating Visio diagrams. When you have Workflow Manager installed and you want to create a SharePoint 2013 workflow, you can create Visio diagrams using the built-in Visual Designer offered by SharePoint Designer, a Visio ActiveX control.

You can design your workflow diagram just like you can with any other Visio diagram by using the drag-and-drop functionality to create a nice layout. Once the diagram is complete, the user can run the validation provided by Visio to ensure that no branches or paths have been missed. Next, you create the Visio diagram file, which can be imported into SharePoint Designer. If you create a Visio workflow diagram, then you cannot configure the conditions and actions within Visio, you need to complete the configuration of the SharePoint 2010 workflow within SharePoint Designer.

You cannot import the .vwi file into Visual Studio; however, once you configure the workflow in SharePoint Designer, you can then save the workflow as a workflow template solutions file (.wsp), which can then be imported into Visual Studio.

Creating a Visio diagram

To create a SharePoint workflow using Visio 2013, perform the following steps:

1. Open Visio 2013 to display the Backstage view. On the New tab, click Categories and then click Flowchart.

2. Click either Microsoft SharePoint 2013 Workflow or Microsoft SharePoint 2010 Workflow, as shown next.

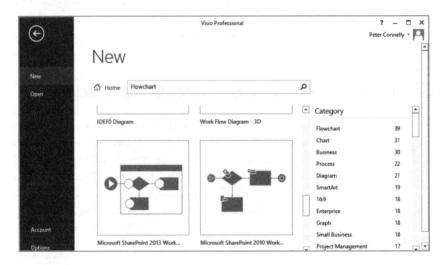

3. In the Microsoft SharePoint 2013 Workflow dialog box, click Create, as shown next.

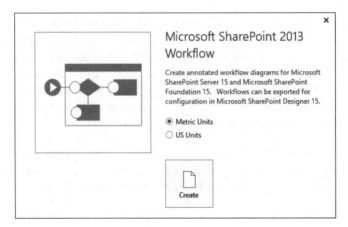

A Visio drawing opens that contains one stage, a start shape (blue cycle with white arrow), a stage enter shape (green-filled arrow), and an exit shape (red-filled square)

with the shapes connected by a blue line. In the left Shapes pane, three stencils are displayed, such as SharePoint 2013 Workflow, Conditions–SharePoint 2013 Workflow, and Components–SharePoint 2013 Workflow, as shown next.

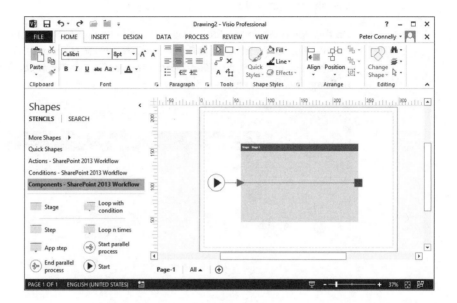

Adding conditions and actions to a Visio diagram

You can now add conditions and actions that represent the tasks of your business process that you wish to automate. For example, you can add a condition that checks whether a calendar item is set to a category of holiday and then creates a task item for the team leader.

To add a condition or action to a Visio diagram, follow these steps:

1. In the Shapes pane, under Conditions–SharePoint 2013 Workflow, click If Any Value Equals Value, drag it to the drawing area to the right of the Enter shape and place it on the line connecting the Enter shape to the Exit shape.

2. In the Shapes pane, under Actions–SharePoint 2013 Workflow, click Start a Task Process. Drag it to the drawing area to the right of the If Any Value Equals Value and place it on the line connecting the If Any Value Equals Value shape to the Exit shape.

3. Right-click the line connecting the If Any Value Equals Value shape and the Start A Task Process shape, and then click Yes.

4. On the Home tab, in the Tools group, click Connector, click the bottom corner of the If Any Value Equals Value shape, and then drag a line to the Exit shape so that a red square appears on the leftmost edge of the Exit shape. Right-click the connecting line, and then click No.

5. On the Home tab, in the Tools group, click the Pointer tool. Double-click If Any Value Equals Value, and then type **Is Calendar Category = Holiday?** Double-click Start A Task Process, and then type **Send email to employee's Team Leader to approve holiday.** This step is illustrated next.

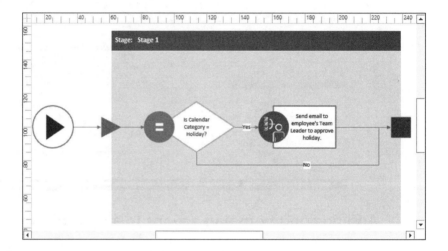

INSIDE OUT Visio workflow actions and condition limitations

The SharePoint Designer workflow conditions and actions that are displayed in Visio are coded into Visio. Visio does not connect to a SharePoint installation to find which SharePoint Designer conditions and actions are installed. So, if you use Visual Studio to develop any custom conditions and actions, they will not be visible in Visio unless you develop your own Visio shapes and validation rules. Perhaps even more important, there are some action shapes displayed in the Shapes pane that are installed only if you have SharePoint Server 2013. The action shapes that you cannot use with SharePoint Foundation are:

- Start approval process

- Start custom task process

- Start feedback process

- Send approval for document set

- Send document set to repository

- Set content approval status for document set

- Lookup manager of a user

- All SharePoint 2013 conditions and actions

If you do add one of these actions to your Visio diagram, when you import the .vwi file into SharePoint Designer, it will throw the error message, "Could not deserialize object." The <*object name*> could not be resolved, where <*object type*> varies depending on the shape you added in Visio. For example, when you add the Lookup Manager of a User action, the type is Microsoft.Office.Workflow.Actions.LookUpManagerOfActivity.

Validating and exporting a Visio SharePoint workflow diagram

Once you have created a diagram of your workflow and modified the text for each shape to document the details of the process, you need to validate the drawing before you can export the diagram and give it to the person who will create the workflow as either a SharePoint Designer or Visual Studio workflow.

To validate and export a Visio SharePoint workflow, complete the following procedure:

1. On the Process tab, in the Diagram Validation group, click Check Diagram, as shown next.

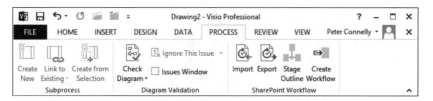

A Microsoft Visio dialog box opens (as shown next), stating "No issues were found in the current document." If your workflow has issues, an Issues task pane opens at the bottom of the Visio window. The erroneous component is highlighted. The Issues pane can be opened or closed by using the Issues Window check box in the Diagram Validation group on the Process tab.

2. Click OK to close the Microsoft Visio dialog box.

3. To create a Visio file that can be used with SharePoint Designer, complete one of the following tasks:

   - If you are creating a SharePoint 2013 workflow, select the File tab, and then, on the backstage, click Save As. Under Computer, click Browse to open the Save As dialog box. Navigate to where you want to save the .vsdx file.

   - If you are creating a SharePoint 2010 workflow, then on the Process tab, in the SharePoint Workflow group, click Export. The Export Workflow dialog box opens so that you can navigate to where you want to save the .vwi file.

4. In the File Name text box, type the name of the file, and then click Save to save the file and close the dialog box. Close Visio.

> **Note**
>
> If you are creating a SharePoint 2010 workflow, then you can choose to save the .vsdx file of your workflow for documentation purposes, if needed.

Importing a Visio diagram into SharePoint Designer

To import a .vwi or a .vsdx file into SharePoint Designer, follow these steps:

1. Using SharePoint Designer, open a SharePoint site for which you want to develop a SharePoint Designer workflow.

   If you want to create a globally reusable workflow from the file, the site must be a top-level site of a site collection.

2. In the Navigation pane, click Workflows. On the Workflows tab, in the Manage group, click the Import From Visio split button and select either Import Visio 2010 Diagram for a .vwi file or Import Visio 2013 Diagram for a .vsdx file, as shown next.

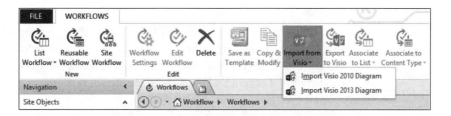

3. In the Import Workflow From Visio Drawing dialog box, click Browse, navigate to the location where you stored the .vsdx or .vwi file, click Open to display the Create Workflow dialog box.

4. In the Workflow Name text box, type the name of the workflow as it will be seen by users on a SharePoint site, and then select List Workflow, Site Workflow, or Reusable Workflow, as shown next.

   If you select List Workflow, you need to select a list with which to associate the workflow defined in the file. If you select Reusable Workflow, then you will be creating a workflow template that you can associate with any content type.

Chapter 7

5. Click OK.

   If this is the first time you've created a workflow, a dialog box opens asking you to wait while SharePoint Designer downloads the necessary information from the SharePoint site you have open, concerning the SharePoint Designer workflow conditions and actions that are installed, as shown next.

   If you import a Visio 2013 diagram, then the workflow opens in the SharePoint Designer Visual Designer; otherwise, the diagram opens in the Text-Based Designer, also known as the *Declarative Designer.*

   You can find more information about SharePoint Designer in the next section and in Chapter 20, "Creating, managing, and designing sites."

Creating, editing, and managing custom workflows with SharePoint Designer

The workflow templates provided with SharePoint 2013 may not be sufficient for many of the tasks related to business processes that you want to automate. This is when you will use SharePoint Designer to create workflows. SharePoint Designer provides a Workflow Editor that allows you to create no-code, rules-based declarative workflows. SharePoint Designer 2013 provides the following new features:

- A Visual Designer that uses a Visio 2013 ActiveX control

- New actions, such as the Call HTTP Web Service action, which enables no-code web service calls from within a workflow, and the new coordination actions, which let you start a workflow built on the SharePoint 2010 Workflow platform from a workflow built on the SharePoint 2013 Workflow platform

- New workflow building blocks such as Stage, Loop, and App Step

Creating workflows and workflow templates

There are three types of workflows that you can create with SharePoint Designer:

- **List workflows** Also known as *content workflows,* these workflows are created to automate tasks associated with content stored in lists and libraries.

- **Site workflows** These workflows are not associated with specific SharePoint objects and are started manually at the site level.

- **Reusable workflows** These are workflow templates that can subsequently be added to (associated with) a list or library on the site for which the reusable workflow is created. You create reusable workflows by binding them with content types. Reusable workflows can be published to the global workflows catalog, which makes it reusable on every site in the site collection, and visible to all users. Only reusable workflows at the top-level site of a site collection can be published as globally reusable workflows.

INSIDE OUT   Creating workflows using SharePoint Designer on a client operating system

To create workflows by using SharePoint Designer, you must have .NET Framework 3.5 installed on your computer to create SharePoint 2010 workflows or .NET Framework 4.5 to create SharePoint 2013 workflows. It is extremely likely that unless you are a developer with your own copy of a SharePoint installation, you will be running SharePoint Designer on a computer that does not have SharePoint installed on it. If that is the case, you will be running a client operating system such as Windows 8, Windows 7, Windows Vista, or Windows XP. Windows 7 includes .NET Framework 3.5; however, if you are using Windows Vista or Windows XP, you might need to install .NET Framework before you can work with workflows in SharePoint Designer. The .NET Framework is available from the Microsoft Download Center at *www.microsoft.com/downloads*.

When you create a workflow with SharePoint Designer, you can modify the workflow using two pages:

- Workflow Settings
- Workflow Editor

Creating list and site workflows

Perform the following steps to create a list workflow for a list or library:

1. Using the Navigation pane in SharePoint Designer, click Workflows.

2. On the Workflows tab, in the New group, click List Workflow, and then click the name of the list or library (such as Holiday Request) to display the Create List Workflow dialog box, as the following graphic shows.

    You can also display the Create List Workflow dialog box by using the List Workflow command in the New group on the Site tab and the List Settings tab.

3. In the Name text box, type **Holiday Request Approval**, and then click OK, as shown next.

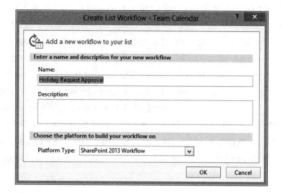

If the Downloading Data dialog box opens, wait for it to close.

A new tab named Holiday Request Approval opens with an asterisk, indicating that the workflow is not saved. The Text-Based Designer contains one stage, Stage 1, and a flashing orange horizontal line where the first condition or action can be inserted, as shown next.

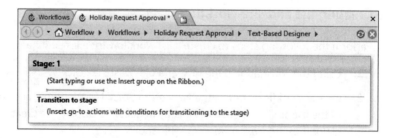

4. On the workspace breadcrumb, click Holiday Request Approval to navigate to the Workflow Settings page.

5. On the Workflow Settings tab, click Save.

   The Microsoft SharePoint Designer dialog box temporarily opens as the workflow is saved back to the SQL content database.

Checking and publishing workflows

Once you have created or modified a workflow, you should use the commands in the Save group on the Workflow tab to check for errors, save, and then publish the workflow. The Publish command also checks for errors and saves the workflow. Use the following steps to publish your workflow:

1. If you are on the Workflow Settings page, then on the Workflow Settings tab, click Edit Workflow in the Edit group. On the Workflow tab, click Check For Errors in the Save group.

   A Microsoft SharePoint Designer dialog box opens, stating that the workflow contains no errors. Click OK. If errors are reported, then this is usually because you have failed to complete link values in conditions or actions or with a SharePoint 2013 workflow that the Transition section is empty. Review and correct any errors, and then recheck your workflow.

2. On the Workflow tab, click Publish in the Save group.

   A Microsoft SharePoint Designer dialog box displays as the workflow files are saved to the server. You can publish a workflow that contains errors; however, the errors may prevent it from functioning correctly, and therefore it will be saved in a draft state.

You can now test your solution by creating a holiday request in the Holiday Schedule list. You might need to initiate a workflow instance manually on your list item, depending on the workflow start options that you set on the Workflow Settings page.

INSIDE OUT   Where are Sharepoint Designer workflows saved?

SharePoint 2010 workflows created by SharePoint Designer are saved in a hidden document library named Workflows that contains a folder for each workflow that you create in SharePoint Designer. This folder contains the declarative workflow files, as well as the workflow initiation page and any task pages. The Workflows library has versioning enabled, and therefore, theoretically you could revert a workflow to a previous state.

SharePoint 2013 workflows are first saved within the content database, where they are often referred to as the "truth" copy, and then transmitted and saved in Microsoft SQL Server databases associated with the Workflow Manager.

Using reusable and globally reusable workflows

Reusable workflows are workflow templates that can be modified in SharePoint Designer. In SharePoint 2010, these were the only no-code workflows created or modified by SharePoint Designer that you could develop in non-production environments and then move to a live environment. Now, in SharePoint 2013, you can develop list, site, and reusable no-code SharePoint 2013 workflows that can be moved between environments. No-code workflows developed in the live environment can be used on other lists and libraries, within the same site, within all sites in a site collection, or on sites within other site collections.

When you create a SharePoint 2010 reusable workflow, you must associate it with a content type—either a specific content type, such as Event, or with all content types. Windows 2013 reusable workflows are not associated with a content type.

With SharePoint 2010 workflows, the advantage of associating a reusable workflow with a specific content type, if you choose your content type carefully, is that the site columns you need to retrieve values for the current item will be present. The disadvantage is that you will be able to use that reusable workflow only with lists or libraries where that specific content type is added.

When you create a SharePoint 2010 reusable workflow associated with all content types, you need to create site columns and use the Association Column command to make columns that you want to work with available to your workflow. This entails more planning and forethought when you create your workflows.

INSIDE OUT There is no Association Column command with SharePoint 2013 reusable workflows

There is no Association Column command with SharePoint 2013 reusable workflows; they assume that all site columns are available at design time. Also, when you create a workflow to be used by other users, with slight variations to your business scenario, you need to create a more robust workflow, more error messages in the history log, and probably additional tests that will cater to values that you had not envisaged. It is usual when such reusable workflows are created that the support and maintenance might be handed over to the central team that supports the SharePoint implementation, thereby allowing you, the business user, to continue with your day job.

If you create a reusable workflow that is not in the top-level site of a site collection, which you then need to use on all sites within a site collection, you will need to export the workflow as a solutions file (.wsp) and then import the .wsp into the site collection's solution gallery.

Packaging workflows

In SharePoint 2010, you could only package and deploy reusable workflows. Now, in SharePoint 2013, you can deploy list, site, and reusable SharePoint 2013 workflows.

Exporting workflows   Before you can export a workflow, first save or publish the workflow, and then save the workflow as a .wsp file, also known as a *template*, by performing the following steps:

1. Open a site that contains the workflow that you have created in SharePoint Designer and then, in the Navigation pane, click Workflows.

2. Click the appropriate workflow to display the Workflow Settings page.

3. On the Workflow Settings tab, in the Manage group, click Save As Template.

   A dialog box appears, stating that the template has been saved to the Site Assets library. The workflow template is saved with a file name that is the same as the name of the workflow.

4. In the Navigation pane, click Site Assets to display the gallery page that displays all the files stored in the Site Assets library. If you do not see the workflow, click the refresh icon or press F5.

5. Click the icon to the left of the appropriate .wsp file, and then, on the Assets tab, in the Manage group, click Export File to display the Export Selected As dialog box.

6. Choose a directory in which to save the file, and then click Save. A Microsoft SharePoint Designer dialog box opens, as shown here, stating that the .wsp has been successfully exported:

Importing a reusable workflow   To use a reusable workflow in a site where it was not created, execute the steps that follow. You can also use these steps if you create a reusable workflow in a subsite of a site collection; therefore, you cannot publish it as a globally reusable workflow.

1. Using the browser, navigate to the top-level site of the site collection where you want to make the reusable workflow available.

2. Click Site Actions, and then click Site Settings.

3. Under Galleries, click Solutions.

4. On the Solutions tab, in the New group, click Upload Solution.

5. Click Browse to open the Choose File To Upload dialog box, navigate to where you saved the .wsp workflow template file, click Open, and then click OK.

    The Solution Gallery–Activate Solution dialog box opens.

6. On the View tab, click Activate.

7. Browse to the site where you want to use the workflow, click Site Actions, and then click Site Settings.

8. Under Site Actions, click Manage Site Features.

9. Click the Activate button to the right of the workflow template.

Using conditions, actions, steps, stages, and loops

The SharePoint 2013 Workflow template that is included in Visio 2013 also uses conditions, actions, steps, stages, and loops as logical building blocks to create workflows. SharePoint 2010 workflows use steps, conditions, and actions.

You can group together actions and conditions, including if-then-else branching, into stages or steps. However, there can be only one path into a stage (and a step) and one path out. Steps represent a grouped series of sequential actions and must be contained in a SharePoint 2013 workflow by a stage.

Conditions are used to create rules that portray the logic of the workflow. Actions are the basic unit of work performed by the workflow. When a condition is true, then all the actions associated with that condition are performed. A condition and its else-if branch conditions must be completed in a single step; that is, they cannot extend from one step to another.

Using a combination of conditions and actions, you can define which actions should be performed under which conditions. A workflow does not need to contain any conditions, but should contain at least one action, such as writing to the history log or sending the creator of a list item an email. If a workflow does not contain any conditions, then all the actions defined in the workflow will be performed.

Loops are a series of connected actions and conditions that will execute as a loop.

> **Note**
>
> When the set of built-in conditions and actions does not meet your business needs, a developer can create new conditions or actions, which are known as *custom activities*, using Visual Studio 2012 or a third-party tool. You can find information on how to create a custom activity by using Visual Studio at *msdn.microsoft.com/en-us/library/ jj163911(v=office.15).aspx*.

Conditions

SharePoint Designer divides the built-in conditions into two categories: Common Conditions and Other Conditions, which are listed in Table 7-1.

TABLE 7-1 Workflow conditions

Condition category	Conditions that can be used in both SharePoint 2013 and SharePoint 2010 workflows	SharePoint 2010–only conditions
Common	If Any Value Equals Value	If Current Item Field Equals Value
Other	Created By A Specific Person Created In A Specific Date Span Modified By A Specific Person Modified in A Specific Date Span Person Is A Valid SharePoint User Title Field Contains Keywords	Check List Item Permission Levels (only available within an Impersonation Step) Check List Item Permissions (only available within an Impersonation Step) The File Size In A Specific Range Kilobytes The File Is A Specific Type

The most used condition in a SharePoint Designer workflow is If Any Value Equals Value, which is a generic condition that you can use to compare two values, where a value can be:

- A metadata value from the list item or file on which the workflow instance was initiated, known as the *current item*

- A metadata value for a list item or file in list or library, where the workflow instance was not initiated

- Workflow variables or parameters, such as initiation form parameters and local variables

- Workflow context, such as the name of the workflow template, the current site URL, or the current user

- A value from items stored in the workflow's associated tasks or history list

When the value that you want to compare is not in the current item, you need to provide logic to specify from which item the workflow can obtain the value.

Actions

A SharePoint 2010 workflow action is a task that needs to be completed. You can choose to run actions serially; that is, an action starts only if the preceding one is complete. Alternatively, you can choose to run actions in parallel, known as a *parallel block,* where all actions start at the same time. SharePoint Designer divides built-in actions into categories, as shown in Table 7-2.

SharePoint Designer does not provide any diagnostic or debug facilities. When your workflow fails to run to completion, the only way to track which branch of a condition or which actions completed successfully is to write many items to the history list.

TABLE 7-2 Workflow actions

Action category	Used in both SharePoint 2013 and SharePoint 2010 Workflows	SharePoint 2013 workflows only	SharePoint 2010 workflows only
Coordination Actions		Start a List Workflow Start a Site Workflow	
Core Actions	Add a Comment Add Time to Date Do Calculation Log to History List Pause For Duration Pause Until Date Send an Email Set Time Portion of Date/Time Field Set Workflow Status Set Workflow Variable	Build Dictionary Call HTTP Web Service Count Items from a Dictionary Get Item from a Dictionary	Send Document to Repository Stop Workflow
Document Set Actions			Capture a version of the Document Set Send Document Set to Repository Set Content Approval Status for the Document Set Start Document Set Approval Process

Action category	Used in both SharePoint 2013 and SharePoint 2010 Workflows	SharePoint 2013 workflows only	SharePoint 2010 workflows only
List Actions	Check In Item Check Out Item Copy List Item Create List Item Delete Item Discard Check Out Item Set Field In Current Item Update List Item Wait For Event In List Item	Translate Document	Declare record Delete Drafts Delete Previous Versions Set Content Approval Status Undeclared Record Wait for Change in Document Check-Out Status Wait for Field Change in Current Item
Relational Actions			Lookup Manager of a User
Task Action		Assign a Task Start a Task Process	Assign a Form to a Group Assign a To-do Item Collect Data from a User Start Approval Process Start Custom Task Process Start Feedback Process
Utility Actions	Extract Substring from End of String Extract Substring from Index of String Extract Substring from Start of String Extract Substring from Index with Length Find Interval Between Dates	Find Substring in String Replace Substring in String Trim String	

Note

SharePoint Foundation does not support document sets or importing user information from Active Directory; this is why you will not see those categories when you work with workflows in SharePoint Designer on a SharePoint Foundation site.

For additional information, read the reference guide to workflow actions in SharePoint Designer 2013, which is available at *msdn.microsoft.com/en-us/library/jj164026(v=office.15). aspx*. Information on the Visio 2013 shapes that refer to SharePoint Designer workflow actions and conditions can be found at *technet.microsoft.com/en-us/library/jj164055(v=office.15).aspx*.

Steps

Use steps to document the major set of activities that need to be completed as part of your workflow. SharePoint Designer workflows can become large; and by grouping conditions and actions into steps, your workflow becomes more readable, which is important if a colleague is asked to maintain a workflow that you have created, or if it has been some time since you last looked at the workflow.

Stages

All actions in a SharePoint 2013 workflow must be placed in a stage, which is a container stage in Visio 2013 and the Visual Designer in SharePoint Designer 2013. Each stage must have a unique name and should be used to document the purpose of the stage.

In the Visual Designer view or in Visio, a Stage shape requires that an Enter and an Exit shape be added to the edges of the container to define the paths in to and out of the stage. The Enter and Exit shapes are added for you when you first drop a stage onto the drawing area of a Visio SharePoint 2013 workflow diagram.

Unlike steps, where the flow of the workflow is sequential from one step to the next, in stages, the follow of the workflow stops at the end of the stage. Therefore, at the end of each stage, there is a Transition To Stage area, as shown in Figure 7-2, where you can configure the workflow to end the workflow or to go to another stage to execute the conditions and actions within that stage. Only conditions can be added to a Transition To Stage area.

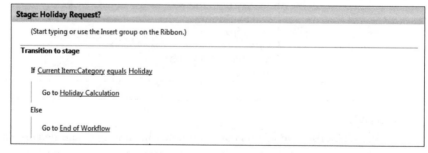

Figure 7-2 Use conditions in the Transition To Stage area to control the flow of your workflow.

A stage must adhere to the following rules:

- All SharePoint 2013 workflows must have at least one stage.

- Stage containers cannot be nested. If you want to nest another subprocess within a stage, use a step.

- Stages in a Visio diagram must conform to the following:

    - They cannot have any connectors coming in or going out other than through the Enter and Exit shapes. Stop Workflow shapes may exist within a stage.

    - They must have an explicit Start shape outside the stage for the entire diagram. An explicit Terminate shape outside the stage is not required.

- At the top level, a SharePoint 2013 workflow can contain only stages, conditional shapes, and Start and Terminate terminators. All other shapes must be contained within a stage.

Loops

Loops are a series of connected shapes that will execute as a loop, returning from the last shape in the series to the first, until a condition is satisfied.

Like stages, loops in Visio are represented by a container shape that includes an Enter and Exit shape (added when the shape is dropped on the drawing canvas). A Loop shape also requires that an Enter and Exit shape be added to the edges of the container to define the paths in to and out of the loop.

Visio 2013 and SharePoint Designer 2013 support two types of loops: loop *n* times and loop until value1 equals value2.

Loops must also conform to the following rules:

- Loops must be within a stage, and stages cannot be within a loop.

- Steps may be within a loop.

- Loops may have only one entry and one exit point.

Using the Workflow Settings page

Use the Workflow Settings page to view and manage settings for the workflow. It consists of a contextual ribbon tab, as shown in Figure 7-3, and five areas, as shown in Figure 7-4.

Figure 7-3 On the Workflow Settings tab, you can save, edit, manage workflows, and create and manage variables.

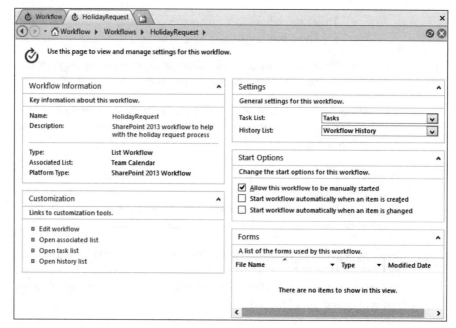

Figure 7-4 Use the Workflow Settings page to configure the workflow.

The five areas on the Workflow Settings page can be used as follows:

- **Workflow information** This area displays basic workflow information, such as the workflow name, description, type (list, site, or reusable) and Platform type (SharePoint 2010 Workflow or SharePoint 2013 Workflow). When the type of workflow is a list workflow, then this area displays the name of the list or library with which the workflow is associated. When the workflow type is reusable, this area displays the name of the content type with which it is associated.

- **Customization** The links provided in this area will differ depending on the type of workflow. For example, for a list workflow, this area contains links to the Workflow Editor page and links to open the associated list, task list, and workflow history list.

- **Settings** Use this area to select the task and workflow history list that the workflow is to use. For list and site workflows when you create a SharePoint 2010 workflow, this area contains a check box that is associated with workflow visualization within the browser. This option is only applicable when you have SharePoint Server 2010 Enterprise edition installed.

- **Start options** Use this area to select the start options for the workflow.

- **Forms** This area displays the pages that SharePoint Designer automatically creates during the publishing process. Depending on the type of workflow and the start option selected, a number of pages will be created. Whenever a workflow can be started manually, an initiation page is created. When you use the task action to collect data from a user, then task pages are created. If you create a SharePoint 2010 workflow in a SharePoint Server 2013 installation, the forms will be created as InfoPath forms; otherwise, the forms will be .aspx files.

Editing workflows

Use the Workflow tab to create and change the workflow. If you are creating a SharePoint 2013 workflow, use the Workflow tab to switch between three editing views of the workflow: Text-Based Designer, Visual Designer, or Stage View. When you create a SharePoint 2010 workflow, you can only use the Text-Based Designer view.

The Workflow tab can consist of up to five tab groups, depending on the view you are using. The Workflow tab when you are using the Text-Based Designer is shown in Figure 7-5. The Clipboard, Modify, and Insert groups are specific to the Text-Based Designer.

Figure 7-5 Use the Workflow tab to create and modify the logic of your workflow.

Save

Use the Save group to check your workflow for errors, save your workflow, and publish your workflow. The Save and Publish commands are the same commands you find in the Save group on the Workflow Settings tab. Use the Save command when you wish to save your amendments but have not completed the workflow, and therefore you do not wish other users on the site to use the workflow. When you click the Publish command, it also saves the workflow.

Clipboard

New to SharePoint Designer 2013, you now have the ability to copy and paste within the Text-Based Designer. You can use the command in the Clipboard group on the ribbon, as well as using keyboard combinations such as CTRL+C to copy, CTRL+V to paste, or CTRL+X to cut. There is no undo or redo capabilities. You can also use the context menu of any selected item, as shown in Figure 7-6.

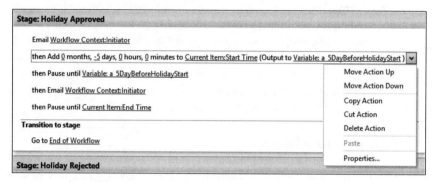

Figure 7-6 Use the context menu on actions and conditions to copy and paste.

You can copy Stages, Steps, or individual actions or condition blocks, as well as selecting multiple lines of actions, steps, condition blocks, or stages. Selected items will be highlighted in a sky-blue color.

Modify

Use the commands in the Modify group to move and delete conditions, actions, and steps, as well as to modify the advanced properties of conditions and actions. Actions can be moved between steps and within steps, whereas conditions can only be moved up or down within their condition block. A condition block starts with an If statement, and subsequent conditions within that condition block start with an and or an or.

Insert

Use the commands in the Insert group to insert conditions, actions, steps, and, if it is a SharePoint 2013 workflow, stages. Use the else-if branch commands to add another condition block so that you can define actions to be performed, if the conditions of the first condition block are not true.

Use the Parallel Block command when you want a set of actions to execute at the same time and not in sequence. Parallel actions may not be performed absolutely simultaneously. The exact order cannot be specified and can vary each time a workflow instance runs.

Use steps to document the major set of activities that need to be completed as part of your workflow.

If you are using a SharePoint 2013 workflow, the Insert group will contain the Impersonate Step command, which you can use to add a special step to your workflow that allows the conditions and actions within that step to execute using the security credentials of the workflow author.

Manage

The Manage group contains three commands that are the same as those in the Manage group on the Workflow Settings tab. The commands available on the Workflow tab allow you to publish a reusable workflow as a globally reusable workflow, export the workflow as a Visio file, and to switch to the Workflow Settings page. You can also switch to the Workflow Settings page by using the workspace breadcrumb and clicking the name of the workflow, which appears in the workspace breadcrumb to the right of Workflows.

Variables

Variables provide temporary storage that persists for the lifetime of the workflow. This tab group contains two or three commands, depending on whether you are working with a SharePoint 2013 or SharePoint 2010 workflow. These commands are the same as those in the Variables group on the Workflow Settings tab. The three commands are:

- **Initiation form parameters** Use when a workflow instance is to be manually started; thus, the initiator of the workflow can provide values stored in initiation variables, which can then be used in the workflow. The values entered by the workflow initiator are only available for the lifetime of the workflow instance.

- **Local variables** Use to pass values from one condition or action to another condition or action (for example, to save the Task ID created from the Collect Data From A User action so that a subsequent action can use the values that a person entered into the task).

- **Association columns** This command is available only with SharePoint 2010 workflows and is used with reusable workflows to add site columns to the list or library when the workflow is associated with that list or library. You should review existing site columns before you create new site columns within the Association Columns dialog box. With a SharePoint 2013 workflow, if you need to use workflows on other sites, then you should create a list or library workflow where the list or library contains the columns needed by your workflow. You can then save those workflows as workflow templates.

With SharePoint 2013 workflows, you can create a new type of variable that can hold an array of values, known as a *dictionary*. These are created using the Build Dictionary action and are used in conjunction with the loop actions.

More information on dictionary actions in SharePoint Designer 2013 can be found at *msdn.microsoft.com/en-us/library/jj554504(v=office.15).aspx.*

Authoring work using the Visual Designer

You can use the Visual Designer within SharePoint Designer only when you are creating a SharePoint 2013 workflow. You can use the Visual Designer once you create a workflow from a Visio diagram, as described in the previous section, or you can create a SharePoint 2013 workflow within SharePoint Designer and then switch to use the Visual Designer by using the Views split button in the Manage group on the Workflow tab, as shown in Figure 7-7. The Visio diagram displayed is also known as the Workflow Outline.

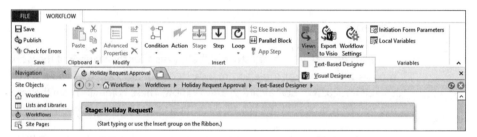

Figure 7-7 Use the Views split button to switch among the three views for a SharePoint 2013 workflow.

You can use the content area of the workspace and Workflow tab as you would within Visio. In the content area, you have a Shapes pane and a drawing area. When using the Visual Designer, the Workflow tab is displayed and consists of four groups:

- Save

- Modify

- Manage

- Variables

The Modify group is specific to the Visual Designer and contains commands similar to those that you would see in Visio: Pointer tool, Connector tool, and Text. The other ribbon groups are the same as you would see when using the Text-Based Designer and are described later in this chapter.

In the Modify ribbon group, you have the Advanced Properties command, which provides a way of displaying the Properties dialog box. You also can display this box by using the Action Tags menu, shown as a workflow settings type icon that appears on the lower-left side of the shape when you pause over or select the action, as shown in Figure 7-8.

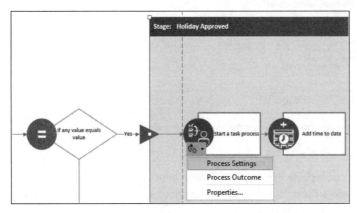

Figure 7-8 Shapes displayed in the Visual Designer have Action Tags.

The Action Tag, a drop-down menu, displays the attributes for that action or condition in the workflow and as a link—Properties—that opens a dialog box allowing you to modify parameter values to be used for that action.

Action Tag attributes

In many cases, the attribute links on the Action Tag drop-down menu are also provided in the Properties dialog box; however, the Action Tag attributes provide a friendlier input mechanism than the Properties dialog box. The Action Tags attribute dialog boxes are the same as the dialog boxes that you would see if you used the Text-Based Designer. For example, the Start A Task Process shape has two attributes, Process Settings and Process Outcome, which you can use to configure the Start A Task Process action, as in the following procedure:

1. From the Action Tag menu, select Process Settings to display the Select Task Process Participants dialog box.

2. Configure the recipient or recipients of the task item by clicking the ellipsis icon to the right of the Participants text box to open the Select Users dialog box. Under Or Select From Existing Users And Groups, select User Who Created Current Item, click Add, and then click OK. The following graphic shows an example.

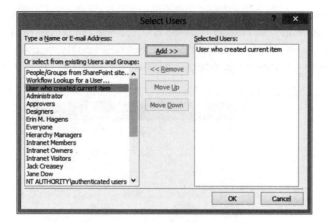

3. Enter a task title line for the task item.

   You can include dynamic data within your workflow. For example, if you have associated your workflow with a calendar list, you can get the workflow to dynamically obtain the start date that a user has entered when he or she created the calendar item. To the right of the Task Title text box, there is an ellipsis button (also known as the Display Builder button), and the Define Workflow Lookup button, as shown next.

4. Click the ellipsis button to open the String Builder dialog box and then, in the Name text box, type **Holiday request.** At the lower left side of the String Builder text box, click Add Or Change Lookup to open the Lookup For String dialog box.

5. As shown in the following graphic, leave the Data Source as Current Item to tell the workflow to use the list item which was used to start the workflow instance, and then, from the Field From Source list, select Start Time.

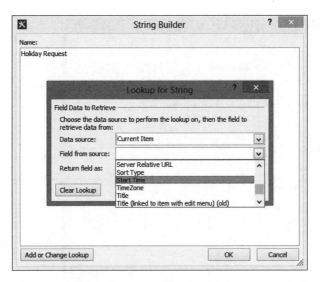

In the Return Field As list, you can choose how you want the date/time field to be displayed. Select Long Date and then click OK twice to close the Lookup For String dialog box and the String Builder dialog box.

6. Use the Description text box of the Select Task Process Participants dialog box, to type the main message of the task item, as shown next. You can also use the Open Editor For Body button to open a String Builder dialog box, which allows you to include dynamic text. For example, type **Team member,** and then click Add Or Change Lookup to open the Lookup For String dialog box. In the Field From Source list, select Created By, and in the Return Field As List, click Display Name. Click OK to close the Lookup For String dialog box.

In the String Builder dialog box, on a new line, under Team, type **has submitted a holiday request to**, and then click Add Or Change Lookup to open the Lookup For String dialog box. In the Field From Source list, select Location. Click OK to close the Lookup For String dialog box.

Workflows developed by using SharePoint Designer are human centric, and therefore, as the workflow progresses, you will need to communicate with users of the site, either to complete a task or to obtain additional information. SharePoint 2010 workflows provided a number of task actions, the Start A Task Process action is similar to the Start Approval Process action that you may have used in SharePoint 2010 workflows. The sections Assignee Options, Email Options, and Outcome Options allow you to further configure this action, as shown next.

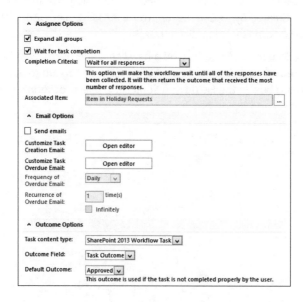

If you choose to send an email to the participants in the approval process, you can use the Open Editor button to open the Define Email Message dialog box, where you can enter the subject and the body of the email. The dialog box provides buttons that allow you to format the body of the email message.

7. Click OK to close the Define Email Message dialog box.

Action tag properties

You could use the Properties dialog box to configure the action. When you choose Action Tag, Properties, a Start A Task Process Properties dialog box appears that displays all of the parameters for the action, as shown in Figure 7-9.

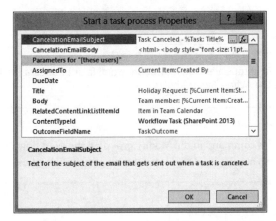

Figure 7-9 Use the Properties dialog box to alter the attribute settings of the action.

In the Define Email Message dialog box, you are limited to how to format the text by the button shown above the Body text box. Notice that the Properties dialog box exposes the body of any email properties as HTML tags. For example, by clicking AssignmentEmailBody and then clicking the ellipsis button that appears, the String Builder dialog box opens, where you can modify the HTML source code, as shown in Figure 7-10. Unfortunately, there is no IntelliSense provided, and you cannot copy and paste HTML text from your favorite HTML editor because you would lose any lookup values that you may have included in the message.

Figure 7-10 Using Action Tag properties, you may be shown data or have data displayed differently than when you use Action Tag attributes.

> **Note**
>
> The Advanced Properties command in the Modify group on the Workflow tab is not available in Visio and can also be used to display the Properties dialog box.

Working with the Text-Based Designer

The Text-Based Designer, similar to the Visual Designer, allows you to see how stages, steps, actions, and conditions are associated with each other. The Workflow Editor surrounds conditions and their associated actions with a gray rectangle. Action and condition attributes are displayed as underlined text, which you use to configure them. Any dialog boxes that are displayed are the same dialog boxes that you see when you configure the actions and conditions using the Visual Designer.

Stage outline

Stage outline provides a high-level view of your SharePoint 2013 workflow, as shown in Figure 7-11. It shows the stages within your workflow, not the individual conditions and actions.

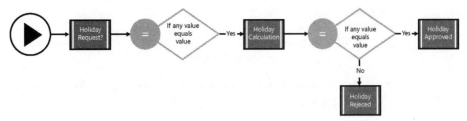

Figure 7-11 Use the Stage View to show the stages and how they are connected.

To use the Stage View within SharePoint Designer, Visio needs to be installed as well, and you have to display the workflow using the Visual Designer, before you can select the Generate Stage Outline from the Manage group on the Workflow ribbon tab. To switch to the Workflow Outline (that is, the first diagram displayed when you click Visual Designer), click Generate Workflow Outline in the Manage group on the Workflow ribbon tab.

Obtaining data not saved in the current item

There will be circumstances in which you find yourself in need of information, but it is not saved in the list where the workflow is associated nor in other lists or libraries in your site. However, the information can be calculated from the information in your site. SharePoint also allows you to specify a condition, so you are able to match retrieved data from a list item within another list or library; however, it will return only the first item that matches your condition.

The best way to understand these workflow calculations and obtaining data from another list is to use a specific scenario. In the following example, a holiday request scenario uses two related lists, as shown in Figure 7-12.

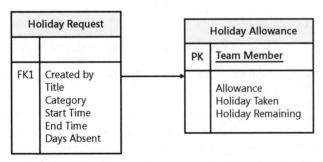

Figure 7-12 The relationship between the Holiday Request, Holiday Allowance, and Teams lists.

The two lists are:

- **Holiday Request** This list is based on a Calendar list template with content approval enabled and one additional column:

  - **Days Absent** This column is a number column with a default value of 1 and a minimum value of 1.

- **Holiday Allowance** A list created from the Custom list template, which has a list item for each employee in a team and consists of four columns. Because you will not be using the Title column, this field should be set as Not Required. All other columns should be configured as Required. The four columns are:

  - **Team Member** A People Or Group field.

  - **Allowance** A number field with a default value of 20, a minimum value of 0, and a maximum value of 50.

  - **Holiday Taken** A number field with a default value of 0, a minimum value of 0, and a maximum value of 50.

  - **Holiday Remaining** A calculated column with a formula, `[Allowance]-[Holiday Taken]`.

In the following steps, you will find the list item in the Holiday Allowance list that matches the team member who created the holiday request. You will then calculate the number of days a team member plans to take when adding the new holiday request to the number of days the team member has taken as holidays previous to this request.

1. In the Text-Based Designer, click where you would like the calculation action to appear. On the Workflow tab, in the Insert group, click Actions, and then, under Core Actions, click Do Calculation.

   The words "Then Calculate Value Plus Value (Output To Variable: Calc)" appear.

2. Click Variable: Calc, and then click Create A New Variable to open the Edit Variable dialog box.

   You can also create new variables by using the Local Variables command on the Workflow tab in the Variables group. It is good practice to not use the variables that SharePoint Designer creates because they might not be of the correct data type for your calculation, and the name will not indicate the information stored in the variable. You should use the variable name as a mechanism to document your workflow, and in large workflows where there are many variables using an appropriate name, this can save you time when you need to change your work-flows. When you create a new workflow variable, create it before completing any links within an action or condition. When you create a variable after completing the links, then the links will clear and you will need to complete them again.

3. In the Name text box, type **a_HolidayTaken**, and then, in the Type list, select Number, as shown here. Click OK to close the Edit Variable dialog box.

Some actions, such as the SharePoint 2010 workflow actions, Start Approval Process, or the Start Feedback Process available in SharePoint Server 2013, will create their own variables when incorporated into your workflow; therefore, when you create a variable, it is advisable to devise a naming standard so that you can quickly identify the variables that you generated.

4. Click the first occurrence of Value, and then click Define Workflow Lookup to open the Lookup For Number dialog box.

5. Leave Current Item as the selected item in the Data Source list, and then, in the Field From Source list, select Days Absent. Click OK to close the Lookup For Number dialog box.

6. Click the remaining Value link, and then click Define Workflow Lookup again to open the Lookup For Number dialog box.

7. In the Data Source list, scroll down and click Holiday Allowance.

The Lookup For Number dialog box expands to include a second section, Find The List Item.

8. In the Field Data To Retrieve section, click Field From Source, and then select Holiday Remaining.

9. In the Find The List Item section, click the down arrow to the right of Field, select Team Member, and then in the Value, click the ellipsis button to open the Select User dialog box, as shown in the following graphice.

10. Under Or Select From Existing Users and Groups, select User Who Created Current Item, and then click Add. Click OK to close the Select Users dialog box.

11. Click OK to close the Lookup For Number dialog box.

    A Microsoft SharePoint Designer dialog box opens, stating that the lookup you defined does not guarantee to return a single value, and that if more than one value is returned, only the first value will be used. Therefore, when you use SharePoint Designer to join two lists or libraries, you should verify that your workflow design ensures that only one value is returned. In this scenario, there should only be one list item in the Holiday Allowance list for each team member. Unfortunately, you cannot use the Enforce Unique Value option when you create a column of type People or Group.

12. Click Yes to close the Microsoft SharePoint Designer dialog box.

INSIDE OUT   Using the Impersonation Step

When a workflow instance starts, it runs under the identity of the user who starts the workflow instance—the initiator; therefore, the actions that the workflow can execute is limited by the actions that the workflow initiator can perform. If you want to move an item from a list (source) to another list (destination), then the workflow initiator must have contribute rights on the destination list. However, in many scenarios, you do not want to give the workflow initiator access to the destination list. When you create a SharePoint 2010 workflow, you can use the Impersonation Step that allows the workflow instance to execute actions and conditions under the security permissions of the user who authored the workflow.

There are four additional actions that are available within the Impersonation Step. These are:

- Add List Item Permissions

- Inherit List Items Parent Permissions

- Remove List Item Permissions

- Replace List Item Permissions

When you use the Add List Item Permissions action, you are breaking the inheritance of the item from the security settings of the list. This is known as using unique permissions within a list or library. In SharePoint 2010, this could result in performance implications, such as long page load times across the farm, and cause high load on the SQL servers, which could result in page request timeouts. In SharePoint 2010, it was recommended that lists and libraries have no more than 50,000 unique permissions. SharePoint 2013 has increased the number of unique permissions per list, and so breaking inheritance at item levels should not be an issue.

The Impersonation Step comes with its own set of limitations that you must be aware of before you use it. Unlike the default step, the Impersonation Step cannot be nested within an existing step; therefore, the Impersonation Step command in the Insert group on the Workflow tab is active only when the insertion point is outside all steps in the Workflow Editor workspace. When the workflow author leaves the company and his or her user account is removed from the system, the workflow terminates when the Impersonation Step is executed. The termination of workflows due to this scenario can cause organizations major support issues, especially if the support team is unaware of the implications of using the Impersonation Step. Similarly, if the Impersonation Step moves an item from one list to another and the workflow author does not have contribute permissions on the destination list, then the Impersonation Step will fail. This is most likely to happen when using the Impersonation Step within reusable and globally reusable workflows.

It is important to document the permissions the workflow author must have to ensure that the Impersonation Step will work as designed. You can use the Add A Comment action to include documentation within your workflow.

Summary

SharePoint 2013 provides two workflow platforms: the SharePoint 2010 workflow platform and the SharePoint 2013 workflow platform. The SharePoint 2010 workflow engine is installed automatically with SharePoint 2013. SharePoint 2013 workflows become available only when you install and configure the Workflow Manager. The Workflow Manager can be used only with editions of SharePoint Server 2013 and is not available with SharePoint Foundation 2013. All of your workflows that were built using SharePoint 2010 will continue to work in SharePoint 2013; however, SharePoint 2010 workflows do not use the Workflow Manager and are hosted within SharePoint.

The SharePoint 2010 workflow templates provided out of the box with SharePoint 2013 can be used to meet many customer requirements with no further effort. If they don't meet your specific requirements, you can design your own workflows by using Visio 2013, which can then be imported into SharePoint Designer 2013, where the configuration of the workflows can be completed.

SharePoint Designer 2013 includes new functionality designed specifically for the Workflow Manager, which includes a visual workflow development environment that uses a Visio 2013 add-in. Workflow Manager is built on .NET Framework 4.5 and provides additional workflow actions and conditions and includes the notions of stages and loops, as well as steps.

SharePoint Designer also gives you an expanded capability to design workflows and reusable workflows within a site and to promote those workflows to globally reusable workflows so that they can be used by any site in a site collection. You can also save list and site workflows as templates and use them on other sites. In addition, you have the ultimate flexibility to design your own workflow components and SharePoint Designer activities within WF by using Visual Studio 2012.

CHAPTER 8

Planning site content

C ONTENT is the heart of a Microsoft SharePoint 2013 site. Organizing content and using the web parts available to you in a way that is accepted by those you work with on the site is the best way to provide value to your organization through SharePoint.

How do you plan SharePoint site content? Understanding why this question is important is a little bit of a conundrum. Until you have enough content in your sites to make managing it an issue, you really can't have a full appreciation for the full breadth of the concerns involved in getting that content under control. On the other hand, planning site structure and strategy is more efficiently applied at the beginning of any site content undertaking.

Where is the middle ground? The practical approach to managing site content requires both ongoing content creation and ongoing planning around the existing content and for future content. It is only through the experience of creating the content that you can truly appreciate why planning is a benefit. Some amount of planning must be done up front, but it also must be revisited throughout the creation process to fine-tune the architecture and rules of the road to match what you've put in place and can envision down the road.

The other chapters of this book provide the tools you need to create and publish content into SharePoint sites effectively. After reading this book, you will have a good view of the breadth of features and functionality of SharePoint 2013. You will know how to navigate and manipulate the views and interactions of web applications, site collections, sites, lists, libraries, and pages. Creating sites and workspaces, designing lists and libraries, and creating and formatting webpages are all content creation processes. Adding, editing, connecting, and managing web parts add even more content to your sites.

SharePoint has no lack of options for getting content on the site. With a great SharePoint infrastructure in place, you and your colleagues in your organization are doing just that; you're creating content, and lots of it. However, like any great endeavor undertaken by a group of people, all that content—and you and your colleagues as the content consumers—will benefit from structure, strategy, and some rules of the road. You don't just want to create and consume content. You want to do it effectively.

This chapter provides the tools and strategies for designing a well-organized SharePoint site. You will learn how information architecture (IA) and governance can be applied to web content creation and management. This chapter also provides techniques for content planning, including identifying a content manager and protecting content via Information Rights Management (IRM). Using the strategies described here, you will find effective ways to present information that is up to date and relevant in your sites.

An introduction to information architecture

The following quote from the Wikipedia article (located at *en.wikipedia.org/wiki/Richard_ Saul_Wurman*) about Richard Saul Wurman is a good introduction to IA:

In 1976, Wurman coined the phrase "information architect" in response to the large amount of information generated in contemporary society, which is often presented with little care or order. Wurman said, "I thought the explosion of data needed an architecture, needed a series of systems, needed systemic design, a series of performance criteria to measure it."

You might have experienced an "explosion of data" in your organization. SharePoint can play a role in helping to increase the amount of content publishing; therefore, it must also be a part of this needed architecture to help control it. If you have ever seen file shares that seem unmanageable or hundreds of abandoned SharePoint sites that are out of date, you have a great reference point for understanding the architecture tools and strategies that are introduced in the following sections.

Start with purpose

Starting from a blank site, your potential to create is mostly limited by your imagination. But before you create your first list or add your first web part, you have the opportunity to design your solution to fit your end purpose for the site. If you don't have a purpose in mind for your site, this would be a good time to reconsider what you hope to gain from your use of SharePoint.

The simplest purpose for a SharePoint site might be sharing documents with others in your organization. In fact, document sharing is a valid and well-received feature of SharePoint, and many organizations start there. If this is the case with your organization, the simplest information architecture is one site with one document library. The only page needed to start the site, and possibly the clearest view to a new user of such a site, is to present the document library front and center. It might be that in your organization, this is the case for departmental sites—for example, Human Resources. If so, state the purpose clearly on the page. A description of roles and responsibilities for the site helps to reinforce the IA and introduce documentation of governance, as explained later in this chapter. An example of the simple site is shown in Figure 8-1.

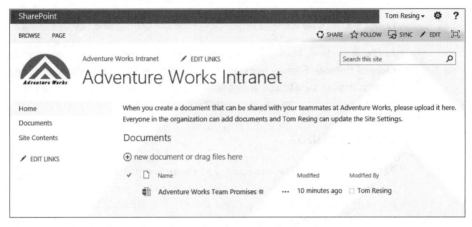

Figure 8-1 The simplest IA for a SharePoint document sharing site.

INSIDE OUT   The new and improved Team Site template in SharePoint 2013

Note that Figure 8-1 shows a site set up for document sharing, one of the most popular uses of SharePoint. It was created using the Team Site template, which historically is probably the most popular site template. The Team Site template has changed in SharePoint 2013. In previous versions of SharePoint, if you didn't intend to use the calendar, tasks list, and team discussion list that were created with the Team Site template, we recommended starting with the Blank Site template to improve your IA. Limiting choices for the user to those that are the most important is an improvement in usability of your site. Now, the Team Site template comes with only the bare minimum for document sharing and is the better choice over the Blank Site in many situations.

You still may choose to use the Blank Site template in SharePoint 2013. For example, you may not want a document library or some of the features activated by default in the Team Site template. If you do, the first change you might want to make is to activate the Wiki Page Home Page feature in Site Settings under the Site Features list. This will switch your home page to a wiki page from a Web Part page, which is the default on the blank template. Wiki pages have enhanced functionality and are the default on the Team Site template starting with SharePoint 2010 and moving forward. Figure 8-2 shows the Wiki Page Home Page row on the Site Features page.

Figure 8-2 Activate the Wiki Page Home Page site feature when using a Blank Site template.

At any given time, your purpose might simply be to play or experiment with some new piece of the tool. Even in this case, you could take a little extra time to exercise your IA process in your sandboxed environment. Like everything else, practice makes perfect, and you can't expect to design the perfect solution on your first try.

Use a sandbox

Because SharePoint sites are so easy to create and just as easy to delete, you can really feel free to experiment with your SharePoint sites before you share them with others. Once you populate your site with content and share it with others, it becomes much more important to plan structural changes ahead of time and communicate them to the site's audience early. However, before you have others that depend on your site, it is important to try out the various tools that are at your disposal.

Figure 8-3 shows the picker for adding an app to a blank site. Using each app and web part at least once will give you a basis for making architectural decisions. Before you create your next SharePoint site for use with others, try playing a little in a sandbox to inform your decisions and add confidence to your choices. How long do you think it would take to create one site of each of the template types available to you? On the other hand, if you don't create one of each type and explore it, how sure will you be that you are choosing the right template?

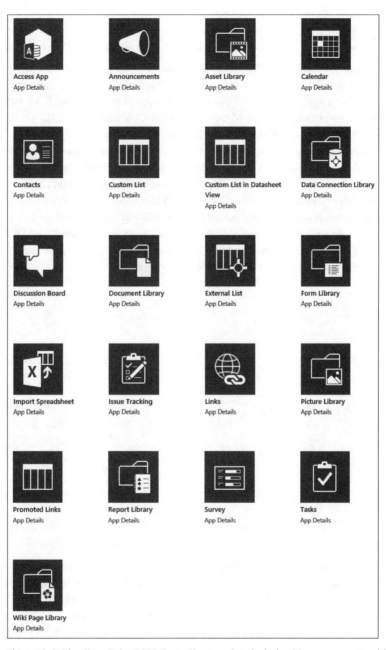

Figure 8-3 The SharePoint 2013 Team Site template includes 21 apps you can add out of the box.

INSIDE OUT

Modern HTML and apps change the way we add content

Do you remember the table of list, library, and site templates from SharePoint 2010, shown here? It served a similar function, but you'll notice a few changes in the App Selection page in SharePoint 2013. The list of apps shown in Figure 8-3 is only part of the story. SharePoint 2010 used Microsoft Silverlight, but SharePoint 2013 has been updated to use more modern HTML that works across browsers and platforms without plug-ins. In addition, the user experience has been improved based on user feedback. SharePoint 2010 presented list, library, and site templates together, in one selection dialog box. Based on interviews with users, they found this confusing and didn't really care about the differences between lists and libraries. In SharePoint 2013, what were called List and Library templates are now grouped apps, simplifying the terminology. Site template selections have been separated and can be selected from the new Subsite button on the Site Contents page. Showing apps without the site templates in SharePoint 2013 reduced the number of choices to 21 on the Add An App page.

To expand your knowledge of SharePoint 2013, try creating a blank site and adding all the types of apps and web parts to it. Even the most advanced SharePoint user can benefit from occasional review. And again, if you start here with the purpose to discover, the experience you gain will help you design your next site or manage an existing site with confidence. Keep in mind that you can also create a site template from any site that you originally create as a sandbox. If you accidentally happen upon the perfect site structure while playing, you can capture that structure and reuse it where others can benefit.

Figure 8-4 shows the last page of the Web Part Gallery of a site created with the Team Site template. Notice that there are 70 web parts out of the box. In addition, you will see one instance of the List View Web Part in the Add New Web Part dialog box for every instance of a list or library that exists on your site. Experimenting with web parts continues to be important in SharePoint 2013.

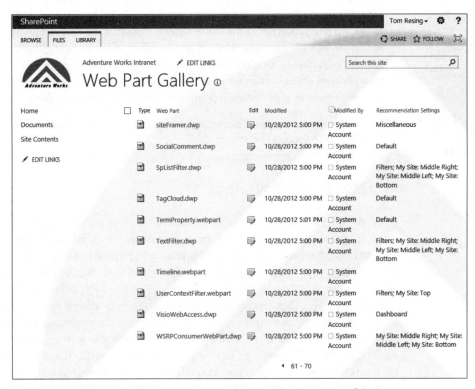

Figure 8-4 The Web Part Gallery on a team site has 70 web parts out of the box.

The type of SharePoint content that you can experiment with doesn't stop with apps, sites, and web parts. List columns, content types, list views, terms, and workflows are just as simple to create and delete. Don't be afraid to create what you can easily remove later. Without the ability to create these types of content, SharePoint would be no different than any other website. When mastered, creating the right type of content for your needs allows you to reach the full potential of SharePoint planning and management. Experience leads to mastery, and a sandbox is a great place to gain experience.

INSIDE OUT Using security trimming to hide your sandbox

You can standardize by creating one sandbox in every site collection when you use this method. SharePoint's security trimming will hide your sandbox site from search results and features like the Site Content page if you use unique permissions to remove most security groups. However, in most cases, the links will not be trimmed if you add them to the top navigation bar or the Quick Launch toolbar, so it's best not to list a sandbox in navigation. Each site collection and web application can be configured with different features activated, so it's often helpful to create one sandbox per site collection or at least per base site collection template. If you use a common address, such as /sandbox, you won't need to guess where it is when it's not in the navigation bars.

For more information about managing permissions settings, refer to Chapter 3, "Working with list and library apps."

Prototypes or wireframes

While not strictly an IA tool, drawings or sketches of page prototypes can help solidify the vision for a site's content. Sometimes these prototypes are called *wireframes* or *storyboards*, in reference to the processes used in engineering and movie making to envision a project. When starting your drawing, you might find it helpful to start as simple as possible. Sit down with pencil and paper to create a black-and-white rough sketch quickly, just to capture some ideas. Don't worry about making it pretty or adding color. The benefit in this process is in committing the ideas in your head to a rough visualization that can be perfected with time and effort later. If you're not comfortable with your artistic skills with a pencil, or you simply prefer an electronic method, products such as Microsoft Visio or Microsoft PowerPoint can help you to create visuals of your site content visions. While not required to wireframe with PowerPoint, developers with Microsoft Visual Studio will appreciate the added SharePoint storyboard shapes.

Read more about PowerPoint storyboarding added with Visual Studio 2012 Premium at *msdn.microsoft.com/en-us/library/hh409276.aspx.*

INSIDE OUT   A software tool for that hand-drawn look

There is a middle ground between hand-drawn sketches and professional-looking mock-ups. The benefit of a hand-drawn look is that it suggests that change is as easy as an eraser and pencil. Mock-ups that too closely resemble an end product might confuse the design process with actual implementation and move the viewer too far, too fast. Remember, the goal here is planning and refinement, not an exact blueprint for building. As an example, refer to the following graphic for a typical first draft of an intranet portal that was drawn by using the rapid wireframing tool Balsamiq Mockups.

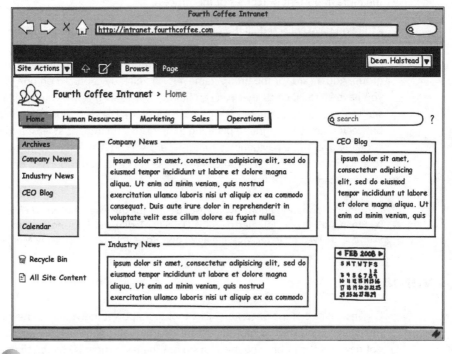

Read more about Balsamiq Mockups and use the free, web-based version of the drawing software at *www.balsamiq.com*.

Card sorting

Often, when starting a site, you have many ideas for the types of things that should go on the site, but no concrete way to arrange it. Card sorting is a technique that will help you to organize your content. For example, if you want to determine the navigation headings for your site, card sorting can help start the process.

The most common way to perform card sorting is to use stacks of 3 x 5-inch index cards. Think through every type of content that you have in mind for your site. Write these out on the cards, with one type of content per card. You can use a short title and add a sentence or two of description to clarify.

If you can get a group of people together to plan a site, everyone can contribute cards and participate in the sorting. Multiple minds contributing ideas and multiple eyes on the cards for sorting can yield stronger results than performing a card sort alone. However, even if you don't have a group, taking the time to commit each concept to paper requires thinking about each concept's uniqueness and importance. That thinking alone can often be one of the more important outcomes of this process.

After you have collected all the unique, important types of content on the cards, you can begin the sorting. Group the cards by common concepts. For example, if you see many items that represent events to happen in the future, they might fit nicely in a calendar group. Add a card for the group name if it isn't already captured on one of your cards. If you have 20 to 30 cards that you can fit into four to six groups, you have likely found your site's top navigation structure. If you have more total cards or you can't find commonalities between them, you might be planning a multisite structure, or at least a top navigation structure and a side navigation structure. Card sorting is an exercise that commits site plans to a first informal structure. You can use these concepts and groups to plan your navigation, lists, and pages.

For more information about IA and user design for the web, read *Head First Web Design* by Ethan Watrall and Jeff Siarto (2009, O'Reilly Media) and *Information Architecture for the World Wide Web* by Peter Morville and Louis Rosenfeld (2002, O'Reilly Media).

Governance

Organizations can use SharePoint as a tool to empower individuals in new ways through the creation and sharing of web content. Sharing information within an organization is not new, but the publishing mechanism is. Whenever there is change that fosters growth, there is a corresponding challenge to the organization to respond to the change in positive ways. Governance is directly related to managing site content because it is the agreements, written or understood, between the participants in the websites.

How you decide on and document the governance of the SharePoint sites and content in your organization depends on many factors. Microsoft has built many capabilities into SharePoint that can help build strong communities. Understanding the tools at hand will help you better highlight the positive aspects of the SharePoint content for which you are responsible.

The Wild West of SharePoint

Governance comes up as a topic in many SharePoint implementations because the freedoms that it gives users to create can result in chaos and unmet expectations when not properly managed. In some ways, a new SharePoint installation can be compared to a wide open frontier. There is freedom and potential, but there is also the potential for lawlessness and failure due to the unknown. In theory, the tools that SharePoint gives you are like any other tools you are given to use within your organization. Their use falls under the expectations of professionalism. However, there is potential for abuse and unintentional harm caused by misunderstanding.

Your SharePoint installation is not the Wild West, but it might benefit from some documented agreements on use and operation. As you begin to rely more and more on the servers hosting your content, your dependency on those same servers' consistent responsiveness and reliability grows. It is in your best interest to look out for the maintenance and upkeep of this resource. It is a given that SharePoint will be used by you and others because of the nature of web collaboration. Governance will help to ensure that the shared resources that deliver your information will meet the demand.

What is SharePoint governance?

The Microsoft TechNet library provides guidance on many aspects of SharePoint planning and operations management, including resources on governance. In the article "Governance Overview (SharePoint Server 2010)," the following definition is given:

Governance is the set of policies, roles, responsibilities, and processes that guide, direct, and control how an organization's business divisions and IT teams cooperate to achieve business goals. A comprehensive governance plan can benefit your organization by:

- *Streamlining the deployment of products and technologies, such as SharePoint Server 2010.*

- *Helping protect your enterprise from security threats or noncompliance liability.*

- *Helping ensure the best return on your investment in technologies, for example, by enforcing best practices in content management or information architecture.*

The full TechNet overview of SharePoint governance can be found at *technet.microsoft.com/en-us/library/cc263356.aspx.*

You might find other definitions that suggest governance is generally applied at a higher level than most management and operations. However, for the purposes of this book, the broader definition given earlier is sufficient. Including the management and operational implications of a proper governance strategy is important. Not only must the strategy for governance be in place, but the strategy must be implemented effectively and followed up.

How to govern SharePoint

If you don't personally govern your organization, you probably also won't be solely responsible for setting the strategy and implementation of governance for SharePoint. Organization-wide governance of any resource is usually an executive-level task, incorporating the concerns of all affected parties. However, that isn't to say that you cannot influence the direction of SharePoint use, management, and operations. As a business user, you have a stake in the outcome of governance decisions. As an advanced user of SharePoint, you might be looked upon as a thought leader in what is sure to be a new initiative within your organization.

TechNet provides some valuable resources for governance planning. The sections that follow contain a review of the highlights of the online material from the advanced user's perspective. Also included is analysis of the content and suggestions for their use in your work.

Governance by site audience

SharePoint sites can serve many purposes. You might find it helpful to tailor your governance to the use of the site. In general, the broader the target audience of a site, the more tightly controlled is the content publishing process.

Audience size growth

As a modern business professional, you share information electronically as part of your workday. You write emails, author documents, build spreadsheets, and produce slides. When you think about the process of writing a Microsoft Word document, do you believe that you approach the work a little differently than when you are writing an email? Traditional documents stored on your hard disk are hidden from others unless they have access to your computer. SharePoint provides a new opportunity to share, and along with that should come a different approach. The opportunity is to share information securely with a broader network of people who you think might benefit from your hard work. And, unlike the network file shares that might be available to you, SharePoint can provide information securely to others beyond your work location without special secure connections like a virtual private network (VPN). When the audience is broadened, your approach to authoring and sharing should and will change.

Consider Figure 8-5. It shows the amount of effort and rigor around the editorial process growing as the audience size grows. This is a visualization of one aspect of a good governance strategy, and it really represents something you do naturally and might consider to be common sense. You focus your effort where it will have the greatest effect. The width of the pyramid represents the total content at each level of a typical SharePoint installation. Your organization might have some or all of these levels of sites. Generally, the more people in the target audience of one site, the more effort you should consider putting into the production of the content.

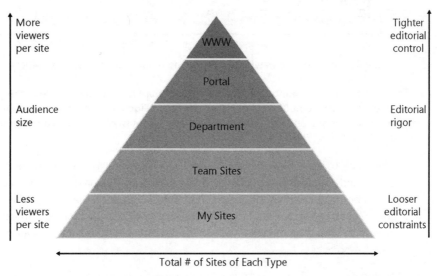

Figure 8-5 Editorial rigor increases as audience size grows. Sometimes a large amount of content will have a small audience. For example, My Sites overall represent a large amount of content. Each My Site is viewable by only the individual My Site owner by default. Sites with small audiences require and receive less editorial control than sites with large audiences.

Large audience governance

Audience size and site type are strongly related. Figure 8-6 shows the typical amount of governance in a selection of site types. This isn't a hard-and-fast rule, but it does closely follow the editorial rigor pyramid of Figure 8-5. A central published site will have more eyeballs on it than a My Site and therefore warrants closer scrutiny.

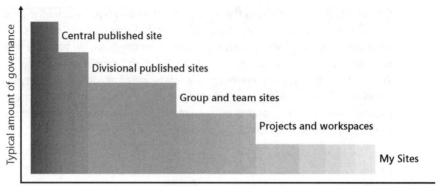

Figure 8-6 Some site types typically receive more governance effort than others.

TechNet includes a number of nice wall poster graphics. You can download the governance model for SharePoint Server 2010 that's shown in Figure 8-6, along with supporting visualizations and text (for Visio or PDF version) from *www.microsoft.com/download/en/details.aspx?id=13594.*

When web content is expected to be read by a large audience, the effect of the content's quality and compliance with guidelines are magnified. The payoff for care in creating and publishing the content is bigger when the audience is large. Intrinsically, there is an agreement between the publisher and the reader. By broadcasting your message wide and far, you are implying that your material is relevant and appropriate for everyone that the broadcast reaches.

SharePoint supplies a few tools that support a more thorough content creation process. Check-in and checkout help allow edits to be submitted with less conflict between versions. Similarly, revision history provides traceability regarding who added what, and when. And finally, you can take advantage of minor versions for drafting content before publishing a major version that can be seen by the wider audience.

Personal site governance

Going to the other extreme, a personal site might defer all content addition decisions to the individual's discretion. When the permissions match the use, these types of guidelines can be applied to good effect. For example, on a personal site where only one user has access, the same guidelines that apply to personal computer use might apply with slight adjustments, based on storage or network bandwidth needs. When you save a document to your computer's local storage, only you are affected by the reduction in available space for other new documents. On a SharePoint site, storage is most likely shared. One benefit in a shared space such as this is that storage space can be added without taking apart your personal computer. Another benefit is that if your hard disk fails, your important documents stored online are safe.

INSIDE OUT   **Behavior within your organization is governed by written and unwritten agreements with others. Behavior on the web is no different in that respect.**

Many organizations new to SharePoint lack agreements on proper use. If web publishing is a new medium for communication within your organization, managing web content will involve many new experiences. Before you accept responsibility for a SharePoint site, take a minute to assess the agreements, formal or informal, that you've made about the site's use. If you don't have them already, can you find some agreements with others with little effort? For example, if you have permissions in SharePoint, you could create a new site of any type, including a blog site. A blog can be a great platform for sharing unique, individual viewpoints, including opinion. However, are all others in your organization willing and eager participants in the broad publication of your individual viewpoint? In many organizations, a brief discussion with a manager can help inform these types of governance decisions. Will your manager support, or even better, praise your content publishing efforts? A really good sign could be a performance goal around the type, quality, or quantity of your content creation efforts. Governance takes many forms, but agreed-upon performance goals are one example of a method of encouraging content management agreement and compliance.

Search

Search presents opportunities to measure governance and highlight achievements of the shared community of electronic content. If you've agreed to present relevant, timely, and appropriate content to others, SharePoint Search will help reveal how well you've delivered on those goals. Some website visitors find information through browsing the site, but many will find what they need through Search. In addition to the standard search box and results page, SharePoint Search results can be exposed through Search Web Parts and in custom solutions. SharePoint sites that are shared publicly will also be crawled by public search engines such as Bing and Google. Your document, page, or list item title will be the most prominent wording displayed in search. If you have input on documented governance, you can include tips on creating good titles to help in the discovery of all the valuable web content in your organization's SharePoint sites.

Search can also expose items that previously were thought to be hidden from others. New discoveries in old content are common in initial implementations of SharePoint.

Out of the box, SharePoint 2013 Search will provide search ability into the full contents of Microsoft Office documents stored across all site collections, into network file shares, and to non-SharePoint websites. While the results are trimmed according to SharePoint security, incorrect application of security can result in exposing information that might not be appropriate for the full organization. For example, if your Social Security number is contained in documents uploaded to a SharePoint site, you want to ensure that those documents have the proper security settings. While document permissions are important beyond search, probably no other tool within your organization will provide such broad discovery capability. To comply with corporate governance that likely includes privacy and other compliance required outside of your organization, review of content added to your sites is important. If you make it available to browse, it can be made available to search. And if it's available to search, all of the text within the content and even some graphics can be exposed to those with permissions to view the content.

INSIDE OUT Use Search to validate your personal documents before sharing

To use Search to measure compliance of content that hasn't been exposed by it before, you could set up a test. Would you like to be able to search your files, but you can't guarantee that the information is safe for everyone? You can create a site and break permission inheritance temporarily. After the documents in question are uploaded and the search engine has incorporated them into its index, you can safely search the documents without exposing the contents to everyone else. Over time you may become comfortable sharing the whole site with more people. Or if searching turns up documents that you would like to share before you become comfortable sharing the entire site, you can upload the individual documents that you're comfortable sharing to a site with broader permissions.

Search alerts

Any account associated with an email address can be notified of new or changed keyword results through search alerts. To create a new alert, type your keywords into the Search box and look for the link "create a search alert." Search alerts are a great tool for monitoring compliance when your governance agreements contain items that match a specific pattern. For example, if you work for a company that develops and sells Windows Phone apps, you might add an alert for the keyword iPhone. When reviewing the information shared with that keyword, you might find content that's not appropriate for general consumption in your company. With the alert, you have access to the item's location and creator information. You could have the item removed or contact the creator of the item to discuss it.

Choosing a content manager

When you look at a freshly created, out-of-the-box webpage in SharePoint, can you tell who is responsible for updating the content? Knowing who authored the content gives you more security in the accuracy of the information. It also gives you someone to contact if you'd like to follow up on something you see that interests you. Identification could be grouped with governance, but it is worthwhile to identify the content manager of any given SharePoint site, regardless of the rules, policies, and organization-wide strategy in place. You care who the content manager is because you want quality information. Your audience cares for the same reason.

Identifying the content manager on the page

On an internal website, you are more likely to know the owners of site content personally. To take advantage of your in-person social relationships, it can be very helpful to identify the site owner on most sites by name. This way, when you have a question about the site, not only can you look up the name and contact information easily if you are not close by, if you are close by, you can just walk over and talk to your colleague about an item that strikes you as interesting.

One way to easily identify the content manager of a page is to take advantage of a SharePoint Security group and the Site Users Web Part. Figure 8-7 shows an example of this setup.

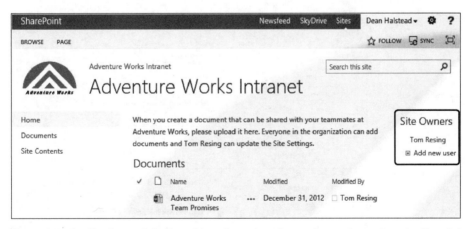

Figure 8-7 The Site Owner is indicated in a dynamic web part that updates when the SharePoint Security group is updated.

The steps to achieve the same setup follow:

1. Ensure that your content manager is in the group with Full Control of the site.

   Often this is a group with the word "owners" in it. For example, the Adventure Works Intranet Owners group in the following example was created with a site called Adventure Works Intranet.

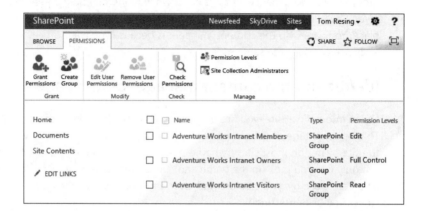

2. Modify the Security Group Settings to allow Everyone to see the membership of this group, as shown in the following graphics.

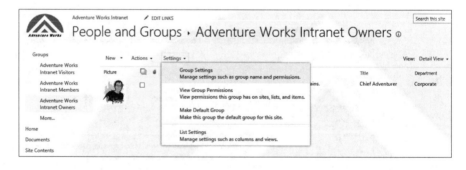

The Site Collection Administrators setting, shown in the following graphic, is a list of users who are not part of the standard SharePoint Security groups. For this method, don't consider a user in the Site Collection Administrators list a content manger unless the user is also in a standard Security group that also has full control.

Occasionally, there might be a need for a user to belong to the Site Collection Administrators group serving a support or auditing role that is not related to directly managing the content.

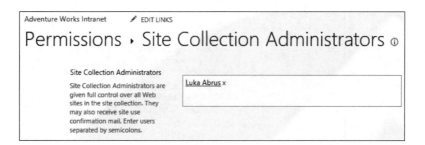

Chapter 3 includes more information on site permissions and site collection administration.

3. Insert a Site Users Web Part on the Home page for the site, as shown here.

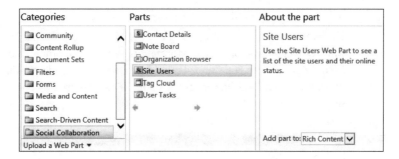

Look in Chapter 9, "Creating and formatting content pages," for more detail about editing a webpage.

4. Edit the Site Users Web Part. Select the Show People In The Group option and browse for the SharePoint Security group with Full Control that contains your content manager or managers. Modify the web part title to something appropriate, such as Site Owners or Content Managers, as shown in the following graphic.

The site owner's name links through to the My Site page for the owner, shown here, with contact and biographical information. When the membership of the SharePoint Security group with Full Control is modified, the name and link will change on the page, keeping all the viewers of the page up to date on the content manager for this site.

TROUBLESHOOTING

Standard users can't see the members of the Site Owners group

If a user viewing a site that you control sees the message in the Site Users Web Part shown here, review step 2 to ensure that it was completed successfully.

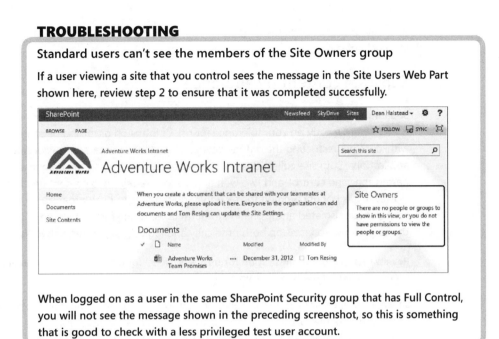

When logged on as a user in the same SharePoint Security group that has Full Control, you will not see the message shown in the preceding screenshot, so this is something that is good to check with a less privileged test user account.

Planning content for Internet sites

Special consideration must be taken when managing site content to be shared with the general public. For the most part, the techniques you've learned for editing lists, pages, and web parts in previous chapters apply equally well to public and internal sites. However, if you are planning content with SharePoint for Internet sites, take into consideration the information presented in the sections that follow.

Tight governance for public messaging

Generally speaking, the governance for this type of website will be tightly controlled because of the potential impact on the organization. In smaller organizations, content publishing might be handled directly by the person who is responsible for the public image of the organization. In many large organizations, an entire group is dedicated to publishing any content for public consumption. As an example of tighter governance on content management, a public website is one case for which you most likely will not be putting the All Authenticated Users Active Directory group in the Contributors SharePoint Security group. While contributions might be more limited than on an internal site, a public site uniquely grants broad viewing permissions to another set of users—unauthenticated or anonymous users. A discussion of managing site content for anonymous users follows later in this chapter.

Separate content by audience

Separation of public site content from internal sites is common. The level of separation is dependent mostly on your tolerance for risk of intrusion or mixing of content. To start with, consider restricting the different types of content to separate site collections and web applications. Both site collections and web applications can provide unique administrative permissions and control, and two web applications require two content databases. However, it is not uncommon for security requirements to push organizations to keep some content types isolated at the SharePoint farm level. At the furthest extreme is separating the content out to farms on both physically and logically separated networks.

Review Chapter 2, "Administration for business users," for more details on SharePoint farms, servers, content databases, and security.

At whatever level you choose to separate your content, keep in mind that it is important to treat the site that allows anonymous access as inherently more risky for intrusion by unwanted visitors—more risky than internal anonymous sites are those that allow anonymous, public access. One example of public website intrusion is automated spam bots. A vigilant website manager will quickly detect and remove spam content. An even more proactive approach can keep the likelihood of unwanted content low.

TechNet has large sections on logical architecture planning for SharePoint. "SharePoint 2013 Design Samples: Corporate Portal and Extranet Sites," located at *technet.microsoft.com/en-us/ library/cc261995.aspx*, includes helpful information for governance and information architecture decisions. The chapter includes many helpful tips on extranet design.

Open to the public with anonymous permissions

For a public site, you generally don't want to require all visitors to log on to view the content. If you don't want an authentication prompt to appear, you want to enable anonymous access. Enabling anonymous access is at least a two-part process that requires one change at the Web Application Zone level and one change at the Site level. Additionally, there are options to set anonymous access for lists, libraries, and individual items.

Enabling anonymous access in Central Administration

You might be asking an IT professional to make this change for you, but the check box that needs to be selected is shown in Figure 8-8. This check box is found on the Edit Authentication Providers dialog box for the Web Application Settings in Central Administration. Selecting the Enable Anonymous Access option in Central Administration is a required preliminary step toward enabling anonymous access on each individual site collection in the web application. If you don't see the anonymous settings described in the sections that follow, it is likely that this check box has not been selected for the Web Application Zone with which you are working.

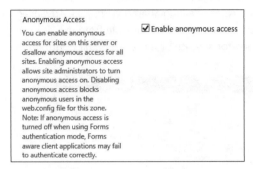

Figure 8-8 The Enable Anonymous Access check box must be selected before site-collection administrators can enable anonymous access for site collections in this web application zone.

For your IT professional administrators, the name of the zone is the link to the Edit dialog box. Figure 8-9 shows the zone selection dialog box for Authentication Providers from the Central Administration site. You might never view Central Administration, but when your IT staff accesses the dialog box the first time, it can be easy to miss the link. The administrator must know to click the hyperlink over the name of the zone to open the Edit dialog box for that zone.

Figure 8-9 Default is the name of the zone and the link to the Edit dialog box.

If you want a refresher, Chapter 2 covers SharePoint architecture terminology, such as what a farm is, what a web application is, and how sites fit into site collections. Visit the TechNet article "Plan Authentication Methods," at *technet.microsoft.com/en-us/library/cc262350.aspx* for more details, including planning web application zones and an explanation of web application zones in SharePoint.

Enabling anonymous access in Site Settings

After Anonymous Access has been enabled for the web application, site administrators will see a new option on the Site Permissions page ribbon, as shown in Figure 8-10. One way to access the Site Permissions page is via the Shared With link from the Settings menu, as shown in Figure 8-11. After selecting Shared With, click Advanced to see the Site Permissions page. Site Permissions is also easily accessible from the Users And Permissions section of the Site Settings page for any site by a user with Full Control of the site.

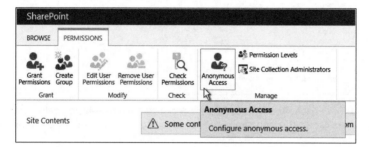

Figure 8-10 The Anonymous Access button is highlighted in this example from a Site Permissions page.

Figure 8-11 The Shared With link from the Settings menu is available on any SharePoint page.

From the Anonymous Access dialog box (see Figure 8-12), you can choose to expose the entire website or individual pieces of the site. Selecting the Entire Web Site option is the best option for publishing a public website if you want it to be available without specifying a list or library path. The next section explains the difference in more detail.

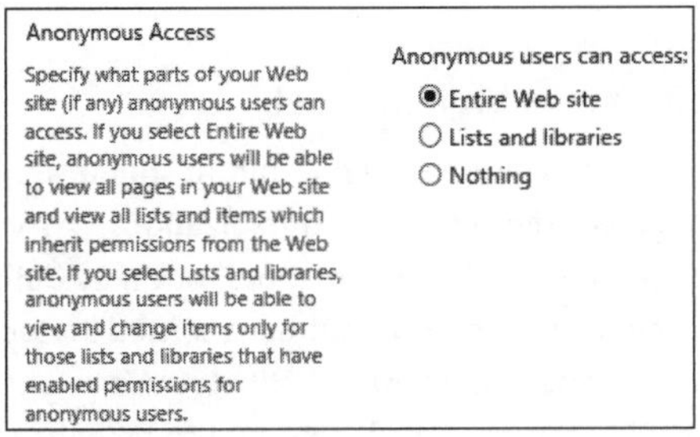

Figure 8-12 You have two anonymous access options at the site level: Entire Web Site and Lists And Libraries.

> **Note**
>
> **If you select the Lists And Libraries option, all users viewing your site will be prompted for authentication unless navigating directly to a list, library, or individual item that has been configured for anonymous access.**

Chapter 12, "Designing web content management sites," is all about publishing sites. Publishing sites are the kind of SharePoint site most likely to be used on a public Internet site, so if you're planning to deploy a public Internet site on SharePoint, take a look at Chapter 12.

Advanced planning considerations

Many features of SharePoint require advanced planning by an organization before they can be effectively used by individuals. Some planning information for features not covered earlier in this chapter are provided in the sections that follow.

IRM

IRM features allow you to protect documents stored in SharePoint. With an IRM-protected SharePoint Document library, you can control what users can do with Office documents and PDFs. You can limit printing and saving, and you can put an expiration date on the files downloaded from the document library. All of this functionality is meant to help restrict sensitive information to those who need to see the information only.

INSIDE OUT   What's sensitive enough to protect

Deciding what requires protection from features like IRM might sound subjective, but in many cases, it's clear what is sensitive. For many organizations, passwords and corporate strategic initiatives are required to be documented, but they definitely require protection. For others, personal information can be recorded in documents and forms, but it definitely should not be widely shared. Whatever it might be in your organization, don't overlook the IRM features, which continue to be enhanced across the entire product portfolio from Microsoft, including Office, Windows, Windows Azure, and SharePoint.

IRM must be enabled by a Farm Administrator through Central Administration before it can be enabled on a document library or list. For SharePoint Online, the setting is in Tenant Administration rather than Central Administration, and it is available only for Enterprise Office 365 subscription levels that include IRM.

Note

Enabling IRM protection for a list will protect documents that are attached to list items only. IRM doesn't place restrictions on list items outside of documents in attachments.

Data protection, recoverability, and availability

Are your SharePoint sites reliable? Can you be sure that information stored in SharePoint will always be there for you? Part of the answers to those questions depends on the infrastructure. The infrastructure is the computer and network hardware, power, and Internet connections. Each piece of the infrastructure will likely fail over time. And part of the answer depends on you and others in your organization using and supporting SharePoint and the SharePoint infrastructure. You plan to store important information in SharePoint, and the following considerations will help your piece of mind.

Service-level agreement

For peace of mind, consider asking for the service-level agreement for your SharePoint installation. When you have a service-level agreement with your SharePoint host, you are looking out for the reliability of your information and platform. Your SharePoint host can be your IT group or a paid provider of infrastructure, but either can enter into an agreement with the users of the SharePoint sites. A service-level agreement should define the percentage of time that your environment is available for use. It should also define how much information loss is acceptable. Maximizing availability and minimizing loss are goals, but often the tradeoff is the cost of infrastructure and people resources.

Chapter 2 discussed some considerations that may affect service levels for your SharePoint installation. Organizations that amass large amounts of information in one SharePoint content database, for example, may be down longer if infrastructure fails or lose more data due to long backup times for the database. Planning for content database growth requires business decision makers and IT professionals to come together for accurate projections of use. Agreements about availability and data loss are sometimes forgotten about in SharePoint planning. Even a little bit of thought in this area may result in more efficient use of infrastructure resources and increased faith in SharePoint as an information repository.

Two-stage recycle bins

When you delete a document from a document library, you are prompted by a question asking if you'd like to move the file to the Recycle Bin. This is similar to the Recycle Bin you're used to on your desktop file system, but there are some differences. The first difference is that when you delete an item from the Recycle Bin, it is not completely gone. It goes first to a second-stage Recycle Bin, as shown in Figure 8-13. Items in both Recycle Bins are removed after a set amount of time. The default retention period in the Recycle Bin is 30 days, but it can be changed by a Farm Administrator. The second-stage Recycle Bin is also subject to a file-size limit. Items are removed automatically when a storage-size quota for the site collection Recycle Bin is reached.

Figure 8-13 A Site Collection Administrator can restore list items, documents, and sites deleted by users before they are cleared from the second-stage Recycle Bin.

INSIDE OUT   Site and Site Collection Recycle Bin

Accidental deletions can be considered a people problem that causes loss of data. People make mistakes, and in a shared collaboration environment, the results of accidental deletion are multiplied. If you permanently delete a file that you've created and stored on your computer, it mostly affects you. However, if you delete an important site shared by hundreds or thousands of people in your organization, it will be noticed. The Site and Site Collection Recycle Bin were much-demanded features added in Service Pack 1 of SharePoint 2010 and retained as features in SharePoint 2013. As shown in Figure 8-13, a Site Collection Administrator can restore a site, much like restoring an item deleted from the user Recycle Bin. To restore a site collection, an IT Pro must run a Windows PowerShell command against the SharePoint server.

Summary

From one perspective, almost any act of creation, deletion, or editing on a SharePoint site can be seen as a part of affecting site content. The area of planning covered specifically by this chapter is the more strategic, higher-level approach to all of those other pieces of site interaction that you are learning about in detail in the other chapters of this book.

In this chapter, you learned how identifying the purpose of your site is critical to planning its architecture effectively. You learned how to experiment safely with all the SharePoint tools that you've learned about already and will continue to explore throughout the rest of the book. Visualizations of site content are useful, and not just at the beginning of a new site content project; you can revisit and refactor your site's layout and organization at any point in time. When users of your site can benefit from better organization, look to prototypes, wireframe diagrams, storyboards, and card sorting to help put the pieces in place.

Governance is a hot topic in many organizations using or planning to use SharePoint these days. SharePoint has empowered the members of the organizations who have implemented it. In many organizations—maybe in yours—SharePoint users have been creating and filling SharePoint sites for years. With so much content sprawl, the shared principles of fellow users must now be considered, if they weren't at the initial implementation of the product. This chapter explained what governance is and how you and your organization can benefit from it. Governance strategies for different types of site audiences were covered. Also covered was taking advantage of Search for governance.

By all means, use the wealth of references presented in this chapter to follow up on the topic of governance. Take advantage of the excellent free electronic books and posters available for download from Microsoft.com on the topics of planning and governance. In many cases, the material documents lessons learned from customers, Microsoft partners, and the internal implementations of SharePoint within Microsoft. Use this information to help your organization to harness the spread of information across SharePoint sites more effectively.

Planning content for Internet sites is a practical example of IA and governance. SharePoint is an effective tool for creating a public Internet presence for your organization. However, when you open the doors of your site to the general public, make sure that the proper controls are in place. Like any public space, proper manners are common, but vandalism can happen. Use the anonymous permissions settings to open your site at the right level. Consider the specific features in SharePoint Server for publishing information to broad audiences.

When planning SharePoint sites with sensitive information, consider using the IRM features. Also take into consideration your service-level agreement with your SharePoint host. A good service-level agreement spells out the business needs to the provider and sets the expectations of the business correctly. Only when you can trust your information to reside in SharePoint, will you encourage others to participate in collaborating with you using the platform.

As you read the remaining chapters of this book, you will pick up even more advanced ways you can interact with the content of your sites. Using what you learn, you will extend sites and customize them to meet your needs and the needs of the consumers of your sites. Whether you are adding content from external data sources or adding automated workflows to content creation, keep in mind the content management strategies and tools introduced in this chapter. Plan, create, and seek agreement for your site content's use with your fellow participants in your organization's SharePoint implementation.

Creating and formatting content pages

IN previous chapters of this book, you considered the organization of content within site collections, sites, lists, libraries, and on pages. In this chapter, you will learn how users create and format their own unique content on pages. Microsoft SharePoint Server 2013, like previous versions, contains a number of types of pages.

When using SharePoint Server within an organization, where many sites are based on the Team Site template, users will be most familiar with creating and modifying wiki pages. When you create a new Team Site, SharePoint creates a Wiki Page library, named Site Pages, where the webpages are stored and where new pages are stored when created. Users find it easy to add content to these pages and modify the layout of the page by using the browser. Wiki pages should be used when users wish to share content that does not require an approval mechanism and the site contains many content authors.

For public-facing sites or for company portals, where content does need to go through a formal approval process, web content management (WCM) sites are used. In SharePoint 2013, the WCM capabilities are significantly enhanced. In SharePoint 2010, WCM functionality was largely unchanged from Microsoft Office SharePoint Server (MOSS) 2007. Content was structured into WCM pages within sites, and that structure was the basis for navigation and the organization information architecture (IA). WCM pages, known as *publishing pages,* are created from publishing templates, known as *page layouts.*

In SharePoint 2013, the emphasis is now on displaying content based on search as well as the structure of the site, and the way the navigation is organized can be based on managed metadata. SharePoint 2013 introduced a new type of content page: category pages. You can use category pages when you want to aggregate content that meets certain criteria or parameters. These pages use a new feature introduced in SharePoint 2013: cross-site publishing (XSP). XSP lets you store and maintain content in one or more authoring site collections, while content can be displayed and surfaced in different target site collections. When the content is changed in an authoring site collection, those changes are displayed on all site collections that are reusing that content.

> **More information on WCM, category pages, and XSP can be found in Chapter 12, "Designing web content management sites."**

Pages that display the contents of list or libraries use Web Part pages. Such pages can be changed using the browser, but many users do not find the mechanism of changing such pages easy. Using the browser, these pages can only contain web parts; therefore, the addition of static text and images is possible only by adding web parts, such as the Content Editor Web Part (CEWP) or the Image Web Part. Web Part pages are still a popular choice for creating interactive dashboards or pages that aggregate information from several resources.

> **More information on web parts can be found in Chapter 10, "Adding, editing, connecting, and maintaining web parts."**

Another type of page that you will see on SharePoint sites is application pages, also known as *system pages,* which are those pages with _layouts in their URL. Application pages cannot be changed using the browser or SharePoint Designer 2013. They contain the same information or type of links no matter which site you are on and can be shared across all sites on the server. The Site Settings page is an example of an application page. Application pages are stored on the SharePoint server file system and are never stored in a SharePoint content database.

This chapter introduces the basic concepts of content pages and application pages. Using the browser, you will learn how to view content pages in different ways, as well as how to change the appearance of these pages by adding and removing static text and images.

INSIDE OUT   What is a content page?

Wiki pages, publishing pages, and Web Part pages are known as *content pages, site pages,* or *authoring pages.* They contain content that is unique to a site and content that you wish to share with visitors either (1) on your site, (2) on other sites in the same site collection, or (3) on other site collections in the same web application or in other web applications.

Creating and modifying content pages using a browser

The first page you see on a SharePoint site is known as the *home page* because as with any website, this is the page where all site visitors start. In your organization, the home page is also known as the *welcome page, the default page,* or the *landing page.* Home pages tend to aggregate information from elsewhere, and as you click links, you are directed to other pages that display content. For instance, on a Team Site when you click the Shared Documents link on the Quick Launch toolbar, you are taken to the All Documents view. This page will dynamically change as you upload, modify, and delete files in the Shared Document library.

You may also have pages that contain static text and images that describe, for example, the company's expense policy and contain links to other pages that are related to information. The approach of thinking of your site as a number of pages is natural and in line with websites not based on SharePoint, where each site is a collection of webpages and those webpages are interconnected.

In SharePoint Server, you can use four types of content pages: wiki pages, publishing pages, category pages, and Web Part pages. In Microsoft SharePoint Foundation 2013, as in SharePoint Foundation 2010, you are limited to using wiki pages and Web Part pages. When you display these pages in the browser, you will find it hard to differentiate between these page types. However, if you place the pages in edit mode, then you will be able to tell the difference. You may also be able to differentiate between the three types of content pages, if you know the type of site you are working with.

Wiki pages are the default pages when a site is created from the Team Site template. Wiki pages consist of a mix of free-format static text and images, in addition to web parts. Web parts are reusable components that can contain any type of web-based information, including analytical, collaborative, and database information.

You can dynamically display data from many lists or libraries, using content rollup web parts, such as the Content Query Web Part (CQWP); however, those lists and libraries had to be stored within sites in the same site collection. A new web part introduced with SharePoint 2013, the Content Search Web Part (CSWP) allows you to aggregate content across sites from many site collections or web applications. The CSWP and other search-related web parts introduced in SharePoint 2013 are instrumental to the implementation of XSP.

INSIDE OUT How to reuse content on pages in other site collections

To reuse content on pages in other site collections, first enable the XSP site collection feature and then enable the list or library as a catalog.

Publishing pages are only available on sites, which reside in site collections where the SharePoint Server Publishing Infrastructure site collection feature and the SharePoint Server Publishing site feature are activated. These two features are activated by default when you create a site using one of the publishing site templates, such as the Publishing Portal, Enterprise Wiki, Product Catalog, Publishing Site, Publishing Site with Workflow, and Enterprise Search Center.

INSIDE OUT Site templates used at the top level of site collections

The Enterprise Search Center, Publishing Portal, and Product Catalog Site templates can only be used to create a site at the top level of a site collection.

The three types of pages are flexible and highly customizable using three types of tools:

- A browser

- A SharePoint Foundation–compatible webpage editing tool, such as Microsoft SharePoint Designer 2013 or SharePoint Designer 2010

- A professional development tool, such as Microsoft Visual Studio 2012

Note

SharePoint Designer is a free product that can be downloaded from the download center at *www.microsoft.com/en-us/download* using the search keywords "SharePoint Designer."

No one tool can do everything; therefore, it is likely that in any deployment of SharePoint, all three types of tools will be used at some point.

Whatever type of content page you display in the browser, the ribbon will display at least two tabs:

- **Browse** You can use this tab when you do not wish the ribbon to be displayed. To make the ribbon visible again, click one of the other tabs.

- **Page** Use the Page tab to manage the pages on your site. More information on this tab is detailed later in this chapter.

The composition of a SharePoint page

When you enter the URL of a SharePoint site into a browser's address input box, the browser contacts the SharePoint server, which duly responds with a number of components that the browser then uses to present the information to you. These components can include an HTML file that contains content and instructions on the data structure, CSS files that contain format and layout instructions, and JavaScript files that contain client-side code that the browser will use to respond to the interaction you will have with the page. On the SharePoint server, the HTML file is created from the combination of two Microsoft ASP.NET pages: a master page and a content page. The content page contains static content that you may have entered, such as text and images, web part details, and list and library content that you may have included on your page, as shown here.

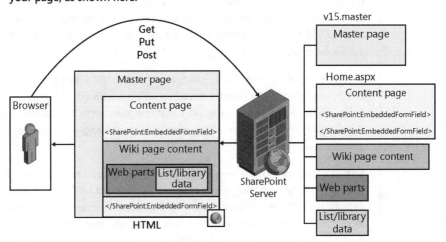

A *master page* is a special ASP.NET 2.0 page that is used to provide a consistent appearance and navigation for each page within one or more sites. A master page cannot be viewed using a browser, but you can view and customize a master page using SharePoint Designer.

On a wiki page, the wiki page content that you enter in the browser is placed in an EmbeddedFormField SharePoint control. A Web Part page is composed using similar components, except it will have no wiki page content and therefore no EmbeddedFormField SharePoint control. When you use the browser and add, delete or modify web parts, those web parts are placed in the WebPartPages WebPartZone control. On a publishing page, the content is added as page properties or as web parts within a web part zone.

Using SharePoint Designer, you can only modify wiki pages and Web Part pages. In normal edit mode, you can modify the content inside the EmbeddedFormField and WebPartPages WebPartZone controls, and when you are in advanced edit mode, you can modify content that resides elsewhere on the page. (You'll find more on this later in this chapter.)

Sites are grouped into a site collection, and the content for all sites in a site collection are stored in one content database. A content database can contain content from one or more site collections. The content database contains a number of tables. For example, the AllDocs table is the main table that contains the information about files, such as webpages and documents that you may attach to list items or upload into libraries. This table contains the contents of the file as well as the file's properties, such as file size, the person who created the file, whether the file is checked out, and if so, the name of the person who checked out the file. The Sites table stores information about sites, and when you add a web part to a page, then that information is stored in another SQL table—AllWebParts. The information for lists and libraries is stored across a number of tables.

In SharePoint 2010, many times when a user interacted with a page, the whole page was downloaded to the client, even when only a portion of the page changed. Share-Point 2013 includes a new framework that improves page load performance by only downloading those portions of the page that have changed [known as the minimal download strategy (MDS)].

MDS is implemented as a new SharePoint feature scoped at the web level and works with the AjaxDelta control, which is added to the head section of master pages. By default, the MDS feature is activated on the Team, Community, Wiki, Projects, App, and Blog Site templates. When activated, it sets the web object EnableMinimalDownload property. It is not enabled on publishing sites.

When the site uses MDS and a page is requested, you will see in the address bar of the browser a URL similar to:

http://intranet.adventure-works.com/_layouts/15/start.aspx#/SitePages/Home.aspx.

The Start.aspx file contains a JavaScript object, asyncDeltaManager, which parses the URL and dynamically loads the page that follows the # sign. When subsequent requested pages contains the query string parameter AjaxDelta=1, only the changed portions are downloaded to the client's browser.

When SharePoint loads a content page, such as the Home.aspx page for a Team Site, the following events occur:

1. The Home.aspx page is retrieved, as well as any files that the Home.aspx page references, such as the master page that the Home.aspx page uses.

2. The business logic for controls that the Home.aspx and the master page contain is executed, which may produce additional HTML and links to files such as CSS, JavaScript, and image files.

3. The site properties are retrieved. The properties include the site title, permissions, and the links that should be shown on the Quick Launch tool bar.

4. The Home.aspx page properties are retrieved, including its title, the information of the data stored in the EmbeddedFormField control, and whether it contains any web parts.

5. If the page contains any web part zones, information of the web parts they contain is retrieved.

6. The web parts' properties and any data they contain are retrieved. If the data to be presented in the web part is stored in lists and libraries, then that data and associated properties, such as permissions, is also retrieved.

7. The master page, the Home.aspx page, and all the data retrieved (taking into account the security settings of the user) are merged to form one HTML page.

8. The merged HTML page, together with any other files such as CSS and JavaScript files, is sent to the browser.

9. The browser parses and interprets the content of the files it has received, executes any client-side code, which may produce additional HTML and page content, and then renders the page.

The logic that is executed on the SharePoint server is called *server-side code,* and the logic that the browser interprets and executes is called *client-side code.*

Modifying wiki pages

On a Team site, the default webpages are wiki pages and the home page of such sites is a wiki page. Wiki pages are stored in a wiki library, named Site Pages, which by default inherits its permissions from the site. Therefore, anyone who is mapped to the Contribute permission level at the site level — that is, anyone who is a member of the site's Members SharePoint group — is allowed to change any wiki page or create new pages. If a page is found to be incomplete or poorly organized, any member of the site can edit it as he or she sees fit. Therefore, as users share their information, knowledge, experience, ideas, and views, the

content evolves. Site members can work together to change or update information without the need to send emails or attend meetings or conference calls. This is known as "open
editing." All users are allowed to control and check the content because open editing relies on
the assumption that most members of a collaboration site have good intentions.

INSIDE OUT   Wiki sites

**You can create new Wiki Page libraries on any site. SharePoint Server provides a second
type of wiki page that you can create when you create a site based on the Enterprise
Wiki Site template. These wiki pages are a type of publishing pages.**

You can edit a wiki page using one of the following three methods (see Figure 9-1):

● On the Page ribbon tab, click Edit in the Edit group.

● Click Settings icon in the upper-right corner and then click Edit Page. When you use
this method to open a wiki page into edit mode, the ribbon will not automatically
display. To display the ribbon, you need to click the Page ribbon tab.

● On the far right of the tabs, click Edit.

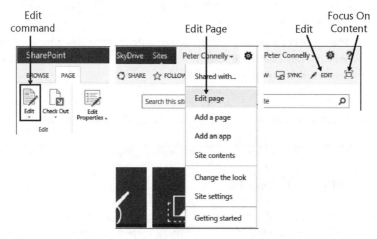

Figure 9-1 A wiki page may be edited in one of three ways.

When a wiki page is in edit mode and the ribbon is displayed, a tab set appears that
contains two tabs: Format Text and Insert, as shown in Figure 9-2. These tabs also appear
when you enter content in a CEWP, and just as with the CEWP, you are provided with a
What You See Is What You Get (WYSIWYG) environment for adding content to your page.

These tabs allow you to format the text and control the layout of the page, as well as insert tables, images, and hyperlinks.

Figure 9-2 The Format Text and Insert tabs enable you to format text and insert components.

You should always try to create content so that it conforms to accessibility guidelines. The additional benefit is that it helps to ensure that your website is compatible and interoperable with any assistive technologies that visitors to your site may use. However, do not rely on testing your pages against accessibility guidelines. Testing of your page by disabled users should take place.

Using the Format Text tab

To format your text, use the Format Text tab. Select the text that you wish to format and then click the appropriate command on the ribbon. To include new static text on your page, place the insertion point in the area of the page where you want the text to appear and then start typing. The Format Text tab contains seven ribbon groups: Edit, Clipboard, Font, Paragraph, Styles, Layout, and Markup.

Edit   Use the commands in this group to save and close the page, save and keep editing the page, and stop editing the page, which means that any changes you make to the page will be lost. The other two commands in the Save drop-down list, Edit and Edit In Share-Point Designer, are inactive. These commands are available on the Page tab when the page is not in edit mode.

When you create a Team Site, by default the Site Pages library has major versions enabled. In this configuration, the Save And Publish command (when clicked) is the same as the Save command. However, if you enable the Site Pages library to support major and minor (draft) versions, the Save command saves the page as a minor version, and the Save And Publish command saves the page as a major version.

INSIDE OUT   When does the Publish tab appear?

When the major and minor version is enabled, a third tab, Publish, will be displayed. The Save And Publish command on the Format Text tab is new on wiki pages in SharePoint 2013, as is the display of the Publish tab. This duplicates the experience that users have on the Page tab on publishing pages.

The third command in the Edit group is Check Out. Any team member mapped to the Contribute permission level, which on most Team sites is most users, can amend the wiki pages of the site. When you edit a page, you should always check it out before you modify the content. This is to prevent other users in your team from editing the page at the same time. Once the page is checked out, the Check In, Discard Check Out, and Override Check Out commands are available.

Check Out locks the page so other contributors cannot edit the page; however, while the page is checked out to you and in edit mode, you will be the only person to see the amendments that you are making to the page.

Clipboard   Use the commands in this group to cut, copy, paste, undo, and redo your modifications. These commands are placed in a group named Clipboard, as they will be using your computer's Clipboard feature; therefore, you are able to copy and paste content from other applications and websites.

When you paste content from other websites, the Paste command will maintain the formatting from the copied or cut source by default. When pasting contents from other programs, such as Microsoft Word, by default the content is unformatted, semantically correct HTML markup. This is known as Paste Clean, as shown in Figure 9-3, and is a new option in SharePoint 2013.

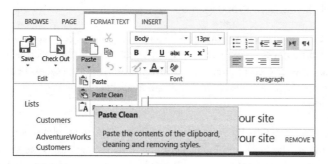

Figure 9-3 Paste Clean is a new option in SharePoint 2013.

If the text contains links or is categorized as a heading 1, heading 2, or bold, those categories are translated to <h1>, <h2>, and <strong> HTML tags; however, if the text is styled, such as red font, the style will not be copied to the page. To paste the unformatted text, use the down arrow for the Paste command and click Paste Plaintext.

As with other Microsoft applications, you can use the standard shortcut keys to complete these commands, for example, use Ctrl+C to copy selected text, and Ctrl+V to paste the copied text. Use Ctrl+Z (Undo) and Ctrl+Y (Redo) to cycle through the history of changes. If you do inadvertently paste content with the format and later decide that you wish to remove that format, use the Clear Format (Ctrl+Spacebar), command in the Font group.

Font Use the set of commands in this group as you would in other Microsoft Office applications, such as you would in Word to change the font face, font size, font color, as well as formatting text to a specific style—bold, italics, underline, strikethrough, subscript, or superscript.

Paragraph Use the commands in this group, again similar to those you would find in Word, to arrange the text on the page as bulleted lists, number lists, to increase or decrease the indent level, and align a paragraph Left, Center, Right, or Justify. You can also choose to display the paragraph for the selected text so that it displays in left-to-right or right-to-left reading order. (The latter is primarily used for languages that read right to left.)

Styles Select the text you wish to format, then select a style in the Styles group. More styles are available by using the Styles drop-down list. Similar to Office 2010 and 2013 applications, a preview of the styling is provided when you pause the mouse over the style command, as shown in Figure 9-4. Use this method of formatting text in preference to the commands in the Font group to apply styles consistently across all wiki pages in your site.

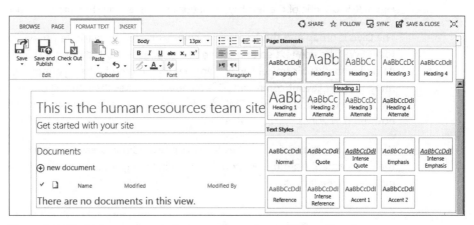

Figure 9-4 The Styles command allows you to preview text formatting.

The drop-down option for the Styles command is populated dynamically by client-side code.

Layout When you create a Team Site, the home page has one rich text editing area. In SharePoint 2010, the rich text editing areas appeared as two columns. Use the Text Layout command in the Layout group to change the structure of your page. You can reformat the page using any of the eight options shown in Figure 9-5. A thumbnail to the left of each option provides a view of the editing areas and structure that will be applied to the rich content area when selected.

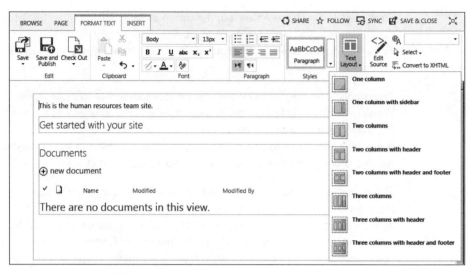

Figure 9-5 Use one of the Text Layout options to change the structure of the page.

The Layout group and the Text Layout command are not available when you add content to a CEWP. The rich text editing area of a wiki page is created using a SharePoint control named EmbeddedFormField, which enables you to modify the layout of the wiki page using the Text Layout command. This command creates the rich text editing areas and the layout you choose by using HTML <table> and <div> tags. The rich text editing areas are not web part zones.

When you select a layout that has fewer rich text editing areas than the current layout, then the content from the area not included in the layout is combined into an area that is included in the layout.

> **Note**
> If you are working on a publishing or enterprise wiki page, then the Format Text tab that you see on the ribbon is very similar to the Format Text tab on wiki pages. However, on publishing and enterprise wiki pages, there is no Text Layouts command but a Page Layout button.

Markup   This ribbon group provides four commands:

- **Edit source** This option opens a plain-text box in a dialog box that displays HTML code in a fixed-width font. The HTML for the whole wiki page is not displayed, only the HTML that is displayed in the EmbeddedFormField SharePoint control where you had placed the cursor. For example, when you have a two-column layout and you place the cursor in the left column, only the HTML for the left column is displayed in the dialog box. The commands available on the ribbon support only a number of features; for example, you cannot format the line type of a table. Unfortunately, no IntelliSense is provided; therefore, it may be easier to use the Code View of SharePoint Designer to modify the contents of the EmbeddedFormField control if you have limited knowledge of HTML or you have a considerable amount of HTML code to write. The section, "Using SharePoint Designer 2013 to create and modify webpages," later in this chapter, details the code that you can enter in this text box and the validation process that occurs when you save the page.

- **Languages** When a SharePoint site is created, it has a default language. A lang attribute appears in the <html> tag for each page of the site—this is the webpage's primary language. When you incorporate text in your page that is of a different language, select the text and then use this command to identify the language of the text. This surrounds your text with a <span> HTML tag with the lang attribute. The HTML lang attribute, whether it is applied to a webpage or a portion of a page, is used by search engines to identify pages that include text in specific languages. Therefore, when a user specifies in a search engine to return only pages of a specific language, your page could appear in the search results if it meets the search criteria. The lang attribute is also used by some screen reader software, such as Job Access With Speech (JAWS), so that it can pronounce words correctly when it reads them out loud.

- **Select** Use this command to select all the text of the parent HTML tag. For example, you may have created a table and wish to select a row in that table. Place the insertion point in a cell in the row, use the Select command to highlight the row, and then format or style the row. A red dotted line surrounds the area related to the HTML tag when you pause the mouse over the tag, as shown in Figure 9-6.

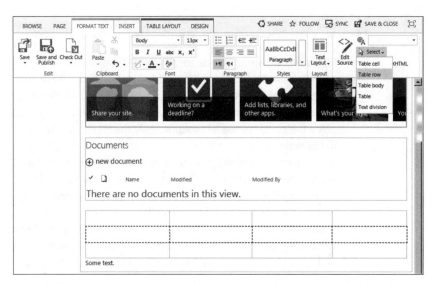

Figure 9-6 A red dotted line surrounds the area related to the parent HTML tag.

The inner tags are listed at the top of the drop-down list, and the most outer parental HTML tag—Text Division—is listed as the last item on the drop-down list. The Text Division tag represents the column that the select text appears in.

- **Convert to XHTML** This converts the HTML text within the EmbeddedFormField control to be Extensible HTML (XHTML) compliant. XHTML is a stricter and cleaner version of HTML and attempts to reduce the need for browsers to correct invalid client-side code.

When you save a page, you may see a warning message similar to the one shown in Figure 9-7. To prevent the entry of malicious code, SharePoint sanitizes HTML content that is entered in the wiki page EmbeddedFormField control, publishing pages field controls, and the CEWP when you use the browser or SharePoint Designer.

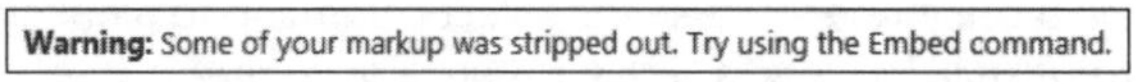

> **Warning:** Some of your markup was stripped out. Try using the Embed command.

Figure 9-7 SharePoint validates user-entered HTML.

If the user enters JavaScript as well as HTML, then the JavaScript is removed. If you have used a CEWP on your wiki page and entered HTML and JavaScript in the CEWP, then SharePoint will sanitize the code in the CEWP but will not remove the JavaScript code. However, by sanitizing the HTML code, the JavaScript may not continue to work. This can cause problems, especially with users who may not understand the difference between HTML and XHTML and copy HTML and JavaScript code from samples they find on the Internet. The workaround in SharePoint 2010 was to use the HTML Form Web Part or copy the JavaScript into a file that you load into a library such as the Site Assets library, and then within the CEWP link to the file, as SharePoint does not follow the link and therefore will not validate the code within the file.

In SharePoint 2013, there is a new web part, the Script Editor Web Part that has been specifically created so that you can add script on pages. If your users wish to enter HTML, JavaScript, styles, or other markup, you should tell users to use the Script Editor Web Part, which can be inserted on the page using the Embed Code command on the Insert tab.

> **Note**
>
> As SharePoint sanitizes the code, extra spaces may appear. This usually occurs when an HTML object is inserted in the middle of an opening <p> and a closing </p> tag, such as when a table is inserted on the same line as some text. SharePoint tries to amend the code so that the paragraph is added below or above the enclosed HTML object. In the HTML source window, you will see the inclusion of <p> </p> where the spaces are included.

For users who wish to learn more about HTML and XHTML, the w3schools website has free tutorials. To check your code against the formal standards, you can use validation services such as those that can be found at *www.htmlhelp.com/tools/validator/* or at *validator.w3.org*. Common errors that are found in HTML code are detailed at *www.htmlhelp.com/tools/validator/problems.html.en*.

Using the Insert tab

When the wiki page is in edit mode, a second Editing Tools tab, Insert, is displayed as shown in Figure 9-8. The Insert tab displays a number of objects that you can now add to a wiki page. You can intermix these objects with text anywhere within a wiki page.

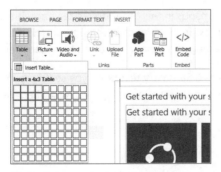

Figure 9-8 Use the Insert tab to add other objects to your wiki page.

The Insert tab contains five ribbon groups: Tables, Media, Links, Parts, and Embed. The Embed group is new for SharePoint 2013.

Tables   Use the down arrow on the Table command to add an HTML table. You can use the grid provided to create a table quickly by dragging the mouse across the grid to select the number of columns, and then dragging the mouse down the grid to select the number of rows. From the Table drop-down menu, you can also click Insert Table, which displays a dialog box where you can type the number of columns and rows that the table should contain.

Note

The number of cells in the table—that is, the number of rows multiplied by the number of columns—is limited to 625.

Once the table is created, an additional ribbon tab set is added to the ribbon that contains two tabs: Table Layout and Design, as shown in Figures 9-9 and 9-10.

Figure 9-9 The Table Layout tab.

The Table Layout tab consists of four groups:

- **Merge** Use the commands in this group to combine or split cells. You can merge only two cells to a single cell.

- **Rows & Columns** Use this group to add and remove rows and columns. You also use the Delete drop-down menu to delete the table.

- **Width & Height** Use the commands in this group to resize your table or resize a column or row. The controls provide an up and down arrow to select a size. However, you can type a number and **%** or **px** to change the unit of measurement.

- **Properties** This group contains a Summary text box. Type summary information that will be displayed to site visitors and screen reader applications when the table is not visible.

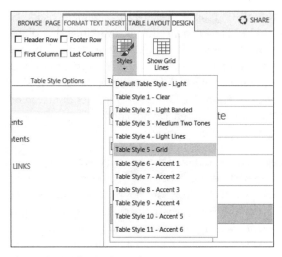

Figure 9-10 The Design tab.

The Design tab contains three groups:

- **Table Style Options** Use the four check boxes to select the table components, where the special formatting selected in the Table Styles group should be applied. For example, select Header Row and Footer Row to apply the special formatting to the first and last rows of your table.

- **Table Styles** Use this command to format the entire table by using one of the preformatted table styles. In SharePoint 2010, only four preformatted table styles were provided. As you pause your mouse over each style, the style is applied to the table in preview mode.

- **Table** The Show Grid Lines command can be used to display the cell boundaries of the table, when the table is not configured with borders. (In SharePoint 2010, this group was originally on the Table Layout tab.)

Media The Media group provides two split buttons for Picture and Video And Audio that you can use to insert images, video, or audio in your page. On both split buttons, three of the commands are similar: From Computer, From Address, and From SharePoint. These commands allow you to add media objects from your computer or reference a web address where the object is currently stored. You do not need to upload your media objects prior to editing the page. On the Video And Audio split button, there is a fourth option, Embed. The four commands in the Media group are:

- **From Computer** Using this option, the Upload Image dialog box opens and you can both upload and add an image to the page with one click of the mouse. The Upload Image dialog box allows you to navigate to the location on your computer where the picture is stored. You can then select a library on your site where you want to upload the picture. By default, the Site Assets library is chosen. The Site Assets library is the location where site supporting files, such as images displayed on pages, CSS files, or JavaScript files should be stored. Do not combine team documentation with files that are needed to brand a site.

- **From Address** Use this option if the media object is already uploaded onto a website. In the Select Picture dialog box, you need to type or paste the URL of the image manually. The dialog box does not provide any browse button that enables you to navigate to the library where the picture is stored. To guard against your typing the URL of the image incorrectly, resulting in a broken link, it is easier to open another browser window, navigate to the picture, and copy and paste the URL into the Select Picture, Address text box.

- **From SharePoint** Use this option if the media object is already uploaded into a library. In the Select An Asset dialog box, you can navigate to any library in your site. If the media object is in a library in another site, then you will need to use the From Address option.

- **Embed** SharePoint 2013 also provides the ability to embed HTML code to play audio and video that is not stored in SharePoint. The Insert Ribbon tab contains two new commands: the Embed command on the Video And Audio split button and Embed Code. These commands allow you to embed external sources like Bing Maps, Vimeo videos, YouTube videos, and other resources directly to the HTML content on an article page. (In SharePoint 2010, you had to use the HTML Form Web Part or other web parts.)

> **Note**
>
> The new Embed feature inserts an iFrame in the page, which can be seen as a potential scripting security risk. A site collection administrator can prevent users from using these commands. More information on HTML field security can be found in Chapter 10.

Once an image is added to a page, then when that image is selected, another contextual ribbon tab, Image, appears as shown in Figure 9-11. In SharePoint 2010, this tab was labeled Design. Once a picture is selected, you can press the Delete key to remove it from the page.

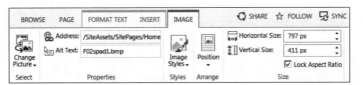

Figure 9-11 The Image tab.

The Image tab contains five ribbon groups:

- **Select** This group contains the Change Picture split button, which allows you to change the image that is displayed on the page and provides you with the same options as the Picture command on the Insert tab.

- **Properties** Use the commands in this group to replace the image on the page by typing the URL of an image and to set the alternative text for the image. Alternative text allows you to type text that displays if an image does not load or provides text for screen reader software. Append a period to the end of the words you enter so that users who listen to screen readers are able to understand your content more easily, especially when two alternative text tags are next to each other.

- **Styles** Use this command to format the borders of the image by using one of five preformatted image styles.

- **Arrange** Use the Position split button to arrange the image on the page. The drop-down list provides two Float styles, Left and Right, and three Inline Styles, Top, Middle, and Bottom.

- **Size** Use the commands in this group to reduce the size of the image on the page. These commands do not alter the image file but place width and height attributes on the <img> tag. The browser uses these attributes to display the image file differently than the physical size of the image, as stored in the image file. For prototyping purposes, this may be adequate. The image file still has to be stored on the server and requires network bandwidth when it is downloaded from the server to the client machine, even if the browser then displays the picture less than its original size. So if users to your site complain that a page takes more time to load than other pages, you may need to look at the size of the image files.

Chapter 9

When you use the Insert tab to insert media files, a Media Web Part is inserted on the page. When the web part is selected, then two contextual ribbon tabs, Web Part and Media, appear as shown in Figure 9-12.

Chapter 10 contains information on the Media Web Part.

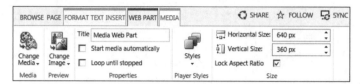

Figure 9-12 Use the Web Part and Media tabs to configure how you want the audio or video file to play.

INSIDE OUT   Optimizing images for websites

In SharePoint 2010, many users loaded images they had taken with their camera or phone and then reduced the size of the image on the page. On WCM sites, content authors were trained to optimize images before they were uploaded into SharePoint. In many cases, they had to produce a number of different sizes for the same picture, known as *renditions*. In SharePoint 2013, you can use image renditions to display uploaded images in predefined sizes, widths, and crops. You can create more than one rendition of a source image file, which means that you can set the display characteristics once and apply them to any number of images. For example, a rendition named "Article_image" displays a full-sized image in an article, while the rendition called "Thumbnail_small" displays a smaller version of the image. Before image renditions can be used in SharePoint 2013, the SharePoint server administrator has to enable Binary Large Object (BLOB cache) caching. More information on BLOB caching can be found at *technet.microsoft.com/en-us/library/ee424404.aspx*.

Links   On the Insert tab, in the Links group, two commands are provided: the Link split button and the Upload File command.

The Link split button allows you to associate a hyperlink with text on the page, so when you click the text, you are directed to the page associated with the hyperlink.

The Insert Hyperlink dialog box does not provide you with any options to configure the hyperlink to open in a new browser window; therefore, when the user clicks the hyperlink, he or she will be redirected from the wiki page and the user will need to use the browser's back button to return to the wiki page. However, once you add a link to the page, the Link tab is displayed, which allows you to remove the link, edit the URL, display an icon to the left of the hyperlink, and configure the hyperlink so that when a user clicks it, the page that the hyperlink is pointing to is displayed in a new tab and the user is not redirected from the page. You can also associate a description with the hyperlink, which is displayed when a user pauses over the hyperlink. This is sometimes known as a Screen Tip, and it is something that you should configure for accessibility reasons.

INSIDE OUT   Opening a new browser window

You could use the Edit Source command in the Markup group on the Format Text tab to add a target="_blank" attribute to the <a> tag, if you want a new browser window to open. Your organization may have a policy as when to open a new browser window. Generally, you should only open a new browser window in scenarios such as displaying a printable version of a webpage and large images. You can find expert usability references on this topic at *www.sitepoint.com/article/beware-opening-links-new-window/*, and by using the search keywords *opening, new, browser, window,* and *usability.*

The second command in the Links group, Upload File, allows you in one action to upload a file and store that file by default into the Site Assets library. It then creates a hyperlink pointing to the file that you have just uploaded. An icon appears to the left of the hyperlink indicating the type of file the hyperlink points to.

If you want to create a link to an existing wiki page, it is easier to use a method known as wiki links or forward links, than it is to use either of the two commands on the Links tab. See the "Creating wiki links" section later in this chapter.

Parts   The Parts group provides commands to insert app parts and web parts into your wiki page. When you click App Part, the Parts pane is displayed at the top of the page below the ribbon, as shown in Figure 9-13. This displays lists and libraries from the current site. When you click Web Part, the Web Parts pane is displayed.

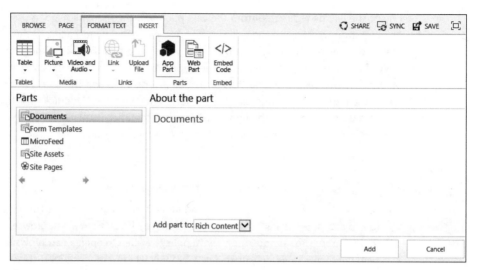

Figure 9-13 Select App Part from the Insert tab to insert an app part onto a wiki page.

More details on web parts can be found in Chapter 10.

Embed Code When you use the Embed Code command, the Embed dialog box opens and allows you to embed HTML, JavaScript, styles, and other markups into your page using the Script Editor Web Part. This is a new Web Part with SharePoint 2013. You can add the Script Editor Web Part to your page by clicking Embed Code on the Insert tab. The Script Editor Web Part is also available in the Web Part pane under Media And Content, as shown in Figure 9-14.

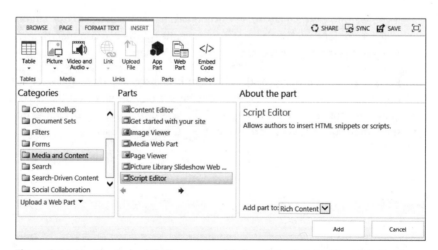

Figure 9-14 Use the Embed Code command to insert the Script Editor Web Part into your page.

INSIDE OUT How to display the Web Part Maintenance page

Web parts, if not fully tested, can cause a page not to display in the browser. If this occurs, append **?contents=1** to the page's URL to navigate to the page's Web Part Page Maintenance page, where you can close, reset, or delete the offending web part. You can use this page to delete all web parts from the page. The reset option is on the personal view of a page. The Web Part Page Maintenance page does not allow you to change the web part properties. To change web part properties, you must edit the page. If the web part is closed, you must first add the closed web part back on the page and then change the web part properties.

Modifying publishing pages

Web content management figures prominently in SharePoint 2013, where the content displayed in sites can be based on search and the structure of the site and the way the site is organized can be based on managed metadata. Using these two methods, WCM pages can contain content that rolls up content from anywhere within your SharePoint implementation, including external content. As far as the visitor to your site is concerned, the location of where the content lives is not important. Visitors will land on pages whose content is dynamically displayed as the result of indexing the content and how the content is tagged. Such pages are sometimes known as *landing pages* or *detailed pages* and will need to be configured only once as they dynamically obtain their content based on the properties of the web parts and controls that they contain. If your organization intends to use this method of sharing content, then it will be important that content authors categorize or tag the content they create appropriately.

The content author will need to know where the content is stored so she can modify it and decide where to create new content. However, this search-based approach of presenting content will allow the content owners to reorganize where the content is stored, either within the site or between sites, without affecting how the content is displayed to visitors to the site. There are restrictions as to where images can be added if you wish users to find them using a search-based approach.

More details on WCM can be found in Chapter 12. Information on how to use Search to expose content can be found in the search-related chapters, and details on managed metadata can be found in Chapter 11, "Managing documents."

WCM uses the document management features to manage pages and places the content pages in a document library called Pages, so that you can check pages in and out, as well as use the Approval workflow. One of the key constructs of publishing sites is the ability to control the strict layout of content on a page, known as a *page layout* or *publishing template*. A page based on a page layout is known as a *publishing page*.

Each page layout is associated with a master page, so the branding and navigation is the same on WCM pages as it is on ordinary content pages. When a publishing page is created from the page layout, you can restrict the content that the content author can create to be just text or not to include images. These features are available because a page layout is associated with page controls, and it is the properties of the page control that dictates the content rules and the look and feel in that particular portion of the page. SharePoint Server provides a number of page layouts.

When you modify a publishing page, you are not modifying a live page, where your changes are immediately visible to visitors; you can modify properties of the page to specify when the page should be visible to visitors once the page is approved. You can also specify when a page should be removed from common view. This does not override the security trimming that has been applied to the content. If you visitor does not have permissions to see content, then the search process and the WCM process will not make that content available to the visitor.

To edit a publishing page, you have the same three methods that you use on wiki pages: the Edit command on the Page tab, the Edit Page option on the Site Action menu, and the Edit command to the far right of the tabs. When the page is in edit mode and the cursor is in a rich text field control, you will see the Format Text and Insert tabs. This is very similar to editing wiki pages. The differences are listed as follows:

- **Format text** When ending content in a field control based on the Publishing HTML site column, then the Format Text tab contains no Edit or Layout group. It does contain a Spelling command, which allows you to check the spelling of the text that you enter.

- **Insert** The commands on this tab are the same for a publishing page as on a wiki page.

Creating wiki pages

There are three methods of creating a new page using the browser:

- Use wiki links, also known as *linking* or a *forward link*. This is the recommended method of creating new wiki pages, as this method creates a hyperlink to the new page on an existing wiki page and users find it easier to find a page when another page is linked to it.

- Click the Settings icon and then click New Page.

- On the All Pages view of the Site Pages library, click New Wiki Page above the list of pages or click New Document on the Files tab. If you click the down arrow on the New Document split button, you can create Web Part pages as well as wiki pages, as shown in Figure 9-15.

Figure 9-15 Use the File tab to create a new Web Part page.

Creating wiki links

You can create hyperlinks that point to wiki pages using wiki links. This is a quicker and easier method than using the Links command on the Insert tab. The very first wiki site, WikiWikiWeb, was created for the Portland Pattern Repository in 1995 by Ward Cunningham, who devised a system that created webpages quickly—and this method is what is now called *wiki links*. You can create a wiki link to an existing page or you can create a wiki link to a wiki page that is not created. You can then click the wiki link to create a new wiki page.

Wiki is the Hawaiian word for quick, and as Hawaiian words are doubled for emphasis, *wiki wiki* means very quick. Ward Cunningham used double characters as formatting clues. These formatting clues are standard to many wiki applications. To create a wiki link, you type the name of the page within two sets of double square brackets. To display double open or closed square brackets without making a link, type a backslash before the two brackets, such as **\[[or \]]**.

To create a wiki link to an existing page, follow these steps:

1. Open a wiki page in edit mode and place the insertion point where you would like a hyperlink to the new page to be displayed.

2. Type **[[**.

   A list of pages that exist in the Site Pages wiki library are displayed.

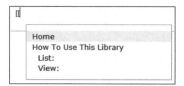

3. If the Site Pages library contains a large number of pages, you can filter the list of pages by typing the first few characters of the page name. You can then use your mouse or the Up and Down arrow keys to select the correct wiki page. You can also type the first characters for the name of the wiki page until only one page remains in the list and then press Tab. You do not need to type the page name in full, only sufficient characters to uniquely identify the page. Press the Enter key to close the brackets.

To create new wiki page using the forward link method, follow these steps:

1. Open a wiki page in edit mode and place the insertion point where you would like a hyperlink to the new page to be displayed.

2. Type **[[** and then type the name of the new page.

   The page name needs to be unique within the Site Pages library and will form part of a URL. When you have typed sufficient characters of the page name to make it unique, a message appears stating that the item does not exist.

   Webpage names are usually short and terse, yet the text on the wiki page that represents the hyperlink is descriptive, so a user who reads the page can make a decision whether to click the link or not.

3. To create descriptive text that is displayed as the text for the link, type **|** followed by the descriptive text and then type **]]**, such as **[[NewTravelPolicy|New Travel Policy]]**.

4. On the Format Text tab, click Save & Close in the Edit group.

   The descriptive text, such as training material, is underlined with dashes. This indicates that the wiki link points to a non-existent page, as shown in the next graphic.

How To Use This Library

New Travel Policy

5. Click the wiki link. A New Page dialog box appears, stating that the page NewTravelPolicy does not exist and asks whether you want to create a new page. Click Create, and the page is created in the Site Pages library.

> **Note**
>
> The naming convention for wiki pages, known as *WikiWords* or *WikiNames,* is to concatenate two or more words, where each word is composed of two or more letters with no spaces between words and where the first letter of each word is capitalized and the remaining letters are in lowercase. This formatting is known as *Camel case.* However, you may have your own naming standard for URLs.

Creating publishing pages

There are two methods of creating a new publishing page using the browser:

● Click the Settings icon and then click New Page to display the Add A Page dialog box. Type the name of the page. If you type spaces in the name of the page, they will be replaced with hyphens. The URL of the page is displayed below the Give It A Name text box. Notice that although the page will be created in the Pages library, as shown in Figure 9-16, the URL does not reflect this—that is, the page URL is *http://internet. adventure-works.com/new-travel-expenses.* This is known as the *friendly URL,* and it is not *http://intranet.adventure-works.com/Pages/new-travel-expenses.aspx,* which is known as the *physical page address.* The "friendly" URL is new in SharePoint 2013. Such URLs are also search engine optimization (SEO)–friendly, and friendly URLs will appear in search results.

Figure 9-16 Publishing pages are created with friendly URLs.

> **Note**
>
> Using this method does not allow you to choose the page layout for the new publishing page. You can change the page layout for the publishing page using the Page tab.

- In the All Pages view of the Pages library, click New Document on the Files tab. This will select the default page layout to create the publishing page. If you click the down arrow of the New Document split button, you can choose to create your publishing page based on a page layout other than the default one, as shown in Figure 9-17.

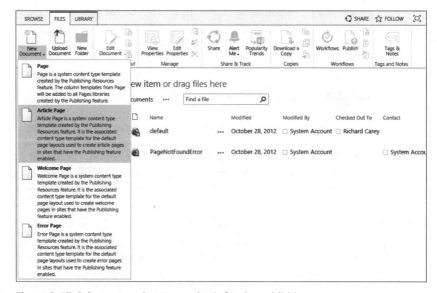

Figure 9-17 Select a page layout as a basis for the publishing page.

Managing pages

Once you have created your pages, in order to ensure the accuracy of your content, you will need to manage them. This is where the Page tab is useful. For wiki pages, the Page tab consists of six groups. For publishing pages, the Page tab contains those six groups plus an additional group, Publishing. The groups are:

- **Edit** This group contains two split buttons, Edit/Save and Check Out, and on publishing pages, the command Save And Publish:

    - **Edit/Save** When the page is in edit mode, the command dynamically changes to Save. Use this to save and close the page, save and keep editing the page, and stop editing the page, which means that any changes you make to the page will be lost. The other two commands in the Save drop-down list, Edit and Edit In SharePoint Designer, are inactive. These commands are available on the Page tab when the page is not in edit mode.

    - **Check Out** Use to check out, check in, discard checkout, and to override checkout.

    - **Save And Publish** Use this command to save and publish the page in one action.

- **Manage** Use the commands in this group to edit the page's properties, rename the page, view the page history, manage the page's permission, and delete the page. You cannot rename a site's home page. The Edit Properties command will be inactive if you have not created any additional columns in the Site Pages library. When editing publishing pages, this group does not contain a rename option, but contains a Page URLs and Revert option:

    - **Page URLs** This allows you to see the physical page address and all the terms that are associated with this page. Each URL list loads the page in the context of the corresponding term. You can also add friendly URLs to the page.

    - **Revert** This allows you to revert the page to the currently published version of the page. A page is just a file in a library and therefore can be deleted and have item-level permissions, as can any file in any library. Also similar to other files, once a page is deleted, it will move to the site's recycle bin.

- **Share & Track** This group contains three commands: the E-mail A Link and Popularity Trends commands and a split button labeled Alert Me.

    - **E-mail A Link** This command, when clicked, opens a new Mail message and creates a hyperlink to the wiki page in the body of the email message.

    - **Alert Me** This split button allows you to either set an alert on the page or manage your alerts. By setting an alert on a wiki page, you can receive an email or a text message (SMS) when the page changes and you can choose when to receive that message: immediately, daily, or weekly. If your SharePoint

Foundation installation, at the farm level, does not have the outgoing email settings configured, then the Alert Me split button will not be displayed. If the mobile account settings are not configured, the SMS option cannot be used. Use the Central Administration website to configure outgoing email settings and mobile accounts, which can be found on the System Settings page.

- **Popularity Trends** This command, when clicked, will prompt you to open a Microsoft Excel spreadsheet file, Usage.xlsx, that shows daily and monthly count per usage event for the page, as shown in Figure 9-18. This is new in SharePoint 2013.

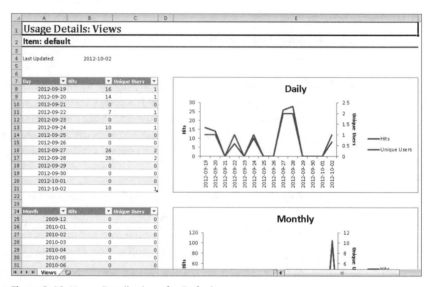

Figure 9-18 Usage Details views for Default.aspx.

- **Page Actions** This group consists of two commands on wiki pages: Make Homepage and Incoming Links. If a user types the URL of a site and does not specify a webpage, then the home page of the site is displayed. Use this command to replace the site's current home page with the current wiki page. When you click Incoming Links, you are redirected to a page that displays all pages that link to the current page.

Publishing pages also contain the commands to preview the page as seen on a device, change the page layout, and complete a draft check. A draft check is when you check for unpublished items on a page. For example, you may have inserted an image in the page, and the image may be stored in a library that has major and minor versioning enabled. If the image is a minor version, and therefore still in draft mode, when the publishing page is published, then the image will show as a broken link to visitors to the site.

- **Page Library** Depending on the type of page, this group consists of two or three commands:

  - **Library Settings** This command redirects you to the list settings page for the Site Pages library. You can use the list settings page as you can other libraries. For example, you can use content approval and workflow with the Site Pages library.

  - **Library Permissions** This command redirects you to the library permissions page for the Site Pages library that you can use to restrict the rights as to who can create and edit wiki pages. This option is not displayed on wiki pages.

  - **View All Pages** This command redirects you to the All Pages view for the Site Pages library.

- **Tags & Notes** You can add tags and notes to documents and pages on a SharePoint site, and even pages on the Internet. You can view your tags and notes on your profile, on other people's profiles that you have permission to view, and on the SharePoint pages that you have added tags and notes to. You use tags to classify and remember pages. Use Notes to comment on a page.

Working with Page History

The Pages and Site Pages libraries have all the features of a document library, such as history and version management. Therefore, no amendments are lost. Major versioning is turned on by default when you create a wiki page library, and both major and minor versioning is turned on by default for publishing sites.

On the Page tab, click Page History in the Manage group to display the History page. In the left pane is a list of all the versions for the page, together with the date and time that the versions were created. You have the option to choose which two versions of the page to compare, as shown in Figure 9-19. In the content area, content that is deleted from the older of the two versions appears on the page but has a strikethrough red font. Content that is added since the older of the two versions has a green background color. The History page does not show changes in web parts, images or client-side code, such as changes to HTML tags or their attributes.

The Page History page provides links to edit the properties of the page, delete the page and all its versions, manage its permissions, check it out, and create an Alert Me for the page, as well as a link to manage the versions of the page.

Figure 9-19 Use the Page History page to delete or restore versions.

Managing versions

The Versions Saved page is displayed when you click Version History on the Page History page. The Versions Saved page is displayed as a dialog box when you have Microsoft Silverlight installed. You can also display the Versions Saved page from the All Pages view of the Site Pages library: click Version History in the Manage group on the Documents tab. Similarly, the Versions Saved dialog box is displayed when you use the Version History command on the list item menu.

You can use the Versions Saved page to replace the current version of a page with the selected version. When the previous version of the page is restored as the current version of the page, a yellow status bar appears. The message in this status bar is different for publishing pages as compared to wiki pages.

On a publishing page, it will state that the page is still checked out to you and only you can see the recent changes. You will need to check the page in for other authors to see it, and then publish it for all visitors to see it.

On wiki pages, the yellow status bar states that the current page has been customized from its template, as shown in Figure 9-20. This occurs when you restore a previous version of a page using the browser or when using a program such as SharePoint Designer 2010 or SharePoint Designer 2013. Click Revert To Template, and then click OK to revert the page to its template.

Figure 9-20 Restoring a wiki page version customizes the page.

> **Note**
>
> You cannot restore the state of only one web part on the page.

For more information on customizing pages, see the "Site template pages" sidebar later in this chapter.

Using Web Part pages

On sites such as the Group Work Site, Meeting Workspaces, and Blog sites, Web Part pages are the default type of page. Lists and libraries also use this page type to display their contents. Web Part pages consist only of web part zones and do not contain the Embed-dedFormField SharePoint control, as shown in Figure 9-21. Therefore, they cannot use wiki links to create new pages quickly and easily. You cannot mix text and web parts anywhere on the page. They can contain only web parts quickly and easily. To add static text or images to a Web Part page, you must first add either the CEWP or the Image Web Part, and then use the Web Part tool pane to alter the properties of the web part and to add text or images.

Figure 9-21 A Web Part page containing one web part zone: Main.

Using the browser, you can only add web parts to web part zones. Using SharePoint Designer, you can add web parts outside web part zones on a Web Part page, when the page is opened in advanced edit mode. With SharePoint Designer 2013, you will use the code view of the page to do this, as the Design View is no longer available. Web parts added to outside web part zones and outside the EmbeddedFormField control on wiki pages are called *static web parts*, whereas web parts added to web part zones or the EmbeddedFormField control are called *dynamic web parts*. The properties of a static web part are stored on the page and not in the Web Parts Microsoft SQL Server table. Inserting a static web part in a page allows users to view the contents of the web part, but prevents them from using the browser to modify the web part or the way that it is displayed on the page.

More details on web parts can be found in Chapter 10.

There are two types of a Web Part pages: Shared and Personal versions. All Web Part pages have a Shared version, but not all Web Part pages have a Personal view. Wiki pages and publishing pages only have a Shared version.

Shared version

The Shared version of a Web Part page is displayed for all users who have at least the view permission. To modify the Shared version, you must have the following rights, all of which are included in the Design and Full Control permission levels by default:

- Manage Lists

- Add And Customize Pages

- Apply Themes And Borders

- Apply Style Sheets

A member of a website's Site Owners group has Full Control permissions and therefore is able to customize the Shared version of all Web Part pages. To edit the Shared version of a Web Part page, use the Edit Page option on the Site Actions menu or on the Page tab, click Edit Page. If the Edit Page command is not active, then you do not have permissions to edit the page.

Personal version

The Personal version of a Web Part page is displayed for the person who created the page and cannot be viewed by others. To create a Personal version of any Web Part page, the Web Part page must be designed to be personalized. In addition, you must have the following rights, all of which are included in the Contribute, Design, and Full Control permission levels by default:

● Manage Personal Views

● Add/Remove Personal Web Parts

● Update Personal Web Parts

The site's Members group is mapped to the Contribute permission levels, and therefore any member of that group is able to customize the Personal version of a Web Part page if it is designed to be personalized.

To edit your Personal version of a Web Part page, click the down arrow to the right of your name in the upper-right corner of the page, and then click Personalize This Page, as shown in Figure 9-22.

Figure 9-22 Select Personalize This Page to edit your Personal version of a Web Part page.

A yellow status bar below the ribbon is displayed, stating that you are editing the Personal version of this page. This will always be displayed when you are editing the Personal version of a Web Part page.

Once you have personalized a page, then the upper-right corner menu will contain two other options, Show Shared View and Reset Page Content. To remove the Personal version of a Web Part page, use the Reset Page Content option.

When you have a personal view of a Web Part page, then it will be displayed by default when you first visit the page. This can be confusing to some users, who then do not see the same components on the page as other users.

> **Note**
> When a Web Part page is designed to be personalized, editors of the Shared version of the page can disable the personalization of web parts on an individual basis by using the Web Part tool pane to configure the web part properties.

How to control page personalization

You can control page personalization using the following methods:

- **Permissions** By default, the Manage Personal Views, Add/Remove Personal Web Parts, and Update Personal Web Parts permissions can be enabled or disabled in permission levels at the site and site-collection level. However, at a web application level, you can configure whether sites and site collections within the web application can use these permissions in permission levels. To configure whether to allow the use of these permissions, navigate to the Web Application page within the Central Administration website. Select the web application, and then, on the Web Application table, click User Permissions in the Security group. Then clear the check boxes of the permissions that you do not want to be enabled within permission levels.

- **Web part property** There are two supported types of web parts in SharePoint. They are referred to as *SharePoint* and *ASP.NET Web Parts*. ASP.NET Web Parts use the System.Web.UI.WebControls.WebParts.WebPart base class, while SharePoint Web Parts use the Microsoft.SharePoint.WebPartPages.WebPart base class. Both types are supported, but the ASP.NET Web Part is recommended for all web parts. When a developer creates a SharePoint Web Part, the web part property definitions use WebPartStorageAttribute and PersonalizableAttribute attributes to decide whether a value for a Web Part property is stored the same for all users or is stored on a per-user basis. When a developer creates an ASP.NET Web Part, then the Personalizable property attribute should be used. Information on the web part personalization can be found at *msdn.microsoft.com/en-us/library/ms178182.aspx*. Information on WebPartStorageAttribute can be found at *msdn.microsoft.com/en-us/library/microsoft.sharepoint.webpartpages.webpartstorageattribute.aspx* and on the PersonalizableAttribute at *msdn.microsoft.com/en-us/library/system.web.ui.webcontrols.webparts.personalizableattribute.aspx*.

- **Web part zones** By default, most web part zones placed on Web Part pages allow users to change personal settings for any web part within the web part zone, if the web part is designed to be personalized and the user has the permission to personalize web parts. However, a developer can create a Web Part page and disable web part personalization on a per-web-part-zone basis. You can also use SharePoint Designer in advanced edit mode to modify the settings of web part zones to disable personalization of web parts. Therefore, by configuring web part zones differently, you can allow users to personalize some parts of a Web Part page and prevent them from personalizing or modifying other parts of a page. To disable personalization on a web part zone in SharePoint Designer, click the web part zone label, and then, on the Format tab, click Properties in the web part zone group. The Web Part Zones Properties dialog box is displayed, where you can select or clear the check box to the right of Allow Users To Change Personal Web Part Settings. This adds the attribute allowpersonalization="false" to the WebPartPages:WebPartZone control.

- **Pages**   Web parts personalization is enabled by default on Web Part pages. On websites where you do not want users to personalize or modify pages, you can disable personalization for the whole page by using the personalization-enabled:"false" attribute on the ASP.NET control:webpartmanager. This control is present in all out-of-the-box master pages, and therefore when the personalization-enabled attribute is set to false on the master page, all pages associated with that master page cannot be personalized.

Editing Web Part pages

You can edit a Web Part page using the Edit Page option on the Settings icon menu. On Web Part pages that are displaying views of lists or libraries, there is no Page tab. On Web Part pages that are the default page of sites, such as meeting workspaces and project sites, there is a Page tab, which contains two extra groups:

- **Approval**   The commands, Approve and Reject, are active if content approval is enabled at the library level.

- **Workflow**   The Workflows command is enabled if the Web Part page is stored in a library and a Workflow template has been associated with the library.

Some of the commands in the other groups will be inactive. For example, when you initially create a project site, the home Web Part page is stored in the root of the site and not in a library. When the Web Part page is in edit mode, no Format Text or Insert tabs are displayed. These will appear only when you are typing content into the CEWP.

Creating Web Part pages

Using the browser, there are a number of methods of creating Web Part pages:

- If you are on a site that uses wiki pages, such as a Team Site, navigate to the Site Pages library, click the New Document split button, and then select Web Part Page.

- Create a document library and use the Advance Options to specify Web Part Page as the library's document template. Then, to create a new Web Part page, click New Document on the Documents tab.

- On Meeting Workspaces, from the Settings icon menu, click Add Pages. The current page is open in edit mode and a Pages task pane is displayed, as shown in Figure 9-23. In the Page Name text box, type the name of the new page and then click Add. The three-column Web Part page is created in a hidden library, named Workspace Pages, with a URL of pages.

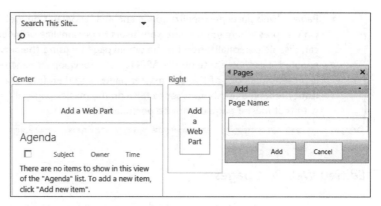

Figure 9-23 Type the name of the new page you want to create in the Pages task pane.

● Create a view for any list or library. The page created is a Web Part page.

When you use one of the first two methods, the new Web Part page is displayed where you type the name of the new Web Part page and choose a layout template and a document library to store the new Web Part page, as shown in Figure 9-24.

Figure 9-24 Choose a layout template for a new Web Part page.

To the left of the Layout Template list box when you select a layout template, a thumbnail preview displays, which shows the web part zones and the organization of the web parts within the zones for the layout. For example, the Header, Footer, 2 Columns, 4 Rows layout option consists of eight web part zones. The four rows of web part zones show the web parts side by side; therefore, if you insert web parts in one of those web part zone rows, the web parts will not be displayed above and below each other, which is the usual configuration, but rather to the right or left of each other. These web part templates do not provide a left navigation area for the Quick Launch links.

Once you have created a Web Part page from a layout template, you cannot change the layout of web part zones on the page using the browser; you need to use a tool, such as SharePoint Designer. You can also use SharePoint Designer on a page-by-page basis to reestablish the Quick Launch link in the left pane.

The implementation of the web part layout templates has not changed from Windows SharePoint Services 3.0. The eight Web Part page templates are located in the SharePoint root directory (%PROGRAMFILES%\ \Common files\Microsoft Shared\Web Server Extensions\15) in the subfolder \TEMPLATE\1033\STS\DOCTEMP\SMARTPGS. These files, named spstd1.aspx through spstd8.aspx, cannot be renamed, as SharePoint still uses a page called spcf.aspx to list the web part layout templates and owssvr.dll to initiate the page. Therefore, you can use the same technique to amend and add your own layout templates to SharePoint 2013 as you may have done when using Windows SharePoint Services 3.0 or SharePoint 2010. A good starting point to add your own custom Web Part page templates can be found at *www.dontpapanic.com/blog/?p=58* and *msdn.microsoft.com/ en-us/library/ms916835.aspx*. However, it does entail updating files provided by Microsoft in the SharePoint root directory for each server in your SharePoint farm, and therefore this method has some severe limitations, such as the possibility that future SharePoint updates could overwrite the changes.

> **Note**
> The New Page option on the Settings icon menu is used to create wiki pages only.

Using mobile pages

SharePoint 2013 provides an improved mobile browser experience, consisting of three views:

- **Contemporary view** A HTML5–optimized mobile browser experience, available for Mobile Internet Explorer 9.0 or later for Windows Phone 7.5, Safari versions 4.0 or later for iPhone 4.0, and the Android browser for Android 4.0 or later versions.

Chapter 9

- **Classic view** Identical to the mobile browser experience of SharePoint Server 2010. Uses HTML or similar markup languages, such as Compact HyperText Markup Language (CHTML) or Wireless Markup Language (WML), to provide backward compatibility for mobile browsers that cannot render the contemporary view.

- **Full-screen user interface** A full desktop view of a SharePoint site on a smartphone device.

The contemporary view is available on sites where the new site level feature, Automatic Mobile Browser Redirection, is activated. This feature checks if the mobile browser can handle HTML5 before sending the contemporary view to the mobile device; otherwise, the classic view is downloaded. By default, this feature is activated on the following site templates: Team Site, Blank Site, Document Workspace, Document Center, and Project Site.

On publishing sites, SharePoint 2013 includes device channels that allow you to use different designs that target different devices based on their user agent string.

The new stand-alone Office Web Apps Server product still provides mobile browser-based viewers: Word Mobile Viewer, Excel Mobile Viewer, and Microsoft PowerPoint Mobile Viewer. These are optimized to render documents for phones.

More information on planning for mobile devices in SharePoint 2013 can be found at *technet.microsoft.com/en-us/library/gg610510(v=office.15).aspx*. Information on how to administer a mobile device in SharePoint 2013 can be found at *technet.microsoft.com/en-us/library/ff393820(v=office.15).aspx*.

Windows SharePoint Services 3.0 supported mobile pages that you could navigate to in your desktop browser by appending **/m** to the end of the website's URL. This displayed links to the site's lists and libraries. SharePoint Foundation 2010 included support for mobile devices by appending **?mobile=1** to the end of the any page's URL. SharePoint 2013 supports both of these methods.

If a mobile device navigates to a SharePoint site's page, it is automatically redirected to these mobile pages, which restructures the requested page for mobile devices and inserts at the bottom of every mobile page links to View All Pages, All Site Content, and the home page of the site. The pages used to redirect the browser are stored in the _layouts/mobile virtual directory and are listed in Table 9-1.

TABLE 9-1 **Redirection mobile pages**

Page type	Redirection mobile page
List and library views	View.aspx
Wiki pages	Mblwiki.aspx
Web Part pages	Mbllists.aspx
Application pages	Mblerror.aspx
Page used to display a list items properties	Dispform.aspx
Page used to edit a list items properties	Editform.aspx

Site template pages

When you create a site from one of the built-in site templates, the pages on the newly created site refer to pages stored in the TEMPLATE subfolder of the SharePoint root directory. No files or pages are created. Instead, table entries are created in a SQL Server content database in the ALLDocs tables, and those table entries point to files in the TEMPLATE folder. Each site appears to have its own pages, but in reality, they all share the same files. The files in the TEMPLATE folder are known as *site definitions*. Site definition files are cached in memory on the server at process startup. As a result, when a user requests a page, such as Home.aspx, which is one of the site definition files, it is retrieved from the server's memory. SharePoint retrieves from the SQL server content database the content entered in the EmbeddedFormField control on wiki pages or web parts inserted in web part zones, as this content is stored separately from the site definition files, as shown here. Therefore, a relatively small set of files can support a large number of SharePoint sites with many pages, resulting in improved performance.

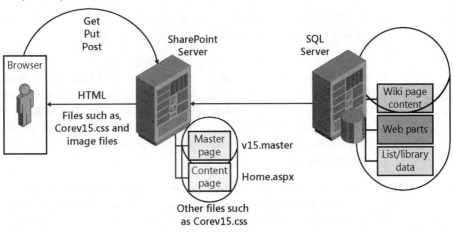

Similar to the browser, when you use SharePoint Designer to modify the contents of the EmbeddedFormField control and web parts in web part zones, only the data in the content databases is being modified. This is SharePoint Designer's default edit mode. However, with SharePoint Designer, when you open a page in advanced edit mode, you can modify content that is defined outside the EmbeddedFormField and web part zone. You are then modifying content that is defined in the site definition files; therefore, SharePoint Foundation saves a copy of the site definition files from the SharePoint root to the SQL server, as shown here. This copy of the site definition file is specific to the site you are modifying; all other sites continue to use the site definition files stored in the SharePoint root.

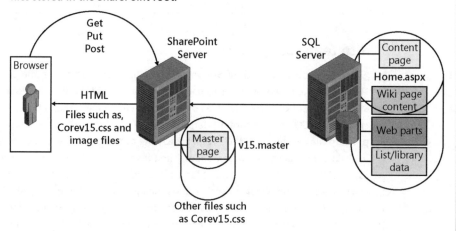

Site definition files amended by SharePoint Designer in advanced edit mode are known as *customized* or *unghosted* pages. Site definition files that have not been customized are known as *uncustomized* or *ghosted* files. The master page, v15.master, CSS files (such as Corev4.css), JavaScript files, and the web part layout template files are all site definition files. Therefore, when you edit these files in advanced edit mode, you are creating customized pages that are unique to your site.

For a site that is frequently visited, and where ASP.NET output cache is enabled and available, the customized page will introduce little significant overhead when the page is requested. However, if page cache is not available and if a large number of users request the customized page, the performance level of the customized page could be significantly affected. Therefore as you plan your solutions, you should take this into account. A common decision is not to customize an organization's master pages or a site's home page.

Customizing pages can also make global changes to all your sites difficult. If your organization has deployed its own site definition files (for example, its own master page, which you customized in SharePoint Designer) and then it subsequently redeploys a new version of that master page, you will not see the changes to the organization's master page. Using the browser or SharePoint Designer, you can reset your customized page to the site definition pages.

Using SharePoint Designer, you can prototype your master page modifications to a specific site. Once the modifications have been approved, you can export your customized master page and either store the master page in the site master page gallery that is located at the top-level site of a site collection, or use Visual Studio 2012 to package the master page in a solutions file and deploy it as a site definition file into the SharePoint root directory. Using the browser to upload the master page into the master page gallery, store the master page in the SQL server content database. Any file that is stored in the content database is considered to be customized.

When you deploy files to SharePoint, you deploy them as features. The feature specifies what to do with the file. If the file is to be stored in the SharePoint root directory as an uncustomized file and cached in memory, then you can use one of two Type attributes, Ghostable or GhostableInLibrary. If you wish to deploy a file, such as a master page as an uncustomized file, but you want the file to appear as if it is stored in a library (such as _catalog/masterpage), use GhostableInLibrary. Users can then see the file in any of the list views and work with the file as they would with any other file. For example, they can check it in, approve it, or reject it. If you deploy a file without the Type attribute Ghostable or GhostableInLibrary, the file is customized—unghostable—and is stored in the content database.

Using SharePoint Designer 2013 to create and modify webpages

The browser is still SharePoint's main web content editing tool for most users; however, in SharePoint 2013, the webpage markup has been re-architected to reduce the number of bytes over the wire and reduce the complexity of the CSS hierarchy. The goal of this release of SharePoint was to make changing the look and feel of SharePoint sites easier for web designers. They do not now have to understand SharePoint as fully as they did with SharePoint 2010. They still have to understand HTML, CSS, and JavaScript, though.

With SharePoint 2013, web designers can continue to use designer tools that they are familiar with, such as Adobe Dreamweaver and Microsoft Expression Studio. SharePoint differentiates logic from the HTML rendering logic. SharePoint pages, the markup, ASP.NET, and SharePoint controls are exposed to generic HTML editors as HTML templates. Web parts and web part zones no longer use tables; they but are rendered using HTML DIV tags.

This change, targeted at publishing sites, provides new ways of building master pages and page layouts. A new tool is available on every publishing site: the Design Manager. (More information on the Design Manager is provided in Chapter 12.) You can still use SharePoint Designer, however. The Design view has been removed in SharePoint Designer 2013 and thus has the split code/design view. Only the code view remains in SharePoint Designer 2013.

> **Note**
>
> Although you no longer need to use SharePoint Designer to design master pages and page layouts on WCM sites, there is no built-in design tool for collaboration sites. This would not be significant if you could still use SharePoint Designer 2013 for developing and prototyping web design solutions. However, the Design view (and therefore also the Split view in SharePoint Designer 2013 Preview) have been removed. This signifi-cantly complicates the management and further development of existing SharePoint Designer customizations, such as mashups, and interactive solutions that made use of the Data View Web Part. This will severely affect super users or user champions who build business solutions and are not comfortable working in code view. You may be able to use SharePoint Designer 2010 as a workaround to this problem; however, to enable generic HTML editors to modify pages, a new SharePoint control, SPHtmlTag, encapsulates all the controls on a SharePoint page and hides the rendering information from the Design view of SharePoint Designer 2010.

You can use SharePoint Designer 2010 or SharePoint Designer 2013 on SharePoint 2013 sites. Before you can modify any pages, you must open a SharePoint site with SharePoint Designer. Then you can open individual files, whether they are stored within the SharePoint site or out-side the site, such as your computer's hard disk. You should never use SharePoint Designer to amend files on the SharePoint server's file system. Modifications or the creation of files on SharePoint servers should be tightly managed and deployed with SharePoint solution files, which you create using Visual Studio 2010.

When you open a SharePoint site with SharePoint Designer, the Navigation pane is displayed, which focuses on SharePoint objects and not where the objects are stored. Previously in this chapter, you worked with webpages stored in the site object's Site Pages, Site Assets, and Master Pages, which are listed on the Navigation pane.

When you click the first site object in the Navigation pane, the site's information is displayed in the SharePoint Designer's workspace, as shown in Figure 9-25.

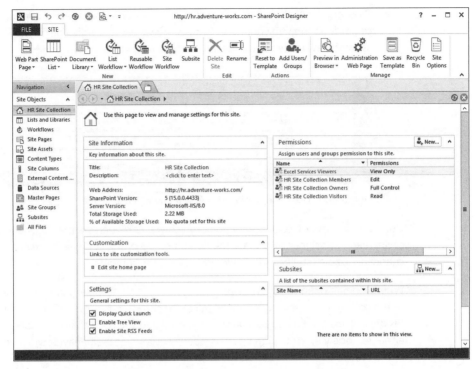

Figure 9-25 SharePoint Designer's ribbon, Navigation page, and workspace.

You can then navigate to the home page of the site by clicking Edit Site Home Page in the Customization area. A new tab opens, displaying the Editor page for the site's home page, which for a Team Site is the wiki page, Home.aspx. In the Navigation pane, below the site objects, a mini gallery displays the contents of the Site Pages library. You could also navigate to the home page by clicking Site Pages in the Navigation pane.

With SharePoint Designer 2013 Preview, you are limited to using the Code view. This displays the HTML tags, client-side code, such as JavaScript, and controls, such as the SharePoint control for the ribbon, SPRibbon—if you had opened a master page, or content controls on webpages, where the content for the page is positioned. The Code view provides you with a number of features that help you write code, such as the following:

- The Code view uses colors to identify different code elements so that you can quickly identify coding errors.

- IntelliSense is also included in Code view. As you type, it detects what you are writing and provides suggestions. The IntelliSense in Code view is not limited to HTML tags; it is also provided when writing CSS or selecting parameters.

- The Code View also offers snippets of code. These snippets are predefined, and you can include them in your code by pressing Ctrl+Enter, which displays a drop-down list of the available code snippets, as shown in Figure 9-26.

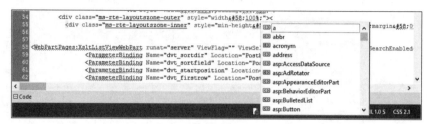

Figure 9-26 Use code snippets for frequently typed-in code.

Use the Page Editor Options dialog box, which you can open via the Backstage view of SharePoint Designer, to change the default colors of the code elements that can be changed, disable IntelliSense, or add your own code snippets.

When you first open the Home.aspx page, you are in Code view, and you will see that some of the code in the Home.aspx page is yellow, as shown in Figure 9-27. This is the code that resides outside the EmbeddedFormField control and the code that you cannot modify either in Code view or Design view. This behavior mimics the behavior when editing a page in the browser.

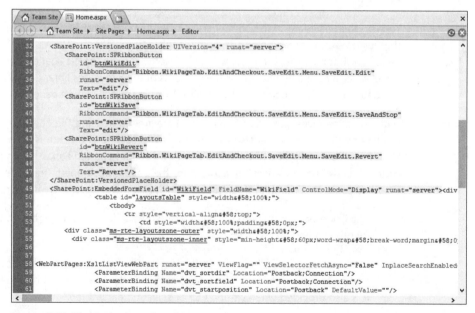

Figure 9-27 The Code view of a wiki page.

By looking at the Code view for Home.aspx, you can see that the code that is used to present content on a wiki page is

```
<SharePoint:EmbeddedFormField ID="WikiField" FieldName="WikiField"
    ControlMode="Display" runat="server" />
```

INSIDE OUT   Web part zones on wiki pages

As you look at the controls on the Home.aspx page in Code view, you may also discover that the page contains a web part zone named Bottom, and the web part zone's properties are set to allow users with a browser to interact with web parts placed in the zone, as shown here. On wiki pages, only content within the EmbeddedFormField can be modified with a browser. With SharePoint Designer, you can add web parts to the bottom web part zone. You can add other web part zones to a wiki page; however, these and any web parts that they contain, like the Bottom web part zone will not be visible when the page is in edit mode when using the browser.

```
 98            </tr>
 99          </tbody>
100        </table>
101        <span id="layoutsData" style="display:&58;none;">false,false,1</span></div></SharePoint:EmbeddedFormField>
102        <WebPartPages:WebPartZone runat="server" ID="Bottom" CssClass="ms-hide" Title="loc:Bottom"><ZoneTemplate></Z
103 </asp:Content>
```

Saving modifications

When you save your webpage, if your page contains an EmbeddedFormField, then a SharePoint Designer dialog box is displayed, stating that the content may be changed by the server to remove unsafe content. This is the same sanitization process that occurs when you save a wiki page using the browser. When you click Yes in the dialog box, the page is reloaded so that you can see the result of the save.

Managing pages

To manage pages using SharePoint Designer, in the Navigation pane, click Site Pages to display the pages gallery and to display the Pages tab, as shown in Figure 9-28. The Pages tab contains an Edit group that allows you to delete and rename a page, navigate to the page settings, and edit the page in Safe Mode or Advanced Mode. The Actions group allows you to reset a page to its site definition or set a page as the home page for the site.

Figure 9-28 Use the Pages tab to manage files in the Site Pages library.

Use the Manage group to do the following:

- Preview the page in the browser.

- Open a browser window to display the administration webpage for a page.

- Check out, check in, or undo checkout.

- Import or export files from the Site Pages library.

- Open the Site Pages settings page in SharePoint Designer.

Creating pages

With SharePoint Designer, you can create a number of file types of different files including .ASPX and Web Part pages. You cannot create a wiki page or site definition files. The browser is the best method for creating wiki pages and you should use Visual Studio to create and deploy site definition pages.

To create a Web Part page, perform the following steps:

1. In the Navigation pane, click Site Pages to display the site pages gallery.

2. On the Pages tab, click Web Part Page and then select the web part zone layout for the page.

   These are the sample template layouts that you used in the browser when you created a Web Part page. A file, Untitled-1.aspx, is created and displayed in the Site Pages gallery, with Untitled_1.aspx selected.

3. Type the name that you wish to call the page and then press Enter to rename the page.

4. To edit the page, on the Pages tab, click Edit File in the Edit group.

To create an ASPX or HTML file, perform the following steps:

1. In the Navigation pane, click Site Pages to display the site pages gallery.

2. On the Pages tab, click Page and then select either ASPX or HTML.

   A file, Untitled-x.aspx, is created, where x is a number that makes the page name unique.

Using this method of creating ASPX or HTML files, they will not contain any controls. Specifically, they will not contain the EmbeddedFormField control or web part zones; therefore, they do not contain any regions that are editable in Safe Mode. You will have to edit the pages in Advanced Mode; that is, these pages are not associated with a site definition file and the entire contents of the page is stored in the content database.

To create a file from a master page, follow these steps:

1. In the Navigation pane, click Master Pages to display the master pages gallery.

2. On the Master Pages tab, click Page From Master in the New group.

   A Select A Master Page dialog box opens, where you can select to create a page from the master page designated as the site's master page or a specific master page. Custom master pages are used on publishing sites, which is a SharePoint Server feature.

   Alternatively, in the master page gallery, right-click the appropriate master page and then click New From Master Page.

Alternatively, to create webpages as well as other file types, use the following steps:

1. Click the File tab and then click Add Item.

2. In the middle pane, you can create a Web Part page or a New Page From Master. For other file types, click More Pages, as shown next.

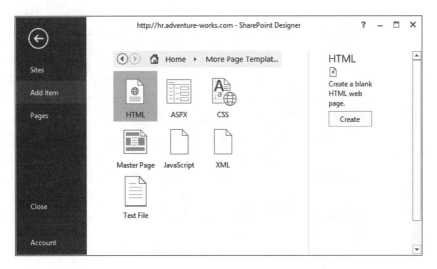

3. Select the page type that you wish to create and then click Create.

INSIDE OUT   Site definition pages and SharePoint Designer

Using SharePoint Designer, you cannot create a site definition page, but you can create a page from a site definition by copying an existing site definition page. This allows you to have the same performance benefits as the original file. Another benefit is you can maintain the same look and feel across a set of pages. For example, if you added a completely new page to your original site—if you replaced Default.aspx with a different file rather than making changes to the existing Default.aspx file—the new page has no site definition association. If for any reason the site definition file changes, such as when your company upgrades to the next version of SharePoint, then the new page might not look like the other pages in the upgraded site, nor can it be reset to look like them.

Working in Advanced Mode

Up to this point in this chapter, you have opened the webpage in Safe Mode, where you are unable to modify specific areas of the page. In Safe Mode, you can only edit the content in the EmbeddedFormField control or modify and insert web parts in web part zones. Both of these components are placed into an area of the page called PlaceHolderMain. On the Home tab, in the Editing group, there is a command called Advanced Mode.

In Safe Mode, you are amending content that is not stored within the page but is stored in tables in the content databases. In Advanced Mode, you can modify content that is stored in other areas of the page. Therefore, if the page is a site definition page, SharePoint will take a copy of that file from the SharePoint server's file system (usually the subfolder in the SharePoint root directory), apply your amendments, and store the file in the content database. This process, known as customizing a page, was described earlier in this chapter in the "Site template pages" sidebar.

If you edit a site template page in Advanced Mode, modify content outside the EmbeddedFormField or web part zones, and then save the file, the Site Definition Page Warning dialog box is displayed, as shown in Figure 9-29.

Figure 9-29 The Site Definition Page Warning dialog box appears so you can confirm that you want to make changes to a site template page.

> **Note**
> You should not customize pages whenever possible. You can always create web parts or apps on new pages or on other sites and then add them to the default uncustomized pages using the browser. You should encourage your users to use SharePoint as an out-of-the-box application with the browser whenever possible. When you find it necessary to produce custom work, then you should be thorough in your web design, development, and testing. See the great SharePoint deployment section in the Microsoft SharePoint Team blog, "The New SharePoint," at *sharepoint.microsoft.com/ blog/Pages/BlogPost.aspx?pID=1012.*

In the Site Pages gallery, a blue circle surrounding a white *i* character is displayed to the left of the page. This indicates that the page is a site definition file that has been customized. To reset the page to the site definition file, right-click the file and click Reset To Site Definition, as shown in Figure 9-30.

Figure 9-30 Select Reset To Site Definition to reset a page to its Site Definition file.

When you reset a page to its site definition page, the contents of the page will be replaced with the original contents of the site definition file and a backup copy of the current page is created. However, remember that content in areas of the page (for example, in the Embed-dedFormField control and web part zones), are not stored on the page; therefore, when the page is reset to the site definition file, if the site definition file contains those areas of the page, then the content for those areas is still retrieved from the content database.

If a web part zone exists in a customized (unghosted) page but not in the site definition, on Reset To Site Definition, the web parts from that web part zone may have been moved into the bottom zone on the page.

Unfortunately, there is no ribbon command to switch the editing mode from Advanced to Safe Mode. If you have the page in Advanced Mode, you will need to close the page and then open it again to edit the page in Safe Mode.

Creating application pages for SharePoint sites

SharePoint provides some flexibility when developing pages for your SharePoint environment. One of the nice features about SharePoint is the ability to create application pages. An *application page* is a page that contains *_layouts* in its URL, such as the site settings page. Application pages are deployed once per SharePoint server and have the ability to be shared across all sites and site collections in the farm. They also have the ability to contain code that runs behind the page that is compiled into a single dynamic-link library (DLL), which improves performance.

Most of the typical pages are content pages. Content pages can be customized with an application like SharePoint Designer, whereas application pages cannot be customized. Also, application pages can include inline code and page markup, whereas content pages cannot because this could be manipulated by users with SharePoint Designer so that it does not work correctly or has malicious intent.

Therefore, if you want to create a page that will contain some heavy custom code and you want that capability across all sites, application pages are the way to go. Visual Studio 2012 provides out-of-the-box templates that allow developers to create an application page quickly in Visual Studio.

For more information on using Visual Studio to create SharePoint 2013 solutions, and how to set up your development environment, see Chapter 23, "Introduction to custom development."

Summary

This chapter explained the basics of webpages used by SharePoint Server 2013. The main types of webpages that can be created using the browser are publishing pages, wiki pages, and Web Part pages. Each publishing page, wiki page, or Web Part page contains unique content; each type is created from a template stored in a specific location on the SharePoint server file system, known as the *SharePoint root directory.*

The chapter then explained how to create and format these pages using SharePoint Designer, where you saw that you can modify the same content area as you can using the browser. But with SharePoint Designer, when you use Advanced Mode, you can edit content outside the main content area. However, this resulted in a customized page, which may cause performance problems. Finally, we described how to create application pages (that is, those pages with *_layouts* in their URL).

The next chapter will provide details on how to add, edit, connect, and maintain web parts on pages.

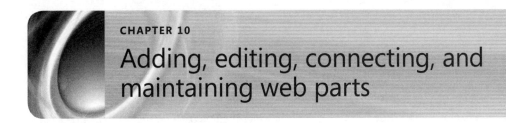

I N the previous chapter, you learned the ins and outs of creating and formatting webpages. Now that you have learned how to create and manage pages, it is time to learn about Microsoft SharePoint web parts. This chapter introduces you to the web parts in SharePoint 2013, details the deprecated web parts, and discusses the changes and improvements to existing web parts.

Web parts overview

What is a web part? If you are new to SharePoint, you have probably never heard the term *web parts*. However, even if you are new to web parts, you may be familiar with something called *widgets*. Widgets, in a way, are similar to web parts. A web part is an ASP.NET server control that can be added to a Web Part zone or Web Part pages by users at run time in SharePoint. The web parts run in the context of the page. SharePoint has out-of-the-box web parts, and developers can write custom web parts that can be deployed to on-premises and SharePoint online environments.

Web parts were first introduced in Windows SharePoint Services (WSS) 2.0 to allow users to add or remove content on a webpage. In WSS 2.0, web parts were used for displaying list content. Web parts enable users who have the appropriate permission to modify the content, appearance, and behavior of web parts directly on SharePoint pages. As mentioned in Chapter 9, "Creating and formatting content pages," web parts can be added to Web Part zones on a page or on Web Part pages. Modifications to web parts can be applied to individual users on the site or to all users on the site through personal and shared views.

All web parts share a common set of properties that control their appearance, layout, and advanced characteristics, which can be accessed from the Web Part Tool pane. The common web part properties available in the tool pane can vary depending on the type of web part, due to permissions and properties hidden by a developer. Table 10-1 details the common web part properties.

TABLE 10-1 Common web part property options

Section	Property	Description
Appearance	Title	Specifies the title of the web part that appears in the web part title bar.
	Height	Specifies the height of the web part.
	Width	Specifies the width of the web part.
	Chrome State	Specifies whether the entire web part appears on the page. By default, the chrome state is set to Normal and the entire web part appears. When the state is set to Minimized, only the title bar appears.
	Chrome Type	Specifies whether the title bar and border of the web part frame are displayed.
Layout	Hidden	Specifies whether the web part is visible. If the check box is selected, the web part is visible only when you are editing the page. You can hide a web part if you want to use it to provide data to another web part through a web part connection, but you don't want to display the web part on the page.
	Direction	Specifies the direction of the text in the web part content. For example, Arabic is a right-to-left language; English and most other European languages are left-to-right languages. This setting may not be available for all web parts.
	Zone	Specifies the zone on the Web Part page where the web part is located.
	Zone Index	Specifies the position of the web part in a zone when the zone contains more than one web part. To specify the order, type a positive integer in the text box. If the web parts in the zone are ordered from top to bottom, a value of 1 means the web part appears at the top of the zone. If the web parts in the zone are ordered from left to right, a value of 1 means that the web part appears on the left of the zone.
Advanced	Allow Minimize	Specifies whether the web part can be minimized.
	Allow Close	Specifies whether the web part can be removed from the Web Part page.
	Allow Hide	Specifies whether the web part can be hidden.

Section	Property	Description
	Allow Zone Change	Specifies whether the web part can be moved to a different zone.
	Allow Connections	Specifies whether the web part can connect to other web parts on the page.
	Allow Editing in Personal View	Specifies whether the web part properties can be modified in a personal view.
	Export Mode	Specifies the level of data that is permitted to be exported for this web part. Depending on your configuration, this setting may not be available.
	Title URL	Specifies the URL of a file containing additional information about the web part. The file is displayed in a separate browser window when the user clicks the web part title.
	Description	Specifies the ScreenTip that appears when the user rests the mouse pointer on the web part title or web part icon.
	Help URL	Specifies the location of a file containing Help information about the web part. The Help information is displayed in a separate browser window when the user clicks the Help command on the web part menu.
	Help Mode	Specifies how a browser will display Help content for a web part.
	Catalog Icon Image URL	Specifies the location of an image to be used as the web part icon in the Web Part list. Image size must be 16 x 16 pixels.
	Title Icon Image URL	Specifies the location of an image to be used in the web part title bar. Image size must be 16 x 16 pixels.
	Import Error Message	Specifies a message that appears if there is a problem importing the web part.

The new app model and app parts

If you have a smart phone, you are already familiar with apps and how to obtain them. iPhone, Android, and Windows phones all have marketplaces where you can buy, download, and install apps for your phone. Microsoft has taken a similar approach with SharePoint 2013. The company has introduced a new app model in SharePoint 2013 that essentially has reinvented how third-party software can plug into SharePoint.

The architecture of SharePoint apps includes the following:

- Self-contained, stand-alone applications of functionality. The back-end code for SharePoint apps can run outside of SharePoint (on other web servers, Windows Azure, and so on) and can be written using a number of web standards such as HTML, JavaScript, ASP.NET, and PHP. The connectivity and authentication back to SharePoint is handled by the SharePoint client-side object model (CSOM) and oAuth.

- Mounted on SharePoint pages via iFrames that point to a domain other than the SharePoint server's domain, which ensures complete client-side isolation between SharePoint and the nested app. The URL for the iFrame contains information the app uses on the back end to connect to SharePoint via the SharePoint CSOM.

- Can be published to the public SharePoint Store or hosted in a private store.

Developers can write custom apps using the SharePoint app model. Apps can be added by users who have the appropriate permissions so long as the web application is configured in Central Administration to support apps.

The link to the SharePoint Store is located in the left navigation of the Your Apps settings page, as shown in Figure 10-1. The SharePoint Store is shown in Figure 10-2.

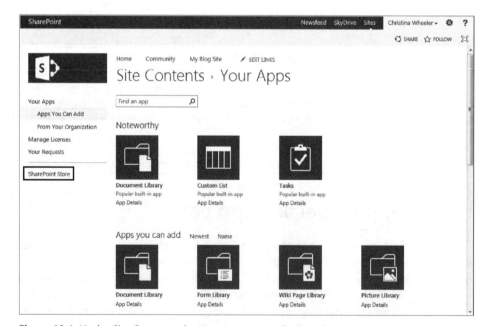

Figure 10-1 Under Site Contents, the Your Apps page displays the SharePoint Store link.

Figure 10-2 You can publish apps to the SharePoint Store.

More details on the app model are covered in Chapter 23, "Introduction to custom development."

When an app is not an app

When is an app not an app? In SharePoint 2010, lists and libraries had associated web parts. In SharePoint 2013, lists and libraries are associated with apps. This means when a new list or library is created, SharePoint automatically creates a corresponding app for the list or library. The Site Contents page for SharePoint 2013 displays a link to Add An App, the list of existing site content, and a subsites section at the bottom, which lists all existing subsites along with a New Subsites link.

Figure 10-3 displays the Site Contents page showing the Add An App link and some existing content of a site.

Figure 10-3 The Site Contents page displays the Add An App link and existing site content.

When users want to add new content to a site, they Add An App from the Your Apps page within Site Contents, as displayed in Figure 10-4.

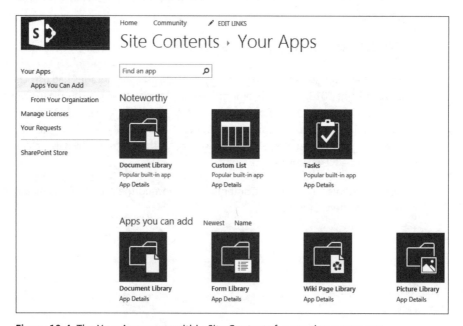

Figure 10-4 The Your Apps page within Site Contents for creating a new app.

Web parts in SharePoint 2013

Every time a new version of SharePoint is released, new web parts are introduced and changes to some of the existing web parts are made. In SharePoint 2013, Microsoft has provided some new and exciting web parts and has made great improvements to existing web parts. This section looks at the new and existing web parts in SharePoint 2013.

Blog web parts

In the past, SharePoint was not the best option for creating blog sites; therefore, companies often would integrate a third-party solution or site outside of SharePoint. When SharePoint 2010 was released, more organizations started using SharePoint for blog sites. SharePoint has three blog web parts available: the Blog Archives Web Part, the Blog Notifications Web Part, and the Blog Tools Web Part, each of which are detailed in Table 10-2. A blog site displaying the Blog Tools Web Part and the Archives Web Part is shown in Figure 10-5.

TABLE 10-2 Blog web parts in SharePoint 2013

Web part	Description
Blog Archives	Provides quick links to older blog posts.
Blog Notifications	Provides quick links to register for blog post notifications using alerts or Really Simple Syndication (RSS) feed.
Blog Tools	Provides blog owners and administrators with quick links to common settings pages and content lists for managing a blog site. Also, includes a drop-down menu to change the post layout to Basic, Boxed, or Inline.

Figure 10-5 A blog site displaying Blog Tools and Archives Web Parts.

Business data web parts

SharePoint 2013 includes five default business data web parts: the Business Data Actions Web Part, the Business Data Connectivity Filter Web Part, the Business Data Item Web Part, the Business Data Item Builder Web Part, the Business Data List Web Part, and the Business Data Related List Web Part. These web parts rely on the Business Connectivity Services (BCS). The full list of web parts available in SharePoint 2013 is displayed in Table 10-3.

TABLE 10-3 Business data web parts in SharePoint 2013

Web part	Description
Business Data Actions	Displays a list of actions from Business Data Connectivity. An action is something that can be performed on a single row of a business data item.
Business Data Connectivity Filter	Filters the contents of web parts using a list of values from Business Data Connectivity. This filter web parts adds a picker dialog box that enables the user to use a drop-down list to search for the specified entity.
Business Data Item	Displays one item from a data source in Business Data Connectivity.
Business Data Item Builder	Creates a Business Data item from parameters in the query string and provides it to other web parts.
Business Data List	Displays a list of items from a data source in Business Data Connectivity.
Business Data Related List	Displays a list of items related to one or more parent items from a data source in Business Data Connectivity.
Excel Web Access	Uses the Excel Web Access Web Part to interact with an Excel workbook as a webpage.
Indicator Details	Displays the details of a single Status Indicator. Status Indicators display an important measure for an organization and may be obtained from other data sources including SharePoint lists, Microsoft Excel workbooks, and Microsoft SQL Server 2005 Analysis Services key performance indicators (KPIs).
Status List	Shows a list of Status Indicators. Status Indicators display important measures for your organization, and show how your organization is performing with respect to your goals.
Visio Web Access	Enables the viewing and refreshing of Microsoft Visio Web Drawings. For more information, please see Chapter 17, "Working with Visio Services."

For more information on Excel Web Access, Indicator Details, and the Status List, see Chapter 15, "Implementing better business intelligence with Excel Services and SQL Server 2012."

Community web parts

Remember the discussion boards in previous versions of SharePoint? One of the biggest complaints with older versions of SharePoint was the lack of features in the discussion boards. Most companies would not use the built-in discussion boards and instead would turn to third-party offerings. Fortunately, discussion boards are greatly improved in SharePoint 2013.

Similar to the MSDN forums, SharePoint 2013 now has community sites and a feature that can be activated on a site that provides a forum experience unlike it was before. This interactive forum includes the ability of "likes," ratings, badges, and reputation scores. Table 10-4 lists the web parts that are a part of the community feature. A community site main page is shown in Figure 10-6. Figure 10-7 shows the members page.

TABLE 10-4 Community web parts in SharePoint 2013

Web part	Description
Tools	Provides community owners and administrators quick links to common settings pages and content lists for managing a community site.
Manage	Available for site owners and community moderators to manage discussions and categories, assign badges to members, and update reputation settings and community settings.
About This Community	Displays the community description and other properties such as date established.
Join	Provides the ability for nonmembers of a community site to join the community. The button hides itself if the user is already a member.
What's Happening	Available for visitors and members to display the number of members, discussions, and replies within the community.
Top Contributors	Available for visitors and members to display the members who contribute to the community the most.
My Membership	Displays reputation and membership information for the current visitor of a community site.

Figure 10-6 A discussion thread and a list of the top contributors appears on the main page of a community site.

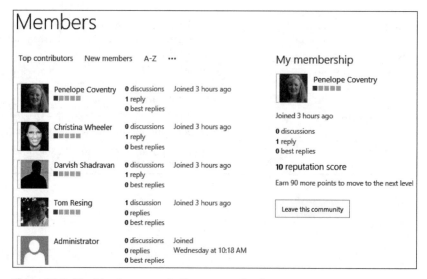

Figure 10-7 The Members page in the community site.

Content rollup web parts

When web content management (WCM) and the publishing feature were integrated into previous versions of SharePoint, content rollup web parts were introduced. Content rollup web parts are useful for displaying dynamic content on a SharePoint page. This section covers all the available content rollup web parts in SharePoint 2013.

Content Query Web Part

The Content Query Web Part (CQWP) is an out-of-the-box web part that was introduced in Microsoft Office SharePoint Server 2007. The core benefit of the CQWP is to aggregate content from all the subsites, lists, or libraries within a site collection so that content can be displayed in a single view. In the beginning, there was very minimal documentation on the CQWP; therefore, not many organizations used the web part because either they did not know about the web part or they did not know how to customize it. This web part is still a part of the publishing feature and becomes available when the publishing feature is activated.

Besides the need to aggregate content over multiple lists and libraries, there has been a need to display content from a single source across multiple subsites. For organizations that were not aware of the CQWP, it was common to see lists and libraries duplicated in various subsites to make the organization's content available in all locations. Of course, that approach easily became a maintenance nightmare and was easily solved by implementing the CQWP to query the single list or library and place the web part in the subsites that needed to display the content.

Even though the CQWP is an out-of-the-box web part, it does require some customization for the query. When using the CQWP the first options that need to be configured are the options in the Query section. Table 10-5 provides the details of the available query options.

TABLE 10-5 CQWP Query Options

Property	Description
Source	Select the source where you want to query the data from. Options include querying content from the entire the site collection, query from a specific site and all subsites, or query items from a specific list.
List Type	Select the list type you want to pull data from.
Content Type	Select the content type group and content type you want to query. When creating content it is recommended to use custom content types for content you intend to roll-up as it provides better filtering.

Property	Description
Audience Targeting	Select this option to use audience targeting. If the "Include items that are not targeted" option is selected then the items that do not have a target audience value will also display in the results.
Navigation Context	Setting that allows the ability to filter the content results by the page navigation term.
Additional Filters	Include any additional fields you want to filter on. The list of available fields change based on the content type selected for the querying.

INSIDE OUT   Can the Content Query Web Part query content across multiple site collections or is it limited to a single site collection?

Unfortunately, the CQWP is limited to querying items within a single site collection only. If you have a need to query across multiple site collections the Content Search Web Part can be used to accomplish this which is discussed later in this chapter. There is also a third-party web part I recommended for more advanced roll-ups called the Lightning Conductor Web Part from Lightening Tools. More information is available at *http://www.lightningtools.com.*

The Presentation section of the CQWP contains the properties to configure the grouping, sorting, and styling of the results. Table 10-6 displays the available options.

TABLE 10-6 CQWP Presentation Options

Property	Description
Grouping and Sorting	Settings for grouping and sorting. Select the drop-down list value for the field you want to group the items by. To group by site select the Site option in the Group items by drop-down list. Grouping is optional. The Sort items by option defaults to Created in descending order with the limit of displaying 15 items in the display. You can change the field to sort the items by and also change the limit on the items displayed.

Property	Description
Styles	The Group style is used for changing the styling of the grouped items. The value is set to Default and is not used unless the Group items by option is set. The Item style is used for the styling of the individual items that are returned in the results. These styles are XSL styles, not CSS styles. Please see Table 10-7 to learn more about the XSL style sheets.
Fields to display	Setting to specify what fields you want to map to the item styles. Type the name of the field you want to map to each available field slot. The fields available for mapping change based on the Item style that is selected in the Item style setting.
Feed	Setting to indicate whether or not a RSS feed will be generated for the results of the query.
Additional Filters	Include any additional fields you want to filter on. The list of available fields change based on the content type selected for the querying.

The CQWP use XSLT to render its content. The three XSL files used to render the fields in the styles are the same files used in SharePoint 2010. These files can be modified in Microsoft SharePoint Designer to include additional templates to use in the CQWP. The three XSL files used by the CQWP are described in Table 10-7.

TABLE 10-7 CQWP XSL files used for rendering

File	Location	Description
ContentQueryMain.xsl	\Style Library\XSL Style Sheets\ContentQueryMain.xsl	Contains logic that receives all the content, parses it, and sends the appropriate calls to the Header and Item templates for each item.
ItemStyle.xsl	\Style Library\XSL Style Sheets\ItemStyle.xsl	Contains style definitions that apply to row items. One row of data is processed at a time to ensure that the style and data in the item rows are consistent.
Header.xsl	\Style Library\XSL Style Sheets\Header.xsl	Contains Group style definitions that define how to display a header.

For more details on the XSL templates, go to the MSDN article, "How to: Customize XSL for the SharePoint Content by Query Web Part (ECM)," located at *http://msdn.microsoft.com/ en-us/library/bb447557.aspx.*

INSIDE OUT

Why is the CQWP called an out-of-the-box web part if modifications are made to the XSLT?

There have been debates online within the SharePoint community on what "out-of-the-box" (OOTB) means. In SharePoint terms, *OOTB* refers to the functionality of what the platform can provide using all of its built-in tools and features when it is installed without writing custom code. One of the challenges some developers have is not understanding the difference between customizations for web parts OOTB versus custom code. There are also people who see XSLT as custom coding and think if you make changes to the XSLT for a built-in SharePoint web part, then the web part is not OOTB. This is false. Making changes to the XSLT without writing custom code in Microsoft Visual Studio is only considered customizing, not coding.

Now if you were to subclass the CQWP in Visual Studio to extend the features and override the methods, then that would be considered a custom web part, not the OOTB CQWP. Andrew Connell has an older blog post about creating a subclass for the CQWP that is still helpful in showing an example, even though the post was written for SharePoint Server 2007.

To read Andrew Connell's post, go to "Subclassing the Content Query Web Part: Adding Dynamic Filtering," located at *www.andrewconnell.com/blog/archive/2008/02/18/Subclassing-the-Content-Query-Web-Part-Adding-Dynamic-Filtering.aspx*.

Even though the CQWP was a powerful web part in SharePoint Server 2007, there were still some improvements that needed to be made. When SharePoint 2010 was released, Microsoft improved the CQWP, which made it even more powerful.

The improvements made to the CQWP in SharePoint 2010 included:

- **Fields to display**

    - *Slots* A slot is a marker in the Item Style template that is filled with the content at run time. The mappings between the slots and the fields to display can be set in the property pane of the CQWP, which is shown in Figure 10-8.

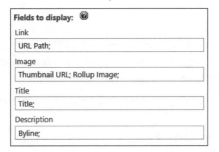

Figure 10-8 The CQWP Fields To Display property pane.

- **Dynamic filtering**

  - *PageFieldValue* A token that allows users to specify fields on a page layout and dynamically replaces the value of the filter with the current page's field value to filter query results.

  - *PageQueryStringValue* A token that allows users to specify query string parameters to filter query results, as shown in Figure 10-9.

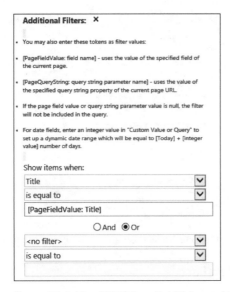

Figure 10-9 The CQWP PageFieldValue and PageQueryString filters.

For more details, go to the MSDN ECM Team Blog, "What's New with the Content Query Web Part," located at *http://blogs.msdn.com/b/ecm/archive/2010/05/14/what-s-new-with-the-content-query-web-part.aspx*.

> **Note**
>
> The recommended best practice for modifying the XSL templates for the CQWP is to create your own custom XSL files (instead of overwriting the existing XSL files) and link them to your CQWP. Remove sentence. Adding new section.

Another new feature in the CQWP is the ability to filter the content results by the page navigation term. This means that you can create your site navigation within the Term Store and use it within your sites. Figure 10-10 displays the property added to the CQWP Edit mode panel, and Figure 10-11 shows the Managed Metadata Term Store, displaying the settings for Site Navigation and Intended Use properties.

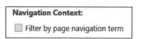

Figure 10-10 The Filter By Page Navigation Term property is added to the CQWP Edit mode panel.

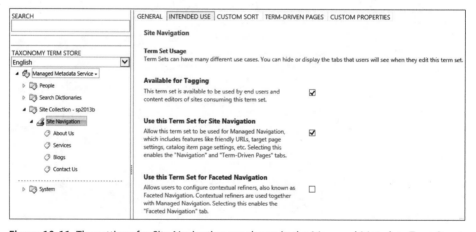

Figure 10-11 The settings for Site Navigation are shown in the Managed Metadata Term Store.

Content Search Web Part

The most used rollup web part has been the Content Query Web Part (CQWP). In SharePoint 2013, Microsoft has introduced a powerful and versatile web part called the Content Search Web Part (CSWP). This new Content Search Web Part is similar to the CQWP; however, it displays items that are results of a search query that you specify. When you add the part to the page, it will show recently modified items from the current site; however, you can change this setting to show items from another site or list by editing the web part and changing its search criteria. When new content is discovered by search, the CSWP will display an updated list of items each time the page is viewed.

One of the limitations of the out-of-the-box CQWP is that it is only able to query content within a single site collection. CSWP, however, can be a more powerful search tool when a feature called cross-site publishing is used. *Cross-site publishing* allows content to be displayed and maintained in one or more authoring site collections and in one or more publishing site collections. When the publishing feature is activated, lists and libraries can be enabled as *catalogs*, which allows the content to be reused in other site collections. The content can be displayed in a publishing site collection when the content of the list or library catalogs has been crawled and added to the search index.

For more details, go to the Microsoft TechNet article, "What's new in web content management for SharePoint 2013 Preview publishing sites," located at *http://technet.microsoft.com/ en-us/library/jj219688(v=office.15)#BKMK_Catalog_enabled.*

Choosing which web part is best to use, CQWP or CSWP, depends on your requirements. Table 10-8 lists the differences between these two web parts.

TABLE 10-8 Differences between the CQWP and the CSWP

	CQWP	CSWP
Content returned	Returns any content from several scopes (site collection, site, or list) based on the selected content type and filters to display results.	Returns any content from the search index.
Accuracy	Instant content.	Returns content as fresh as the latest crawl.
Versions display	Major and minor versions are displayed.	Because search crawls only major versions, only major versions are displayed in the results.
Results availability	Displays content regardless of whether the site is marked to not be indexed.	Does not display content from sites marked to not be indexed.

For more information on the Content Search Web Part, see Chapter 12, "Designing web content management sites."

Project Summary and Timeline Web Parts

The Project Summary Web Part provides a high-level view of events and tasks involved in a project and is included by default on the home page of Project sites. This web part can also be added to any other site that includes a task list. The Project Summary Web Part displays information about a project in an easy-to-read overview, as shown in Figures 10-12 and 10-13.

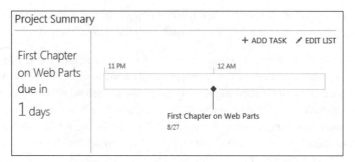

Figure 10-12 The default view of the Project Summary Web Part provides an easy-to-read overview of a project.

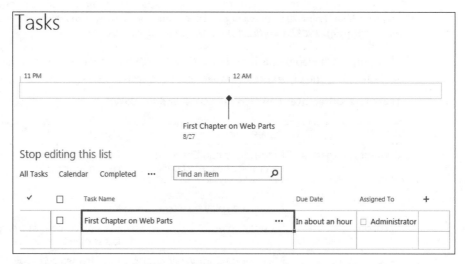

Figure 10-13 A new task is added in the Edit Task screen in the Project Summary Web Part.

The Timeline Web Part, which is included in the Project Summary Web Part, was added in SharePoint 2013 to provide new functionality taken from Microsoft Project Server to display a timeline of tasks. The Timeline Web Part also allows users to display or remove tasks or subtasks from the timeline. Figure 10-14 displays what the web part looks like when it's first added to a page. Figure 10-15 shows the property options that can be set.

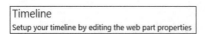

Figure 10-14 The Timeline Web Part is added to a SharePoint page.

Figure 10-15 The Timeline Web Part properties settings.

Relevant Documents Web Part

The Relevant Documents Web Part is an out-of-the-box web part used for document management to help create a personalized view of the documents you (as the current logged-on user) are working on (see Figure 10-16).

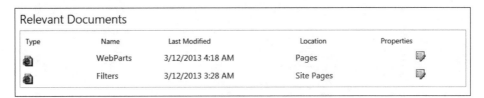

Figure 10-16 The Relevant Documents Web Part enables a user to see the current documents he or she is working on.

The Relevant Documents Web Part allows you to do the following:

- Display documents that were last modified by the current user.

- Display documents that were created by the current user.

- Display documents that are checked out to the current user.

- Display a link to the folder or list containing a particular document.

RSS Viewer Web Part

The RSS Viewer Web Part can be used to display RSS feeds in your SharePoint site. The web part can subscribe to RSS feeds from SharePoint lists and libraries or from another website.

Once the RSS Viewer Web Part is added to a page, you can set the following properties:

- **RSS feed URL** Input the URL to SharePoint list or library or to an external website.

- **Feed refresh time (in minutes)** The amount of time that you want the feed to refresh. The default is set to 120 sections.

- **Feed Limit** The limit on how many items you want to display from the feed. The default setting is 5.

- **Show feed title and description** A check box option disabled by default, to hide and show the feed title and description.

- **Data view properties** Located in the Data View Properties section, the XSL Editor can be used to modify the transformation of data, as shown in Figure 10-17.

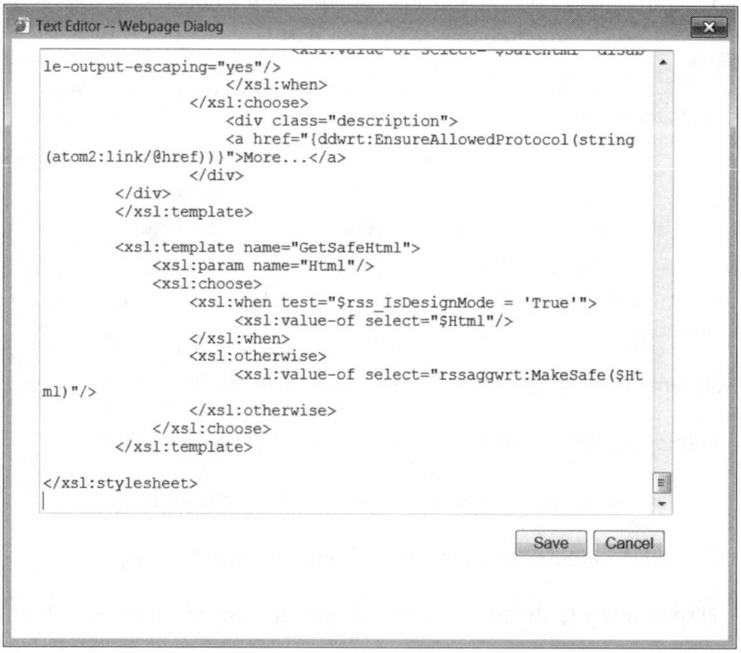

Figure 10-17 The XSL Editor can be accessed by clicking the XSL Editor link in the Data View Properties section of the RSS Viewer Web Part Tool pane.

WSRP Viewer Web Part

The WSRP Viewer Web Part displays portlets from websites using WSRP 1.1. Web Services for Report Portals (WSRP) is an OASIS network protocol standard designed for communications with remote portlets. The WSRP Viewer was in MOSS 2007 and is not a common web part used by organizations.

For more information, see the MSDN article, "Interoperability Scenarios and Technologies for SharePoint Server 2007," located at *http://msdn.microsoft.com/en-us/library/ ee230448(v=office.12).aspx.*

XML Viewer Web Part

The XML Viewer Web Part can be used to display structured data and XML-based documents and forms and display it in SharePoint. This web part can be used to display structured data from database tables or queries, XML-based documents, and XML forms that combine structured and unstructured data.

Content can be added to the XML Viewer Web Part in the following two ways:

- **XML and XSL editors** The XML and XSL source editors, located on the Web Part Tool pane, are plain-text editors that are intended for users who have knowledge of XML and XSLT syntax.

- **XML and XSL links** Instead of editing the XML and XSLT, you can enter a hyperlink to a text file that contains the XML and XSLT source code. The two valid hyperlink protocols that can be used are http:// and https://. An absolute URL or a relative URL can be used; however, you cannot use a file path.

The XML Viewer Web Part is often used for displaying a Twitter feed, as shown in Figure 10-18.

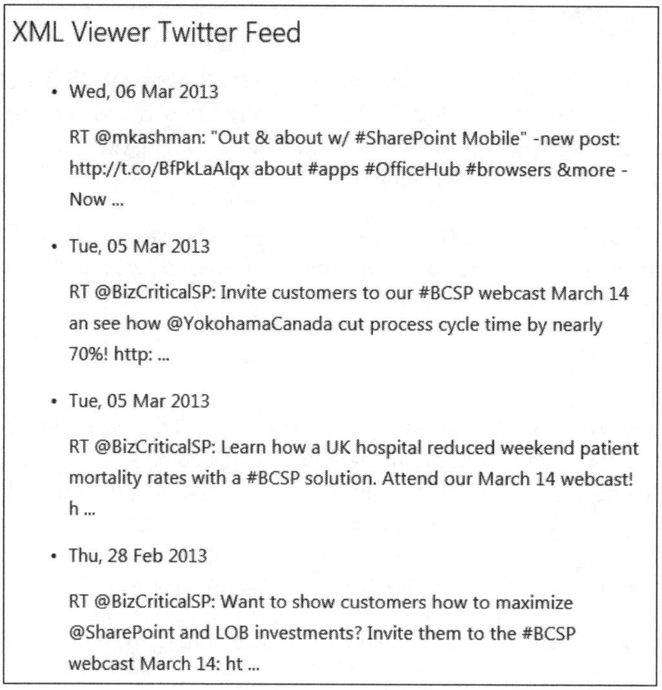

XML Viewer Twitter Feed

- Wed, 06 Mar 2013

  RT @mkashman: "Out & about w/ #SharePoint Mobile" -new post:
  http://t.co/BfPkLaAlqx about #apps #OfficeHub #browsers &more -
  Now ...

- Tue, 05 Mar 2013

  RT @BizCriticalSP: Invite customers to our #BCSP webcast March 14
  an see how @YokohamaCanada cut process cycle time by nearly
  70%! http: ...

- Tue, 05 Mar 2013

  RT @BizCriticalSP: Learn how a UK hospital reduced weekend patient
  mortality rates with a #BCSP solution. Attend our March 14 webcast!
  h ...

- Thu, 28 Feb 2013

  RT @BizCriticalSP: Want to show customers how to maximize
  @SharePoint and LOB investments? Invite them to the #BCSP
  webcast March 14: ht ...

Figure 10-18 XML Viewer Web Part configured to pull the SharePoint Twitter feed.

Filter web parts

Filter web parts, which are a part of SharePoint Server 2013, connect to web parts that contain one or more sets of data and filter that data based on user input. Some of the filter web parts filter data automatically, and others enable people viewing a page to enter values or select values from a list. The types of filter web parts you may want to use depends on the data source, type of interaction you want from a user for the data source, and the desired results that you want displayed for the data source. Table 10-9 displays the filter web parts available in SharePoint 2013, grouped by the type of filter.

TABLE 10-9 Filter web parts available in SharePoint 2013

Web part	Description
ALLOWS USERS TO SPECIFY VALUES MANUALLY	
Date Filter	Filter contents by allowing users to enter or pick a date.
Query String (URL) Filter	Filters using values passed via the query string.
Text Filter	Filters by allowing users to enter a text value.

Web part	Description
ALLOW USERS TO PICK FROM A LIST OF VALUES	
Choice Filter	Filters using a list of values entered by the page author.
Business Data Connectivity Filter	Filters using a list of values from the Business Data Connectivity.
SharePoint List Filter	Filters using a list of values.
SQL Server Analysis Services Filter	Filters using a list of values from SQL Server Analysis Services cubes.
FILTER THE WEB PART PAGE AUTOMATICALLY	
Current User Filter	Filters using properties of the current user.
Query String (URL) Filter	Filters using values passed via the query string.
Page Field Filter	Filters using information about the current page.

> **Note**
> The Apply Filters button can be added to a page to let users decide when to apply their filter choices; otherwise, each filter is applied when its value is changed.

Forms web parts

SharePoint includes two types of web parts for forms: the HTML Form Web Part and the InfoPath Form Web Part. This section provides the details of these two web parts.

HTML Form Web Part

The HTML Form Web Part can be used to connect to and pass data to other web parts. This web part uses a standard text box and a Go button that can be used as is or customized. For example, you can use the default HTML Form Web Part to pass the value, such as region, to a List View Web Part to filter the data by that region. You can customize the HTML Form Web Part by using the Source Editor located on the tool pane. The elements that you can use are the standard text box, options buttons, check boxes, multiline text boxes, and list boxes. You can also add labels and assign default values to the controls.

When you add the HTML Form Web Part to a page, you get the default standard text box and Go button, as shown in Figure 10-19.

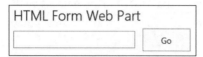

Figure 10-19 The HTML Form Web Part.

Figure 10-20 displays the Source Editor dialog box containing the default source for the text box and Go button.

Figure 10-20 This HTML Form Web Part Source Editor dialog box contains the default code for the text box and Go button.

The following must be considered when customizing the HTML Form Web Part:

- Only one Go button can be used to pass data to another web part.

- The HTML Form Web Part uses the FORM element, and certain HTML elements cannot be used inside the FORM element. This includes HTML, BODY, and FORM elements.

- All form field names must be unique. Each form field name value is used to connect to a corresponding column name in the web part you are connecting to.

- You can have more than one element (text box, option buttons, and so on) on your form; however, only one field can be connected to a web part. However, different fields from the same form can be connected to different web parts on the page.

- Two or more fields can be connected to another web part if the web part can accept multiple parameters.

- The HTML Form Web Part only provides data to another connectable web part and cannot get data from another connectable web part.

To use the HTML Form Web Part, you must have the list you want to filter—with the column you want to filter on—visible on the same page as the HTML Form Web Part.

Follow these steps to connect an HTML Form Web Part to another web part:

1. Browse to the page that contains the web part that you want to filter or go to the location where you want to create a new page.

2. From the Settings menu, click Edit Page or Add A Page.

   If the Edit command is disabled, then you may not have the appropriate permissions to edit the page and need to contact your administrator to get the appropriate rights.

3. Locate the HTML Form Web Part on the page or add the HTML Form Web Part to the page.

   To add the HTML Form Web Part to your page, select the Insert tab, and then click Web Part. Select Forms in the Categories list. Select HTML Form Web Part, and then click Add.

4. From the HTML Form Web Part, click the down arrow, and then select Connections | Provide Form Value To.

5. Select the name of the web part you want to connect to.

   Only the web parts that allow connections will show up in the list.

6. From the Choose Connection dialog box, select the Choose Connection tab (selected by default).

7. Make sure that the Connection Type drop-down has Get Filter Values From selected, and then click Configure, as shown here.

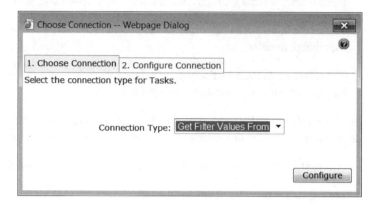

8. Select the field you want to use to filter for the HTML Form Web Part.

Because the values sent from the HTML Form Web Part are text values, the fields do not have to have the same names, nor do they have to be the same data type.

9. Click Finish, then click Exit Edit mode or Save/Check In/Publish if you are using a publishing page.

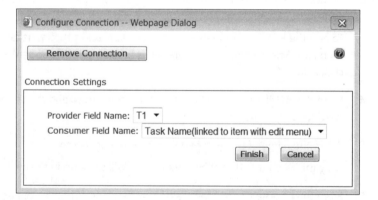

10. Test your HTML Form Web Part to see if the connected web part updates with the filtered data by searching a value on the field and then click Go.

InfoPath Form Web Part

The InfoPath Form Web Part can be used to display a Microsoft InfoPath browser-enabled form that is published to a form or document library. You can also display a browser form that has been associated with a SharePoint list form that has been customized using InfoPath 2013. Once you add an InfoPath Form Web Part to a page, you can connect the web part to other web parts on the page or send or receive data from the web part. The InfoPath Form Web Part is linked to the employees list default InfoPath form modified using InfoPath 2013.

Follow these steps to connect an InfoPath Form Web Part to another web part:

1. Browse to the page that contains the web part that you want to filter or go to the location where you want to create a new page.

2. From the Settings menu, click Edit Page or Add A Page.

3. Locate the InfoPath Form Web Part on the page or add the InfoPath Form Web Part to the page, as shown in the following graphic.

   To add the InfoPath Form Web Part to your page, select the Insert tab, and then click Web Part. Select Forms in the Categories list. Select InfoPath Form Web Part, and then click Add.

   ### InfoPath Form Web Part

   Select a Form

    To display an InfoPath form, open the tool pane and specify the location of the form.

   Click here to open the tool pane

   ---

4. From the InfoPath Form Web Part, click the down arrow and select Edit Web Part.

5. Set the desired properties, as detailed in Table 10-10.

   TABLE 10-10 InfoPath Form Web Part properties

Property	Description
List or Library	Specify the list or library that contains the published InfoPath form.
Content type	Specify the content type of the form. This is required if more than one InfoPath form has been published as a content type or added as a library template. If no selection is made, a default content type is selected.

Property	Description
Display a read-only form (lists only)	Option to prevent or allow data entry in list form.
Show InfoPath Ribbon or toolbar	Option to display or hide the InfoPath ribbon or toolbar. If cleared, make sure that the user can use the InfoPath form by adding a Submit button to the form.
Send data to connected web parts when page loads	Option to send or not send the first row of data to one or more connected web parts when the page first displays and to show or hide any default values.
Select the form view to display by default	If the form has two or more views defined, select the view to display from the drop-down list.
Select the action to perform after a form has been submitted	Select one of the following options: **Close The Form** Closes the form and displays the following message: "The form has been closed." **Open A New Form** Opens a new blank form. **Leave The Form Open** Keeps the form open.

6. Once the web part is configured, click the menu of the InfoPath Web Part and select Connections.

7. Select one of the following commands:

   a. **Send Data To**   Displays a list of web parts on the page that can receive form data. The InfoPath Form Web Part can be a library form that has output parameters defined or a list form.

   b. **Get Form Data**   Displays a List View Web Part based on a list or library. Users can select forms from the List View Web Part to display a specific form in the InfoPath Form Web Part.

   c. **Get Data From**   Displays another web part that sends one or more fields of data to the InfoPath Form Web Part, which must have input parameters defined and can be a library form or a list form.

Media and content web parts

The media and content web parts in SharePoint 2013 include some existing and new web parts. This section covers both the new and existing web parts.

Content Editor Web Part

The Content Editor Web Part (CEWP) is intended for adding HTML content to a SharePoint page. This web part was included in previous versions of SharePoint; however, many organizations overused this web part and did not understand when they should and should not use it for their site. Before we talk about the recommendations on when to use it, let's first discuss *how* to use it. The CEWP can be added to a page and then modified to contain the desired content.

Content can be added to the CEWP in the following three ways:

- **Rich text editor** When the CEWP is added to a page, the user can click the Click Here To Add New Content link inside the web part to enable the rich text editor. The FORMAT TEXT tab becomes active on the ribbon so that the text can be formatted.

- **HTML source editor** Another option is to use the source editor, which can be accessed from the Edit Source ribbon button located in the Markup section of the FORMAT TEXT tab. Clicking this button will open the HTML Source dialog box, which is a plain-text control.

- **Content link** Instead of editing content directly in the web part, you can link to existing content by entering a hyperlink to the text file containing the HTML source code. This setting is located in the Content Editor Tool pane. It is recommended to use this option when you want to reuse HTML content throughout the site. This is a common approach for linking to HTML source code that contains jQuery scripting.

The CEWP ended up getting a bad name because of how many people misused the web part in the past. Some organizations used the CEWP to contain all their content in their site instead of using actual content pages. This is not recommended because the CEWP is not actual SharePoint content, which means there is no metadata. However, it is recommended to use the CEWP when doing such things as CSS spot treatments, loading jQuery, and adding items to the site that aren't specific content. A common example is using the CEWP to add some CSS to hide the Quick Launch menu. By adding the inline style to the CEWP, the user can hide the Quick Launch menu for a particular page instead of affecting the rest of the site.

Getting Started With Your Site Web Part

The Getting Started With Your Site Web Part displays a set of tiles with common SharePoint actions. Figure 10-21 shows how this web part looks when it is added to a page.

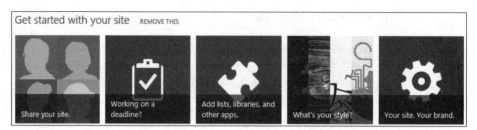

Figure 10-21 The Getting Started With Your Site Web Part as it appears on a page.

> **Note**
>
> This Getting Started With Your Site Web Part does not have any customization options except for the standard web part properties.

Image Viewer Web Part

The Image Viewer Web Part is used to display a specified image on a page. This web part can be configured to control the alternate text, vertical/horizontal alignment, and the web part background color.

An image can be displayed in the Image Viewer Web Part in two ways:

- URL to the image file

- Connect the Image Viewer Web Part to another web part.

  For example, you can connect a List View Web Part (which contains contacts) to an Image Viewer Web Part. Each time a row is selected in the List View Web Part (that contains a column with a hyperlink to a file that contains a picture of the contact), the picture of the contact will display in the Image Viewer Web Part.

Page Viewer Web Part

The Page Viewer Web Part is used to display a webpage, file, or folder that is presented in an iFrame. The linked content of the Page Viewer Web Part is isolated, which ensures that any of the HTML elements displayed as content in the web part through the iFrame do not conflict with other HTML elements on the page. The web part displays the content asynchronously, which means the users can view the page and use the other web parts even if the content in the Page Viewer Web Part takes a long time to load.

Picture Library Slideshow Web Part

The Picture Library Slideshow Web Part is used to display a slideshow of images and photos from a picture library. The pictures can be displayed in sequential or random order and transitioned based on the duration setting. The Title and Description can also be displayed and configured based on a Display With Drop-Down List setting.

Embed code and media and the Script Editor Web Parts

A new embedding feature was added to the SharePoint 2013 ribbon that allows the embedding of media or scripts. The Video and Audio menu section labeled "Embed" allows users to paste iFrame code for embedding YouTube videos and other video and audio media. The Embed Code button allows users to paste HTML and JavaScript code. No matter which button will be used for embedding, a modal dialog box opens containing an input to paste the script or embedded code. A preview of the content will display below the input box, and once submitted, the source is added to the rich text editor called "Snippet." The Script Editor Web Part works the same way; however, it is a web part, so it can be exported and reused.

Because allowing every iFrame to be added to a page can lead to potential scripting security problems, there is an option to change the security settings for what you want to allow. Allowed sources can be configured under the site collection administration setting called HTML Field Security. This setting offers the following configuration options:

- Do not permit contributors to insert iFrames from external domains into pages on this site.

- Permit contributors to insert iFrames from any external domain into pages on this site.

- Permit contributors to insert iFrames from the following list of external domains into pages on this site (Figure 10-22).

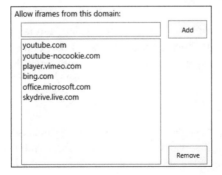

Figure 10-22 Add allowed domains for the iFrames in the Script Editor Web Part dialog box.

Social collaboration web parts

The social collaboration features in SharePoint 2013 offer an improved administration and user experience. The Newsfeed page in My Site continues to provide an aggregated view of activities; however, the feed is improved, with new microblogging functionality. The Newsfeed, previously referred to as the "activity feed" in SharePoint 2010, offers a Facebook-style activity feed that enables users to post messages, "like" posts, and follow contacts or documents. Users also have the ability to receive email alerts when there is new activity on a subject the user has subscribed to. The Site Feed Web Part is the web part associated with the Newsfeed feature that can be added to any site.

A new memory cache called the Distributed Cache has been implemented in SharePoint 2013 to maintain the Newsfeed. This new memory cache uses AppFabric for Windows Server, which better supports the read and write operations generated by users' activities and participation in microblogging.

Deprecated web parts

Every time a new version of SharePoint is released, there are always at least a few web parts that end up either being deprecated or completely removed.

The following web parts have been deprecated in SharePoint 2013:

- Recent Activities Web Part

- Chart Web Part

- Status Indicator and Status List Web Parts

- Web Analytics Web Part

Recent Activities Web Part

The Recent Activities Web Part, which is a part of the My Site features, has been replaced with the new Site Feed Web Part. The Site Feed Web Part is part of the Newsfeed feature that supports multithreaded conversations and dynamic feed retrieval.

Chart Web Part

The Chart Web Part is no longer available; however, similar features can be exposed from service applications such as Excel Services. If you used the Chart Web Part in SharePoint 2010 and migrate to SharePoint 2013, you will still be able to use the existing Chart web parts.

Status Indicators and Status List Web Parts

Status Indicators and Status Lists are no longer available in SharePoint 2013. If you used them in SharePoint 2010 and migrate to SharePoint 2013, then you can still continue to use the existing Chart Web Parts. If you did not use Status Indicators and Status Lists, you can use other functionality such as Excel Services to create KPIs.

KPIs are a part of the business intelligence features and are covered more in Chapter 15 and Chapter 16, "Building powerful dashboards with PerformancePoint Services."

Web Analytics

The Web Analytics service has been discontinued in SharePoint 2013, as Web Analytics processing is now a component of the Search service. The new analytics infrastructure encompasses SharePoint, and the Analytics Processing Component runs analytics jobs to analyze content in the search index and on user actions performed on SharePoint sites.

When upgrading to SharePoint 2013 from SharePoint 2010, the Web Analytics service is not upgraded to the Analytics Processing Component, and the databases containing the Web Analytics from SharePoint 2010 are not removed. However, the databases are not used or maintained by the Analytics Processing Component. Therefore, documents on sites upgraded from SharePoint 2010 will show a hit count of 0.

Reports from Web Analytics that get carried over are the top items in a site; however, reports that show referring URL, browser traffic, and top users of a site are not carried forward and used by the Analytics Processing Component in SharePoint 2013. Because SharePoint 2013 does not support the Web Analytics Web Part, all pages in the upgraded site that contain this web part will render, and a message will display informing the user that the web part is no longer supported.

INSIDE OUT   Upgrade recommendation

The recommendation for upgrading from SharePoint 2010 is to turn off Web Analytics in SharePoint 2010 before copying the content databases that you want to upgrade to SharePoint 2013. Do not attach and upgrade the databases containing the Web Analytics data.

Summary

This chapter provided a high-level overview of web parts and the new app model in SharePoint 2013, as well as the different types of web parts available for use. This includes the blog web parts, community web parts, content rollup web parts, form web parts, media and content web parts, and many others. There are so many ways to use the various out-of-the-box web parts to create an eye-pleasing, content-rich, dynamic site.

Managing documents

COMPANIES used to share important information with staff by creating copies and placing them on the employees' desks. This worked so long as there were no mistakes. If a mistake was found, then another round of copies would have to go out. Then, rich email systems allowed for digital copies to be sent to employees. While the document would have to be re-sent if there were mistakes, it would take only a few seconds instead of hand-delivering each copy. However, sending a large file throughout a large organization could have a negative impact on the email system's storage capacity. As an example, assume a 10-MB file was sent to all 100,000 employees in the company. Each time this file was sent, if there were revisions, it would require 1 GB of storage.

Microsoft SharePoint Server 2013 offers a far more efficient solution to this common occurrence: Save the document in a document library and send the link to the document! Even if multiple versions must be created because of mistakes, they are only created on the single document in SharePoint. In addition, the link will still be valid after all of those revisions, thus eliminating multiple emails needing to be sent about said revisions. SharePoint Server 2013 introduces Shredded Storage, which means that files will be broken into smaller parts in the database. If certain parts don't change, then those parts will not have new versions created.

This example is just one of the many benefits an organization can realize when using SharePoint for document management. Document management has been a core feature of the platform since its inception. Document management in SharePoint is not just about storing files in a virtual file system, though. For the purpose of this chapter, the terms *document* and *file* are synonymous. There are different types of storage locations, including the Document Library. There are additional ways to categorize and group documents, such as document sets and content types. SharePoint Server 2013 also grants the ability to associate additional information about the document through use of the Managed Metadata Service. This gives the user the option to "tag" the document with descriptive keywords, such as "Employee Insurance Form" or "Annual Shareholder Report." All of these features of the SharePoint Document Management capability provide the organization the ability to build a reusable information architecture that can show relationships between items across the various repositories in the farm. These relationships also lead to an increase in the findability of the documents.

Document management locations

There are several locations for document storage and management in SharePoint. There are three major site templates available for document management: Team Site, Document Center, and Records Center. Each of these is designed with different types of storage in mind. At the heart of these site templates is the document library. A *document library* is a collection of files and folders where files are primarily stored in SharePoint.

Team Site

In many organizations, the Team Site is the site definition for a large quantity of sites in the farm. A Team Site is used for collaborative purposes between members of the site. In terms of document management, a Team Site might be created for a project when several files are being modified as part of the project deliverables. Document coauthoring (allowing more than one user to edit the document) may be used in the Team Site document libraries to allow different users to update their sections within these documents without locking other team members out of the document.

INSIDE OUT   Requirements of coauthoring

Coauthoring has a detailed list of requirements. First, only Microsoft Word 2010 and 2013, Microsoft PowerPoint 2010 and 2013, Microsoft OneNote 2010 and 2013, Microsoft Visio 2010 and 2013, and Microsoft Excel 2010 and 2013 files can be coauthored. Second, it is allowed in both the web app and the client app of the product, except Excel files. Excel files can only be coauthored in the Excel Web app.

Coauthoring requires versioning to be enabled and file checkout to be disabled. Draft versions will be automatically created at specific intervals to ensure that changes are not lost. Checkout must be disabled because that allows only one person to edit the file at a time.

Users will be notified of changes in the application of changes. They may choose to load the changes into their session or ignore it. Either way, their changes will still exist.

Document Center

A Document Center site is intended for large-scale storage. Document editing will not be as heavy as in a Team Site because documents should be here for archiving, knowledge base, or other, read-only reasons. Because they contain large quantities of files, Document Centers come with web parts configured for searching and navigating these files.

Creating a Document Center is the same as creating other sites, such as Team Sites, as outlined in Chapter 4, "Working with collaboration sites." While Document Centers can be created as child sites, that may not be the most optimal solution because of the potentially large storage footprint involved in storing that many files. Also, your information architecture may dictate different security requirements for Document Centers (particularly ones for archival purposes) than other sites in the site collection. By creating a Document Center in a new site collection, the security requirements can be more easily met and the site collection can be moved to its own content database so that the storage can be managed independently of the other data in the original site collection.

When it is time to move documents to a Document Center, say from a team site library, there are a few ways to do it. First, a workflow on a document could move it once a certain step is reached in the process. Second, a developer could create a custom solution to move the file. This may be used instead of a workflow if there is not a business process centered on the document, but it still needs to be moved at a certain time or when certain criteria are met. Third, it can be done manually by configuring the Send To action for the web application.

For more information about workflows, see Chapter 7, "Using and creating workflows," and for more information about custom development, see Chapter 23, "Introduction to custom development."

To configure the Send To action, follow these steps:

1. Open the Document Center, click the Settings icon, and select Site Settings.

2. Select Manage Site Features under Site Actions. Ensure that the Content Organizer feature is Activated.

3. Under Site Settings, select Content Organizer Settings under Site Administration.

4. Copy the web service URL under Submission Points.

5. Open Central Administration, and under General Application Settings, select Configure Send To Connections.

6. Configure the settings as follows:

- **Web Application** Select the Web Application where you want the Sent To option to be available. In the example shown here, the Contoso website is the selected Web Application.

- **Tenant Settings** By selecting this, the connections will be available to other tenants' services, as shown here.

- **Send To Connections** Select New Connection. If there are other options, they have already been created and can be edited. The following graphic shows only the New Connection option.

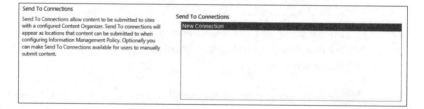

7. Connection Settings:

- **Display Name** Provide a descriptive name, as this is what will be seen in the Send To menu in the library.

- **Send To URL** Paste the web service URL from step 4.

8. Select Allow Manual Submission from the Send To menu if you want users to be able to send the document to the Document Center.

9. Send To actions:

- **Copy** This will create a copy of the document in the Document Center.

- **Move** The file will be deleted from the current library and created in the Document Center.

- **Move And Leave A Link** This will move the file, but a link will be left in the current library that will send users to the Document Center.

- **Explanation** Provide some text that will explain how the document was moved. This will show in the audit logs and will show on the redirection page.

10. Click Add Connection once you have completed the settings, as shown next.

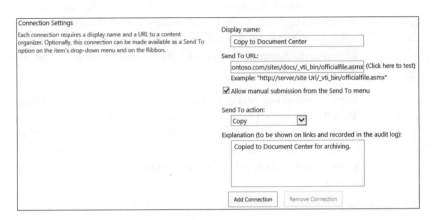

11. You may repeat steps 6-10 for additional connections. Click OK when finished.

12. In your document library, select a document.

13. On the File ribbon, under the Copies section, click Send To.

You will see the options that you created in steps 6-10. All three possible actions are shown next.

Records Center

The Records Center is also a large-scale storage location for data retention. These sites are used to store documents long-term because of legal compliance or some other necessity. Records moved here will keep associated metadata and audits. Record Centers are not meant to be used for any type of document editing, as litigation would require the document to appear as it was when it was moved to the Records Center.

For more information about Records Centers, see Chapter 13, "Implementing compliance, records management, and eDiscovery."

INSIDE OUT   eDiscovery

There is a new site collection template introduced in SharePoint Server 2013 called eDiscovery. With this template, eDiscovery sites use Search to discover documents, email (through Microsoft Exchange), and Microsoft Lync conversations (through settings in Exchange to save conversations) related to cases under the legal discovery process.

Most advanced business users can create new sites, but new site collections require a SharePoint administrator to create them in Central Administration. Document Centers and Record Centers are created as sites. However, the eDiscovery Center can only be created as a site collection. Using a separate site collection for this template makes sense because access to legal discovery cases should not be easily given or widely spread.

Document library

Document libraries offer several features that can enhance the documents stored within it. Document versioning will keep multiple copies of the document and its associated metadata in the database. Workflows can be associated with a library to automate a business process in documents. Finally, additional columns can be added to the library to relate descriptive information to the document.

Versioning

Document versioning can keep multiple major and minor versions of a document in storage. There are three options for versions: no versioning, create major versions, and create major and minor (draft) versions. A major version is created when a document is published. A minor version is created when changes to the document have been checked in. These differ because while a minor version has been checked in, it has not been published. Only users with the ability to modify documents will be able to see the minor version changes. Users with only view access will see the last major version. If there is no prior major version, then the document will not appear in the library.

INSIDE OUT
Planning document versioning

While it is possible to preserve all versions of a document, this is not suggested. In SharePoint Server 2010, each version would create a new copy of the document and associated metadata in the database. Shredded Storage in SharePoint Server 2013 will create only new versions of the changed parts of the document, thus potentially shrinking the storage footprint of each version. Even with this improvement in storage efficiency, this could still cause the storage footprint of the database to grow astronomically if files in the library are edited often.

A common suggestion is to limit both major and minor versions to the last three. This is configurable at any time in the library settings, so if that isn't enough, increasing the limit is a simple task.

To create major versions, content approval can be configured to ensure that the appropriate people support the changes before they're made available to the rest of the users. For example, the Director of Human Resources may be required to approve of all changes to employee benefits documents before the rest of the company may view them.

To set or change versioning, follow these steps:

1. In the Document Library, click Library on the ribbon. Then select the Library Settings icon in the Settings section. The following graphic shows the Settings section of the Library ribbon.

2. Under General Settings, select Versioning Settings.

3. Configure the settings as desired:

    - **Content Approval** By selecting Yes when a version is published, it will send an alert to approvers to approve the changes. If approved, a major version will be published. If it's rejected, it will remain a draft, and the person who submitted it will receive notification of the rejection, along with any comments the approver supplied (see the following graphic).

Content Approval

Specify whether new items or changes to existing items should remain in a draft state until they have been approved.   Learn about requiring approval.

Require content approval for submitted items?
⦿ Yes ○ No

- **Document Version History** Three types of versioning are available: no versioning, create major versions, and create major and minor (draft) versions. If either of the last two options is selected, version limits are available for both major and minor versions. Select the check box next to either or both and enter a numerical value into the associated text box or boxes. Major and minor versioning are enabled here, with a retention limit of the past three major and minor versions.

Document Version History

Specify whether a version is created each time you edit a file in this document library.   Learn about versions.

Create a version each time you edit a file in this document library?
○ No versioning
○ Create major versions
   Example: 1, 2, 3, 4
⦿ Create major and minor (draft) versions
   Example: 1.0, 1.1, 1.2, 2.0

Optionally limit the number of versions to retain:
☑ Keep the following number of major versions:
   `3`
☑ Keep drafts for the following number of major versions:
   `3`

- **Draft Item Security** If content approval is required, this setting controls who has access to see drafts.

- **Any User Who Can Read Items** By selecting this option, anyone who can access the list will be able to see the draft. This may be desired when the library is used for documents where the users know they are being changed, but changes can be viewed before finalized.

  For instance, system documentation is being created for a new version of a product. The product is currently in a beta testing phase, but the technical writers are making changes to the user manual. Training staff viewing the document would know that the product hasn't been released so that the document may change, but they could start building their training courses for the new version based on the drafts.

  Note that, by selecting this option, the draft will be the latest version returned in search results, not the most recent major version. While it might be acceptable for any readers to see it in the library, having a potentially incomplete document returned in search results may not be desired.

- **Only Users Who Can Edit Items** This option gives all contributors access to drafts, but those who can only read will see the last major version. This may be appropriate in situations where several contributors are making changes to a large document, but the rest of the organization should only see the final product.

Take employee annual reviews as an example. A manager, human resources (HR) specialist, and an executive may be required to contribute to the employee's review paperwork, but the employee should not see the document until all the contributors have finished their parts and it has been approved.

- **Only Users Who Can Approve Items (And The Author Of The Item)** This limits access to only those with approval rights and the author. All other contributors and readers will see the last major version. This would be used where the document needs to be kept secret until the final product is complete.

  Assume that a company is planning to announce the purchase of its top competitor. If this news were to leak early, it could cause the company legal and financial issues. Thus, only the person writing the press release and the approvers should have access to drafts to ensure that the fewest number of people would be aware of the pending merger. In the following graphic, all contributors are given the ability to see drafts.

- **Require Check Out** Selecting Yes, as shown here, will cause contributors to apply a lock to the document where other contributors cannot edit the docu-ment until the user currently editing checks it back in, thus removing the lock. If this is enabled, coauthoring will not be available on documents in the library. However, this may be desired if the library contains documents where this level of control is needed. If the library was filled with webpages for an Internet site, only one developer or designer should be making changes to avoid mistakes or duplications in code changes.

   4. Click OK, and the changes will be committed.

Workflows

Workflow presents a way for automated business processes to execute on documents when certain criteria are met. For example, when an employee review is saved to the library by the manager, a workflow could notify HR of the submission. Once HR reviews and approves it, the manager's executive would then receive it for final approval. Once the review approvals have been completed and closed, the workflow will then archive it to a Document Center.

For more information about associating workflows with document libraries, see Chapter 7.

Site columns, content types, and the content type hub

The various locations for document storage provide basic storage options for your organization. However, many companies use several types of documents throughout the organization. These documents likely have additional data that should be tracked, much as with columns in a list or library. Site columns are reusable templates that can be used in those libraries to relate to different document types.

Some document types are even commonly used across an organization where several site columns are needed to fully describe the documents. Content types are templates for list and library items that contain site columns. A document template can be associated to create a uniform look in the document, along with the data associated with it via the content type.

Site columns

In the document library, you can add additional columns to provide more information about the documents. This is good if those fields are only needed in that single library. If other libraries need the same field, they could be created in each of the additional lists, but that would require much more work, and it wouldn't truly create relationships between the documents because while the names of the columns are the same, the database sees them as different columns. This could affect search results based on these fields' values.

By creating a site column and using it in each of those libraries, those documents will be linked through that field. If you want to surface all documents where this field is used with a specific value, you can now configure a Content Search Web Part (CSWP) to do this in a matter of minutes, whereas before, it would have been difficult, if not impossible, with a single web part.

See Chapter 10, "Adding, editing, connecting, and maintaining web parts," for more about the Content Search Web Part.

Creating a site column requires Design or Full Control permissions. The standard Contributor role does not have either of these permissions. Site Owners and Site Collection Administrators have the ability to grant these permissions.

To create a site column, follow these steps:

1. Click the Settings icon and select Site Settings.

2. Under Web Designer Galleries, click Site Columns.

3. Click the Create button near the top of the page.

4. Configure the settings as appropriate:

    - Name and Type:

        - **Column Name**   This field, which is required, should be a descriptive name of the data to be stored. If the documents pertain to a client, then Client Name would be a good choice.

        - **Type**   Select the type of field for the column, as shown here. The screen will refresh for several of the fields to give additional settings.

Name and Type	Column name:
Type a name for this column, and select the type of information you want to store in the column.	Client Name
	The type of information in this column is:
	◉ Single line of text
	○ Multiple lines of text
	○ Choice (menu to choose from)
	○ Number (1, 1.0, 100)
	○ Currency ($, ¥, €)
	○ Date and Time
	○ Lookup (information already on this site)
	○ Yes/No (check box)
	○ Person or Group
	○ Hyperlink or Picture
	○ Calculated (calculation based on other columns)
	○ Task Outcome
	○ Full HTML content with formatting and constraints for publishing
	○ Image with formatting and constraints for publishing
	○ Hyperlink with formatting and constraints for publishing
	○ Summary Links data
	○ Rich media data for publishing
	○ Managed Metadata

- **Group** There are several existing groups available out of the box with SharePoint Server 2013. Groups allow for easier navigation of the list of site columns. There may be other groups that have already been created by other users as well. Alternatively, a new group can be created. The following graphic shows a new group being created for the Contoso site columns.

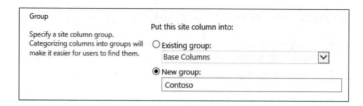

- **Additional Column Settings** This section is similar to the same section in the Add List Or Library Column page.

- **Column Validation** This section is also similar to the same section in the Add List Or Library Column page.

Refer to Chapter 3, "Working with list and library apps," for more about Column Validation.

5. Click OK.

Content types

Content types, like site columns, are ideal if the document type is being used in multiple libraries. In fact, a library can use more than one content type. This is especially important in Document Centers and Record Centers, where documents are typically archived. Even in Team Sites, multiple content types in a single library are also useful. As an example, a library may store documents based on several tax forms. Even though the content types are different, storing them together may be a sensible idea because security access would likely be similar.

Content types have additional points of integration with other SharePoint Server 2013 features:

- Workflows can be associated with them. This is useful in situations like the tax forms. Different forms may need different business processes to be enacted as new items are created.

- Information management policies can also be targeted at content types. This allows data retention and legal holds to be placed on different tax forms.

- A document template can be added to a content type to provide a Microsoft Office document type that has a format applied to it, thus giving all new items created from the content type a similar design. Tax forms have a specific format for each type, so providing a document template will make it easier for users to submit a completed form.

- A Document Information Panel can be linked to the content type. The panel is a Microsoft InfoPath form that will be available in Office documents that are associated with the content type. This form will allow the users to set the metadata of the document from the Office client application. This allows the user to avoid editing the properties of the document in SharePoint after saving. The form needs to be created using Microsoft InfoPath Designer 2010 or 2013.

- Custom events can be developed and attached to a content type. A developer can build a solution to perform additional actions when an item from the content type is added, updated, or deleted. (Refer to Chapter 23 for more information on custom solutions.)

Content type creation requires Design or Full Control permissions. If a user does not have those permissions, browsing the Content Type Gallery will not be possible, either.

To create a content type, follow these steps:

1. Click the Settings icon and select Site Settings.

2. Under Web Designer Galleries, click Site Content Types.

3. Click the Create button near the top of the page.

4. Supply information about the content type:

   - Name and Description:

     - **Name**   Provide a descriptive name for the content type. For the purposes of this tutorial, we'll create a content type for a personal income tax form and call it **Personal Income Tax**.

     - **Description**   A description can be provided to explain the use of the content type. This will appear to users who are adding content types to a list or library.

   - Parent Content Type:

     - **Select Parent Content Type From**   The values of this box are group names of different types of content types. Selecting one of these, for instance Document Content Types, will change the values in the Parent Content Type control.

- **Parent Content Type** Every custom content type must be derived from an existing content type. The custom type will then have all of the columns, workflows, and other characteristics of the parent type. For the Personal Income Tax content type, select Document, as shown in the following graphic.

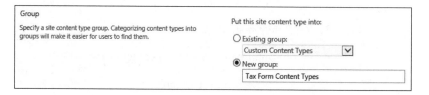

- **Group As** With the site columns, there are several existing groups with which a new content type can be associated. These are not the same groups as in the first menu in Parent Content Type, as those refer to functional groups and this group is purely for organizational purposes. A new group can be created, as well. The following graphic shows a new group being created as Tax Form Content Types.

5. Click OK to create the content type.

Once the content type is created, the user is sent to a page where it can be managed. This is also the same page that the user will be sent to when clicking an existing content type in the gallery. From here, the user can add existing site columns, create new ones, associate workflows, configure information management policies, and add a document template or document information panel.

Content types can be created at the site level. Sites below this site (child sites or other descendants) can also use the content type in their libraries. However, parent and other ancestor sites will not be able to access it. If it needs to be used throughout the site collection, create the content type at the topmost, or root, site.

Content type hub

If there is a need for the content type to be available across multiple site collections, and even across multiple web applications, creating it manually would cause them not to be related—in much the same way as the library column issue discussed earlier in the chapter. There is a way to deploy it across the farm. The content type hub is associated with the managed metadata service. A particular site collection's content type gallery becomes the master, or "hub," where content types to be shared across the farm are created. A scheduled job in SharePoint will run regularly to publish content types from this gallery to all the other galleries in web applications that are being targeted by this job. Consult your SharePoint administration team about configuring a content type hub.

Managed metadata service for documents

In addition to the content type hub, the managed metadata service manages taxonomies. *Taxonomies* in SharePoint are simply the grouping of similar terms. These can be used by metadata fields in lists and libraries, where one or more values can be selected to describe the list item or document. By defining these terms in the Managed Metadata Service, any web application and its descendant site collections and sites can consume them in fields.

There are actually two locations where metadata taxonomies can exist. The service application is the first. Alternatively, each site collection can have its own term store. These terms will be available only to that single site collection and will be managed through the Site Settings Term Store Management page. However, if the Managed Metadata Service is configured to be the default storage location for the site collection terms, Site Collection Administrators will be able to manage their subset of taxonomies through Central Administration.

There is a hierarchy of objects in the service. Groups, Term Sets, and Terms are available for creation in the service application settings, called Term Store Manager.

- **Group** A group is a logical container for Term Sets, where security can be customized. Contributors and Group Managers can be assigned. Both can create new terms and edit existing ones. Group Managers can also grant additional users the Contributor role. This is desirable, as groups may be defined to separate organizational terminology by department, product line, or some other major boundary where certain users would have the knowledge to manage the terms properly.

  For example, a company's Information Technology (IT) department may have a group called IT, where department management are the Group Managers and team leads have been granted Contributor roles. These users will know what terms should be part of the IT taxonomy. However, it doesn't make sense that they should be able to manage Human Resources' taxonomies.

- **Term Set** Term Sets do contain terms, but they also can be configured for easy notification of term suggestions, stakeholder alerts, and submission policy. The submission policy can be closed or open. If it is open, then any user with access to a field that implements the Term Set can create new terms inside of it. If it is closed, then only the service administrator, Group Contributors, and Managers can create new terms. Stakeholders can be added to a Term Set as people who should be notified when changes are made to the Term Set. Finally, if a Term Set is closed, users may want to submit suggestions for additional terms. Providing an email address will send suggestions to that mailbox. Term Sets can be used in metadata columns and all terms beneath it will be available for selection in those list or library items.

- **Term** A term is a value that can be assigned as a descriptive attribute of an item or document. Terms can have child, or nested, terms, but there is a seven-level limit of term nesting. For instance, if a Term Set was called Location, the nested hierarchy couldn't go any further than what is shown in Figure 11-1.

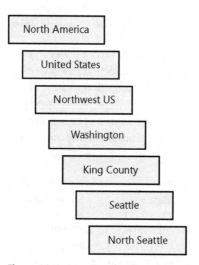

Figure 11-1 An example of maximum term nesting.

Adding Managed Metadata fields to libraries or content types creates data relations. Because the data is hosted in the service application, any web application that is connected to this service application can use the terms. Any document libraries or content types that use the same Term Sets will share a level of commonality. By creating this relationship between two or more documents, it "opens" access to other relationships.

INSIDE OUT   Closed vs. open Term Sets

Terms in the Managed Metadata Service application are centrally located and usable across all web applications that consume the same instance of the service application. However, because the application is managed in Central Administration, direct access is usually limited to the administration team.

SharePoint Server 2013 offers two types of Term Set management access: open and closed. A closed Term Set can only have terms added or changed from Central Administration. These Term Sets typically represent tightly managed terms that are limited and have a distinct, corporate purpose. A company may create a term set of clients or internal business units and mark the set as closed because users don't need to add to these lists. The company must choose, at a higher level, to add clients or business units. If the Term Set is configured to allow suggestions to be submitted, users can do so through email submission.

Alternatively, an open Term Set can be managed through columns that implement the Term Set. These Term Sets are usually highly dynamic and thus require constant change. For example, a firm may have an internal help forum where users can tag a post or questions with terms to increase the chance of other users finding the post. It would be a slow process if a user wanted to submit a new post, but a term that is integral to the topic is not available and the Term Set was closed. They would have to submit a suggestion and potentially wait several days before the term being added. The open Term Set will add the term when the new post is created.

The example shown in Figure 11-2 includes four content types: Corporate Document, Project Document, Contract, and Case Study. Each of the columns listed are metadata columns. Lines are drawn to show relationships between the fields because the columns share the same Term Set. While Corporate Document only has a single relation to Project Document, it now has a connection, albeit not as strong, to Contract and Case Study. Assume that a user selects a Corporate Document where the Document Type field is set to Press Release in a web part. In a connected web part, related documents will be shown as a way to help drive idea generation for current and future projects. Additional Corporate and Project Documents with similar traits would show in this web part, but so would Case Studies and Contracts based on the shown Project Documents. They would just be less relevant because there isn't a direct correlation with the Corporate Document.

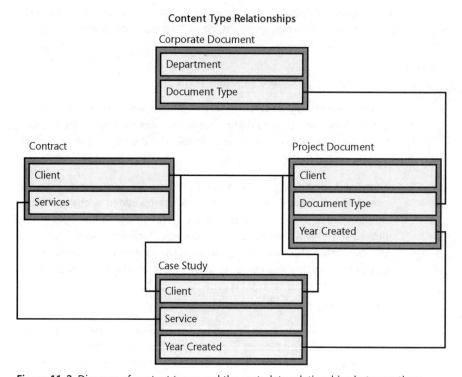

Figure 11-2 Diagram of content types and the metadata relationships between them.

To create a metadata group, term set, and term, follow these steps:

1. In Central Administration, select Manage Service Applications under Application Management.

2. Click the Managed Metadata Service application.

   This sends you to the Term Store Management tool.

3. Select the topmost node of the tree and click the drop-down to the right of the name. The following graphic shows the topmost node as Managed Metadata Service. Select New Group.

   A new group icon will appear near the bottom of the list.

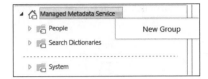

4. Provide a name and press Enter. As shown here, you name the group **Wingtip**.

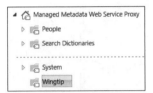

   The right side of the page will now load some additional settings such as Description, Group Managers, and Contributors.

5. Right-click the Wingtip group and select New Term Set, as shown next.

6. Enter a name for the new Term Set and press Enter. As shown here, you name it **Client**.

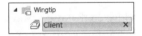

   The right side of the screen will now display four tabs and the General tab properties. The General tab is where the terms Suggestion Contact, Stakeholders, and Submission Policy are set. The Intended Use tab offers settings to use the Term Set for tagging and for navigation. The Custom Sort tab allows the user to change how the terms will be ordered when displayed in fields. Finally, the Custom Properties tab provides a way to store additional information about the Term Set. This could be useful for custom-developed applications.

7. To add a term to this Term Set, right-click the Term Set and select Create Term, as shown next.

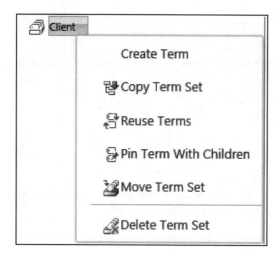

8. Enter a name for the term and press Enter.

   It will start a new term. This is expected as it makes it easier to add several terms consecutively. In the following graphic, the Term is added as Fabrikam.

9. Select Fabrikam and notice the properties available.

   Additional labels, or synonyms, can be added so that users who use some other word or phrase will still set the right term for the record. For example, Fabrikam's stock symbol, FBKM, would be a good synonym. Terms also have Custom properties. Shared properties will be associated with all pinned instances of the same term, whereas local properties will only be associated on the current instance.

Managing document sets

Document sets are specialized folders that contain multiple documents as part of a single package. They contain columns of data, much like a list item or document, to describe the collection. Document Set content types can be built to add these additional columns as well as use other benefits of content types. In addition to these features, Document Set content types can have default content associated with them. This content is not the same as a document template; it is an actual spreadsheet, image, and other file.

As an example, a public relations (PR) team is building an initiative for a client around Wingtip Toys' new product. This project requires several different documents as part of the deliverables: a press release, demo video, several print advertisements, and a PowerPoint presentation. Because the team provides all of Wingtip's PR services, they have a Document Set content type called Wingtip Project Deliverables that has several columns of data associated with it. It also contains several of Wingtip's logo files, corporate branding files, and a list of important contacts in the organization, as default content.

To create a Document Set content type, follow these steps:

1. Click the Settings icon and select Site Settings.

2. Select Site Content Types under Web Designer Galleries.

3. Click the Create button near the top of the page.

4. The following graphic uses these settings:

   - Name: Project Deliverables

   - Select Parent Content Type From: Document Set Content Types

   - Parent Content Type: Document Set

   - Group: Wingtip

5. Press OK.

The content type will now be available in the Content Type Gallery under the Wingtip group.

To create a document set, follow these steps:

1. Open a document library, click the Library tab on the ribbon, and select Library Settings in the Settings section.

2. If Content Types are not enabled, select Advanced Settings under the General Settings section.

3. Change the Content Types section to Yes and click OK.

4. On the Library Settings page, select Add From Existing Site Content Types under the Content Types section, as shown next.

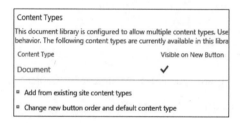

5. Change the Select Site Content Types From drop-down to Wingtip.

This will filter the list of Available Site Content Types.

6. Select Project Deliverables and click Add, as shown next.

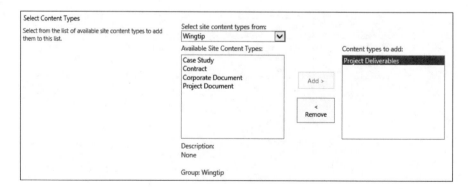

7. Click OK.

8. Click Documents at the top of the screen and to the left of Settings to get back to the library record entry page.

9. Click the Files tab and select the New Document drop-down menu (shown here). Select Project Deliverables.

10. Provide information for the various fields and press Save.

The following image shows a Fabrikam Widget Rollout document set.

The document set page will now be displayed. New documents can be added here in the same way as the document library.

The importance of SharePoint Search in document management

Organizations can generate large quantities of documents across their farms. When there are so many, it's difficult to just look through a document library or the Document Center for a single record. SharePoint Search can simplify the process. Search indexes column data and the content inside the files.

You can read more about the Search Service application in Chapter 18, "Discovering information with SharePoint 2013 Search."

Search pages and Search Center sites are highly customizable. Query results, refinements, and display templates are just three of the most useful ways of configuring search results to get a more effective document search result set. The Search Results Web Part displays returned results. By default, it will return everything that the search query matches. When building a Search Center for documents, it would make sense to limit results to documents, thus eliminating other types of data like people, sites, and list items. In fact, the web part query builder is very robust and allows for far more granular boundaries, like filtering on a specific Managed Property, a column that is registered with Search to be crawled. While this could potentially return a very small subset of all the organization's documents, it could be useful where the property is Project Document, with a value of Contract. A Contract search would be useful to both the Sales and Legal departments. Sales would be able to use previous contracts to judge how much should be charged for new contracts. Legal would need the search should there be a contract dispute or other relevant litigation. This legal search is used in an eDiscovery site to group all of these files into cases for easy reference during the evidence discovery process.

INSIDE OUT   Result Sources

Result Sources also provide a way to limit the type of results returned during a search. Result Sources can be configured in Central Administration, the site collection, or the site level. There are 16 prebuilt sources that come in SharePoint Server 2013. One of these is a Document source that only allows document items to be returned. Other sources include Conversations, Pictures, and People. Chapter 18 details Result Sources in more detail.

Refiners, or more specifically the Refinement Web Part, give users a quick way to explore a large set of search results to find the desired document. Typically displayed on the left side of a search results page, the web part contains refiners for common data like result type, author, and modified date. However, in the web part properties, additional fields can be added. If the environment has a rich taxonomy story, adding metadata refiners will allow users to explore data based on what are typically the most important attributes of a document. It's important to provide only the refiners that make the most sense given the context of the search page as Search performance starts to degrade once the Refinement panel exceeds 10 refiners.

Display Templates allow the layout of search results to be changed so that the items are rendered in a different way depending on the type of result. Result Types define a rule for a specific kind of result. The Result Type then implements an Item Display Template that configures the result, corresponding hover panel, and even refinement controls. Now, Wingtip Toys can display Contract results with certain fields showing and in a specific format, while Case Studies are displayed in a completely different manner.

Display Templates are discussed in more detail in Chapter 19, "Creating a customized SharePoint 2013 search experience."

INSIDE OUT   Notes on Search Center

The Enterprise Search Center is a powerful site definition. It can access all search results from the Search application associated with the current web application. If there is only a single application, then all crawled data is available.

More pages can be added to the site so different types of search can be configured for the user. This means that not only the out-of-the-box Search can be performed, but a document search, people search, or other custom data search pages can be created to restrict the records returned. Users will appreciate this because it lessens the number of refinements they have to perform on a search.

Summary

This chapter discussed the capabilities of SharePoint Server 2013 as a document management solution. Team Sites, Document Centers, and Record Centers are document repository locations with different storage designs. One or more document libraries are used in each of these sites and are where the documents are actually stored. Libraries can implement versioning and coauthoring to improve simultaneous productivity and maintain historical data. Site columns, content types, and document sets enhance libraries by grouping similar records together. The Managed Metadata Service can synchronize content types across multiple web applications, as well as provide a centralized store of terms that can be used in columns to describe a document more accurately. The attributes associated with a file through metadata and other columns give the SharePoint Search application more data to build and return meaningful results.

The next chapter will explore utilizing SharePoint as a web content management system. It will cover topics such as branding, mobile support, and content publishing.

Designing web content management sites

B EFORE Microsoft Office SharePoint Server (MOSS) 2007, Microsoft SharePoint was used primarily for document management. However, since the integration of content management server (CMS) 2002 into MOSS 2007, web content management (WCM) has become an integral component of SharePoint. If you have experience with WCM in previous versions of SharePoint, the changes in 2013 may come as a shock to you. Andrew Connell said it best in his blog post, "SP2013 WCM: Forget Everything You Knew About SharePoint WCM" (*www.andrewconnell.com/blog/archive/2012/07/16/sp2013-wcm-forget-everything-you-knew-about-sharepoint-wcm.aspx*). The title alone says it all. WCM has drastically changed in this release and the approach is significantly different than before. In SharePoint 2013, the content-creation workflow is revamped so that content can be created using any tool and branding a site no longer requires the use of writing custom .NET code nor requires the use of Microsoft SharePoint Designer. This chapter focuses on the new and improved changes of WCM for SharePoint 2013.

Designing and branding

In this section, you will learn about Design Manager, the new WCM toolset included with SharePoint 2013 for designing and branding web content management sites. As you will see, even if you do not possess SharePoint-specific web design skills, Design Manager allows anyone with basic HTML skills to create attractive WCM sites.

An overview of Design Manager

In previous versions of SharePoint, branding was not easy for designers because it required technical knowledge beyond HTML and CSS. This was challenging for many because the skills required were beyond common web design skills. Many companies had to have a developer implement the branding or have the designer go to training to learn how to implement the branding. SharePoint Designer or Microsoft Visual Studio were the only tools that could be used to brand SharePoint sites. All of that has changed in SharePoint

2013 with a new feature called Design Manager. Design Manager is a publishing feature that is available on publishing sites or sites with publishing enabled in both SharePoint Server 2013 and Microsoft Office 365.

The new Design Manager interface and central hub help separate the design aspects from the technical requirements to create a master page. The designer no longer needs to know which components are necessary on a page and only has to worry about the design and conversion into HTML, CSS, and images. The purpose of Design Manager is to provide a new and easier way to brand SharePoint using existing tools that designers are familiar with, such as Adobe Dreamweaver. With Designer Manager, you can import design elements and create an HTML-based master page to define the chrome (shared framing elements) that all of the site's pages and page layouts share. If preferred, you can still write custom code to brand your site by using the publishing and taxonomy libraries.

Design Manager enables a step-by-step approach for creating design assets such as master pages and page layouts used for the branding of your site. In addition, with Design Manager, you can:

- Create design assets—images, HTML, CSS, and JavaScript files—using Expression Web, Dreamweaver, or other tool of choice.

- Upload design files.

- Convert HTML pages into page layouts and master pages.

Design Manager is located at the top level of the site collection. It is a publishing feature that is available in both SharePoint Server 2013 and Office 365 for publishing sites or sites that have the Publishing Infrastructure (site collection) feature and the SharePoint Server Publishing (site) feature activated. To use Design Manager, the user must be assigned the designer permission level.

Understanding the SharePoint page model

Before creating a site design, it is important to understand the SharePoint page model. This model includes master pages, page layouts, and pages:

- **Master pages** Define the shared framing elements of the site. This includes such things as the logo, header, search box, footer, and content placeholders.

- **Page layouts** Define the layout for a specific class of pages that contains the content for the content placeholders. Controls are added to the page layouts based on the content type being used.

- **Pages** Created from the page layouts by content authors, which become the publishing content pages.

Master pages

Master pages define the chrome of the site, such as the site logo, header, footer, search box, breadcrumb, and other shared site elements. The master page remains consistent throughout the site. Master pages also define regions called *content placeholders* that get filled in by the content from the matching regions on the page layouts, as shown in Figure 12-1. The common placeholder in the body of a master page is called the PlaceHolderMain. The PlaceHolderMain is created automatically, and all of the content from inside the page layout appears inside this single content placeholder.

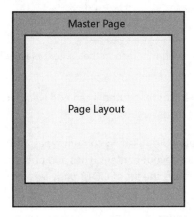

Figure 12-1 A master page is filled in by content from page layouts.

When previewing a master page in Design Manager, you will see the message shown in Figure 12-2.

This div, which you should delete, represents the content area that your Page Layouts and pages will fill. Design your Master Page around this content placeholder.

Figure 12-2 This message appears inside the PlaceHolderMain content placeholder when previewing a master page from Design Manager.

Page layouts

Page layouts are templates that define the layout or structure for the body of the pages. In a page layout, regions or content areas are defined that map to the content placeholders contained in the master page (see Figure 12-3). SharePoint has existing out-of-the-box page layouts, such as Article page or Welcome page, that can be used; however, it is more common to create your own custom page layouts for your site.

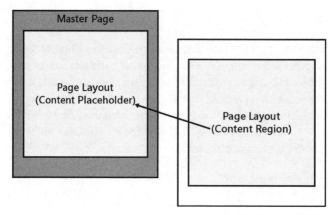

Figure 12-3 Regions or content areas are defined that map to the content placeholders contained in the master page.

Page layouts can include web part zones, so content authors can add web parts to the zones. Page layouts can also contain page fields.

Page layouts are based on the page layout and publishing content types. Figure 12-4 displays the list of out-of-the-box (OOTB) page layout content types and publishing content types for a publishing site. Figure 12-5 displays the list of OOTB page layouts in SharePoint Designer 2013.

Page Layout Content Types		
Article Page	Page	SharePoint
Catalog-Item Reuse	Page	SharePoint
Enterprise Wiki Page	Page	SharePoint
Error Page	Page	SharePoint
Project Page	Enterprise Wiki Page	SharePoint
Redirect Page	Page	SharePoint
Welcome Page	Page	SharePoint
Publishing Content Types		
ASP NET Master Page	System Master Page	SharePoint
Html Master Page	ASP NET Master Page	SharePoint
Html Page Layout	Page Layout	SharePoint
Page	System Page	SharePoint
Page Layout	System Page Layout	SharePoint

Figure 12-4 A list of the OOTB page layout content types and publishing content types.

Name	Title	Content Type	Size	Modified Date	Modified By
Display Templates					
Editing Menu					
en-us					
Preview Images					
Themable					
ArticleLeft.aspx	Image on left	Page Layout	5KB	2/12/2013 2:49 ...	SPDEV\admi...
ArticleLinks.aspx	Summary links	Page Layout	4KB	2/12/2013 2:49 ...	SPDEV\admi...
ArticleRight.aspx	Image on right	Page Layout	5KB	2/12/2013 2:49 ...	SPDEV\admi...
BlankWebPartPage.aspx	Blank Web Part page	Page Layout	6KB	2/12/2013 2:49 ...	SPDEV\admi...
CatalogArticle.aspx	Catalog Item Image o...	Page Layout	7KB	2/12/2013 2:49 ...	SPDEV\admi...
CatalogWelcome.aspx	Blank Catalog Item	Page Layout	7KB	2/12/2013 2:49 ...	SPDEV\admi...
EnterpriseWiki.aspx	Basic Page	Page Layout	6KB	2/12/2013 2:49 ...	SPDEV\admi...
ErrorLayout.aspx	Error	Page Layout	3KB	3/6/2013 12:35 ...	SHAREPOINT...
PageFromDocLayout.aspx	Body only	Page Layout	4KB	2/12/2013 2:49 ...	SPDEV\admi...
PageLayoutTemplate.aspx	_catalogs/masterpag...	Page Layout	2KB	2/12/2013 2:48 ...	SPDEV\admi...
ProjectPage.aspx	Basic Project Page	Page Layout	7KB	2/12/2013 2:49 ...	SPDEV\admi...
RedirectPageLayout.aspx	Redirect	Page Layout	3KB	2/12/2013 2:49 ...	SPDEV\admi...
VariationRootPageLayou...	Variations Root Page	Page Layout	1KB	2/12/2013 2:48 ...	SPDEV\admi...
WelcomeLinks.aspx	Summary links	Page Layout	5KB	2/12/2013 2:48 ...	SPDEV\admi...
WelcomeSplash.aspx	Splash	Page Layout	5KB	2/12/2013 2:49 ...	SPDEV\admi...

Figure 12-5 A list of OOTB page layouts in SharePoint Designer 2013.

In addition to web part zones, page layouts can include page field controls, which will contain content when an author creates a page based on a page layout and fills in the content for the controls. The page fields available are based on the selected content type used when creating each page layout. For example, the ArticleLeft.aspx page layout used the Article Page content type. The Article Page (Page Layout content type) which includes specific fields for the content type. Every page layout is associated with a content type in the Pages library of the site. For any page layout, the page fields that become available for the layout corresponds to the columns defined for the content type used for the page layout.

Figure 12-6 displays the list of columns for the Article Page content type and the Toolbox in SharePoint Designer for the ArticleLeft.aspx page layout. Notice that the page fields and content fields that are available in SharePoint Designer match the fields listed for the Article Page content type.

Columns				Page Fields (from Article Page)
Name	Type	Status	Source	Browser Title
Name	File	Required	Document	Comments
Title	Single line of text	Optional	Item	Contact
Comments	Multiple lines of text	Optional	System Page	Contact E-Mail ...
Scheduling Start Date	Publishing Schedule Start Date	Optional	System Page	Contact Name
Scheduling End Date	Publishing Schedule End Date	Optional	System Page	Contact Picture
Contact	Person or Group	Optional	System Page	Content Type
Contact E-Mail Address	Single line of text	Optional	System Page	Document Cre...
Contact Name	Single line of text	Optional	System Page	Document Mo...
Contact Picture	Hyperlink or Picture	Optional	System Page	Hide from Inter...
Rollup Image	Publishing Image	Optional	System Page	Hide physical ...
Target Audiences	Audience Targeting	Optional	System Page	Meta Descripti...
Hide physical URLs from search	Yes/No	Optional	System Page	Meta Keywords
Page Image	Publishing Image	Optional		Name
Page Content	Publishing HTML	Optional		Page Layout
Summary Links	Summary Links	Optional		Rollup Image
Byline	Single line of text	Optional		Scheduling End...
Article Date	Date and Time	Optional		Scheduling Sta...
Image Caption	Publishing HTML	Optional		Target Audienc...
Browser Title	Single line of text	Optional	Page	Title
Meta Description	Single line of text	Optional	Page	Refresh
Meta Keywords	Single line of text	Optional	Page	**Content Fields** (from Article Page)
Hide from Internet Search Engines	Yes/No	Optional	Page	Article Date
				Byline
				Image Caption
				Page Content
				Page Image
				Summary Links
				Refresh

Figure 12-6 Article Page content type site columns and the SharePoint Designer Toolbox, displaying the ArticleLeft.aspx page layout page fields and content fields.

INSIDE OUT   What is the recommendation for creating site column names?

SharePoint has two names for columns: Internal Name and Display Name. The Internal Name is generated automatically based on the Display Name that is input during the creation of the column. The best practice recommendation in creating column names is not to use spaces or special characters. After the column is created, you can then go back and change the Display Name, adding spaces or special characters. Once the Internal Name is created, it cannot be changed without deleting and re-creating the column.

If special characters or spaces are used, then the Internal Name will contain internal hex codes. For example, if a space is used in the creation of the name, then the space would be replaced with "_x0020_" (that is, "Left Column Story Image" would create an Internal Name of "Left_x0020_Column_x0020_Story_x0020_Image"). Keeping the Internal Name "clean" and simple will make it easier for developers to use the columns in code, and will aid in troubleshooting any issues that may arise.

Pages

In Chapter 9, "Creating and formatting content pages," you learned how to create and format various types of content pages, including publishing pages. When authors go to create a publishing page, they are presented with a list of available page layout templates. Once the content page is created, authors can fill in the content for the page field controls or add web parts to the web part zones that are dependent on the available options for the page layout template being used. The rendered page is what the visitors will see. When the page is requested by the user in the browser, the master page merges with the page layout and the authored content for the page loads in the page fields of the page layout.

Themes and composed looks

Themes are nothing new to SharePoint; however, how themes work in SharePoint has changed with each new release. In previous versions of SharePoint, themes were not the easy to work with until a new theming engine was introduced in SharePoint 2010. It was better, but it still was not great. Thankfully, Microsoft has made some huge improvements to theming in this release. SharePoint 2013 introduces another new theming engine that provides an easy and simple way to change the look and feel of your site.

Themes

What is a theme? If you have not worked with themes before it is important to understand what a theme is. A *theme* is a set of colors and fonts that can be applied to provide a quick and easy way for site owners or site designers to do lightweight branding. Themes are defined in XML files that are uploaded to the Themes gallery. If the custom master page being used is enabled for themes, the theme elements will replace the elements that have special markups (token names) in the CSS.

The three token names are:

- **ReplaceColor** Used to replace background color and font color

- **ReplaceFonts** Used to replace fonts

- **RecolorImages** Used to recolor images using a tint, blend, and fill method

The 12 theme colors are represented by the following tokens:

- Dark1, Dark2

- Light1, Light2

- Accent1, Accent2, Accent3, Accent4, Accent5, Accent6

- Hyperlink

- Followed Hyperlink

The theming engine works with these colors and produces five additional permutations of each one, which are Lightest, Lighter, Medium, Darker, and Darkest. The engine works by reading your comments in the CSS file and replacing any styles that have a theming token directly before the style. For example, if you want the background color of an element in your CSS to use the Light2-Darker token, you would include the comments as

```
/* [ReplaceColor(themeColor:"Light2-Darker")] */ background-color:#C0C0C0;
```

In the default theme, the background color would appear as #C0C0C0, and when a theme is applied, the background color would be replaced with *Light2-Darker*.

Composed looks

In SharePoint 2010, themes were created by using Microsoft PowerPoint 2010 or Theme Builder to customize the theme file. In SharePoint 2013, the theming experience and theming interface has been completely redesigned. Themes are no longer created using the Office client; instead, the elements are configured and added to a Composed Looks list. A *composed look* is an association between a design (master page), theme (fonts and colors), and a background image. A composed look takes these predefined design elements (master pages, themes, and background images) and enables them to be used in many different combinations, so publishing sites have more design options. The Composed Looks list, as shown in Figure 12-7, is located at Site Actions | Site Settings | Composed Looks and contains all predefined designs.

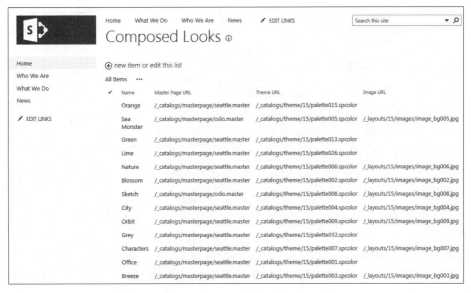

Figure 12-7 A Composed Looks list displays predefined composed looks.

The edit properties page of a composed look, shown in Figure 12-8, consists of the following:

- **Name** Defined name of the composed look.

- **Master Page** Location of the master page to use for the design.

- **Theme URL** Location of the XML file that defines the colors that you want to apply to the different CSS. It works similar to SharePoint 2010, except that instead of using Accent1, Accent2, and so on, you create your own theme IDs.

- **Image URL** Location of the background image to use for the site.

- **Font Scheme URL** Location of the XML font scheme file that defines the fonts used for the site. Seven font schemes are included in SharePoint 2013.

- **Display Order** Order in which to make the available composed looks.

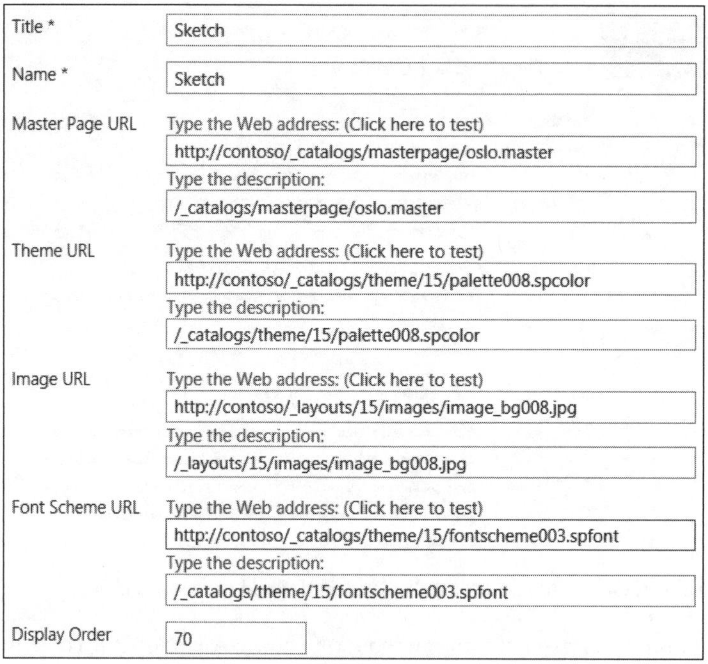

Title *	Sketch

Name *	Sketch

Master Page URL	Type the Web address: (Click here to test)
	http://contoso/_catalogs/masterpage/oslo.master
	Type the description:
	/_catalogs/masterpage/oslo.master

Theme URL	Type the Web address: (Click here to test)
	http://contoso/_catalogs/theme/15/palette008.spcolor
	Type the description:
	/_catalogs/theme/15/palette008.spcolor

Image URL	Type the Web address: (Click here to test)
	http://contoso/_layouts/15/images/image_bg008.jpg
	Type the description:
	/_layouts/15/images/image_bg008.jpg

Font Scheme URL	Type the Web address: (Click here to test)
	http://contoso/_catalogs/theme/15/fontscheme003.spfont
	Type the description:
	/_catalogs/theme/15/fontscheme003.spfont

Display Order	70

Figure 12-8 The edit properties page of the "Sketch" predefined composed look.

> **Note**
>
> Themes created in SharePoint 2010 cannot be used in SharePoint 2013.

Changing the look

You can use the preinstalled themes or create your own custom theme by creating additional color palettes and font schemes and uploading them to the Theme gallery. When a preinstalled theme is modified, a new theme, called *Current*, is created automatically after the theme changes are applied. There is only one Current theme used for a site, which means if you modify a preinstalled theme, apply the changes (creates Current), and then modify a second preinstalled theme, the second preinstalled theme becomes the Current theme when the settings are applied. To save a modified theme, you can create a list item in the Composed Looks list that contains the same master page, color palette, font scheme, and background image URLs that match the values of your Current theme. You can create new designs by creating a new list item in the Composed Looks list specifying the master page, color palette, font scheme, and background image for the new design.

The SharePoint 2013 new theme interface provides a wizard for changing the composed look, which can be accessed by going to Site Actions | Site Settings | Change The Look. This will take you to the Change The Look interface, which is shown in Figure 12-9.

Figure 12-9 The Change The Look page, which lists preinstalled composed looks.

As shown in Figure 12-10, when you select a design, this takes you to another page that allows you to change the background image, colors, site layout (master page), and fonts.

Figure 12-10 The Change The Look page for the selected design, with options to change the background, colors, site layout, and fonts.

When you make changes to the selected design, the preview image updates with the new look, as shown in Figure 12-11.

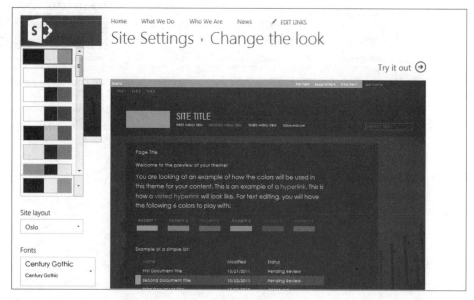

Figure 12-11 The view after changing the background image, color scheme, and fonts.

Once you have made all desired changes to the settings, you can click Try It Out to preview the new look on the site before committing the changes as shown in Figure 12-12.

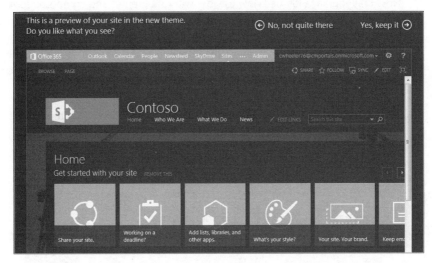

Figure 12-12 A preview of the site design before the new theme is applied.

Once Yes, Keep It is selected, the new theme is applied to the site, as shown in Figure 12-13.

Figure 12-13 The new theme, with the new background image, colors, master page, and font changes, is applied to the site.

Creating site design

Now that you have learned how to work with the themes and composed looks, the next step to learn is how to create your own custom master pages and page layouts. When creating the HTML and CSS design files, you can use any HTML editor to work with the files locally. Once the design files are ready to be converted, upload the files to the Master Page gallery of the SharePoint site and then use Design Manager to convert, preview, and polish the design.

Before using Design Manager, you must create a design for your site, which is most commonly made up of the following files:

- An HTML file to be converted to a SharePoint master page

- One or more CSS files

- Images (such as a logo and header graphic)

- JavaScript files

- Other supporting files (based on requirements)

When creating a mockup of your site in HTML and CSS, you will most likely have multiple HTML files that implement designs for the different pages you want to appear. If you create more than one HTML file, only one HTML file will be converted to a SharePoint master page unless you are using device channels. After Design Manager is used to create other site elements, such as page layouts, you can transfer the markup from the HTML mockups to the HTML and CSS associated with the desired page layout.

Supporting mobile devices

Before designing your site, you need to take into consideration what types of mobile devices you want to support and how you want the user experience to be for each device. The use of mobile devices for browsing the web has grown exponentially; however, the support for mobile devices on the web have been lacking for most public-facing websites. With technology changing rapidly, there are still factors that differentiate mobile device scenarios from desktop computers for web browsing. These factors include limited screen size, touch screen, limited bandwidth, platform capabilities, and animation technologies, such as Adobe Flash. The concept of supporting mobile devices is not new to SharePoint; however, it was not as easy to control and customize in previous versions of SharePoint. A single default mobile view was autogenerated based on the existing site and making modifications to the view was not easy. Because customizing was somewhat difficult, this caused some companies to either not support or delay implementing support for mobile devices.

In SharePoint 2013, mobile support has drastically improved, which makes it easier to design for mobile devices in the beginning of the design phase versus delaying the implementation.

One of the big improvements to the mobile look and feel is the introduction of new mobile views. The different types of mobile browser experience view options are:

- **Classic view** Lightweight mobile view for interacting with lists and libraries using a hyperlink navigation model. This view was used in SharePoint 2010 and is for smartphone devices only. It renders in HTML format and provides backward compatibility for mobile browsers that cannot render the new contemporary view.

- **Contemporary view** A modern UI optimized for touch that renders in HTML 5. It provides an intuitive navigation experience that supports full-screen UI view. This view is for smartphone devices only and is activated by default on the Team Site, Blank Site, Document Workspace, Document Center, and Project Site templates. It is available for the following browsers and devices:

  - Mobile Internet Explorer version 9.0 or later

  - Safari version 4.0 or later (iOS 5.0+)

  - Android browser for Android 4.0 or later

- **Full-screen UI view** A full desktop view for smartphones and tablet devices that has the same navigation experience as the desktop experience. This contemporary view has a menu option to switch to the full-screen UI view.

- **Device channels** This is only used with publishing sites for smartphone and tablet devices. The next section provides more details about device channels.

Understanding device channels

A new concept in SharePoint 2013, called *device channels,* allows you to target areas of content on pages using designs created for specific mobile devices. If you are supporting mobile devices, you may want to create HTML mockups for the device channels so that they can also be converted to separate master pages.

Device channels can render a single publishing site in multiple ways by mapping different designs to different types of devices. Channels can be created in Design Manager and each channel can use its own master page that references a different style sheet optimized for the specific device. Channels are mapped to mobile devices or browsers by using substrings of each incoming device's user agent string, such as "Windows Phone 8." These rules are what determine which devices belong to each channel. SharePoint knows which device is being used and uses the information to perform different tasks based on the device by the user agent. When visitors browse the site from the device, each channel captures the traffic for each of the specified devices, and the visitors see the site in the design optimized for the specific device.

For example, you can define a channel for a tablet, the Windows Phone, the iPhone, or the Android phone, then create four separate master pages and assign a master page to the desired channel. Some devices do not support Flash content; however, you can put the Flash content in a Device Channel and the content will render only on the device that has been targeted. Figure 12-14 shows the use of two device channels to provide two different displays for a Windows Phone and an iPad.

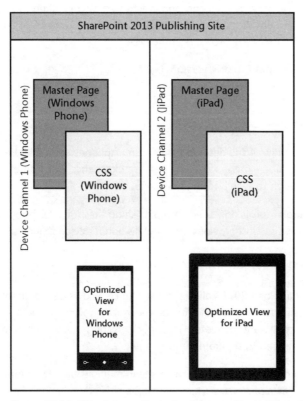

Figure 12-14 This diagram illustrates the use of two different device channels.

Device channel rankings   *Device channels* are created and stored in a SharePoint list and contain orders that are necessary for ranking. Channels can be ranked in order from top to bottom, and the inclusion rules are processed in the ranked order. This means that device channels with the highest number of specified rules need to be on the top. For example, a channel targeting "Windows Phone 8" should precede a channel targeting "Windows Phone OS."

Device channel panels   *Device channel panels* are a control that can be added to a master page, page layout, or display template to control what content is rendered in each channel. In essence, a device channel panel is a container that specifies one or more channels and can include any other type of content. If one or more channels are active that are in the container when the page is rendered, all of the content of the channel panel is rendered. For example, you may have a page layout that contains separate text fields, such as a long text field for desktops and a short text field for mobile devices.

Mobile fallback device channel   If you want to target all mobile devices for a single channel, you can insert the following Device Inclusion Role:

`$FALLBACKMOBILEUSERAGENTS;`

Whether a device is recognized as a mobile device or not is determined by the *HttpContext. Current.Request.Browser.IsMobileDevice* property, which is driven by the browser definition file schema (*.browser*) for the web application.

For more information on browser definition files, see the MSDN article "Browser Definition File Schema (browsers Element)," located at *http://msdn.microsoft.com/en-us/library/ ms228122(v=vs.90).aspx.*

Working with device channels

To configure device channels, you must first define new channels. When defining a new channel, you must define a number of fields. These fields are shown in Table 12-1.

TABLE 12-1 Device channels required and optional fields

Field name	Required	Description
Name	Yes	Friendly name of device channel to identify the channel.
Alias	Yes	Alias to identify the device channel in code, device channel panels, previews, and other contexts.
Description	No	Field to contain general information about the device channel.
Device Inclusion Rules	Yes	Field to contain the user agent substring that will be matched against the user agent string of the visitor's browser, such as "Windows Phone 8." Device redirection to a specific master page depends on the value entered in this field.
Active	No	An enable/disable flag for the particular device channel. If working on a live site, it is recommended not to activate the channel until the design is finished. To test, you can use the Query String value (*?DeviceChannel=aliasname*) within the browser to preview the site for the specific channel.

Creating device channels   To create a new device channel, follow these steps:

1. Select Site Actions | Site Settings | Device Channels.

   You can also access Device Channels from Design Manager by clicking Manage Device Channels.

2. Click New Item.

   The New Item window appears, as shown in the following graphic.

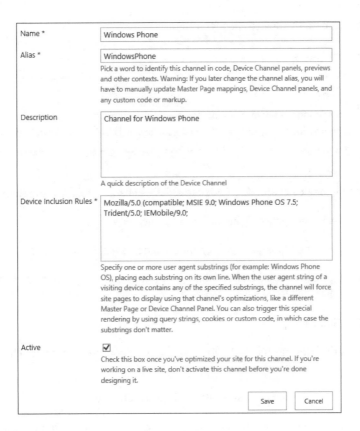

3. Fill in values for all the required fields and then click Save.

> **Note**
>
> When defining Device Inclusion Rules, you can create a fallback channel for all mobile devices that do not match specific Device Inclusion Rules.

Modifying existing device channels   To make changes to an existing device channel, follow these steps:

1. Select Site Actions | Site Settings | Device Channels.

2. From the Manage Device Channels page, select Edit Or Reorder Existing Channels.

3. Select the device channel that you want to modify, and then select Edit Item from the Items tab.

4.   Update the device channel settings.

5.   Click Save.

> **Note**
>
> If you change the alias for a device channel, you must also manually update the mappings for the alias in all the places where it is being used, such as master pages.

Deleting device channels   To delete a device channel, follow these steps:

1.   Select Site Actions | Site Settings | Device Channels.

2.   From the Manage Device Channels page, select Edit Or Reorder Existing Channels.

3.   Select the device channel that you want to delete, and then, from the Items tab, select Delete Item.

4.   Click OK.

Reordering device channels   To change the order of existing device channels, follow these steps:

1.   Select Site Actions | Site Settings | Device Channels.

2.   From the Manage Device Channels page, select Edit Or Reorder Existing Channels.

3.   Select the device channel that you want to delete, and then, from the Items tab, select Reorder Channels.

4.   Reorder the channels by selecting Move Up or Move Down.

5.   When finished, click OK.

Mapping a network drive

This section provides the instructions to map a network drive to a SharePoint Master Page gallery so that you can use Design Manager to upload design files into SharePoint Server 2013. Before you can map a network drive, you must find the location of the Master Page gallery for your site. Perform these steps to find the correct location:

1. From your publishing site, open Design Manager.

2. In the numbered list, select Upload Design Files, as shown here.

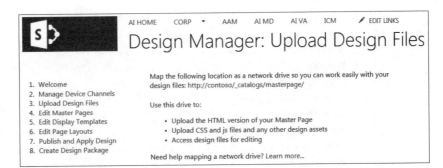

3. Note the location of the Master Page gallery or copy the location to the clipboard.

Continue with the following steps to map a network drive to the location of your Master Page Gallery, depending on the operating system:

- **Windows 8** Follow the steps from the article "Create a shortcut to (map) a network drive," located at *http://windows.microsoft.com/en-US/windows-8/ create-shortcut-to-map-network-drive*.

- **Windows 7** Follow the steps from the article "Create a shortcut to (map) a network drive," located at *http://windows.microsoft.com/en-US/windows7/ Create-a-shortcut-to-map-a-network-drive*.

- **Windows Vista** Follow the steps from the article "Create a shortcut to (map) a network drive," located at *http://windows.microsoft.com/en-US/windows-vista/ Create-a-shortcut-to-map-a-network-drive*.

Once the drive is mapped to the Master Page gallery, the mapped drive should open in Explorer view, as shown in Figure 12-15.

> **Note**
> If mapping the drive does not work or you prefer not to map a drive, you can still navigate to the Master Page gallery from the browser and open the library in Explorer view.

Name	Date modified	Type
Display Templates	2/12/2013 2:39 AM	File folder
Editing Menu	2/12/2013 2:49 AM	File folder
en-us	2/12/2013 2:48 AM	File folder
Forms	2/12/2013 2:39 AM	File folder
Preview Images	2/12/2013 2:39 AM	File folder
Themable	2/12/2013 2:49 AM	File folder
__DeviceChannelMappings.aspx	2/12/2013 2:49 AM	ASP.NET Server Pa...
AdvancedSearchLayout.aspx	2/12/2013 2:39 AM	ASP.NET Server Pa...
ArticleLeft.aspx	2/12/2013 2:49 AM	ASP.NET Server Pa...
ArticleLinks.aspx	2/12/2013 2:49 AM	ASP.NET Server Pa...
ArticleRight.aspx	2/12/2013 2:49 AM	ASP.NET Server Pa...
BlankWebPartPage.aspx	2/12/2013 2:49 AM	ASP.NET Server Pa...
CatalogArticle.aspx	2/12/2013 2:49 AM	ASP.NET Server Pa...
CatalogWelcome.aspx	2/12/2013 2:49 AM	ASP.NET Server Pa...
DefaultLayout.aspx	2/12/2013 2:39 AM	ASP.NET Server Pa...

Figure 12-15 A mapped network drive connected to a Master Page gallery, seen in Explorer view.

Once your drive is mapped, you can move on to creating and uploading your design files.

How to upload design files

The following steps describe how to upload your design to Design Manager:

1. Open up the mapped network drive.

2. Upload your design to SharePoint by copying the design files to the folder on the mapped drive.

You can create your own folder structure on the mapped drive that will synchronize the files automatically. It is recommended to keep all files related to one design in a single folder and then copy the folder containing the design files to the mapped drive.

Converting HTML to a master page

Once the design files are uploaded, you can use Design Manager to convert the HTML files to a SharePoint 2013 master page. After the conversion, the HTML file and master page file are associated so that when you edit and save the HTML file, the changes are synced to the associated master page. In SharePoint 2013, master pages work exactly as they do in ASP.NET; however, SharePoint also requires that certain elements specific to SharePoint be present on the page for SharePoint to render the master page correctly. The required elements include such things as controls and content placeholders. By converting an HTML file to a SharePoint master page using Design Manager, you do not have to know ASP.NET or the SharePoint-specific markup, as you did in previous SharePoint versions. Instead, you can focus on designing the site in HTML, CSS, and JavaScript.

When you convert an HTML file to a SharePoint master page, the following will occur:

- A master file (*.master*) is created with the same name as your HTML file in the Master Page gallery.

- All required SharePoint markup is added to the *.master* file.

- Markup is added to the original HTML file, such as <div> tags, comments, snippets, and content placeholders.

- The HTML file and master page are associated so that any edits made to the HTML file are synced to the *.master* file when the HTML file is saved.

> **Note**
> The syncing is completed in one direction only, which means changes to the HTML page are synced to the associated *.master* file. If you modify the *.master* file directly, the changes are not synced to the HTML master page. Every HTML master page has a property named Associated File that is set to True by default, which creates the association and syncing between the two files.

If you have a pair of associated files (HTML and *.master*) and you edit the *.master* without breaking the association, the changes to the *.master* file will be saved; however, you cannot check in or publish the *.master* file. Any changes to the HTML file will override the *.master* file, and any changes made directly to the *.master* file will be lost.

Preparing the HTML file for conversion

Before converting your HTML file, there are some recommendations to consider:

- The HTML file must be XML-compliant in order for the conversion to work. This requirement overrides some of the HTML 5 standards. For example, HTML 5 can have doctype specified in lowercase; however, in XML, doctype must be uppercase.

- All <FORM> tags must be removed from your HTML file.

Additional considerations must be made regarding CSS references:

- Do not put <STYLE> blocks in the <HEAD> tag because these styles are removed during the conversion. Instead, link the CSS from your HTML file to an external CSS file.

- Add `ms-design-css-conversion="no"` to the <CSS LINK> tag if you are using a web font.

- Be cautious applying styles to general HTML tags such as <BODY> and <IMG>. Everything within SharePoint is in the <BODY> tag, so for styles where you would normally apply the <BODY> tag, use something like `<div id="s4-bodyContainer">` instead.

- SharePoint uses dynamic navigation controls that have styles applied by using the <UL> and <LI> tags; therefore, if you use these tags, you will need to override the default styles being applied.

- If you are using JavaScript, make sure that the <SCRIPT> start tag is on its own line.

- References to jQuery libraries should go before the </HEAD> tag.

Converting the HTML file to a master page

Before you can convert an HTML file to a master page, you must upload all your design files to the Master Page gallery.

To convert the HTML file to a *.master* file, follow these steps:

1. From your publishing site, open Design Manager.

2. In the left navigation, click Edit Master Pages.

3. Choose Convert An HTML File To A SharePoint Master Page.

4. From the Select An Asset dialog box, browse to and select the HTML file that you want to convert.

5. Choose Insert.

   SharePoint 2013 converts your HTML file into a *.master* file with the same name. In Design Manager, your HTML file will now appear with a Status column showing one of two statuses:

   - Warnings And Errors

   - Conversion Successful

6. Click the link in the Status column to preview the file and to view any errors or warnings for the master page.

    The preview page is a live, server-side preview of the master page, and the top of the preview will display any warnings or errors that you may have to resolve by editing the HTML file. All errors must be fixed in the HTML file before the preview will display the master page correctly.

7. To fix any errors, modify the HTML file that resides on the server by using an HTML editor to open and edit the file on the mapped drive.

    Each time you save the HTML file, the changes are synced to the associated *.master* file. Once the master page previews successfully, you will see a <DIV> tag that resides in the ContentPlaceHolderMain.

    More information about ContentPlaceHolderMain is found in the following section, "Understanding the HTML markup after conversion."

Understanding the HTML markup after conversion

When you convert an HTML file to a master page, various types of markup is added to the HTML file automatically. The markup that is added includes tags before and inside the <HEAD> tag, snippets, and content placeholders. Most of the added markup is enclosed with comment tags, and when a change is saved to the HTML file, the conversion strips out the comments to use the ASP.NET markup within.

Document properties

The <MSO> tag contains SharePoint metadata, which includes information about the file itself, as well as some of the properties needed for the successful conversion to the *.master* file.

SharePoint markup

The <SPM> tag, which stands for "SharePoint markup," is added automatically with a line registering the SharePoint namespace.

Comments

The <CS> and <CE> ("comment start" and "comment end") tags are for comments that help parse the lines of markup. These tags are ignored during the conversion process.

Markup (snippets)

The <MS> and <ME> ("markup start" and "markup end") tags denote the beginning and end of a snippet. A *snippet* is a SharePoint control, such as the search box, ribbon, or page contents.

Preview blocks

The <PS> and <PE> ("preview start" and "preview end") tags contain a section of HTML code used for design-time preview. These preview sections are a snapshot in time of the SharePoint control that the snippet is inserting.

SharePoint IDs

During the conversion process, the two snippets added to the HTML file are the SharePoint Ribbon and the Page Head Contents snippet. These snippets have an associated SharePoint ID, or SID, which makes it possible to shorten the snippets to make the HTML in the page easier to read.

- **The ribbon** This is added automatically and contained in a security-trimmed snippet with restrictions set so that the ribbon is displayed only for authenticated users. The ribbon can be moved around to a different position, and it can be styled by overriding the default CSS classes for the ribbon. However, it is not recommended you move or reorder the components such as the Site Actions menu that are contained inside the ribbon.

- **ContentPlaceHolderMain** The content placeholder named ContentPlaceHolder-Main is added at the bottom of the `<div id="s4-bodyContainer">` tag before the closing </BODY> tag. Inside this snippet is a yellow <DIV> tag that represents the area where the content specified by the page layout will go.

Updating the site master page

Once your master page is created, you can assign your master page to your publishing site by following these steps:

1. From your publishing site, go to the Site Settings page by selecting Site Actions | Site Settings.

2. Under Look And Feel, select Master Page to open the Site Master Page Settings page.

3. In the drop-down list, select the desired master page for the Site Master Page and System Master Page.

4. If you want to update all subsites below this site, select the option for Reset All Subsites To Inherit This Site Master Page setting.

5. Click OK.

Creating page layouts

Page layouts work hand in hand with master pages. The role of page layouts is to define the layout for a specific class of pages for your site.

To create a new page layout, follow these steps:

1. From your publishing site, open Design Manager.

2. In the numbered list, select Edit Page Layouts.

3. Select Create A Page Layout.

4. Type in a value for the Name.

5. From the Master Page drop-down list, select the desired master page.

    The selected master page will be used for the preview of the page layout. The master page also determines what content placeholders will be added to the page layout.

6. From the Content Type drop-down list, select the desired content type.

    The content type for the page layout determines what page fields will be available for the page layout in the Snippet gallery.

7. Click OK.

    SharePoint 2013 converts your HTML file to a *.master* file with the same name. In Design Manager, your HTML file will now appear with a Status column showing one of two statuses:

    - Warnings And Errors

    - Conversion Successful

8. Click the link of the Status column to preview the file and to view any errors or warnings about the page.

9. To fix any errors, modify the HTML file that resides on the server by using an HTML editor to open and edit the file on the mapped drive.

    Each time that you save the HTML file, the changes are synced to the associated *.aspx* file.

INSIDE OUT What is the relationship between master pages and page layouts?

A master page and page layout must have the identical set of content placeholders for the page layout to render correctly for the specified master page. In previous versions of SharePoint, custom master pages and page layouts were created manually through SharePoint Designer (or Visual Studio), so the relationship between the two was maintained manually. If a page layout was using a manually added content placeholder but the placeholder did not exist in the specified master page, the page would not render correctly and would display an error about the missing content placeholder. This meant that any time a custom page layout was created and a content placeholder was added manually, the creator had to remember to update all master pages that the site was allowed to use to contain the content placeholder. This manual process is no longer a problem when you use Design Manager to create master pages and page layouts because the correct set of content placeholders is added to every file when it is created.

When you create styles for page layouts, the styles can reside in the same style sheet that is linked to the master page file, or the styles can be in a separate style sheet linked to the page layout. To minimize the weight of the CSS that is loaded per page, it is recommended to use different style sheets for different page layouts. To do this, the reference to the style sheet cannot go into the <HEAD> tag of a page layout; instead, it must go into the content placeholder named PlaceHolderAdditionalPageHead. The additional page head merges into the end of the head of the master page so that the styles for the page layout are applied after the styles for the master page.

For supporting mobile devices, each page layout can have device channel–specific style sheets. This is done by including one or more device channel panels inside the additional page head where each channel panel includes a link to a style sheet with channel-specific styles.

For examples of the SharePoint markup, see the MSDN article "Reference: Examples of SharePoint markup added to the HTML file," located at *http://msdn.microsoft.com/en-us/library/jj822370.aspx#Reference*.

Using image renditions

As mentioned in Chapter 9, image renditions can be used to display uploaded images in predefined sizes—which is useful for reducing the size of the images that are downloaded to the client. This feature is especially useful for mobile devices because different versions of the same image can be displayed based on the device used.

To use image renditions, you must do the following:

- Enable the binary large object (BLOB) cache on the web application (if not already enabled).

For more information on how to configure cache settings, see "Configure cache settings for a web application (SharePoint Server 2010)," at *http://technet.microsoft.com/en-us/library/ cc770229.aspx.*

- Define the image rendition sizes (that is, specify width and height for all images that use the image rendition).

- Generate the default image preview by uploading an image.

- Add the image to a page and specify which image rendition to use on that page.

When adding an image to a page in a SharePoint publishing site, you can specify the image rendition to use for the image that is rendered in the browser so that the correct image size is displayed.

Image renditions can be specified in the following ways:

- **Rich text editor** You can specify the image rendition in the rich text editor only for images that are stored in the same site collection as the page that is being modified.

- **Image URL** You can specify the image rendition by adding the RenditionID, Width, or Height parameters to the image URL. The following is an example using the RenditionID query string value and one using the width and height query string value:

```
<img src="/sites/pub/Assets/Image.jpg?RenditionID=2" />
<img src="/sites/pub/Assets/Image.jpg?Width=400&Height=200" />
```

- **Image field control** Through custom development, you can specify the image rendition to use in the image field control by using the *RenditionID* property to set the ID of the image rendition.

Using content rollup web parts

As mentioned in Chapter 10, "Adding, editing, connecting, and maintaining web parts," content rollup web parts were introduced in previous versions of SharePoint. The main out-of-the-box web part that was used was the Content Query Web Part (CQWP). Styling for the CQWP was a bit challenging because of the technical skills required. Specific XSL files had to be updated in order to change the styling for the CQWP.

Using the CSWP and display templates

As discussed in Chapter 10, the CSWP is a powerful web part that uses various styling options to display dynamic content on SharePoint pages. The CSWP can return any content from the search index. Therefore, it makes sense to use it on your sites when you want to return indexed search results in your pages.

You can easily configure and alter how a CSWP displays search results on a page. Each CSWP is connected with a search query, thus displaying results for that search query. To format how search results appear on the page, you can use display templates which are comprised of snippets of HTML and JavaScript. This section focuses on the steps to use the CSWP and display templates.

> **Note**
>
> Display templates can only be used with Search Web Parts. The Content Query Web Part is not search-driven therefore it cannot use display templates.

Display templates

In SharePoint 2010, if you wanted to style an item differently, you had to modify XSLT to change the item's look and feel. A new feature in SharePoint 2013 that eliminates the need to modify the XSLT is display templates. The feature is used in web parts that use search technology to show the results of the query made to the search index. Display templates control which managed properties are shown in the search results and also control how they appear in the web part. Each display template consists of an HTML file (.html), which is where the display pattern resides, and a JavaScript file (.js), which is generated automatically when the HTML file is uploaded.

Display templates are part of Design Manager and there are three contexts in which you may use them: with search results, with groups of results, and with item results. Display templates can also be used to style the rendering of the items of the Content Search Web Part (CSWP). Creating display templates is different than how you create master pages and page layouts.

Display templates and search web parts

The relationship between display templates and search web parts, such as the CSWP, are as follows:

- **Control template** This template determines the overall structure of how the results are presented, which includes lists, lists with paging, and slide shows.

- **Item template** This template determines how each result in the set is displayed. This includes text, images, videos, and other items.

Once a CSWP is added to a page, the edit tool pane for the web part has a configurable section called Display Templates, which has the Control and Item drop-down lists, as shown in Figure 12-16.

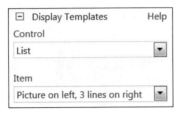

Figure 12-16 The Display Templates section of the Content Search Web Part edit tools pane is configurable.

The control template provides the HTML to structure the overall layout of the presentation of the search results for the heading. The item template provides the HTML structure of the display for each item and is rendered one time for each item in the result set. So if the result set contains five items, the item display template will create a section of the HTML that is rendered five times. When used together, the control template and item template combine to create a cohesive block of HTML that renders in the web part, as shown in Figure 12-17.

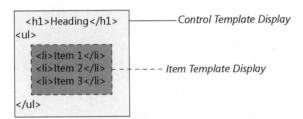

Figure 12-17 The combined HTML output of a control template and item template display.

Adding and configuring the CSWP

The following example demonstrates how to add and configure the CSWP.

Add a CSWP to your desired page by performing these steps:

1. Browse to the page where you want to add the web part.

2. From the Settings menu, choose Edit Page.

3. From within the zone where you want to add the CSWP, click Add A Web Part. Alternatively, from the Insert tab, click Web Part.

4. From the categories list, select Content Rollup.

5. In the parts list, click Content Search, and then click Add.

   The CSWP is in the same category as the CQWP in the Content Rollup grouping. When you add it to the page, it should display as shown here.

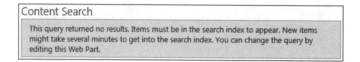

The next step is to configure the CSWP by editing the web part, which you do as follows:

1. Select the Settings menu, and then click Edit Page.

2. Inside the CSWP, click the menu arrow, and then click Edit Web Part.

3. In the tool pane, look for the Properties section. Then, in the search criteria category, as shown here, click Change Query to open the Build Your Query dialog box.

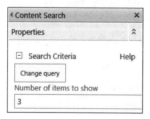

4. On the Basics tab, define your query by using "quick mode."

By using quick mode, you can focus the CSWP on the content source of your choice by using the following options:

- Using an existing result source using the Select A Query menu

- Restrict the targeted content to a specific app (site, list, library, etc.)

- Restrict content by tag (metadata terms)

- Choose how you want to sort the results

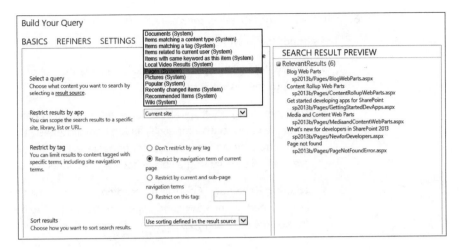

5. On the Refiners tab, select the desired refiner (filter) on the left and click Apply to add.

The Refiners tab provides the enabled managed properties that are enabled as refiners (filters) in the search schema.

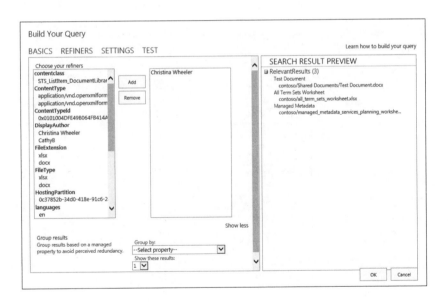

6. On the Settings tab, select the desired performance settings.

The settings tab provides the following options:

- **Query Rule**   The option to disable or enable the use of query rules from Site Settings for this web part.

- **URL Rewriting**   Select if the URL rewrite to the item details page should continue to be relative for each catalog item as defined when setting up the connection. If *Don't rewrite URLs* option is selected, the URLs for catalog items are pointed directly to the library item of the connected catalog.

- **Loading Behavior**   Controls the loading behavior when the search results are returned by the CSWP and appear on the page. The default option is *Display the page and web part simultaneously* however you can change it to the asynchronous option which is *Display the page and web part independently*. The asynchronous option may be considered for secondary content on a page such as recommendations or popular items.

- **Priority**   Select the importance of the web part's query in relation to other Search web parts. If SharePoint 2013 is running under a heavy load, the queries will run according to their set priority.

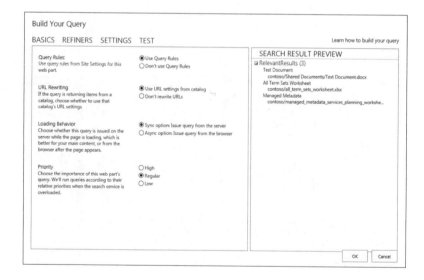

7. Select the Test tab to see the actual query text that is used behind the scenes to create the query.

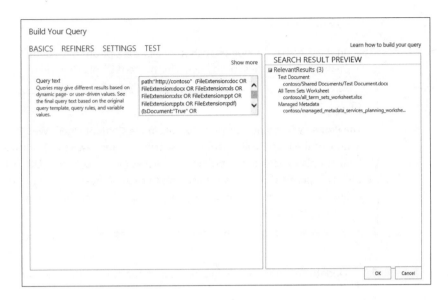

8. Once you have completed all of the desired settings for the Build Your Query options, click OK.

9. Set the Number of items to show. The default value is 3.

10. In the Display Templates section, select one of the following Control options:

- **List** This is the default value and is most commonly used

- **List with Paging** Same as List but with paging added

- **Slideshow** Image rotator

11. For the Item property, select the Item display template by changing the drop-down list to one of the following:

This setting dictates the style applied to each item displayed.

- Diagnostic

- Large picture

- Picture on left, 3 lines on right

- Picture on top, 3 lines on bottom

- Recommended Items: Picture on left, 3 lines on right

- Two lines

- Video

12. In the Property Mappings section, select the option for Change the mapping of managed properties for the fields in the Item Display Template.

> **Note**
>
> The Property Mappings is similar to slots in the Content Query Web Part. They are a feature of the Item Display Template (specified in the JavaScript) which is selected. Item Templates use generic properties (such as Picture URL, Link URL, Line 1) that you can map specific fields from the list item to each of these properties. You can input a single value or specify multiple values for each property by using a semi-colon (PublishingImage;PictureURL).

13. Update any other remaining optional properties for the web part.

14. Once complete, click OK.

How to create a display template

You can view existing display templates in Design Manager; however, to create them, you do the following:

1. Open the mapped network drive to the Master Page gallery.

2. Open one of the four folders in the Display Templates folder.

The folder you select depends on the type of display template that you want to create. For example, if you want one for cross-site publishing, you would copy a display template from the Content Web Parts folder.

For more information on the different display templates available, see the article "Display template reference in SharePoint Server 2013," located at *http://technet.microsoft.com/en-us/library/jj944947.aspx*.

3. Copy the HTML file for an existing template similar to what you want to the Master Page gallery.

4. Open and modify the copy in any preferred HTML editor.

   By using a copy of an existing display template as a starting point for your new display template, this helps guarantee that your template uses the correct basic page structure. The comments in the display template provide helpful information about the customization process.

   When you create a new display template by copying an existing template to the Master Page gallery, the following occurs:

   - A *.js* file with the same name is created in the location where you copied the HTML file.

   - All required SharePoint markup is added to the *.js* file so the display template will render correctly.

   - The HTML file and *.js* file become associated so when edits to the HTML file are saved, the changes are synced with the *.js* file.

5. From your publishing site, open Design Manager.

6. In the left navigation, click Edit Display Templates.

   Your HTML file now appears with the Status column showing one of the following two statuses:

   - Warnings And Errors

   - Conversion Successful

7. To fix any errors, modify the HTML file for the display template that resides on the server by using an HTML editor to open and edit the file on the mapped drive.

8. Save the display template and then reload the page that contains the CSWP that uses the display.

9. Modify the web part properties of the CSWP and change the Item drop-down list to your new display template.

> **Note**
>
> Display templates cannot be previewed like master pages and page layouts. To preview the display template, you must add an CSWP to a page and then apply the customized templates.

Using the Content Query Web Part

As mentioned in Chapter 10, "Adding, editing, connecting, and maintaining web parts," both the CQWP and the CSWP are very powerful web parts that can be used to aggregate content in SharePoint. Determining which one to use depends on your requirements. This section provides the steps to configure and customize the CQWP.

Adding and configuring the CQWP

The following example demonstrates how to add and configure the CQWP.

Add a CQWP to your desired page by following these steps:

1. Browse to the page where you want to add the web part.

2. From the Settings menu, choose Edit Page.

3. From within the zone where you want to add the CQWP, click Add A Web Part. Or from the Insert tab, click Web Part.

4. From the categories list, select Content Rollup.

5. In the parts list, click Content Query, and then click Add.

6. Inside the CQWP, click the menu arrow, and then click Edit Web Part.

7. In the Query section of the Web Part, select the source you want to query data from.

8. Select the List Type, Content Type, Audience Targeting, and desired Additional Filters settings.

9. In the Presentation section of the Web Part, select the desired Grouping and Sorting options.

10. If the Group items by option was set, select the desired style in the Group style drop-down list.

11. From the Item style drop-down list, select the desired style.

12. Under Fields to display, type the field name of each field in the desired text boxes to map the fields to the slots.

How to create customized XSL files for the CQWP

The following example demonstrates how create custom XSL style sheet for the CQWP.

To create a custom XSL style sheet file for the Item styles by following these steps:

1. From SharePoint Designer 2013, navigate to the Style Library | XSL Style Sheets.

2. Make a copy of the Itemstyle.xsl and rename the file (IE. CustomItemStyle.xsl).

3. Right-click on the new file and select Edit File in Advanced Mode.

4. Identify the style that is similar to the one you want to create and then copy/paste the style before the closing **</xsl:stylesheet>** tag or in between an of the existing templates.

5. Change the **name** and match **property** values.

    ```
    <xsl:template name="CustomName" match="Row[@Style='CustomName']"
    mode="itemstyle">
    ```

6. Make any desired changes and additions to your new custom template.

7. Once complete, check in the file and select Publish a major version.

8. From the browser, navigate to the page where you want to configure an existing CQWP or add a new CQWP to desired page.

9. Inside the CQWP, click the menu arrow, and then click Export.

10. Save the file to your local computer.

11. Open the saved file on your local computer in desired text editor.

12. Find the ItemXSLStyle property and replace with the line below:

    ```
            <property name="ItemXslLink" type="string">/Style Library/
    XSL Style Sheets/CustomItemStyle.xsl</property>
    ```

    You can also create custom XSL style sheet files to replace the Header.xsl and the ContentQueryMain.xsl using the same steps above. For the Header.xsl you will need to set the HeaderXslLink property and for the ContentQueryMain.xsl you will need to set the MainXslLink property and point it to your new custom XSL files.

13. Save the .webpart file and upload to your Web parts gallery which is located in the Web Designer Galleries section on the Site Settings page. Navigate to Site Actions | Site settings | Web parts.

> **Note**
>
> You can either save the web part to your Web part gallery or just upload the web part to your desired page. Uploading to the Web part gallery is recommended so the web part can be reused.

14. Add the newly exported web part to a page and then inside the CQWP, click the menu arrow and then click Edit Web Part.

15. Under the Presentation settings, select the desired template in your Item style drop-down list. Map any necessary fields in the Fields to display and make any other desired changes and then apply the changes.

16. Click OK.

Metadata and navigation

In SharePoint 2010, Managed Metadata and the Term Store were introduced to provide a hierarchical collection of centrally managed terms that could be defined and used as attributes for items in SharePoint.

Prior to SharePoint 2013, the only out-of-the-box dynamic navigation option available was Structural Navigation, which based its navigation model on the hierarchical structure of the site collection. Customization options were limited; therefore, many companies would decide to implement their own custom navigation solution or purchase a third-party solution to overcome the limitations, especially for public-facing websites. A common question that was asked by customers was, "Can we use Managed Metadata for SharePoint navigation out of the box?" The answer for SharePoint 2010 was always no. Now when that question is asked, the answer is, "You can absolutely do that in SharePoint 2013."

For more information on Managed Metadata, see "Plan managed metadata in SharePoint Server 2013," located at *http://technet.microsoft.com/en-us/library/ee530389.aspx.*

Managed navigation

Microsoft has added the ability to use Managed Metadata for navigation, called managed navigation. SharePoint 2013 navigation now has two different options: the old structural navigation way and the new managed navigation way. Managed navigation uses a Managed Metadata term set to populate the items within the navigation control.

Figure 12-18 shows the options available from the Navigation Settings page, which can be accessed from Site Actions | Site Settings | Navigation.

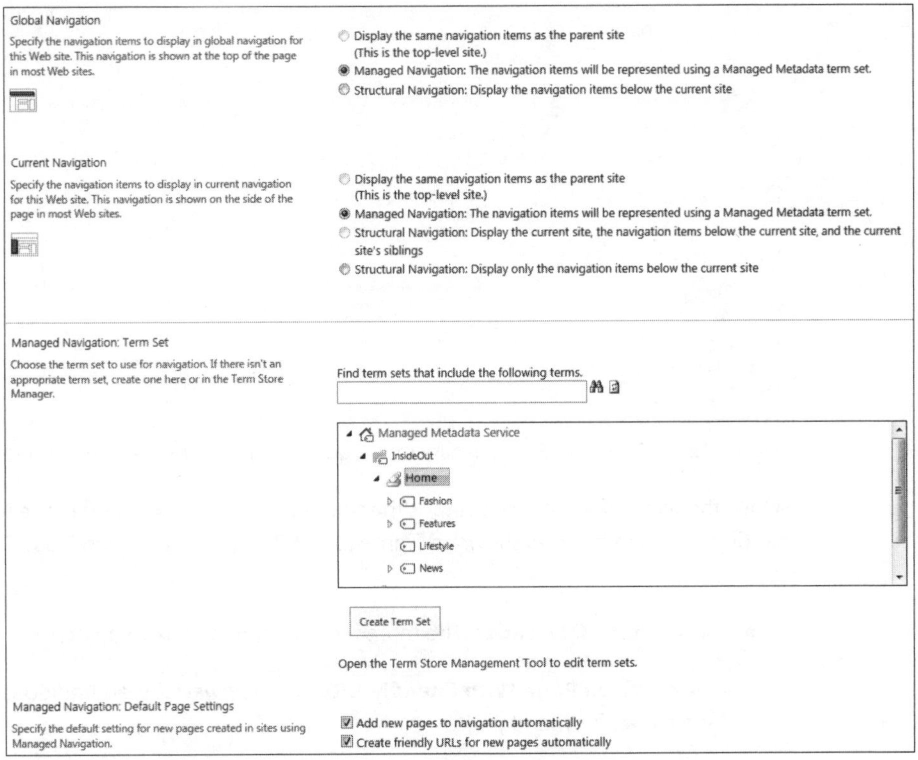

Figure 12-18 The Navigation Settings page provides multiple configuration options.

When you change the Global Navigation or Current Navigation option to Managed Navigation, you then have the option to select from an existing Term Store or to click the Term Store Management Tool link located below the Create Term Set button.

Chapter 12

> **Note**
>
> Navigation settings for Global and Current Navigation are available only on sites that have the publishing features enabled.

Figure 12-19 shows the Intended Use options for the Term Set. To use the Term Set for navigation, you must first enable the Use This Term Set For Site Navigation option.

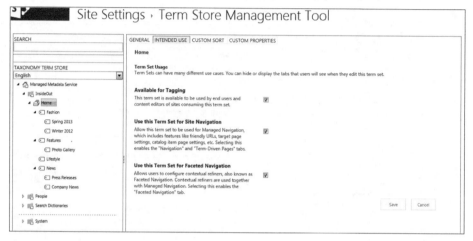

Figure 12-19 The Term Store Management Tool – Term Set Intended Use settings.

Once the navigation option is set for the term set, you can then modify the Navigation settings for each term, as shown in Figure 12-20. The two Navigation Node Type options are:

- **Simple Link Or Header** The more traditional hyperlink to an item

- **Term-Driven Page With Friendly URL** More powerful than traditional hyperlinks and allows for friendly URLs

The friendly URL can be set from the Term-Driven Pages tab, shown in Figure 12-21. Options available include friendly URL, as well as the ability to set the target page for the hyperlink. There is also an option to set search engine optimization (SEO) properties.

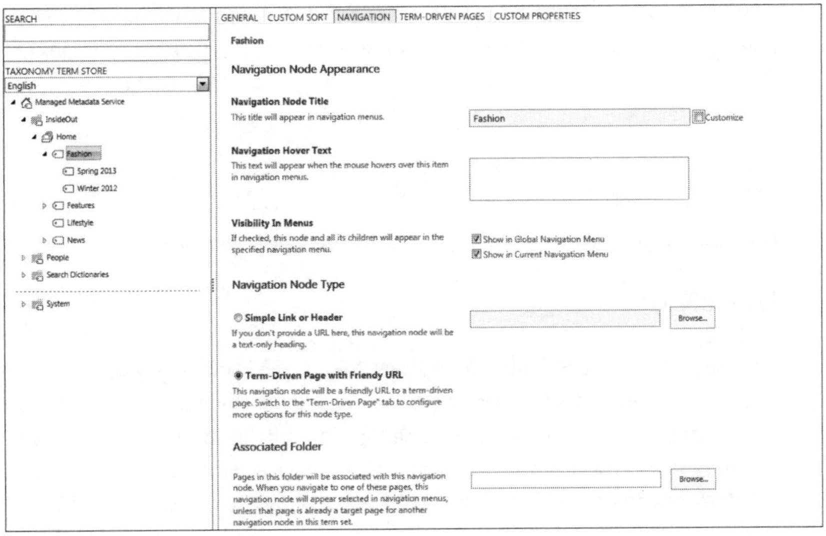

Figure 12-20 The Term Store Management Tool – Term Navigation settings.

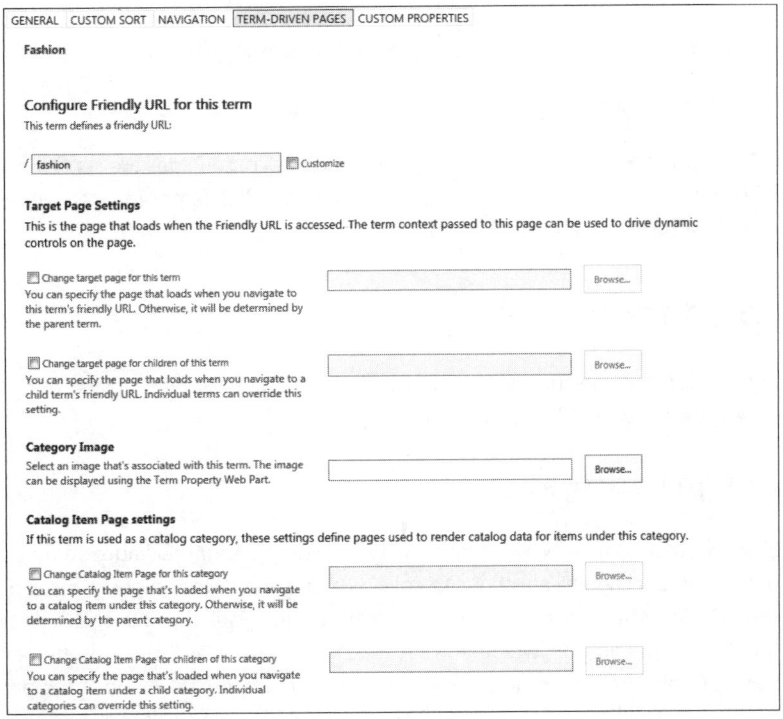

Figure 12-21 The Term Store Management Tool – Term-Driven Pages settings.

With managed navigation, you also have the ability to modify links anywhere without having to use the Navigation Settings page. You simply click the Edit Links button next to the top links on the site, as shown in Figure 12-22, or the links on the left of the page. You can add, remove, edit, and hide/show the links.

Figure 12-22 Click Edit Links to add, remove, edit, or hide/show links.

Friendly URLs

Another new navigation feature in SharePoint 2013 is friendly URLs. In SharePoint 2010, when you navigate to a publishing page, the URL in the address bar is typically /Pages/default.aspx, and there is no separation of URLs from the site hierarchy. This was a common complaint from customers, especially for public-facing websites. One of the great improvements in SharePoint 2013 is the ability to use friendly URLs. With the use of managed navigation and friendly URLs, navigation for items no longer have to be long URLs and can be configured so that they can be referenced more easily. Here is an example of SharePoint 2013 friendly URLs in practice:

- **SharePoint 2010** *www.contoso.com/Pages/AboutUs.aspx*

- **SharePoint 2013** *www.contoso.com/AboutUs*

URLs no longer contain */Pages/* and .aspx and Welcome Pages are served from the web URL and no longer display */Pages/default.aspx,* nor 302 Temporarily Moved redirects. This is a huge improvement in SharePoint!

Publishing content

This section provides the information on how to publish content using the SharePoint 2013 enterprise content publishing model.

Design packages

SharePoint 2013 now provides the ability to export design packages so that you can import the design package to another site collection or server. Design packages can be created from Design Manager by clicking the Create Design Package link. This will take you to the Create Design Package, where you set the Design Name and choose whether to Include Search Configuration in this package. As shown in Figure 12-23, once the package is created, you will see the message, "Your package is ready. Click here to download." Clicking this link will generate the .WSP design package.

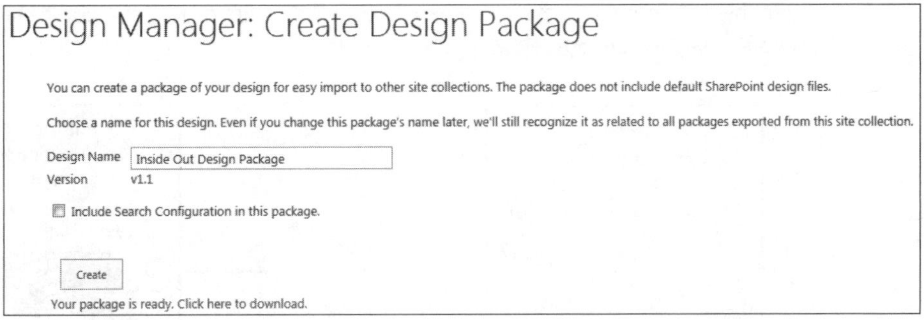

Design Manager: Create Design Package

You can create a package of your design for easy import to other site collections. The package does not include default SharePoint design files.

Choose a name for this design. Even if you change this package's name later, we'll still recognize it as related to all packages exported from this site collection.

Design Name   Inside Out Design Package

Version   v1.1

☐ Include Search Configuration in this package.

Create

Your package is ready. Click here to download.

Figure 12-23 Click Create to generate the .WSP Design Package.

A design package can be imported by selecting Site Actions | Site Settings | Import Design Package. From there, you browse to your .WSP design package and click Import, as shown in Figure 12-24.

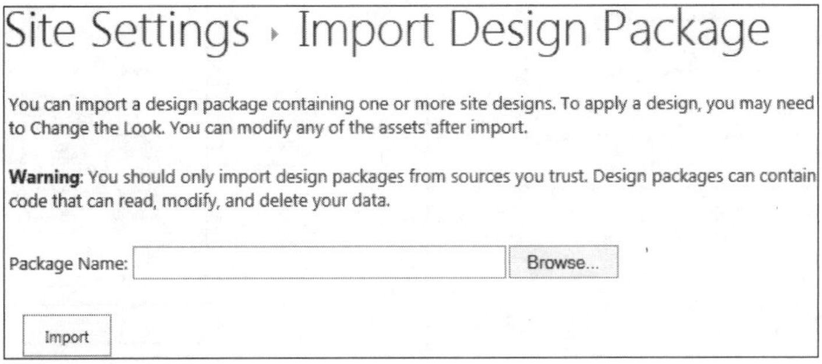

Site Settings ▸ Import Design Package

You can import a design package containing one or more site designs. To apply a design, you may need to Change the Look. You can modify any of the assets after import.

Warning: You should only import design packages from sources you trust. Design packages can contain code that can read, modify, and delete your data.

Package Name: Browse...

Import

Figure 12-24 Click Import to import your design package.

Cross-site collection publishing

Although previous versions of SharePoint had great WCM features, one of the problems was the inability to share content between site collections. Because many organizations require multiple site collections, they ended up duplicating content between the site collections. That has now changed in SharePoint 2013 with the new concept of cross-site publishing.

The cross-site collection publishing feature in SharePoint 2013 enables organizations to use one or more site collections to create content and use one or more site collections to control the site design and content display. When content is changed in an authoring site collection, the content changes are displayed on all site collections that are reusing the content, as shown in Figure 12-25. Cross-site publishing uses search technology to retrieve the content from site collections that have the cross-site collection publishing feature enabled. Before the content can be reused in other site collections, libraries and lists must be enabled as catalogs.

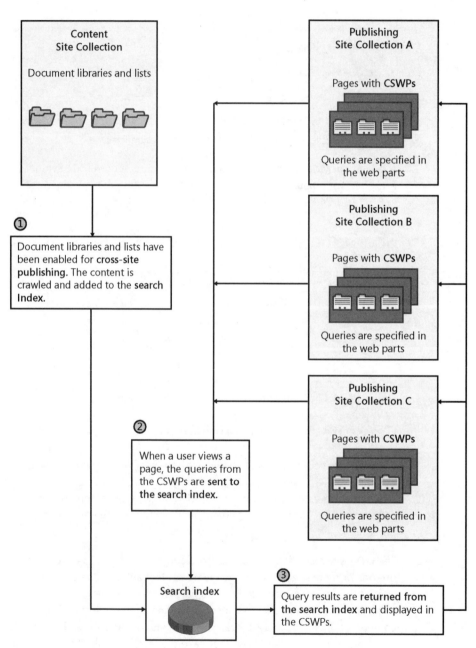

Figure 12-25 A diagram of cross-site collection publishing.

> **Note**
> Lists and libraries can be designated as catalogs on any site collection that has the
> cross-site collection publishing feature enabled so that it can be reused on publishing
> site collections. You can surface content stored in catalogs across site collections by
> using the CSWP, as demonstrated earlier in this chapter.

WCM considerations

There are many things to consider before implementing WCM for SharePoint 2013, such as
the following:

- Are you upgrading from SharePoint 2010 or creating a new SharePoint 2013 site?

- Is your site external or internal? What type of authentication are you using?

- Does your site need to be multilingual?

Usage analytics

Usage analytics is a new feature in SharePoint 2013 that, in essence, is an improved version
of Web Analytics that was a part of SharePoint 2010. This new feature provides informative
site use analytics and statistics.

The two analytics components introduced in SharePoint 2013 are:

- **Search analytics** This component analyzes content in the search index. The set of
  analyses extracts information such as links and anchor text from content as it is being
  crawled and processed. The extracted information is stored in the Link database, and
  the results from the search analyses are used to enrich items in the search index with
  information to help improve relevance and recall.

- **Usage analytics** This is a set of analyses that receive information about user actions
  or usage events, such as clicks and viewed items on the SharePoint site. Usage
  analytics combines the set of analyses with information about crawled content
  from the search analyses and processes the information. The data in the reporting
  database can be used to generate popularity trends and most popular item reports.

Variations and multilingual sites

Many organizations operate globally, and even domestic markets have the need to support users who speak multiple languages or have specific information based on regional differences. This diversity of users often requires publishing sites to be tailored to suit different cultures, different markets, and different geographic regions. Producing and maintaining different versions of a site can be difficult and time consuming. SharePoint has the ability to support multilingual sites through a Multilingual User Interface (MUI) and variations that can simplify the process of producing and maintaining multilingual sites.

Understanding variations

Variations, first introduced in MOSS 2007, constitute a SharePoint feature that enables users to create, manage, and translate locale-specific content for publishing sites. The MUI feature is used to create sites in different languages than the default language of the SharePoint installation, and the feature works with your site's user interface. Variations, which include enhanced translation workflow and machine translation services, are used to create a source publishing site that makes copies of the content, which then can be translated into different languages. The way it works is if the language packs are installed on the SharePoint environment and the MUI has been set up, the UI will appear for the selected language based on the default language setting of the user's browser.

In SharePoint 2010, building multilingual sites using variations was supported; however, the translation of the content on the pages for the other languages had to be done manually. Variations were used exclusively for multilingual sites, and content was made available to specific audiences on different sites by copying content from a source variation site to one or more target variation sites and tracking the relationships between source and target content. Users visiting the multilingual site would be redirected to the appropriate variation site based on the language setting in their browser. Since the implementation of multilingual sites for the previous versions of SharePoint required content to be duplicated and manually translated, this steered away some companies from implementing a global site.

The variations feature in SharePoint 2013 has been greatly improved with a new translation service that provides the ability to automate the creation, management, synchronization, and translation of sites, pages, and lists, eliminating the need to manually create a site and all associated lists and pages for each instance of a needed variation. However, if needed, content can still be exported for human translation. Bulk export of pages was added to the variations feature to improve performance, logging functionality has been updated to improve the usefulness of error messages, and the logs can now be exported to Microsoft Excel.

For more information on variations, see the MSDN article "Variations overview in SharePoint Server 2013," located at *http://technet.microsoft.com/en-us/library/ff628966.aspx.*

Machine Translation Services

Translating content to other languages in SharePoint 2013 no longer needs to be done manually. Machine Translation Services is a new service application that allows content and sites to be translated automatically in the cloud, or you can export the translated content to an XLIFF package and send it over for the translator to review, and then once translated, it will be imported back into SharePoint.

To provision and use the Machine Translation Service, the environment must meet the following requirements:

- The App Management Service is started in Central Administration.

- Server-to-Server and App Authentication is configured.

- The User Profile Service Application Proxy must be in the Default Proxy Group, and the User Profile Service must be provisioned and configured.

- Internet connectivity must be available on the server from which the machine translations are run.

To learn more about provisioning and configuring Machine Translation Services for SharePoint 2013, please visit *http://technet.microsoft.com/en-us/library/jj553772(v=office.15).aspx.*

Summary

WCM has been completely revamped in SharePoint 2013. The big overhaul that Microsoft did with WCM makes branding and design much easier for designers. With Design Manager, introduction of the CSWP, cross-site publishing, and other new and improved features, SharePoint can be a powerful WCM solution for your organization. Not only have the enhancements closed the gaps from the previous versions of SharePoint, the new features also allow for much better ability to build truly dynamic SharePoint sites. Search also plays a significant role in WCM, which is covered in Chapter 18, "Discovering information with SharePoint 2013 Search," and Chapter 19, "Creating a customized SharePoint 2013 search experience."

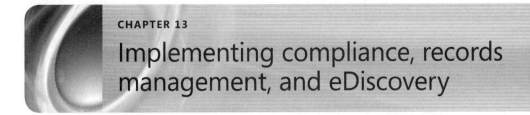

Implementing compliance, records management, and eDiscovery

N ow that you have learned about web content management (WCM) in Chapter 12, "Designing web content management sites," this chapter discusses the Microsoft SharePoint features that can help with compliance, records management, and eDiscovery. In today's world of technology, organizations are increasingly subject to state and federal regulations that govern the retention of electronic records, including what records must be retained and how readily records should be accessible to regulators. In addition to the rules and regulations that some organizations must comply with for legal reasons, organizations have found that defensive business practices also call for good data management to protect the organization from potential litigation. This chapter focuses on the compliance features in SharePoint, the planning process for records management, and how to use SharePoint for eDiscovery.

Compliance

What is compliance? *Compliance* is the state of being in accordance with federal and regional authorities and their requirements. In other words, compliance is when organizations have regulations that they must abide by according to their specific industry, such as HIPAA/HITECH, DOD 5015, Section 508, WCAG 1.0/2.0, and SOX. The three most common sets of regulations used today are the Health Insurance Portability and Accountability Act (HIPAA), the Health Information Technology for Economic and Clinical Health Act (HITECH Act), and SOX (Sarbanes-Oxley Act).

HIPAA and the HITECH Act

In 1996, the Health Insurance Portability and Accountability Act (HIPAA) was enacted by Congress for the healthcare industry in response to issues faced with health care coverage, privacy, security, and fraud. Before HIPAA, rules and regulations varied by state and by organization, and there was no standard authority for the enforcement of fraud and abuse protections applied to state and federal health care programs. With the increasing use of electronic technology, Congress recognized a need to establish security and privacy standards due to the risk of potential abuse or compromise. HIPAA requires organizations that have access to personal health information to adopt security policies to safeguard the confidentiality of patients' data. The access to this data must be monitored by the organization and must be controlled, as well as have an audit trail available for regulators.

In 2009, another act was introduced, called the Health Information Technology for Economic and Clinical Health Act. The HITECH Act became part of the American Recovery and Reinvestment Act of 2009 (ARRA), which stated that beginning in 2011, healthcare providers were offered financial incentives for demonstrating meaningful use of electronic health records. The HITECH Act widens the scope of privacy and security protections available under HIPAA. It also increases the potential liability for noncompliance and provides more enforcement.

HIPAA-Compliant SharePoint sites

In today's healthcare industry, SharePoint adoption is on the rise as the medical industry realizes the great potential to streamline and organize business processes and data in SharePoint. Many healthcare organizations require HIPAA-compliant SharePoint solutions to store and process electronic protected information. In order to make a SharePoint site HIPAA-compliant, these guidelines must be followed:

- Secure Transmission   The site content must always be encrypted as it is transmitted over the Internet. This can be accomplished by using Secure Sockets Layer (SSL).

- Integrity   The data should be backed up and must be recoverable. Every SharePoint environment should have a disaster recovery (DR) plan, part of which should include how often backups are performed and the acceptable potential loss of data in a disaster.

- Access Control (Authentication)   The data should be accessed only by authorized personnel. The governance planning should include user security, password policies, procedures when bringing in new employees, and the procedures when an employee leaves. Windows Rights Management and Information Rights Management (IRM) can help handle how content is downloaded and secured on users' computers inside and outside the network. Rights for opening, modifying, printing, and forwarding files can be configured for each Active Directory user.

- Audit Controls (Integrity)   The records should be backed up and must be recoverable.

- To get around the HIPAA Notification Clause   All data should be encrypted if it is being stored or archived. There is a clause in HIPAA documentation that requires organizations to notify each patient if there is a security breach in the system. When documents are stored in SharePoint, they are stored in Microsoft

> SQL Server as Binary Large Objects (BLOBs) or elsewhere if Remote Backup Service (RBS) is enabled. SQL Server 2008 R2 and SQL Server 2012 have a feature called *transparent database encryption* that will encrypt the databases automatically. To get around the HIPAA clause, the organization can implement encryption for files stored in the environment because the information is still secure. If FILESTREAM RBS data is used, please be aware that FILESTREAM data is not encrypted even when transparent data encryption is enabled.
>
> - **Retention for six years**   Health records must be kept for six years and can be permanently disposed of when no longer needed.

SOX

In 2002, Congress introduced legislation called the Sarbanes-Oxley Act (SOX), which requires businesses operating in the financial industry to maintain documentation through a set of internal controls that prove the effectiveness of its reporting systems. SOX applies to publicly traded companies. It requires business owners and executives to sign off on internal controls as defined by standard operating procedures (SOPs), and the SOPs define the controls that the business puts in place to meet the requirements.

Two key sections of SOX help define these requirements:

- **Section 302**   Requires executives to sign off directly on financial statements.

- **Section 404**   Requires all internal controls and SOPs are documented along with evidence of assertions made in the SOP. It requires all documentation be adequately audited and reviewed.

Site-based retention

The compliance features in SharePoint Server 2013 have been extended to sites. Retention policies can be created and managed in SharePoint and the policies can be applied to SharePoint sites and any Microsoft Exchange Server 2013 team mailboxes associated with the sites. For example, compliance officers may create policies that define:

- The retention policy for the entire site and Exchange Server 2013 team mailbox (if one is associated)

- What causes a project to close

- When a project should expire

The two main drivers for compliance in SharePoint are records management and eDiscovery.

Records management

Before we talk about records management, we must first talk about records. What is a record? Well, the first thought that may come to mind is a round disk made from vinyl plastic that sound was recorded on, which is now a thing of the past. As vinyl records are now part of vintage collections, records in another sense are still produced. A *record* is a document or other electronic or physical entity serving as evidence of an activity or transaction performed in an organization that requires retention for a period of time. Records management is the practice of maintaining records from the time of their inception to the time of their disposal in accordance with applicable laws. *Records management* is the process by which an organization defines what type of information needs to be classified as a record, whether it be a physical or electronic document, an email message, or some other form of digital information that serves as evidence of an activity or transaction performed by the organization.

Records management is also the process by which an organization:

- Determines how to handle the active documents that will become records while they are being used and determines how the documents should be collected once they are declared records

- Determines the retention period for each record to meet legal, business, and regulatory requirements

- Researches and implements technological solutions and business processes to ensure that the organization complies with the records management requirements

- Performs records-related tasks, such as locating and protecting records that are related to external events, such as lawsuits, or handles disposing expired records

Records management systems help the organization demonstrate compliance with regulatory obligations, help protect organizations legally, and increases organizational efficiency by promoting the disposition of out-of-date items that are not records. Who is responsible for determining which documents and other electronic or physical items are records? Records managers, lawyers, and compliance officers are the ones responsible, and they help ensure that documents are retained for the appropriate period of time by carefully categorizing all enterprise content within the organization. Figure 13-1 illustrates the records management application process.

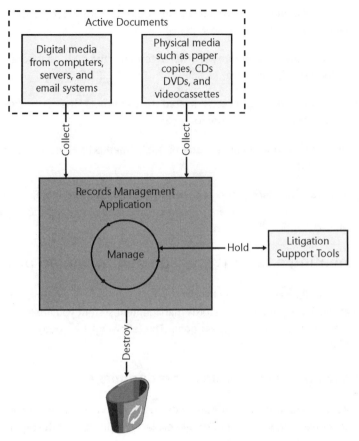

Figure 13-1 A diagram of a records management application process.

A records management system typically includes the following features:

- **Content analysis**   Describes and categorizes content that becomes records, provides the source locations, and describes how content will move to the records management application

- **File plan**   Indicates for each record where they should be retained as records, the policies that get applied, the retention period time, how they are disposed, and who is responsible for managing them

- **Compliance requirements document**   Defines the rules that the organization must follow to ensure compliance and which methods are used to ensure participation by the organization

- **Method for collecting inactive records** Collects from all record sources (such as servers, email systems, and file systems)

- **Method for auditing active records** Determines the method for auditing records when the records are active

- **Method for capturing records' metadata** Determines the method for capturing the metadata and audit history for records

- **Process for holding records** Determines the method to follow when events occur, such as litigations

- **Process for monitoring and reporting the records handling** Ensures that employees within the organization are filing, accessing, and managing the records according to defined policies and processes

Implementing a records management planning process

This section describes an example of a records management planning process to help ensure that the SharePoint Server records management system you implement will achieve the organization's record management goals. The following steps outline the records management planning process.

Review the compliance requirements document

The compliance standards that must be followed depend on the type of industry. A compliance requirements document should explain the purpose of the organization's compliance program and its benefits, and the essential components should identify the legal or business criteria to which the compliance plan must adhere. The document should also include the metrics or other objective criteria that will be used to measure the effectiveness of the compliance plan and the formal policies that represent the organization's internal statement of the regulatory rules that must be followed. In addition, the compliance requirements document should include specifications for ongoing training for employees and the guidelines for the roles and involvement in the compliance process. For some organizations, it may also be practical to carry out a formal compliance audit at regular intervals to ensure that the records management plan is meeting its objectives.

Identify the records management roles

When developing a records management plan, it is important to consider who is responsible for the various roles involved in the creation and implementation of the records management solution.

Some of the common roles defined are:

- **Compliance officers and records managers** These employees categorize the records in the organization and run the records management process.

  - Compliance officers are often lawyers who are associated with the legal department of the organization. They are responsible for understanding and interpreting the rules and regulations that the organization must follow. The compliance officers also develop the formal compliance policies that will be implemented, and because they are the primary authors, they will be the ones to perform the internal auditing and monitoring when necessary to ensure that the organization is following the records management plan.

  - Records managers are responsible for developing the file plan that applies the compliance requirements to the data specified as records. The records managers may be senior staff members or members of the legal department who have a thorough understanding of the organization's business practices and workflow. They are the ones responsible for configuring the document libraries and retention rules in the SharePoint Records Center site. Records managers should be part of the design of the records management solution.

- **IT personnel** These employees implement the systems that support records management. The SharePoint administrators will be responsible for the installation and configuration of the SharePoint servers that provide the records management services to the enterprise.

- **Content managers** These managers work on the teams that create the content that will be designated as records and are the ones who ensure that their teams follow the records management practices.

Analyze the organizational content

Records managers and content managers survey document usage in the organization to determine which documents and other items will become records. This step is done before creating a file plan.

Develop a file plan

Once the records managers and content managers analyze the content and determine the retention schedules, the file plan is developed. File plans can differ from organization to organization. The file plan is a written document or set of documents that generally describe the kinds of items the organization determines to be records, specifies where they will be stored, describes the retention time, and provides other information, such as who is responsible for managing them. Table 13-1 lists the common file plan elements.

TABLE 13-1 File plan elements

Plan element	Purpose
Record type	The classification of the item. Each record type corresponds to a set of typical documents or messages that need to be tracked and managed the same way.
Required fields	Additional information that will be required when a document is submitted into the repository.
Retention	The length of time the document will be retained.
Disposal	How the document will be handled or disposed when the item expires.
Audit	Whether access to the document will be tracked and logged along with the types of actions on the document that have to be logged.

It is important to understand the difference between documents that are retained as records and documents that are retained in an archive. Archived information is not classified as a record after the period of time the record must be retained has expired. Normally at this point, the expired information is usually transferred to tape backup or printed out and placed in long-term storage with the expectation it will be kept mainly for historical purposes. Unless it is electronic, expired archived data is generally not readily available for search and retrieval and is not expected to be required for legal discovery or current research. However, even though it is not required, the legal discovery process can request any information deemed appropriate for the matter at hand that provides the reason that expired data should be properly archived. If you have ever called your doctor's office and asked for information older than six years, chances are that the information is not readily available and the office has to request the retrieval of the information from where the data is archived. The most common form of backup the medical industry uses is tape backup for archiving expired information.

Identifying the kinds of records   Determining which type of active documents in your organization might be declared as records requires the collaboration of records managers, lawyers, compliance officers, and content managers. Even if your enterprise is not in a highly regulated industry, there are general laws that may obligate your enterprise to keep records. Along with general business laws, you must evaluate the legal requirements specific to your enterprise. Most likely, your enterprise is doing some form of records management and has filled most of the records management roles that you need, and you might already have a taxonomy of records.

To determine what are considered records in your organization, follow these steps:

1. Understand the legal obligations and business needs of your enterprise.

2. Analyze how active documents are used in a collaborative effort across the divisions of the organization.

3. Develop a list of the kinds of documents that should become records, such as documents related to employees' benefits or to product research and development.

4. Categorize the records. Records in the same category often have the same retention periods and other similar policies applied.

A Records Category worksheet template is available in Microsoft Excel format at *http://go.microsoft.com/FWLink/p/?LinkID=179987&clcid=0x409.*

Creating information management policies   Information management policies are sets of rules governing the automated management of the documents. This includes how long a document should be retained and which actions on the document should be applied. Each rule in an information management policy is called a *policy feature.* The records managers are the ones who configure the policies in the records management system to reflect the file plan requirements.

The two recommended approaches for implementing polices into a document repository are the following:

- Create individual policies for each document library if the requirements are unique to the content in each library.

- Create site-collection policies to cover an entire set of record types and apply them to several document libraries as needed. One policy can be applied for an entire document library or, if multiple content types are configured for the document library, then you can apply a separate policy for each content type.

After creating a policy, it is implemented by associating it with a site collection, content type, list, or library in SharePoint. The association to the content type, list, or library can be accomplished by the following three methods:

- **Site collection policy** Associate the policy features with a site collection policy and then associate the policy with a content type, list, or library.

- **Content type policy** Associate a set of policy features directly with a content type and then use the content type for one or more lists or libraries. Content type policies can be specified within a content type hub so that the policies will follow the content types down into the consuming locations.

- **List or Library policy** Associate a set of policy features directly with a list or library when multiple content types are not configured for the list or library.

> **Note**
>
> A policy feature may use one or more policy resources that provide functionality to a policy feature. An example would be a custom policy resource for a barcode policy feature could be used to generate a unique barcode value for a document.

Completing the file plan   Once the records have been identified and the record categories sets have been determined, you can now complete the file plan by providing additional information about each kind of record. The following is the additional information that must be indicated:

- What is the retention time for each record?

- How will the records be disposed when the retention period ends?

- Who is the primary records manager for the records?

- What is the media the records will be stored in?

Develop the retention schedules

Develop retention schedules for each record type, determining when a record is no longer active, how long it should be retained after it is no longer being used, and how the record should be disposed of.

Evaluate and improve the document management practices

To improve the document management policies that have been implemented, it is important to evaluate and ensure that the required policies for the document repositories are being applied by the organization.

Design a records management solution

Determine if an archive will be created, if the records will be managed in place, or if a combination of both will be used. Based on the desired file plan, design the record archive or determine how to use the existing sites to contain the records. Define content types, libraries, policies, and metadata (when required) that determine the routing location for a document.

Plan how content becomes records

After the file plan has been developed and the records management solution has been designed, the next step is to plan how active documents in the organization will become records. In SharePoint Server 2013, there are two ways you can manage records: managing the records in an archive or managing the records in the same document repository as active documents. The in-place approach is when a document has become a record in the same document repository, the record remains in place but SharePoint now manages the record. For example, a document may have a retention policy that when it becomes a record, it can no longer be edited. Another approach is hybrid in nature, such as keeping records in place with active documents for three years and then moving the records to a records archive once the project is complete.

Should the records be managed in a records archive or managed in place? The answer to this question varies per organization, and there are some considerations to help determine the answer. Consider the following when trying to determine if records should be managed in a separate Records Center site or in the same collaboration site in which the document is created:

- Is the collaboration site governance appropriate for managing records? Is your industry subject to regulatory requirements mandating that records be separated from active documents? Should the site collection administrator of the collaboration site be trusted to manage a site containing records?

- How long will the SharePoint collaboration site be used? If the records have to be kept longer than the project, then selecting an in-place records management strategy means that the collaboration site must be maintained even after the project is over.

- Will the project members need continual access to the documents once they become records? If so, then an in-place records management strategy would be the more desired approach in this situation.

- Are record managers responsible for all information regardless of whether they are active or not, or are they responsible for just records? If they are responsible for just the official records, then having a separate Records Center site might be the better option.

The differences between what can be done with records in a Records Center site and records managed in place may help determine what is better for your organization. Table 13-2 describes the differences between a records archive and in-place records management.

TABLE 13-2 Differences between a records archive and in-place records

Factor	Records archive	In-place records
Managing record retention	Content organizer automatically puts new records in the correct folder based on metadata in the archive's file plan.	There may be different policies for records and active documents based on the location or current content type.
Restricting which users can view records	Yes. The records archive specifies the permissions for the record.	No. The permissions do not change when a document becomes a record; however, you can restrict which users can edit/delete records.
Ease of locating records (for records managers)	Easier because all records are in one location.	Harder because records are spread across multiple SharePoint sites.
Maintaining all document versions as records	The user must explicitly send each version of a document to the records archive.	Automatic if versioning is turned on.
Ease of locating information (for team collaborators)	Harder; however, a link to the document can be added to the site when the document becomes a record.	Easier.
Clutter of collaboration site	The site contains only active documents.	The site contains active and inactive documents (records). However, views can be created to display only records.
Ability to audit records	Yes.	Dependent on the audit policy of the site.
Administrative security	Records managers can manage the records archive.	Site administrators have permission to manage records and active documents.

Table 13-3 details the differences between the two that may affect how IT resources are managed.

TABLE 13-3 Resource differences between a records archive and in-place records

Factor	Records archive	In-place records
Scalability	Relieves database size pressure on sites containing active documents.	Maximum site-collection size reached sooner because it contains both records and active documents.
Ease of administration	Additional provisioning work for separate sites or farms.	No additional site provisioning work beyond what is already needed for the sites that have active documents.
Storage	Records can be stored on different media.	Records and active documents are stored together.

Convert active documents to records

The section provides information on the techniques that can be used to declare and convert active documents to records.

Creating records manually   Users can declare a document to be a record manually in one of the following ways:

- **In-place records management** If in-place records management is enabled on a document library, then users can explicitly declare a document in the library to be a record by editing the document's compliance details.

- **Records archive** If there is a connection to a Records Center site, then users can send documents to the Records Center site manually by using the Send To command. Depending on how the connection to the Records Center site is configured by the farm administrator, documents can either be copied, moved to the Records Center site, or moved to the Records Center site with a link to the document maintained from the document library where it originated.

> **Note**
> Manually sending records to the Records Center site is not practical for large-scale solutions; however, you can still use it to supplement other methods of creating records.

Defining a policy   A retention policy can be defined that declares a document to be a record or sends a document to a Records Center site at a specified time. Policy actions occur automatically, and users do not have to start the action.

Two policy actions that relate specifically to managing records are:

- **Transferring a document to another location** If a connection to a Records Center site exists, a policy can be created that sends documents to the Records Center site, and the policy also specifies whether to copy, move, or move and leave a link in the document library which it was moved from.

- **Declaring a document to be an in-place record** If in-place records management is enabled for the site, a policy can be created that declares a document to be a record. A custom action can also be created by custom developers using the SharePoint object model. If in-place is used, the site can contain both active documents and records, and you can specify different retention policies for both. For example, a policy can be created that declares an active document to be a record three years after the document is created, and a second policy is created that deletes the record seven years after it has been declared a record.

Creating a workflow   If SharePoint Server 2013 is being used for both active document management and records management, custom workflows can be created to move documents to a records archive. A workflow can be created either in Microsoft SharePoint Designer or through a Microsoft Visual Studio workflow that contains an action to send a document to a Records Center site. Other action items can also be included, such as the workflow sends an email message to the document's author requesting approval and then sends the document to the Records Center site once it is approved.

INSIDE OUT
Is it recommended to create SharePoint Designer workflows or Visual Studio workflows?

If you have worked with workflows in the past, you may have experienced some of the instabilities of SharePoint workflows. Workflows are known to be buggy in SharePoint, whether they are created through SharePoint Designer or Visual Studio.

One of the problems I have encountered with SharePoint Designer workflows is that if I created a workflow and then kept making changes to the workflow, eventually the workflow would have issues. For example, email alerts would randomly not send when the workflow was started. The issue I have found is that if there are a lot of changes made to an existing SharePoint Designer workflow, you are better off re-creating the workflow from scratch. Once the workflow was recreated to match exactly how the changed workflow was, everything worked properly and all email alerts were being triggered. It is unknown what the reasoning is behind the issue. It may be caused if

SharePoint Designer is not cleaning up the workflow markup when major changes or too many changes are being made.

Deciding between using SharePoint Designer and Visual Studio for workflow can vary based on your organization's needs. Therefore, it is recommended you read "What's new in workflows for SharePoint 2013," located at *http://msdn.microsoft.com/library/ sharepoint/jj163177%28v=office.15%29.aspx*. This article provides the comparison between the differences of the capabilities and features of SharePoint Designer and Visual Studio 2012, which will help you to determine what the best workflow solution is for your organization.

Using custom solutions   If external document management systems are being used, you can plan and develop custom solutions that move the content from the systems to the records archive.

Plan the email integration

Determine if you will manage email records within SharePoint Server 2013 or manage email records within the email application itself, such as Exchange.

Plan compliance for social media content

If the SharePoint social media features are being used within the organization, determine what blogs, wikis, and My Sites content will become records.

Plan compliance reporting and documentation

Document your records management plans and processes to communicate the required practices. Also, documenting will help verify the organization is performing the required records management practices. The records management guidelines, implementation plans, and metrics on effectiveness may have to be produced if your organization becomes engaged in a records-related litigation.

Using the Records Center Site template

The Records Center site template is intended to serve as a central repository in which an organization can store and manage all records. The Records Center supports the entire records management process, from records collection to the disposition of the records. In SharePoint 2010, the site template was updated with new functionality, such as the Content Organizer to route incoming documents, which gave records managers faster access to common tasks and actions.

When you create a Records Center site, the following site-collection features are enabled:

- **Disposition approval workflow** Manages document expiration and retention by allowing participants to decide whether to retain or delete expired documents.

- **Document ID service** Assigns IDs to documents in the site collection, which can be used to retrieve items independent of their current location.

- **Document sets** Provides the content types required for creating and using document sets. Create a document set when you want to manage multiple documents as a single work product.

- **In-place records management** Enables the definition and declaration of records in place.

- **Library- and folder-based retention** Allows list administrators to override content type retention schedules and set schedules on libraries and folders.

- **SharePoint Server Enterprise** Features such as InfoPath Forms Services, Visio Services, Access Services, and Excel Services Application are included in the SharePoint Server Enterprise license.

- **SharePoint Server Standard** Features such as user profiles and search are included in the SharePoint Server Standard icense.

- **Site policy**   Allows site collection administrators to define retention schedules that apply to a site and all its content.

In addition, the following site features are enabled:

- **Content organizer** Creates metadata-based rules that move content submitted to this site to the correct library or folder.

- **Following content** Enables users to follow documents or sites.

- **Hold** Tracks external actions such as litigations, investigations, or audits that require you to suspend the disposition of documents.

- **Metadata navigation and filtering** Provides each list in the site with a Settings page for configuring that list to use metadata tree view hierarchies and filter controls to improve the navigation and filtering of the contained items.

- **SharePoint Server Enterprise** Features such as Visio Services, Access Services, and Excel Services Application are included in the SharePoint Server Enterprise license.

- **SharePoint Server Standard Site features** Features such as user profiles and search are included in the SharePoint Server Standard license.

- **Team collaboration lists** Provides team collaboration capabilities for a site by making standard lists, such as document libraries and issues, available.

- **Workflow Task content type** Adds the SharePoint 2013 Workflow Task content type to the site.

Create a Records Center site

Follow these steps to create a Records Center site:

1. From Central Administration, click Application Management located in the left navigation.

2. Under Site Collections, click Create Site Collections.

3. In the Web Application drop-down list, select the desired web application you want to use to create the Records Center site, as shown here.

Web Application
Select a web application.

To create a new web application go to **New Web Application** page.

Web Application: http://spdevsolutions.com/ ▾

4. Input the Title and Description (optional), as shown here.

Title and Description
Type a title and description for your new site. The title will be displayed on each page in the site.

Title:
Records Center

Description:

5. For the Web Site Address, select the desired drop-down path or click the Define Managed Paths link to create a new managed path, as shown in the following graphic.

For more information on managed paths, visit *http://technet.microsoft.com/en-us/library/ cc261845.aspx.*

6. In the Template Selection, click the Enterprise tab and select Records Center, as shown here.

7. Assign at least one Site Collection Administrator for the site, as shown here, then scroll down to the bottom and click OK.

> **Note**
>
> Because the site collection is going to be a Records Center site, it is recommended that the Quota Template property be set to No Quota. It is also recommended to use a separate database for the Records Center site collection for ease of management, which includes maintenance, growth monitoring, and business continuity.

Access the Records Center dashboard

To access the dashboard in the Records Center site, follow these steps:

1. In the browser, open the newly created Records Center site (such as *http://contoso/recordscenter*).

2. Click the Site Settings icon, and then click the Manage Records Center link, as shown here.

3. Proceed with all necessary steps to configure your Records Center site. Configure tasks and set up Content Organizer Rules based on your file plan.

Manage connections to a Records Center

A *connection* is a path used for sending documents to a Document Center or Records Center site and is created by a farm administrator. The farm administrator configures the connection to copy, move, or move the content and leave a link in the source site collection. This section provides the details of creating, modifying, and deleting connections from a web application to a SharePoint 2013 Document Center or Records Center site.

Creating a connection   To create a connection, ensure that you have the appropriate permissions to continue with these steps. If you are not a farm administrator, then your farm administrator can follow these steps to configure the connection on your server farm:

1. From Central Administration, click General Application Settings.

2. Under External Service Connections, click Configure Send To Connections, as shown here.

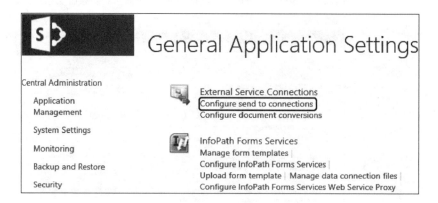

3. From the Configure Send To Connections page, select the Web Application that contains the Records Center site.

4. In the Tenant Settings area, leave the Allow Sites To Send To Connections Outside Their Tenancy option checked (as shown in the graphic on the next page) to allow the site to send content to other tenants on the farm.

Configure Send To Connections

Web Application

Select a web application.

Web Application: http://spdevsolutions.com/ ▾

Tenant Settings

Choose whether tenants on this farm can send content to other tenants on this farm.

☑ Allow sites to send to connections outside their tenancy

5. The Send To Connections list will automatically have New Connection listed and selected, as shown here. If other connections have been created, then all connections will show up in the list.

Send To Connections

Send To Connections allow content to be submitted to sites with a configured Content Organizer. Send To connections will appear as locations that content can be submitted to when configuring Information Management Policy. Optionally you can make Send To Connections available for users to manually submit content.

Send To Connections

New Connection

6. In the Connections Settings section, set the Display Name and the Send To URL.

7. Leave the Allow Manual Submission From The Send To Menu checked if you want to allow manual submission.

8. In the Send To Action drop-down list, select the desired option:

a. **Copy**   Select this option to create a copy of the document and send the copy to the destination repository.

b. **Move**   Select this option to delete the document from its current location and move the document to the destination repository. Users will no longer be able to access the document from its original location.

c. **Move And Leave A Link**   Select this option to delete the document from its current location, move it to the destination repository, and leave a link at the current location indicating that the document has been moved. When a user clicks this link, a page will appear that displays the URL of the document and the document's metadata.

9. In the Explanation (To Be Shown On Links And Recorded In The Audit Log) multiline text box (shown here), type the information to be added to the audit log when users send a document using this connection.

   If you selected Move And Leave A Link, the page that appears when the user clicks the Send To link will also display the explanation.

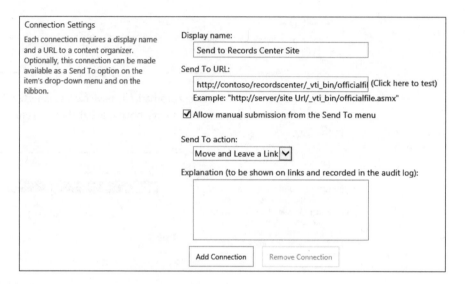

10. Click Add Connection to create the connection.

    Notice that the new connection is now in the Send To Connections list.

11. Configure or add any additional connections, and once finished, click OK.

Modifying connections   To modify the connection, follow these steps:

1. From Central Administration, click General Application Settings.

2. Under External Service Connections, click Configure Send To Connections.

3. In the Web Application drop-down list, select the desired Web Application that contains the site collections that use this connection.

4. In the Send To Connections list, select the connection you want to modify.

5. Modify the settings, and then click Update Connection, as shown in the following graphic.

Connection Settings

Each connection requires a display name
and a URL to a content organizer.
Optionally, this connection can be made
available as a Send To option on the
item's drop-down menu and on the
Ribbon.

Display name:

Send to Records Center Site

Send To URL:

http://contoso/recordscenter/_vti_bin/officialfil   (Click here to test)

Example: "http://server/site Url/_vti_bin/officialfile.asmx"

☑ Allow manual submission from the Send To menu

Send To action:

Move and Leave a Link ∨

Explanation (to be shown on links and recorded in the audit log):

[Update Connection]   [Remove Connection]

6. Click OK.

Deleting connections   To delete a connection, follow these steps:

1. From Central Administration, click General Application Settings.

2. Under External Service Connections, click Configure Send To Connections.

3. In the Web Application drop-down list, select the desired Web Application that contains the site collections that use this connection.

4. In the Send To Connections list, select the connection you want to modify.

5. Click Remove Connection to delete the connection.

6. Click OK.

eDiscovery

What is eDiscovery? *eDiscovery* is the process of collecting and analyzing content in electronic format for record managers and litigators. eDiscovery typically requires searching for documents, websites, email messages, file servers, and other sources, and then collecting and acting on content that meets criteria for a legal case.

eDiscovery in SharePoint 2013 helps reduce the cost and complexity of discovery in the following new ways:

- **eDiscovery Center** A central SharePoint site used to manage the preservation, search, and export of content stored in Exchange across Exchange servers and in SharePoint across SharePoint farms

- **SharePoint in-place hold** Preserves entire SharePoint sites and protects all documents, pages, and list items within the site but allows users to continue to edit and delete preserved content

- **Exchange in-place hold** Preserves Exchange mailboxes and protects all mailbox content through the same UI and APIs used to preserve SharePoint sites

- **Query-based preservation** Allows users to apply query filters to one or more Exchange mailboxes and SharePoint sites and restricts the content that is on hold

How eDiscovery works

eDiscovery works by using Search Services applications (SSAs) to crawl SharePoint farms. SSAs can be configured many ways for eDiscovery. The most common way is to have a central Search Services farm that crawls multiple SharePoint farms. This one Search Service can be used to crawl all SharePoint content or used to crawl specific regions, such as all SharePoint content in the United States.

To crawl, the eDiscovery Center uses a proxy connection to query and send preservations to SharePoint sites in other SharePoint farms. When a hold is initiated, Hold actions are created and passed to the Search Service. In the case of Exchange, the Hold action is immediately federated to the Exchange server. This triggers an asynchronous Hold operation on the Exchange side in which the status will not be immediately known. In the case of SharePoint, the Hold actions are stored in the content database. The source system/ farms have the "Preservation Processing" Timer Job, which runs periodically and retrieves the hold commands from the Search server. For the intended sites, it updates the metadata, marking them as Hold. The eDiscovery Center has a timer job that periodically refreshes the status of the pending actions. After the various source systems have acted on the hold commands and updated the status in the Search Service, the eDiscovery Center will reflect the updated status.

To learn more about SharePoint Search, see Chapter 19, "Creating a customized SharePoint 2013 search experience."

Site holds

Site holds preserve content on the site level, so when you preserve a site, its lists and subsites are preserved. If you preserve a site collection, all subsites, documents, lists, and pages within the site collection are preserved. To hold a site, create a Discovery Case in the eDiscovery Center.

eDiscovery Center Site Collection template

The eDiscovery Center site collection is used to perform discovery actions. It allows the ability to create cases (which are SharePoint sites) to identify, hold, search, and export content from Exchange mailboxes, SharePoint sites, and file shares for civil litigation or investigations.

Creating an eDiscovery Center site collection

Follow these steps to create an eDiscovery Center site collection:

1. From Central Administration, click Application Management located in the left navigation.

2. Under Site Collections, click Create Site Collections.

3. In the Web Application drop-down list, select the desired web application that you want to use to create the site.

4. Input the Title and Description (optional).

5. For the Web Site Address, select the desired drop-down path or click the Define Managed Paths link to create a new managed path, as shown here.

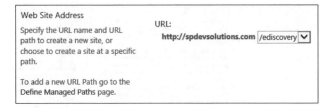

6. In the Template Selection, click the Enterprise tab and select, eDiscovery Center as shown here.

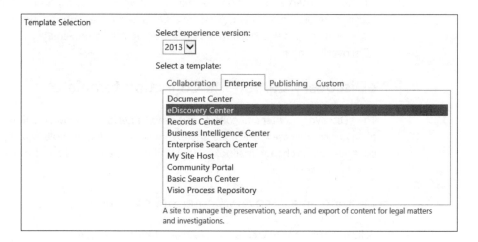

7. Assign at least one Site Collection Administrator for the site, as shown here, then scroll down to the bottom and click OK.

Creating an eDiscovery case

To create an eDiscovery case, follow these steps:

1. In the eDiscovery Center site, click Create New Case.

2. Type a Title and Description (optional) for the case.

3. In the Web Site Address, type the last part of the URL you want for the case (such as **Contoso vs Adventure Works**), as shown here.

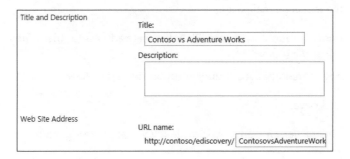

4. Under Select A Template, click eDiscovery Case, as shown here.

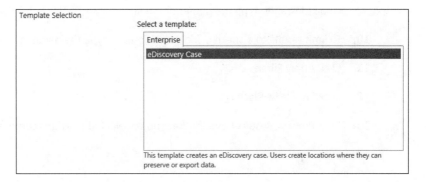

5. For the User Permissions, select whether to keep the same permissions as the parent site or use unique permissions.

   If specific people need access to this case but not to other cases, choose Use Unique Permissions.

6. Change the Navigation settings if desired, and then click OK.

Adding sources and placing them on hold

To add a source to an eDiscovery case and place it on hold, follow these steps:

1. In the eDiscovery Center, open the case you want to add a source to.

2. Click eDiscovery Sets and then type a name for the eDiscovery set.

3. Next to Sources, click Add & Manage Sources.

4. In the dialog box, under Mailboxes, type the account names or email addresses for the Exchange mailboxes.

5. Under Locations, type the URL or file share address for the content that you want to use as the source.

    Any content that you include must be indexed by Search.

6. Click Save.

7. Under Filter, type any keywords that you want to use to narrow down the source.

8. To narrow content by a date range, enter the Start Date and End Date.

9. To limit results to the author of a document or list item or to a specific sender of email messages, type the names or email addresses in the Author/Sender box.

10. To limit results to a specific Exchange domain, type the name in the Domain box.

11. Click Apply Filter.

12. Click Enable In-Place Hold.

13. Click Preview Results to verify that you've selected the right content.

14. Click Save.

Preserving content

When content is placed on hold, it is preserved, but users can still continue to work on it. The state of the content at the time of the preservation is recorded so that if a user modifies or deletes the content, the original version is preserved and is still available.

Preserving content is similar to placing the content on hold with the following enhancements:

- Documents, list items, pages, and Exchange 2013 mailboxes can be preserved.

- Preservation is done at the site level, and preserving a site preserves the content of the site.

- Users can continue to work on the preserved content because an original version at the time of the preservation still exists.

- Users with the permission to perform eDiscovery can access the original version of the preserved document.

- The entire site or mailbox does not have to be preserved. You can define specified queries for the preservation scope to preserve only the content that matches the query.

Exporting eDiscovery search results

The eDiscovery Download Manager is an application used to export the results of an eDiscovery search and can export all the content associated with a case to produce to authorities. The format of the export is compatible with the Electronic Discovery Reference Model standard.

Summary

In this chapter, you learned about the integrated records management features of SharePoint that can help your organization store and protect business records based on industry compliance requirements. You also learned about the eDiscovery Center site collection and features that can help organizations place content on hold during litigation or investigations, conduct queries, and export content. Now, even if your organization may not require a SharePoint solution that follows some type of industry standard compliance, you can still benefit from the records management features for other options, such as setting up policies and rerouting documents based on metadata to prevent users from creating or uploading content to the incorrect lists or libraries. The next chapter focuses on the business intelligence capabilities in SharePoint 2013, along with the software requirements for implementation.

Planning for business intelligence and key performance indicators

MODERN business intelligence (BI) has come a long way from when it started as a back-office function; it is now utilized by both consumers and IT decision makers alike. BI refers to the systems and tools used by an organization to consolidate and maintain large amounts of information. Generally, these systems illustrate business intelligence in areas such as inventory, product profitability, market research, customer profiling, and customer support.

Two primary programs exist for BI: strategic planning and tactical implementations. Strategic planning encompasses the long-term vision of the enterprise and plays a key role in the processes of the corporation. Strategic plans set the boundaries for tactical implementations, as well as provide guidelines around how the business will be governed in the long term. Data warehouses become a single source of reliable data delivered through dashboards and portals, and business analysts are able to get deeper custom analysis through business intelligence analytical tools.

Traditionally, these tools were available only to people with years of experience in data warehousing and data mining, and they were used to access large amounts of unstructured data for the purpose of analysis. Many companies collect the large amount of data from their business operations and then keep track of the information through a wide range of tools used throughout the organization. Using multiple software programs can make it difficult to retrieve the information in a timely manner and perform the analysis of the data. Because this process is more manual, it can lead to errors, making the data untrustworthy. This is no longer the case today. BI applications and tools in Microsoft SharePoint 2013 enable organizations to capture and present data in an organized and meaningful way to help promote the organization's goals, processes, and performance measures. This chapter looks at the improvements in the BI capabilities in SharePoint 2013, along with the software requirements for implementation.

Software requirements for business intelligence

Planning for business intelligence in SharePoint 2013 requires specific installations and settings for SharePoint and Microsoft SQL Server to be implemented first. The next part of this chapter focuses on the software requirements for implementation.

SQL Server 2012 for SharePoint business intelligence

Analysis Services, Integration Services, Reporting Services, PowerPivot, Master Data Services, and several client applications are part of the Microsoft BI platform as features in SQL Server 2012. This section focuses on the requirements for these features.

Reporting Services and Analysis Services can be set up on stand-alone servers, in scale-out configurations, or as shared service applications within a SharePoint farm. Installing these services enables PowerPivot and Power View for SharePoint and the new Reporting Services ad hoc interactive report designer, which runs on PowerPivot or Analysis Services tabular model databases.

PowerPivot software requirements

The following requirements are necessary to run PowerPivot for SharePoint 2013:

- **SQL Server 2012 SP1 CTP3** To use the new Microsoft Excel Services advanced data models feature, an instance of SQL Server 2012 SP1 CTP3 Analysis Services must be installed in SharePoint Deployment mode.

- **Excel Services and SQL Server Analysis Services (SSAS) server** Excel Services must be configured on a farm that has at least one SSAS server in SharePoint mode and must be registered in the Excel Services configuration. If using multiple SSAS servers, all SSAS servers must be running SQL Server 2012 SP1 CTP3.

- **Secure Store** Must be configured on the farm in order to configure scheduled data refreshes of PowerPivot workbooks.

> **Note**
> PowerPivot for SharePoint 2013 must be installed from either SQL Server SP1 CTP3 setup or from the SQL Server 2012 SP1 Feature Pack (*http://www.microsoft.com/en-us/download/details.aspx?id=35580*). If your organization is not planning to immediately use PowerPivot for SharePoint, it is still recommended to set up the servers for PowerPivot if the organization would like to use PowerPivot in the future. This will eliminate difficulties with post-implementation. The primary MSDN documentation for installing and configuring PowerPivot for SharePoint 2013 may be found at *http://msdn.microsoft.com/en-us/library/jj218792.aspx*.

Reporting Services software requirements

The following requirements are necessary to run Power View, start Report Builder from SharePoint, and view SQL Reporting Services reports on SharePoint 2013:

- **SQL Server 2012 SP1 CTP3** An instance of SQL Server 2012 SP1 CTP3 is required in order to start Report Builder from SharePoint and for viewing Reporting Services reports from SharePoint Server 2013.

- **SSAS server** To view Power View from Microsoft Excel worksheets in SharePoint, Excel Services must be configured and at least one SSAS server in SharePoint mode must be registered in Excel Services.

> ### Note
> The SQL Server 2012 SP1 CTP3 Reporting Services in SharePoint Deployment mode includes all required web front-end components, so the Report Viewer component is no longer needed.

Excel Services advanced scenarios software requirements

The requirements are as follows for Excel Services in advanced scenarios:

- **SSAS server** At least one SSAS server must be registered in Excel Services in order to use Excel Services with advanced data models.

- **Secure Store Service** Must be configured in the farm in order to store encrypted credentials for data refresh scenarios or if you want to use the Excel Services unattended service account.

> ### Note
> The SQL Server 2012 SP1 CTP3 Reporting Services in SharePoint Deployment mode includes all required web front-end components, so the Report Viewer component is no longer needed.

PerformancePoint Services (PPS) software requirements

The requirements are as follows for PPS:

- **ADOMD.NET V10** The Microsoft ADOMD.NET client library must be installed so PerformancePoint can connect to any SSAS data source.

- **Secure Store Service** Must be configured in the farm in order to store encrypted credentials for data refresh scenarios or if you want to use the PPS unattended service account.

- **Kerberos** If you want to delegate user credentials to an external data source for data refresh scenarios, the Kerberos constrained delegation must be configured.

> **Note**
>
> For SSAS data, the EffectiveUserName option is an alternative method to access data from PerformancePoint Service. When enabled, all connections to SSAS for individual users will be made using the EffectiveUserName connection string property instead of using Windows delegation.

Visio Services software requirements

The requirements are as follows for Visio Services:

- **Secure Store Service** Must be configured in the farm in order to store encrypted credentials for data refresh scenarios or if you want to use the Visio Services unattended service account.

- **Kerberos** If you want to delegate user credentials to an external data source for data refresh scenarios the Kerberos constrained delegation must be configured.

Business intelligence in SharePoint Server 2013

SharePoint 2013 business intelligence applications provide the ability to create powerful data mashups, data models, ad-hoc reporting, and sophisticated dashboards capable of integrating reports and metrics from multiple data sources that can be customized for difference audiences. The BI tools available in SharePoint Server 2013 include Excel Services, PPS, and Visio Services.

Excel Services

Excel business intelligence provides the capability to explore and analyze data of any size and integrate and show interactive solutions of the data. In SharePoint 2013, Excel Services BI offers the following new features:

- **Power View ("Crescent") add-in for Excel** Powered by the BI Semantic Model and IMBI, Power View enables users to visualize and interact with modeled data by using interactive visualizations, animations, and smart querying. Rich storyboard presentation capabilities provide the user the ability to present and share insights with others.

- **Decoupled PivotChart and PivotTable reports** Enables users to create PivotChart reports without the need to include a PivotTable report on the same page.

- **In-Memory BI Engine (IMBI)** Also known as *Vertipaq Engine,* IMBI is a fully integrated feature in Excel that allows almost instant analysis of millions of rows of data.

Excel Services, introduced in Microsoft Office SharePoint Server (MOSS) 2007, is a business intelligence tool that allows the sharing of data-connected workbooks and is used primarily for business intelligence scenarios. In SharePoint 2013, Excel Services is a shared service and is only available in the Enterprise edition of SharePoint. Excel 2013 workbooks can be connected to external data sources and then published to a SharePoint library so the workbooks can be rendered through the browser. The workbook is rendered through the browser via Excel Services and the external data connection is maintained and the data is refreshed when necessary. The published workbooks allow broad sharing of reports through the organization and can be managed and secured according to the organizational needs.

Excel Services consists of the following:

- **Excel Calculation Services** Used to load, calculate, and call custom code (user-defined), and refreshes the data.

- **Excel Web Access Web Part** Web part used to display Excel workbooks through the browser.

- **Excel Web Services** Used for programmatic access.

Excel Services improvements

Excel Services has come a long way from when it started. The improvements in SharePoint 2010 included better handling of unsupported features. Some of the unsupported features include Microsoft Visual Basic for Applications (VBA) macros and form controls will not load in Excel Services. In MOSS 2007, Excel Services would not open a file that contained an unsupported feature. This improved with the updates to Excel Services in SharePoint 2010 and with each release, the functionality gap between Excel and Excel Services becomes narrower and the number of unsupported features gets reduced.

The new features in Excel Services for business intelligence include the following:

- **Business Intelligence Center update** Improvements to the Business Intelligence Center Site template include a new look and easier use.

- **Improved data exploration** Using SSAS data and PowerPivot data makes it easier for data exploration and data analysis.

- **Field list/field well support** Enables the ability to change easily which items are displayed in rows, columns, values, and filters in PivotChart and PivotTable reports that have been published to Excel Services.

- **Calculated measures and members** Support for calculated measures and calculated members created in Excel.

- **Enhanced timeline controls** Support for timeline controls that render and behave the same as in the Excel client.

- **Application business intelligence servers** Allows the support of more advanced analytic capabilities in Excel Services by allowing administrators to specify SSAS servers.

PPS

PPS is a service application in SharePoint 2013 that enables users to create rich interactive, context-driven business intelligence dashboards that aggregate data and content. These dashboards can display key performance indicators (KPIs) and data visualizations in the form of scorecards, reports, and filters. PPS allows for robust security to the user and can integrate with multidimensional data sources.

PPS improvements

PPS in SharePoint 2013 has the following new features and improvements:

- **Business Intelligence Center update** Cleaner and easier to use, with folders and libraries configured for each use.

- **Dashboard migration** Enables the ability to copy complete dashboards and dependencies to other site collections, users, or servers. Single items can be migrated to other environments and content can be migrated with Windows PowerShell.

- **Filter enhancements and filter search** Improved UI allows users to view and manage filters easily. Items can be searched within filters without navigating through the tree.

- **Support for Analysis Services effective user** Eliminates the need for Kerberos delegation when per-user authentication is used for Analysis Services data sources.

- **iPad support** PerformancePoint dashboards can now be viewed and interacted with on iPads through the Safari browser.

Visio Services

Visio Services enables users to share and view Visio diagrams through a web browser and mobile devices without the need for Visio or Visio Viewer. The Visio-rendered diagrams are rendered within a Visio Web Access Web Part. Visio Services enables published diagrams to refresh connections to various data sources and update the visuals of the Visio diagram.

Visio Services improvements

The improvements to Visio Services in SharePoint 2013 include the following:

- **New file format** Visio 2013 introduces a new file format (.vsdx) that replaces the Visio binary (.vsd) and Visio XML Drawing (.vdx) file format. This new file format is supported in Visio Services and eliminates the need to convert the file before publishing to a SharePoint site.

- **Comments on diagrams** Comments can be added to diagrams and associated with specific shapes to a diagram when in Full-Screen mode. Where are the comments stored? The comments on the diagrams are not attached to the metadata as most would expect—they are actually embedded in the document.

- **Business Connectivity Services (BCS) support** Visio shapes can now be connected to data contained in external lists.

- **Maximum cache size parameter** Central Administration now contains a new service parameter for the maximum cache size located in the Visio Graphics Service Application Global Settings. The value can be set between 100 MB and up to 1,024,000 MB, and the default value set is 5,120 MB.

- **Updated Windows PowerShell Set-SPVisioPerformance cmdlet** This cmdlet has been updated to include the new maximum cache size parameter.

- **New Health Analyzer rules** New Health Analyzer rules have been added to reflect the new maximum cache size parameter.

Creating and configuring Excel Services service applications

Before Excel Services can be used on your SharePoint farm, Excel Services must be enabled by creating an Excel Services service application from Central Administration. This section walks through the steps to set up and deploy Excel Services for your SharePoint farm.

Configuring Excel Services

Before configuring Excel Services, the following prerequisites are required:

- **SharePoint 2013 Enterprise edition** Required to run Excel Services.

- **Domain account** Required to run the Excel Services application pool. It is recommended that you use a separate domain account when running the Excel Services application pool. This account does not require any specific domain privileges.

- **Farm Administrators group permissions** You must be a member of the Farm Administrators group to perform the configuration and setup of Excel Services.

Configuring an application pool account

Excel Services uses an application pool account to run Excel Services. Once a domain account is created, before it can be used as an account to run an application pool, it must first be registered as a managed account in SharePoint.

> **Note**
>
> Using a separate domain account for the Excel Services application pool is recommended for better security. Have your domain administrator create a domain account for Excel Services. As mentioned earlier, this account does not require any specific domain privileges.

Registering the managed account   To register the managed account in SharePoint Server, follow these steps:

1. From Central Administration, click Security, located in the left navigation.

2. Under General Settings, click Configure Managed Accounts | Register Managed Account.

3. Type the user name and password of the preferred domain account, and then click OK.

> **Note**
>
> Optionally, you can select Enable Automatic Password Change if you want SharePoint Server to manage password changes for the domain account that is being registered.

Granting the managed account access to the content database   The managed account used to run the Excel Services application pool must also be granted access to the SharePoint content database. Use the following Windows PowerShell steps to grant access to the managed account:

1. On the Application Server, click Start | All Programs | Microsoft SharePoint 2013 Products.

2. Right-click SharePoint 2013 Management Shell, and then click Run As Administrator.

3. Type the following in to the Windows PowerShell command prompt:

   ```
   $webApp = Get-SPWebApplication -Identity http://<WebApplicationURL>
   $webApp.GrantAccessToProcessIdentity("<Domain>\<Username>")
   ```

Starting Excel Calculation Services

The Excel Calculation Services service must be started on at least one application server in the farm in order to use Excel Services.

To start an Excel Calculation Services service, follow these steps:

1. From Central Administration, click Manage Services on a server located in the System Settings group.

2. Select the desired server you want to start the service on by selecting Change Server from the Server drop-down list.

3. Click Start next to Excel Calculation Services.

Creating an Excel Services service application

Once the application pool account has been granted access to the content database, follow these steps to create an Excel Services service application:

1. Navigate back to the Manage Services application in Central Administration.

2. Click New, and then Excel Services Application. The Create New Excel Services Application window appears, as shown here.

Chapter 14

Create New Excel Services Application

⬜ Specify the name, application pool, and default for this Application.   Help

Name   [Excel Services Application Service]

Application Pool   ○ Use existing application pool
Choose the Application Pool to use   [SearchAppPool   ⌄]
for this Service Application. This
defines the account and credentials   ● Create new application pool
that will be used by this web   Application pool name
service.
                                          [Excel Application Pool]
You can choose an existing
application pool or create a new   Select a security account for this application pool
one.   ○ Predefined
                                             [Network Service ⌄]

                                          ● Configurable
                                             [DC07\SPFarm ⌄]
                                             Register new managed account

Add to default proxy list   ☑ Add this service application's proxy to the farm's default proxy
The setting makes this service   list.
application available for use by
default for web applications in this
farm. Do not check this setting if

---

3. Select an existing application pool or create a new one.

To create a new one, select the Create New Application Pool option and type in the Application pool name. Select the Configurable option, and select the account to be used to run the application service. It is recommended to create a new application pool for the Excel Services Application.

4. Click OK.

Data authentication for Excel Services

Retrieving data from a data source requires a user to be authenticated by the data source before the user is provided authorized access to the data. In the case of a workbook, Excel Services authenticates to the data source connected to the workbook on behalf of the user viewing the file. Excel Services supports connections with SQL Server databases, SSAS, and custom Object Linking and Embedding Database (OLE DB) or Open Database Connectivity (ODBC) providers.

Data sources and authentication methods for Excel Services

The authentication method used with Excel Services to retrieve data depends on the type of the underlying data source. Table 14-1 lists the Excel Services data source options and their associated authentication methods.

TABLE 14-1 Excel Services data source options and supported authentication methods

Data source	Authentication method
SQL Server databases	Windows authentication (integrated security) using: ● Constrained Kerberos delegation ● Secure store ● Unattended service account ● EffectiveUserName connection string property
SSAS	Windows authentication (integrated security) using: ● Constrained Kerberos delegation ● Secure store ● Unattended service account ● SQL Server Authentication ● EffectiveUserName connection string property
Custom OLE DB or ODBC data providers	Varies based on the data source, but typically uses a connection string that stores the user name and password.

Excel Services does not support connecting to the following data sources:

● Access databases

● Text files

● Web content

● Windows Azure

● XML data

Connecting to external data with Excel Services

Excel Services can connect to various data sources by using a specific data provider for each data source. As a security measure, before using the data providers, Excel Services must explicitly trust data providers. Trusted data providers can be configured for Excel Services, which is covered later in this chapter in the section, "Managing Excel Services."

Data connections for Excel workbooks

Excel workbooks allow the following two kinds of connections:

- Embedded connections

  - Stored as part of the Excel Services workbook.

  - Used in scenarios when you need a data connection that will not be widely used.

- Linked connections

  - Stored externally to a workbook in Office Data Connection (ODC) files. A workbook must reference an .odc file stored in the same farm as the workbook in a trusted data connection library. Trusted data connection libraries are covered later in this chapter in the section, "Managing Excel Services."

  - Most useful in scenarios when the connections will be shared across many users and when control by an administrator for the connection is important. Use in scenarios when you must have a data connection to an enterprise-scale data source.

The two data connection options are compared in Table 14-2.

TABLE 14-2 Excel Services data connection comparison

Connection type	Advantages	Disadvantages
Embedded connections	Connection information is stored in the workbook. Little administration required. Easy to create.	If data connection details change for the data source, all workbooks with embedded connections must be updated and republished. More difficult for administrators to audit.
Linked connections (ODC files)	Connections can be centrally stored, managed, audited, shared, and accessed using a data connection library. Workbook authors can use existing connections. If the data connection details change, the administrator needs to update the connection only in the one ODC file. All workbooks will use the updated connection information when refresh occurs.	May require help from a SharePoint administrator to share, manage, and secure the linked connection. Linked connections are stored in clear text, so extra care must be taken to help secure these files because they may include database passwords.

> **Note**
> The linked connections ODC files must be created in Excel and exported to the Share-Point server before they can be used with Excel Services.

Managing Excel Services

The options for managing the Excel Services Application Service settings are shown in Figure 14-1 and include the following:

- **Global Settings**   Defines the load balancing, memory, and throttling thresholds. Also includes the option for setting the unattended service account and data connection timeouts.

- **Trusted File Locations**   Defines where the spreadsheets can be loaded from in SharePoint.

- **Trusted Data Providers**   Adds or removes data providers that can be used when data connections are refreshed.

- **Trusted Data Connection Libraries**   Defines the SharePoint document library where data connections will be stored and loaded from.

- **User-Defined Function Assemblies**   Settings for registering managed code assemblies that can be used by Excel spreadsheets.

- **Data Model Settings**   Registers SSAS servers that Excel Services can use for advanced data analysis functionality.

Manage Excel Services Application ⓘ

Global Settings
Define load balancing, memory, and throttling thresholds. Set the unattended service account and data connection timeouts.

Trusted File Locations
Define places where spreadsheets can be loaded from.

Trusted Data Providers
Add or remove data providers that can be used when refreshing data connections.

Trusted Data Connection Libraries
Define a SharePoint Document Library where data connections can be loaded from.

User Defined Function Assemblies
Register managed code assemblies that can be used by spreadsheets.

Data Model Settings
Register instances of SQL Server Analysis Services servers that Excel Services Application can use for advanced data analysis functionality.

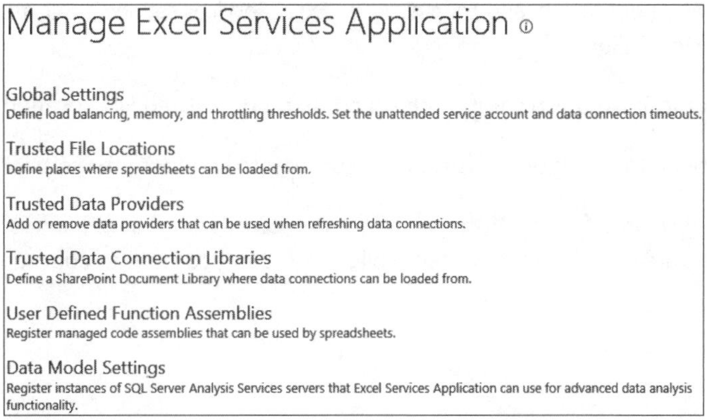

Figure 14-1 The service settings for the Excel Services Application are changed in Central Administration.

Global settings for Excel Services

The global settings for managing workbooks includes settings for external data connections, load balancing, session management, memory utilization, workbook caches, and security.

Follow these steps to edit the Excel Services global settings:

1. From Central Administration, click Manage Service Applications in the Application Management group, and then click the Excel Services service application that you want to configure.

2. From the Manage Excel Services page, click the Global Settings link.

3. Update the desired settings and then click OK.

Trusted file locations

A *trusted file location* is a SharePoint server location, a network file share (UNC path), or a web folder address that enables workbooks to be loaded from it and is required because Excel Services loads workbooks only from trusted file locations. By default, Excel Services automatically creates a trusted file location (http://) that trusts the entire SharePoint farm and enables any file to be loaded from the SharePoint farm. Administrators can define new trusted file locations as needed to tighten security and expand workbook capabilities.

Adding trusted file locations   Follow these steps to add a trusted file location in Excel Services. To perform these steps, you must be a member of the Farm Administrators group or an administrator of the Excel Services service application that you are configuring.

1. From Central Administration, click Manage Service Applications in the Application Management group, and then click the Excel Services service application that you want to configure.

2. Click the Trusted File Locations link and then Add Trusted File Location.

3. Continue to Configure A Trusted File Location to configure the settings.

Configuring trusted file locations   Follow these steps to configure the trusted file locations. (If you are already in the trusted file location that you want to edit, continue to step 3.)

1. From Central Administration, click Manage Service Applications in the Application Management group, and then click the Excel Services service application that you want to configure.

2. Click the Trusted File Locations link, and then, in the Address column, click the file location that you want to configure.

3. Configure the settings as described in Table 14-3 and then click OK when finished.

TABLE 14-3 Trusted file location setting options

Option	Description
Address	Location of the Excel documents that you want Excel Services to trust.
Location Type	Select Microsoft SharePoint Foundation if the document library is stored in the SharePoint 2013 content database. Select UNC if the document library is stored in a network file share. Select HTTP if the document library is stored in a web folder address.
Trust Children	Select Children Trusted if you want to trust all child libraries or directories.
Description	Text description of the file location that you specified.
Session Timeout	Value in seconds that an Excel Calculation Services session can stay open and inactive before it is shut down, as measured from the end of each open request. The default is 450 seconds.
Short Session Timeout	Value in seconds that an Excel Services session stays open and inactive, before any user interaction, before it is shut down. This is measured from the end of the original open request. The default is 450 seconds.
New Workbook Session Timeout	Value in seconds that an Excel Calculation Services session for a new workbook stays open and inactive before it is shut down, as measured from the end of each request. The default value is 1,800 seconds (30 minutes).
Maximum Request Duration	Value in seconds for the maximum duration of a single request in a session. The default is 300 seconds.
Maximum Chart Render Duration	Value in seconds for the maximum time that is spent rendering any single chart. The default is 3 seconds.
Maximum Workbook Size	Value in megabytes for the maximum size of workbooks that Excel Calculation Services can open. The default size is 10 MB.
Maximum Chart Or Image Size	Value in megabytes for the maximum size of charts or images that Excel Calculation Services can open. The default size is 1 MB.
Volatile Function Cache Lifetime	Value in seconds that a computed value for a volatile function is cached for automatic recalculations. The default is 300 seconds.

Chapter 14

Option	Description
Workbook Calculation Mode	Select File to perform calculations as specified in the file. Select Manual if you want recalculation to occur only when a Calculate request is received. Select Automatic if you want any change to a value to cause the recalculation of all other values that depend on that value. Also, volatile functions are called if their time-out has expired. Select Automatic Except Data Tables if you want any change to a value to cause the recalculations of all other values dependent on that value (the values cannot be in a data table). Also, volatile functions are called if their time-out has expired.
Allow External Data	Select None to disable all external data connections for the trusted file location. Select Trusted Data Connection Libraries only to enable using connections to data sources that are stored in a trusted data connection library. The server will ignore settings embedded in the worksheet. Select Trusted Data Connection Libraries and embedded to enable connections that are embedded in the workbook file or connections that are stored in a trusted data connection library. If you do not have to have tight control or restrictions on the data connections that are used by workbooks on the server, consider selecting this option.
Warn On Refresh	Select the Refresh Warning Enabled check box to display a warning before refreshing external data for files in this location. This option will make sure that external data is not automatically refreshed without user interaction.
Display Granular External Data Errors	Select the Granular External Data Errors check box to display specific error messages when external data failures occur for files in this location. Displaying specific error messages can help troubleshoot data connectivity issues if they occur.
Stop When Refresh On Open Fails	Select the Stopping Open Enabled check box to prevent users from viewing files that are configured to refresh on open, if the refresh fails. This prevents users from seeing cached information in the workbook. This option is effective only if the user does not have Open Item permissions on the workbook. (A user with Open Item permissions on the workbook can open the workbook in Excel and thus has access to any cached information.)
External Cache Lifetime (Automatic Refresh)	In the Automatic Refresh (periodic/on-open) box, type a value in seconds for the maximum time that the system can use external data query results for automatically refreshed external query results. The default is 300 seconds.
External Cache Lifetime (Manual Refresh)	In the Manual Refresh box, type a value in seconds for the maximum time that the system can use external data query results for automatically refreshed external query results. To prevent data refresh after the first query, type **-1.** The default is 300 seconds.

Option	Description
Maximum Concurrent Queries Per Session	Type a value for the maximum number of queries that can run at the same time during a single session. The default is 5 queries.
Allow External Data Using REST	Select the Data Refresh From REST Enabled check box to use all requests from the REST application programming interface (API) to refresh external data connections. Note this setting has no effect if Allow External Data is set to None. Also, this setting has no effect if Warn On Refresh is enabled.
Allow User-Defined Functions	Select User-defined Functions Allowed to allow user-defined functions in Excel Calculation Services for workbooks from this location. See the "User-defined function assemblies" section, later in this chapter, for more details on user-defined functions.

Deleting trusted file locations   Follow these steps to delete a trusted file location in Excel Services:

1. From Central Administration, click Manage Service Applications in the Application Management group, and then click the Excel Services service application that you want to configure.

2. Click the Trusted File Locations link.

3. Point to the trusted file location you want to delete, click the arrow that appears, and then click Delete.

4. Click OK in the Delete Confirmation message box.

Trusted data providers

As mentioned earlier in this chapter, trusted data providers are part of a security measure because Excel Services must explicitly trust data providers before they can be used. Trusted data providers can be configured for Excel Services through Central Administration.

Adding a trusted data provider   Follow these steps to add a trusted data provider in Excel Services:

1. From Central Administration, click Manage Service Applications in the Application Management group, and then click the Excel Services service application that you want to configure.

2. Click the Trusted Data Providers link and then click Add Trusted Data Provider.

The Excel Services Application Add Trusted Data Provider window opens, as shown here.

Excel Services Application Add Trusted Data Provider

☐ Provider

An external data provider that workbooks
opened in Excel Services Application are
permitted to use.

Provider ID
The identifier for this data provider.

Provider Type
Data provider type:
- ◉ OLE DB
- ○ ODBC
- ○ ODBC DSN

Description
The optional description of the purpose of this data provider.

3. Type the Provider ID in the Provider section (for example, **SQL Server**).

4. Select the Provider Type to be one of the following:

   - **OLE DB**   Object Linking and Embedding (OLE) provider type

   - **ODBC**   Open Access Connectivity

   - **ODBC DSN**   Open Database Connectivity (ODBC) with Data Source Name

5. Type in Description (optional), and then click OK.

Configuring a trusted data provider   Use the following steps to configure an existing trusted data provider in Excel Services:

1. From Central Administration, click Manage Service Applications in the Application Management group, and then click the Excel Services service application that you want to configure.

2. Click the Trusted Data Providers link, and then click Edit on the menu of the data provider that you want to configure.

Deleting a trusted data provider   Use the following steps to delete an existing trusted data provider in Excel Services:

1. From Central Administration, click Manage Service Applications in the Application Management group, and then click the Excel Services service application that you want to configure.

2. Click the Trusted Data Providers link, and then click Delete on the menu of the data provider that you want to delete.

3. Click OK in the Delete Confirmation message box.

Trusted data connection libraries

Excel Services provides the ability to connect to external data sources and uses data connection files that are stored in a trusted data connection library. Follow the steps in this section to add and configure a trusted data connection library.

Adding a trusted data connection library   Follow these steps to add a trusted data connection library in Excel Services:

1. From Central Administration, click Manage Service Applications in the Application Management group, and then click the Excel Services service application that you want to configure.

2. Click the Trusted Data Connection Libraries link, and then click Add Trusted Data Connection Library.

3. Type in the address of the trusted data connection library in the Location section and input a Description (optional), as shown here.

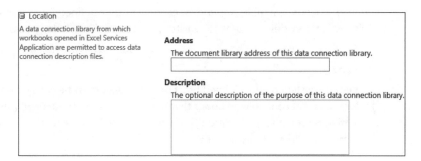

4. Click OK.

Configuring a trusted data connection library   Follow these steps to update the configuration of an existing trusted data connection library in Excel Services:

1. From Central Administration, click Manage Service Applications in the Application Management group, and then click the Excel Services service application that you want to configure.

2. Click the Trusted Data Connection Libraries link.

3. Click the data connection library that you want to configure or point to the name and click the arrow that appears, and then click Edit.

4. Modify the settings and then click OK.

Deleting a trusted data connection library   Follow these steps to delete an existing trusted data connection library in Excel Services:

1. From Central Administration, click Manage Service Applications in the Application Management group, and then click the Excel Services service application that you want to configure.

2. Click the Trusted Data Connection Libraries link. Point to the data connection library that you want to delete, click the arrow that appears, and then click Delete.

3. Click OK in the Delete Confirmation message box.

User-defined function assemblies

User-defined functions in Excel Services is supported if your deployment scenarios include workbooks that contain user-defined functions to extend the capabilities of Excel Calculation Services. In order to use user-defined functions, you must register the user-defined function assemblies on the Excel Services user-defined function assemblies list. This section provides the steps to register your user-defined function assemblies.

> **Note**
>
> Before registering, user-defined function assemblies must be enabled on trusted file locations that contain workbooks that require access to user-defined functions. This setting is set in the global settings, which is discussed in the section, "Trusted file locations," earlier in this chapter.

Adding a user-defined function assembly   Follow these steps to add a user-defined function assembly in Excel Services:

1. From Central Administration, click Manage Service Applications in the Application Management group, and then click the Excel Services service application that you want to configure.

2. Click the User-Defined Function Assemblies link, and then click Add User-Defined Function Assembly.

3. In the Assembly section, shown here, type in the Assembly box the assembly name or full path of an assembly that contains the user-defined functions.

```
☐ Assembly details
Settings for a .NET assembly that contains
User-Defined Functions.                    Assembly
                                           Strong name or full path of an assembly that contains user-defined
                                           functions, which Excel Calculation Services can call. Examples:
                                           SampleCompany.SampleApplication.SampleUdf, C:\UDFs\SampleUdf.dll,
                                           \\MyNetworkServer\UDFs\SampleUdf.dll.


                                           Assembly Location
                                           Location of the assembly:
                                           ● Global assembly cache
                                           ○ File path

                                           Enable Assembly
                                           Allow this user-defined function assembly to be loaded and used by Excel
                                           Calculation Services. Turning off this option disables the assembly without
                                           having to completely remove the entry from the list.
                                           ☑ Assembly enabled

                                           Description
                                           The optional description of this user-defined function assembly.


```

4. For Assembly Location, select one of the following options:

   - **Global Assembly Cache**   The global assembly cache (GAC) is the global place where signed assemblies can be deployed and run with full trust by default.

   - **File Path**   A local or network file location.

5. In the Enable Assembly section, select the Assembly Enabled check box to enable Excel Services to call the assembly. You can also clear this check box to disable the assembly without removing the function from the list.

6. Click OK.

Editing a user-defined function assembly   Follow these steps to edit an existing user-defined function assembly in Excel Services:

1. From Central Administration, click Manage Service Applications in the Application Management group, and then click the Excel Services service application that you want to configure.

2. Click the User-Defined Function Assemblies link, point to the user-defined function assembly that you want to edit, click the arrow that appears, and then click Edit.

3. Update the assembly details, and then click OK.

Deleting a user-defined function assembly   Follow these steps to unregister (delete) a user-defined function assembly in Excel Services:

1. From Central Administration, click Manage Service Applications in the Application Management group, and then click the Excel Services service application that you want to configure.

2. Click the User-Defined Function Assemblies link, point to the user-defined function assembly that you want to delete, click the arrow that appears, and then click Delete.

3. Click OK in the Delete Confirmation message box.

Data model settings

The data model settings in Excel Services are used to register one or more instances of SSAS. It can be used in Excel Services for processing data models created in Excel 2013 to perform advanced data analysis calculations. SSAS provides the back-end service for Excel Services to load, query, and refresh the data models so that users can interact with the workbook through SharePoint.

When multiple tables in the same import operation in Excel are selected, Excel Services will automatically create the data models. SSAS is required if you want to build workbooks that store imported data in multiple tables and interact with this data through SharePoint.

In order to use SSAS with SharePoint, SSAS must be on the same network and domain as the SharePoint farm, and SSAS must be installed and managed using the SQL Server installation and media tools. After SSAS is installed, the only additional configuration required is to configure Excel Services to point to the SSAS server instance.

Multiple instances of SSAS can be specified in Excel Services, which then makes the data models stream to the instances in a round-robin fashion for load balancing. Additional SSAS servers are used for greater capacity when the resource usage is excessive on the SSAS server or SharePoint becomes slow in the browser when working with the data models.

Registering SSAS with Excel Services   To register an SSAS server to Excel Services, follow these steps:

1. From Central Administration, click Manage Service Applications in the Application Management group, and then click the Excel Services service application that you want to configure.

2. Click the Data Model Settings link.

3. Click Add Server, and then type in the instance of the SSAS server in the Server Name and the Description (optional), as shown here.

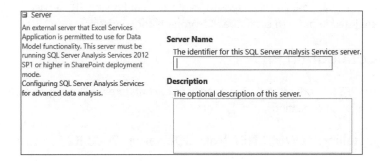

4. Click OK.

Editing SSAS details   Follow these steps to edit the details of registered SSAS servers in Excel Services:

1. From Central Administration, click Manage Service Applications in the Application Management group, and then click the Excel Services service application that you want to configure.

2. Click the Data Model Settings link.

3. Pause the mouse over the server that you want to edit, click the arrow that appears, and then click Edit.

4. Update the Server Name and Description as needed, then click OK.

Deleting SSAS in Excel Services   Follow these steps to remove an instance of SSAS servers from Excel Services:

1. From Central Administration, click Manage Service Applications in the Application Management group, and then click the Excel Services service application that you want to configure.

2. Click the Data Model Settings link.

3. Pause the mouse over the server that you want to unregister, click the arrow that appears, and then click Delete.

4. Click OK in the Delete Confirmation message box.

Creating and configuring PPS service applications

This section describes the steps to create and configure a PPS service application. The steps are listed in order to configure PPS properly for SharePoint.

Configuring PPS

For PPS to work properly, it is important to configure it following all required installs and configuration settings.

Installing ADOMD.NET from SQL Server 2008 R2 feature pack

ADOMD.NET is a Microsoft .NET Framework object model used to enable client-side applications to access data stored in SSAS. The PerformancePoint Dashboard Designer uses ADOMD.NET to browse and query data in SSAS, so ADOMD.NET must be installed. The stand-alone package installation instructions are available for download from the Microsoft website located at *http://www.microsoft.com/en-us/download/details.aspx?id=16978*. Download and follow the instructions provided to install ADOMD.NET to your environment before moving on to the next steps.

INSIDE OUT Why does the SQL Server 2008 R2 ADOMD.NET version have to be installed instead of the version from the SQL Server 2012 SP1 feature pack?

When writing Chapter 16, "Building powerful dashboards with PerformancePoint Services," I encountered an issue with not being able to connect Dashboard Designer to my SSAS server and cube. I had installed ADOMD.NET from the SQL Server 2012 SP1 feature pack and was able to connect through SQL Server 2012 with no problem, but I could not get the connection to work in Dashboard Designer. After I spent hours and hours of troubleshooting, it turned out that Dashboard Designer 2013 was written for SQL Server 2008 R2 Analysis Services clients. Thanks to the help of a blog post by my friend Chris McNulty, I found that the solution was to download and install the ADOMD version 10 client support SQL Server 2008 R2 ADOMD.NET from the SQL Server 2008 R2 feature pack on my SSAS 2012 server. After it was installed, I did an IISReset on my server farm and then was able to connect successfully through Dashboard Designer.

Configuring the application pool account

To run the PerformancePoint Services service application, the application pool account requires a managed account, which is typically an Active Directory account. This account must have access to the PerformancePoint data content databases.

Registering the managed account   To register the managed account in SharePoint Server, follow these steps, which are the same as the steps you followed for Excel Services:

1. From Central Administration, click Security, located in the left navigation.

2. Under General Settings, click Configure Managed Accounts, and then click Register Managed Account.

3. Type the user name and password of the preferred domain account and then click OK.

> **Note**
>
> Optionally, you can select Enable Automatic Password Change if you want SharePoint Server to manage password changes for the domain account that is being registered.

Granting the managed account access to the content database   The managed account used to run the PPS application pool must also be granted access to the content databases where the PerformancePoint data will be stored. Use the following Windows PowerShell steps to grant access to the managed account for each web application that contains a content database where PerformancePoint Services data will reside:

1. On the Application Server, click Start | All Programs | Microsoft SharePoint 2013 Products, right-click SharePoint 2013 Management Shell, and then click Run As Administrator.

2. Type the following into the Windows PowerShell command prompt:

   ```
   $webApp = Get-SPWebApplication -Identity http://<WebApplicationURL>
   $webApp.GrantAccessToProcessIdentity("<Domain>\<Username>")
   ```

Starting PPS

Once the application pool account has been granted access to the content database, you can proceed to start PPS on the application server where you want PPS to run. For better performance, you can start the service on multiple application servers. It is not required to start the PPS service on all application servers; however, it is required to be started on at least one application server.

Follow these steps to start PPS:

1. From Central Administration, click Manage Services on a server located in the System Settings group.

2. Select the desired server that you want to start the service on by clicking the Server drop-down list and then click Change Server.

3. Click Start next to PerformancePoint Services.

Creating a PPS service application

Follow these steps to create a PPS service application:

1. Navigate back to the Manage Service Applications in Central Administration.

2. Click New, then PerformancePoint Services Application.

3. Type in the Name and select the box for Add This Service Application's Proxy To The Farm's Default Proxy List.

4. Update the Database Name (optional).

> **Note**
>
> The database name will be autogenerated with the name of the type of service application and a GUID. It is recommended to change the database name to something that follows your company's naming conventions.

5. Select an existing application pool or create a new one.

   To create a new one, select the Create New Application Pool option and type in the Application Pool name. Select the Configurable option and select the account to be used to run the application service.

6. Click Create.

> **Note**
>
> If you need to create a new managed account, click the Register New Managed Account link before clicking Create.

Once the PPS application is created, a module window will pop up with the information regarding the service application. If you have not installed PowerPivot, you will receive the message shown in Figure 14-2.

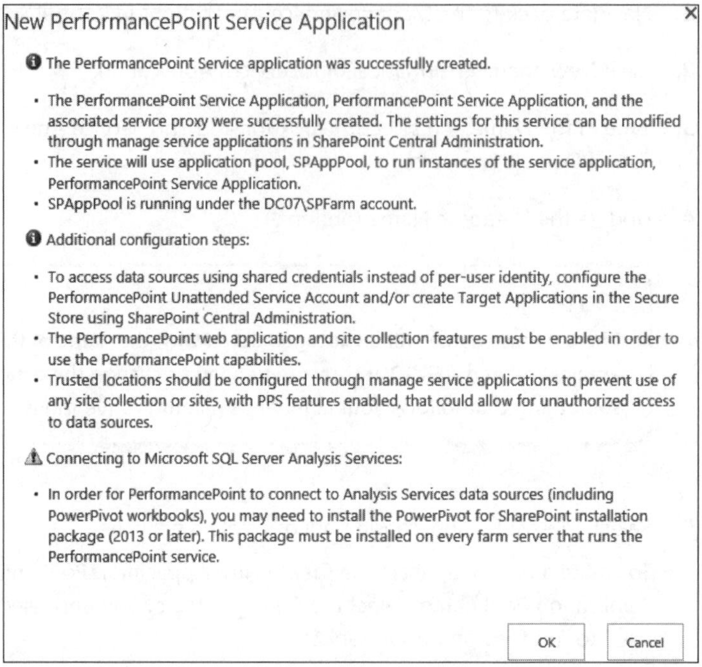

New PerformancePoint Service Application ✕

ⓘ The PerformancePoint Service application was successfully created.

- The PerformancePoint Service Application, PerformancePoint Service Application, and the associated service proxy were successfully created. The settings for this service can be modified through manage service applications in SharePoint Central Administration.
- The service will use application pool, SPAppPool, to run instances of the service application, PerformancePoint Service Application.
- SPAppPool is running under the DC07\SPFarm account.

ⓘ Additional configuration steps:

- To access data sources using shared credentials instead of per-user identity, configure the PerformancePoint Unattended Service Account and/or create Target Applications in the Secure Store using SharePoint Central Administration.
- The PerformancePoint web application and site collection features must be enabled in order to use the PerformancePoint capabilities.
- Trusted locations should be configured through manage service applications to prevent use of any site collection or sites, with PPS features enabled, that could allow for unauthorized access to data sources.

⚠ Connecting to Microsoft SQL Server Analysis Services:

- In order for PerformancePoint to connect to Analysis Services data sources (including PowerPivot workbooks), you may need to install the PowerPivot for SharePoint installation package (2013 or later). This package must be installed on every farm server that runs the PerformancePoint service.

| OK | Cancel |

Figure 14-2 A New PerformancePoint Service Application summary appears once the PPS application is created.

INSIDE OUT   Should I use spaces in the database names?

I recommend not using spaces in the database names, nor keeping the autogenerated GUID. For example, upon creation, I changed the database name from PerformancePoint Service Application_c59e4eaf13bb4e81b45fc77b9dcb874d to PerformancePoint_Service_Application. I replaced the spaces with underscores (_) and removed the autogenerated GUID.

INSIDE OUT Do I need to create a new application pool for my service applications?

Unless you are setting up and configuring your staging and production environment, I recommend using the same application pool for the service applications for your development environment. In most cases, your development environment will not have the same amount of resources as your production environment. The more application pools you use, the more resources are being used. Therefore, in order to get better performance from your development environment, select the Use Existing Application Pool option instead of the Create New Application Pool option. In this case, I would select the same application pool that I created for Excel Services.

The PPS service application proxy must be associated with the default web application in order for PPS to function. If you did not select the Add This Service Application's Proxy To The Farm's Default Proxy List option in the previous steps, then you can confirm that the association is configured between the web application and the PPS application proxy by following these steps:

1. From Central Administration, click Application Management.

2. Click Configure Service Applications Associations, located in the Service Applications section.

3. Under the Application Proxy Group column, click Default and ensure that the PerformancePoint Services box is selected. Click the box if it is not selected, then click OK.

Enabling trusted locations for PPS

PPS objects are made available for others to use on any site within the site collection after the feature is enabled on a site collection. Administrators can limit the PPS features that use trusted locations by allowing one or more sites, document libraries, or lists rather than allowing the entire site collection.

Enabling trusted locations for data sources and dashboard content

Specified locations can be set where dashboard content and data sources are secured for PPS. The default is to trust all locations; however, the following other trusted locations can be specified by the administrator:

- **PerformancePoint content list** Stores the elements used to construct a PerformancePoint dashboard.

- **PerformancePoint data source library** Contains data-source definitions that identify a source of business data. May include cubes or perspectives based on online analytical processing (OLAP) cubes, relational databases, Excel Services worksheets, or Comma-separated values (CSV) files.

- **Trusted data sources and trusted content locations** Both have two options, which are All SharePoint Locations or Only Specific Locations. When Only Specific Locations is selected, the list of trusted locations is enabled.

Adding a trusted data source location

Follow these steps to add a trusted data source location:

1. From Central Administration, click Manage Service Applications in the Application Management group, and then click the PerformancePoint Services service application that you want to configure.

2. Click Trusted Data Source Locations, then select either All SharePoint Locations or Only Specific Locations (Current Setting), as shown here.

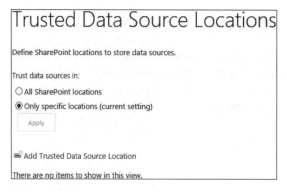

Trusted Data Source Locations

Define SharePoint locations to store data sources.

Trust data sources in:

○ All SharePoint locations
◉ Only specific locations (current setting)

Apply

🖼 Add Trusted Data Source Location

There are no items to show in this view.

If Only Specific Locations (Current Setting) was selected, the Add Trusted Data Source Location window appears.

3. Click Add Trusted Data Source Location and specify the URL and Location, as shown here.

4. Enter the full web address (site collection, site, or document library).

5. Select Location Type, type a Description (optional), and then click OK.

Adding a trusted content location

Follow these steps to add a trusted content location:

1. From Central Administration, click Manage Service Applications in the Application Management group, and then click the PerformancePoint Services service application that you want to configure.

2. Click Trusted Content Locations, then select All SharePoint Locations or Only Specific Locations.

   If Only Specific Locations was selected, the Add Trusted Data Source Location window appears.

3. Click Add Trusted Data Source Location and specify the URL and Location.

4. Enter the full web address (site collection, site, list address).

5. Select Location Type, type a Description (optional), and click OK.

Creating and configuring a Visio Graphics Service service application

This section provides the steps to create and configure Visio Graphics Service service applications for SharePoint Server 2013 through Central Administration.

Creating a Visio Graphics Service service application

Follow these steps to create a Visio Graphics Service service application:

1. From Central Administration, click Managed Services on a server located in the System Settings group.

2. On the ribbon, click New, then click Visio Graphics Service.

3. Input the name for the new Visio Graphics Service service application.

4. Choose an existing application pool or create a new one.

    To create a new one, select the Create New Application Pool option and type in the Application Pool name. Select the Configurable option and select the account to be used to run the application service.

5. Leave the Create A Visio Graphics Service Application Proxy and add it to the default proxy group box checked.

6. Click OK.

Configuring the global settings for a Visio Graphics Service

The global settings for a Visio Graphics Service include managing settings for performance, security, and refreshing data connections.

Follow these steps to configure the Visio Graphics Service global settings:

1. From Central Administration, click Manage Service Applications in the Application Management group, and then click the Visio Graphics Service service application that you want to configure.

2. From the Manage Visio Services page, click the Global Settings link.

3. Configure the settings as described in Table 14-4 and click OK when finished.

TABLE 14-4 Visio Graphics global settings

Parameter	Description
Maximum Diagram Size	• Maximum size in megabytes of a diagram that can be rendered. If the server is under heavy load, a larger size limit may lead to slower performance and a smaller limit may prevent more complex diagrams from being rendered.
	• Valid values range from 1 to 50; default value is 25 MB.
Minimum Cache Age	• Minimum number of minutes that a diagram is cached in memory. Smaller values increase CPU and memory usage on the server but allow more frequent data refresh operations for users.
	• Value is per user per diagram. Interval begins when a user views a diagram and the user cannot refresh the diagram until the interval expires. Interval begins for other users when they first view the diagram.
	• Applies to diagrams with data connections and diagrams with recalculations based on shape sheet functions. For Visio Web Parts, the automatic refresh setting is also constrained by this setting.
	• Valid values range from 0 to 34,560 minutes; default value is 5 minutes.
Maximum Cache Age	• Number of minutes that pass before cached diagrams are purged. Larger values increase memory usage on the server but decrease file I/O and CPU load.
	• Valid values range from 0 to 34,560 minutes; default value is 60 minutes.
Maximum Recalc Duration	• Number of seconds before data refresh operations time out. Longer timeouts will use more processing power but will allow for more complex data connected diagrams to be recalculated. This setting applies only to data connected diagrams.
	• Applies to diagrams with data connections and diagrams with recalculations based on shape sheet functions.
	• Valid values range from 10 to 120; default value is 60 seconds.

Chapter 14

Parameter	Description
Maximum Cache Size	• Maximum cache size in megabytes (between 100 and 1,024,000) that can be used. A larger size limit may lead to more disk resource usage by the service and a smaller limit may affect performance. • Valid values range from 100 to 1,024,000; default value is 5,120 MB.
External Data	The Target application ID in the registered Secure Store Service used to reference Unattended Service Account credentials. The Unattended Service Account is a single account that all documents can use to refresh data. Required when you connect to external data sources outside of SharePoint.

Creating trusted data providers for a Visio Graphics Service

Settings to add or remove data providers can be used when refreshing data connections through a Visio Graphics Service. Follow these steps to create a trusted data provider for a Visio Graphics Service:

1. From Central Administration, click Manage Service Applications in the Application Management group, and then click the Visio Graphics Service service application that you want to configure.

2. From the Manage Visio Services page, click the Trusted Data Providers link.

3. Click Add A New Trusted Data Provider. The Add Trusted Data Provider window opens, as shown here.

Add Trusted Data Provider

Trusted Data Provider ID
The identifier for this data provider.

Trusted Data Provider Type
The type of this data provider. Must be one of the following values: 1 for OLEDB, 2 for SQL, 3 for ODBC, 4 for ODBC with DSN, 5 for SharePoint Lists and 6 for Visio Custom Data Providers.

Trusted Data Provider Description
The description of the purpose of this data provider.

4. Enter the values for the parameters as described in Table 14-5 and click OK.

TABLE 14-5 **Trusted data provider parameters**

Parameter	Description
Trusted Data Provider ID	The data provider ID is the name of the driver that acts as the data provider. This ID must be the same ID used to reference the data provider in the connection string. The driver for the data provider must be installed on all application servers running the Visio Graphics Service.
Trusted Data Provider Type	The data provider type must be one of the following values: 1 - OLEDB 2 - SQL 3 - ODBC 4 - ODBC with DSN 5 - SharePoint Lists 6 - Custom Data Provider
Trusted Data Provider Description	Friendly name that appears in the Trusted Data Providers section.

Creating and configuring a Business Intelligence Center

The Business Intelligence Center provides a central location to store reports and dashboards. When Excel Services and PPS are enabled, a location to store reports and dashboard content will already exist.

> **Note**
>
> Before you can create and configure a Business Intelligence Center, a Secure Store Service must be configured first. Please see the article "**Configure the Secure Store Service in SharePoint 2013,**" located at *http://technet.microsoft.com/en-us/library/ee806866.aspx.*

Creating a Business Intelligence Center

A Business Intelligence Center is created by using the Business Intelligence Center enterprise template and creating a new site collection. To create a Business Intelligence Center, follow these steps:

1. From Central Administration, click the Application Management group, and then click Create Site Collections.

2. Input the Title, Description, and set the Web Site Address for the site collection.

3. Click the Enterprise tab located in the Template Selection section, and then click Business Intelligence Center.

4. Set the Primary Site Collection Administrator, and then click OK.

5. When the top-level site is successfully created, click OK.

6. Set the user permissions for the new site collection.

Setting permissions for a Business Intelligence Center

To set permissions for a Business Intelligence Center, follow these steps:

1. From the browser, open the newly created Business Intelligence site collection.

2. In the upper-right corner, click Settings | Site Settings, and then click Site Permissions.

3. On the ribbon, click Grant Permissions.

4. In the Share Central Administration Invite People To box, type the name of the account to which you want to assign permissions, and then click Show Options and select a group or permission level.

5. Click Share.

Summary

In this chapter, you learned what improvements were made to the business intelligence features in SharePoint Server 2013, along with the requirements for implementing BI for SharePoint Server 2013. Excel Services new features include the Power View, IMBI and decoupled PivotChart and PivotTable reports. Some of the new and improved features of PPS include dashboard migration, support for SSAS Effective User, and iPad support. You learned that Visio Services has a new file format, the ability to comment on diagrams, and also added BCS support for external lists. The Business Intelligence Center has also been updated in this release.

This next chapter will continue with a deeper dive into Excel Services and the ways to work with Excel Services and SQL Server 2012. Chapter 16 focuses on PPS, and in Chapter 17, "Working with Visio Services," you will take a more detailed look at Visio Services.

Implementing better business intelligence with Excel Services and SQL Server 2012

IN the previous chapter, you learned about the administration side of planning for business intelligence (BI) and key performance indicators (KPIs) for your Microsoft SharePoint 2013 environment. Now that you have your environment ready for BI, you can focus on using the BI features of SharePoint. This chapter focuses on the steps to implement better BI solutions using the features and capabilities of Microsoft Excel 2013, Excel Services, and Microsoft SQL Server 2012. You will learn about the different data sources you can use in Excel 2013 and Excel Services, along with how to use the new features in Excel Services, including Excel Services data connections, and creating reports and scorecards using PowerPivot, PivotTables, and Power View. Finally, this chapter looks at the enhanced Excel Services technologies for developers in SharePoint 2013.

Excel Services features overview

Excel BI provides the capability to explore and analyze data of any size and integrate and show interactive representations of the data. In SharePoint 2013, Excel BI offers the following new features:

- **External data connections** As mentioned in the previous chapter, most external data connections are supported in Excel Services. This includes SQL Server Analysis Services (SSAS), SQL Server databases, OLE DB, and ODBC data sources.

- **Data models** Data models are supported, so long as an instance of SSAS is registered in Excel Services.

- **Reports and scorecards** Reports, dashboards, and scorecards created in Excel are supported in Excel Services. PivotTable reports can be viewed, sorted, filtered, and interacted with in the browser through SharePoint. This includes views created by Power View.

- **Field List and Field Well (PivotChart and PivotTable reports)** Opening and using Field List and Field Well are supported through the browser in Excel Services.

- **Timeline controls** Timeline controls are supported in Excel Services. Before an existing timeline control in Excel Services can be used, the timeline control must be added to a workbook through the Excel client.

- **Slicers** Slicers are supported in Excel Services, but they must be added to a workbook through the Excel client.

- **Quick Explore** Quick Explore is supported and is used to browse up and down to view higher or lower levels of information; however, new views cannot be created using Quick Explore through the browser.

- **Calculated measures and calculated fields** Calculated fields and calculated measures are supported in Excel Services; however, they must be created from the Excel client.

Excel Services, introduced in Microsoft Office SharePoint Server (MOSS) 2007, is a BI tool that allows the sharing of data-connected workbooks and is used primarily for BI scenarios. In SharePoint 2013, Excel Services is a shared service and is only available in the Enterprise edition of SharePoint. Excel 2013 workbooks can be connected to external data sources and then published to a SharePoint library so that the workbooks can be rendered through the browser. The workbook is rendered through the browser via Excel Services and the external data connection is maintained and the data is refreshed when necessary. The published workbooks allow broad sharing of reports through the organization and can be managed and secured according to the organization's needs.

Excel Services consists of:

- **Excel Calculation services** Used to load, calculate, call custom code (user-defined), and refresh the data.

- **Excel Web Access Web Part** Used to display Excel workbooks through the browser.

- **Excel Web services** Used for programmatic access.

> **Note**
>
> The tutorials in this chapter use the *AdventureWorksDW2012* database and *AdventureWorksDW2012Multidimensional-EE OLAP* cube, which are available at *http://msftdbprodsamples.codeplex.com/releases/view/55330*. The instructions, "Configure AdventureWorks for Business Intelligence Solutions," are available at *http://technet.microsoft.com/en-us/library/jj573016.aspx*.
>
> SQL Server Data Tools are required to perform the steps in this chapter. The SQL Server Data Tools can be downloaded from *http://msdn.microsoft.com/en-us/data/hh297027* and installed separately, instead of using the SQL 2012 DVD install.

External data connections

External data connections are used by Excel to connect to various data sources, and many of the data connections used are supported in Excel Services. As mentioned briefly in Chapter 14, "Planning for business intelligence and key performance indicators," the connections supported by Excel Services include SQL Server, SSAS, and custom OLE/ODBC data providers. The external data connection must be created from the Excel client first and then the Office Data Connection (ODC) file can be uploaded into a trusted data connection library in SharePoint. Data connections stored in a trusted data connection library provide reusability so users can create multiple reports and workbooks using the available data connections. When the data connections are updated, the reports and workbooks using these connections are updated with the current information.

Configuring the authentication settings

Before a data model can be created, the authentication settings need to be determined and configured. This section details the various authentication methods for Excel Services in preparation for the creation of the ODC file from the Excel client. The different authentication settings that are available when creating the ODC file from the Excel client are listed in Table 15-1.

TABLE 15-1 **Excel Services authentication settings options**

Authentication setting	Details
Use a stored account	Use when Excel Services is configured for authenticating through the Secure Store Service. The user name and password are retrieved from a target application in the Secure Store Service, which then performs a Windows logon.
None	Use when Excel Services is configured to use the Unattended Service Account. This setting is similar to using a stored account except that Excel Services uses the target application registered under the Unattended Service Account.

Creating a data access account

To move forward with the Use A Stored Account option, an account must be granted access to the data source for use with the Excel workbook. This account can be a SQL Server logon, an Active Directory account, or another set of credentials, as required by the data source. This account will be stored in the Secure Store. In this tutorial, an Active Directory account is being used. Once the data access has been established for the account, the next step is to create a SQL Server logon using the Active Directory account for data access.

Follow these steps to grant access in SQL Server:

1. Open Microsoft SQL Management Studio and connect to the database server that contains the *AdventureWorksDW2012* database.

2. From the Object Explorer, expand Security | Logins.

    If your account is not already in the list, continue to step 3.

3. Right-click Logins and select New Login.

4. Type in the Active Directory account name for the Login Name or click Search to find the user account. Leave the Windows Authentication option selected.

> **Note**
> Instead of typing the name directly into the Login Name text box, I typically click Search, type in the name, and click Check Names, so the name will get resolved properly. This small extra step will prevent you from getting errors when trying to add the account if it is typed in incorrectly.

5. Select User Mapping, located under the Select A Page option, and then check the Map box for the database you want to provide access to. For this example, select the *AdventureWorksDW2012* database, as shown in the following graphic.

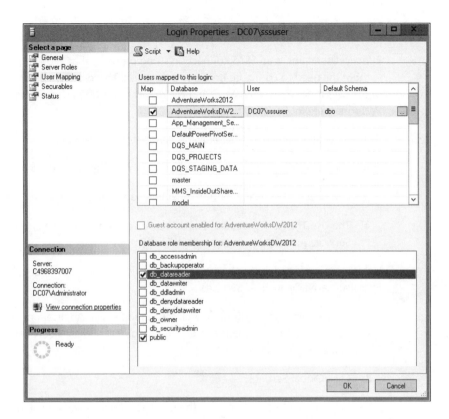

6. Check db_datareader in the Database Role Membership options and then click OK.

> **Note**
>
> Once the account is added, it will show up in the list in the Logins section. Even though the db_datareader option was selected when the setting was created, it may not have been set properly. It is recommended to check the User Mapping for the newly added account to verify that the property is set.

7. From the Logins section, double-click the account that was just added to reopen the properties.

8. Click User Mapping, then click AdventureWorksDW2012 under the Database column to make the options active for that database.

9. If the option is not set, click the db_datareader check box, then click OK.

Using Analysis Services EffectiveUserName

EffectiveUserName is an SSAS connection string property that allows a per-user identity without the need to configure Kerberos delegation. This property passes the value of the user to SSAS, which is accessing the report or dashboard in Excel Services or PerformancePoint Services.

To use EffectiveUserName, the following parameters are required:

- The Excel Service application pool account must be an SSAS administrator.

- The EffectiveUserName option must be enabled in the Excel Services Global Settings.

- The Use The Authenticated User's Account option must be enabled in the Excel Services Authentication Settings in Excel.

If this is the preferred authentication method, follow these steps to enable EffectiveUserName in Excel Services:

1. From Central Administration, click Managed Service Applications, located in the Application Management section, and then click the Excel Services service application that you want to configure.

2. Click Global Settings.

3. In the Excel Data section, click the Use The EffectiveUserName Property check box, and then click OK.

Using Secure Store with SQL authentication

This section provides the steps to use the Secure Store in SharePoint to store SQL Server credentials for use with Excel Services or Visio Services. It is recommended to store credentials in Secure Store over storing them in an Excel workbook file or an ODC file because credentials in Secure Store are not stored in plain text. By storing the credentials in the Secure Store, you provide a central location that is easier to manage and update than credentials stored directly in workbook or ODC files.

The following parameters are required in order to use Secure Store with Excel Services or Visio Services to access data sources through SQL Server authentication:

- A Secure Store target application containing SQL Server credentials with access to the data source must be configured.

- The Unattended Service Account must be configured.

In previous steps in this chapter, the data access account was granted access to the SQL Server database and was given db_datareader permissions. The next step is to create the Secure Store target application.

Creating a target application for SQL Server authentication   Follow these steps to create a target application for SQL Server authentication:

1. From Central Administration, click Managed Service Applications, located in the Application Management section, and then click the SSS service application that you want to configure.

2. On the ribbon, click New, and then fill in the following in the Create New Secure Store Target Application window:

    a. Target Application ID: Type a unique identifier for this target application. For example, this tutorial uses ExcelServicesSQLAccount.

    b. Display Name: Type a friendly name or short description.

    c. Contact E-mail: Type the email address for the contact used for this target application.

3. For Target Application Type, select Group from the drop-down list, as shown here.

    The two Target Application Type options are:

    - **Individual**   Each user connecting to SharePoint will be mapped to a unique set of credentials to connect to the Target Application.

    - **Group**   All users connecting to SharePoint in a specific group will be mapped to a shared set of credentials to connect to the Target Application.

4. Click Next to move to the Credentials Fields page.

Leave the default credential fields if you are using Windows credentials. If you are using other credentials, change the Field Type drop-down menus to the appropriate credentials that you are using.

5. Click Next to go to the Specify The Membership Settings page and enter the following, as shown next.

a. Target Application Administrators: Type in the account of the user who will be the administrator of this target application. In this example, the default administrator account will be added.

b. Members: Type the users to whom you want to grant the ability to refresh the data. To give access to all users, type **Everyone.**

6. Click OK.

Setting credentials for the SQL Server authentication target application   To set the credentials for the Secure Store Target Application, follow these steps:

1. From the SSS service application management page, select the check box next to the newly created Target Application ID and select Set Credentials on the ribbon.

2. Set the Windows User Name, Windows Password, and Confirm Windows Password of the data access account, as shown here, and then click OK.

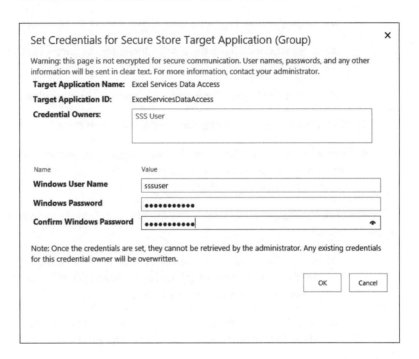

Creating a target application for the Unattended Service Account   Use the following steps to create a target application for the Unattended Service Account. If you currently have an Unattended Service Account configured, then the following steps can be skipped.

> **Note**
>
> To determine if an Unattended Service Account has been configured, check the External Data settings in the Excel Services Global Settings.

1. From Central Administration, click Managed Service Applications, located in the Application Management section, and then click the SSS service application that you want to configure.

2. On the ribbon, click New, and then fill in the following:

    a. Target Application ID: Type a unique identifier for this target application. For example, this tutorial uses ExcelServicesUnattendedAccount.

    b. Display Name: Type a friendly name or short description.

    c. Contact E-mail: Type the email address for the contact used for this target application.

    d. Target Application Type: Select Group from the drop-down list.

3. Click Next to move to the Specify Credentials Fields page.

4. Leave the default credential fields if you are using Windows credentials. If you are using other credentials, change the Field Type drop-downs to the appropriate credentials that you are using.

5. Click Next to go to the Specify The Membership Settings page and enter the following:

    a. Target Application Administrators: Type in the account of the user who will be the administrator of this target application. In this example, the default administrator account will be added.

    b. Members: Type the users to whom you want to grant the ability to refresh the data. To give access to all users, type **Everyone.**

6. Click OK.

Setting credentials for the Unattended Service Account target application   To set the credentials for the Unattended Service Account target application, follow these steps:

1. From the SSS service application management page, select the check box next to the newly created Target Application ID and select Set Credentials on the ribbon.

2. Set the Windows User Name, Windows Password, and Confirm Windows Password of the data access account and then click OK.

Configuring the Unattended Service Account   To configure the Unattended Service Account for the Secure Store Target Application, follow these steps:

1. From Central Administration, click Managed Service Applications, located in the Application Management section, and then click the Excel Services service application that you want to configure.

2. Click Global Settings.

3. From the External Data section, select the Use An Existing Unattended Service Account option, and in the Target Application ID text box, input the name of the target application that you created for the Unattended Service Account, as shown here.

Unattended Service Account

The Unattended Service Account is a single account that all workbooks can use to refresh data. This account is required to refresh data when workbook connections specify "Use the Unattended Service Account" without using Windows Credentials.

Secure Store Service Association:

> Secure Store Service Application

○ Create a new Unattended Service Account:

> ⚠ This page is not encrypted for secure communication. The User Name and Password will be sent in clear text.

User Name: (Domain\UserName)

Password:

Confirm Password:

◉ Use an existing Unattended Service Account:
Target Application ID:

> ExcelServicesUnattendedAccount

| OK | Cancel |

---

4. Click OK.

Configuring Secure Store settings in Excel

This section covers the steps to configure Secure Store settings in Excel using the AdventureWorksDW2012 sample database and sample tables.

To configure the Secure Store settings in Excel, follow these steps:

1. Open Excel 2013 and click Blank Workbook to create a new workbook or open an existing workbook.

2. Click the Data tab, and in the Get External Data group, click From Other Sources | From SQL Server, as shown here.

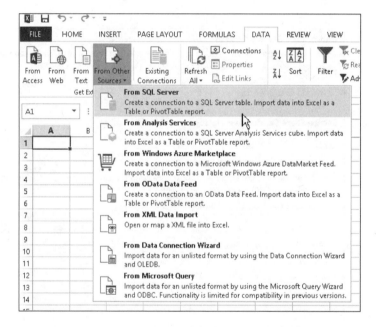

3. In the Data Connection Wizard, input the name of the server where the AdventureWorks data resides in the Server name box.

4. Select the Log On credentials according to your organization based on the following:

   a. For Windows Authentication, choose Use Windows Authentication and click Next.

   b. For specific user credentials, choose Use The Following User Name And Password, input the appropriate credentials and click Next.

5. From the Select The Database That Contains The Data That You Want list, select the AdventureWorksDW2012 database.

6. Select both the Connect To A Specific Table and the Enable Selection Of Multiple Tables check boxes.

7. Select the check box for each of the following database tables:

- DimProduct

- DimPromotion

- DimSalesTerritory

- FactInternetSales

- FactResellerSales

8. Verify that Import Relationships Between Selected Tables is selected, as shown here, and click Next.

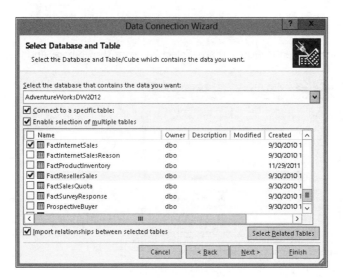

9. Optional: Change the File Name, input a Description, and modify the Friendly Name to the desired settings, as shown here.

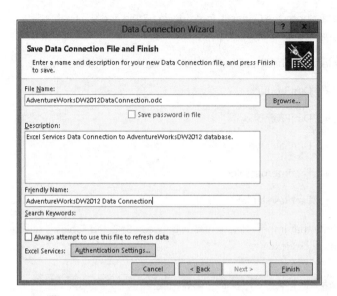

10. Click Authentication Settings. Select None, as shown here, and then click OK.

The entire options available are as follows:

- Select Use The Authenticated User's Account if Excel Services is using Claims to Windows Token Service.

- Select Use A Stored Account if Excel Services is configured to use SSS.

- Select None if Excel Services is configured to use the Unattended Service Account.

See Table 15-1 for more details on authentication setting options.

11. Click the Browse button next to the File Name text box. Note the location where the data source is being saved or change the location.

12. Click Save, and then click Finish.

13. From the Import Data dialog box, click Only Create Connection and then click OK.

> **Note**
>
> Secure Store is used by Excel Services when the workbook is rendered from a SharePoint site. The Excel client does not use Secure Store and connects to the database directly. Once the workbook is connected to the data source, you can complete changes to the workbook and then publish to a SharePoint site so that it can be rendered with Excel Services. The connection information to the Secure Store target application will remain embedded in the workbook file.

Exporting the ODC file

The Secure Store connection information can be exported as an ODC file, which allows easier management and distribution of data connections so it can be used by additional Excel workbooks.

Follow these steps to export the ODC file:

1. In Excel, click Connections located in the Data tab.

2. Select the connection that you just created in the previous steps and then click Properties.

3. Click Definition | Authentication Settings.

4. Confirm the Use A Stored Account option is selected and the correct Application ID is specified, and then click OK.

5. Click Export Connection File.

6. Keep the workbook open.

Adding the ODC file to the BI Center trusted data connection library

Before uploading the ODC file to the BI Center trusted data connection library, the next step is to add the data connection library to the Excel Services Trusted Data Connection Libraries settings.

Follow these steps to add the ODC file to the trusted data connection library:

1. From Central Administration, click Managed Service Applications in the Application Management group, and then click the Excel Services service application that you want to configure.

2. Click the Trusted Data Connection Libraries link and then click Add Trusted Data Connection Library.

3. Type in the address of the BI Center site data connection library (for example, *http:// contoso/sites/bicenter/Data%20Connections*) in the Location section and input a Description (optional).

4. Click OK.

INSIDE OUT   Why is there a "%20" in my URL for my data connection library?

You will notice in the URL for the data connections library there is "%20," which is the HTML conversion of a space. Because the BI Center site was created using the out-of-the-box (OOTB) Business Intelligence Center template, it created all the list and libraries necessary for the site, and the libraries were created by default with spaces. The recommendation for creating lists and libraries is to use neither spaces nor special characters for the initial creation and then modify the Display Name after creation. For example, if a library name was created without spaces, the URL path would be cleaner than the way it was created containing spaces. The URL path for lists and libraries cannot be changed OOTB after it has been created; however, the URL path for sites can be changed. Typically, I will still leave as is the OOTB lists and libraries that were created automatically, but when I create new lists and libraries, I follow the recommended best practice for creation.

Uploading the ODC file to the data connection library

This section provides the steps to upload the ODC file that was created in the previous steps.

To upload an ODC file, follow these steps:

1. Open your BI Center site.

2. Click Data Connections | New Item.

3. Browse to the ODC file created from the previous steps and then update any necessary information and click Save, as shown here.

Working with data connections

When using Excel to access data, you can create your own data connections or use an existing data connection. When creating new data connections for SharePoint Server 2013, the connection must be created from Excel 2013 first, and then the ODC file can be uploaded into a trusted data connection library in SharePoint and be used to create reports, scorecards, and dashboards. Before the file can be uploaded, Excel Services must be configured to include a trusted data connections library and a trusted documents library. If Excel Services has not been configured, please refer to Chapter 14 to configure Excel Services. When SSAS retrieves the value when the call is being made, SSAS returns the results of the query, which are security-trimmed based on the user.

Using existing data connections in Excel

Follow these steps to use an existing data connection in Excel:

1. In Excel, click the Data tab, and then choose Existing Connections.

2. Choose Browse For More to open the Select A Data Source dialog box.

3. Select the existing data source that you want to use, and then click Open.

4. From the Import Data page, select how you want to view the data, and then click OK.

Creating new data connections in Excel

Follow these steps to create a new data connection in Excel:

1. In Excel, click the Data tab and then pick one of the From Other Sources options that is available in the Get External Data group:

    - SQL Server

    - SQL Analysis Services

    - Windows Azure

    - OData

    - XML file

    - Or data accessed through a custom data provider

> **Note**
>
> The From Access, From Web, and From Text options in the Get External Data group are not supported in Excel Services.

2. Follow the steps of the Data Connection Wizard and specify all required information, and then click Finish.

3. From the Import Data page, select how you want to view the data and then click OK.

Collecting data through data models

As mentioned in Chapter 14, Excel Services enables the ability to view and use Excel workbooks that have been published to SharePoint. One of the ways to collect data is through data models. A *data model* is a useful way for gathering a collection of data from a variety of sources that you create and organize by using PowerPivot for Excel. These sources include SQL Server, Microsoft Access, OData feeds, Windows Azure, XML files, and other custom providers. You can sort, organize, and create relationships between different tables in Excel, and once the data is imported and organized into a data model, you can use it as a source for creating powerful reports, scorecards, and dashboards.

The advantages to using data models over connecting to external data sources are as follows:

- You can gather data from multiple sources and put it together as a single data set.

- Flash Fill functionality is supported to format columns.

- You can view, sort, and organize the data.

In SharePoint 2010, data models were queried, but they could not be refreshed interactively. The most significant improvement for PowerPivot in SharePoint 2013 is the ability to refresh data models interactively all the way down from the original data sources. Excel Services in SharePoint 2013 retains the connection to the external data sources so that the data stays updated. Excel Services first sends processing commands to the SSAS that is hosting the data model and then queries the data model to update the workbook. The update is processed when you click the Refresh Selected Connection or Refresh All Connections command from the data menu in the browser for the Excel workbook.

> **Note**
>
> **Data models interactive refresh only works for workbooks created in Excel 2013. Excel Services will display an error message if you try to refresh an Excel 2010 workbook.**

Two options are available to refresh a data model in Excel Services: interactive and scheduled, which are outlined in Table 15-2.

TABLE 15-2 Data model refresh options

Refresh option	Details
Interactive Data Refresh	Available out-of-the-box when a SQL Analysis server is registered in Excel Services. Only refreshes the data in the current user's session and does not save the data back to the workbook. Can use the identity of the current logged-on user or use stored credentials to connect to the data source. Only works for workbooks created in Excel 2013.
Scheduled Data Refresh	Requires the deployment of the PowerPivot add-in for SharePoint. Opens workbook in a separate refresh session and saves the updated version back to the content database. Uses stored credentials. Works for workbooks created using SQL Server 2012 PowerPivot add-in for Excel 2010 or workbooks created in Excel 2013.

In Excel 2013, much of the functionality from Excel 2010 to import and relate large amounts of data from multiple sources is built directly into the data model. Without installing a separate add-in, you can do the following:

- Import millions of rows from multiple data sources.

- Create relationships between data from different sources and between multiple PivotTable tables.

- Create implicit calculated fields (previously called *measures*).

- Manage data connections.

Now data models can be used as the basis for PivotTables, PivotCharts, and Power View reports. Excel automatically loads the data into the xVelocity in-memory analytics engine, which used to be available only with the PowerPivot add-in.

Creating reports and scorecards

SharePoint 2013 provides the ability to create powerful reports and scorecards for data analysis. This section provides the functionality for PowerPivot and Power View to create dynamic reports and scorecards for your BI Center.

Using PowerPivot

You may or may not be familiar with PowerPivot. What is PowerPivot? PowerPivot for Excel is an add-in used to perform powerful data analysis that extends the capabilities of PivotTable data summarization and cross-tabulation by having the ability to import data from multiple sources. PowerPivot provides a richer modeling environment allowing more experienced users to enhance their data models. The add-in was available for download for Excel 2010 and is built into Excel 2013 in Microsoft Office Professional Plus. Although this add-in is built into Excel 2013, it is not enabled by default; therefore, it will need to be enabled in order to use this feature.

Even though PowerPivot was available in SharePoint 2010, most organizations did not use nor implement the feature. Organizations wanted reporting features, but the implementation and SQL Server requirements for PowerPivot were different than they are now for SharePoint 2013. SQL Server had Excel add-ins for building data models in Excel 2010 and were not part of an internal SharePoint feature.

In SharePoint 2013, there has been a paradigm shift in that Excel 2013 and Excel Services now fully integrate data models as an internal feature. The new architecture for SQL Server 2012 SP1 PowerPivot supports the ability to have a PowerPivot server outside of a SharePoint 2013 farm. Even though it is not required, the PowerPivot server can still be installed on a SharePoint server. Excel Services in SharePoint 2013 includes data model functionality to enable interaction with PowerPivot workbooks through the browser without the need to deploy the PowerPivot for SharePoint add-in to the farm. However, this add-in does provide additional functionality and features to your SharePoint farm.

Deploying the PowerPivot for SharePoint 2013 add-in enables the following additional features:

- PowerPivot Gallery

- Schedule Data Refresh

- PowerPivot Management Dashboard

> **Note**
>
> The PowerPivot for SharePoint 2013 add-in is available for download at
> *http://www.microsoft.com/en-us/download/details.aspx?id=35577.*

PowerPivot features

This section reviews the PowerPivot features available in SharePoint 2013 that are supported in Excel Services.

Filters and timeline   Excel and PowerPivot both allow data to be imported, and Power-Pivot provides the ability to filter out unnecessary data for the import. The timeline control, shown on the ribbon in Figure 15-1, is a new time filter that makes it easier to compare PivotTable and PivotChart data over different time periods. Instead of grouping by dates, you can create a PivotTable timeline to filter dates interactively or to move through data in sequential time periods.

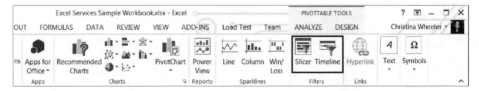

Figure 15-1 The Excel 2013 Slicer and Timeline ribbon buttons are on the PivotTable Tools tab.

Figure 15-2 shows a sample workbook that includes a slicer and a timeline control. When the user clicks a value on the slicer or the timeline, the PivotTables update accordingly.

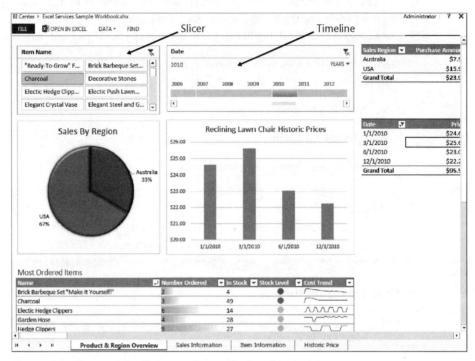

Figure 15-2 Slicer and timeline examples are displayed in the browser.

Field List and Field Well support   Excel Services enables the ability to open the Field List and Field Well for PivotChart and PivotTable reports through the browser, as shown in Figure 15-3. This added capability makes it easy to change the displayed information temporarily in a PivotChart or PivotTable report without having to open the Excel client.

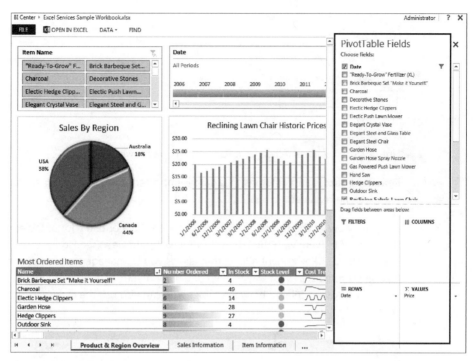

Figure 15-3 With Excel Services, the Field List and Field Well for PivotChart and PivotTable reports can be opened through the browser.

If you are not using the Excel Access Web Part to render the workbook, the Field List and Field Well can be disabled through the Excel client. Once it is saved into the document library, the Field List will no longer show up. To re-enable the Field List, make the update on the ribbon in the Excel client, as shown in Figure 15-4, and then save it back to the document library.

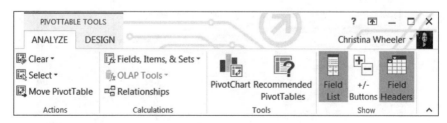

Figure 15-4 The Excel Client Field List ribbon buttons are shown.

If you are using the Excel Access Web Part to render the workbook, the PivotTable and PivotChart Modification property can be set on the web part, as shown in Figure 15-5.

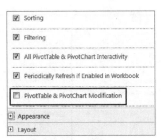

Figure 15-5 The Excel Access Web Part settings are shown.

Renaming tables and columns   As data is imported through PowerPivot, tables and columns can be renamed.

Diagram view   When working with data models that contain a lot of tables, it is sometimes easier to work with the tables through Diagram view (see Figure 15-6). Diagram view is an Excel 2013 PowerPivot add-in that allows you to manage the data models. Diagram view also provides a great way to help understand your entire data model by being able to see what fields are related between tables. You can also use the drag-and-drop feature to create new relationships in the Diagram view.

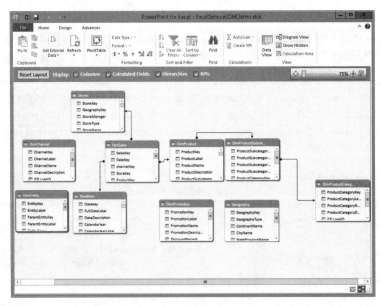

Figure 15-6 An example of a Diagram view in Excel 2013 displayed through the PowerPivot for Excel window.

Formatting   You can apply various types of formatting to Power View and PowerPivot reports. This includes styling of the workbook, charts, and other elements.

Calculated fields   Calculated fields, previously known as *measures,* are calculations used in data analysis, such as sums, counts, averages, and minimum/maximum values. Excel Services supports the ability to define custom calculated fields, as shown in Figure 15-7.

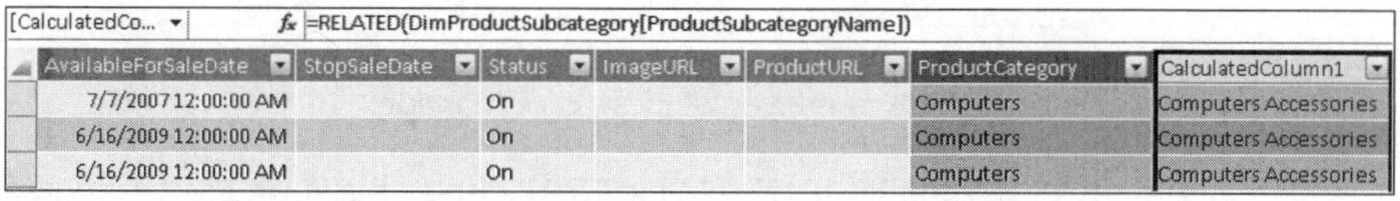

Figure 15-7 An example of a calculated column that uses a related formula.

Key performance indicators   KPIs, in essence, are quantifiable measurements for gauging business objectives. A KPI in PowerPivot is based on a specific calculated field designed to help evaluate current value and current status of a metric against a defined target. KPIs can be defined and used in PivotTables.

KPIs are covered in Chapter 16, "Building powerful dashboards with PerformancePoint Services."

Perspectives   Perspectives in PowerPivot are custom views that can be defined for a particular business scenario or user group that make it easier for users to navigate through large data sets. Perspectives can include any combination of tables, columns, KPIs, and multiple perspectives can be created.

Advanced formulas   Author custom calculations by writing advanced formulas that use the Data Analysis Expressions (DAX) expression language.

Enabling PowerPivot in Excel

Before we can begin to work with PowerPivot, we need to enable PowerPivot for Excel and SharePoint. To enable PowerPivot in Excel 2013, follow these steps:

1. In Excel, go to File | Options | Add-Ins.

2. In the Manage drop-down, select COM Add-ins, and then click Go.

3. Click the Microsoft Office PowerPivot for Excel 2013 check box and then click OK.

4. Click the PowerPivot tab get to the PowerPivot options, as shown next.

Chapter 15

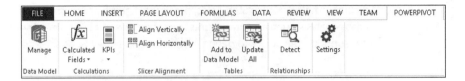

5. To open the PowerPivot window, click Manage.

Figures 15-8, 15-9, 15-10, 15-11, and 15-12 display the PowerPivot window and tab options for a workbook that was created using the existing data connection from the section "Configuring Secure Store settings in Excel" earlier in this chapter.

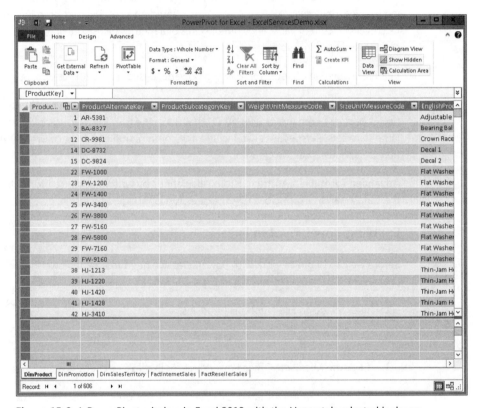

Figure 15-8 A PowerPivot window in Excel 2013 with the Home tab selected is shown.

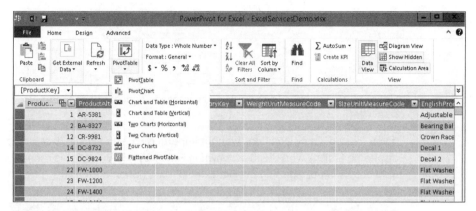

Figure 15-9 The PowerPivot window Home tab options display the available options in the drop-down menu for the PivotTable command.

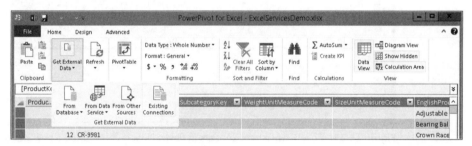

Figure 15-10 The PowerPivot window Home tab options display the available drop-down menu items for Get External Data.

Because this workbook is already connected to an existing data connection, it displays the imported data with a tab at the bottom for each table that is part of the data connection query. The PowerPivot options for this data can be updated accordingly (Figure 15-11), and then a PivotTable of choice can be generated by using the PivotTable ribbon button, or you can connect to more data sources by using the Get External Data ribbon button shown in Figure 15-12.

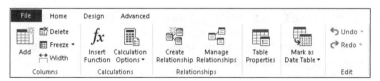

Figure 15-11 The PowerPivot window Design tab options ribbon buttons are viewable in Excel 2013.

Figure 15-12 The PowerPivot window Advanced tab options ribbon buttons are viewable in Excel 2013.

If you created a new workbook without importing data, the PowerPivot window opens displaying a blank worksheet, as shown in Figure 15-13. A PivotTable cannot be created until data is imported using the Get External Data ribbon button.

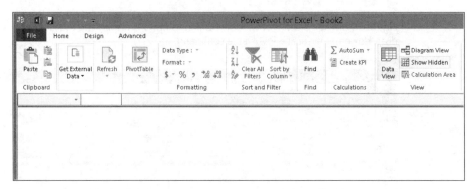

Figure 15-13 A blank worksheet appears in PowerPivot if you created a new workbook without importing data.

Enabling PowerPivot in SharePoint

Before working with PowerPivot, the PowerPivot Feature Integration for Site Collections feature must be activated. To enable PowerPivot in SharePoint, follow these steps:

1. Open the browser and navigate to your SharePoint site.

2. Click Site Actions | Site Settings.

3. Under the Site Collection Administration section, click Site Collection Features.

4. Click the Activate button for the PowerPivot Feature Integration for Site Collections feature, as shown here.

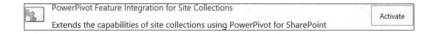

Creating a PowerPivot Gallery

Once the PowerPivot Feature Integration for Site Collections feature is activated on the site collection, the PowerPivot Gallery becomes available in the list of available apps.

Follow these steps to create a PowerPivot Gallery library:

1. From the BI Center site, click the Site Settings icon | Site contents.

2. Click Add An App, and then click the PowerPivot Gallery tile.

3. Click Advanced to go to the advanced settings creation page.

4. Set the following:

   a. Name: Type a friendly name for your library, or use PowerPivotDocuments.

   b. Description: Type a description. (This setting is optional).

   c. Document Version History: Default value is No; however, change to Yes if you want versioning turned on for this document library.

   d. Document Template: Set the drop-down value to Microsoft Excel Spreadsheet.

> ### Note
> By setting the Document Template value to Microsoft Excel Spreadsheet, this makes Excel the default template type so that when a user clicks New From This Document Library, the New Document defaults to an Excel document, as shown here.
>
>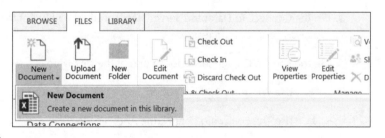

5. Click Create.

INSIDE OUT   What is the recommendation for naming libraries and fields?

As mentioned in the INSIDE OUT sidebar, "Why is there a '20%' in my URL for my Data Connection library," earlier in this chapter, the recommended practice for naming libraries and fields is to use neither spaces nor special characters for the initial creation. For example, for this library, the name was set to **PowerPivotDocuments** for the initial creation, and then the Display Name was changed through the **Library Settings | List name, description, and navigation** after creation to **PowerPivot Documents.** By doing this, the URL becomes *http://contoso/sites/bicenter/PowerPivotGallery* instead of *http://contoso/sites/bicenter/PowerPivot%20Gallery*.

Creating an Excel Services dashboard using SSAS data

This section provides the steps to create a basic sales dashboard that contains several reports using an external data connection pulling from SSAS data.

Creating Data Connection to Analysis Services data

In order to create a dashboard from Excel, a data connection must be created first, as follows:

1. Open Excel 2013 and choose Blank Workbook.

2. From the Data tab, choose From Other Sources (located in the Get External Data group) and then select From Analysis Services.

3. In the Connect To Database Server step, specify the name of the server where the Analysis Services data resides.

4. In the Log On Credentials, choose one of the following:

   a. Use Windows Authentication

   b. Use The Following User Name And Password

5. From the Select Database And Table dialog box, select AdventureWorksDW2012Multidimensional-EE from the drop-down list.

6. Select the Adventure Works cube and then click Next.

7. From the Save Data Connection File And Finish step, shown in the following graphic, update the File Name, Description (optional), and Friendly Name.

8. Click Authentication Settings, set the authentication to None, and then click OK.

Note

Setting the authentication to None, as shown here, will use the credentials stored for the Excel Services in the SSS application.

9. Click Finish.

10. From the Import Data dialog box, select Only Create Connection, and then click OK.

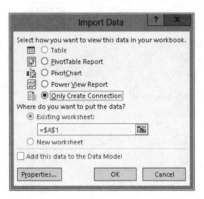

11. Keep Excel open and save the workbook locally.

12. Name the file (for example, Adventure Works Sales) and leave the workbook open.

Creating the PivotTable and PivotChart reports

Now that the data connection has been created, the next step is to create the PivotTable and PivotChart reports. The following dashboard reports will be created:

- **ProductSales PivotChart report** A bar chart report to show sales amounts across different product categories.

- **GeoSales PivotChart report** A bar chart report to show sales amounts across different sales territories.

- **ChannelSales PivotTable report** A table to show order quantities and sales amounts across the Internet and reseller channels.

- **OrderSales Pivot Table report** A table to show order quantities and sales amounts across different product categories.

Creating a ProductSales PivotChart Follow these steps to create a PivotChart report called ProductSales:

1. In Excel, select cell A9 and then click the Insert tab. In the Charts section, choose PivotChart.

2. In the Create PivotChart dialog box, select Use An External Data Source, as shown in the following graphic, and click Choose Connection.

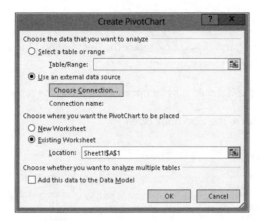

3. In the Existing Connections wizard, select AdventureWorksDW2012Multidimensional-EE, and then click Open.

4. In the Create PivotChart dialog box, leave the Existing Worksheet option checked and click OK.

5. In the Analyze tab, in the Chart Name box (PivotChart group), change the name from Chart1 to **ProductSales** and press Enter.

6. From the PivotChart Fields panel, shown here, select the following:

    a. In the Sales Summary section, select Sales Amount.

    b. In the Products section, choose Product Categories.

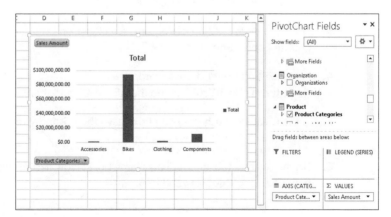

Next, sort the bars in descending order by following these steps:

7. From the PivotChart, select the down arrow on the Product Categories control.

8. In the Select Field dialog box, click More Sort Options.

9. From the Sort (Category) dialog box, select the Descending (Z to A) By option and set the drop-down value to Sales Amount.

10. Click OK. The bar graph should now be updated according the sort order, as shown here.

11. Save the file and leave the workbook open.

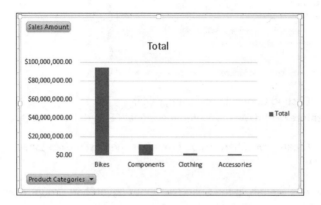

Creating a GeoSales PivotChart report   Follow these steps to create a PivotChart report called GeoSales:

1. In the existing workbook, choose an empty cell where you want to add a new PivotChart report, such as G9.

2. On the Insert tab, choose PivotChart.

3. In the Create PivotChart dialog box, select Use An External Data Source and click Choose Connection.

4. In the Existing Connections wizard, select AdventureWorksDW2012Multidimensional-EE, and then click Open.

5. In the Create PivotChart dialog box, leave the Existing Worksheet option checked and click OK.

6. On the Analyze tab, in the Chart Name box (PivotChart group), change the name from Chart2 to **GeoSales** and press Enter.

7.   In the PivotChart Fields panel, shown here, select the following options:

    a.   In the Sales Summary section, select Sales Amount.

    b.   In the Sales Territory section, drag Sales Territory to the Legend section.

8.   Save the file and leave the workbook open.

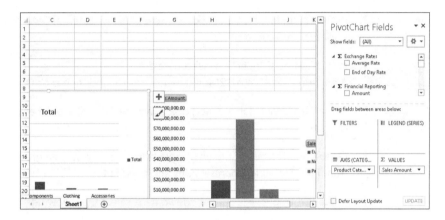

9.   Select and move the PivotCharts down to leave some empty cells at the top. The empty cells at the top will be where the Timeline control will be added later in this chapter.

Setting the sizing for the PivotCharts   To ensure that the PivotCharts will not have sizing issues, we will specify the size settings for the report. To do this, follow these steps for each of the PivotChart reports:

1.   In an empty section of the PivotChart report, right-click and select Format Chart Area from the select menu.

    The Format Chart Area list opens.

2.   Below the Chart Options, choose the Size and Properties icon.

3.   Expand the Size section and check the Lock Aspect Ratio option.

4.   Expand the Properties section and check the Don't Move Or Size With Cells option.

    If you want to specify alternate text for the report, expand the Alt Text section and type the text that you want to use for the report.

5.   Repeat these steps for all PivotCharts. Once complete, close the Format Chart Area panel by clicking the Close button in the panel.

6.   Save the file and leave the workbook open.

Creating a ChannelSales PivotTable report   Follow these steps to create a PivotTable report called ChannelSales:

1. In the existing workbook, choose an empty cell where you want to add a new PivotTable report, such as A25.

2. On the Insert tab, choose PivotTable.

3. In the Create PivotTable dialog box, select Use An External Data Source, and click Choose Connection.

4. In the Existing Connections wizard, select AdventureWorksDW2012Multidimensional-EE, and then click Open.

5. In the Create PivotTable dialog box, leave the Existing Worksheet option checked and click OK.

6. On the Analyze tab, in the PivotTable Name box (PivotTable group), change the name from PivotTable3 to **ChannelSales** and press Enter.

7. In the PivotTable Fields panel, shown here, select the following:

    a. In the Sales Orders section, select Order Count.

    b. In the Sales Summary section, select Sales Amount.

    c. In the Sales Channel section, select Sales Channel.

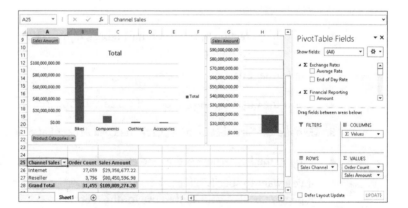

8. In the ChannelSales PivotTable, select the cell that says Row Labels. On the Formula bar at the top for the selected cell, change the text Row Labels to **Channel Sales.**

9. Save the file and leave the workbook open.

Creating an OrderSales PivotTable report   Follow these steps to create a PivotTable report called OrderSales:

1. In the existing workbook, choose an empty cell where you want to add a new PivotTable report, such as G25.

2. On the Insert tab, choose PivotTable.

3. In the Create PivotTable dialog box, select Use An External Data Source, and click Choose Connection.

4. In the Existing Connections wizard, select AdventureWorksDW2012Multidimensional-EE, and then click Open.

5. In the Create PivotTable dialog box, leave the Existing Worksheet option checked and click OK.

6. On the Analyze tab, in the PivotTable Name box (PivotTable group), change the name from PivotTable4 to **OrderSales** and press Enter.

7. In the PivotTable Fields panel, shown in the following graphic, select the following:

    a. In the Sales Orders section, select Order Count.

    b. In the Sales Summary section, select Sales Amount.

    c. In the Product section, select Product Categories.

8. In the OrderSales PivotTable, select the cell that says Row Labels. On the Formula bar at the top for the selected cell, change the text Row Labels to **Products**.

9. Save the file and leave the workbook open.

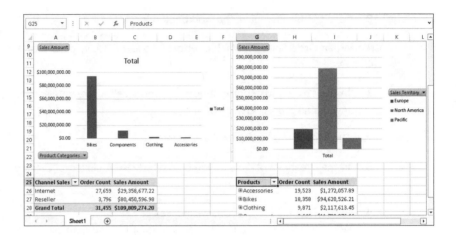

Creating a Timeline control filter   This section provides the details to create a Timeline control to enable the users to filter the data for a particular time.

To create a Timeline control, follow these steps:

1. In the existing workbook, choose an empty cell where you want to add the Timeline, such as A1.

2. On the Insert tab, in the Filters section, select Timeline.

3. In the Existing Connections dialog box, select AdventureWorksDW2012Multidimensional-EE, and then click Open.

4. Select Date, and then click OK.

5. Move the Timeline control to a preferred location in the workbook.

6. To resize, drag the resizing handles on the right side of the control to the desired size.

7. Select the Timeline control to make it active, and then click the Options tab. In the Timeline group, select Report Connections.

8. The Report Connections dialog box appears.

9. Select all four reports (ChannelSales, GeoSales, OrderSales, and ProductSales), and then click OK.

10. Save the file and leave the workbook open.

Improving the look and feel of the dashboard

Before publishing the workbook, we will make some minor adjustments to it to improve the look and feel of how the dashboard will be displayed in the browser. By default, the dashboard displays gridlines on the worksheet; therefore, we will hide the gridlines to make it look cleaner. We will also rename the worksheet tab from Sheet1 to something else.

1. To remove the gridlines, select the View tab and clear the Gridlines check box located in the Show section.

2. To remove row and column headings, clear the Headings check box.

3. To rename the worksheet tab, right-click Sheet1 and select Rename.

4. Type a name such as **Sales Dashboard,** as shown here, and press Enter.

5. Save the file and leave the workbook open.

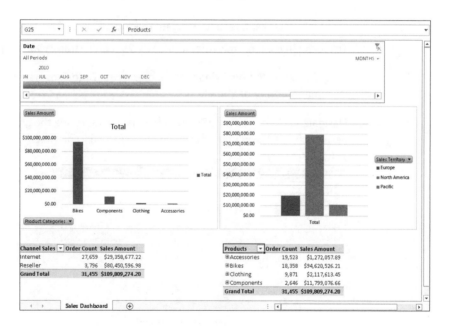

Uploading to your BI Center site

The next step is to upload your data connection file and Excel workbook dashboard to your BI Center site.

To upload your data connection file to your BI Center, follow these steps:

1. Open the BI Center site.

2. Click Data Connections.

3. Open Windows Explorer and navigate to your saved
   AdventureWorksDW2012Multidimensional-EE.odc file.

   The location used for this tutorial is C:\Users\Administrator\Documents\My Data
   Sources.

4. Drag the AdventureWorksDW2012Multidimensional-EE.odc file from Windows
   Explorer to the Drag Files Here section of the Data Connections library on the site.

Now upload your Excel workbook to your trusted documents library used for your Excel
Services workbooks. To upload your Excel workbook to your BI Center, follow these steps:

1. From the BI Center site, click Libraries in the left navigation pane, and then click the
   PowerPivotGallery tile.

2. Open Windows Explorer and navigate to your saved workbook file.

   The location used for this tutorial is C:\Users\Administrator\Documents.

3. Drag the Excel file from Windows Explorer to the Drag Files Here section of your
   Documents library on the site.

4. Navigate back to the PowerPivotGallery main page to see the graphical list of your
   newly uploaded workbook, as shown in the following graphic.

5. Click the newly uploaded file to render the file through the browser using Excel Services, as shown here.

You can browse through, filter, and interact with the data to see the charts change based on your selections.

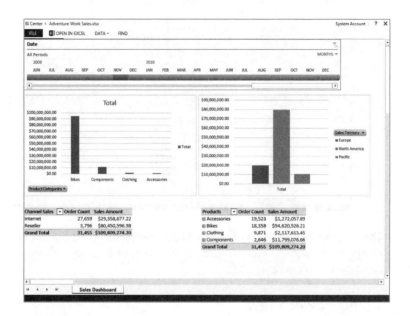

6. Right-click the PivotTable or PivotCharts and select Show Field List to display the Fields panel.

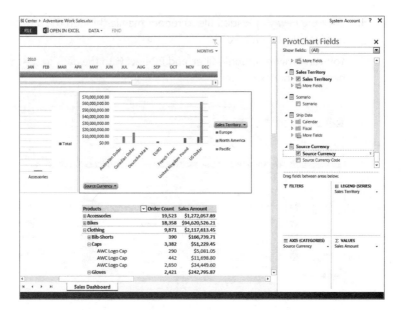

The previous image displays the PivotChart Fields panel for the workbook that is being displayed through the browser. The Source Currency field was selected, which changed the GeoSales PivotChart dynamically.

Using Power View

Power View is an add-in for Excel 2013 and a SharePoint feature that provides an interactive data exploration, visualization, and presentation experience to create mashups and interactive dashboards that encourages intuitive, ad-hoc reporting. With Power View, you can interact with data in the same Excel workbook as the Power View sheet, in data models in Excel workbooks published to PowerPivot galleries, and in tabular models deployed to SSAS instances.

> **Note**
>
> To use Power View, the SQL Server Reporting Services service application must be configured on the SharePoint farm. The instructions "Install Reporting Services SharePoint Mode for SharePoint 2013" are available at *http://msdn.microsoft.com/en-us/library/jj219068.aspx*.

Excel 2013 workbooks with Power View sheets can be saved to SharePoint Server 2013 on-premises or SharePoint Online in Office 365. Users can view and interact with the reports; however, the Power View sheets created from the Excel client can be edited only from the Excel client. The interaction in SharePoint includes visualization interactions such as filtering, sorting, highlighting data in charts, and slicers. The reason why Power View sheets cannot be modified directly from SharePoint if the Power View was created through the Excel client is that Power View sheets are part of the XSLX file and Power View reports created from SharePoint are RDLX files, not XLSX files. When creating Power View reports directly from SharePoint instead of the Excel client, the reports are saved directly on the server, where others can view and interact and those who have permissions can also edit the Power View reports.

Enabling Power View in Excel

To enable Power View in Excel 2013, follow these steps:

1. From Excel, go to File | Options | Add-Ins.

2. In the Manage drop-down, select COM Add-ins, and then click Go.

3. Click the Power View check box, and then click OK.

4. Click the Insert tab, and the Power View button should now be available and enabled, as shown here.

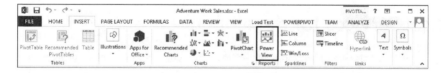

5. Click Power View to open Power View, as shown in the following graphic.

> **Note**
>
> **Microsoft Silverlight is required for Power View. If this is the first time that you are using Power View, you will be prompted to install Silverlight.**

Chapter 15

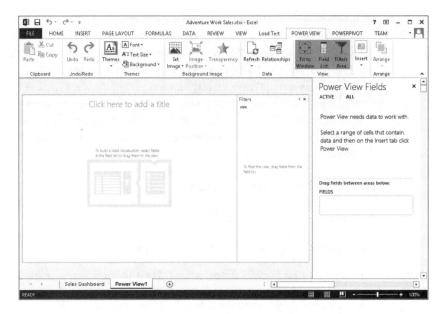

For more information on Power View, see "Power View: Explore, visualize, and present your data," located at *http://office.microsoft.com/en-us/excel-help/power-view-explore-visualize-and-present-your-data-HA102835634.aspx*.

Excel Services for developers

This section provides a high-level overview of the Excel Services additions and enhancements for developers in SharePoint 2013. Excel Interactive view and ECMAScript (JavaScript, Jscript) user-defined functions (UDFs) are two of the new technologies added to Excel Services.

Excel Interactive view

Excel Interactive view is a new technology that uses HTML, JavaScript, and Excel Services to generate table and chart views contemporaneously in the browser from an HTML table hosted on a page. Using Excel Interactive view enables the users to harness the analytical power of Excel for use on any HTML table on a page without having to install Excel.

To enable Excel Interactive view, simply insert two HTML tags on your page in your site. The first tag inserted into the HTML of the page is a standard HTML <a> tag that has attributes that you can configure in Excel Interactive view. You insert the <a> anchor tag above the HTML for the table that has the data you want to use to create the Excel Interactive view, as highlighted in Figure 15-14. Table 15-3 lists the Excel Interactive view tag attributes.

```
<a href="#" name="MicrosoftExcelButton"
    data-xl-buttonStyle="Small"
    data-xl-tabletitle="My Table Title"
    data-xl-fileName="MyExcelWorkbook"
    data-xl-attribution="Data provided by Contoso.com">
</a>
<table cellpadding="4" cellspacing="0" border="0" width="100%">
        <tr>
            <td id="_invisibleIfEmpty" name="_invisibleIfEmpty"
            <WebPartPages:WebPartZone runat="server" Title="loc
        </tr>
        <script type="text/javascript" language="javascript">if
</table>
```

Figure 15-14 An example of an Excel Interactive view HTML <a> tag.

TABLE 15-3 Excel interactive view tag attributes

Attribute	Description	Default value	Required?
data-xl-dataTableID	Unique identifier for the table.	N/A	No
data-xl-buttonStyle	Sets the button graphic style. Two style options are *standard* and *small*.	Standard	No
data-xl-fileName	Sets the name of the workbook that the user can download by clicking the Download button in the Excel Interactive view.	"Book1"	No
data-xl-tableTitle	Sets the title of the table. This attribute can be set to up to 255 characters long. Something to consider when naming the title is that if the table is small but the title is long, the display of the title could be cut off.	Same as the webpage title.	No
data-xl-attribution	Sets a message used to describe the source for the view that displays within the workbook when viewed. This attribute can be set to up to 255 characters long.	"Data provided by [website domain]"	No

The second tag that needs to be inserted into the HTML of the page is a standard HTML <SCRIPT> tag that references the JavaScript file that creates the Excel Interactive view. In Figure 15-15, the script is added to the PlaceHolderAdditionalPageHead content placeholder of the page.

```
<asp:Content ContentPlaceHolderId="PlaceHolderAdditionalPageHead" runat="server">
    <meta name="GENERATOR" content="Microsoft SharePoint" />
    <meta name="ProgId" content="SharePoint.WebPartPage.Document" />
    <meta http-equiv="Content-Type" content="text/html; charset=utf-8" />
    <meta name="CollaborationServer" content="SharePoint Team Web Site" />
    <script type="text/javascript">
// <![CDATA[
    var navBarHelpOverrideKey = "WSSEndUser";
// ]]>
    </script>
    <script src="http://r.office.microsoft.com/r/rlidExcelButton?v=1&kip=1"
    type="text/javascript"></script>
    <SharePoint:UIVersionedContent ID="WebPartPageHideQLStyles" UIVersion="4" runa
        <ContentTemplate>
<style type="text/css">
body #s4-leftpanel {
    display:none;
}
.s4-ca {
    margin-left:0px;
}
</style>
        </ContentTemplate>
    </SharePoint:UIVersionedContent>
</asp:Content>
```

Figure 15-15 An example of an Excel Interactive view HTML <SCRIPT> tag.

> **Note**
>
> To add the tag to a site that uses SSL, change the src attribute to also use https://, such as *https://r.office.microsoft.com/r/rlidExcelButton?v=1&kip=1*.

JavaScript Object Model

The JavaScript Object Model (JSOM) in Excel Services enables developers to automate, customize, and create mashups and other integrated solutions to interact with Excel Web Access Web Parts. JSOM also enables the ability for developers to add more capabilities to workbooks.

The JSOM has some enhancements to the Excel Services JSOM application programming interface (API), which includes the following:

- **Reloaded embedded workbooks** The ability to reload embedded workbooks has been added, which allows the user to reset the embedded workbook to the data in the underlying workbook file.

- **User-created floating objects** The EwaControl object has new methods that allow the ability to add/remove floating objects that you create. There is also more control over the viewable area of the Ewa control.

- **SheetChanged event** This new event raises when something has changed on the sheet, such as updating/deleting/clearing cells, copying/cutting/pasting ranges, and undo/redo actions.

- **Data validation** Enabling data validation is now supported, so you can validate data entered by the user.

For more information on working with Excel Services and JSOM, see "Working with the Excel Services JavaScript Object Model," located at *http://msdn.microsoft.com/en-us/library/ jj907313.aspx.*

JavaScript UDFs

JavaScript UDFs are similar to regular UDFs that you can create in the Excel client. UDFs are a user-defined function that can be added to the list of available functions in Excel when Excel does not provide the type of function you want out-of-the-box. JavaScript UDFs are similar to UDFs; however, the difference is that the JavaScript UDF are only used in the embedded workbooks and the JavaScript UDFs only exist on the page rendering the workbook. When the page rendering the workbooks is closed, the JavaScript UDF is no longer available.

You can use JavaScript UDFs on workbooks that are either rendered through SharePoint using the Excel Web Access Web part or on a hosted page that has the embedded workbook that is stored on SkyDrive.

OData in Excel Services

What is OData? OData is an open web protocol for querying and updating data that uses a Uniform Resource Identifier (URI) with query parameters included to get information about a specific resource. In the case of Excel Services, OData provides a simple way to get data from Excel workbooks that is stored in SharePoint libraries. The syntax for OData is based on web standards such as HTTP and REST through the Excel Services REST API.

For more information about OData, see the MSDN article "Open Data Protocol specification," located at *http://msdn.microsoft.com/en-us/library/jj163874.aspx.*

Summary

The data exploration improvements, along with the various feature enhancements in SharePoint 2013, provide an easy way to implement powerful BI solutions for your organization. In this chapter, you learned how to implement BI using Excel 2013, Excel Services, and SQL Server 2013. You learned about the different data sources that you can use in Excel 2013 and Excel Services, along with how to use the new features in Excel Services.

Now that you have explored Excel Services, the next chapter focuses on the BI features of PerformancePoint Services and also includes information on how to integrate Performance-Point dashboards for creating powerful reports.

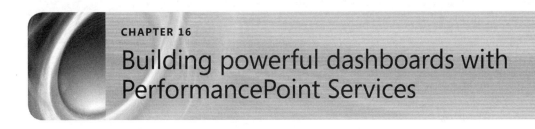

Building powerful dashboards with PerformancePoint Services

I N the previous chapter, you learned how to use Microsoft Excel Services and Microsoft SQL Server 2012 to provide business intelligence (BI) for your organization. Although Excel Services is powerful on its own, you can take it further by using PerformancePoint Services. This chapter reviews the features of PerformancePoint and demonstrates the steps to build powerful, rich dashboards to display key performance indicators (KPIs) and data visualizations in the form of scorecards, analytic reports, and filters.

PerformancePoint overview

PerformancePoint (formerly ProClarity) enables users to create BI dashboards that provide insight into an organization's performance. PerformancePoint was first offered in November 2007 as an independent BI product called PerformancePoint Server 2007, which could be set up to be used with Microsoft Office SharePoint Server (MOSS) 2007. Before its initial release, Microsoft offered the product as Community Technology Preview releases starting in mid-2006. That same year, Microsoft acquired ProClarity Corporation, which enabled Microsoft to add deep analytics for reports. In April 2009, the development of the separate product stopped; the dashboard, scorecard, and analytic reporting components were incorporated into Microsoft SharePoint Server 2010 and the product then became known as PerformancePoint Services. In SharePoint 2013, there are both UI enhancements and server-side improvements to PerformancePoint Services, which are discussed in the following sections.

UI enhancements

With the introduction of Dashboard Designer in SharePoint Server 2010, the BI user interface was a big improvement from Microsoft SharePoint Server 2007. However, there still were some features that were lacking, which usually led organizations to implement other third-party BI solutions. With the improvements in SharePoint Server 2013, organizations are starting to realize that a third-party solution may not be necessary anymore. This section covers the high-level UI enhancements that have been implemented in this new release.

Themes

Themes have been somewhat of a challenge in the past in Microsoft SharePoint, and it was nearly impossible to change the look and feel of core PerformancePoint functionality. This has changed in SharePoint 2013 with better theme support. Now when a dashboard is published from the Dashboard Designer to SharePoint, the dashboard for the most part will adopt the new theme configured for the site. Because the dashboard is a set of pages with web parts, the site owners can change the theme or create new themes to apply to the dashboards without touching Dashboard Designer. There is one caveat, however. Chart web parts do not conform to the applied theme because the graphics are created on the server and displayed as images to the browser.

iPad support

Even though there are other devices on the market, one of the common devices that some companies use within their organization is the iPad. iPads were a challenge compared to other tablet devices because iPads use the Safari browser instead of Windows Internet Explorer or the other common browsers used on other tablet devices. When SharePoint Server 2010 was released, PerformancePoint content could not be viewed on iPads until the December 2011 Cumulative Update (CU) was released. Even though this release provided the support for PerformancePoint content to be viewed on iPads, there were still many drawbacks, which led companies to either pursue or keep a third-party BI solution instead of using the built-in SharePoint BI features. One of the big drawbacks was that only certain types of reports could be viewed on the iPad and Reporting Services reports were not supported. In the release of SharePoint Server 2013, Microsoft has implemented better iPad support so that PerformancePoint dashboards can be accessed from iPads through the Safari browser and the user has the ability to use touch to interact with the form intuitively and effectively.

Filter enhancements and filter search

The filter control is also improved in SharePoint 2013, which includes the ability to select all, clear all, reset to default, select children, get all filter items (when the 5,000 limit is reached), dynamically size, apply bolding, and use measure-based filtering, as well as other performance improvements. The filter search now works in similar ways because search is implemented in the PivotTable filter in Microsoft Excel. There are search filters, data sources, member selection, and MDX queries.

Business Intelligence (BI) Center

Enhancements have been made to the BI Center with integrated support for PowerPivot, Power View, and Excel Services.

Dashboard Designer

Dashboard Designer can now be started from the SharePoint ribbon without having to navigate to the old BI Center landing page. The appearance of the PerformancePoint ribbon tab is based on content type, so it appears in document libraries where the "Web Part page" content type is present and in lists where any of the PerformancePoint content types have been added.

Server-side improvements

In addition to the UI enhancements, the server-side improvements in SharePoint Server 2013 also play a part in why more organizations are deciding to implement the built-in SharePoint BI features instead of using a third-party solution. This section covers the server-side improvements of the BI features that have been implemented in this new release.

Dashboard migration and deployment

In previous versions, dashboard creators had to create and publish dashboards from Dashboard Designer for each environment. There was no way to deploy from server to server, and each dashboard had to be manually created. This provided challenges because the SharePoint administrators had to do the work of creating each new dashboard for production environments. This has all changed with SharePoint 2013. PerformancePoint now has better migration support, which fits into the software development lifecycle (SDLC) models, providing the ability to migrate dashboards from SharePoint 2010 to SharePoint 2013 and copy and move PerformancePoint Services content between SharePoint sites. Dashboards can now be bundled into a single file, which can be handed off to the SharePoint administrator to deploy, eliminating the need for manual deployment. Furthermore, users with appropriate permissions can now connect to production environments using Dashboard Designer.

> **Note**
>
> Even though users with the appropriate permissions can connect to production environments using Dashboard Designer, it is not recommended to take this approach because dashboards can now be exported and imported across environments. The recommended approach is to have the users connect directly to QA instead and then export the dashboards from QA and import them into production.

Analysis services support for the "effective user"

PerformancePoint now integrates more smoothly with SQL Server Analysis Services (SSAS) by supporting the concept of the "effective user." Effective user and SSAS is a more advanced feature, which saves the SharePoint administrator from having to set up Kerberos constrained delegation in order to use per-user authentication.

Using Dashboard Designer

The PerformancePoint Dashboard Designer included with PerformancePoint Services is a tool used to create powerful dashboards for your organization. If PerformancePoint Services is configured, users with the necessary permissions can create a wide variety of PerformancePoint items such as data sources, dashboards, scorecards, KPIs, indicators, filters, and reports, as listed in Table 16-1.

TABLE 16-1 PerformancePoint Dashboard Designer items

Items	Description
Data sources	Data sources are connections to databases that can be used for scorecards, reports, and filters created in Dashboard Designer.
Dashboards	Dashboards are containers used to display scorecards and reports. When creating dashboards, you start by selecting a page template. Page templates contain one or more dashboard zones, which can be added, removed, and configured to different zone sizes. Reports, scorecards, and filters can be added to the page template zones.
Scorecards	Scorecards are dashboard items that show performance for one or more metrics, which compare actual results to specified goals and display the results by using graphical indicators.
KPIs	KPIs are metrics used in scorecards that include target and actual values, and graphical indicators that show whether performance is on or off target.
Indicators	Indicators are graphical symbols that are used in KPIs to show whether performance is on or off target. Stoplight symbols are the most commonly used indicators. Green circles indicate performance is on target, yellow triangles indicate performance is not far off target, and red diamonds indicate poor performance.
Filters	Filters are individual dashboard items that enable users to focus on specific information.
Reports	Reports are dashboard items that display information in tables or charts. A variety of reports can be created, such as bar charts, pie charts, line charts, and tables, otherwise known as grids. Some reports can be created directly in Dashboard Designer and web parts can be created to display existing reports that are hosted on other servers.

The advantages of using Dashboard Designer instead of other methods such as Excel include the following:

- **Reusability** Improvements to the BI Center Site template include a new look and easier use.

- **Copy/Paste** Dashboard Designer includes the ability to copy/paste dashboard items, which saves time and rework for dashboard authors.

- **Linking** When creating dashboards, dashboard items (such as scorecard KPIs) can be linked to other reports, such as SQL Server Reporting Services reports and analytic charts and grids.

- **Time Intelligence** Timeline Intelligence functionality can be included in dashboards that can easily display time periods such as Year to Date or Last Six Months.

- **Drilling** Depending on how the dashboard is set up, users can drill up and down within the data to see higher or lower levels of information. The drilled reports and scorecards can be exported by the user to Microsoft PowerPoint or Excel.

Authenticating Dashboard Designer

When getting Dashboard Designer up and running for the first time, a few considerations must be made to set it up properly. One consideration is whether you are using a computer that is on the same domain as the SharePoint environment or using a computer that is not on the same domain, as the set-up steps are slightly different for each situation.

Setting user authentication for a computer on the same domain

When using a computer that is on the same domain (that is, the same Active Directory forest) as the SharePoint site, the user authentication process is better than not being on the same domain. Instead of being prompted for credentials each time, users will be automatically authenticated from their computers using their Windows domain accounts, providing a seamless experience. Additional settings are required through the browser for the user authentication to be passed automatically. Internet Explorer includes predefined security zones that enable you to set security options for each zone and add and remove sites depending on the level of trust in a website. If you are a local administrator of your computer, you can update the settings yourself; however, if your organization does not allow the properties to be changed, the administrator would need to update the settings for you.

For more information on Internet Explorer security zones, go to: *http://support.microsoft .com/kb/174360.*

If the SharePoint URL has not already been set in the local intranet or trusted sites zone, follow these steps to set user authentication:

1. Open Internet Explorer, and then navigate to the Internet Explorer option settings by clicking on Tools (icon) | Internet Options.

2. Click the Security tab. Add the site to either the Local Intranet zone or the Trusted Sites zone, as follows:

   a. For local intranet (as shown here): Click local Intranet, click Sites, and then click the Advanced button.

   b. For trusted sites: Click Trusted Sites, and then click Sites.

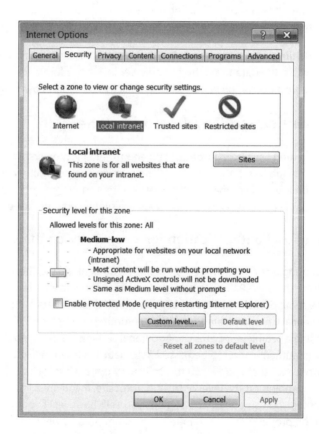

3. Input the SharePoint URL, if it is not already in the text box, as shown in the following graphic, and then click Add.

4. Once complete, click Close and then click OK.

Setting user authentication for a computer not on the same domain

When you try to start Dashboard Designer from the browser of a computer that is not on the same domain or not on a domain at all, you will encounter an authentication error. Even through you input your SharePoint credentials when prompted for the SharePoint site, your local NT credentials will automatically get passed to the Dashboard Designer, causing a permission issue, as shown in Figure 16-1.

Figure 16-1 An authentication error appears when Dashboard Designer is started from a computer that is not on a domain.

To get around this issue, the credentials need to be stored in the Windows Credential Manager so that the local NT credentials will not be passed to Dashboard Designer. Credential Manager is a "digital locker" that Windows uses to store logon credentials (for example, user name and password) for websites, servers, or other computers on your network. The credentials are split into three categories:

- **Windows credentials**   Used by Windows and its services.

- **Certificate-based credentials**   Used with smart cards in more complex business network environments.

- **Generic credentials**   Defined and used by some installed programs, such as Windows Live ID, which is stored and used in Windows Live Security Essentials.

> **Note**
> Windows 8 contains one more set of credentials, called web credentials. Web credentials are used by Internet Explorer to log on automatically to specified websites.

To add a Windows credential for your SharePoint site, follow these steps:

1. Open up the Credential Manager.

2. Click Start | Control Panel | User Accounts And Family Safety | User Accounts, then click Credential Manager or click Manage Windows Credentials.

3. Click Add A Windows Credential.

4. Type in the Internet address, User Name, and Password, as shown here, and then click OK.

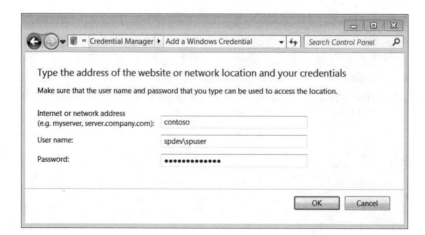

You should now see your newly added credentials in the list of Windows credentials. If you made a mistake, simply expand the credential to access the options to Edit or Remove From Vault, as shown here.

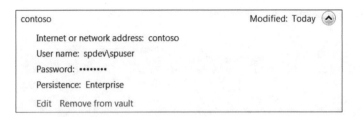

Starting Dashboard Designer

Now that the authentication settings have been configured for your environment, the next step is to start Dashboard Designer.

> **Note**
> When starting Dashboard Designer for the first time, it is recommended that you use Internet Explorer. If using Mozilla Firefox, make sure that the Microsoft .NET Framework Assistant 1.1 is installed before attempting to install Dashboard Designer and Safari is not supported. When starting the Dashboard Designer, you may be prompted to install it the first time. If that happens, click Run to install. Once installed, you can start Dashboard Designer by using the Start Menu (Start | All Programs | SharePoint | PerformancePoint Dashboard Designer).

To start Dashboard Designer, follow these steps:

1. From the browser, open your BI SharePoint site.

2. Click PerformancePoint Content in the left navigation.

3. Click New Item to start Dashboard Designer. The progress window appears, as shown here.

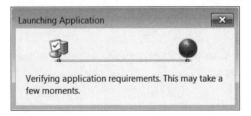

Once Dashboard Designer is started and started, Dashboard Designer will open on your desktop. As shown in Figure 16-2, in the lower-left corner of the Dashboard Designer workspace, the site shows Unconnected for both User and Connected To. The unconnected status means Dashboard Designer does not have an existing connection to any SharePoint sites and needs to be configured.

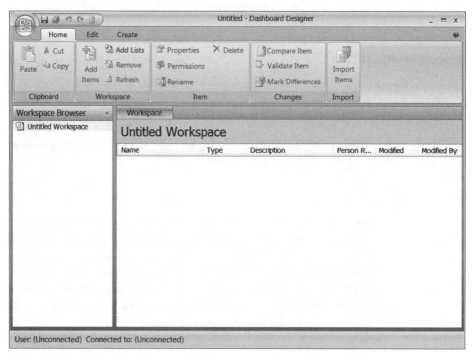

Figure 16-2 Dashboard Designer is not connected to a SharePoint site.

Configuring Dashboard Designer to a SharePoint site

Because Dashboard Designer is unconnected, the next step is to configure Dashboard Designer to connect to the SharePoint site. Follow these steps to create the connection in Dashboard Designer:

1. In Dashboard Designer, click File menu, and then click Designer Options.

2. Click the Server tab.

3. Set the SharePoint URL to your SharePoint site, as shown in the following graphic, and then click Connect.

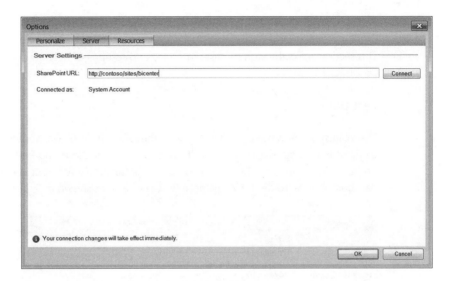

4. Click OK.

Once successfully connected, Dashboard Designer will open an Untitled Workspace and display the libraries that are a part of the Business Intelligence site, as shown in Figure 16-3.

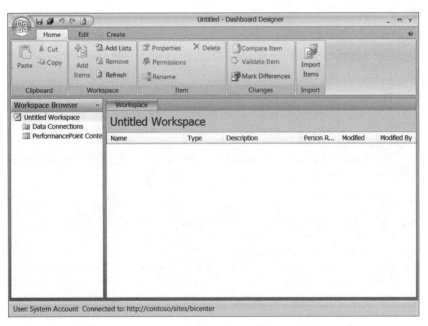

Figure 16-3 Dashboard Designer is connected to a SharePoint Server site.

Exploring the Dashboard Designer interface

This section walks through the user interface and settings to help you become familiar with Dashboard Designer.

Left pane

The Workspace Browser pane is located on the left side of the Dashboard Designer and contains two categories of dashboard items: Data Connections and PerformancePoint Content. The Workspace Browser uses right-click functionality to perform tasks for the dashboard items inside the Workspace Browser pane, as shown in Figure 16-4.

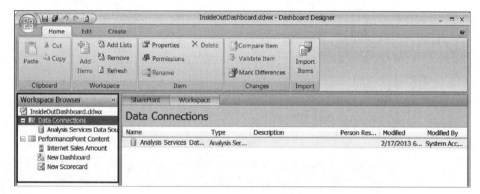

Figure 16-4 Options for Data Sources are revealed by right-clicking in the Workspace Browser pane.

The ribbon

The Dashboard Designer ribbon includes three main tabs: Home, Edit, and Create.

Home tab The Home tab includes toolbar commands used to view and open dashboard items, as shown in Figure 16-5.

Figure 16-5 The Home tab in Dashboard Designer includes commands to view and open Dashboard items.

Edit tab   The Edit tab includes toolbar commands used to change dashboard items, as shown in Figure 16-6. The items in the Edit tab are dynamic, meaning only commands and buttons that are specific to the particular dashboard items that you want to edit are enabled or disabled based on the type of dashboard item that is open in the center pane of the workspace.

Figure 16-6 The Edit tab in Dashboard Designer changes depending on the Dashboard item open in the center pane.

The ribbon buttons for the Edit tab are split into the following groups: Font, Header, View, Settings, and Comments, as shown in Figure 16-7. The buttons will be enabled or disabled based on what is selected in the center pane of Dashboard Designer.

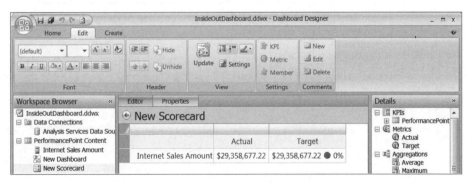

Figure 16-7 The Edit tab View commands are enabled when a scorecard is the center pane workspace item.

The Settings ribbon button in the View group opens the View Settings dialog box for Interactivity, Display, Toolbar, and Filters. Figure 16-8 illustrates the Interactivity options.

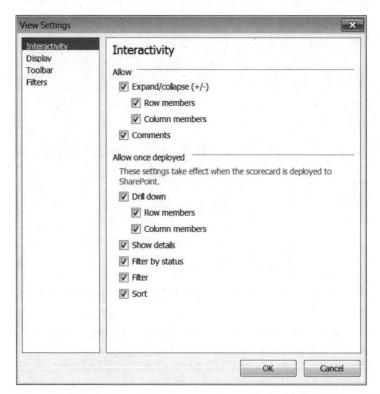

Figure 16-8 The Interactivity options may be enabled or disabled based on how you want the user to interact with the scorecard.

The Interactivity settings are the options you can enable and disable based on how you want the user to be able to interact with the scorecard. Table 16-2 lists the details of the Interactivity setting options.

TABLE 16-2 Dashboard Designer interactivity setting options

Section	Option	Description
Allow	Expand/Collapse (+/-)	Enable dashboard authors and users to expand and collapse scorecard rows and columns.
	Row Members	Enable dashboard authors and users to expand and collapse all scorecard rows.
	Column Members	Enable dashboard authors and users to expand and collapse scorecard columns.
	Comments	Enable dashboard authors and users to leave comments in scorecard cells. To use this option, Enable Comments must be selected in the Central Administration settings for the PerformancePoint Services.
Allow Once Deployed	Drill Down	Enable dashboard users to drill down to see lower levels of detail in scorecard rows and columns.
	Row Members	Enable dashboard authors and users to drill down on data in scorecard rows.
	Column Members	Enable dashboard authors and users to drill down on data in scorecard columns.
	Show Details	Enable dashboard authors and users to view transaction-level details for a particular scorecard value.
	Filter By Status	Enable dashboard authors and users to filter information displayed in a scorecard by KPIs.
	Filter	Enable dashboard authors and users to apply filters to a scorecard such as Top 10 and Value Filters.
	Sort	Enable dashboard authors and users to sort scorecard rows and columns.

The Display settings shown in Figure 16-9 are the options for rendering the scorecard, such as show/hide the actual and target headers, whether you want the text in the cells to wrap, show/hide gridlines, whether you want to display a message in the cells that return empty cells, and the message you want to display in the cells that have an error. Table 16-3 lists the details of the Display setting options.

Figure 16-9 The Display options enable you to configure how you want the scorecard to appear.

TABLE 16-3 Dashboard Designer display setting options

Section	Option	Description
Show	Actual And Target Headers	Enable to display actual and target headings in the scorecard.
	Wrapped Text In Cells	Enable to wrap text in scorecard cells. This is useful for scorecards where row or column members have longer names.
	Gridlines	Enable to display gridlines in scorecard.
Messages	Empty Cells	Use this option to specify what should display in the empty scorecard cells.
	Error Cells	Use this option to specify what should display in the scorecard cells that have errors.

The Toolbar settings are the options for the actual toolbar of the scorecard. When creating a scorecard, these options are not enabled by default; however, to enable them, check the desired settings for the toolbar in the View Settings dialog box shown in Figure 16-10. Table 16-4 lists the details of the Toolbar setting options.

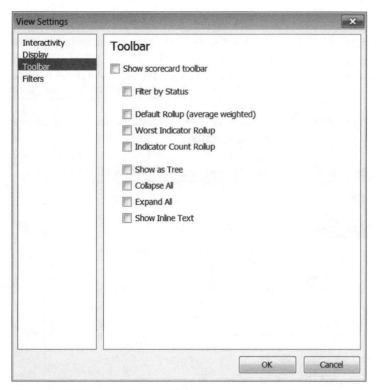

Figure 16-10 You can adjust options for the scorecard toolbar in this dialog box.

TABLE 16-4 Dashboard Designer toolbar setting options

Option	Description
Show Scorecard Toolbar	Select to display the toolbar in the scorecard.
Filter By Status	Select to display the Filter By Status toolbar command in the scorecard toolbar.
Default Rollup (average weighted)	Select to display the Default Rollup toolbar command in the scorecard toolbar.
Worst Indicator Rollup	Select to display the Worst Indicator Rollup toolbar command in the scorecard.
Indicator Count Rollup	Select to display the Indicator Count Rollup toolbar command in the scorecard.
Show As Tree	Select to display the Show As Tree toolbar command in the scorecard.
Collapse All	Select to display the Collapse All toolbar command in the scorecard.

Option	Description
Expand All	Select to display the Expand All toolbar command in the scorecard.
Show Inline Text	This option does not work in the current version of PerformancePoint Services; therefore leave it cleared.

The Filter settings shown in Figure 16-11 are the options for filtering a scorecard. Table 16-5 lists the details of the Filter setting options.

Figure 16-11 You can adjust scorecard filtering options in this dialog box.

TABLE 16-5 Dashboard Designer filter setting options

Option	Description
Filter Empty Rows	Select to prevent empty rows from displaying in the scorecard.
Filter By Status	Select any of the options (On Target, Slightly Off Target, Off Target) to display only the KPIs that have the status that you select.

Create tab   The Create tab includes toolbar commands used to create dashboard items, and each toolbar command opens a wizard that guides you through the creation of the item.

When Data Connections is selected in the Workspace Browser, the Edit tab will enable the Data Sources ribbon button, as shown in Figure 16-12.

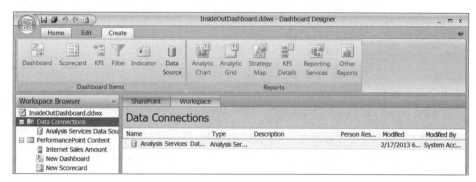

Figure 16-12 The Data Source ribbon button is enabled when Data Connections is selected in the Workspace Browser.

When PerformancePoint Content is selected in the Workspace Browser, the Edit tab will disable the Data Sources ribbon button and the rest of the buttons will become enabled, as shown in Figure 16-13.

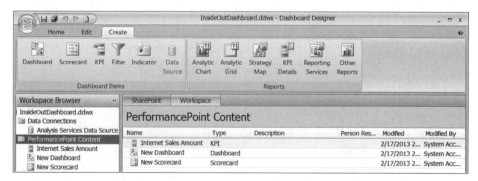

Figure 16-13 The Create tab ribbon buttons change when PerformancePoint Content items are selected in the Workspace Browser.

Center pane

The center pane has specific tabs available based on what is selected in the Workspace Browser.

SharePoint and Workspace tabs   The SharePoint and Workspace tabs are available when one of the category items is selected in the Workspace Browser. These tabs are used to view lists of dashboard items created by yourself and other dashboard authors.

Editor tab   The Editor tab, shown in Figure 16-14, is available for most dashboard items, including dashboards, scorecards, KPIs, filters, indicators, and reports (except analytic charts and grids). The Editor tab is used to add or change data that you use for your dashboard items. The Editor tab can also be used to preview scorecards and reports.

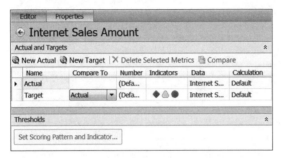

Figure 16-14 The Dashboard Designer Editor tab is used to add or change data that you use for your dashboard items.

Properties tab   The Properties tab, shown in Figure 16-15, is available for all types of dashboard items and is used to specify the item's name, description, owner (referred to as Person Responsible), and the display folder for the item that is in the SharePoint list or library.

Figure 16-15 Use the Dashboard Designer Properties tab to identify the general properties of dashboard items.

Time tab   The Time tab, shown in Figure 16-16, is available for the data sources and is used to configure a data source to work with Time Intelligence by specifying time period levels such as days, months, or years.

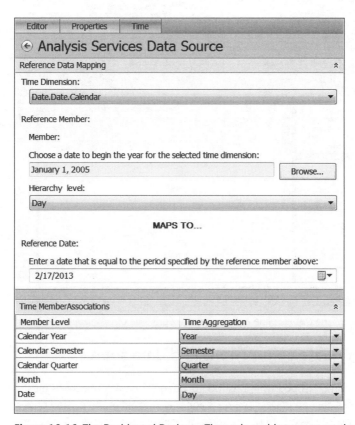

Figure 16-16 The Dashboard Designer Time tab enables you to set timeframe options.

View tab   The View tab is available for some types of data sources, such as tabular data sources. The view tab is used to preview the data or to specify column definitions.

Right pane

The right pane of Dashboard Designer includes the Details pane, shown in Figure 16-17, which is only visible when creating, viewing, or modifying specific dashboard items. You use the Details pane to add, remove, or change the content that you display in the dashboard. The items displayed in the Details pane vary according to the specific dashboard that is selected. When a scorecard is open, the Details pane lists items such as KPIs, Metrics, Aggregations, Dimensions, and other items relevant to the scorecard. When an Analytic

Chart or Grid is open, the Details pane lists items such as Dimensions, Measures, and Named Sets.

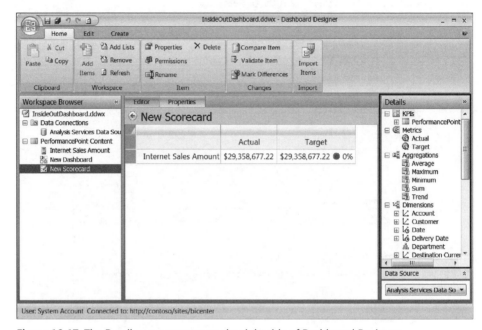

Figure 16-17 The Details pane appears on the right side of Dashboard Designer.

Creating data connections and data sources

Before creating dashboards in Dashboard Designer, data connections must be created first. Data sources defined in Dashboard Designer are stored in the trusted data connection library of the site. The data source template options for creating data sources for PerformancePoint Services in Dashboard Designer are shown in Figure 16-18 and include the following:

- **Analysis Services** Connects to multidimensional cube data in SSAS

- **Excel Services** Connects to an Excel Services file

- **Import From Excel Workbook** Connects to fixed values imported from Excel

- **SharePoint List** Connects to a SharePoint list

- **SQL Server Table** Connects to a SQL Server table

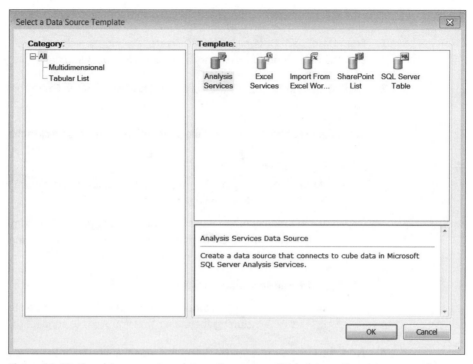

Figure 16-18 Five data source template options are available for creating data sources for PerformancePoint Services in Dashboard Designer.

Analysis Services data source

Analysis Services is a more advanced implementation for PerformancePoint Services. This section covers how to create an Analysis Services data source in Dashboard Designer. SSAS must be configured in order to complete the steps in this section.

When creating a data connection to Analysis Services, you have three authentication options:

- **Unattended Service Account** All users connect by using the Unattended Service Account that has been defined for the PerformancePoint shared service when the data source is accessed.

- **Credentials stored in a Secure Store target application** All users connect using the credentials from the specified Secure Store target application when the data source is accessed.

- **Per-user identity** The current user's identity will be used to access the data source. Requires Kerberos or the EffectiveUserName property set in the PerformancePoint Application Settings in Central Administration.

Chapter 16

Follow these steps to create an Analysis Services data source in Dashboard Designer:

1. From Dashboard Designer, click the Create tab, and then click Data Source (or right-click the Data Connections library and select New Data Source).

2. Click Analysis Services, and then click OK. This will open the Editor for the new data source.

3. In the Connection Settings, select the preferred method to connect to the data source.

    a. For Use Standard Connection:

        i. Type the full path for the server, then select the database name from the Database drop-down list.

        ii. (Optional) In the Roles text box, type the name of an administrator or database role. For multiple roles, type the names of the roles and separate them with commas.

    b. For Use The Following Connection:

        i. In the Connection String text box, type the connection string to the server—including the cube name you want to connect to.

4. From the Cube drop-down list, select the cube that you want to use as the data source.

> **Note**
>
> If Dashboard Designer is not connected to SSAS, the issue is related to the incorrect ADOMD.NET feature being installed. Refer to "Installing ADOMD.NET from SQL Server 2008 R2 Feature Pack" in Chapter 14, "Planning for business intelligence and key performance indicators."

5. In the Data Source Settings, select the desired authentication method.

    a. Unattended Service Account: Leave this option selected if you set the Unattended Service Account in the PerformancePoint Services Application Settings.

    b. Use A Stored Account: Enter the Application ID of the Secure Store target application.

    c. Per-User Identity

6. In the Formatting Dimension drop-down, select the desired dimension formatting needed for the report.

7. For Cache Lifetime, type the refresh rate (in minutes) for the cache for the desired time you would like the data source to update at this interval.

8. Click Test Data Source to confirm that the data connection is configured correctly, as shown here.

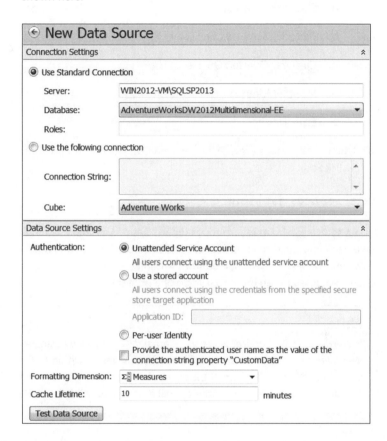

9. On the Properties tab, set the Name to "Adventure Works Data Source."

10. (Optional) Set the Description, Person Responsible, and Display Folder of the data source.

11. Switch to the Time tab.

12. Choose Date.Date.Calendar in the Time Dimension drop-down list, and then click the Browse button for the Member control.

13. In the Select Member dialog box, select January 1, 2005.

14. Choose Day in the Hierarchy Level drop-down list.

15. Set the Reference Date to the first day of the latest year available from the data (for example, 1/1/2010 if it is 2010).

16. Choose the time member associations for each member level, as follows:

   a. Calendar Year: Year

   b. Calendar Semester: Semester

   c. Calendar Quarter: Quarter

   d. Month: Month

   e. Date: Day

17. In the Workspace Browser, under Data Connections, right-click the data source and click Save.

Excel Services data source

A data source can be made from Dashboard Designer to data within Excel files that have been published to Excel Services and are stored in a SharePoint site. The published parameter values can be modified from within PerformancePoint Services and are useful when a parameter is an input to a value of a published cell.

> **Note**
>
> PerformancePoint Services accesses external data sources by using a delegated Windows identity and external data sources must reside within the same domain as the SharePoint 2013 server farm. If the external data sources do not reside within the same domain, the authentication to the eternal data source will fail.

To create an Excel Services data source connection, follow these steps:

1. In Dashboard Designer, click the Create tab and then click Data Source (or right-click the Data Connections library and select New Data Source).

2. Click Excel Services, and then click OK. This will open the Editor for the new data source.

3. Input the SharePoint URL for the Excel Services site.

4. From the Document Library drop-down, select the document library where the workbook is located.

5. From the Excel Workbook drop-down list, select the workbook you want to connect to.

6. In the Item Name, select or type in the Name Range or table value.

> ### Note
> **A Named Range is required for connecting to an Excel Services data source in Dashboard Designer. Steps to define a named item in Excel 2013 can be found at *http://office.microsoft.com/en-us/sharepoint-server-help/share-workbooks-using-excel-services-HA102772301.aspx*.**

7. In the Data Source Settings, select the desired authentication method:

    a. Unattended Service Account: Leave this option selected if you set the Unattended Service Account in the PerformancePoint Services Application Settings.

    b. Use A Stored Account: Enter the Application ID of the Secure Store target application.

    c. Per-User Identity.

8. Click Test Data Source, shown here, to confirm that the data connection is configured correctly.

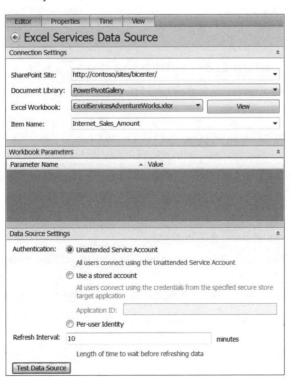

9. From the Properties tab, set the Name, Description, Person Responsible, and Display Folder of the data source.

10. From the Time tab, select the desired Time options for this data source.

11. Click the View tab, then click the Preview Data button to preview the results, as shown here.

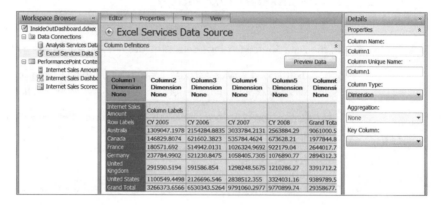

12. In the Workspace Browser under the Data Connections, right-click the data source and click Save.

Import from an Excel workbook data source

To create a data connection in Dashboard Designer to an Excel workbook, follow these steps:

1. From Dashboard Designer, click the Create tab, and then click Data Source (or right-click the Data Connections library and select New Data Source).

2. In the Select A Data Source Template dialog box, select Import From Excel Workbook, located in the All or Tabular List category pane.

3. Click OK.

4. In the center pane, click Import.

5. In the Workspace Browser, rename your data source, and then right-click the data source and click Save.

SharePoint list data source

Data from a SharePoint list can be used as a data source for PerformancePoint Services, and the connection can be made to any kind of SharePoint list.

> **Note**
> The data from the SharePoint list in PerformancePoint Services is read only.

To create a SharePoint list data source connection, follow these steps:

1. From Dashboard Designer, click the Create tab, and then click Data Source (or right-click the Data Connections library and select New Data Source).

2. In the Select A Data Source Template dialog box, select the SharePoint list located in the All or Tabular List category pane and then click OK.

3. In the Connection Settings of the center pane Editor tab, select the preferred method to connect to the data source.

4. In Cache Lifetime, type the refresh rate (in minutes) for the cache.

    Data from this data source will update according to the interval that you specify.

5. In the Connection Settings section, type the URL of the SharePoint site.

6. In the SharePoint Site List drop-down menu, select a List collection.

7. In the List drop-down menu, select the SharePoint list that you want from the collection.

8. Click Test Data Source to confirm that the data connection is configured correctly.

9. In the Workspace Browser, rename your data source, and then right-click the data source and click Save.

SQL Server table data source

A SQL Server table or view can be used as a data source in PerformancePoint Services. Only tables and views can be used, and the SQL data is read only from Dashboard Designer.

To create a SQL Server table data source connection, follow these steps:

1. From Dashboard Designer, click the Create tab, and then click Data Source (or right-click the Data Connections library and select New Data Source).

2. In the Select A Data Source Template dialog box, select the SQL Server table located in the All or Tabular List category pane. Click OK.

3. In the Connection Settings, select the method to connect to the data source:

   a. For Use A Standard Connection:

      i. Type the full path for the server to which you want to connect.

      ii. In the Database drop-down list, select the database name you want to use.

   b. For Use A Specific Connection String:

      i. Type a connection string with the full path of the server and database to which you want to connect.

      ii. In the Table drop-down list, select the specific table that you want to use.

4. In Data Source Settings, select the desired authentication method.

   a. Unattended Service Account: Leave this option selected if you set the Unattended Service Account in the PerformancePoint Services Application Settings.

   b. Use A Stored Account: Enter the Application ID of the Secure Store target application.

   c. Per-User Identity.

5. Click Test Data Source to confirm that the data connection is configured correctly.

6. In the Workspace Browser, rename your data source, and then right-click the data source and click Save.

Dashboard items

This section covers all the available dashboard items that can be created using PerformancePoint Services Dashboard Designer.

Scorecards

Scorecards are dashboard items that show the performance of one or more metrics and can be created using the PerformancePoint Dashboard Designer within SharePoint. Score-cards are used to compare actual results to specified goals, and the results are displayed in graphical indicators. Scorecards resemble a table that typically has Target and Actual value columns and one or more KPIs.

Scorecards can be created from the following two methods using the PerformancePoint Dashboard Designer:

- **Scorecard Wizard** A basic scorecard can be created quickly and easily by using the wizard. This method is useful for users who are new to the Dashboard Designer and do not have many existing dashboard items that are available for reuse. When using the wizard, you select a data source that will be used by at least one KPI in the scorecard, and then create the scorecard and finish configuring the workspace.

- **Blank Scorecard** Instead of using the wizard, you can create a blank scorecard and then manually add the KPIs and other graphical indicators. This method is useful when dashboard authors have created one or more KPIs.

Toggling the Dashboard Designer Scorecard Wizard

The PerformancePoint Dashboard Designer can be configured to default the creation to use the wizard or to create a blank scorecard every time you create a scorecard. To update the setting, follow these steps:

1. In Dashboard Designer, click File and then click Designer Options.

2. On the Personalize tab, select (or clear) the option for the Use Wizards To Create Scorecards. Click OK.

Creating a blank scorecard

Follow these steps to create a blank scorecard using Dashboard Designer:

1. In Dashboard Designer, click PerformancePoint Content in the Workspace Browser.

2. On the Create tab, click Scorecard (or right-click PerformancePoint Content and select New | Scorecard).

3. If the Scorecard Wizard appears, select the Blank Scorecard template located in the Standard category and then click OK.

4. In the center pane, click the Properties tab and set the Name of your scorecard to Performance By Country.

5. (Optional) For Display Folder, specify a location for the scorecard by selecting or creating a folder.

6. In the Workspace Browser, right-click the scorecard and click Save.

Creating KPIs for a scorecard

Follow these steps to create a KPI for a scorecard:

1. In Dashboard Designer, click PerformancePoint Content in the Workspace Browser.

2. From the Create tab, click KPI (or right-click PerformancePoint Content and select New | KPI).

3. In the Select A KPI Template dialog box, choose Blank KPI and click OK.

   The next step is to define the actual value as Year to Date (YTD).

4. Click the Name for Actual and rename it **YTD.**

5. Click the 1 (Fixed values) link in the Data Mappings column for YTD.

6. In the Fixed Values Data Source Mapping dialog box, click Change Source. Select the Adventure Works Data Source data connection and click OK.

7. Choose Reseller Sales Amount in the Select A Measure drop-down list and click New Time Intelligence Filter.

8. Enter a time formula of YearToDate, as shown here, and click OK.

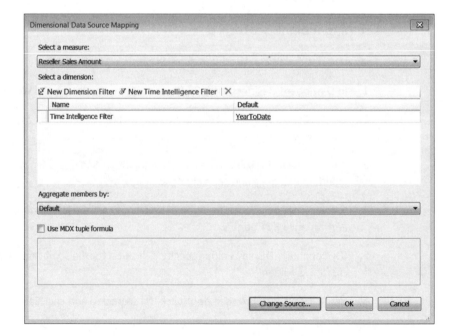

9. Click the (Default) link in the Number column for YTD, shown here. Choose Currency in the Format drop-down list and then click OK.

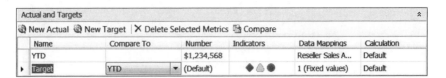

Next, we define the target value as last year's sales plus 25 percent.

10. Click the 1 (Fixed values) link in the Data Mappings column for Target.

11. In the Fixed Values Data Source Mapping dialog box, click Change Source and switch to the Calculated Metric tab. Select Blank Calculation, as shown here, and click OK.

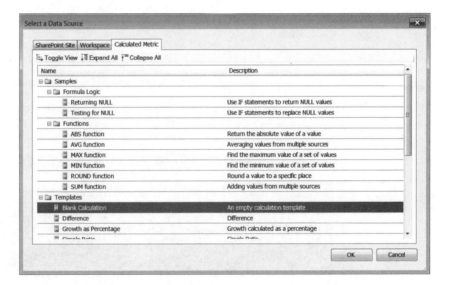

12. In the Calculated Metrics Data Source Mapping dialog box, delete Value2 and rename Value1 to **LastYearsSales.**

13. Click the 1 (Fixed Values) link for LastYearsSales.

14. On the Fixed Values Data Source Mapping, click Change Source and select the Adventure Works Data Source data connection. Click OK.

15. Choose Reseller Sales Amount in the Select A Measure drop-down list and click New Time Intelligence Filter.

16. Enter Year-1 for the time formula, as shown here, and click OK.

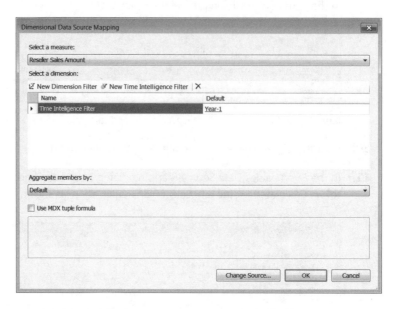

17. Click OK to close the Dimensional Data Source Mapping dialog box. Enter **LastYearsSales*1.25** for the formula, and then click OK.

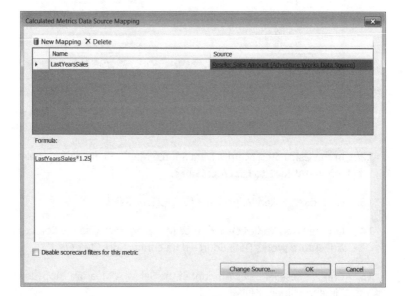

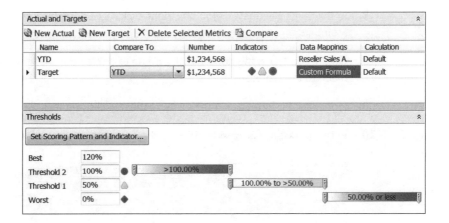

18. Click the (Default) link in the Number column for Target.

19. Choose Currency in the Format drop-down list and click OK.

20. Click the Properties tab, and then rename the New KPI to **Performance**.

21. In the Workspace Browser, right-click the scorecard and click Save.

Adding KPIs to a scorecard

A scorecard typically contains at least one KPI but can contain multiple KPIs that use the same or different data sources. Follow these steps to add KPIs to a scorecard:

1. In Dashboard Designer, under the PerformancePoint Content in the Workspace Browser, click the Performance scorecard that was created in the earlier procedure.

First, place performance KPIs on the scorecard.

2. With the Editor tab active in the center pane, locate the KPIs in the Details pane on the right.

3. Expand the KPIs and then drag the Performance KPI onto the Drop Items Here block on the left side.

4. On the Edit tab in the ribbon, click Update to display the changes that have been made to the scorecard.

Next, we add geography dimensions to the scorecard.

5. In the Details pane, expand the Dimensions node.

6. Drag the Geography dimension to the right side of the Performance cell.

7. In the Select Members dialog box, right-click All Geography and select Autoselect Members, and then select Country.

8. On the Edit tab in the ribbon, click Update to display the changes that have been made to the scorecard.

9. Right-click Performance in the center pane and click Hide.

10. In the Workspace Browser, right-click the Performance scorecard and click Save.

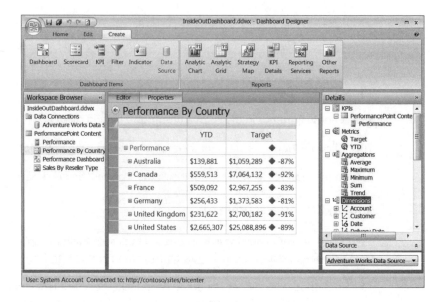

Reports

Dashboard Designer provides the ability to create various PerformancePoint Services reports. These reports include Analytic Chart, Analytic Grid, Excel Services, KPI Details, Reporting Services, and Strategy Map.

Analytic Chart and Analytic Grid reports

In Dashboard Designer, you can create analytic reports for your dashboards that are dynamic, visual representations of data displayed as interactive line charts, bar charts, pie charts, or tables (grids). Analytic Chart and Analytic Grid reports use data stored in SSAS.

To create an Analytic Chart report to display the sales by year, follow these steps:

1. In Dashboard Designer, click PerformancePoint Content in the Workspace Browser.

2. On the Create tab on the ribbon, click Analytic Chart.

3. In the Select A Data Source window, select the Adventure Works Data Source data connection that you want to use. Click Finish.

   The analytic report opens for editing in the workspace center pane.

4. In the Details pane, expand the Measures node.

5. Drag Reseller Sales Amount into the Bottom Axis section of the center pane.

6. Expand Dimensions, and then expand the Reseller nodes in the Details pane.

7. Drag Business Type to the Series section.

8. From the center pane, click the Properties tab and rename the report to **Sales By Reseller Type**.

9. (Optional) To specify a location for the report, click Display Folder and select or create a folder.

10. In the Workspace Browser, right-click the report, and click Save.

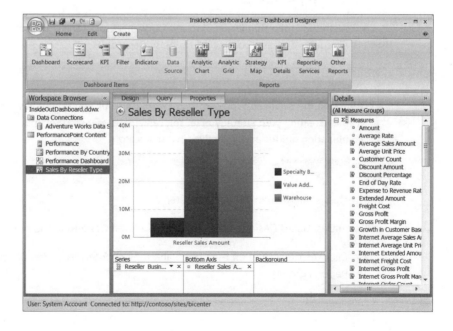

Strategy map reports

Strategy map reports can show relationships between objectives, goals, and KPIs. Strategy maps have their roots in the Balanced Scorecard framework, which defines organizational performance by using the following four perspectives:

- **Financial** Perspective that typically includes metrics such as revenue, cost, and profit.

- **Customer** Also known as the *customer satisfaction perspective,* this perspective typically includes metrics such as customer counts, market share, and number of complaints.

- **Internal process** Also known as the *operations perspective,* this perspective typically includes metrics such as time to market for new products, service error rates, and quality control measures.

- **Learning and growth** Also known as the *human resources perspective,* this perspective typically includes metrics such as employee turnover rates, the number of new employees, and hiring data.

A Balanced Scorecard is typically a dashboard page consisting of the following:

- A scorecard displaying performance metrics across the organization using the four perspectives described previously and contains four groups of KPIs that correspond to those perspectives.

- A strategy map that includes four groups of shapes (one group of shapes for each perspective) that is connected to the scorecard KPIs.

> **Note**
> Although the Balanced Scorecard framework is useful, you do not have to follow it when creating your strategy map. You can create your strategy map using any combination of KPIs and objectives in a scorecard.

To create a strategy map, follow these steps:

1. In Dashboard Designer, click PerformancePoint Content in the Workspace Browser.

2. Click the Create tab on the ribbon and then click Strategy Map (located in the Reports group).

3. In the Select A Scorecard step wizard, select the scorecard that you want to use and click Finish.

The strategy map opens in the Workspace center pane.

4. Click the Edit tab on the ribbon, and then click Edit Strategy Map.

5. In the Strategy Map Editor dialog box, do one of the following:

a. If you have an existing Microsoft Visio diagram, click Import Visio File. Browse to the location where the Visio diagram is saved and then click Open.

b. If you want to create a new Visio diagram, click Stencil. Browse to the location where the Visio stencils are located and then click Open.

6. Use the stencil shapes to create your Visio diagram in the Strategy Map Editor dialog box.

7. Click a shape in the Visio diagram and click Connect Shape.

8. In the Connect Shape dialog box, click the cell that you want to connect to the shape that you selected.

> **Note**
>
> If you want the color of the shape to update automatically (to indicate whether performance is on or off target), click in a cell that is in the Target column. (The Target column is the column containing the graphical indicator.)

9. Click Connect.

10. (This step is optional.) To replace the text inside a shape with the text that is used for the scorecard KPI, select Show KPI Name In Shape Text.

11. Repeat steps 4–6 for each shape in the Visio diagram that you want to connect to the scorecard KPIs.

12. When finished connecting shapes to KPIs, click Close, and in the Strategy Map Editor dialog box, click Apply.

13. From the center pane, click the Properties tab and type the name that you want to use for the report.

14. (Optional) To specify a location for the report, click Display Folder and select or create a folder.

15. In the Workspace Browser, right-click the strategy map and click Save.

KPI Details reports

Using Dashboard Designer, you can create a KPI Details report that is a view type used to show additional information about scorecard values and properties. The KPI Details report serves as a companion to a scorecard and is not used in a dashboard without its corresponding scorecard on the same dashboard page. When users click the cells in a scorecard, the KPI Details report updates to display the particular information about the value clicked.

To create a KPI Details report using Dashboard Designer, follow these steps:

1. Click the Create tab on the ribbon and click KPI Details (located in the Reports group).

2. Click the Editor tab in the center pane, as shown here, and specify the information that you want to display in the report.

Table 16-6 lists the information that you may include in the KPI Details report.

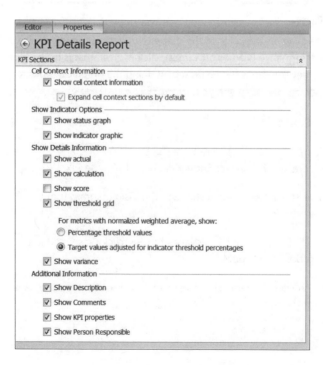

3. In the center pane, click the Properties tab and type the name that you want to use for the report.

4. (Optional) To specify a location for the report, click Display Folder and select or create a folder.

5. In the Workspace Browser, right-click the report, and click Save.

TABLE 16-6 KPI Details report options showing KPI section, option, and description

KPI section	Option	Description
Cell Context Information	Show Cell Context Information	Select this option to display the following: • Metric • Measure • Row Path (corresponds to clicked scorecard row) • Column Path (corresponds to clicked scorecard column)
	Expand Cell Context Sections By Default	This option is selected by default. It sets the KPI Details report to be expanded to display the specified information.
Show Indicator Options	Show Status Graph	This option does not work in the current version of PerformancePoint Services.
	Show Indicator Graphic	This option does not work in the current version of PerformancePoint Services.
Show Details Information	Show Actual	Option to display actual values when cells in the scorecard's Target column are clicked.
	Show Calculation	Option to display how scores are calculated and what banding method is used by the clicked KPI.
	Show Score	Option to show raw scores when cells in the scorecard's Target column are clicked.
	Show Threshold Grid	Option to determine whether to show the threshold grid when cells in the scorecard's Target column are clicked.

KPI section	Option	Description
	For Metrics With Normalized Weighted Value, Show Percentage Values	Option to display performance in percentages in the threshold grid.
	For Metrics With Normalized Weighted Value, Show Target Values Adjusted For Indicator Threshold Percentages	Option to display performance in numeric values in the threshold grid.
	Show Variance	Option to show the variance from the next status threshold.
Additional Information	Show Description	Option to display any text entered in the Description box for a KPI (visible on the Properties tab for KPI).
	Show Comments	Option to display any comments or annotations added to a scorecard.
	Show KPI Properties	Option to display any custom properties that have been created for each KPI (visible on the Properties tab for KPI).
	Show Person Responsible	Option to display information about the person responsible for the KPI status (visible on the Properties tab for KPI).

Creating a dashboard

Now that you have created reports and scorecards, the next step is to create a dashboard to display the dashboard items. When creating dashboards, a page layout template must be selected to create pages to contain the dashboard items. Dashboard pages can be created using Dashboard Designer. You start by selecting a page template and then add the dashboard items to the page.

Seven page layout templates are available for dashboards, as shown in Figure 16-19, and are listed as follows:

- 1 Zone
- 2 Columns
- 2 Rows
- 3 Columns

- 3 Rows

- Column, Split Column

- Header, 2 Columns

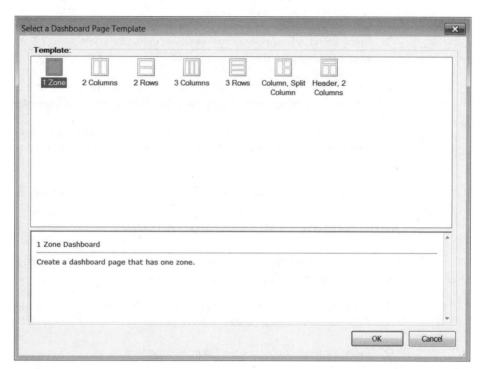

Figure 16-19 The Select A Dashboard Page Template dialog box for creating a new dashboard.

> **Note**
>
> Select the page layout template that best suits the content that you want to display. It is recommended not to display too many items in a single page, or else the individual items on the page may not display properly. You can easily add more pages to the dashboard to display a large number of reports and scorecards.

Creating a dashboard page

In this task, you will create a dashboard to display the performance scorecard and Analytic Chart report to connect the content created earlier in this chapter. The connection will allow filtering of the report by using the currently selected country from the Performance scorecard.

To create a dashboard page, follow these steps:

1. In Dashboard Designer, click PerformancePoint Content in the Workspace Browser.

2. On the Create tab, click Dashboard (or right-click PerformancePoint Content and select New | Dashboard).

3. In the Select A Dashboard Page Template dialog box, select the 2 Columns page layout template for the dashboard.

4. On the Properties tab in the center pane, update the Name for your dashboard by setting it to **Performance Dashboard**. Set all other optional properties if desired.

5. On the Editor tab in the center pane, rename the dashboard page by clicking the dashboard page name to highlight and then type a new name for the page. Set the name to **Country**.

6. In the Workspace Browser, right-click the dashboard and click Save.

Adding items to the dashboard page

Next, you will add the dashboard items to the newly created dashboard page. To add the dashboard items to the Country page, follow these steps:

1. In Dashboard Designer, under PerformancePoint Content in the Workspace Browser, click the Performance Dashboard to edit.

2. In the Pages section, click the Country page to edit.

3. In the Details pane, expand the Scorecards | PerformancePoint Content nodes.

4. Drag the Performance By Country scorecard into the left column.

5. In the Details pane, expand the Reports | PerformancePoint Content nodes.

6. Drag the Sales By Reseller Type report to the right column, as shown in the following graphic.

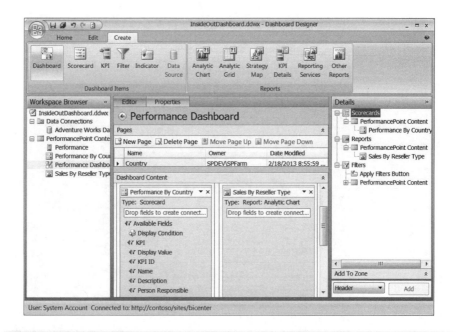

> **Note**
>
> It is recommended to put dashboard filters in a separate zone from the scorecard and reports to keep chart legends and reports from not displaying correctly. Also, consider using the Header, 2 Columns page layout template for pages that will include dashboard filters. You can place the filters in the Header zone and put the scorecards and reports in the other zones.

Setting autosize for Excel Services dashboard reports

If adding an Excel Services report, be sure to use the autosize setting, or else additional scrollbars may display in the deployed dashboard. To specify the autosize setting, perform these steps:

1. Once the Excel Services report has been added to the dashboard, click the Edit tab on the ribbon and click Edit Item.

2. On the Size tab, select Auto-size Width and Auto-size Height, as shown in the following graphic, and then click OK.

Connecting the selected country in the scorecard to the Analytic Chart report

Next, we need to connect the selected country to the Analytic Chart report. To do so, perform these steps:

1. In the center pane, drag the Row Member | Member Unique Name item from the scorecard to the report.

2. In the Connection dialog box, change the Source drop-down value to Member Row:Member Unique Name, and then click OK.

3. In the Workspace Browser, right-click the dashboard and click Save.

Configuring dashboard zones

Dashboard zones can be configured on pages created from the page templates. This section provides instructions to add or remove zones and to configure the sizing of the zones.

Chapter 16

Adding or removing zones

To add or remove a zone on a dashboard page, perform these steps:

1. On the center pane Editor tab, right-click the Dashboard Content section and click one of the following options:

   - **Add Left**   Adds a new zone to the left of the pointer

   - **Add Right**   Adds a new zone to the right of the pointer

   - **Add Above**   Adds a new zone above the pointer

   - **Add Below**   Adds a new zone below the pointer

   - **Split Zone**   Divides the zone nearest to the pointer into two zones of equal size

   - **Delete Zone**   Removes the zone nearest to the pointer

Changing the zone size

To change the size of the zone on a dashboard page, perform these steps:

1. On the center pane Editor tab, right-click the Dashboard Content section and then right-click the zone that you want to modify.

2. On the Size tab, set the width and height settings for the zone.

Zones can be sized only based on percentage and cannot be autosized or sized to specific pixel counts.

1. On the Orientation tab, arrange the items in the zone.

   The options available are Horizontal, Vertical, or Stacked. Horizontal arranges multiple items in a row. Vertical arranges multiple items in a column. Stacked layers multiple items in the same location on the dashboard page, and dashboard users use a drop-down list to switch between the items.

2. Click OK to save your changes.

Deploying the dashboard

Once you have assembled a dashboard and are ready to view and use it, the next step is to publish or "deploy" it to the SharePoint document library that contains the Performance-Point content.

To deploy a PerformancePoint Services Dashboard, perform these steps:

1. In Dashboard Designer, click PerformancePoint Content in the Workspace Browser.

2. On the Home tab ribbon, click Refresh to refresh the list of dashboard items that you and other dashboard authors have saved to SharePoint.

3. Under PerformancePoint Content in the Workspace Browser, right-click the Performance Dashboard and click Deploy To SharePoint.

4. If you are publishing the dashboard for the first time, the Deploy To dialog box appears, as shown here.

   a. Select the Dashboards library that you want to use.

   b. Select the Master Page template that you want to use for your dashboard.

   c. If the dashboard contains one or more pages, select Include Page List For Navigation.

   d. Click OK.

A Deploy To SharePoint Site dialog box will appear, displaying the status of the dashboard deployment, as shown here.

Once the deployment is successful, the browser window will open automatically to display the dashboard, as shown here.

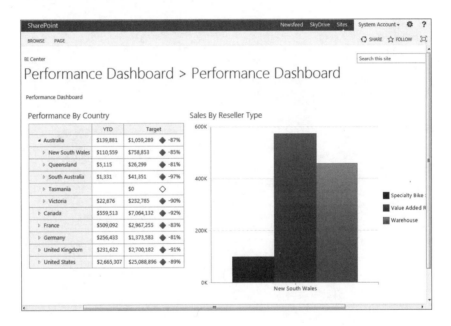

As you drill down into the Performance By Country content, the graph on the right will update dynamically based on the items selected.

Summary

As you have seen in this chapter, PerformancePoint Services is a powerful BI solution for SharePoint 2013. It has come a long way from when it was first integrated into SharePoint. PerformancePoint Services enables users to create BI dashboards that can help provide insight into the organization's performance. This chapter touched on the features and capabilities necessary for creating powerful dashboards, scorecards, and reports. You learned how to create data connections, scorecards, KPIs, and reports and display them in dashboards that you deployed to SharePoint. Now that you have learned about the BI features in SharePoint 2013, the next chapter focuses on working with Visio Services.

Working with Visio Services

Humans have always strived to communicate ideas visually, from the prehistoric era through today. For many complex ideas or systems, there is no alternative but to communicate them visually. Microsoft Visio, originally created in the early 1990s, is an advanced diagraming product that allows you to communicate ideas and systems pictorially across multiple domains, such as engineering, IT, processes, and business intelligence (BI).

Using Visio drawings with Microsoft SharePoint is not new. You have been able to share Visio files among team members by placing them in document libraries since SharePoint Team Services and SharePoint Portal Server 2001. You can then manage the Visio files directly from the SharePoint site, thereby providing checkout, check-in, viewing, editing, alert, content type, and discussion group functionality. However, to share diagrams in earlier versions, you were limited to saving snapshots of the diagrams as image files or Portable Document Format (PDF) files. Also with early versions of Visio, you could create non-SharePoint websites from Visio drawings. However, whichever method you used, there were difficulties managing those files and pages to ensure that users had the latest version of the diagrams.

With the Enterprise edition of SharePoint Server 2010, a new feature—Visio Services—was introduced, which that allows you to share drawings with users who do not have Visio installed on their computers. With Visio Services, the Visio drawings are not static snapshots but instead are dynamic. You can pan, zoom, and navigate around the drawing, plus using a properties window, you can view shape data and any associated hyperlinks.

You do not need to install an ActiveX control to view the Visio drawings in the browser. You create the Visio drawings using Visio and save them in a SharePoint site; then, using Visio Services and the Visio Web Access Web Part, you can view the Visio drawing in the browser. This also allows diagrams to be viewed on mobile devices. You can create connections between the web parts that contain Visio drawings, as well as connecting them to other web parts. Using the Visio Services application programming interface (API), you can program changes to the drawing as the user navigates around a drawing or interacts with other UI objects on the webpage.

> **Note**
>
> In Windows SharePoint Services 3.0 and SharePoint Foundation 2010, you could generate Visio Pivot Diagrams using a command on task and calendar lists. This command is no longer available in SharePoint 2013.

This chapter details Visio Services and the use of the Visio client application to facilitate the development of solutions using Visio Services. This chapter also describes the changes in SharePoint 2013 within Visio Services, which include the following:

- Support for the new Visio 2013 file format.

- Visio 2013 drawings can connect to external lists that are created from external content types (ECTs).

- Programmatic support for the new commenting framework.

- The Visio Process Repository site template is available in SharePoint Server 2013; however, it will be removed in the next major release of SharePoint.

- Visio Services can recalculate formulas in the ShapeSheet.

- Greater extensibility via the ECMAScript (JavaScript or Jscript) object model that allows you to integrate JavaScript code with a Visio Web Access Web Part JavaScript API.

- Additional options when using web part connections with the Visio Web Access Web Part.

If you are new to Visio, there are 24 self-contained videos ranging from five to seven minutes, created by three Visio MVPs that discuss and demonstrate the basics of how to use and apply some of the features and capabilities of Visio available at *visio.microsoft.com/en-us/ Get_Started/How_To/Learn_Visio_2010_from_Visio_MVPs/Pages/default.aspx*. Although these videos are based on Visio 2010, they are useful in learning skills with Visio 2013.

Looking at Visio Services

Visio Services allows users to save and share their Visio drawings to a SharePoint site. You can use Visio Services to render a Visio drawing that people can view in their browser. Since Visio Services does all of the rendering, anyone can view the Visio drawing without having Visio or the Visio Viewer installed on the computer.

The Visio 2013 Viewer can be downloaded at *www.microsoft.com/en-us/download/details .aspx?id=35811*.

The power Visio Services can add to your solutions with very little effort is often overlooked. Simply because the eye is plugged directly into your brain and the eye is our primary sense, users can easily distinguish between differences in color, shape, size, and form. When users are presented with a large list of data, they have to read that data and interpret them and then do some kind of calculation or comparison. By default, SharePoint tends to present data in a tabular form; however, it is far easier if someone else has already done the calculations/comparison and presents the results visually so that users can see what the data is telling them quickly, with a single look.

> **Note**
>
> Visio Services can be used to display visualizations of SharePoint 2010 workflow instances in the browser. Visio visualizations cannot be used with SharePoint 2013 workflow instances. However, you can use Visio drawings to create and modify both SharePoint 2013 and SharePoint 2013 workflows using the Visio client application; and in SharePoint Designer, you use the built-in Visual Designer, which is a Visio ActiveX control, to create and modify SharePoint 2013 workflows. More information on both SharePoint 2013 workflows and SharePoint 2010 workflows can be found in Chapter 7, "Using and creating workflows."

When you upload a Visio file into SharePoint and it is presented in the browser using Visio Services, it is considered as a read-only file (except for commenting). You cannot change Visio diagrams using Visio Services, or the data in a Visio file, you need to use the Visio client application to do that; however, the diagrams can react to changes in the data if the data they are based on is external to the file; that is, the diagrams can be data driven. Connecting data to Visio diagrams, known as *data linking*, must be configured using Visio 2010 Professional, Visio 2010 Premium, or Visio Professional 2013.

More information on data linking can be found later in this chapter.

When Visio is teamed with a SharePoint 2010 or SharePoint 2013 environments, users do not need to know how to create the Visio diagrams, nor do the creators of the Visio Services solutions need to write code. By using the standard, out-of-the-box features of both Visio and SharePoint, the creator can create integrated solutions without writing code. The development life cycle of Visio Services solutions involve three basic players:

- **Creator** The creator understands the business data, is aware of the trends and significant changes in the data, as well as knowledge of the overall business process in the organization. Creators may not write code or necessarily understand the technical intricacies of software product development; however, they do know the business systems that host the data for the Visio Services solution. They will create the Visio diagrams, connect those diagrams to business data, and then upload the Visio diagrams to SharePoint and build any dashboards.

- **Consumer** Users of the Visio Services solution must know how to interact with the solution developed by the creator of the solution. In many ways, the solution will be similar to other solutions built with SharePoint, such as the use of web part connections or the solutions built using Business Connectivity Services (BCS) or Excel Services.

- **Developer** A developer extends the out-of-the-box functionality of Visio and SharePoint by using the Visio Services class library, in the Microsoft.Office.Visio.Server namespace and the JavaScript object model in the Vwa namespace in Visio Services, as well as other parts of the SharePoint object model.

In SharePoint Server 2013, Visio Services renders diagrams created in either of the following:

- **Visio 2010** These must be created using Visio 2010 Professional or Visio 2010 Premium and must be published to a SharePoint site as a Visio web drawing (*.vdw) file. Standard Visio 2010 diagrams (.vsd files) are not rendered by Visio Services and require Visio 2010, Visio 2013, or Visio Viewer to be viewed.

- **Visio 2013** These must be created using Visio Professional 2013. The new standard diagram format in Visio Professional 2013 (*.vsdx files) can be rendered by Visio Services, along with web drawings (.vdw) format. You should use the new .vsdx format unless you require compatibility with previous versions of Visio.

> ## Note
>
> Visio 2013 provides several compatibility features to help organizations move to the new file format. You can find more information in the following two blog posts:
>
> - "What IT Pros need to know about the new VSDX file format in Visio 2013," at *blogs.technet.com/b/office_resource_kit/archive/2012/10/26/what-it-pros-need-to-know-about-the-new-vsdx-file-format-in-visio-2013.aspx*.
>
> - "Working with Visio 2013 files in SharePoint 2010," at *blogs.msdn.com/b/chhopkin/archive/2013/02/14/working-with-visio-2013-files-in-sharepoint-2010.aspx*.

INSIDE OUT   The new Visio 2013 file format

Visio 2013 contains new XML-based file formats, known as Office Open XML, based on the Open Packaging Conventions (OPC) standard (ISO 29500, Part2). This makes it possible for Visio to provide new functionality and improve interoperability with other applications. Microsoft Office 2007 introduced new XML file formats for Microsoft Word (.docx), Microsoft Excel (.xlsx), and Microsoft PowerPoint (.pptx). Just as those file formats were a combination of a ZIP archive package and XML content, so too are the new file formats for Visio. In fact, you can save a drawing in Visio 2013 as one of the new file formats, rename the file extension to "*.zip" in Windows Explorer, and then open the file like a folder to see the contents inside.

The benefits offered by the new XML file format include the following:

- Smaller file sizes due to the new compressed format, which can be up to 75 percent smaller than the comparable binary document.

- Greater security. This is the result of data being stored in a standard structure, with a separate file extension for files with executable macro code. The macro-free file extensions are .vsdx for Visio drawings, .vstx for Visio templates, and .vssx for Visio stencils. The equivalent macro-enabled file extensions are .vsdm, .vstm, and .vssm.

- Improved data recovery via segmenting and separating different components within the file.

- Previous to SharePoint 2013, you had to publish a Visio drawing to Visio Services as a Visio web drawing (.vdw); now you can save new Visio XML-formatted files to a document library and the drawings can be viewed natively in the browser by using Visio Services, both with on-premises installations of SharePoint 2013 and Office 365.

- Support for coauthoring when Visio drawings are saved to SkyDrive, SharePoint, or SharePoint Online in Office 365.

The new XML files can be read and updated without the need of a client application; for example, a developer could write code to selectively read one item out of a Visio .vsdx file without having to extract the whole file, or they could change the logo in all the background pages of all .vsdx files in a SharePoint library to reflect new branding guidelines.

Although Visio is part of the Office product, it is slightly different from other Office applications, and hence some Visio functionality has been shoehorned in the XML file to look like Office format. For example, the previous version of Visio also included an

XML-based file format, the Visio XML drawing format or .vdx, as well as XML template, .vtx, and XML stencil formats, .vsx. Therefore, for example, some of the Visio XML schema from the .vdx file has remained the same in the .vsdx format.

There is a software development kit (SDK) for Open XML; however, at this time the current SDK contained no Visio-specific examples. The best source of information can be found in the Visio 2013 SDK, which can be downloaded from *www.microsoft.com/en-us/download/ details.aspx?id=36825,* or use the information on the MSDN site at *msdn.microsoft.com/ en-us/library/office/jj684209.aspx*, where you can find more information on the Visio 2013 file format (.vsdx) and how to manipulate the file programmatically. The Visio product team also has a blog post, "10 tips for developers working with the Visio VSDX file format," at *blogs.office.com/b/visio/archive/2013/01/29/10-tips-for-developers-working-with-the-visio-vsdx-file-format.aspx*.

Displaying Visio drawings in Visio Services

When you click a Visio file in a SharePoint library, by default the Visio diagram opens in a webpage for a full-screen viewing experience, as shown in Figure 17-1.

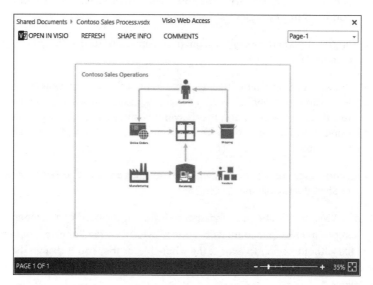

Figure 17-1 The Visio Web Access page displays the drawing in a Visio file.

The SharePoint page hosts an instance of the Visio Web Access Web Part, where the URL of the page is *<SharePointSiteURL>/_layouts/15/VisioWebAccess/VisioWebAccess.aspx?id=*<fileURL>*& Source=*<pageURL>, where:

- *<file URL>* is the relative address of the location of the Visio file, such as */sites/IT/ Workflow/Shared%20Documents/Contoso%20Sales%20Process.vsdx.*

- *<pageURL>* is the URL of the page where you clicked the name of the Visio file, such as the All Items view of a document library: *http%3A%2F%2Fintranet%2Eadventure% 2Dworks%2Ecom%2Fsites%2FIT%2FWorkflow%2FShared%2520Documents%2FForms %2FAllItems%2Easpx.*

At the top of the Visio Web Access page is a breadcrumb that allows you to navigate to the page you were previously on, *<pageURL>*. If you click the cross (x) in the upper-right corner of the Visio Web Access page, you will also be redirected to *<pageURL>*. Below the breadcrumb are four links:

- **Open in Visio** Click this link to open the Visio drawing in the Visio client application. This requires that Visio or Visio Viewer is installed on your computer. A Microsoft Office dialog box opens, warning you that some files can contain viruses that are harmful and that it is important to be certain that the file is from a trustworthy source. Once you have clicked Yes in the dialog box, Visio will open. You can also click the file name in the breadcrumb to open the file in Visio.

- **Refresh** Use this link to refresh the page. When the Visio diagram is linked to an external data source and that content has changed since the last refresh, the new data appears in the diagram. Changes in the data source might not be immediately reflected by refreshing the diagram, depending on the data caching settings for Visio Services. In SharePoint 2013, refreshing can now alter all shapes, shape styling, and calculated shape data during a refresh, and that BCS is now a supported data source for refreshable data.

- **Shape info** Click this link to open the Shape Information pane and then select a shape in the drawing to view detailed information about the shape, as shown in Figure 17-2.

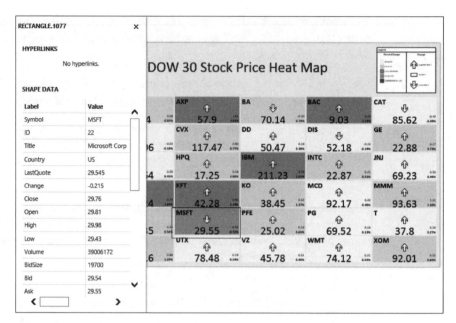

Figure 17-2 Use the Shape Information pane to display detailed information about a shape.

The pane can be repositioned by dragging the title bar of the pane using the left mouse button (floating), or it can be docked. You can also resize the window by grabbing one of the borders of the pane and dragging it. If a shape has a hyperlink, when you pause the mouse over the shape, the Pointer tool changes to show that it can be clicked. Select the shape, and then click it again to follow the link. Hyperlinks are also displayed in the Shape Information pane, which is useful for shapes that contain more than one hyperlink.

- **Comments** Use this link to open the Comments pane. When the drawing is saved in SharePoint and viewed in the browser by using Visio Services, users who do not have the Visio client application can add comments to a shape or at the page level which are indicated by a cloud icon, as shown in Figure 17-3. Commenting is not supported for .vdw or the older binary Visio file formats.

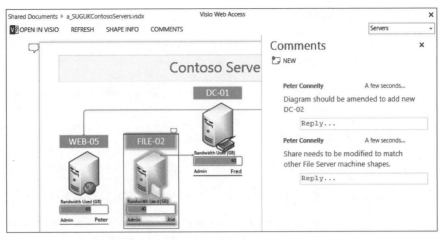

Figure 17-3 You can attach comments to a page or to shapes.

You can view all comments in the Comments pane. You can add, edit, and delete comments within the Visio client application. Comments are stored as part of the Visio file (.vsdx); therefore, you need to save the file to save your comments, and therefore comments in Visio files are similar to using comments in other Office applications, such as Word. Depending on the configuration of your SharePoint library, when you are editing a draft version, then comments may only be seen by other contributors and would only be seen by all users when the .vsdx file is published as a major version. To display the Comments pane in Visio, click Comments Pane on the Review Ribbon tab in the Comments group.

Visio Services includes new JavaScript APIs to read comments from a page or shape in a diagram.

Visio diagrams can have multiple pages, and in the footer of the webpage is the number of pages in the diagram. At the top of the page, to the right of the breadcrumb, is a Page Navigation box, which you can use to view the page you want to see, as shown in Figure 17-4. Selecting a different page will cause Visio Services to load and render that page, as well as update and link data and data graphics.

Figure 17-4 Use the Page Navigation box to view pages in a multipage diagram.

You can click and drag the diagram around the webpage to view specific parts of the diagram. Use the zoom tools in the footer to change the size of the diagram and to make the entire diagram visible in the browser window.

Adding a Visio Web Access Web Part to a page

Visio diagrams can be embedded on SharePoint pages using the Visio Web Access Web Part, using the following steps:

1. Navigate to the site that contains the page that you want to add a Visio Web Access Web Part.

2. Place the page in edit mode.

3. To display the Web Part page, complete one of the following actions:

   - On a wiki page, on the Insert tab, click Web Part in the Parts group.

   - On a Web Part page, in the web part zone where you want to add the Visio Web Access Web Part, click Add A Web Part.

4. Under Categories, click Business Data, and then, under Parts, click Visio Web Access, as shown next.

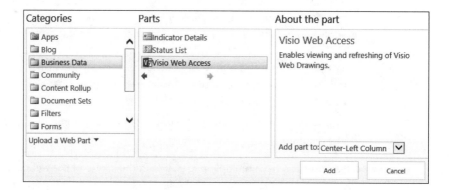

5. Click Add.

> More information on editing pages can be found in Chapter 9, "Creating and formatting content pages." Information on web parts can be found in Chapter 10, "Adding, editing, connecting, and maintaining web parts."

You can customize the Visio Web Access Web Part by using the Visio Web Access tool pane, as shown in Figure 17-5. You can open the tool pane for a newly added Visio Web Access Web Part by clicking Click Here To Open The Tool Pane. Alternatively, on the Web Part Ribbon tab, click Web Part Properties in the Properties group.

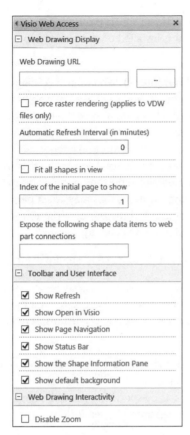

Chapter 17

Figure 17-5 Use the Visio Web Access tool pane to customize display options for the Visio diagram and the refresh interval for data-connected diagrams.

The Visio Web Access tool pane contains the standard three web part headings (Appearance, Layout, and Advance) and three Visio Web Access–specific headings:

- **Web Drawing Display** This section allows you to specify which Visio drawing to display and how to display it, by modifying the following options:

    - **Web drawing URL** In the text box, either type the URL to the Visio file whose diagrams you want to display in the web part, or click the ellipsis button to navigate to the SharePoint library where the file is stored. When you are using web part connections to provide the URL of the Visio file, leave this text box blank.

    - **Force raster rendering (applies to VDW files only)** If the person viewing the Visio web drawing has Silverlight 3.0 or later installed, the web drawing will be rendered using Silverlight. Otherwise, it is rendered as an image file in Portable

Network Graphics (PNG) format. If you would prefer that the web part never use Silverlight, even if Silverlight is installed on the viewer's computer, select this option.

- **Automatic refresh interval (in minutes)** When the Visio diagram is connected to an external data source, you can have the web part check the data source periodically to get the latest data. Type the number of minutes you would like for the interval between data refresh attempts. By default, the data is not automatically refreshed. Values must be integers and greater than or equal to 1. Leave this option set as 0 (zero) if you prefer that users refresh the data manually by clicking the Refresh button on the diagram viewer. As high refresh rates on frequently visited pages may affect performance, a SharePoint server administration can throttle this on a per Visio Services service application level by using the Minimum Cache Age setting.

- **Fit all shapes in view** Use this option to make the entire diagram visible in the browser window.

- **Index of the initial page to show** Use this text box to type the page to display in a multi-page diagram when the page is first displayed in the browser. By default, the value is 1.

- **Expose the following shape data items to web part connections** When you configure the web part connection, you can send the shape data of selected shapes to other web parts by specifying in this box the data fields to send. Type the data field names separated by semicolons.

- **Toolbar and User Interface** The options available in this section of the tool pane are tools that are available to the diagram user, with the exception of the Show Default Background option. When Show Default Background is selected, the background of the web diagram is gray. When the option is cleared, the background is transparent. The other options in this section are:

  - Show Refresh

  - Show Open In Visio

  - Show Page Navigation

  - Show Status Bar

  - Show The Shape Information Pane

Users will still be able to perform some of the actions using the mouse or keyboard shortcuts. To disable functionality completely, use the options in the Web Drawing Interactivity section.

- **Web Drawing Interactivity** Use the options in this section to remove tools from the UI that you don't want users to see by clearing the check box beside those items. The option in this section are:

  - Disable Zoom

  - Disable Pan

  - Disable Hyperlink

  - Disable Selection

INSIDE OUT   Coauthoring Visio files

Coauthoring Visio files is an exciting new Visio functionality that uses the same Office Document Cache as Word and PowerPoint. When more than one user is editing a Visio file when the Visio file is stored in SharePoint (on-premise or SharePoint Online) or SkyDrive, the Visio client application displays an icon on the status bar that indicates the number of users editing the file.

When the icon is clicked, the list of authors is displayed, as shown here. By pausing over the author names, you can display contact information along with the options to call, send an instant message, or email a contact. You can see similar information in the Backstage view, on the Info tab.

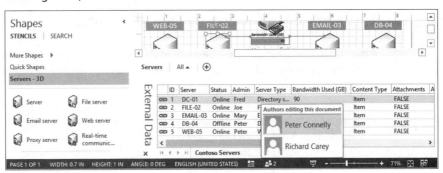

When a user is editing a shape, the shape is not locked against editing; instead, a person icon is added to the upper-right corner of the shape, as shown in the image that follows, to inform you that someone else is editing the shape.

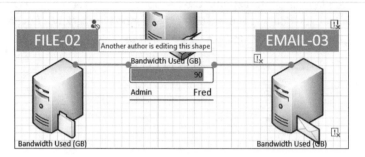

When you pause over the icon, a ScreenTip is displayed. When you click the icon, the name of the person is displayed. You can then contact that individual by clicking the name. Visio does not prevent either user from editing the shape; therefore, a more correct name for this feature would be *collaborative authoring*. Shapes that have been deleted by someone else display an exclamation mark in a square box along with a small red cross in the lower-right corner of the box.

Developers can create Visio templates that do not allow coauthoring by using the NoCoauth cell on the Document ShapeSheet. Developers also have access to the Document.AfterDocumentMerge event, which provides information about diagram changes due to coauthoring.

Visio Graphics Service service application

Visio Services, much like Access Services and Excel Services, is implemented as a service application, named Visio Graphics Service. As the service application architecture has not changed in SharePoint 2013, you install Visio Services as you would in SharePoint Server 2010. Visio Services is still an Enterprise feature; therefore, you cannot use it if you only have SharePoint Foundation installed or you have only purchased SharePoint Server Standard Client Access Licenses (CALs).

To use Visio Services, create a Visio Services service application on a SharePoint Server farm and purchase an Enterprise CAL for each user who uses it; then on a site to use the features included in the Enterprise license, you need to activate the following:

- The site collection feature—SharePoint Server Enterprise Site Collection Features.

- The site feature—SharePoint Server Enterprise Site Features.

If these features are not enabled, then when a Visio Web Access Web Part is added to a page or the Visio Web Access page is displayed, an error message is displayed, as shown in Figure 17-6. This is important to remember, as these features can be deactivated and yet the web part is still on the page and new Visio Web Access Web Parts can be added to pages.

Figure 17-6 Here is the "Visio Web Access is not available" error message.

Visio Services system performance

SharePoint servers running the Visio Graphics Service may be affected by various factors, such as:

- The size of the diagrams being rendered

- The number of diagrams connected to a data source

- The performance of the data sources to which diagrams are connected

- The frequency of data refresh for data-connected diagrams

- Peak loads of users who are accessing diagrams

- Peak loads on external data sources accessed by diagrams

- Complexity of diagrams

- Visio Services cache settings

Your SharePoint server administrators should monitor the performance of servers in your SharePoint farm. More information on planning Visio Services deployment can be found at *technet.microsoft.com/en-us/library/ff356849.aspx.*

Visio Services security considerations

When Visio drawings are connected to external data and the elements in the drawings can be updated based on that data, security is an important consideration. Users must have permission to view the diagram and the data that the diagram is connected to.

Visio files, as they are stored in document libraries, can be secured using the native security mechanisms of lists and libraries. To access external data, Visio Services uses a delegated Windows identity, and therefore, external data must reside within the same Active Directory domain as the SharePoint Server 2013 farm or you must configure Visio Services to use the Secure Store Service (SSS).

The SSS is used to map a user's credentials or a group of users to a different credential that has access to the external data source. Visio Services also uses SSS to configure an unattended service account that can be used to associate all users to a single account. This is always used in diagrams that are connected to Microsoft SQL Server databases that do not use Office Data Connection (ODC) files. If SSS is not used and external data does not reside within the same domain, authentication to the external data sources will fail.

You can also control access to specific data sources by explicitly defining the data providers that are trusted and configuring them using the Visio Graphics Service Trusted Data Providers page, as shown in Figure 17-7.

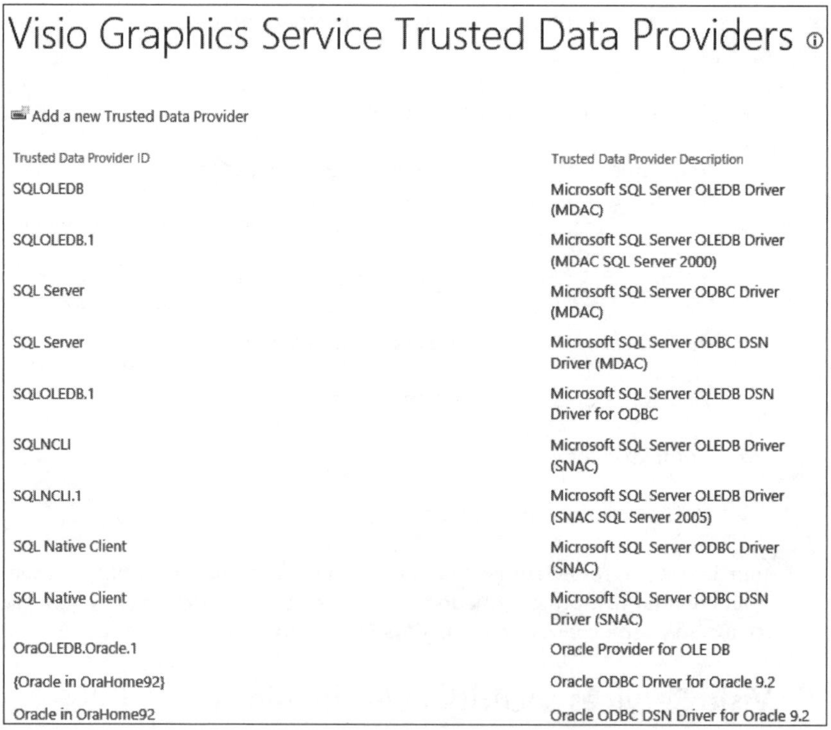

Visio Graphics Service Trusted Data Providers ⓘ

📃 Add a new Trusted Data Provider

Trusted Data Provider ID	Trusted Data Provider Description
SQLOLEDB	Microsoft SQL Server OLEDB Driver (MDAC)
SQLOLEDB.1	Microsoft SQL Server OLEDB Driver (MDAC SQL Server 2000)
SQL Server	Microsoft SQL Server ODBC Driver (MDAC)
SQL Server	Microsoft SQL Server ODBC DSN Driver (MDAC)
SQLOLEDB.1	Microsoft SQL Server OLEDB DSN Driver for ODBC
SQLNCLI	Microsoft SQL Server OLEDB Driver (SNAC)
SQLNCLI.1	Microsoft SQL Server OLEDB Driver (SNAC SQL Server 2005)
SQL Native Client	Microsoft SQL Server ODBC Driver (SNAC)
SQL Native Client	Microsoft SQL Server ODBC DSN Driver (SNAC)
OraOLEDB.Oracle.1	Oracle Provider for OLE DB
{Oracle in OraHome92}	Oracle ODBC Driver for Oracle 9.2
Oracle in OraHome92	Oracle ODBC DSN Driver for Oracle 9.2

Figure 17-7 Control access to specific data sources by managing trusted data providers.

You navigate to this page by clicking Trusted Data Providers on the Manage The Visio Graphics Services page on the SharePoint Central Administration website. You can also manage trusted data providers using the Windows PowerShell cmdlets: New-SPVisioSafe-DataProvider, Set-SPVisioSafeDataProvider, and Remove-SPVisioSafeDataProvider.

More information on how to manage Visio Services can be found in Chapter 14, "Planning for business intelligence and key performance indicators." Information on SSS can be found in Chapter 14 and Chapter 15, "Implementing better business intelligence with Excel Services and SQL Server 2012."

Supported data scenarios

When diagrams link to data external to the Visio file, and then that file is presented in Visio Services, that data can be refreshed only when using the following data sources:

- SQL Server databases hosted on SQL Server 7.0 or later, including SQL Azure. Visio Services can connect to tables and views, but not stored procedures.
  If you want to use stored procedures, then you need to use BCS, or you can write your own code.

- Sheet information that is stored in Excel workbooks (.xlsx files) published from Excel 2007, Excel 2010, or Excel 2013 stored on the same SharePoint Server 2013 farm with Excel Services enabled.

- SharePoint lists and libraries that are hosted on the same farm as the library when the Visio drawing is stored.

- External lists exposed in SharePoint Server through BCS. In order for a user to access data in an External List, the user must have permissions to access the ECT and permissions to access the external data source. This is new in SharePoint 2013 and means that your developers should not need to create new custom data providers. More information on BCS can be found in Chapter 22, "Working with external content."

- Databases using Object Linking and Embedding Database (OLE DB) or Open Database Connectivity (ODBC) APIs. The only limitation of using these data source types is obtaining and deploying the drivers on the SharePoint servers.

- Custom data providers implemented as Microsoft .NET Framework assemblies.

Using these data providers, a wide range of data sources can be used, such as Power View, System Center, SAP, Dynamics Web Services, Windows PowerShell, and BCS.

> **Note**
>
> If you are using Office 365, then you are limited to Excel Services, SharePoint lists, and external lists.

Designing dashboards

Combining a number of Visio Services web parts together, and also with other web parts, on one page brings data to life. These pages are known as *dashboards*. Users understand data presented as diagrams and charts much easier than when data is presented in a tabular view. It also helps to have related data all on one page.

As you design these dashboards, you must try to make the presentation of data meaningful for users who are not necessarily technical people but can understand what the data means quickly and easily. Users need not understand that the data is stored separately; they expect related data to be incorporated into one or more pages. For example, most users are familiar with mapping applications, such as Google maps and Bing maps. The sophistication of such applications have grown in power as the power of satellites has grown or the data from satellites have become more available using the Internet and global positioning satellite (GPS). Users can now display their current location and nearby facilities on mobile phones with ease, and thereby they can make better decisions quicker. Now, with Visio Services, you can build similar dashboards, especially where the data is not suited to be displayed in a graph or is too complex or too boring to be displayed in a grid.

Visualization of data makes decision making quicker and easier. However, Visio Services is just the presentation layer for your data. Before creating your dashboards, you must get the data in the format you want, the format that makes sense, and the format that is easy to present using diagrams and shapes. To use the power of Visio Services, the data will be stored externally to the Visio file, and therefore, to get the data in the necessary format, you may have to work with a number of data source owners. Visio is not an analysis tool, other tools, such as Excel Services, may be suited if you need to slice, dice, aggregate, or use formulas.

Building dashboards is not new to Visio Services in SharePoint Server 2013, you could build dashboards in Visio Services in SharePoint Server 2010. However, the following features are new with Visio 2013:

- Updated drawing templates with a more Windows 8–centric look, with improved containers and callouts.

- New themes, each offering four unique variants that you can use to fine-tune your drawings. A set of Quick Styles, which is a style and color pairing, is provided for each theme. You can use these to format at the page, shape, or selection level. You can also customize the default themes. You can apply themes by using the Quick Styles split button, which is on the Home tab, in the Shape Styles group.

- The ability to exchange one shape with another by using the Change Shape split button in the Editing group on the Home tab. The new shapes can retain the position, connections, formatting, shape text, and/or shape data of the originals. If another shape in the drawing references the original shape in a formula, Visio restores this reference after the operation and updates the reference to point toward the resulting shape. Hyperlinks, connections, callout associations, shape comments, container membership, and list membership are likewise restored.

> **Note**
> 2-D shapes can only be replaced by other 2-D shapes, and single-dimension shapes by other single-dimension shapes. For example, a connector cannot be replaced with a rectangle.

- Additions to the shape sheet, including a range of visual effects such as 3-D Rotation, that gives height to a two-dimensional shape, and the sketch effect, that gives a drawing a more "penciled-in" look. Other effects include reflection, glow, and gradients.

Visio is a very quick and easy diagramming tool. As the dashboard designer, you should build as much as possible in Visio that is supported by Visio Services, before uploading it into SharePoint and building your dashboards. In this way, your dashboard will not be as complex to build, nor will you need to use as many web part connections or write client-side code, such as JavaScript or HTML.

Within the Visio file, you will define how to obtain the external data (known as *data linking*), display information about the data within shapes, and then apply data graphics to those shapes so that you can visualize the data behind them without having to modify the shape. In the previous release of Visio Services, it was only when you combined data graphics with the shapes that you could enhance the visual behavior of those shapes. In SharePoint 2013, shape behavior has been enhanced so that you can build custom shapes that respond to changes in the shape properties, allowing you to build really powerful diagrams that present the data in a manner that is attractive to the eye.

Data linking

As already stated earlier in this chapter, Visio supports the refresh of data from multiple data sources. You link the external data to the Visio diagrams and connect the individual data records or rows to specific shapes in your diagram. The external data fields are mapped to the shape's properties and as the values of those properties change so the visualization of the shapes changes.

For many diagrams, once they are created, you may only need to delete, add, or move a shape occasionally, but typically the diagram remains the same—it is the data that changes. When you connect data to diagrams, it is all about visualizing that data.

Obtaining external data

Complete the following steps to obtain external data within your Visio file:

1. Open Visio and use a Visio template to create a Visio diagram. You can also base your Visio diagram on other drawing products, such as AutoCAD, by using the Open Backstage View option.

2. Put shapes on the page if the template does not include any shapes.

3. On the Data tab, click Link Data To Shapes in the External Data group, as shown next.

4. On the first page of the Data Selector wizard, select the data connector which matches where the external data is stored, and then click Next, as shown in the following graphic.

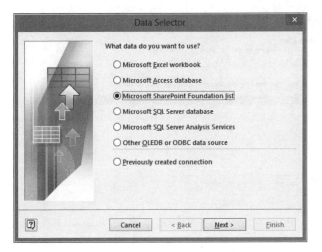

> **Note**
>
> Access data sources are not supported by Visio Services. To use Visio Services to refresh data from an Excel workbook or a previously created connection, then the workbook or the data connection (*.odc) file must be located on the same SharePoint site as the drawing. For an Excel workbook, that site must also have Excel Services enabled since Visio Services uses Excel Services to pull the data from the workbook into the Visio file. The Data Selector wizard will ask you to select a data source from the workbook, such as a range and columns. You will be asked which column in the workbook provides the unique ID so that Visio Services can reconcile the row in the workbook that matches a specific shape in the Visio diagram.
>
> When an Excel workbook is linked to data in a SQL Server database, and the data in the database changes, these data changes do not trigger a data refresh in Visio Services. The data must be stored in the Excel workbook to update data in the Visio diagram. To connect to an External List in Visio, select Microsoft SharePoint Foundation List.

5.   Subsequent pages of the Data Selector wizard will be different depending on the data connection selected. When Microsoft SharePoint Foundation List is selected, on the Select A Site page, in the Site input box, type the site that contains the list that contains the data, and then click Next, as shown next.

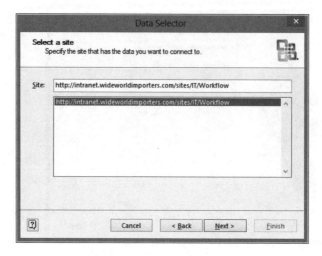

6. On the Select A List page, in the List combo box, click a list and select either Link To A List or Link To A View Of A List and then click Next, as shown next.

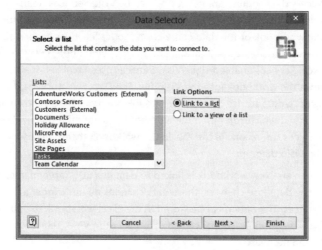

7. Click Finish. Note that you can have multiple data sources in a drawing, and those data sources can be applied to the same shapes or different shapes.

Refreshing external data

Visio Services will then contact that external source and run a query that asks for the data set, which is cached together with the schema of the external data into the Visio diagram. Visio Services then disconnects from the data source and presents the data at the bottom of Visio in the External List Window as a record set. The data in the External List Window is not a live link—for performance reasons, and also to allow you to send the diagram to users who may be offline and do not have access to the data source. You can refresh the data by right-clicking anywhere in the External Data Window and selecting Refresh Data, or using the Refresh Data split button on the Data tab in the External Data group. The Refresh Data dialog box opens, which lists all the data sources linked to your drawing, as shown in Figure 17-8.

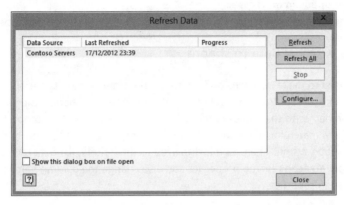

Figure 17-8 Use the Refresh Data dialog box to refresh your linked data or to see the data and time when the data was last refreshed.

You can configure a linked data source by selecting the data source in the Refresh Data dialog box and clicking Configure to display the Configure Refresh dialog box, as shown in Figure 17-9.

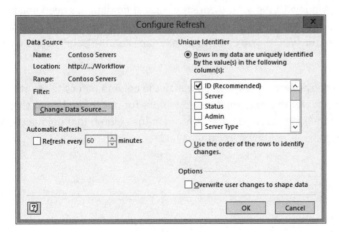

Figure 17-9 Use the Configure Refresh dialog box to change the data source, configure automatic refresh, and set the unique identifier.

> **Note**
>
> The Overwrite User Changes To Shape Data option is not selected by default; therefore, if you want to change the data for a shape property using the Shape Data pane, that value will not be overwritten if you later refresh the data from the external data source. Usually you want your diagrams to change as the external data changes, so it is best to select this option in most cases.

Mapping external data to shapes

Next, you need to make decisions on how to link the external data to the shapes in your Visio diagram. You can drag each data row onto the matching shape. Visio will try to match data column names to the names of the properties in the shape. With properties that Visio does not find a match for, it will create new shape properties. As each row in the data set is linked to a shape, a small chain icon is displayed to the left of each data row in the External Data Window. You can rename properties and also change the column names associated with the shape properties.

Once you drag a row of data from the External Data Window onto a shape, a set of data graphics is created in the Data Graphics gallery and the first data graphic in the gallery is automatically applied to the data-linked shape. You can change this graphic, create a new data graphic, or edit one of the data graphics that Visio built for you in the gallery.

Alternatively, you can use the Automatically Link wizard in Visio to link the data in the External Data Window to the Visio diagram shapes. If no data has been imported by using the Data Selector wizard, the Automatic Link command on the Data tab is unavailable. On the first page of the wizard, you can choose all shapes on the page, as shown in Figure 17-10.

Next, you can decide how to tell Visio to match the column names to the shape properties. The wizard allows you to create multiple conditions for matching data to shapes by clicking And. However, in many cases, you need only map the column that uniquely identifies a data row with a shape, as shown in Figure 17-11.

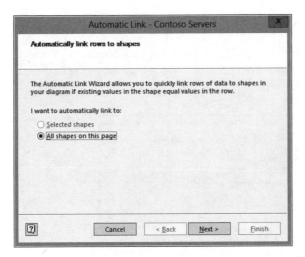

Figure 17-10 Use the Automatic Link wizard to link rows of data to shapes in your diagram quickly.

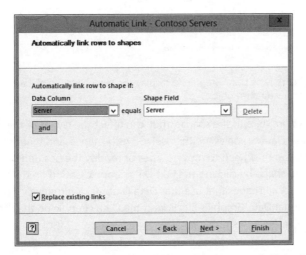

Figure 17-11 Use the second page of the Automatic Link wizard to tell Visio how to match data with shapes by indicating the column name in the data and the property name in the shapes that are equivalent.

The final page summarizes your choices. When you click Finish, Visio will then match the rows in the data set with the shapes in the diagram.

Adding data graphics

Optionally, you can remove, modify, or apply new data graphics to shapes in the Visio diagram by using the Data Graphics menu on the Data tab in the Display Data group, as shown in Figure 17-12.

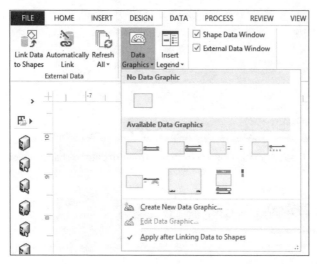

Figure 17-12 Click Create New Data Graphic to display the New Data Graphics dialog box, where you can create new data graphics.

When you apply data graphics to the shapes, they can affect the layout of the shapes in your diagram because Data Graphics are themselves Visio shapes, and therefore, as you apply Data Graphics, you may need to move shapes or modify the position of the Data Graphic relative to the shape by clicking the Edit Data Graphic option on the Data Graphics menu. This would affect all shapes that use that Data Graphic. Alternatively, you modify the position of individual Data Graphics by clicking the Data Graphic on the drawing and moving it as you can with any Visio shape.

Inserting a legend

You can add a legend to your diagram to help users understand the meaning of your Data Graphics. To add a legend to your shape, use the Insert Legend split button on the Data tab. Automatically, all Data Graphics that are associated with shapes on your diagram are added to the legend. The legend is also a Visio shape, so you can change text, format, and position.

When you have completed the diagram, you can save it to a SharePoint document library and render it with Visio Services so that it can be used as a basis for your dashboards.

Web part connections

You can transfer data between drawings displayed in a Visio Web Access Web Part and other web parts. For example, you can create a Web Part page with a library app web part that displays a filtered list of Visio drawing files and connects to a Visio Access Web Part. As users click the double arrow icon to the left of the Visio file name, the diagram in the Visio file is displayed in the Visio Web Access Web Part.

To add a web part connection, place the page in edit mode and then click the down arrow to the right of the web part title, point to Connections, and then click the connection option you want, as shown in Figure 17-13.

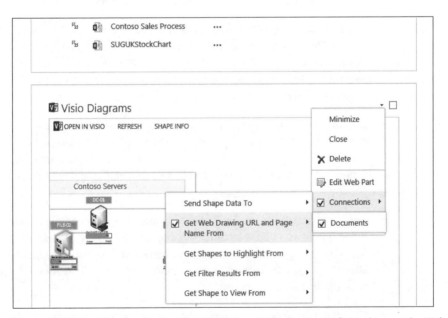

Figure 17-13 In this example, the Visio Web Access Web Part is configured to get the Web Drawing URL and Page Name for files from a library app web part named Documents.

> **Note**
> In this particular example, the browser UI allows you to pick only one property. Additional properties can be passed between the two web parts by using SharePoint Designer to configure the web part connection.

There are five Visio Web Access Web Part connection options:

- **Send Shape Data To** When a shape is selected in the web diagram, data from the shape data fields are sent to the specified web part. By default, the following items are sent:

  - Shape name

  - Shape ID

  - URL of the web drawing

  - Name of the page that the selected shape is on

  To specify additional shape data items to send, open the web part tool pane. Type the labels of the shape data items as a comma-delimited list in the box labeled Expose The Following Shape Data Items To Web Part Connections.

- **Get Web Drawing URL And Page Name From** When the Visio Web Access Web Part gets the URL and page name from the specified web part, it loads the Web Drawing and displays the named page. The URL must point to a Visio file that can be rendered by Visio Services. The page name must be formatted as it appears in the pages list of the Visio diagram.

- **Get Shapes To Highlight From** When the specified web part sends the name of a shape, that shape is highlighted in the diagram. The web part can send a list of names to highlight as a comma-delimited list without spaces (for example, *Shape1, Shape2, and Shape3*), as well as specifying the highlight color as a separate parameter.

- **Get Filter Results From** The connected web part must contain a SharePoint list that is being used as a data source for the diagram. When the SharePoint list is filtered, the diagram highlights the shapes that correspond to visible results in the filtered SharePoint list. The diagram must be connected to the SharePoint list that the connected web part is displaying.

- **Get Shape To View From** When the specified web part sends the name of a shape, the diagram view zooms and centers on that shape. You can also specify the zoom percentage as a separate parameter.

An interactive course offering Visio developer-focused training can be found *at msdn.microsoft.com/en-us/office/fp161532*. Other examples of no-code mashups with Visio Services and web part connections can be found at *blogs.msdn.com/b/visio/archive/2010/02/05/no-code-mashups-with-visio-services-and-web-part-connections.aspx*. This is a blog post using Visio Services 2010; however, the post is still valid for Visio Services 2013.

Customizing Visio Services solutions

There are two ways of customizing the out-of-the-box experience of Visio Services solutions:

- Creating custom data providers using server-side code

- Enhancing the interactivity of your dashboards that include the Visio Web Access Web Part by manipulating the different Visio diagram objects programmatically using browser client-side code

The following two sections detail the options that developers have for writing code against Visio Services.

You can also create client application-level add-ins for Visio. However, such solutions that are data driven within Visio, if they are not using the Data Linking feature, may be data driven when displayed in Visio Services. For a top-level view of the enhancements and additions for developers in Visio 2013, see "What's new for Visio 2013 developers," at *msdn.microsoft.com/ en-us/library/office/ff767103.aspx*, and the blog with the same title, at *blogs.msdn.com/b/ officedevdocs/archive/2012/10/29/what-s-new-for-developers-in-visio-2013.aspx*.

Server-side customizations

Custom data providers can be created to allow data linking to external sources where an out-of-the-box data connector is not provided. In SharePoint 2013, where BCS and External Lists can be used with Visio Services, the need to develop custom data providers should be less than in SharePoint Server 2010. Of course, you cannot build and deploy custom data providers in a multitenant solution, such as Office 365.

Custom data providers require the development of a custom .NET assembly that implements the Visio Services Data Provider Interface, Microsoft.Office.Visio.Server.Addon-DataHandler. Once created, the assembly needs to be deployed into the global assembly cache (GAC) on each server in the SharePoint farm. The custom data provider then needs to be added within the SharePoint Central Administration website as a Visio Graphics Service trusted data provider.

An example of a custom data provider can be found at *blogs.msdn.com/b/chhopkin/ archive/2011/01/24/extendingdata-linking-to-external-lists-in-visio-2010-and-visio-services. aspx*. This example created a BCS custom data provider for SharePoint Server 2010, which is no longer needed in SharePoint 2013; however, the method used to create a custom data provider is still valid in SharePoint 2013.

Visio Services JavaScript mashup APIs

You can enable rich interactivity on your Web Part page by manipulating the different Visio diagram objects programmatically. A typical example of this type of interactivity is to show custom visual overlays when the person viewing the diagram pauses over a particular shape. You should use these APIs when:

- Functionality is needed that cannot be handled by web part connections. Web part connections do not provide the user experience that is expected today.

- Using JavaScript or HTML 5 canvas provides extra visualization to your diagram.

Before your solution can interact programmatically with a Visio drawing on the Web Part page, you must add a Visio Web Access Web Part. This automatically adds the Visio Services JavaScript API to the page. This API is an embedded resource in the dynamic-link library (DLL), not on the file system.

Create a JavaScript (.js) file that contains the code you want to interact with the Visio drawing and save it to the same SharePoint library where the Visio diagrams are stored. Next, add a web part to the page that can be used to link the .js file to the page. Typically, a Content Editor Web Part is used to link the .js file, but you can use the HTML Script command.

The mashup API has a basic hierarchy that consists of four main classes:

- **Vwa.VwaControl** Use this class to control Visio objects at the Visio drawing level, where the drawings are those contained in the file displayed associated with the Visio Web Access Web Part. You can access the web part properties, assign which diagram in the file to display, iterate and display a page in a multipage diagram, manage user interaction with the drawing by adding or removing event handlers, and also show and hide custom HTML error messages. When a diagram is visible, the only page object that can be accessed is the page that is displayed in the web part. The JavaScript cannot iterate through all page objects – there are developer tricks that can be used to load each page and cache the page objects and then iterate through the page objects in the cache.

- **Vwa.Page** Use this class to access a page object within the Visio drawing and not the web page. You can change the zoom center, zoom percentage, change the currently selected shape, and get a reference to the collection of shapes in the currently displayed page.

- **Vwa.ShapeCollection** Use this class to iterate through all the shapes on a page. Some diagrams may take a while to display; therefore, before iterating through all the shapes in a shape collection object, you need to wait for the diagram complete event.

- **Vwa.Shape** Use this class to manage a single shape, such as drawing a colored rectangle around the bounding box of the shape—known as highlighting or overlaying the shape with a particular shape (for example, a pushpin icon placed on top of a map).

> **Note**
>
> You can find a Visio Services Mashup starter project template for Visual Studio 2012 at *blogs.msdn.com/b/chhopkin/archive/2012/08/17/updated-mashup-project-template-for-visual-studio-2010-2012.aspx*. This project template includes some helper JavaScript functions that Chris Hopkins has written over the years for Visio Services in SharePoint Server 2010 and that are still valid with SharePoint 2013. It also covers other coding patterns from the Visio Services product team, such as using a separate JavaScript file and setting up the initial add_load event on the ASP.NET Sys.Application class so that the JavaScript code gets a reference to the drawing (VwaControl) linked to the Visio Web Access Web Part, once the drawing has been rendered.

Validation

Visio 2010 Premium introduced an extension to the Visio Type Library called the Validation API. On the Ribbon Process tab, there are commands in the Validation group that provide access to the visible parts of the Validation API. Users can click Check Diagram to analyze a diagram to verify that the diagram is properly constructed and complies with a set of rules. If there are any errors or issues with various aspects of the diagram, such as layout, connectivity, data values, or formatting, then they are listed in the Issues Window.

In Visio 2013 Professional, templates with built-in rules include Basic Flowchart, Cross-Functional Flowchart, Business Process Modeling Notation (BPMN), Six Sigma, and SharePoint workflows. These templates can be used to create diagram, ensuring diagram consistency against industry-standard diagram rules, or custom rules designed for a particular company or government regulations, such as Sarbanes–Oxley (SOX), BASEL II, and quantity assurance (QA).

Chapter 7 details the use of the SharePoint 2010 and SharePoint 2013 workflow templates and is a good example of templates that enforce rules and show what can be done with Visio 2013. Rules can be added to the built-in rules provided by the templates, and you can also remove the built-in rules using the validation tools.

Information on creating custom validation rules in Visio 2013 can be found at *blogs.msdn .com/b/chhopkin/archive/2013/01/03/creating-custom-validation-rules-in-visio-2013.aspx.*

Summary

This chapter detailed Visio Services and the client application Visio 2013, in both the on-premise SharePoint Enterprise feature set and Office 365. Visio has been around for over 20 years and allows you to produce diagrams easily. When teamed with Visio Services, you can now share diagrams without the need of the client application. By connecting the diagrams with data, the data is cached, and using the refresh functionality, diagrams, data graphics, and shape behavior can be updated. Diagrams can be stored and displayed in one place, and users can view the diagram and know that they are viewing the latest version.

With SharePoint 2013, the diagrams are no longer dependent on Silverlight. They are rendered as a set of HTML and PNG files, which because of the improvements in Visio Services, are rendered as high-quality, full-fidelity images. This opens up the display of Visio diagrams to a larger number of browsers and devices, as well as organizations that did not allow the installation of Silverlight.

Using Visio Services allows you to integrate with the other SharePoint features, which can be enhanced with visualization from Visio. There are many web parts that allow you to present data in many different formats. You can use Visio shapes and data graphics the same way as in Visio 2010; however, Visio 2013 has better support for custom shapes, thereby allowing you to easily build dynamic data-driven dashboards where you can add custom JavaScript to control the experience.

Another benefit of SharePoint 2013 is Visio diagram collaboration. When Visio diagrams are stored in a central location, users in your team can contribute comments to the diagrams all at the same time using either a browser or Visio. When users have Visio, the diagrams can be coauthored by multiple users.

In addition, you can easily connect SharePoint lists to Visio diagrams, allowing you to move away from the tabular representation of data on webpages to a visual display that uses shapes and diagrams.

In the next chapter, you will learn how to discover information with SharePoint 2013 Search and review a high-level overview of the new search architecture for SharePoint.

Discovering information with SharePoint 2013 Search

W ITH the power of the new Microsoft SharePoint 2013 Search, you can search and discover information you need at precisely the time you need it from nearly any modern computing device. In SharePoint 2013, you have a similar level of power and flexibility for finding information that Internet-based search engines deliver—and beyond! The search architecture of SharePoint 2013 now allows you to connect to the data sources you require and present the information you need in a rich, interactive user interface unlike anything SharePoint possessed previously. Moreover, search in SharePoint 2013 is not merely about getting a list of results; now search actually powers many of the core user experiences, such as social, videos, web content management, navigation, and more. In many cases, users are presented with *actionable* items when they perform searches, enabling them to perform pertinent, useful actions to obtain the information they need.

In the first half of this chapter, you will learn the basics of how to find information using the new SharePoint 2013 Search interface. Then, you will receive a high-level overview of the new search architecture in SharePoint. To wrap things up, you will come to understand some of the configuration and customization power that is now available to site owners.

What's new in SharePoint 2013 Search

The short answer to the question "What's new?" is, a lot! There are massive improvements to the entire search engine—all the way from the UI to the relevancy ranking and tuning model to the physical and logical SharePoint farm architecture. One of the most significant changes is that SharePoint 2013 now has a unified search architecture. In SharePoint 2013, the search architecture is updated and includes components that were previously available only when you installed FAST Search Server 2010 in addition to SharePoint 2010. There is no longer a need to do a separate installation of FAST Search Server for a SharePoint farm, as was the case in SharePoint 2010. Now, when you install SharePoint 2013, you get 100 percent of the search features "in the box."

Some of the new capabilities of SharePoint 2013 Search include the following:

- **User experience** A new HTML5-based search results framework that includes enhanced results pages, hover panels, richer previews, and result counts.

- **Search administration** Enhanced search management, including a number of new Windows PowerShell commands.

- **Developer capabilities** New developer capabilities, including REST web service support, a new client-side object model for returning search results to mobile and other client applications, and a new search results framework allowing customization of the UI with HTML, JavaScript, and CSS.

- **eDiscovery** Closer integration with Microsoft Exchange, allowing eDiscovery of email data.

- **Continuous crawling** SharePoint administrators can now enable *continuous crawling* for content. What this means for users is that new content will be added to the search index and thus show up in search results very quickly.

- **Cloud readiness** SharePoint 2013 search was designed with the cloud in mind for those customers who prefer to outsource the hosting of their SharePoint environments.

- **Search refinements** Site owners can define search refiners that are specific to the needs of their site, thus allowing users to refine search results by using tags and metadata terms that are relevant to their business.

- **Result sources** Site administrators now have the ability to manage result (content) sources for their sites.

- **Query rules** Site owners can add query rules to help guide users to the best results by dynamically reformulating the user's search queries and then promoting the most relevant results on the search page by using *promoted results* (formerly known as *best bets*).

Exploring the new search user interface

SharePoint 2013 has a sleek and modern search interface that represents a significant step forward in ease of discovering and acting upon all types of information. Usability of the search results page and related components was one of the primary investment areas during product development. Some of the most prevalent changes include the following:

- An HTML5- and JavaScript-based interface

- In-document library search

- Rich preview panes and interactive hover panels

- Deep refinement of results

- Visual refinements with counts

- A Results tab for videos and reports

- Language selection

> **Note**
> For this next section, it is assumed that you have a SharePoint 2013 environment in place with some documents that have been crawled and added to the search index.

Now we will explore each of these new interface aspects in more depth, starting with the out-of-the-box search experience. When you enter a search site, as shown in the example in Figure 18-1, you will notice that the interface is clean and simple.

Figure 18-1 The Search page is clean and simple.

When you enter a term in the Search box and execute it, you are directed to a search results page. This is where you will begin to get a full appreciation for the major usability enhancements in the new interface. The page that you see should look similar to Figure 18-2. You should immediately notice some changes in the refinement options in the left navigation pane. You will see that you can refine your content in a variety of ways, including file type and author.

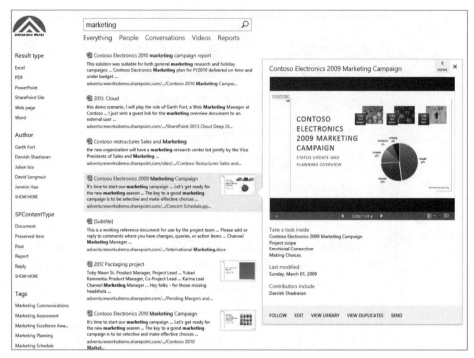

Figure 18-2 The new search results page in SharePoint 2013 includes refiners and rich document previews.

Notice the rich thumbnail previews of the Microsoft PowerPoint files. If you pause over one of the search results, a hover panel appears that shows the file in the Office Web Apps. Depending on the type of file, several options are available for interacting with the document. In Microsoft Word documents, you can scroll or click headings. In PowerPoint, you can toggle between the slides.

Much of the richness of the new SharePoint 2013 search results page is due to the new *display template* technology, which is discussed in more detail in Chapter 19, "Creating a customized SharePoint 2013 search experience."

INSIDE OUT   Display templates

Display templates is a new HTML-based technology in SharePoint 2013 that allows you to customize the look and feel of your search results page easily. You can see which display template your search results page is using by going into page edit mode on your search results page. Once you are in page edit mode, choose Edit Web Part On Your Search Results Web Part in the main zone. The Search Results Web Part has an option to configure the properties of the display template.

From the hover panel, you can easily interact with a search result. You can follow, edit, or view the library in which the file resides. The hover panel also gives you the option to send the file via email to a colleague. If you click one of the links under "Take A Look Inside," you are redirected to a new browser tab in which SharePoint presents that particular location in the document. This requires that Office Web Apps is installed in your environment.

Note

As mentioned in Chapter 6, "Sharing information with SharePoint social networking," Office Web Apps Server is a new server product that delivers browser-based versions of Word, PowerPoint, Microsoft Excel, and Microsoft OneNote. To provide document previews in the hover panel of SharePoint 2013 search results pages, Office Web Apps must be configured and installed correctly in your environment. For details on installing and configuring Office Web Apps, refer to the following Microsoft TechNet article: *technet.microsoft.com/en-us/library/jj219455(v=office.15).aspx*.

The refiners on the left navigation pane give you the ability to limit your results to only the types of results you want. There are many refiners available out of the box, and the good news is that you can now easily select and add refiners to your site under the Schema section of Search Within Site Settings. You will notice each of the refiners has a Show More option under it if there are more options available. The Author refiner, shown in Figure 18-3, has a useful feature in that when you click the Show More option, you are able to type in a user name, and you can refine down to only documents by that person.

Chapter 18

Figure 18-3 With the Author refiner, you are able to refine a list of results by author name.

Another useful feature of using the refinement panel is that you are presented with counts at the bottom of the search results list. In Figure 18-4, the user refined the search results down to include only those with extensions that match "PDF." The set of results went from hundreds down to three with one click.

Figure 18-4 On this search results page, the user refined the search results down to PDF files.

When performing a document search, you probably also noticed near the bottom of the refinement panel the interesting new interactive *Created* refiner, as shown in Figure 18-5. This interactive histogram control allows you to refine your results by either clicking one of the bars on the chart or using the slider to select the date range you are interested in.

Created

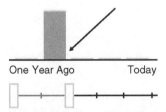

One Year Ago   Today

Earlier than One Month Ago

Figure 18-5 The Created refiner allows you to refine search results further by moving a slider bar.

If you enter page edit mode on the search results page and then edit the Refinement Web Part, the Choose Refiners button appears in the properties for the Search Refinement Web Part. Once you select this, a window appears that allows you to add, modify, or remove refiners, as shown in Figure 18-6.

For a deeper look at adding your own custom refiners, see Chapter 19.

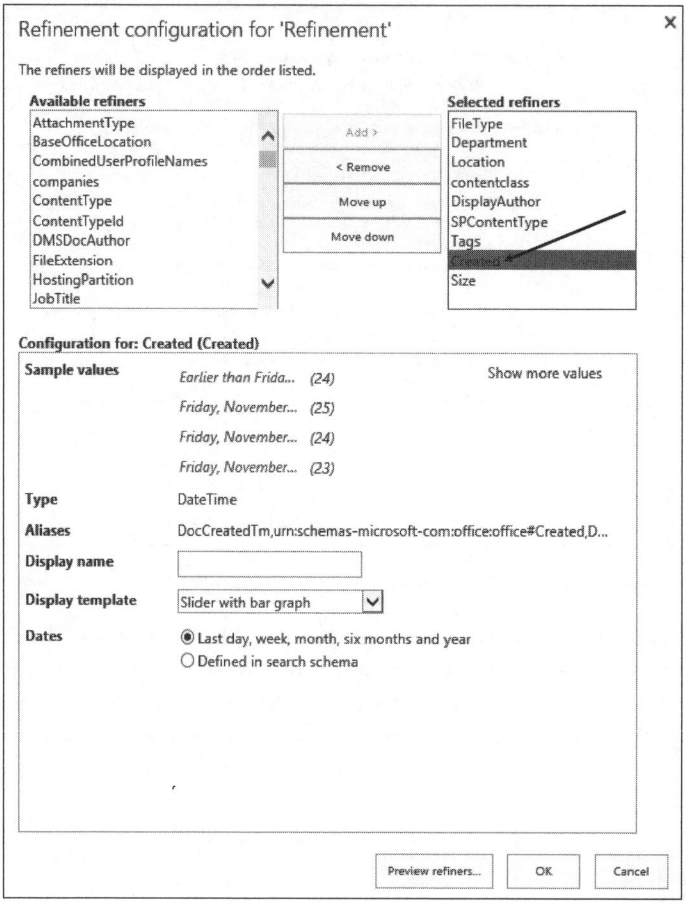

Figure 18-6 On the search refinement configuration page, you can add, modify, or remove refiners.

Searching from an Enterprise Search Center is useful when you want your search to span a large set of enterprise content. However, there are times when you simply need to find a specific item within a document library rather than searching the entire index. SharePoint 2013 has made that task possible by placing a search box inside each library. This capability is called *In Line Search*. In Line Search is scoped to only the items within that particular library.

Figure 18-7 shows a document library with several documents in it, before any search is performed. Figure 18-8 shows the same document library immediately after the user typed "Q3."

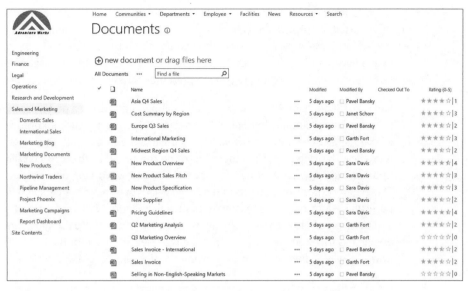

Figure 18-7 The documents library before search shows dozens of documents.

Figure 18-8 The documents library is narrowed after a search is performed.

Discovering social and people information

As you have seen, in SharePoint 2013, document search is greatly improved. Along with that improvement comes a new concept known as *search verticals*. Search verticals were known as *search scopes* in SharePoint 2010. Search verticals are categories of information types that your users may want to search on, such as people, videos, and conversations. Social information, such as discussions in community sites, is now easily searchable, thanks in part to search verticals.

In SharePoint 2010, the option existed to do people searches for those times when you were looking for information related to a person rather than a document (such as skills, projects, location, etc.). That capability still exists in 2013—and is greatly enhanced. To test this yourself, simply do a search for a generic term in your environment (such as marketing, project, etc.). Make sure you select the People tab on the search results page. If you pause over a person's name in the results list, you are presented with a rich set of information in a hover panel, similar to the way you are presented a hover panel for document results.

Similar to SharePoint 2010, the information about a person in a people search result comes from the SharePoint user profile. In SharePoint 2013, one significant improvement is that the people search checks to see which documents a user has authored when determining relevancy. This is important because it is often the case that the user's profile may not be updated regularly, but that person may still be actively working on new content. Therefore, SharePoint surfaces documents in the hover panel that make the person relevant to a particular search query. For example, as shown in Figure 18-9, we searched for "marketing and packaging." Notice that Dorena has items with the term "packaging," and the search engine has therefore determined that she is a relevant result for the query. This is a powerful way to find the right person and the right document at the same time!

Figure 18-9 A people search also returns relevant documents.

Along with people search, SharePoint 2013 now has two additional search verticals: conversations and videos. Each of these verticals allows users to target their search to a category of information. For example, if you know that what you are searching for is related to a conversation on a community site microblog, you can target your search by choosing conversations as the scope, as shown in Figure 18-10.

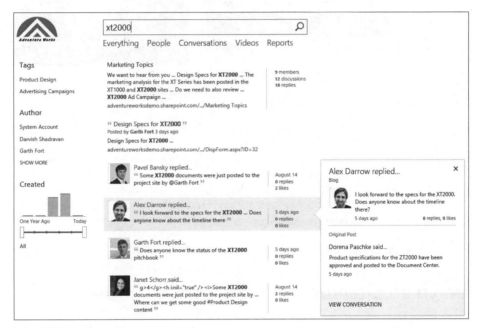

Figure 18-10 On the conversation search results page, I can target my search by choosing conversations as my scope.

The video search works much the same way. The video search is a good example of a *search-based application*. It combines many of the SharePoint Search customization capabilities to deliver a rich video experience. If you have videos in your SharePoint to search, you can select the videos search vertical, as shown in Figure 18-11. Not only will you get video results, but also you can get a hover panel that actually plays the video for you without having to leave the search results page.

Figure 18-11   The video search results page includes playback in the hover panel.

If you want to add your own search vertical with custom data, you can accomplish this with the Site Search Settings page.

> See Chapter 19 for more information about how to add your own search vertical.

Search architecture and site administration

As a site or site-collection owner in SharePoint, you most likely do not need to be concerned with the SharePoint farm administration aspects of search. However, there are now several important and powerful aspects of search administration that can be delegated to site-collection administrators and site owners. This next section will help you become familiar with the new SharePoint 2013 search architecture at a high level. Then you will learn about some of the specific site owner administrative tasks that you can perform to ensure a fruitful search experience for the users of your site.

Overview of the new search architecture

While this book does not cover the farm-level administration of search, it is still important to understand the primary components of a search topology so that when you are discovering information in SharePoint or configuring a site's search settings, you will have a full appreciation and understanding for what is happening behind the scenes.

As was mentioned earlier in this chapter, SharePoint 2013 Search is now consolidated into a single architecture. This is useful from a business standpoint because your organization no longer needs to make the decision of whether to acquire the extra FAST Search option that existed in 2010. All the functionality for Enterprise Search exists in the Standard version of SharePoint 2013.

From a technical point of view, this is also advantageous because now SharePoint administrators no longer need to install a separate farm to support the additional capabilities that a FAST server brought to the table. All of the tools to build, develop, manage, and deliver a rich and modern search experience are available in the Standard edition of SharePoint Server 2013.

As shown in Figure 18-12, SharePoint Search consists of six primary components:

- Crawl

- Content Processing

- Analytics Processing

- Index

- Query Processing

- Search Administration

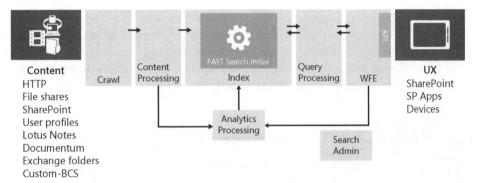

Figure 18-12 Shown in this figure is a high-level view of the SharePoint 2013 search architecture.

Each of these components has a valuable role to play in ensuring that SharePoint Search is able to deliver the information you request rapidly when you perform a search query. When SharePoint administrators configure the SharePoint farm, one of the administrative tasks they undertake is to define result (content) sources. Result sources generally include content that resides in SharePoint, but often include many other sources as well, such as email, databases, business applications, and other websites. After the content sources are defined in SharePoint Central Administration, the SharePoint Search Admin component guides crawling of the content on whatever schedule the administrators have defined.

The Search component responsible for crawling is simply referred to as the *crawl component*. The crawl component does not actually parse through the content; rather, the crawl component hands off the content to the content processing component.

The *content processing* component actually processes the crawled items and their associated metadata. Format handlers within the content processing system actually sift through items such as documents and PDF files to extract the text and other important properties, such as language detection and metadata. Content processing is at the core of the search indexing system in SharePoint. It is the part of the search system where artifacts are actually extracted and prepared for consumption into the search index.

INSIDE OUT PDFS and format handlers

SharePoint 2013 is the first version to contain out-of-the-box support for the crawling and indexing of files that have been saved in the popular Portable Document Format (PDF) format. SharePoint 2013 utilizes a technology called *format handlers* when parsing different types of files in order to make the content inside them searchable. SharePoint now has format handlers for many popular file formats including XML, PDF, HTML, Joint Photographic Experts Group (JPEG), and of course, all of the various Microsoft Office file types (.docx, .pptx, etc.).

Once the content processing function is complete, the *analytics processing* component can begin its work. This includes analyzing the crawled results and making determinations about how the users interact with the content and analyzing usage statistics, such as page views and recommendations. The analytics information is available for reporting in a SharePoint database named Analytics Reporting.

INSIDE OUT Search databases

During a standard SharePoint 2013 installation, four Microsoft SQL Server databases are created that SharePoint uses to store search related information:

- **Admin**   The various search services use the Admin database to store important system information related to search, such as the search configuration, feature data, and topology configurations.

- **Analytics**   The Analytics database stores results of search usage and recommendation analytic data.

- **Crawl**   The Crawl database is used by the crawler/gatherer to manage crawl operations and for storing items, such as history, URL, errors, and so on.

- **Links**   The Links database is the storage location for data about links (click-through statistics, etc.). This information is used by the relevance engine to assist in determining how high any particular document should be ranked.

It is unlikely you will ever need to interact with these databases directly; however, it is useful to understand that SharePoint Search is heavily dependent upon the information stored in these databases.

The next major component in the search architecture is the index. This is a unique part of the SharePoint search architecture in that the index both "eats" and "feeds." The index ingests information provided to it from the previously discussed content processing component and writes that information to the physical index files. The index also provides responses to incoming queries coming from the query processing component, which is discussed next.

INSIDE OUT   Index files: Let's get physical

The search index files are the only part of the search architecture that is stored on the file system; everything else is in one of the aforementioned SQL databases related to search. Your SharePoint administrator has the capability of creating the index files in whatever file location he or she likes by using a Windows PowerShell command called *New-SPEnterpriseSearchIndexComponent*. This command has an optional *RootDirectory* parameter, which allows the administrator to specify the location. Often it makes sense to move the index to a dedicated disk partition for performance optimization and management.

If you want to understand all the details of the SPEnterpriseSearchIndexComponent Windows PowerShell command, there is an article on TechNet located at *technet.microsoft.com/en-us/library/jj219721(office.15).aspx*.

The last major component involved in the handling of user search queries is the *query processing* component. This extremely important last step of the search process is responsible for taking the data from the user's search input, handing it off to the search index, and then returning the results to the user once the query is processed. The query process is much more than merely returning a set of matching results. At the time a query is submitted, the query processing component analyzes the input for linguistics information, checks the input against the thesaurus, spell-checks the input, and performs several other important functions. As part of the query analysis, this component also checks to see if there are any query rules that are applicable to the search.

INSIDE OUT   Query rules

Query rules are a new administrative search tool in SharePoint 2013 that enables a site owner to help guide users to the correct content. A query rule uses conditions and actions (provided by the site owner) to reformulate users' queries dynamically to help them discover the most relevant content based on their queries.

The *administrative* component of SharePoint search focuses primarily on system management of the search components and processes. The administrative component has multiple duties, including:

- Managing search topology on the SharePoint farm

- Coordinating all of the previously mentioned search components

- Running system processes related to search, such as Noderunner.exe and Mssearch.exe

- Reading and writing configuration information to the Search Admin SQL database

INSIDE OUT   Noderunner.exe

On the servers that host the search components, SharePoint will start one Noderunner.exe process for each search component. If you have a single server install for testing purposes, you will see at least five Noderunner.exe processes when you look at Task Manager. One of these processes is managing the crawling, content processing, indexing, analytics processing, and query processing, respectively.

Creating a search center

The first task in providing a rich search experience to users in SharePoint 2013 is to create a special site-collection type called a SharePoint Enterprise Search Center. If you do not already have one created on your SharePoint farm, you will need to create one or work with your SharePoint administrator to put a search site in place. It is a simple process to add a search center; when you create the site collection, simply choose the Enterprise Search Center template, as shown in Figure 18-13.

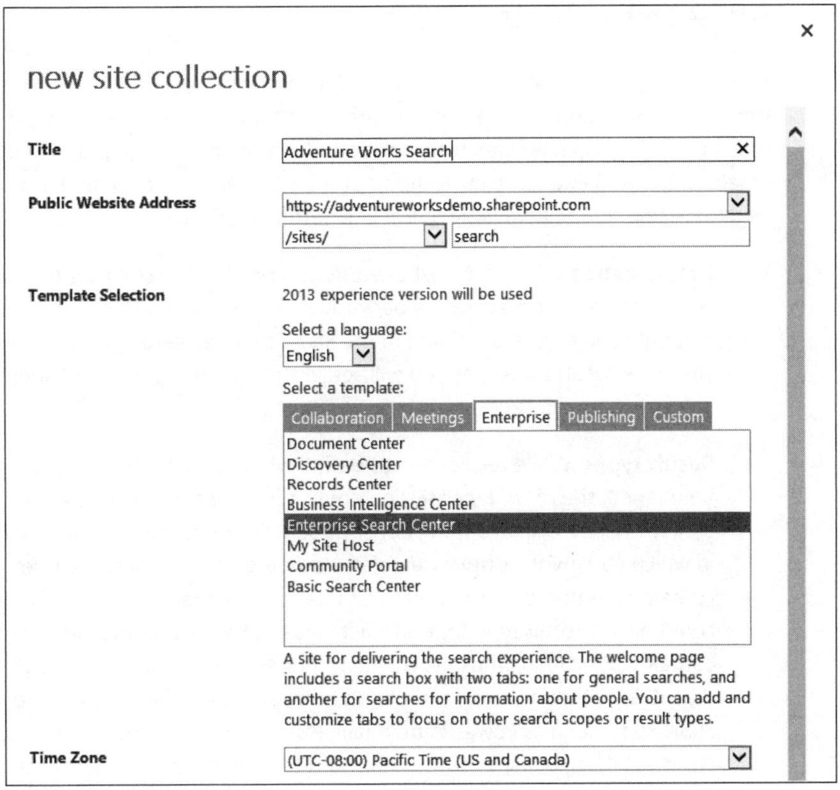

new site collection

Title	Adventure Works Search

Public Website Address

https://adventureworksdemo.sharepoint.com

/sites/   search

Template Selection

2013 experience version will be used

Select a language:

English

Select a template:

| Collaboration | Meetings | Enterprise | Publishing | Custom |

Document Center
Discovery Center
Records Center
Business Intelligence Center
Enterprise Search Center
My Site Host
Community Portal
Basic Search Center

A site for delivering the search experience. The welcome page includes a search box with two tabs: one for general searches, and another for searches for information about people. You can add and customize tabs to focus on other search scopes or result types.

Time Zone

(UTC-08:00) Pacific Time (US and Canada)

Figure 18-13 An Enterprise Search Center template is selected.

Once you have created a search center, you can configure your site collections to use this search center as the users' "fallback" location to search from if they do not find the results they need. If they do not find what they were looking for in your site, they will be prompted to try their search again from that Search Center. This setting is under the Search portion of Site Collection settings, as shown in Figure 18-14. Therefore, by ensuring a properly configured environment, your users will be more likely to find the content they need.

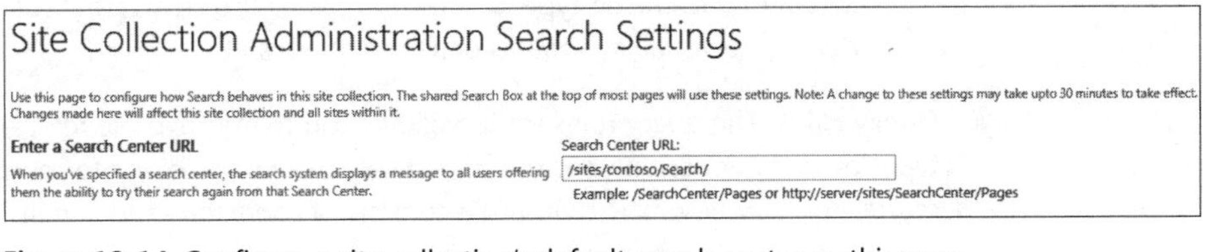

Site Collection Administration Search Settings

Use this page to configure how Search behaves in this site collection. The shared Search Box at the top of most pages will use these settings. Note: A change to these settings may take upto 30 minutes to take effect. Changes made here will affect this site collection and all sites within it.

Enter a Search Center URL

When you've specified a search center, the search system displays a message to all users offering them the ability to try their search again from that Search Center.

Search Center URL:

/sites/contoso/Search/

Example: /SearchCenter/Pages or http://server/sites/SearchCenter/Pages

Figure 18-14 Configure a site collection's default search center on this page.

Site search settings

If you are a SharePoint 2013 site or site-collection owner, you now have a significant amount of power and control over the search settings for your site(s). In this version of SharePoint, the search architecture is designed in such a way that much of the search experience is available to be customized at the site level. A site owner has the following search-specific settings available in the Site Settings for a site:

- **Result sources** This is the list of content repositories a site uses to provide search results when a search query is performed. By default, it will use the same set of content sources as are defined in the Site Collection settings. However, you can add your own result source, as you will see in the upcoming section, "Adding a result source, query rule, and result type to your site."

- **Result types** While result sources define what content repositories are available to be queried, the *result types setting* defines the rules for the way a particular type of content will be displayed on your site's search results page. Result types are the way in which you invoke display templates that are based on a set of rules. The rules can contain common operators that test against managed properties. For example, you could have a result type that only activates if the JobTitle managed property field contains "Executive," thus providing a different experience for the users that have that term in their title. Several common result type definitions are provided with SharePoint, such as PowerPoint, email, PDFs, and so on. You can add custom result types to meet your specific business and technical requirements. Each result type is an aggregation of the following components:

  - **Conditions** Result type conditions define what content sources and specific types of content comprise that result type.

  - **Properties** Properties is an optional part of a result type condition that allows you to restrict the search results to content that has been flagged with the managed property you specified.

  - **Display templates** Display templates are how you define a specific visual layout of each result type. Display templates use HTML, JavaScript, and CSS to define the visual layout and behavior of a result.

- **Query rules** The query rules setting allows you to improve the relevance of certain types of user queries on your site proactively by dynamically reformulating their search at query time. The query rule consists of *conditions* and *actions*. Conditions define when the query rule takes effect, such as when a specific keyword is detected). Conditions also define what content sources the query rule is relevant to when it runs. Actions are what the query rule does with the results. An example would be when someone inputs a query that contains the keywords "customer report," you might return a set of promoted results from a SQL Server Reporting Services content source. We will take a closer look at the details of a query rule in the "Adding a result source, query rule, and result type to your site" section, later in this chapter.

- **Schema** Managed properties (metadata) and crawled properties for the content in your site are configured on the schema page. If you add a custom content type that has some number of data fields (columns), you can work with those columns under the Schema settings. The managed properties will be useful when configuring query rules and custom display templates.

- **Search settings** Configure high-level behavior of your site's search settings here. There is an option that allows you to re-direct searches on your site to an appropriate Enterprise Search Center. You also create custom search navigation links for your site on the Search Settings page.

- **Searchable columns** Here, you have the option to choose any columns of data on your site that you want excluded from the search index.

- **Search and offline availability** If you want your entire site to be excluded from SharePoint search, this is where you make that choice. By default, sites are enabled for display in search results. A similar configuration option exists on this page for allowing users to take files and content from your site offline with them. If you know that you want to disable offline use for everything in your site, you have the option of disabling it on this page.

- **Configuration import and export** If you want to import a search configuration and all its settings from another site where the work has already been done, use the Import option. Likewise, if you need to transport your site's search settings to another site, choose Export.

Adding a result source, query rule, and result type to your site

To help pull together some of the concepts that were discussed in the previous section, we will do a brief walk-through of a real-world use case. In this scenario, our marketing department has requested that whenever someone does a search query for terms such as "marketing news" or "marketing PR," the search results page somehow ensures that documents that are tagged as press releases will be shown as promoted results.

The solution consists of four primary components:

- A press release SharePoint content type.

- A press release result source that narrows the scope of content down to items that match up with the press release content type.

- A press release query rule that will fire whenever a user searches for one of the keywords the marketing team has identified (PR, news, etc.). This query rule helps identify relevant content and promote it to the top of the search results page as a promoted result.

- A press release result type that matches up results from the Press Results content source with a custom display panel that displays extra metadata tags for this specific type of content.

Together, those four items give us the necessary components to achieve the business goal the marketing department defined for us.

The first piece we needed to have in place is a standard SharePoint content type that the marketing team uses when creating press releases. You can see our simple content type in Figure 18-15. It provides all the benefits of SharePoint content types as discussed earlier in the book.

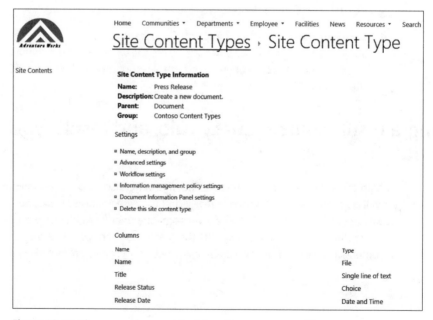

Figure 18-15 The press release content type has many properties.

Once you have the content type in place, you will need to create a result source in your Site Settings. As shown in Figure 18-16, this will help SharePoint identify content that matches our press release content type. The query transformation we use for this content source is simple: {searchTerms} ContentType:Press Release will return results that match the appropriate content type.

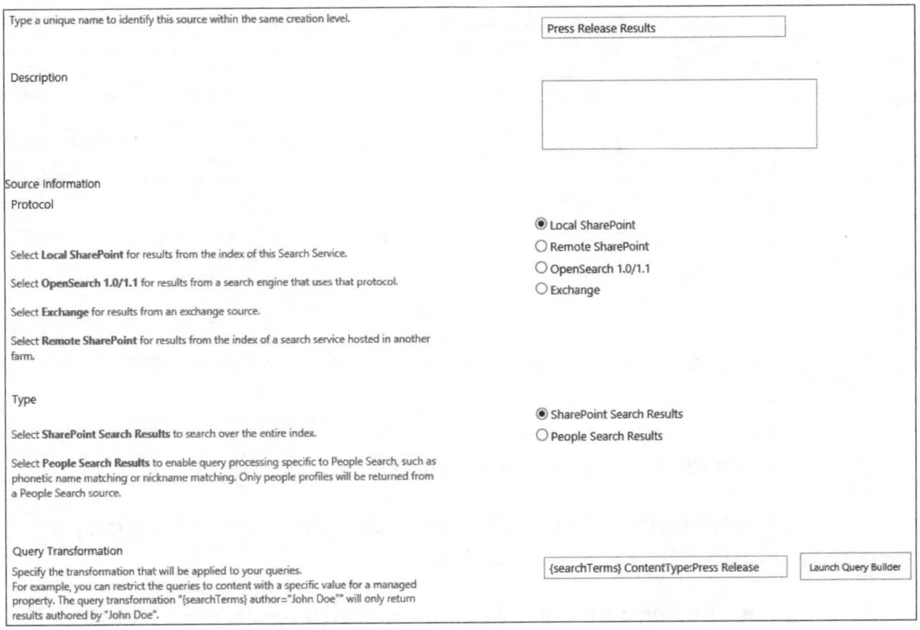

Type a unique name to identify this source within the same creation level.

    Press Release Results

Description

Source Information
Protocol

    ● Local SharePoint
    ○ Remote SharePoint
    ○ OpenSearch 1.0/1.1
    ○ Exchange

Select **Local SharePoint** for results from the index of this Search Service.

Select **OpenSearch 1.0/1.1** for results from a search engine that uses that protocol.

Select **Exchange** for results from an exchange source.

Select **Remote SharePoint** for results from the index of a search service hosted in another farm.

Type

    ● SharePoint Search Results
    ○ People Search Results

Select **SharePoint Search Results** to search over the entire index.

Select **People Search Results** to enable query processing specific to People Search, such as phonetic name matching or nickname matching. Only people profiles will be returned from a People Search source.

Query Transformation
Specify the transformation that will be applied to your queries.
For example, you can restrict the queries to content with a specific value for a managed property. The query transformation "{searchTerms} author="John Doe"" will only return results authored by "John Doe".

    {searchTerms} ContentType:Press Release   Launch Query Builder

Figure 18-16 The values of the press release result source are displayed on this screen shot.

The third component is the query rule. The query rule's primary task is to identify queries that include our keywords and then take appropriate actions. In cases where queries match the query rules, our query rule's main mission is to promote press release results on our search results page. On the query rules page in Site Settings, we added a query rule, as shown in Figure 18-17. In this figure, we are looking at the top portion of the Edit Query Rule page, where the query conditions are identified. In this case, we are looking for text matches of specific terms (such as "PR," "news," "press," and "release").

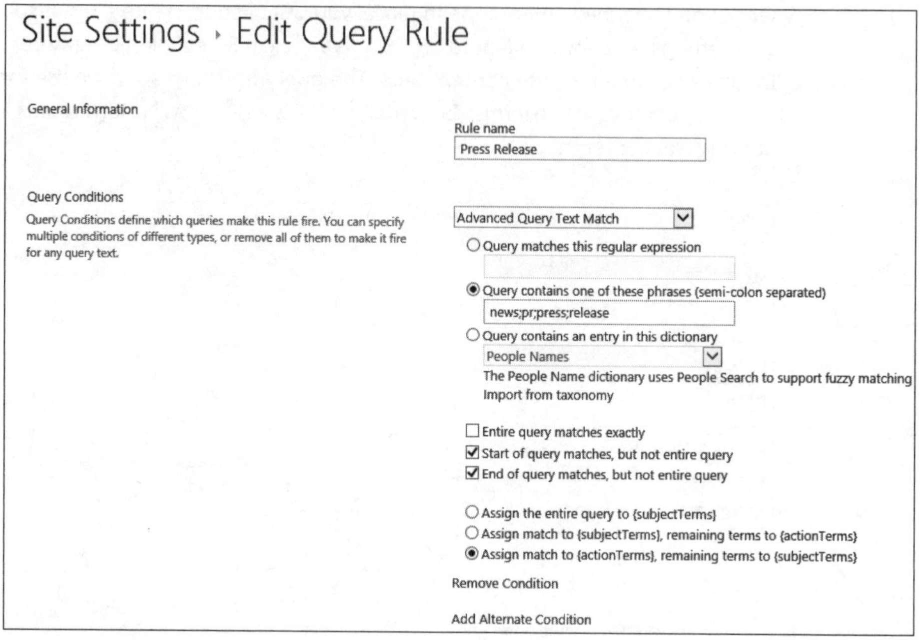

Site Settings ‚ Edit Query Rule

General Information

Rule name

Press Release

Query Conditions

Query Conditions define which queries make this rule fire. You can specify multiple conditions of different types, or remove all of them to make it fire for any query text.

Advanced Query Text Match ▾

○ Query matches this regular expression

◉ Query contains one of these phrases (semi-colon separated)

news;pr;press;release

○ Query contains an entry in this dictionary

People Names ▾

The People Name dictionary uses People Search to support fuzzy matching
Import from taxonomy

☐ Entire query matches exactly
☑ Start of query matches, but not entire query
☑ End of query matches, but not entire query

○ Assign the entire query to {subjectTerms}
○ Assign match to {subjectTerms}, remaining terms to {actionTerms}
◉ Assign match to {actionTerms}, remaining terms to {subjectTerms}

Remove Condition

Add Alternate Condition

Figure 18-17 You can add or edit query rules in Site Settings.

The other part of the query rule that we are concerned with is setting an action. In our example, the actions we provide are:

- **Adding a title to the top of the search results page that says "Marketing Press Releases!!!"** This is added to the results page only when the query rule is actually triggered by a user query.

- **Adding a result block to the search results page** This provides a visual indicator to the user that the results contained in the block are probably the most relevant results.

Figure 18-18 shows the action portion of the query rule. Note the edit link on the result block. That is where you must go to configure the details of the result block.

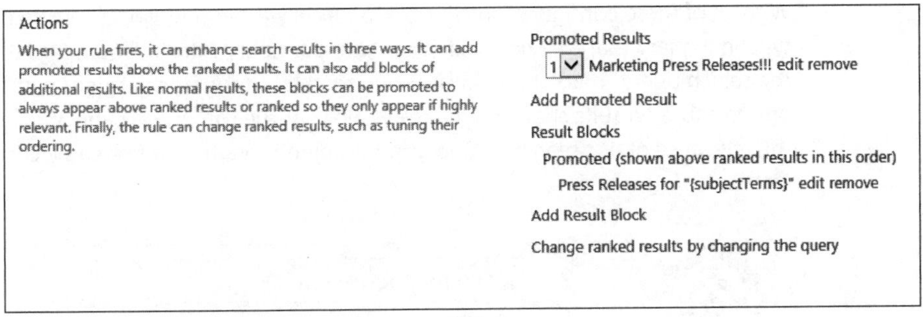

Actions

When your rule fires, it can enhance search results in three ways. It can add promoted results above the ranked results. It can also add blocks of additional results. Like normal results, these blocks can be promoted to always appear above ranked results or ranked so they only appear if highly relevant. Finally, the rule can change ranked results, such as tuning their ordering.

Promoted Results

1 ☑ Marketing Press Releases!!! edit remove

Add Promoted Result

Result Blocks

Promoted (shown above ranked results in this order)

Press Releases for "{subjectTerms}" edit remove

Add Result Block

Change ranked results by changing the query

Figure 18-18 You can add actions for your query rules.

The last major piece of the puzzle is the result type. The primary goal of our result type is to ensure that when search results of a press release result type are put on a search results page, they have a unique display panel that we created just for press releases. As you can see in Figure 18-19, items of press release result type will use a special display template named Word Item - Custom_PR.

For more information about custom display templates, see Chapter 19.

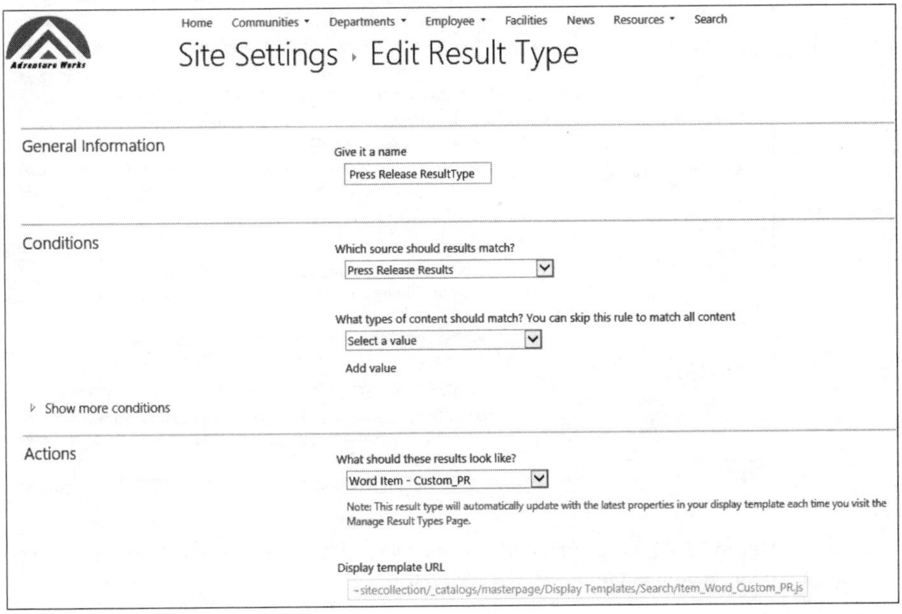

Home   Communities ▾   Departments ▾   Employee ▾   Facilities   News   Resources ▾   Search

Adventure Works

Site Settings › Edit Result Type

General Information

Give it a name

Press Release ResultType

Conditions

Which source should results match?

Press Release Results ▾

What types of content should match? You can skip this rule to match all content

Select a value ▾

Add value

▷ Show more conditions

Actions

What should these results look like?

Word Item - Custom_PR ▾

Note: This result type will automatically update with the latest properties in your display template each time you visit the Manage Result Types Page.

Display template URL

~sitecollection/_catalogs/masterpage/Display Templates/Search/Item_Word_Custom_PR.js

Figure 18-19 When you edit a query rule, you can change the display template under the Actions area.

With all of these configuration changes in place, we can now go to your search box and type in a query that we know will instantiate our query rule. In Figure 18-20, we entered the search query "marketing news," which therefore triggers our query rule. Notice how our promoted results show up in a result block at the top of the page. We have tuned the relevancy of our search engine using nothing more than a few easily configurable site settings!

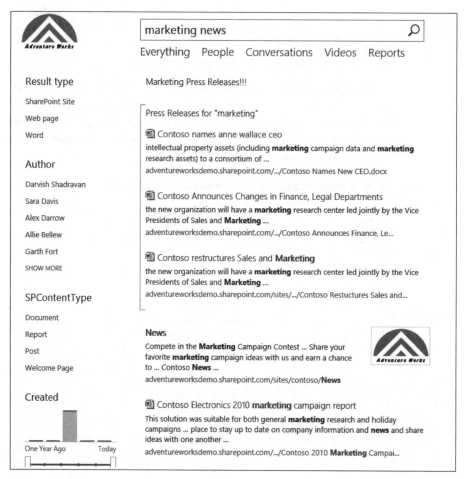

Figure 18-20 When you add a query rule result block, the search results page provides intelligent recommendations to the search user.

When a user pauses over one of the promoted results, the hover panel will use the custom display template that we defined in the result type. Notice that, in Figure 18-21, the hover panel looks similar to the normal document panel except that we have added some extra content such as the Document ID, total views, and so on.

We cover creating custom display panels in depth in Chapter 19.

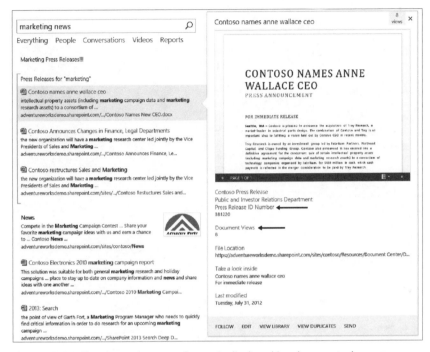

Figure 18-21 The press release result type is displayed in a hover panel.

Summary

As the über-logical Mr. Spock once said, "Insufficient facts always invite danger." Fortunately, you have seen in this chapter that SharePoint 2013 Search is a powerful way to discover information—and to ensure that you have *sufficient facts* to achieve your tasks! Mr. Spock would be so proud.

Through a new relevancy engine, the search system in SharePoint 2013 understands what data a user needs more clearly than ever before. The search engine learns over time with usage and customizes results to a person's unique needs. SharePoint 2013 search has a significantly updated UI, a new unified server architecture, and deep integration with many aspects of SharePoint, including social, reports, people, videos, and so on.

Site owners in SharePoint 2013 have more power than ever before to create a powerful search experience using tools such as query rules, display templates, and result types. Developers can build search-driven applications using powerful new options, such as REST web services. And most important, business users can easily discover and organize essential information, refine the results, and then take appropriate actions.

CHAPTER 19

Creating a customized SharePoint 2013 search experience

Microsoft SharePoint 2013 provides more opportunity than ever before for building custom search experiences that deliver the right information to your search users. Search in SharePoint 2013 graduates to more than just lists of results; Search becomes a practical and powerful data access layer. With several new methods of using Search to access and aggregate information, the search experiences that you can provide your users are undeniably compelling when done properly. Many of the techniques require no code, and in many cases, it is not terribly difficult even when code is required.

In the previous chapter, we introduced some search concepts at a high level. In this chapter, we focus on the most important topics you will need to create your own unique search-based solutions. In the first part of the chapter, we take a deeper look at the primary Search UI building block technologies in SharePoint 2013:

- Keyword Query Language (KQL)

- Search web parts

- Result sources

- Query rules

- Result types

- Display templates

After a deeper look at each of these components, we will walk through a simple search customization that uses each of the items we discussed. After working through this chapter, you should have all the basic knowledge necessary to begin building your own SharePoint 2013 Search solutions.

INSIDE OUT   Testing your search customizations

In scenarios where you need to test your search customization in a question-and-answer or development environment prior to production, you can now use the new Configuration Import and Export feature in SharePoint 2013 Site Settings (in the Search section). The export option sends query rules, result sources, managed properties, and other information to a file named SearchConfiguration.xml. Thus, you are able to get all your settings just the way you want them in a development environment and export them. Then you can use the Import option into a site or site collection in your production environment. In addition, if you are building a search-based app, you can use your export package as part of the app package so that when it is installed in another environment, all the configuration information is installed with the app.

> Search
> Result Sources
> Result Types
> Query Rules
> Schema
> Search Settings
> Searchable columns
> Search and offline availability
> Configuration Import
> Configuration Export

Using the Keyword Query Language (KQL)

Sometimes the best way to provide a "custom" search to users is to arm them with extra knowledge on how they can optimize their search queries. Perhaps the best route for user education is providing them some basic instruction on how to use KQL. When users type a query into a SharePoint Search Box Web Part page, whether they realize it or not, they are taking advantage of KQL.

The following list includes some examples of how you might use KQL to perform better searches.

A full KQL reference is available at *http://msdn.microsoft.com/en-us/library/ee558911.aspx*.

- You want to find all documents that have terms such as "market," "marketing," "markets," and/or the words "distribution," "distributor," and so on. You can use wildcard search to assist in this type of search rather than having to specify an exact match for each of the possible variations of the word. You would enter the following search syntax into the Search Box: **market* dist***, as shown next.

- You want to find only items that match the phrase, "market distribution." To eliminate all other potential matches, enclose the search terms in parentheses. The only results that will be returned are those that have the exact words (in order) in the phrase.

- You want to limit the previous search to now include only items that are authored by Sara Davis. To do this, you can use a property restriction. So, the search syntax you put in the Search box is **"market distribution" author:"Sara Davis."** Notice that there can be no white space between the property name (author), the property operator (:), and the property value (Sara Davis).

- Another example of a property restriction would be to limit your search by the title of the item. You only want to return items that have the exact words marketing campaign in the title. Therefore, your search syntax would be *title:*"**marketing campaign,**" as shown next.

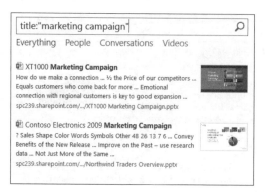

There are many useful properties you can use in your KQL; these are merely a few simple examples. See the link mentioned earlier for even more examples of how to use KQL in your search queries.

INSIDE OUT   Using KQL for search applications

While KQL is simple and accessible for users, it is also an extremely powerful tool for creating custom search applications without code. With some creative use of KQL, you can provide links on team sites that are search URLs with a KQL parameter. For example, the following URL embedded in a link, as shown here, would return all calendar events: *https://adventureworks.sharepoint.com/search/Pages/results. aspx?k=ContentClass%3DSTS_ListItem_Events*.

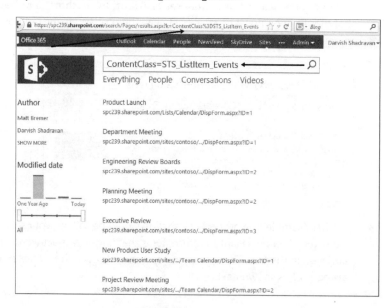

Using Search web parts

The search results page in SharePoint is comprised of four primary web parts:

- Refinement

- Search Box

- Search Navigation

- Search Results

Most of these web parts have properties that can be used to customize the search experience in the browser easily. We will take advantage of the configurable properties of the Search web parts in the walkthrough later in this chapter.

> **Note**
>
> This chapter focuses primarily on the web parts in the search results pages typically found on a SharePoint Search Center. The Content Search Web Part is used most often in publishing scenarios; therefore, it is discussed in Chapter 12, "Designing web content management sites."

Refinement Web Part

As mentioned in the previous chapter, SharePoint 2013 search results pages implement the concept of *verticals* as part of the search navigation. Verticals allow users to target their searches at content, people, videos, and so forth. The Refinement Web Part appears on all the out-of-the-box search vertical pages (such as Results.aspx, Peopleresults.aspx, Conversationresults.aspx, and Videoresults.aspx). The Refinement Web Part helps users narrow search results to a more precise set of content by selecting categories they care about.

Each of the search verticals has its own unique refinement properties that make sense for that context (such as author refiner for documents and expertise refiner for people). When you customize a search results page, you can change properties in the Refinement Web Part and configure the following items:

- Identify a different Search Results web part from which to filter search results.

- Select all the refiners to show in the web part.

- Specify the display template that is applied to the web part if you want to change the way refiners look or how they are ordered.

INSIDE OUT   Managed properties and the Refinement Web Part

The SharePoint 2013 Search schema contains attributes of managed properties and a mapping between crawled properties and managed properties. A crawled property is content and metadata that is extracted from an item (such as a spreadsheet) during an incremental or full crawl. To include the content and metadata of crawled properties in the search index, you simply map crawled properties to managed properties. The managed properties can have many different types of attributes. And it is these attributes that determine how your content is will be shown in search results.

If the managed property you want to add as a refiner is not available in your list of refiners, you first need to ensure that they are configured as a Refined property. This is performed in the Managed Properties area of Search Settings for your site collection, as shown here. (For a complete list of out-of-the-box managed properties, see *http://technet.microsoft.com/en-us/library/jj219630(v=office.15)*.)

Site Collection Administration - Managed Properties

Managed Properties | Crawled Properties | Categories

Use this page to view, create, or modify managed properties and map crawled properties to managed properties. Crawled properties are automatically extracted from crawled content. You can use managed properties to restrict search results, and present the content of the properties in search results. Changes to properties will take effect after the next full crawl. Note that the settings that you can adjust depend on your current authorization level.

Filter

Managed property | attachment

Total Count = 3

Property Name	Type	Multi	Query	Search	Retrieve	Refine	Sort	Safe	Mapped Crawled Properties	Aliases
AttachmentDescription	Text	-	-	-	Retrieve	-		Safe	ows_MediaLinkDescription	
AttachmentType	Integer	-	Query	-	Retrieve	Refine	-	Safe	ows_MediaLinkType	
AttachmentURI	Text	-	-	-	Retrieve	-	-	Safe	ows_MediaLinkURI	

Search Box Web Part

The Search Box Web Part is obviously important, considering that it is the initial point of interaction a user has when typing in a query on a search page. Configuration options for the Search Box Web Part are relatively straightforward. As shown in Figure 19-1, the primary configuration change you might make in the Search Box Web Part settings is to alter the destination of where search results are sent. You have the option to send them to a web part on the same page or to another search results page in cases where you are providing customized search experiences. The Search Box properties also allow you to control whether Query Suggestions are enabled. They are turned on by default.

Figure 19-1 You can alter the destination of where search results are sent in the Search Box Web Part settings window.

Search Navigation Web Part

The Search Navigation Web Part presents the user with the various search verticals configured for the site. Out of the box, the verticals you will see are *Everything*, *People*, *Conversations*, and *Videos*. The primary purpose of this web part is to provide the user interface for search verticals, but the Search Navigation Web Part itself does not have many configurable properties; rather, it directs you to configure the navigation links on the Search Settings page of your site.

As shown in Figure 19-2, on the Search Settings page, you have the option to add your own navigation URLs, which will then appear on the Search Navigation Web Part. Each of the navigation links references a search results page that can be configured with web parts and properties that deliver an experience that is most appropriate for the type of content being searched for. For example, if you added an *Images* search vertical, your navigation link could direct the user to a search results page that has refiners and display templates that make the most sense for picture search results.

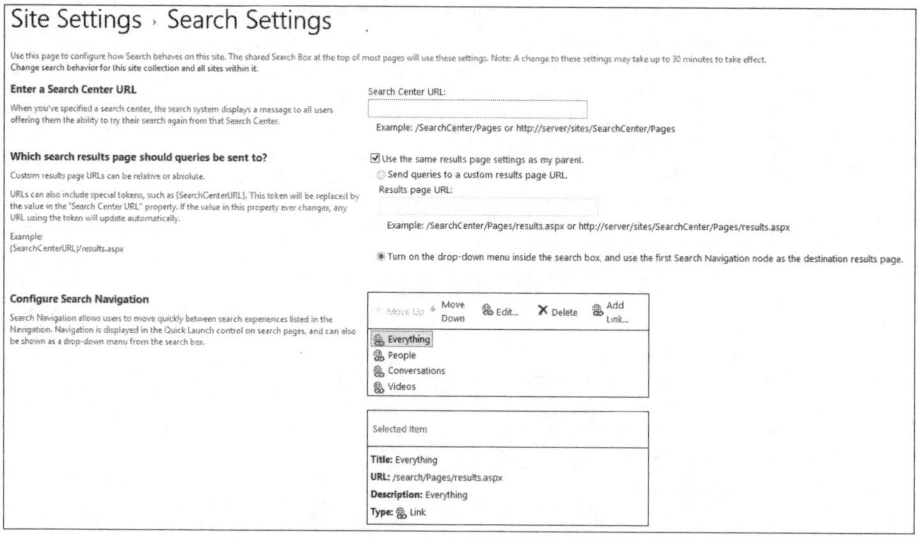

Figure 19-2 You can change properties of the Search Navigation Web Part on your site's Search Settings page.

Search Results Web Part

At its most basic level, the Search Results Web Part provides the UI for displaying results to a user. However, the Search Results Web Part has some important configurable properties that can help provide a very rich and targeted set of results to a person performing a search. As shown in Figure 19-3, the most significant properties on the Search Results Web Part are the Change Query option under Search Criteria and the ability to change the Display Templates used for search results in the Display Templates section. These Search Results Web Part properties allow you to control both the target content sources to which queries are directed and the manner in which the results are displayed.

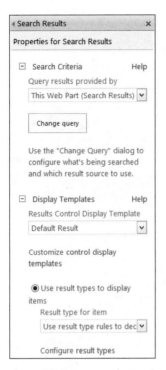

Figure 19-3 You can change Search Results Web Part properties in the Search Results properties window.

Understanding result sources

As discussed in the previous chapter, result sources are the searchable content repositories available in SharePoint 2013. You can see in Figure 19-4 that SharePoint 2013 has 16 result sources out of the box. The default is set as Local SharePoint Results. You can change the default result source for your search pages if you want. If you need to add a custom result source, you may do so at the farm, site-collection, or site level, depending upon how broadly you plan to use the custom result source.

Provided by SharePoint (16)

Conversations

Documents

Items matching a content type

Items matching a tag

Items related to current user

Items with same keyword as this item

Local People Results

Local Reports And Data Results

Local SharePoint Results

Local Video Results

Pages

Pictures

Popular

Recently changed items

Recommended Items

Wiki

Figure 19-4 16 result sources are provided out of the box.

Understanding query rules

In the previous chapter, you were introduced to the basic capabilities of query rules, and you saw an example of a simple one in action. To reiterate, query rules enable a site or site-collection owner to add *conditions,* whereby search results are dynamically reformulated in order to more closely match the intent of the search user and then provide an appropriate *action*. For example, if a user performs a search on a keyword phrase such as "marketing videos," you might give them a promoted result block with items that come from a video repository (result source). In addition, you could then present related actions that the user can perform on the videos.

Another way to think about it is that query rules enable you to "conditionally control" the search experience that a user will have in any given search vertical. Used correctly, query rules substantially increase the likelihood of providing a user with the most relevant information possible.

When you create a new query rule, the action that you configure will create a promoted result, alter the ranked results, or both. *Promoted results* put specific result items that you have selected at the top of the results list in a banner. These were formerly known as "Best Bets" in SharePoint 2010. You can add as many promoted results as you need for any given query rule.

Similar to a promoted result is a result block. A *result block* is essentially the same as a promoted result, but rather than just one promoted item, it is a group of results that match your conditions (such as all items that are on sale today). As with a promoted result, items matching the result block can be configured to return results to the user at the top of the search results page.

Query rules also have the power to dynamically alter the ranked results themselves. Without a query rule in place, the search engine ranking methods of SharePoint will determine what items are most relevant to return to a user's query. But if you have scenarios where you would like to alter the ranked results, you can do that with a *query transform* inside your query rule. An example might be if users search for marketing decks, you might know that they are looking for Microsoft PowerPoint files. So your query rule can have an action that specifies a user who searches for that particular term will get .pptx file type results returned before any other matches. The ability to adjust how ranked results will be returned to the user is a nice step forward in no-code search-relevance tuning in 2013.

Using Query Builder and query transforms

Occasionally, you will want to change a user's query in order to provide the most relevant results. For example, suppose that you create a custom search vertical for HR forms. When someone types a query in the HR forms vertical search page, you can change the query so that it returns only results that are HR forms. In order to give the user's query this sort of nudge in the proper direction, you use the Query Builder to configure a *query transform*.

A query transform can be used to replace properties of a query, such as the result source, or the order that items will be displayed in search results. A query transform replaces the text of the query by using a query template that you can configure. The query template has the text that will replace the user's query, and the template can contain query variables to make it even more flexible. Figure 19-5 shows a simple example of using Query Builder within a result source. The purpose of this transform is simply to take the user's search terms and narrow the results to only items where that user is the author.

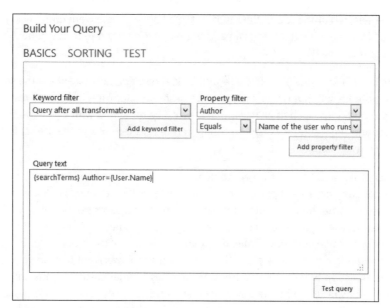

Figure 19-5 You can use Query Builder to narrow search results.

Query transforms can be created in three primary locations:

- **In the result source that the query uses to get its results** Of all the places that you can use query transforms, results sources are the one you should choose if you want to be sure that it takes precedence over any other possible transforms on the content. When you configure a transform in a result source, the transform changes will not be overridden because the result source performs the last transform on the query.

- **The Search Results Web Part** You would typically configure a transform in a web part only when you do not need to make the same changes to queries running beyond the scope of the web part on that page.

- **In a query rule** Here, you can specify that certain actions will be performed only if certain conditions are fulfilled. Two of the query rule actions use a transform to dynamically change the query:

  - *Add A Result Block* on the search results page.

  - *Change The Ranked Results.* This action modifies the query that the user typed, thereby reranking the results at the time the search is performed.

Defining custom result types

Recall from the previous chapter that result types define rules for the way a particular type of content will be displayed in your site's search results page. For example, when you perform a search, the way a Microsoft Excel result type is displayed is different than a Microsoft OneNote result.

Each of the result types are bound to a result source and then configured to match certain types of content with that source. A set of common SharePoint result types are available when you install SharePoint. You can see the list of the out-of-the-box result types in your Search Site settings. Once again, each result type is connected to its own display template. This allows each result type to have a unique appearance and surface properties that are most relevant to a specific kind of document.

In addition to the default result types, you can define custom result types that are relevant to your business. A result type can then be associated with a custom display template, enabling you to surface specific kinds of results that are significant for users. An example might be that when your users search for HR forms, you would like the search results to display some extra fields of metadata information from your forms, such as the human resources contact assigned to the employee performing the search. To accomplish this, you can create a custom result type for human resource result items, as illustrated in Figure 19-6.

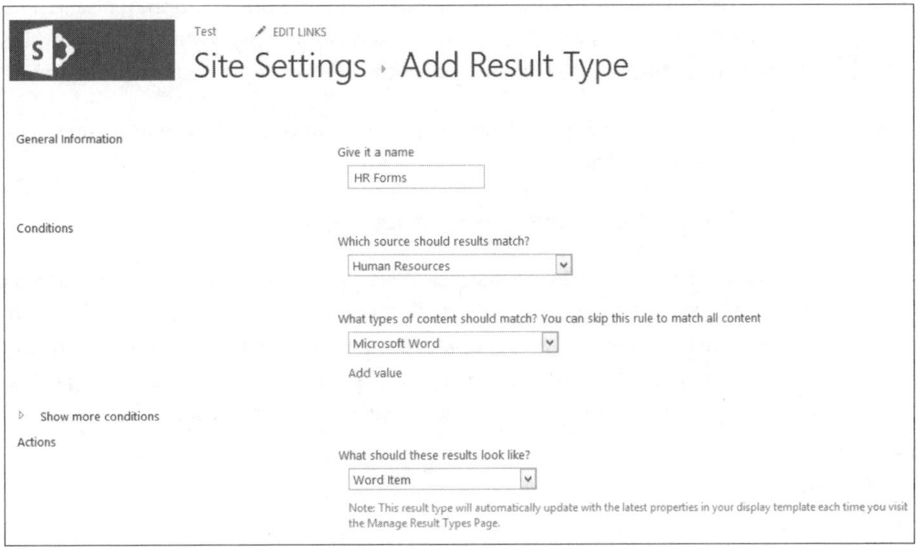

Figure 19-6 An example of a custom human resources result type.

As a real-world example, let us pretend that in your business, HR forms are Microsoft Word documents with a custom property, IsHRform, along with additional metadata: HRContact, EmployeeHireDate, and EmployeeNumber. To create a human resources result type, you would first copy the standard Word result type and add a condition whereby results that match should have the custom property IsHRform equal to True.

Next, you need to build a custom display template for HR forms that surfaces the managed property HRContact and any of the other pieces of metadata you want in your template. The process of customizing display templates is not difficult. The work that you will perform is done in HTML and JavaScript. By far, the best way to do this is to create a new template by copying an existing template. Then add your additional managed properties to the template that is relevant for the respective result type.

Once you complete the result type and template, when a user performs a search, each result is evaluated against the rule for HR results. If the query matches, results are displayed using the HR display template that you created. If the query does not match, it is simply matched to one of the out-of-the-box result types and corresponding template. In the walkthrough later in this chapter, you will have a chance to see some of this in action.

Using display templates

In previous versions of SharePoint, the primary method of customizing search results pages was by adding XSLT to the Search Results Web Part. As mentioned in the previous chapter, the technology for controlling the rendering and presentation of a search result item in SharePoint 2013 is with the HTML5-based Display Template functionality. Display templates provide a much more elegant approach to delivering a customized search result UI.

As you can see in Figure 19-7, one place to view your display templates is in the Design Manager of your Search site.

For full coverage of Design Manager, see Chapter 12.

Display templates provide many useful and flexible options that you can adjust in the HTML and JavaScript code. One of the easiest and most advantageous options is the ability to retrieve managed properties that you have identified in your HTML code and then display them in a search results item. Your users will find great value in having extra bits of highly relevant information displayed along with their search results.

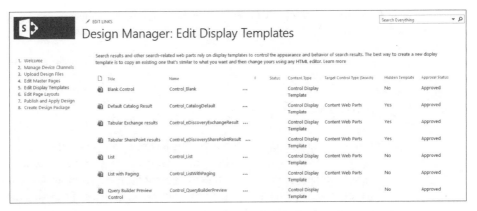

Figure 19-7 You can view your display template settings in Design Manager.

Creating a customized search experience

In this section, we will now put all the components we have discussed thus far together to create a simple, customized search solution. There are limitless examples of when you might want to create a custom search solution. For this exercise, we'll pick a relatively common scenario: users are looking for information contained in product Portable Document Format (PDF) files that are in a corporate repository. Our goal is to make it even easier for them to find the right content.

You might be asking yourself, "That seems like something you could just use standard out-of-the-box SharePoint Search for, right?" Well, yes, that is true, but what we want to illustrate in this section is how to create an enhanced search experience that goes beyond the out-of-the-box interface. Even more important, we want to understand how to customize a search environment so that the probability of users finding the right content on the first search attempt is increased.

The process we use to accomplish our goal consists of six primary steps, each of which requires a number of tasks. In the following pages, we illustrate the steps to take so that you can replicate a similar solution in your environment. The six primary steps are:

1. Create a result source that points at the library holding our PDF files.

2. Generate a search page for the new *Product PDF* vertical.

3. Edit the Search Results Web Part on the new page to point at the PDF result source.

4. Add search navigation so that the new vertical appears on the Search Center.

5. Add a query rule that creates a promoted result anytime someone types "SharePoint," "Business," "Productivity," or "ECM."

6. Create a custom result type and display template that enables a hover panel preview for the PDFs.

Adding a result source

Our first task is to create a result source. The link to create a new result source is in the Site Settings of the Search Center. Create a new result source with the name **Technical PDFs**, and leave all other settings at their default except for the query transform. This is where we tell the result source what its "scope" will be by using search syntax to restrict results to only the library with our technical PDFs in it.

After clicking Launch Query Builder, enter some simple KQL syntax, as shown in Figure 19-8. We use the site property with a prefix match on the library that stores our technical PDFs.

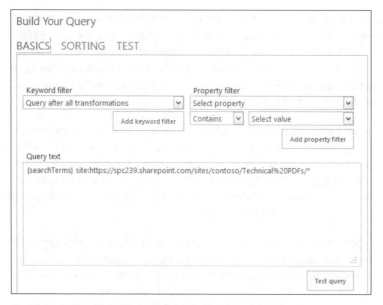

Figure 19-8 Use Query Builder to add a KQL query transform.

Once the KQL is verified using the Test Query button, simply save the result source and exit. The first step is complete.

Adding a search vertical page

The next step is to add a search page that is configured for the new result source. In order to do this, simply go to the Settings menu in your Search Center site and select Add A Page, as shown in Figure 19-9.

Figure 19-9 Add a page from the Settings menu.

After you do this, notice the new page has all the search web parts preconfigured on it. This is because you created the page from within your Search Center. Now that we have a new page, we are ready to configure the Search Results Web Part.

Configuring the Search Results Web Part

Now you need to configure the Search Results Web Part. With the Search Results Web Part in Edit mode, click Change Query and point the result source at the custom Technical PDF source that we added in the previous step. This is shown in Figure 19-10. Providing this configuration will tell the Search Results Web Part for the new Search page to restrict results to only the Technical PDF result source.

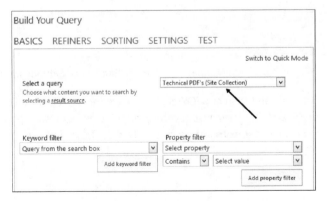

Figure 19-10 Configure the Search Results Web Part to use a custom result source.

At this point, click Apply in the web part settings window. Next, click Save and stop editing your new page. Once you have saved the new page, check it in and publish it to the site. It is time to add a Navigation link for our new PDF vertical.

Adding search navigation

Enter Site Settings in your Search Center and click the Search Settings link under the Search Category. Once we are in Search Settings, click Add Link in the Configure Search Navigation section. Give the new link a name, and then browse to the new PDF search page that we added in the previous step (see Figure 19-11).

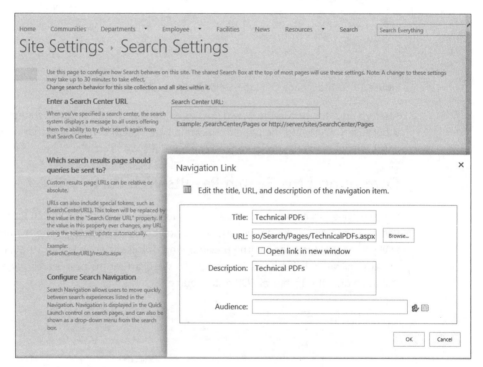

Figure 19-11 Adding a new Search Navigation link in the Site Search Settings window.

Click OK to save the link, and then click OK again to leave the Search Settings page. Now when we perform a search, the new search vertical appears on our results page, and by selecting it, we can restrict results to just technical PDFs, as shown in Figure 19-12.

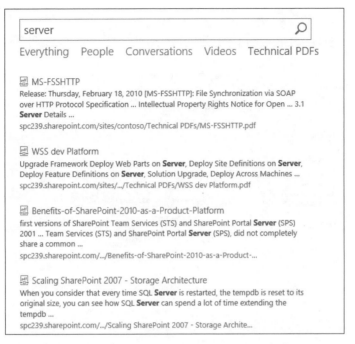

Figure 19-12 The new search vertical appears on our results page.

Using a query rule to provide a promoted result

There are many potential uses for query rules. In our example, we built a search page and added a link to it in the Search Results navigation. But what if the user performing the search is not aware of the Technical PDF Library? Perhaps the user will never use the link that we have provided in the interface. She might never click anything other than the default "Everything" search vertical. Our solution to this is to build a simple query rule that adds a promoted result to the search results page even if the user is performing a search from the Everything vertical. The promoted result that we added is triggered any time the user searches for "SharePoint," "Business," "Productivity," and so on. This ensures that if users type specific search terms indicating that they are likely looking for content that we know is in the Technical PDF Library, they will always get that result at the top of their search results.

In Site Settings, go into Edit Query Rule and create a new query rule for the result source Local SharePoint Results. This will tell the query rule to run any time the user is doing a search for content stored in the "local" SharePoint farm. In the Query Rule Condition, provide all the potential keywords that will trigger your rule, as shown in Figure 19-13. Finally, add a promoted result that simply points to the URL of the Technical PDF Library.

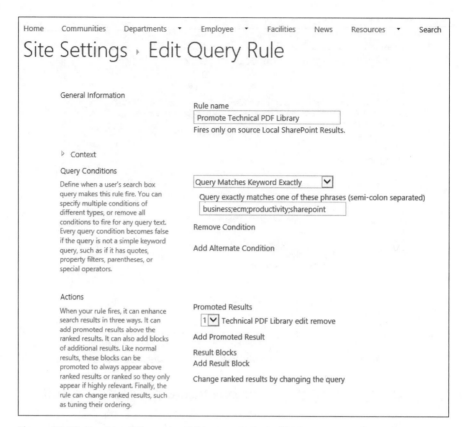

Figure 19-13 Provide all the potential keywords that will trigger your rule.

Now when we run a search from the *Everything* vertical that has one of the keywords defined in our query rule, we will see a promoted result, as shown in Figure 19-14.

At this point, we have a search experience that provides our users much better guidance on finding relevant content in the Technical PDF Library—either by using the new vertical that we created or by using some help from the query rule. In order to do that, we took advantage of result sources, search result pages, Search Results Web Part, search navigation, and a simple query rule. Next, we will show you how to use result types and display templates to improve the look of search results that come from the Technical PDF Library.

Figure 19-14 The Technical PDF Library has been promoted to the top of the results page based on a keyword the user had in his search query.

Creating a custom result type and display template

By default, SharePoint 2013 does not provide a robust display panel for PDF search results because there is no thumbnail preview. The out-of-the-box display panel for PDFs is shown in Figure 19-15. Therefore, to finalize our Technical PDF Library search customization, we chose to use result types and display templates to provide an improved Search interface for results from our library.

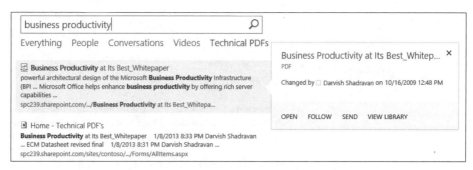

Figure 19-15 The SharePoint 2013 out-of-the-box PDF display panel.

When we are done with our modifications, results from our PDF Technical Library will look like Figure 19-16. Notice the big, beautiful hover panel preview of a PDF search result.

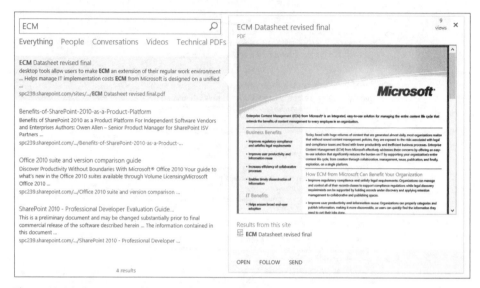

Figure 19-16 Our new and improved version of the PDF display panel.

To create our improved Display Panel template, go into Master Pages And Page Layouts in the Site Settings of the Search Center. Click Display Templates and then Search. When creating a custom Display Panel template, it is best to start with a copy of an existing one, so download a copy of Item_Default.html (this is the Display Panel template for many generic items).

Open the file with your favorite HTML editor. (Notepad will do just fine.) Inside the HTML code, change the title to something like "YourName_PDF." Then change the hoverUrl variable in the body to "~sitecollection/_catalogs/masterpage/Display Templates/Search/Item_Site_HoverPanel.js.

```
<body>
 <div id="Item_Default">
<!--#_
 if(!$isNull(ctx.CurrentItem) && !$isNull(ctx.ClientControl)){
 var id = ctx.ClientControl.get_nextUniqueId();
 var itemId = id + Srch.U.Ids.item;
                  var hoverId = id + Srch.U.Ids.hover;
                  var hoverUrl = "~sitecollection/_catalogs/masterpage/Display
                                  Templates/Search/Item_Site_HoverPanel.js";
```

That change tells our custom Display Panel template to use the SharePoint Site Hover Panel, which is actually quite handy and adept at viewing PDFs. Save your new Display

Panel template file as "PDF_Default.html" or something similar, as shown in Figure 19-17. Now upload the new HTML template to the same place we made the copy from (Site Settings|Master Pages|Display Templates|Search).

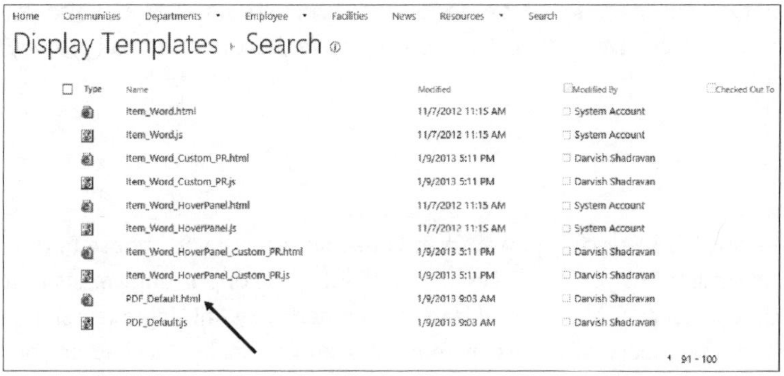

Figure 19-17 Save the new template file as PDF_Default template or something similar.

Last, but not least, we provided a custom result type so that when a user searches for a PDF, search results will know to use your custom Display Panel template for PDF result types. To do this, go into Site Settings and create a new result type. Name it **My PDF Viewer,** set it to match PDF content, and then configure it to match results that look like whatever you named your custom Display Panel template, as shown in Figure 19-18.

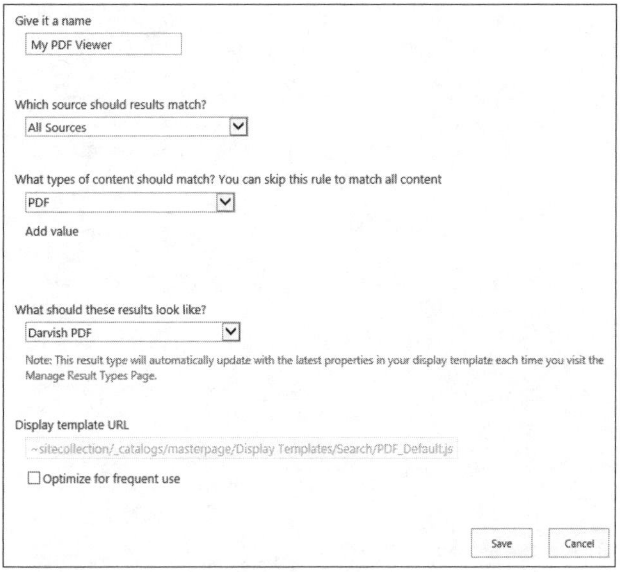

Figure 19-18 Create a new result type in Site Settings.

After saving the new PDF Viewer result type, we went back and edited our Technical PDF Library search page so that the Search Results Web Part specifically uses the new Display Panel template we created. That will force any searches done on the Technical PDF vertical to return results using the correct Display Panel template. Publish your changes and voilà! You not only have made it easier for users to find relevant PDFs, but also you have modified an out-of-the-box Display Panel template to give them a thumbnail preview in the hover panel.

Summary

SharePoint 2013 Search is powerful and effective, even if you choose to use only the default settings. As you have seen in this chapter, the opportunity exists to make the search experience for your organization even better by utilizing a few simple tools, such as result sources, query rules, display templates, and so on. In this chapter, you learned about the basic components that are available to create a customized search experience. With some creative application of these tools, the potential exists to build some truly great and productive search experiences—without very much heavy lifting.

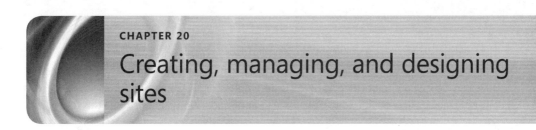

Creating, managing, and designing sites

MICROSOFT SharePoint 2013 is not just another web development platform that IT uses to develop applications that are then handed over to the users. SharePoint changes the game. SharePoint empowers users to do whatever they need to do—for themselves. Users no longer have to send content in an email to someone else for them to add it to a website. When solutions are built on top of SharePoint, the aim is to remove IT staff from the day-to-day tasks, make users self-sufficient, and even to let users build solutions for themselves.

The data and components that are needed for such solutions may not be stored in or be part of SharePoint or Microsoft Office; however, SharePoint enables you to create solutions rapidly by assembling, connecting, and configuring the components. Such solutions are known as *composite solutions* or *mashups*.

Most composites require the generation of a number of pages, sometimes called *forms* or *dashboards* that aggregate the information and are designed to allow the user to dynamically interact with the data. Using the browser and other what-you-see-is-what-you-get (WYSIWYG) tools, such as Microsoft SharePoint Designer 2013, Microsoft Access 2013, Microsoft InfoPath 2013, and Microsoft Visio 2013, the creator of these pages can amend the content visually without learning the different declarative or coding languages. These users can create successful SharePoint noncode solutions because they know what they want to achieve, they understand the business needs, and with a bit of SharePoint knowledge, they can wire together the business processes or sets of tasks. Such users have been termed by technology research firm, Gartner, Inc., as *citizen developers*, also known as the *consumer developer.*

> **Note**
>
> Gartner, Inc. reports that citizen developers will build at least 25 percent of new business applications by 2014 (see *www.gartner.com/it/page.jsp?id=1744514*) and warns that IT departments that fail to capitalize on the opportunities that citizen development presents will find themselves unable to respond to rapidly changing market forces and customer preferences.

SharePoint Designer was once the tool for the citizen developer. With the removal of Design view, SharePoint Designer 2013 is de-emphasized as a no-code forms tool, and business users may decide to use Access web apps and Visio diagrams to fill this gap.

See Chapter 17, "Working with Visio Services," and Chapter 21, "Creating enterprise forms," for more information about using Access web apps and Visio diagrams in SharePoint.

However, you can still build solutions with SharePoint Designer as the Code view remains. This means to achieve many of the same results with SharePoint Designer 2013, that were created using SharePoint Designer 2010, you will need to learn code. For the typical business user, this is not an option. Therefore, for those users, the focus of SharePoint Designer is now on workflows and creating external content types (ECTs), as well as an alternative tool for site collection and site owners to administer and manage sites, thereby allowing them to go beyond what the browser provides.

More information on workflows can be found in Chapter 7, "Using and creating workflows," and information on ECTs can be found in Chapter 22, "Working with external content."

SharePoint 2013 solutions should be more than a collection of lists, libraries, pages, and workflows. Each of these components should be combined to provide users with a holistic solution, where the components work together and not as discrete entities. Using web part connections and adding commands to the ribbon, are examples of how you can improve the user experience (UX). This chapter details a number of techniques that are useful when working with SharePoint Designer 2013 and other design tools to help you create composites.

INSIDE OUT   Using SharePoint Designer

SharePoint Designer adheres to the security settings of the site; therefore, to use SharePoint Designer, you need to be a site collection owner, site owner, or someone who has the Add And Customize Pages, Remote Interfaces, and Browse Directory site permissions. To create and delete lists, add or remove columns in a list, and add or remove public views of a list in SharePoint Designer, you would also need the Manage Lists permission. These permissions are automatically selected in the Full Control and Design permission levels. This is not the first chapter to use SharePoint Designer. Chapter 9, "Creating and formatting content pages," detailed how to use SharePoint Designer for creating and customizing webpages.

Creating and managing sites using SharePoint Designer 2013

You can use SharePoint Designer to edit and build solutions with SharePoint Foundation and SharePoint Server sites. Once connected to a SharePoint site, you can use SharePoint Designer to administer, create workflows, and customize pages. As with the previous release, SharePoint Designer 2013 is free and available from Microsoft's download site, *www.microsoft.com/download/details.aspx?id=35491*.

INSIDE OUT   When to use the 64-bit version of SharePoint Designer

As with SharePoint Designer 2010, SharePoint Designer 2013 comes with two versions: a 32-bit version and a 64-bit version. If you have the 32-bit version of SharePoint Designer 2010 already installed so that you can customize earlier versions of SharePoint, you must download the 32-bit version of SharePoint Designer 2013. Please note that 64-bit Office applications will not run if you have 32-bit versions of SharePoint Designer installed. Also note that unlike SharePoint 2010, which does not support the Edit In Datasheet view functionality if the 64-bit Office client is installed, in SharePoint 2013, the Edit In Datasheet view does not require a client-side control. Therefore, if a user has the 64-bit version of Office 2010 or Office 2013 installed, Edit In Datasheet will work correctly on SharePoint 2013 sites.

Opening sites

You can open a site in SharePoint Designer from the browser or by opening SharePoint Designer first and then opening a site from within SharePoint Designer. You can open a file in SharePoint Designer, such as an .html file, that does not live in a SharePoint site; however, to do so, a SharePoint site must already be open in SharePoint Designer.

> **Note**
>
> If you are using a different authentication authority for your SharePoint sites than the one used when you sign on to your computer (for example, when your SharePoint site is hosted by a third party), then it is easier to open the SharePoint site in the browser and then open SharePoint Designer from the browser.

To open a site within SharePoint Designer, you must first open SharePoint Designer. In Windows 7, click Start | All Programs | SharePoint, and then click SharePoint Designer 2013. In Windows 8, you can find it on the Start screen, as shown in Figure 20-1.

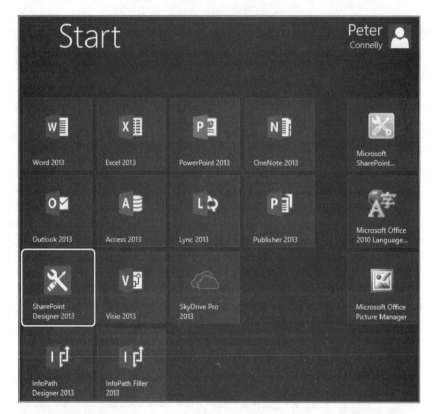

Figure 20-1 On the Start screen of Windows 8, click SharePoint Designer 2013 to open SharePoint.

To open a site from within SharePoint Designer, use the following steps:

1. Open SharePoint Designer to display the Backstage view with the Sites tab highlighted.

    If you previously opened a SharePoint site, these will be listed below Recent Sites, as shown in the following graphic.

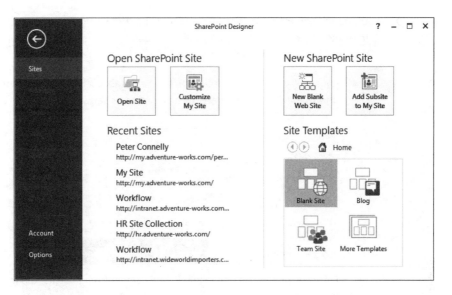

2. To open a site not listed under Recent Sites, under Open SharePoint Site, click Open Site to display the Open Site dialog box.

3. In the Site Name text box, type the URL of your SharePoint site, and then click Open. You may be prompted for your user name and password.

When you have a site already open in SharePoint Designer, you can open subsequent sites by clicking the File tab to display the Backstage view, and then by clicking Sites in the left pane. Then, under Open SharePoint Site, click Open Site. Alternatively, on the Subsites tab, which can be displayed by clicking Subsite in the Navigation pane, you can use the Open Site command in the Edit group. If you have a SharePoint site already open in SharePoint Designer, when you open additional sites, a new SharePoint Designer window opens.

> **Note**
> The focus of SharePoint Designer is still on an individual site in a site collection; that is, when you customize a site, your customizations are applied to the site that you have open. Therefore, if you wish to customize more than one site, SharePoint Designer opens a separate window for each site. As you browse through sites in a site collection, you can open a massive number of instances of SharePoint Designer. As sites can look very similar in SharePoint Designer, to ensure that you do not customize the wrong site, open only one site at a time.

Unlike in SharePoint 2010, in SharePoint 2013, there is no link to open SharePoint Designer from the Settings menu. You can still open a site in SharePoint Designer from the browser, however, by using one of the following methods:

- On a wiki or publishing page on the Page tab, click the Edit command down arrow, and then click Edit in SharePoint Designer, as shown in Figure 20-2.

Figure 20-2 You can open SharePoint Designer from the Page tab in the browser.

- When viewing a list or a library, click either the List or Library tab, and then click Edit List or Edit Library in the Customize List or Customize Library group, as shown in Figure 20-3.

Figure 20-3 You can open SharePoint Designer from the Library tab in the browser.

INSIDE OUT   Site Pages and the Site Assets libraries

No matter which site you open, in the SharePoint Designer Navigation pane, you will always see references to the Site Pages and Site Assets libraries. These libraries are created by default on a Team or a Community site. The Site Pages library contains the home page for the site and any other wiki pages you create. The Site Assets library should be used for files that are referenced within a page, such as images. It should not be used to store files that are used by the members of the team as part of their day-to-day tasks. Use the Documents library or create new libraries for those tasks. CSS or XSL files should be stored in the Style library, which is created when any site is first created.

On sites that do not contain the Site Pages or Site Assets libraries, such as publishing sites, blogs, meeting workspaces, group work sites, or document workspaces, if you click one of these two libraries in the Navigation pane of SharePoint Designer, then they will be created.

Exploring SharePoint Designer

Don't be put off by its name; SharePoint Designer is not aimed at just web designers—with SharePoint Designer, you can carry out similar tasks to the browser; however, you may need to jump back to the browser to complete some tasks.

When you first open a site with SharePoint Designer, you are presented within the SharePoint Designer workspace with a site's summary page, as shown in Figure 20-4. This page provides you with key site information organized in to five areas: Site Information, Customization, Settings, Permissions, and Subsites. You can use this page to change many site settings, manage permissions, and create new subsites. You will see settings pages for other site artifacts, such as for a list, library, master page, and workflow.

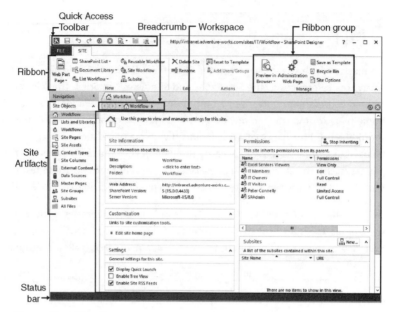

Figure 20-4 The Site summary page appears when you first open a site with SharePoint Designer.

Similar to other Microsoft applications, SharePoint Designer has a Quick Access Toolbar that contains a set of commands that are independent of the currently active Ribbon tab. You can add SharePoint Designer commands that you frequently use to the toolbar, such as creating a Web Part page or creating a list or library. To add commands to the Quick Access Toolbar, use one of the following methods:

- On the ribbon, click the appropriate tab to display the command that you wish to add to the Quick Access Toolbar. Right-click the command, and then click Add To Quick Access Toolbar, as shown in Figure 20-5.

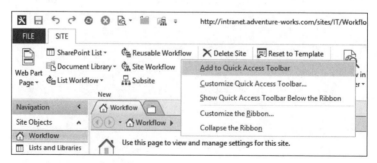

Figure 20-5 Adding a command to the Quick Access Toolbar using the ribbon.

- On the Quick Access Toolbar, click the last icon on the Quick Access Toolbar and then click More Commands, as shown in Figure 20-6.

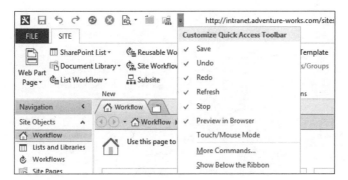

Figure 20-6 Adding a command to the Quick Access Toolbar using the Quick Access Toolbar.

- Click the File tab to display the commands in Backstage view. Click Options to display the SharePoint Designer Options dialog box, and then click Quick Access Toolbar.

> **Note**
>
> The Quick Access Toolbar can be located either in the upper-left corner or below the ribbon.

In the Navigation pane shown in Figure 20-4, selecting the first site object provides a summary of the SharePoint site, and the Site tab on the ribbon is available. When you click the icon to the left of a subsite in the Subsites area, the tab set, Site, appears that contains one tab: Subsites. If you then select the List and Libraries site object in the Navigation pane, a gallery page displays a list of artifacts, which in this case are lists and libraries. On the ribbon, the previous tab dynamically disappears and is replaced with the List and Libraries tab, as shown in Figure 20-7.

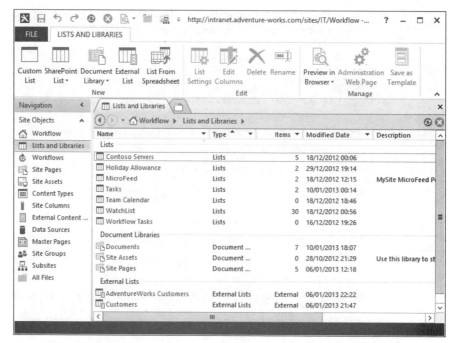

Figure 20-7 The gallery page displays the lists and libraries site objects, and the ribbon displays the List And Libraries tab.

The workspace breadcrumb can be compared to Windows Explorer and allows you to drill down and step upward, as shown in Figure 20-8. Use the back and forward arrow in the breadcrumb as you would use it in the browser to display previous contents.

> **Note**
>
> Although you can upload files into libraries using SharePoint Designer, you cannot associate metadata with those files or create, modify, or delete list items with SharePoint Designer—you must use the browser to complete those tasks.

The status bar is context-sensitive and will provide you with additional tools and information depending on what is displayed in the workspace. In SharePoint 2010, the status bar also contains a Log In command that allows you to log on as a different user. Just as the Sign In As Different User command in the browser was removed from the Settings menu, so the Log In command has been removed from SharePoint Designer 2013.

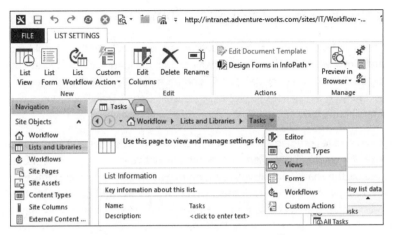

Figure 20-8 Use the breadcrumb to navigate to site artifacts.

When you open a site in SharePoint Designer 2010, you are not presented with the file and folder structure of the site, as with other web editing tools. The URL structure in a SharePoint site does not exist, as it is created from a combination of files from the SharePoint server and content in the SQL content database; however, it is what web developers expect to see in a web editing tool for non-SharePoint sites. The URL structure of a site is still available by clicking All Files in the Navigation pane, as shown in Figure 20-9.

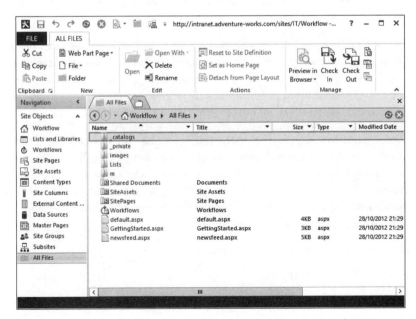

Figure 20-9 Use the All Files object in the Navigation pane to view the URL structure of a SharePoint site.

Chapter 20

Controlling the use of SharePoint Designer

SharePoint Designer has historically been a very powerful and useful tool for customizing SharePoint sites and creating solutions. However, the long-lasting implications of using SharePoint Designer 2007, and its predecessor Microsoft FrontPage 2003 on SharePoint sites, caused organizations to prohibit the installation of SharePoint Designer or to limit its use to all but a few trained users.

When the save command was clicked in SharePoint Designer 2007 or FrontPage 2003, SharePoint would unnecessarily break the link between a page and its site definition file stored on the SharePoint server, resulting in what is known as a *customized* or *unghosted* page. A copy of the page from the SharePoint server would be stored in the SQL Server content database. The customizing or unghosting of a page was not always made obvious to the untrained user. SharePoint Designer 2007 or FrontPage 2003 also did not provide an easy method of controlling the level of modifications users had with SharePoint Designer.

Customizing pages using SharePoint Designer 2013, as in SharePoint Designer 2010 and SharePoint Designer 2007, does not adversely affect the performance of a page in most cases—it is more of a maintenance issue, which is most often experienced when upgrading from one version of SharePoint to another, or when an organization implements a major change to the look and feel of their installation.

More information on customized and unghosted pages can be found in the sidebar, "Site template pages," in Chapter 9.

SharePoint Designer 2013 implements a "safe by default" approach that places reasonable limits around its usage so that citizen developers do not accidentally create solutions that have a negative effect. You can still customize a page in SharePoint Designer; however, first you need to be allowed to customize a page, and second, you have to specifically change your edit mode to advanced mode before you can customize a page.

There are SharePoint Designer usage settings at the web application and site-collection levels that can be used to prevent or restrict the usage of SharePoint Designer. These are not security settings. When configured at the web application level, these settings affect all users, including site collection administrators for all site collections and sites within the web application. When they are configured at the site-collection level, they apply only to site owners and designers for sites within that site collection.

SharePoint Designer usage settings

At both web application and site-collection levels, four settings allow or disallow the following SharePoint Designer uses:

- **Enable SharePoint Designer** If a user has SharePoint Designer open and you clear this check box, it will not close SharePoint Designer for that user; however, the next time the user tries to open the site in SharePoint Designer, the Web Site Editing Is Disabled dialog box opens, stating that the website has been configured to disallow editing with SharePoint Designer, as shown in Figure 20-10.

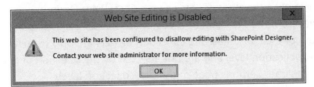

Figure 20-10 Clearing the Enable SharePoint Designer check box or amending attributes in the ONET.XML file can affect the editing of a website using SharePoint Designer.

- **Detach pages from site definitions** Use this option to disallow any pages associated with a site definition file from being customized (unghosted), including master pages and publishing page layouts. Content within web parts or within the EmbeddedFormField can still be modified. This option does not affect pages that are created in the content database and have never been associated with site definition files.

- **Customize master pages and page layouts** This is similar to the previous option; however, by selecting this option, you will only disallow the customization of master pages and publishing page layouts that are associated with site definition files. These are often the types of pages that cause organizations major maintenance problems if they are customized, as it often is with these page types that organizations wish to apply global changes across all sites. If this option is not selected, then the Master Page object will not be available on the Navigation pane in SharePoint Designer. If you are using SharePoint Server and displaying a publishing site in SharePoint Designer, then the Page Layout option will also not be available in the Navigation pane.

- **See the URL structure of the website** Within SharePoint Designer, users will not see the All Files option on the Navigation pane, the All Files gallery page in the workspace, or All Files in the mini-gallery. If this option is enabled but the Customize Master Pages and Page Layouts option is not allowed, then site owners and designers can see the master pages and page layouts, but they are not allowed to amend them.

> **Note**
>
> When a web application is created, all four security settings are selected by default.

You cannot use these options to control the usage of SharePoint Designer for different groups of people or to apply different usage rules on a per-site basis within the same site collection.

When any of the out-of-the-box site templates are used to create the root site of a site collection, site owners and designers can use SharePoint Designer; however, they cannot detach pages from the site definition, customize master pages or page layouts, or see the URL structure of their websites. Site collection owners are only restricted by the settings at the web-application level and are not affected by the selection of check boxes on the SharePoint Designer Settings page at the site-collection level.

If you are using SharePoint Server and the root site of a site collection was created using a publishing site, all four check boxes on the SharePoint Designer settings page at the site-collection level are selected.

INSIDE OUT   Other methods of controlling the user of SharePoint Designer

SharePoint Designer 2010 and SharePoint Designer 2013 can use all of the controlling methods used in SharePoint Designer 2007 and FrontPage 2003, except for contributor settings, including the following:

- Disabling the Add And Customize Pages permission.

- Disabling the Manage List permission.

- Disabling the Browse Directories permission.

- Disabling the Use Remote Interfaces permission.

- Preventing (at the server level) any user, including SharePoint server administrators, from opening sites created from specific site definitions by modifying the Project element to include the attribute, DisableWebDesign Features="wdfopensite" in the ONET.XML file for that site definition. You need to make this change on all SharePoint servers in your farm, and it affects all sites created from the site definition across all web applications created on the farm. You can change the DisableWebDesignFeatures attribute retroactively after a site is created, and SharePoint will not allow the site to be opened with SharePoint Designer. As the site definition files are cached, to make this attribute change take effect, you need to do an IISREST. The DisableWebDesignFeatures attribute can be set to other values, most of which are no longer applicable to SharePoint Designer. For example, sdfbackup and wdfrestore were used to disable SharePoint site backup and restore, but because SharePoint Designer cannot be used to back up or restore SharePoint sites, they have no effect. However, the wdfnewsubsite attribute, can be used to prevent the creation of new subsites using SharePoint Designer. No user feedback is provided when you set the wdfnewsubsite attribute and the user clicks the Subsite command in the New group on the Sites tab. However, when you set the wdfopensite attribute, the Web Site Editing Is Disabled dialog box opens, stating that the website has been configured to disallow editing with SharePoint Designer, as shown in Figure 20-10.

- Per user or per computer, using group policies.

Permissions can be disabled at the web application level and excluded from permission levels at sites or site collections. Information on locking down SharePoint Designer 2007 can be found at *blogs.msdn.com/b/sharepointdesigner/archive/2008/11/25/locking-down-sharepoint-designer.aspx*. However, some of these suggestions can result in upgrade problems and general supportability issues and should be used only if absolutely needed.

Implementing SharePoint Designer settings for a web application

To apply restrictions at the web-application level, complete the following steps. (You will need to be a SharePoint server administrator.)

1. Open the SharePoint Central Administration in the browser and then, in the Application Management section, click Manage Web Applications to display the Web Applications page.

2. Click the web application for which you want to restrict the use of SharePoint Designer. On the Web Applications tab, click General Settings in the Manage group, and then click SharePoint Designer, as shown in the following graphic.

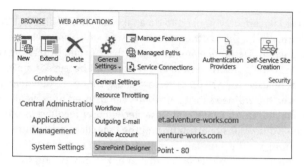

The SharePoint Designer Settings dialog box is displayed, as shown next.

3. Clear or select the check boxes as needed, and then click OK.

Alternatively, in the SharePoint Central Administration website, you can configure SharePoint Designer usage settings at the web-application level by going to the General Application Settings page. Click Configure SharePoint Designer Settings to display the SharePoint Designer Settings page, and then select the appropriate web application in the Web Application section.

Implementing SharePoint Designer settings for a site collection

To configure SharePoint Designer settings at the site-collection level, complete the following steps. (You will need to be a site collection administrator.)

1. Open the root site of your site collection in the browser. Click the Settings icon, and then click Site Settings to display the site settings page.

2. Under Site Collection Administration, if you see only Go To The Top Level Site Settings, you have opened a subsite in the browser. Click the link to go to the root site's Site Settings page. If you do not see the Site Collection Administration section on the Site Settings page, you are not a site collection owner and cannot complete the rest of the steps.

3. Under Site Collection Administration, click SharePoint Designer Settings, as shown next.

Site Collection Administration
Recycle bin
Search Result Sources
Search Result Types
Search Query Rules
Search Schema
Search Settings
Search Configuration Import
Search Configuration Export
Site collection features
Site hierarchy
Site collection audit settings
Audit log reports
Portal site connection
Content Type Policy Templates
Storage Metrics
Site collection app permissions
Site Policies
Popularity and Search Reports
Content type publishing
HTML Field Security
Help settings
SharePoint Designer Settings
Site collection health checks
Site collection upgrade

The SharePoint Designer Settings page is displayed. When one of the four check boxes are not selected at the web-application level, then the matching check boxes at the site-collection level are unavailable and a red text message that each option was disabled by your server administrator is displayed, as shown next.

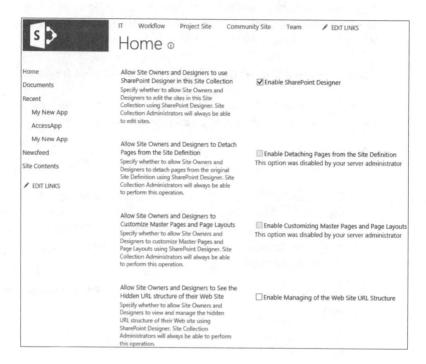

4. On the SharePoint Designer Settings page, select the check boxes as needed, and then click OK.

Using Windows PowerShell to set SharePoint Designer settings

You can enable or disable any of the SharePoint usage settings using Windows PowerShell. For example, to prevent the customization of pages and to disable the view of the URL folder structure at the web-application level, type the following command, using the name of your web application in place of *adventure-works*:

```
Set-SPDesignerSettings -WebApplication http://adventure-works '
    -AllowRevertFromTemplate $False -ShowURLStructure $False
```

To display the SharePoint Designer usage settings for a web application, type the following command:

```
Get-SPDesignerSettings -WebApplication http://adventure-works
```

There is no equivalent specific SPDesignerSettings command for site collections. You will need to use the Get-SPSite command to display the SharePoint Designer usage settings for a site collection. By default, this command displays only the URL property of the site collection. To display all the properties associated with the site collection, you need to pipe the results of the Get-SPSite command into the Select command, as shown in the following example. Use the name of your site collection in place of *adventure-works/sites/hr*:

```
Get-SPSite http://adventure-works/sites/hr | select *
```

The properties concerning the SharePoint Designer usage settings are AllowDesigner, AllowRevertFromTemplate, AllowMastPageEditing, and ShowURLStructure. To prevent site owners and designers from using SharePoint Designer on a site collection, type the following command:

```
(Get-SPSite http://adventure-works/sites/basic).AllowDesigner=$False
```

Windows PowerShell allows you to batch together and automate repetitive tasks, or you can use it to ensure that a set of tasks are completed again exactly as they were the last time they were executed. Therefore, if you have a large number of site collections for which you wish to configure the SharePoint Designer usage settings, create a text file—sitecollection.txt—that contains a list of those site collections, such as

```
http://adventure-works/sites/hr
http://adventure-works/sites/marketing
http://adventure-works/sites/sales
```

Place the text file in your %USERPROFILE% directory, which is the directory that the SharePoint 2013 Management Shell uses, and then type

```
$content = Get-Content sitecollection.txt
$content | ForEach-Object {
   (Get-SPSite $_).AllowDesigner = $False}
```

The contents of the Sitecollection.txt file are stored in the variable $content and the ForEach-Object command acts like a loop, reading a line from the text file one at a time. The variable $_ represents one line from the text file, which in this example is the name of one site collection. To display the AllowDesigner property for each site collection, together with its server relative URL, and use the ForEach alias %, type

```
$content | % {
  Get-SPSite $_ |
  select ServerRelativeUrl, AllowDesigner }
```

More examples of using Windows PowerShell with SharePoint can be found on Gary Lapointe's blog site at *blog.falchionconsulting.com/index.php/category/general/sharepoint-2013/*.

Creating sites

In Chapter 2, "Administration for business users," you learned about web applications and that a web application can consist of one or more site collections; each site collection always has one top-level site and, optionally, one or more subsites, which are also called *child sites*. If you are a SharePoint server administrator, using the browser and the SharePoint Central Administration website, you can create web applications and site collections. Users with the Create Sites permissions right can use the browser to create subsites from the Settings menu. Such users can also use SharePoint Designer to create subsites. You cannot create web applications or site collections using SharePoint Designer.

There are many options to create a subsite using SharePoint Designer:

- From the Backstage view, on the Sites tab, under New SharePoint Site, click New Blank Web Site; or under Site Templates, click Blank Site, Blog, or Team Site. This will create subsites beneath the current site. The Add Subsite To My Site option is applicable only if you are using SharePoint Server.

- From the Backstage view on the Sites tab, under Site Templates, click More Templates to open the Site To Load Templates From dialog box, which allows you to specify a different site than the one currently open. The site templates from that site are then retrieved and displayed in the Backstage view, as shown in Figure 20-11.

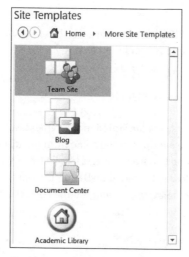

Figure 20-11 More Site Templates displayed in the Backstage view.

- Display the Site Settings page in the workspace, and then click New in the Subsites area title bar.

- In the Navigation pane, click Subsites to display the Subsites gallery in the workspace and then, on the Subsites tab, click Subsite in the New group.

When using the last two options, the New dialog box opens and displays the site templates in the middle pane, as shown in Figure 20-12. The right pane displays a description of the site template selected from the middle pane. If the middle pane does not include any site templates, then, in the Specify The Location Of The New Web Site text box, type the URL of the subsite and then click in the middle pane. SharePoint Designer will communicate with the SharePoint Server hosting your SharePoint site and then populate the middle pane from the information retrieved from the SharePoint server.

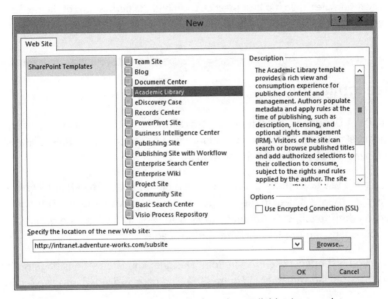

Figure 20-12 The New dialog box displays the available site templates.

When you have a site open already in SharePoint Designer, the new site will open in a new SharePoint Designer window.

> **Note**
>
> Whenever you create a site in SharePoint Designer, it asks you only for the URL of the site and the site template to use. It does not prompt you for any other site properties, such as the title of the site or the permissions to use. The title of the site will be the name of the site template used to create the site, the site will inherit its permissions from its parent site, and the site will not appear as a link in the top navigation bar. Therefore, the first task you should complete once you create a site is to use the Site Settings page in SharePoint Designer to modify the title of the site and, if appropriate, its permissions. If you do not change the title immediately, then you could have many sites with the same name. This can be very confusing for users, as it is the title of the site that is displayed in the browser's user interface. Also, if you plan to use the new site as a basis for creating a solution or customization, which you will then use as a template for new or existing sites, then it is best practice to amend the permissions of the site so that only you and other users who are helping develop the solution have access to the site.

Managing sites

SharePoint Designer is not a tool for general use by all those who visit or have access to a SharePoint site. Rather, it is a tool targeted to site owners, business analysts, project managers, developers, and IT professionals.

There are a few tasks that still cannot be completed within SharePoint Designer. For those tasks, click the site object in the Navigation pane to display the Site Settings page, and then, on the Site tab, click Administration Web Page in the Manage group. A browser window opens and displays the Site Settings page.

When you first open a site in SharePoint Designer, the Site Settings page is displayed in the workspace, as shown earlier in Figure 20-4. The page is divided into five sections:

- **Site information** Use this section to change the site's title and description, which are important properties of a site, as they appear on each page within a site and communicate to users the purpose and function of the site. They are also important as the words in the title and description fields are used to rank content items that are returned in a search result set.

- **Customization** Use this section to open a new workspace tab, when the Home page is displayed in edit mode. In SharePoint Designer 2010, this section also contains a link to display the Site Theme page. This link no longer exists in SharePoint Designer 2013.

- **Settings** Use this section to select the options to display the Quick Launch, enable tree view, and enable site RSS feeds. The Quick Launch and tree view options are the same as you would find in the browser on the Site Settings page, under Look And Feel | Tree View. You can select the RSS feeds option in the browser when on the Site Settings page, under Site Administration | RSS.

- **Permissions** Use this section to assign users and groups permissions to this site. When you click the icon to the left of a user or group, the Site tab set becomes active and displays the Permissions tab, as shown in Figure 20-13, which you can use to add new users and groups, edit permissions, inherit permissions from the site's parent site if the site is using unique permissions, and manage anonymous access, permission levels, access requests, and site collection administrators.

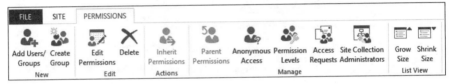

Figure 20-13 The Permissions tab allows you to manage permissions for the site.

- **Subsites** Use this section to list all the subsites created below the site. When you click in the area below Site Name, the Site tab set becomes active and displays the Subsites tab, as shown in Figure 20-14, which you can use to create a new subsite, open, delete, or rename a site, view the subsite in the browser, view the Site Settings page in the browser for the subsite, or save the subsite as a template.

Figure 20-14 The Subsite tab allows you to manage sites created below this site.

INSIDE OUT   Using the Grow Size and Shrink Size commands

You will see the Grow Size and Shrink Size commands in the List View group on many ribbon tabs, especially when a settings page is displayed in the workspace. Settings pages contain many sections, and you can use these two commands to reduce the space taken on the workspace for each section. Alternatively, you can collapse a section, leaving the section title visible by clicking the section title or the up arrow in the title bar.

You can use the SharePoint artifacts listed in the Navigation pane to manage other components of the SharePoint site, such as the following:

- **Lists And Libraries** The List and Libraries gallery, as shown earlier in Figure 20-7, allows you to create new lists and libraries, manage list settings, edit columns, delete or rename a list or library, preview the list or library in the browser, open a browser window and display the List Settings page, and save the list as a template. If you click a list in the workspace, the List Settings page is displayed in the workspace, as shown in Figure 20-15. An alternative method of navigating to this page is to click the icon to the left of the list in the List and Library gallery, and then, on the Lists And Libraries tab, click List Settings in the Edit group.

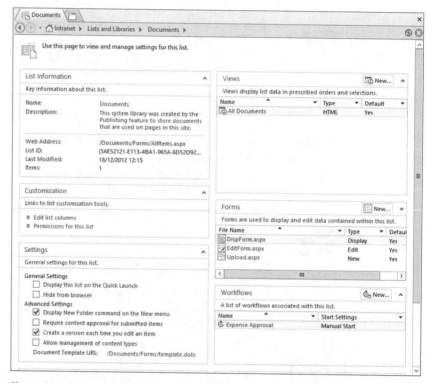

Figure 20-15 Use the List Settings page to view and manage settings for a list or library.

The List Settings page contains eight sections that allow you to view list information, edit list columns and the permissions for the list, manage general settings for the list, such as hiding the list from the browser so that is does not display on the view all sites content page, manage the content types and workflows associated with the list, create and manage list views and forms, as well as create custom actions.

- **Site Groups** When you click this option in the Navigation pane, the Site Groups gallery opens in the workspace and the Site Groups tab is displayed on the ribbon, which allows you to add users to an existing group, create new groups, edit and delete a group, make a group the Default Members group, or view the group permissions. When you click one of the groups, the Settings page for that group is displayed in the workspace, as shown in Figure 20-16.

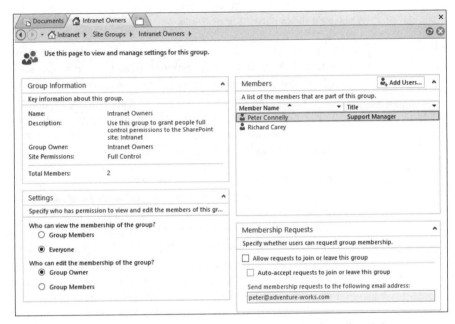

Figure 20-16 Use the Group Settings page to manage settings for a SharePoint group.

Designing sites

The first step in designing your site is to understand your content. Too often, people start designing their sites by creating wireframes without understanding the content. Content is king. You should try and find the answers to the following questions:

- How often is it going to be updated?

- Who is going to update it?

- How often are they going to update it?

- Where is the content coming from?

- What is the main message of the site, of the page or parts of the page? When you design a page, if users to your site could walk away with just one thing from your site, what would it be? What is going to make users come back to your site?

These questions will help you decide which site template to use, the content types, site columns, workflows, lists, libraries, and types of pages to create, as well as which web parts to place on those pages. For example:

- When users have a great deal of static content and images to add to a page, if you design your site so that this content is stored, say, in a Content Editor Web Part (CEWP), then not only will you have to train users on how to use that web part, but users may find this too hard and time consuming to update at the frequency they require. Therefore, the information on the page will become dated and other employees will not visit the site, as it is not a representation of the current business process. Perhaps you should have used a wiki page.

- When content is not going to change frequently, such as company policies, information on company policies must be readily available to all employees. There may also be associated information that you want to be displayed on the page, such as when the policy is to be reviewed; plus, your company's human resources department may own the production of the policy pages and it may also require that part of the page is used to tell visitors of the HR department's plans and an RSS feed of the directors' blog sites, as well as what they are tweeting about. So the page that you design needs to contain both static content that needs to go through an approval process and dynamic content. This affects the page layout and how you lay out the content onto your pages. Is there any special branding consideration that the HR department requires for its site? Is it using any custom web parts that do not follow the same cascading style sheet style as the other web parts?

You need to understand the navigation requirements. You do not want to use a different navigation standard that is used elsewhere on your site. This will confuse visitors to your site. The larger the organization, the more complex the navigation is. If the navigation does not follow a consistent pattern, the users will not know what they are doing or how to get back to where they were originally, or how to get back to a specific step in a business process.

You must also consider the user experience (UX). Although computers have been around for over half a century, there are still many users in organizations who have an aversion to computers, and therefore it is important to gather requirements and understand the skill level of the users who will make use of your solution. Most users of SharePoint are not developers, nor are they administrators—they do not understand the technology behind the pages, lists, and libraries that they need to use and maintain. Many users have experienced many system changes, and to many, your solution is just one more in a very long line of systems they are going to use. They don't have the time to sit down and learn your new system—they've got their day job to be getting on with!

So when you design your site, you have many aspects to consider, and this not only affects the page layout, content types, site columns, lists, and libraries you should use, but it also affects how you want your sites to look. Do you want to move some of the UI objects and want your sites to represent your company's branding? Do you want to brand all sites— sites based on team sites, group work sites, document workspaces, meeting workspaces— or only some of them? Do you want site owners to be able to choose and apply their own branding? This will also help you identify if you need any custom development or whether you can meet your design requirements using the browser and SharePoint Designer or another tool.

> **Note**
>
> If you wish to design or brand Internet-facing websites, where the publishing feature is activated, then you can use any professional HTML editor, such as Microsoft Expression Web or Adobe Dreamweaver—that is, now, a professional web developer, can connect their tool of choice to SharePoint 2013. Then, they can import their HTML files into the publishing site by using the new Design Manager.

Changing the look of your site

In SharePoint 2010, themes reused the theme definition and format defined in the Office Open XML standard that was introduced with Microsoft PowerPoint 2007 to create new themes for slide decks. Using the browser on a SharePoint Server 2010 publishing site, or on a site when the Publishing feature was enabled, you could create your own new themes or you could create a new .thmx file by using Microsoft Word 2010, PowerPoint 2010, or Theme Builder. The .thmx file could then be uploaded into the Theme gallery.

In SharePoint 2013, the theme engine has changed—it is faster and no longer consists of just colors, but also includes fonts and optional background images. It is also based on HTML5; therefore, you are not able to use Office applications to create new themes. It is now easier to change the look of a site or create a new look in the browser by clicking the What's Your Style? tile in Getting Started With Your Site or clicking the Settings icon and then clicking Change The Look. You can also navigate to the Change The Look page, as shown in Figure 20-17, by clicking Change The Look, under Look And Feel on the Site Settings page.

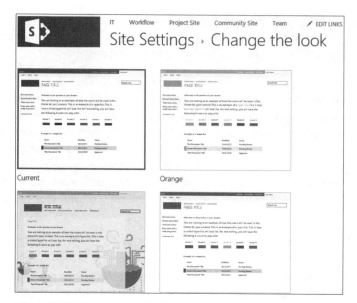

Figure 20-17 You can use the Change The Look page to preview the different looks available.

A total of 18 different looks are available. You can use any of these as a basis for a new look by clicking the preview image to display the second Change The Look page, as shown in Figure 20-18.

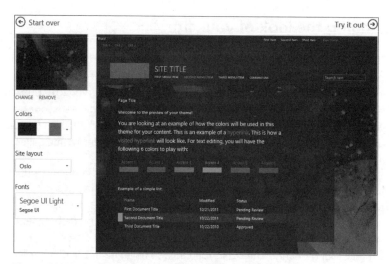

Figure 20-18 Once you have chosen a look, you can change the color scheme, background image, and font.

Most of the Change The Look page is used to display a preview of the look that you have chosen. In the left column, you can modify:

- **The background image** This is displayed in the upper-left corner, and you can use the Change and Remove commands to use your own image as the background or to remove the background image. If you do not like the background image, you can open Windows Explorer and drag a new image over the background image. The file will be uploaded automatically to the Site Assets library of the site. When selecting a background image, you should keep in mind that the content, such as static text, images, tables, and web parts, will be placed over the image, so you should try to select an image that won't make the content difficult to read.

  The supported file types for the background image are .jpg, .bmp, .png, and .gif. You do not have to worry about the size of the image file, particularly of .jpg and .bmp files; for example, the image could be taken with your mobile phone and may be many megabytes or even gigabytes in size. The upload process will compress and scale the image to reduce its size, so that it won't affect the performance of page loads.

- **Colors** When you pause over the colors in the drop-down list, the preview temporarily changes to show the effect that the color palette would look like on your site. Only three colors from the color palette are shown.

- **Site layout** This is the master page. By default, there are two master pages to choose from: Seattle and Oslo; and again, when you pause on it, the preview changes to show the difference between the master pages. The master pages shown are retrieved from the Master Page gallery for the site and only those that have an accompanying preview file.

- **Fonts** The list of fonts can be web fonts, as well as web-safe fonts. Web-safe fonts are those fonts that are guaranteed to be on every computer.

To apply the look to your site, click Try It Out. It is at this point that the theming engine creates new files that contain the CSS and images that match the new look. Your site's Home page is then displayed using the new theme, as shown in Figure 20-19. You then have the options No, Not Quite There to return to the previous page or Yes, Keep It to apply the theme. If you choose Yes, Keep It, the files previously created by the theming engine are used by your site.

Chapter 20

Figure 20-19 Use the Try It Out command to see a preview of your home page.

The different looks displayed on the Change The Look page are a combination of four components: a master page, color palette, font scheme, and background image, which is why the looks are known as Composed Looks. Users can choose any combination of the components. The components are linked together either by using the Composed Looks page or by using Design Manager.

New master pages, color palettes, and font schemes will probably be created by the IT department; however, users can upload new background images that they want for their site.

In SharePoint 2013, SharePoint Designer is no longer needed to build master pages and page layouts for publishing pages. Microsoft has created a new tool available on every publishing site: the Design Manager, which was discussed in Chapter 12, "Designing web content management sites." For collaboration sites, if you do not want to activate the publishing feature, you can use SharePoint Designer to create master pages and the other components and then use the Composed Looks page and Theme Gallery pages, which you can navigate to by using links under Web Designer Galleries on the Site Settings page.

Theme gallery

The color palette and font schemes are XML files that are stored at the top-level site of a site collection in the "15" folder in a document library, as shown in Figure 20-20. They are located in the Theme Gallery and have a URL of _catalogs/theme_. The two file types have the following extensions:

- .spcolor for color palettes files

- .spfont for font scheme files

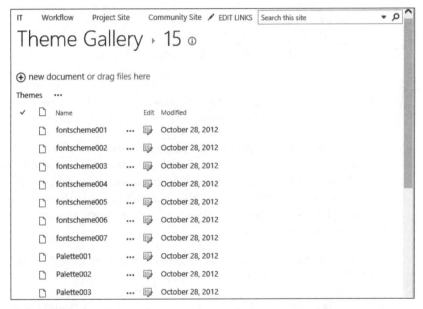

Figure 20-20 The 15 folder in the Theme Gallery stores the theme files.

This library is not configured to use versioning, nor is it configured to require checkout; however, if you do check out any of .spcolor or .spfont files as you modify them, forget to check them back in, and apply a Composed Look to your site that uses them, then the SPTheme logic will not load them properly.

Composed Looks gallery

The four components are associated together to make a Composed Look. The information where to find the four components for each Composed Look is saved at the site level in a list named Composed Look that has a URL of _catalogs/design_. Each Composed Look comprises a name, master page (.master), theme URL (which points to an .spcolor file), image URL, font scheme URL (which points to an .spfont file), and display order, as shown in

Figure 20-21. The font scheme and background image are optional. The two elements that are always required are the color palette and the master page. Although only the master page URL is specified, in the master page gallery where the master page is stored, there must be the associated preview file (.preview).

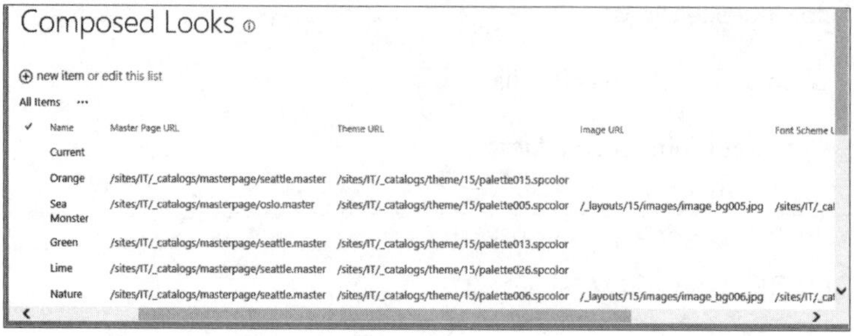

Figure 20-21 You can change the look of your site by choosing a Composed Look.

When a site is first created, the default Composed Look that is applied is Office, which uses the Seattle master page and the palette001 theme, with no font or background image.

When a Composed Look is applied to a site, several images and CSS style sheets based on the .spcolor file are created. Then a new folder is created in the Themed folder in the Themes Gallery and the images and CSS style sheets are put inside it, which is similar to how a theme is applied in SharePoint 2010. Therefore, just as in SharePoint 2010, if you update any of the theme files, you will need to remove the theme and reapply it to a site to see the modifications.

You can view the files created by navigating to the folder using the All Files option in SharePoint Designer, as shown in Figure 20-22.

When a theme is applied to a site, then the ThemedCssFolderUrl property of the site is set to the new folder in the Themed folder, which can be displayed using the following Windows PowerShell commands:

```
(Get-SPWeb http://intranet.adventure-works/sites/IT/Workflow).ThemedCssFolderUrl
/sites/it/_catalog/theme/Themed/D0B0820C
```

You can programmatically apply a Composed Look by using the ApplyTheme method, which now has four parameters:

```
[ClientCallableMethodAttribute]
public void ApplyTheme(
    string colorPaletteUrl,
    string fontSchemeUrl,
    string backgroundImageUrl,
    bool shareGenerated
)
```

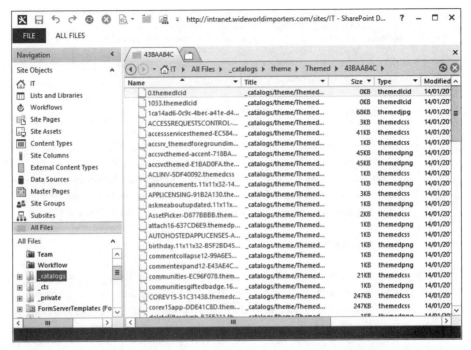

Figure 20-22 To display the files generated by an applied theme, use SharePoint Designer to navigate to the catalog/theme/Themed gallery and click the folder created.

The shareGenerated parameter is used to decide where to store the themed CSS output files. Setting this parameter to:

- True means that the files are stored in the Themed subfolder of the Theme Gallery of the top-level site of the site collection;

- False means that the files will be stored in the _themes folder within the site being themed.

The guidance for this property is the same as it was in SharePoint 2010; that is, use true for SharePoint Server and false in SharePoint Foundation.

However, it is unlikely that you will use the ApplyTheme method in your code since it is more likely that you will only specify the color palette and font using something similar to the following code, where the variable spWeb contains the site where the palette is to be applied:

```
SPFile spColorFile = spWeb.GetFile(spWeb.ServerRelativeUrl +
    "/_catalogs/theme/15/palette001.spcolor");
SPFile spFontSchemeFile = Web.GetFile(spWeb.ServerRelativeUrl +
    "/_catalogs/theme/15/fontscheme001.spfont");
SPTheme spTheme = SPTheme.Open("SPIOTheme", spColorFile, spFontSchemeFile);
spTheme.ApplyTo(spWeb, true);
```

Creating a Composed Look

As a Composed Look is a value in the Name column of the Composed Look list, and the components that are associated with that Composed Look are values in the other columns in the list, it is easy to create or modify new Composed Looks by using the New Item or Edit Item command on the Items tab. Any items that are listed in the Composed Look list are automatically available when you navigate to the Change The Look page.

Color palettes

Both the color palette and font scheme files contain a simple XML format, which you can edit with your favorite text editor. The color palette file contains 89 color slots. This does not mean you have to use 89 colors, but rather that there are 89 different UI objects that form the basis of what you can affect. The main colors that make your planned look will repeatedly be used in the color slots. This gives you the flexibility of specifying which accent colors you want to use and where in the UI you want them to light up, allowing you to create different looks with the same colors. Each color slot has the following format:

```
Color name="BodyText" value="C3C3C3"
```

The color name uses semantic names so that you know where in the UI each color slot is used. Examples of color names are BodyText, SuiteBarBackground, SelectionBackground, ButtonBorder, ButtonBackground, and ButtonBorderOnHover.

You can also specify the opacity/transparency value for background colors, which use RGBA (red, green, blue, and alpha transparency) colors. The HEX values for the background color slots have eight digits and not six. The first two digits are used for transparency and the other digits define the color; for example, 20C3C3C3 has a transparency of 20 and a color of C3C3C3—which is RGBA (195, 195, 195, 0.13). This is important since different colors need different opacity, especially as the background colors are used to overlay the background image of the page and make the content of the page readable.

A hex to and from RGBA calculator can be found at *kilianvalkhof.com/2010/css-xhtml/how-to-use-rgba-in-ie/*.

For each color palette, there are four metadata values specified: the three color slots that will be used in the color picker and an inverted flag. You should choose the three colors that best represent the palette. The inverted flag indicates whether the color palate is a dark or light theme. If the inverted flag is set to true, then the palette is a dark theme where light text is displayed on a dark background. A light color palette is one that has dark text on a light background.

The following is an example of the contents of a color palette file:

```xml
<?xml version="1.0" encoding="utf-8"?>
<s:colorPalette isInverted="false" previewSlot1="BackgroundOverlay"
   previewSlot2="BodyText" previewSlot3="AccentText"
   xmlns:s="http://schemas.microsoft.com/sharepoint/">
   <s:color name="BodyText" value="444444" />
   <s:color name="SubtleBodyText" value="777777" />
   <s:color name="StrongBodyText" value="262626" />
   <s:color name="DisabledText" value="B1B1B1" />
   <s:color name="SiteTitle" value="262626" />
   <s:color name="WebPartHeading" value="444444" />
   <s:color name="ErrorText" value="BF0000" />
   <s:color name="AccentText" value="0072C6" />
   <s:color name="SearchURL" value="338200" />
   <s:color name="Hyperlink" value="0072C6" />
   <s:color name="Hyperlinkfollowed" value="663399" />
   <s:color name="HyperlinkActive" value="004D85" />
   <s:color name="CommandLinks" value="666666" />
   <s:color name="CommandLinksSecondary" value="262626" />
   <s:color name="CommandLinksHover" value="0072C6" />
   <s:color name="CommandLinksPressed" value="004D85" />
   <s:color name="CommandLinksDisabled" value="B1B1B1" />
   <s:color name="BackgroundOverlay" value="D8FFFFFF" />
   <s:color name="DisabledBackground" value="FDFDFD" />
   <s:color name="PageBackground" value="FFFFFF" />
   <s:color name="HeaderBackground" value="D8FFFFFF" />
   <s:color name="FooterBackground" value="D8FFFFFF" />
   <s:color name="SelectionBackground" value="7F9CCEF0" />
   <s:color name="HoverBackground" value="7FCDE6F7" />

   <s:color name="ContentAccent5" value="ED0033" />
   <s:color name="ContentAccent6" value="682A7A" />
</s:colorPalette>
```

Font schemes

This contains seven font slots, again using semantic names so that you know where the fonts will be used: Title, Navigation, Small-Heading, Heading, Large-Heading, Body, and Large-Body. You can also specify a font for a specific language. If you intend to use web fonts, then the URLs to the four web font files (EOT, WOFF, TTF, and SVG) are required. Also, a large preview and a small preview image are needed for the font scheme picker. Web fonts do not provide the hover preview capability. Web fonts are downloaded only when they are chosen and then applied to the instance preview.

An extract of the font scheme file is displayed as follows:

```xml
<?xml version="1.0" encoding="utf-8"?>
<s:fontScheme name="Bodoni" previewSlot1="title" previewSlot2="body"
    xmlns:s="http://schemas.microsoft.com/sharepoint/">
    <s:fontSlots>
        <s:fontSlot name="title">
            <s:latin typeface="Bodoni Book" eotsrc="/_layouts/15/fonts/BodoniBook.eot"
                woffsrc="/_layouts/15/fonts/BodoniBook.woff"
                ttfsrc="/_layouts/15/fonts/BodoniBook.ttf"
                svgsrc="/_layouts/15/fonts/BodoniBook.svg"
                largeimgsrc="/_layouts/15/fonts/BodoniBookLarge.png"
                smallimgsrc="/_layouts/15/fonts/BodoniBookSmall.png" />

            <s:ea typeface="" />
            <s:cs typeface="Segoe UI Light" />
            <s:font script="Arab" typeface="Segoe UI Light" />
            <s:font script="Tibt" typeface="Microsoft Himalaya" />
            <s:font script="Yiii" typeface="Microsoft Yi Baiti" />
        </s:fontSlot>
        <s:fontSlot name="navigation">
            <s:ea typeface="" />
            <s:cs typeface="Segoe UI" />
            <s:font script="Arab" typeface="Segoe UI" />
            <s:font script="Deva" typeface="Nirmala UI" />

        </s:fontSlot>
    </s:fontSlots>
</s:fontScheme>
```

The easiest way to create a font scheme of a color palette is to download one of the out-of-the-box .spfont or .spcolor files from the 15 folder in the Theme Gallery. Make changes and upload it back into the library. There is a tool to help you; which can be found at *www.microsoft.com/en-us/download/details.aspx?id=38182*. The tool will take into consideration accessibility standards and color ratios, and provide a preview of the different UI objects and how the palette looks, thereby reducing the need to upload the files repeatedly into the Theme Gallery and test them using the browser. The tool groups together the color slots according to the type of UI objects they affect, which gives you a better understanding of the relationship of the color slots to each other, helping you create a better palette. The groups are:

- Text

- Backgrounds

- Lines

- Navigation

- Emphasis

- Subtle Emphasis

- Top Bar

- Header

- Buttons

- Suite Bar

- Tiles

- Content Accents

Creating master pages and previews

If color palettes and font schemes do not meet your needs, you will probably need to create your own master pages and CSS files. Both of these processes take some time, especially if you are new to branding and have never tried to change the look and feel of a SharePoint site before, and you have no previous web design or development knowledge. Using a theme can be likened to painting your house; CSS is analogous to moving or hanging new pictures in your house; and using master pages is like adding an extension to your house.

When you want to change the structure of the pages and apply those changes to all pages within a site or across a number of sites, which is when you need to create a new master page. Master pages were introduced in Chapter 9.

For more information about master pages, go to *http://msdn.microsoft.com/en-us/library/ jj191506(v=office.15).aspx.*

When you use a browser to request a page from a site, it combines two Microsoft ASP. NET pages: a master page and a content page. A *master page* is a special ASP.NET 2.0 page that is used to provide a consistent appearance and navigation for each page within one or more sites. Components that are usually placed on master pages are your company's branding images and logo; navigation tabs and links, such as a breadcrumb component and the Site Actions button; footer links, such as Contact Us, Accessibility, and Copyright statements; and links to CSS files and JavaScript files that contain common functions.

Each page in a site is initially configured to use the site's default master page. The @Page directive at the top of the content page specifies the master page to be used. When you first create a SharePoint site, all pages but a select few use the site's default master page. The MasterPageFile attribute of the @Page directive is set to token, *~masterurl/default. master.*

Chapter 20

A master page cannot be viewed in a browser, and although you can create master pages using a web editing tool such as Microsoft Expression Web and then use the Design Manager to import it into SharePoint, you can still use SharePoint Designer to create master pages.

SharePoint Designer is a powerful tool that you can use to customize almost anything. You can create multiple master pages, so that your various sites look different. However, it is almost impossible for users or web designers who know very little about the underlying structure of SharePoint to figure things out. It is also easy to break master pages and content pages using the Code view of SharePoint Designer.

INSIDE OUT   Where are master pages and previews stored?

SharePoint 2013 makes heavy use of master pages to control the general layout of pages within a SharePoint site. When you install SharePoint 2013, the default master page and other master pages are located on the web server, in the %ProgramFiles%\ Common Files\Microsoft Shared\web server extensions\15\TEMPLATE\GLOBAL directory. So long as this master page is not customized, its page definition is cached on the front-end web server and shared across sites. If the master page is edited for a particular SharePoint site, the edited copy of the master page file is stored in the content database. SharePoint Server 2013 contains the following master pages and preview pages:

- app.master

- default.master

- minimal.master

- mwsdefault.master

- mwsdefaultv4.master

- mwsdefaultv15.master

- oslo.master

- oslo.preview

- seattle.master

- seattle.preview

- v4.master

When you open a site in SharePoint Designer, a site's master pages and previews can be found in the Master Page gallery, which is a hidden library. Each site has its own master page gallery. In the browser, you can browse to the Master Page gallery at the top level of the site collection by using the Site Settings page.

Using SharePoint Designer, you can navigate to each site's Master Page gallery by using the Navigation pane and clicking Master Pages or using All Files and navigating to _catalogs/masterpage. The Master Page gallery has major versioning enabled, and therefore, you can restore a previous version of a master page. In SharePoint Server, in a site collection where the SharePoint Server Publishing Infrastructure feature is enabled, this library is also used for page layouts and configured with content approval and major and minor versions.

To set a master page as the site's default master page, perform the following steps:

1. In the Navigation pane, click Master Pages and then click the icon to the left of the master page that you want to use as the site's default master page, as shown next.

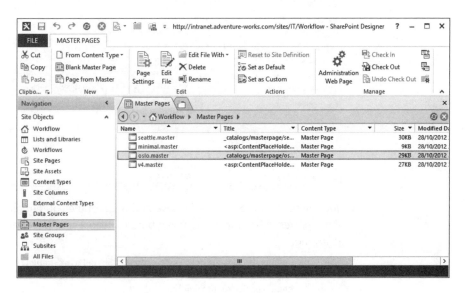

2. On the Master Pages tab, in the Actions group, click Set As Default.

You can modify which master page a content page uses. For example, you can specify whether you want to use the default master page or a different master page. Theoretically, each page within a site collection can use a different master page. Such a scenario would defeat the purpose of using master pages, however, because, as stated earlier, master pages were introduced to support a common look and feel across entire sites. However, making a content page use a specific master page can be very useful when you are developing a new master page because you can test your modification on one page without affecting all pages within a site.

To attach a master page other than the site's default master page to a content page, perform the following steps:

1. In SharePoint Designer, browse to the content page; for example, in the Navigation pane, click Site Pages.

2. Click the icon to the left of the content page. On the Pages tab, click the down arrow on the Edit File command, and then Edit File in Advanced Mode.

For more information on the advanced edit mode, see Chapter 9.

3. On the Style tab, in the Master Page group, click Attach, and then click the master page that you want to attach to the content page, as shown next.

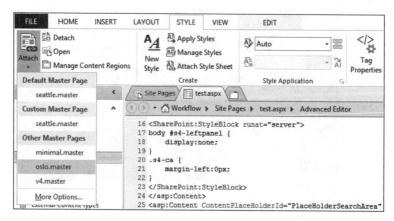

You will see that the @Page directive at the top of the content page no longer uses the *~masterurl/default.master* token but points to a specific master page, such as the following:

```
<%@ Page Language="C#" Inherits=Microsoft.SharePoint.WebPartPages.WikiEditPage"
    MasterPageFile="../_catalogs/masterpage/SPFIIO.master"
    meta:webpartpageexpansion="full"
    meta:progid="SharePoint.WebPartPage.Documet" %>
```

4. Save the content page, and if the content page is a site definition page, you will need to click Yes to the Site Definition Page Warning dialog box that is displayed. View the page in the browser.

> **Note**
> You can also use these steps if you have an .aspx page that is not associated with any master page. This can be very useful if you are migrating pages from a non-SharePoint site and you want the pages to look like all other pages within your site.

You can also create new content pages from a master page, and then add the necessary controls to the content page. However, users will not be able to amend the page in the browser if you do not include web part zones or the SharePoint control EmbeddedFormField. Therefore, especially if you want to create wiki pages, it is easier to create them by using the browser.

To create new content pages from a master page and then add the necessary controls, follow these steps:

1. In the Navigation pane, click Master Pages, and then, on the Master Pages tab, click Page From Master to open the Select A Master Page dialog box, shown next.

2. Select Default Master Page if you want to create the page from the site's default master page, or select Specific Master Page if you want to create a page from a specific master page. Then click Browse to choose the specific master page.

Master pages anatomy

Unlike content pages, master pages contain the tags <html>, <head>, <body>, and <form>. Master page file names have the extension .master, whereas content pages have an extension of .aspx. Master pages can also contain most of the content and functionality of content pages, including JavaScript, web parts (including Data Views and XLV Web Parts), and components such as the Search box and the component that displays the Quick Launch headings and links. Master pages cannot contain web part zones, however.

Each master page contains multiple core controls, which can be divided into four types:

- Controls for links, menus, icons, and navigation components, such as the *SiteMapPath* control that populates the global navigation breadcrumb. SharePoint 2013 also contains a number of new SharePoint controls related to the theme engine, such as ThemedForegroundImage, which together with some CSS, tells the theme engine how to theme an image.

- Content placeholders, such as the *PlaceHolderMain* control, that match areas on the content page where you can enter information.

- Delegate controls, which define a region on the page in which content can be substituted or added by another control driven by feature activation. This allows you to customize your sites, for example, without customizing master pages. Three new delegate controls were added in SharePoint 2013: PromotedActions, *SuiteBarBrandingDelegate*, and SuiteLinksDelegate, which identify regions on the top area of each page, as shown in Figure 20-23.

Figure 20-23 Use the delegate controls to add links to the upper-right section, override content that is displayed, or modify the default link.

- Controls for scripts, which manage the communication of the page and assist with the ribbon, toolbars, and other controls.

You can include style information in a master page, but it's good practice to use a CSS file linked to the master page. The key benefit of using a master page is that any global design changes to your site can be made in one place. By using a master page, you can design your site efficiently and quickly and avoid having to make changes on every page in the site. To locate and edit a master page, perform the following steps:

1. Open your SharePoint site in SharePoint Designer, and then, in the Navigation pane, click Master Pages.

2. Click the icon to the left of the master page that you want to edit, and then, on the Master Pages tab, click Edit File.

   The master page opens in the workspace, and on the breadcrumb, the text Advanced Editor indicates that the page is open in Advanced Edit mode.

3. In the mini-gallery below the Navigation pane, right-click the master page that you want to edit, and then click Check Out. A green check mark appears to the left of the master page, as shown next.

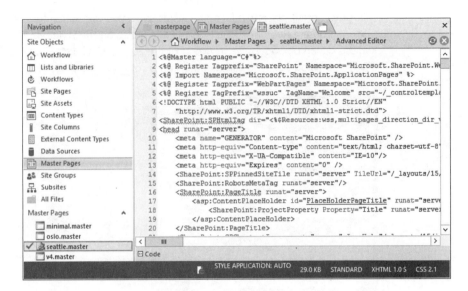

If you want to make a simple customization to a master page, make a copy of the file, or create a blank master page and paste the contents from an existing master page into the blank master page. Make your changes to the copy and test those changes by attaching your copied file to a single page. Then when you have tested your changes, make your copied file the default master page, as described earlier in this chapter. It is good practice to never amend the files provided by Microsoft.

Content placeholders

The key component of a master page is the content placeholder control. It is placed on the master page where content will eventually appear. The content page specifies which content placeholder the components should be placed in, such as

```
<asp:Content ContentPlaceHolderID="PlaceHolderMain" runat="server">

</asp:Content>
```

On the master page, the following code defines the content placeholder and specifies where on the page the content placeholder is located:

```
<asp:ContentPlaceHolder id="PlaceHolderMain" runat="server">

</asp:ContentPlaceHolder>
```

A master page typically has a number of content placeholders, the most important of which is *PlaceHolderMain*, which usually maps to the region on the master page where the elements from the content page should be placed.

To locate content placeholders on a master page, you can search for the control by clicking Manage Content Regions in the Master Page group on the Style tab. The Manage Content Regions dialog box opens, as shown in Figure 20-24, which lists all the regions on the page. Using this dialog box, you can rename, delete, or go to the placeholder.

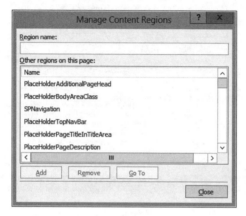

Figure 20-24 Use the Manage Content Regions dialog box to locate, add, and remove content placeholders.

> **Note**
>
> You can use the earlier steps to navigate to content placeholders only when you are working with a master page. On content pages, when you want to find a reference to a content placeholder, and it is not obvious in Design view where that reference is, you need to use the Find functionality in SharePoint Designer.

Other placeholders contain components that you can decide not to incorporate in the page, on a content page–by–content page basis. That is, the components stored within a content placeholder in a master page can be viewed as optional. For example, the components that display the Quick Launch are stored in the master page in the PlaceHolderLeftNavBar content placeholder. When you create a web part page, the templates used has modified the contents of the PlaceHolderLeftNavBar so that the Quick Launch does not appear. Any placeholders you find on a content page do not inherit their content from the master page.

INSIDE OUT ~ Using a starter master page

If you want to create your own master page, then do not start with a blank master page and add the controls yourself. It is likely that you will not include all the controls that are needed, and any content page associated with that master page will not display, and you will get the Sorry, Something Went Wrong page in the browser.

Use the master pages at the following location as starting points for your master page: *startermasterpages.codeplex.com.*

This master page contains comments and the required content placeholders and SharePoint controls on the page. They will be placed in a hidden section on the page. You can move these controls into other locations based on your design.

Creating a preview file

To create a Composed Look, you must have a master page, a preview page, and a color palette. The master page and the preview page are used to populate the layout picker in the Choose The Look page. The preview page must have the same name as the master page; that is, if the master page is named SPIO.master, then the preview page must be named SPIO.preview. Just as it is a good idea not to start with a blank master page, you should also not start with a blank preview page. Use an existing preview page as a basis for your preview page and open it as a text file.

The preview file contains four sections divided by [SECTION] delimiters. The first section points to the color palette to be used. The second section points to the default font scheme. The third section is tokenized CSS, and the last section is tokenized HTML, where class should be used and not IDs. The following is an extract of a preview file:

```
Palette001.spcolor
[SECTION]
SharePointPersonality.spfont
[SECTION]
[ID] .dgp-pageHyperLinkVisited
{
    color: [T_THEME_COLOR_HYPERLINKFOLLOWED] !important;
}
[ID] #dgp-pageContainer
{
    width: 100%;
    height:100%;
    position: relative;
    color: [T_THEME_COLOR_BODYTEXT];
```

```
    background-color: [T_THEME_COLOR_PAGEBACKGROUND];
    font-size: 1.0em;
    font-family: [T_BODY_FONT];
}
. . .
[ID] .dgp-tableheadertext
{
    color: [T_THEME_COLOR_SUBTLEBODYTEXT];
}

[SECTION]
<div id="dgp-pageContainer">
    <div class="dgp-background"></div>
    <div class="dgp-background-ie8"></div>
    <div class="dgp-pageContent">
        <div class="dgp-suiteBar">
            <div class="ms-tableRow">
                <div class="dgp-suiteBarLeft">
                    <div class="dgp-globalleft">
                        [BRANDSTRING]
                    </div>
                    <div class="dgp-globalright">
                        <span class="dgp-spacing">[SUITELINK1]</span>
                        <span class="dgp-spacing">[SUITELINK2]</span>
                        <span class="dgp-spacing">[SUITELINK3]</span>
                    </div>
                </div>
                <div class="dgp-suiteBarRight">
                    <span class="dgp-globalRightLink dgp-globalleft">[WELCOME]</span>
                </div>

                    <div>[CA ACCENT COLORS]</div>
                    <div class="dgp-contentBoxListHeader">[CA LIST TITLE]</div>
                    <table class="dgp-contentTable">[CA TABLE]</table>
                </div>
            </div>
        </div>
    </div>
</div>
```

Working with CSS

Like most industry-standard sites, SharePoint sites use CSS, and SharePoint Designer contains style sheet editors that make it easy to identify and edit the CSS rules and attributes. SharePoint Designer uses a set of configuration options to decide how it should add the CSS tags to your page. You can change these default settings from within the Page Editor Options dialog box, which you can open on the File tab by clicking Options.

CSS separates the look and feel from the content in your webpages. It is a declarative language that browsers use to format fonts, the color within the page, as well as the size and position of elements on the page. All modern browsers support CSS, and CSS functions exactly the same for SharePoint sites as it does with any other websites.

The main CSS file in SharePoint is Corev15.css, which contains over 13,000 lines of code and defines most of the styles you need to customize your site. Corev15.css is stored on the server in the root directory, %ProgramFiles%\Common Files\Microsoft Shared\Web Server Extensions\15\Template\Layouts\<*LCID*>\Styles, where <*LCID*> is the locale for the language packs you have installed. You should not amend this file, but instead create your own style files, which contain only those styles from Corev15.css that you need to modify. All of the CSS files provided by Microsoft are linked into the master page using the SharePoint control:

```
<SharePoint:CssLink runat="server" Version="15" />
```

When the master page is merged with your content page, and the CssLink control is run on the server, one or more HTML <link> statements are generated and sent to the browser, together with the CSS files.

If you want to change the CSS styles for your site or a number of sites, and if you do not have a development environment, then create your own site collection—or if that is not possible, a test site. On your test site, create a new .css file in your site's Style library, add the required CSS styles to your .css file, and then amend your master page and add the following code after the CssLink SharePoint control:

```
<SharePoint:CSSRegistration
    Name="%$SPUrl:~SiteCollection/Style Library/~language/Themable/SPFIO.css"
    After="corev15.css" runat="server" />
```

In the preceding example, SFPIO.css is the name of the custom .css file. The CSSLink control reads the information from the CSSResgistration SharePoint control and inserts a link tag into the page sent to the browser after the link tag for Corev15.css, thereby ensuring that your CSS styles are applied after the styles in Corev15.css. If you create multiple custom CSS files, you can also use the CSSRegistration control to ensure that your custom CSS files are applied in the correct order by using the After attribute.

You might need to reference image files from your CSS files. Upload these into the Style library in a subfolder named Images.

INSIDE OUT   Creating themeable CSS rules

The theme engine looks for CSS files in a set of well-known locations, such as _layouts, both in the localized and unlocalized folders, in the Themeable folder within them. It also looks in the site's Style library in a folder named Themeable. If your files are not in the Themeable folder, then they will not be themed by the engine, which is fine if you do not want your CSS to be themed. If you look inside the Corev15.css file, you will notice that some of the CSS attributes are prefixed by CSS comments, such as in the following example:

```
.ms-descriptiontext
{
 /* [ReplaceColor(themeColor:"SubtleBodyText")] */ color:#777;
}
```

When a theme is applied to your site, the CSSLink control recompiles the CSS files, and for the previous CSS code, it substitutes the color code #777 with the one specified in the theme by SubtleBodyText.

Deploying your design

Earlier in this chapter, we discussed how to customize a master page and CSS files by using SharePoint Designer. You might now want other sites to use a master page, CSS files, and associated files. If you want other site owners in your site collection to use your design, you could export the master page from your site's Master Page gallery and the associated files from your site's Style library, and then upload them to the site collections Master Page gallery and Style library. You might need to change the URL reference specified in the Name attribute in the CSSRegistration control and references to images in your custom CSS file. Using relative URL references to files might overcome this problem.

When the publishing feature is activated, you can use the browser to apply master pages to a site or the whole of a site collection, by using the Master Page link under Look And Feel on the Site Settings page. However, if you want your master page to be available for all sites in all site collections in a web application, or you do not wish to activate the publishing feature on all site collections, then the best option is to deploy the master page plus its associated files as a feature. You will need Microsoft Visual Studio 2010 to create a feature. Visual Studio does not provide a master page designer; however, when teamed with SharePoint Designer, each tool can compensate for the other tool's shortcoming. For example, SharePoint Designer stores any changes to the content database and provides no source code control. Visual Studio supports source control and can deploy files to the SharePoint server's file system.

Saving sites as templates

A site template, also known as a *web template,* is essentially a copy of a site that is saved using the browser and stored in the content database. And because it is stored in the content database and does not need to be stored on SharePoint servers, it is a compelling deployment model for custom SharePoint solutions, both on-premise and in Office 365.

When SharePoint is first installed, the basis for all new sites are files stored on the SharePoint servers, known as *site definitions.* New site definitions are created by developers and packaged as solutions, whereas you can use the browser to create site templates by clicking Save Site As Template under Look And Feel on the Site Settings page. And just like site definitions, site templates are created as solution files and saved in the site collection's Solutions gallery, from which you can download and use them on other site collections.

Chapter 20

> **Note**
>
> When a site template is created, whether it is when you used the Save As Template page or you have uploaded and activated a site template in the Solutions gallery, then for each site template, a new site collection feature is created, named Web Template Feature Of Exported Web Template *<site name>*.

Optionally, you can save content in the site template; however, you do not have the option to save publishing sites as site templates. When a developer creates web templates in Visual Studio, they can be based on publishing sites and use publishing features. Developers can also use a site template created using the browser as a basis for a web template. However, a site template contains many files and each file contains information that is needed to build a site, such as information about all content types defined at the site and site-collection level, even if those content types are not used to create a site from your site template. Developers using Visual Studio can select which information to import from a site template; however, it is difficult to determine the information that is required by a site template to create a site. For this reason, developers will use a site template as a basis for a web template only when small modifications are needed. Typically, developers create new web templates that reference a site definition, scoped at the farm or site-collection level.

In the browser when you create a site, users need not know the difference between site templates and site definitions. In fact, on the New SharePoint Site page, they are referred to as *templates.* However, site templates will be listed only under the Custom tab, whereas site definitions can be listed under any tab and are not usually listed under the Custom tab.

You can control which site templates can be used to create sites in site collections where the publishing feature is activated by clicking Page Layouts and Site Templates under Look And Feel on the Site Settings page.

When a site template is moved to another server or site collection, any features used by that template must be activated in the destination site collection's Solutions gallery. If an out-of-the-box workflow is included as part of a site template, then the site-collection feature that enables the use of the workflow must be activated. SharePoint 2013 workflows are not included, as they are not stored within the site, but rather in the Workflow Manager databases.

Lists, libraries, Web Part pages, wiki pages, custom pages, navigational customizations, and versioning settings are saved within the site template. Content up to a limit of 50 MB can be saved. However, security settings, Web Part page personalizations, and user alerts are not included. Therefore, since no security settings are saved, any sensitive content saved in the site template can be viewed by users on sites created from site templates.

Site templates include references to activated features, both site collection and site features, therefore before you create a site template, it is best to create a site collection with a blank site at the top level of the site collection and then activate those features you need. Using the browser, a site (whether it is a top-level site of a site collection or a subsite) cannot be created using the Blank Site template; you will need to use Windows PowerShell.

Unless you are going to get a developer involved, you will need to document those site-collection features that must be activated and pass that information on to any users who will use the template. If you do not activate a dependent feature prior to using the template, the site creation process will fail. If you try to create a site from a site template when a feature that it is dependent on is not activated, you will see the error message stating that the site template requires a feature, and providing you with the GUID of the feature. The browser error message references a correlation ID, which can be used to find more information from SharePoint's ULS logs, which are located on the SharePoint servers in the LOGs folder. When developers create site templates or site definitions, they can ensure that any dependent components or features are activated as part of the site creation process.

Summary

SharePoint Designer is a tool that you can use when designing SharePoint sites and solutions. It is the tool to use when creating workflows and can be used to create external content types. With the demise of Design view, it no longer is a no-code form editing tool; however, SharePoint Designer can be used as a tool that site or site-collection owners can use to manage their sites.

SharePoint Designer can also be used to help you design your sites when you do not have the Design Manager available or you wish to develop complex master pages. You can also use it to amend XML and CSS files, such as the new color palette (.spcolor) and font scheme (.spfont) files or Corev15.css.

For those organizations that implement development, test, and production environments, SharePoint Designer can be used in the preproduction environments, and amendments can be transferred to the production environment in a controlled manner. SharePoint Designer is safe by default when editing pages and its usage can be controlled at the web-application and site-collection levels.

You can use site templates as a basis for new sites. You can also limit which site templates can be used as a basis for new sites.

Creating enterprise forms

MICROSOFT SharePoint has a long history of being a capable platform for hosting and managing business forms of all types. In the past, these forms fell largely into two categories: declarative (no code) and custom code. Depending on the specific requirements (or skills of the forms designer), SharePoint forms were generally created with Microsoft InfoPath, Microsoft SharePoint Designer, or Microsoft Visual Studio.

These options all still exist in SharePoint 2013, although SharePoint Designer is being deemphasized as a forms tool. InfoPath XML-based forms and Visual Studio 2012 custom forms are still fully supported as form design tools, and the integration they have had with SharePoint in the past is still available. For code-based solutions, your new form projects can piggyback on the support of HTML5 and .NET offered by SharePoint. Visual Studio 2012 is still the flagship tool for creating custom code forms, although with support for HTML5 and JavaScript, several new possibilities exist for responsive design, including TypeScript, jQuery libraries, and so on.

In addition to the aforementioned tools, SharePoint 2013 introduces one compelling, new option for no-code forms: Microsoft Access 2013 form apps. (We'll discuss this more later in this chapter.)

Many factors go into the decision of which tool is best to create your forms with. Some of the factors are technical, some are business-oriented, and some are just pragmatic decisions based on what is possible.

Some of the strengths of InfoPath 2013 forms are:

- Support for offline form-filling scenarios, where users are disconnected from the network

- Deep integration with SharePoint libraries

- Ability to customize SharePoint list forms

- Options for rich-client or browser-based forms

- Support for code-behind solutions using Visual Studio 2012

Some of the strengths of Access 2013 forms are:

- Full support of the new app model

- Integrated with the SharePoint app catalog

- Form data is stored in Microsoft SQL Server

- Inherits SharePoint site permissions and branding

- Cross-browser and mobile support

Some of the advantages of custom code forms are:

- Total control over the UI elements

- Full support of the SharePoint app model

- Ability to connect the form to all the various SharePoint application programming interfaces (APIs) and Web Services

- Allows developers to publish their form to the public SharePoint store for customers to purchase it

- Option to use a variety of industry-standard web-development tools

This chapter primarily focuses on the no-code solutions: InfoPath 2013 and Access 2013. A downloadable custom code example of the sample form written using HTML5 and JavaScript is available for download at *www.* .

For more information on building custom code solutions, see Chapter 23, "Introduction to custom development."

Creating InfoPath forms

InfoPath 2013 is a forms-creation and data-gathering tool that can help you streamline your business processes. It is a flexible, powerful, easy-to-use XML forms editor that's part of the Microsoft Office Professional suite. InfoPath 2013 is well suited for almost anyone that needs to design and deploy form solutions—including information workers, IT pros, and developers. You can use InfoPath 2013 to design sophisticated forms that can quickly and accurately gather information that meet your organizational needs. Moreover, its deep integration with the SharePoint platform opens up a new world of possibilities for your electronic form requirements.

Introduction to InfoPath

InfoPath empowers you to design and fill out electronic forms that are hosted on SharePoint, such as expense reports, event registrations, and other common business forms. When entering data in an InfoPath 2013 form, users are presented with familiar, document-like features. For example, they can change fonts, check spelling, or insert images into certain fields.

If you create your forms as browser-enabled form templates, users who do not have InfoPath installed on their computers can still work with the form in a browser. This lets you share business forms with a variety of users, including employees, customers, and vendors.

The forms that you design can range from simple forms for collecting data from a small group to complex forms that are integral components of a much larger business process. If you use SharePoint Server 2013 and SharePoint Designer, InfoPath 2013 forms can be used as part of a fully automated business process. This can include workflows, such as routing and notification based on information within the form. In addition, the data that users enter in your InfoPath forms does not have to remain sealed inside that form forever; it can be reused in a variety of ways within SharePoint.

InfoPath provides forms design capabilities that include sophisticated logic rules, conditional formatting, and data validation to information workers who may not be programmers. To benefit from these capabilities previously would have required a great deal of technical expertise. A large factor in the power of InfoPath is that the file format of the forms is XML, which provides many inherent benefits in terms of flexibility, power, and standardization. Fortunately, InfoPath forms designers are not required to know much about XML, XML schema definition (XSD) extensible stylesheet language transformations (XSLT), XSLT, and all the other technical details behind the scenes. The UI of InfoPath is essentially the same as the other Office 2013 products. If you are familiar with Microsoft Word, Microsoft Excel, or Access, you probably will feel right at home in InfoPath 2013.

INSIDE OUT   XML 101

XML is perhaps the single most powerful method of storing and sharing structured data to come along since the advent of digital computing. InfoPath uses XML as its primary file/output format. Behind the scenes, when users create an InfoPath form, what they are actually doing is creating an XML document and an associated XML schema. The fact that the file format that InfoPath uses to store and manage data is XML provides you with an amazing amount of power in an easy-to-use tool. InfoPath does an admirable job of allowing everyday business users of Office to take advantage of the plentiful benefits of XML while hiding much of the complexity. We do not need to become experts in XML to create powerful forms, but having a very basic understanding of what XML is and how it works seems a reasonable goal for someone planning to fully employ InfoPath's power. For more information on XML, see the MSDN article "Understanding XML," at *http://msdn.microsoft.com/en-us/library/aa468558.aspx.*

Form design basics

Most InfoPath forms that you create will have several basic design concepts in common. The form design process typically begins with the following two tasks:

1. Building the visual aspects of the form by using tables, themes, and page designs

2. Adding the necessary controls to provide the functionality and data fields that your form requires

Depending on the complexity of the form, you might need to do much more than this, but typically, the creation of most InfoPath forms starts with layout and controls.

As previously mentioned, InfoPath uses XML for storing data and managing the schema of the form for you. Most of the tools that you will use to build the form have a direct correlation to the underlying XML. However, InfoPath removes the need for you to interact with all of the XML "plumbing" behind the scenes. For example, when you add a simple text control, InfoPath automatically generates an XML leaf node (the XML equivalent of an InfoPath field) in the underlying XML schema.

When you open InfoPath on your desktop, the design time visual layout tools that you will use most often can be found on the ribbon, as shown in Figure 21-1.

Figure 21-1 The InfoPath ribbon includes the visual layout tools that you will use most often.

The following tabs on the ribbon are relevant to form layout:

*   **Home** This is where you can find the basic text editing tools that you would find in a word processor. The functionality available on the Home tab is for controlling fonts— size, color, and so forth. These tools are fairly standard and work just as in the other Office products.

- **Insert** This is where you can find the prebuilt table styles. These tables can give your forms a consistent and professional layout.

- **Page Design** This is where you can find InfoPath's predefined page layouts and color themes to quickly give your form a professional look and feel. The color themes are the same ones that are in SharePoint, so it's easy to make your forms blend in nicely on a SharePoint site. Also, on the Page Design tab, you can work with Views and add headers/footers if necessary.

- **Layout** The tools on this tab (also known as the Table Tools tab) are used for modifying properties of the tables in your forms. Tables are the primary structural tool for organizing controls, labels, and images in your forms. This is also the location where you can use the Table Drawing tool if you don't want to use any of the provided table styles.

There are multiple approaches to building InfoPath forms. The one that is most common is to simply begin with one of the built-in page layouts on the Page Design tab of the ribbon, add some tables and a color theme, and then begin adding data controls in order to complete the form's functional requirements.

Along the way of the InfoPath form design process, there are many best practices. A few of the key ones will be highlighted in the next section as we dissect a completed form. If you require a comprehensive tutorial on InfoPath design, Microsoft Press and other publishers have entire books dedicated solely to InfoPath.

Walkthrough of the sample Site Request form

To illustrate the process of designing an InfoPath form, we will walk through the steps to create a sample Records Management Site Request form. This form uses several common InfoPath capabilities that are used when designing enterprise forms that are hosted on SharePoint. The purpose of this form is for employees of the Blue Yonder Airlines company to be able to submit a form to request that a SharePoint Records Management site be provisioned for them.

> **Note**
>
> The completed Records Management SharePoint Site Request form sample is available for download at: *http://aka.ms/SP2013InsideOut/files.*

The form itself is not complex; it really is just gathering some basic information via a series of questions. However, the way in which the form is designed takes advantage of InfoPath's ability to provide business logic, rules, and conditional formatting—all without writing any code. The form is built in a wizard-like approach that walks the user through a series of screens. The functionality in InfoPath that allows this to happen is provided by *views*. After gathering the information from the user, the final screen of the form gives the user a summary of his or her answers.

INSIDE OUT Views

Your forms often will have too many controls to fit cleanly on a single page. One of the worst mistakes novice forms designers can make is putting everything on one page and forcing the user to scroll through an unnecessarily long and complex form—or even worse, creating multiple forms for users to fill out when having one consolidated form is far more efficient and manageable. InfoPath views can help alleviate these problems and solve a few other challenges as well.

A view in InfoPath is simply another view to display data from the same data source, but in a different way. It is perhaps easiest to think of a view simply as another page in the same form. If you create a second view, additional or different fields may be displayed, or even a completely different visual layout; however, underneath the covers, all the views in a form use the same data source(s) and XML schema.

What follows are some common situations where using InfoPath Views make a lot of sense:

- Taking a lengthy or unwieldy form and breaking it into more manageable pieces.

- Building a wizard-like or survey-like interface. Because you can use buttons with rules to switch views, views provide an easy way to build a form with multiple pages that a user clicks through.

- Presenting different views to different users based on role. InfoPath Roles allow you to define which views a user can see depending on which security groups they are in. For example, your form might need to have an extra page of data that only members of the "Managers in Finance" group can see. (Note that Roles are an InfoPath client-only feature.)

- Adding a view that is read-only for the purpose of confirmation when the user is finished with input. An entire view can be set to read-only, which makes it useful for a confirmation when a user is done filling out the form.

- Providing a summary or roll-up view. Some forms need a dashboard that consolidates data from multiple other views into one place. Also, some forms might need a very different visual layout than the input views of the form.

- Providing a print view. Similar to the summary view, a print view can be useful when you want to give users a page to print out data from your form, consolidated in one special view just for printing.

Opening the Site Request form in InfoPath

When you download the Site Request form, you'll notice that the file extension is .xsn. This indicates that the file is an InfoPath template. When you have the form downloaded to your system, you will need to find the file in Windows Explorer, then right-click the file and choose Design, as shown in Figure 21-2. This will open the form in InfoPath 2013 in Design mode. If you were to just double-click the file, the file would open in InfoPath in Filler mode, as if you wanted to submit a new form. However, our goal for now is to take a high-level look at how the form is put together.

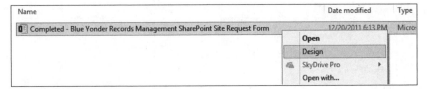

Figure 21-2 The steps to open the Site Request Design form in InfoPath Design mode.

INSIDE OUT   InfoPath templates

When you design a new form, you are actually creating an InfoPath template. The template is saved with an .xsn file extension. After you publish your template to a location that is accessible by your users, that they can create forms that are based on your template, but each instance that they create and save will be saved with an .xml file extension. So to recap, you use InfoPath in Design mode to create .xsn templates, which are published to SharePoint, where your users can go to generate new form instances (.xml files) based on your template.

Understanding the design of the InfoPath Site Request form

In this section, you will learn about the design techniques used to build the Site Request form. The approach we will use is to look at the form's views one at a time and point out the most important design considerations within each view.

View 1 (Home)

When you open the form in Design mode, you should be taken to the first view of the form. To confirm this, you can select the Page Design tab on the ribbon. Once there, you will see a drop-down menu, as shown in Figure 21-3, that lets you navigate quickly between views while in Design mode.

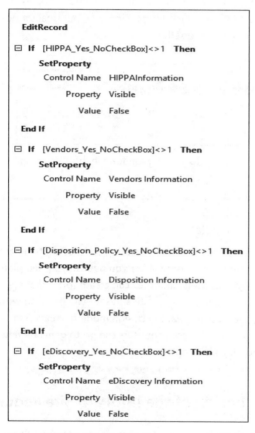

Figure 21-3 The View drop-down menu on the Page Design tab lets you navigate quickly between views in Design mode.

Once you have confirmed that you are seeing the Home view, notice that this initial page of the form is actually quite simple. We are simply asking users to select what type of records they expect to keep in the new site they are requesting. If you look at the properties for the drop-down menu, as shown in Figure 21-4, you will see that they have six options to choose from.

In addition to a drop-down menu for the record type, the consumer of the form is given
a text box in which they can type in some comments about the specifics of their request.
After the user has performed these two tasks on the form, the only other item that's
of interest is the arrow graphic on the lower-right part of the Home view. This arrow is
provided as a way to allow the user to navigate easily to the next screen (view) of the form.
This is the first example in the form of using Rules to provide functionality in the form.

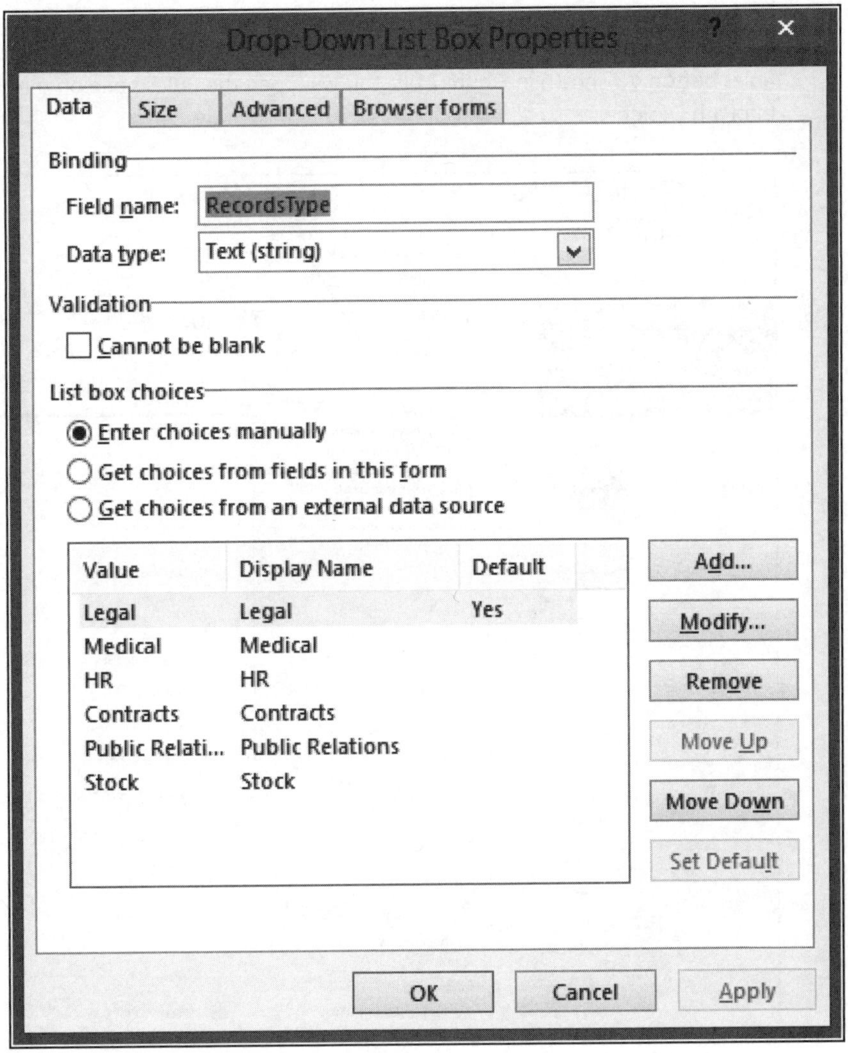

Figure 21-4 The Records Type drop-down has six properties to choose from.

> **Note**
>
> The arrow graphic is a special type of control in InfoPath called a *Picture button*. Picture buttons allow the designer to associate logic and formatting rules with graphics and icons.

Click the arrow graphic so that it is the active selection on the design surface. Once you have done that, ensure that you choose the Home tab of the ribbon and select the Manage Rules button. As shown in Figure 21-5, this will open the Rules pane on the right side of the InfoPath Designer.

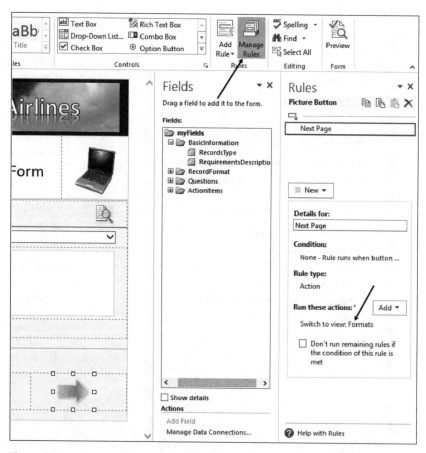

Figure 21-5 Select the Manage Rules button from the Home tab to open the Rules pane on the right side of the InfoPath Designer.

This particular rule is an Action rule —simple, but useful. The rule simply dictates that when the form user clicks the arrow, InfoPath should take the action of moving them to the next view they will be working with. In this case, clicking the arrow will take the form user to the Formats view.

To see this in action, press the F5 key while inside InfoPath Designer. This will put the form into Preview mode so that you can easily see what the user experience will be at run time. When you have the form opened in Preview mode, click the arrow and notice that you are taken forward to the next view in the form.

View 2 (Formats)

If you are not already back in the Designer, close out of Preview mode and, using the Page Design tab on the ribbon, navigate to the *Formats* view. One of the first things you'll notice on the Formats view is that we now have two arrow graphics on the form. Each of these Picture buttons has an Action rule associated with it that allows the user to navigate to either the previous view or the next one.

The primary purpose of the Formats view is to have the user choose whether their records are digital, physical, or both. Each of the icons in the middle of the view is associated (via a rule) with a record format. As with the arrow graphic, if you make one of the graphics the active selection in the Designer and then look at the Rules pane, you will see the details of the rule.

As shown in Figure 21-6, you will be able to see the logic assigned to any particular picture button. Notice that the rule sets both the value of the respective format field and the value of the DisplayLabel field at the same time.

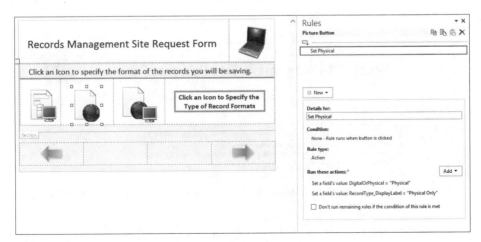

Figure 21-6 In the Rules pane, rules are applied to picture buttons.

Use the F5 shortcut to enter Preview mode while in Formats view. This will allow you to see what this view would do for the form user in Run-time mode.

View 3 (Questions)

If you are not already back in the Designer, close out of Preview mode and, using the Page Design tab on the ribbon, navigate to the *Questions* view. This view asks the user some questions about the nature of their requirements and then displays appropriate information. The method that the form uses to do this is *Formatting Rules*. The formatting rules in this view are primarily to show or hide information depending on the user's answers. As with the previous two views, the Questions view also makes use of picture buttons tied to Action rules, but in a slightly different and creative manner.

Use F5 to enter Preview mode so that you can understand what this view performs when a user is in Run-time mode. After you have familiarized yourself with the functionality of the Questions view, return to InfoPath Designer.

INSIDE OUT   Conditional formatting

A common mistake that forms designers make is to try to display a large amount of information to users, thus overwhelming them and making the form difficult to use. As demonstrated with the Questions view, conditional formatting rules can help overcome this challenge by allowing the interface to dynamically show or hide sections of information, thereby greatly enhancing the form's usability.

With the Questions view open in InfoPath Designer, click the Question Mark picture button, as shown in Figure 21-7.

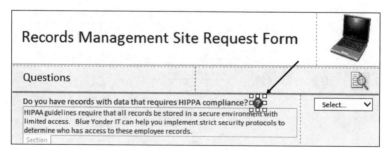

Figure 21-7 When selected, the Question Mark picture button enables further explanatory text to be displayed.

Notice that once you select the Question Mark picture button, you will have a couple of items displayed in the Rules pane. There are two possible rules instantiated when the user clicks the button: a Show rule and a Hide rule. The purpose of the rules are to either show or hide the Help sections for each question. The Help section contains the actual help text. When the user clicks the question mark, the Show rule sets a Boolean field's value to True. When they click it again, it sets the field's value to False, as shown in Figure 21-8.

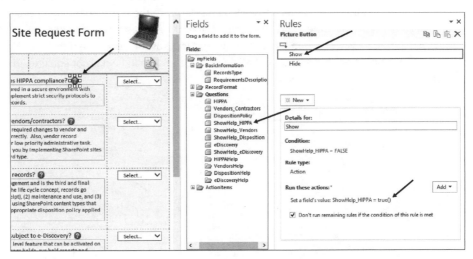

Figure 21-8 The Show Action rule is displayed when the Question Mark picture button is selected.

As you can see in Figure 21-9, each section also has a formatting rule that simply references its respective Boolean field to determine whether it should display the help text on the form.

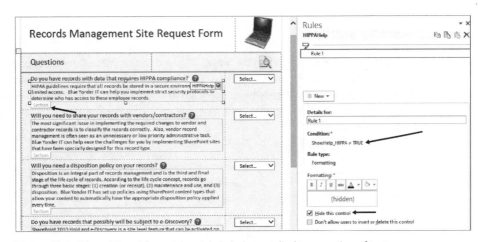

Figure 21-9 A conditional formatting rule is being applied to a section of text.

To summarize, when clicked, the Question Mark picture button runs an Action rule that sets a Boolean field to True or False. The section containing the actual help text then references the hidden field via a conditional formatting rule to determine whether to show itself or not.

In addition to the Help sections, notice at the bottom of the form that additional Action Items informational sections will be displayed to the user depending upon his or her answers. In Figure 21-10, you can see that these Action Item sections will be shown or hidden using the same type of rules and logic as the above Help sections. Notice that the logic here tells the section that if the hidden Boolean field is *not* equal to True, hide the section.

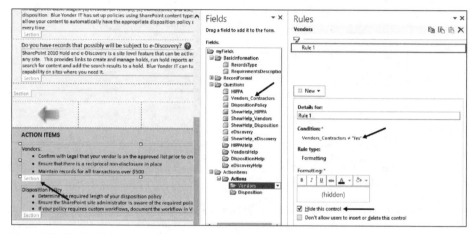

Figure 21-10 At the bottom of the form, additional Action Items informational sections are displayed depending upon users' answers.

View 4 (Summary)

If you are not already back in the Designer, close out of Preview mode and, using the Page Design tab on the ribbon, navigate to the Summary view. This view aggregates and displays information that has already been collected in previous views, as shown in Figure 21-11. It uses the same type of logic as the previous view did to determine whether to display any of the Action Items.

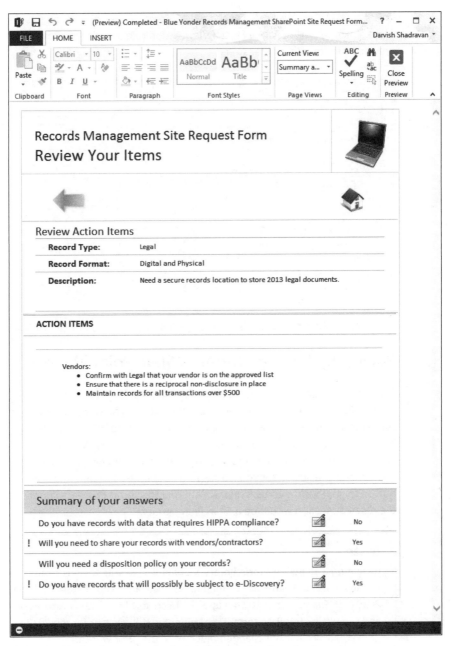

Figure 21-11 The Summary view is shown in Preview (run-time) mode.

In Figure 21-12, you will see that the most interesting use of rules on this view is once again using a picture button with a Switch View Action rule in order to allow users to return to a previous view to edit their answers.

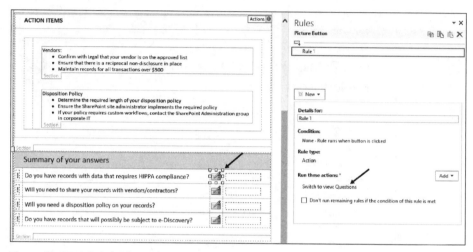

Figure 21-12 A Switch View rule is being applied to a picture button in the Summary view.

Publishing InfoPath forms to SharePoint libraries

One major component is missing in the Site Request form that you will need to add to a form like this in the real world—a Submit button. If you want to have your users easily submit (save) the form to a SharePoint form library once they are done filling it out, the best practice would be to add a nice large SUBMIT THIS FORM button somewhere on the last view. In order to do this, you or your SharePoint administrator will need to create a SharePoint form library for your forms to be published to. And then you will need to add a button to your form that uses an InfoPath rule to submit to a data connection. In our case, the data connection would be a SharePoint library.

> **Note**
>
> If creating a SharePoint form library is unfamiliar to you, there is plenty of information online regarding SharePoint form libraries. Also, an entire chapter in *Using InfoPath 2010 with SharePoint 2010 Step by Step* (Microsoft Press; 2011) focuses on publishing and submitting InfoPath forms. The content is still relevant for the 2013 version of InfoPath, which has not changed much since the prior version.

Creating Access forms

In this section, you will learn about creating SharePoint forms by using Access 2013. You will be given a walkthrough of a Site Request form similar to the previous section, but this time built in Access and using the new SharePoint app model.

Introduction to Access 2013

Access 2013 features a new application model that enables power users and developers alike to quickly create web-based form applications. Most Access databases need a good form in front of them, and fortunately Access 2013 includes a set of templates that you can use to jump-start creating your application. Taking a look at some of the example templates included with Access is a great way to understand how to build your own form app.

> **Note**
>
> To use Access 2013 forms, you must have Access Services enabled on your SharePoint farm. Access Services are part of SharePoint's *Enterprise* features.

As mentioned in Chapter 5, "Using Office applications with SharePoint," when SharePoint 2013 hosts an Access app, SQL Server 2012 is used as its data storage technology. Therefore, Access 2013 significantly improves the manageability and scalability of Access form applications. Availability of Access Services with Office 365 and SQL Azure can significantly increase the reach of your Access forms.

INSIDE OUT   Using SQL rather than SharePoint lists to store form data

As you saw in the last section, InfoPath forms (along with all their data) can be stored in SharePoint lists. This approach has benefits because of the close coupling with SharePoint list features. Access 2013 forms take a different approach by having deep integration with SQL Server (SQL Azure if you're in the cloud). When you use Access 2013 to create a form app on SharePoint, Access Services generates a SQL Server database that stores all the objects and data in the form. This architecture has certain trade-offs when compared with InfoPath—some of which will be addressed in future updates (such as workflow integration). But on the positive side, storing the forms directly in a SQL database increases performance and scalability. Also, SQL developers can work with the Access form data to build rich, highly scalable form applications.

Building a simple Access form app

Building an Access form like the InfoPath example shown in the previous section is similar in terms of effort. Replicating the basic functionality of the Site Request form can be accomplished without any code; however, from a design standpoint, Access 2013 is a different tool than InfoPath. Using some basic design tactics in the Access Designer, we can essentially replicate the form, but now you can also gain all the inherent advantages of a forms tool that conforms with the new app model.

Before we deconstruct the Site Request form built in Access, let's cover a few basic Access forms design concepts.

Views

Access forms also have the concept of views, much as InfoPath does.

For more information, see the MSDN article "What's New for Access 2013 developers," at *http://msdn.microsoft.com/en-us/library/office/jj250134.aspx#ac15_WhatsNew_Views*.

Access automatically generates two views—List and Datasheet—for each table in your form. You can also create blank views if you prefer to start from scratch with your form views. Each view in an Access form automatically gets some useful built-in UI elements, such as the Action Bar, which that is common in each view and shown in Figure 21-13. The buttons, from left to right, perform the following actions:

- Add a new record/form

- Delete the current form

- Edit the current form

- Save your changes

- Cancel your changes

If required for your form, you can add buttons that perform custom actions. You can also delete the default buttons, or hide the Action Bar altogether. In many cases, the default buttons provide the basic editing capabilities that Access form apps need.

Figure 21-13 The default buttons on the Action Bar provide basic editing capabilities.

Macros

There are two types of macros in Access forms: UI macros and Data macros. UI macros will be used extensively in most Access forms because they provide the intuitive navigation guidance of a well-designed form. UI macros perform actions such as navigating to another view or using logic to show or hide various controls. UI macros can be attached directly to objects, such as command buttons or combo boxes.

When you connect a UI macro to an object in the form, the macro is typically triggered by an event. The types of events supported by UI macros include:

- **On Click** Occurs when a control is selected via a mouse click.

- **On Load** When a view is first opened, On Load macros are instantiated.

- **On Current** When the user moves to a different record in a form view.

- **After Update** After you type data into a control or choose data from a control, this type of macro is triggered.

While UI macros focus on the elements that the form user interacts with, data macros provide the capability for implementing business rules at the data layer. Therefore, data macros can create, edit, and delete records.

Understanding the design of the Access Site Request form

In this section, we will explain the Access version of the Site Request form on a view-by-view basis. This will allow you to fully grasp the design principles at work within each page of the form.

> **Note**
> The completed sample form for the following walkthrough is available for download as an .app package at: *www.* . Before you can use the app, you (or your administrator) will need to add the .app package to your app catalog. Instructions to do that are at *http://technet.microsoft.com/en-us/library/fp161234.aspx#AddApps*. Once the app has been added to your app catalog, you need to then add the Records Management Request app to your site. Instructions on how to add an app to your site are located at *http://technet.microsoft.com/en-us/library/fp161231.aspx*.

View 1 (Home)

After you have added the Site Request app to a site in which you are an owner, go ahead and use the Add button on the Action Bar of the form to add a few new records. While navigating through the form and its various views, you should begin to get an understanding of the user experience differences between an Access-based form and InfoPath. When you have created and saved a few new records, then use the Settings icon and choose Customize In Access, as shown in Figure 21-14. This will open Access 2013 and put you in Edit mode, which is similar to Design mode in InfoPath.

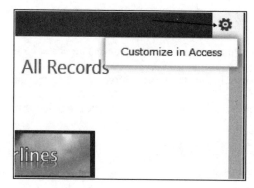

Figure 21-14 Use the Settings icon to edit the form in Access.

Once Access opens the form, ensure that you are in the Home view, as shown in Figure 21-15, and then click the Edit icon.

Figure 21-15 The Home view of the Site Request form.

Now that you have entered Edit mode, we'll take a look at a few of the highlights of this view so that you can understand how to design an elegant, easy-to-use form app using Access 2013.

When you previewed the form in your browser, you may have noticed that the Request Name field contained some text to help the form user. This is called an *input hint*. A best practice is not to use input hints on every field in your form, or else the user will learn to ignore them. But in a required field, such as Request Name, it makes sense to alert users to the fact that they must enter a value. As shown in Figure 21-16, you can see that there is a toolbar with three options on many of the controls in Access forms: Data, Formatting, and Actions. These will help you provide the functionality that each of the fields in your form may need. In the case of the Request Name field, we use the input hint under Formatting to provide the hint.

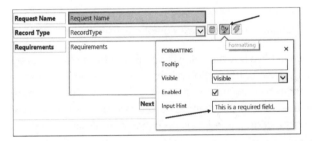

Figure 21-16 An input hint on the Request Name field of the Site Request form.

As users proceed in the Home view of the Site Request form, they are given a drop-down combo box from which to select the desired type of record. The items in the drop-down box can come from either a table in your Access database, or they can be entered manually into the table properties, as shown in Figure 21-17. To access the list of values for a combo box, select the Modify Lookups button on the ribbon.

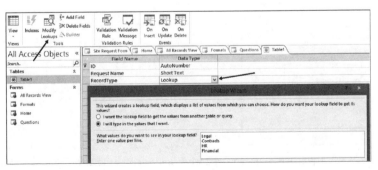

Figure 21-17 The items in the drop-down field can come from a table in your Access database or they can be entered manually into the table properties.

Also on the Home view, there is an arrow graphic similar to the picture button on the InfoPath version of the form. This helps the user easily navigate through the various views of the form in a wizard-like manner, thus eliminating any potential confusion. If you select the Actions property of the arrow graphic, you will notice in Figure 21-18 that the On Click Macro button is green, indicating to the form designer that a macro has been assigned to this particular action.

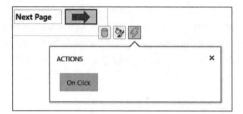

Figure 21-18 The Action property of the arrow graphic is selected.

When you select the On Click button, you will be taken into the Macro Designer in Access. As you can see in Figure 21-19, the action macro in this case performs two quite simple tasks. First, it saves the record when the user selects the arrow. This eliminates the need for the form to ask the user to save the changes before moving to the next view. The macro will perform the Save function immediately on behalf of the user when the user clicks the arrow. Second, the macro performs a ChangeView action to take the user to the Formats view when the arrow is clicked.

Figure 21-19 The macro is instantiated when a user clicks the arrow graphic in the Site Request form.

View 2 (Formats)

As the user progresses to the second view of the form (Formats), the form design approach selected on this view was to simply present the user a series of check box controls to select one or more record formats that will be stored in their SharePoint site. Each of the check boxes will store a Yes or No value as the user fills out this view. You can see in Figure 21-20 that the check boxes are connected to their respective fields in the database schema via the Data properties for each control.

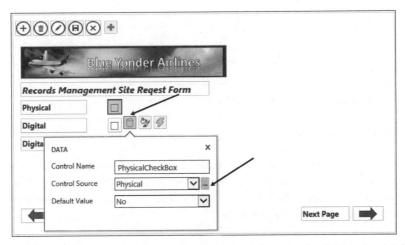

Figure 21-20 The check boxes are connected to their respective fields in the database schema via the Data properties for each control.

One other design tactic worth noting on this view is that the entire view itself has a macro that is instantiated immediately when the view is opened by the form user. The purpose of this On Load macro is to ensure that the form is in Edit mode when the user is moved into the view. If we did not add this macro, the user would have to click the Edit button from the Action Bar—an unnecessary step.

In order to see a macro on a view when in Design mode, you need to click anywhere with some empty space (not on a control) in the view. As shown in Figure 21-21, this will enable the properties for the view. The macros again are under the Actions properties.

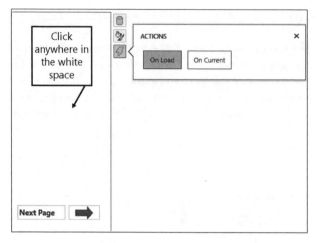

Figure 21-21 An action macro can be applied to the entire view.

View 3 (Questions)

The Questions view, shown in Figure 21-22, is the third view that the user encounters when filling out our simple Site Request form. The purpose of this view is simply to ask the user four questions about the nature of their records content and display extra information about each selection the user makes.

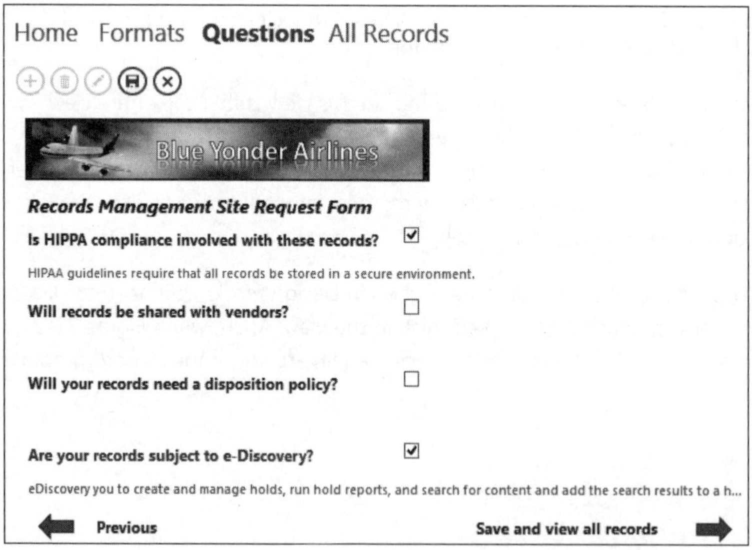

Home Formats **Questions** All Records

Records Management Site Request Form

Is HIPPA compliance involved with these records? ☑

HIPAA guidelines require that all records be stored in a secure environment.

Will records be shared with vendors? ☐

Will your records need a disposition policy? ☐

Are your records subject to e-Discovery? ☑

eDiscovery you to create and manage holds, run hold reports, and search for content and add the search results to a h...

Previous   Save and view all records

Figure 21-22 The third view of the Site Request form is the Questions view.

Similar to the Formats view, the Question view of the form has a macro that runs when the form initially loads. The purpose of this macro, as shown in Figure 21-23, is to ensure that the extra information for each question is set to be hidden. So if the respective item's selection is not equal to 1 (true), then hide the detailed information. This helps reduce clutter when the view is initially displayed to the user.

```
EditRecord

☐ If  [HIPPA_Yes_NoCheckBox]<>1  Then
    ☐ SetProperty
        Control Name  HIPPAInformation
            Property  Visible
               Value  False

   End If

☐ If  [Vendors_Yes_NoCheckBox]<>1  Then
        SetProperty
        Control Name  Vendors Information
            Property  Visible
               Value  False

   End If

☐ If  [Disposition_Policy_Yes_NoCheckBox]<>1  Then
        SetProperty
        Control Name  Disposition Information
            Property  Visible
               Value  False

   End If

☐ If  [eDiscovery_Yes_NoCheckBox]<>1  Then
        SetProperty
        Control Name  eDiscovery Information
            Property  Visible
               Value  False

   End If
```

Figure 21-23 The Form Load macro for the Questions view ensures that the extra information for each question is set to be hidden.

As you just saw, when the Questions view initially loads on a new record, the extra information about each question is hidden until they select it. Once selected, however, then another set of macros (which are tied to each check box's After Update property) take over. The purpose of these macros (see Figure 21-24) is to toggle the extra detailed information on or off, depending on whether the form user has selected that particular item.

The result is that users get a very clean form that only displays extra detail about each question if they need it. If after reading the details they decide they don't need that item checked, they can simply clear it, and the details disappear because the macro returns the Visible value to False.

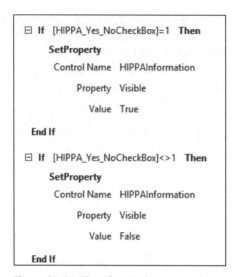

Figure 21-24 The After Update macro is connected to the HIPPA check box control in the Questions view of the form.

View 4 (All Records)

The final view of the form is simply an Access List view that has had the data fields rearranged on it slightly to make it more usable and aesthetically pleasing (see Figure 21-25). From here, the user can easily navigate or search for any of the forms, and then, using the Action Bar, modify the form if necessary. In many form scenarios, this wouldn't be the approach you'd take on the final view, but this is a nice example of using the built-in Access List view to give users a convenient landing spot once they've added a new record.

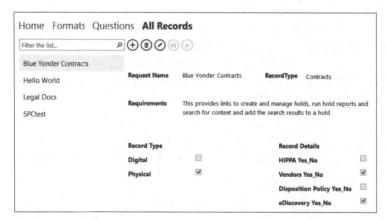

Figure 21-25 The All Records view of the form allows the user to select different records and see the details of a particular site request easily.

INSIDE OUT   Analyzing the Access and InfoPath forms: Behind the scenes

In some instances, you may desire to gain a deeper understanding of what is happening in the background when a browser interacts with your SharePoint farm during the use of a form. InfoPath browser-based forms and Access 2013 form apps can be monitored, dissected, and understood much more deeply if you use the free tool called Fiddler (*www.fiddler2.com*) to analyze your form. When you have Fiddler installed on your desktop, you can use it to peer inside all communication between the client browser and SharePoint, thus allowing you to find performance issues and other potential issues in your form design. Fiddler captures everything, including the JavaScript, form data, images, and all other types of data that flow between the browser and SharePoint when a form is opened and used. Even the JavaScript for the Access macros can be viewed in raw form, as shown here. The authors have found Fiddler to be an invaluable tool when testing, designing, and troubleshooting enterprise forms; we recommend that you take Fiddler along on your next forms design journey.

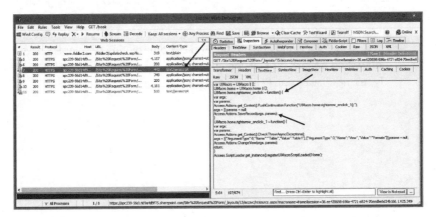

Creating custom forms

If neither InfoPath nor Access 2013 is sufficient to meet the needs of your form, custom development is always an option as well. In Chapter 23, you will learn about SharePoint apps, which are essentially modern web applications. If you know how to build a web application, then you can easily use those skills to build a Form app for SharePoint. And you can use many web-friendly languages such as HTML5, JavaScript, or .NET.

If you are interested in building SharePoint form apps with HTML5 and JavaScript, there are some new options and tools to be aware of, such as Microsoft LightSwitch and TypeScript. For readers of this book, we have provided a sample custom version of the Site Request form that was developed using LightSwitch and JavaScript. It is distributed as an .app package, and you can download the form (including the source code) at *http://aka.ms/SP2013InsideOut/files*.

Summary

Every business and government entity needs forms that enable its users to input and share information. SharePoint 2013 presents a platform that allows for these forms to be hosted and integrated with many other useful technologies, such as workflows and search.

InfoPath and Access 2013 are the two primary tools for creating SharePoint-based electronic forms of all types, without needing to use code. The types of forms that you can create with these two powerful tools are limited only by your imagination. InfoPath has been a popular forms tool for many years and has excellent integration into SharePoint lists. Access 2013 represents the new era of SharePoint digital forms that are adopting the new SharePoint cloud app model. And custom solution developers have never had so many interesting options for building code-based SharePoint forms—HTML5, Visual Studio 2012, TypeScript, JavaScript, PHP, and so on.

Working with external content

Traditionally in Microsoft SharePoint, data are stored in lists and libraries; however, most organizations do not wish to move all their data into SharePoint—nor should they. Most organizations have spent time and money building or purchasing specialized customer relationship management (CRM) software systems such as Siebel and SAP to assist with key business processes. Those users who can access these external systems have to contend with multiple different UIs with an array of terminology. Typically, these users have undergone training in each UI and have developed their own cheat sheets to translate UI terms into their everyday business language. They now wish to integrate the data from those external systems into SharePoint sites and Microsoft Office applications, such as Microsoft Outlook 2013, Microsoft Access 2013, and Microsoft Visio 2013, with an easy-to-use interface and terminology that is familiar to SharePoint users.

Solutions that bring together data from a number of systems to assist in the automation of a business process are known in SharePoint as *composites* or *mashups*. Business Connectivity Services (BCS) is a key SharePoint component in building composites. The BCS stores the definition of the external content—its location, the type of data, and the behavior of the data when it is integrated into SharePoint and Office client applications—centrally, in the Business Data Connectivity (BDC) metadata store. The definition of the external content is known as the *external content type (ECT)*. The definition of the location of the external system, together with the ECT, is known as the *BDC model*. Once an ECT is defined, you can use SharePoint Designer or a browser to manipulate the data from the external system using an external list.

This chapter details the different methods of accessing information external to SharePoint and then describes how to use BCS. You will look at the architecture of BCS, including the security options. You will also look at managing the data connections and how to expose the data from the external systems on webpages and in lists and libraries. Finally, you will learn how to use Microsoft Visual Studio 2012 with BCS.

Using external content in SharePoint

Composite solutions can be divided into the following three types, as shown in Figure 22-1:

- **Simple** Built using the out-of-the-box capabilities within SharePoint. Many of these simple solutions require that the definition of how to connect to the external system is already in existence. The solution is built almost entirely using the ribbon in the browser or Office applications.

- **Intermediate** Built by power users, site owners, or business analysts. Such users, termed "citizen developers" by Gartner, Inc., and also known as *consumer developers*, operate outside the scope of IT, work in the business domain, and can use the What You See Is What You Get (WYSIWYG) tools to create new business applications for consumption by others.

  Citizen developers use a combination of technologies, such as Access web apps, Microsoft InfoPath forms, business intelligence tools, Visio diagrams, webpages, workflows, and integration into Office applications, such as Outlook task panes or Microsoft Word documents. Citizen developers know what they want to achieve, they understand their business needs, and with a bit of SharePoint knowledge, they can wire together the business processes or sets of tasks.

  Intermediate solutions are more complex than simple solutions, and they may involve the use of Office application macros or the manipulation of XSLT using the code view of Microsoft SharePoint Designer. Therefore, citizen developers may initially need some training or help from the organization's central SharePoint team, particularly if they have never used SharePoint Designer, Access, or Visio before.

  > **Note**
  >
  > Gartner, Inc., reports that citizen developers will build at least 25 percent of new business applications by 2014 (*www.gartner.com/it/page.jsp?id=1744514*) and warns that IT departments that fail to capitalize on the opportunities that citizen development presents will find themselves unable to respond to rapidly changing market forces and customer preferences.

- **Advanced** Built by the IT department and professional developers, involving the development of reusable components to augment simple and intermediate solutions or solutions that require a deep knowledge of architectural concerns and a formal code, test, deploy, and support management processes. Such reusable components could include SharePoint Apps, .NET assembly connectors to connect, aggregate, and transform data from external systems, custom web parts, custom workflow actions that can be used from within SharePoint Designer, and extensions to the browser UI. Many of these components will necessitate the use of Visual Studio.

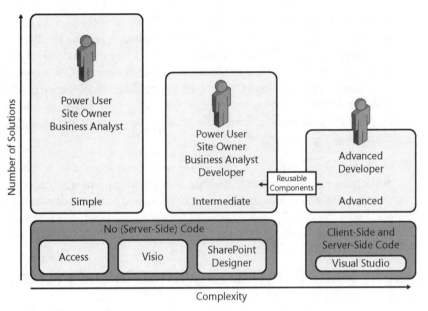

Figure 22-1 The three types of composite solutions are simple, intermediate, and advanced.

IT departments will need to differentiate between the types of solutions that citizen developers can create and those that the IT department should develop. When this identification process is completed successfully, it should free up IT resources for more complex problems.

Although many business users will have developed complex solutions with such programs as Microsoft Excel that involve thousands of rows of data, the simple and intermediate types of BCS solutions will be based around forms or business processes. Many users in an organization may not have the specific data skills to build solutions in Excel or Access, but by taking advantage of their SharePoint skills, solutions involving data from multiple external systems will be more invasive and prolific in an organization.

The shift to citizen developers may be new to an organization and may instigate a user adoption strategy as well as an education program. This education program should be focused more on introducing and managing the changes in the way the business will work going forward rather than enhancing skill sets. Other organizations may assimilate the use of SharePoint and its tools into their formal/informal reengineering processes. The introduction of SharePoint and the use of BCS to hook external data with SharePoint and Office applications should not be seen by users as another task to complete in their already busy day; rather, users should be encouraged to view the use of these technologies as a new way of working so that they can accomplish more in the same amount of time.

Many of the most successful SharePoint solutions are built by the users who use them: the citizen developers. The solutions are successful because the citizen developers know what they want to achieve, they are using the solutions as they develop them, and they can resolve any problems—including issues that can be uncovered only by using the solution. Citizen developers find that there is no need to provide feedback to others or raise incidents with their organization's help desk. These citizen developers are probably very passionate about their own SharePoint solutions. Therefore, when an organization encourages citizen developers to instigate the business reengineering process, it is more likely that other users in the organization will take to the solution, as one of their own developed it and that person knew the business requirements and experienced firsthand the issues of the solution.

Key to the success of this paradigm shift is that organizations need to take the citizen development strategy into consideration with any development process. That is, any SharePoint-related development project needs to add to the list of citizen developer tools, continuing the SharePoint philosophy of self-service for users, content owners, business owners, and site owners.

Connecting SharePoint 2013 with external systems

SharePoint 2013 provides the following methods of integrating with data that are not stored in SharePoint:

- **Access web apps** SharePoint 2013 provides two Access service applications: Access Services 2010, as provided in SharePoint 2010, and Access Services. To use either of these service applications, the Enterprise Client Access Licenses (CALs) are required. Access Services allows users to build quickly no-code, web-based form applications, known as *web apps*. These web apps are SharePoint Apps and can be deployed to SharePoint App stores. Data and Access objects for each Access web app is saved in its own Microsoft SQL Server 2012 database and not in SharePoint lists.

For more information about Access web apps, see Chapter 21, "Creating enterprise forms."

- **Access Services 2010** This service application enables you to publish an Access 2010 database, which creates a web database that is exposed as a SharePoint site where data held in Access tables is moved to SharePoint lists and forms and reports are created as webpages. You can then access the web database using the browser or the Access client application. Access web databases cannot be created using Access 2013. You can still view and edit a web database that was previously created by using Access 2010 and SharePoint Server 2010, and you can republish it to SharePoint Server 2013. You cannot convert a web database to an Access web app automatically; however, you can convert a web database to an Access web app manually by importing the data from the web database into a new Access web app and then re-create the user interface and business logic.

More information on how to configure Access Services 2010 for web databases in SharePoint Server 2013 can be found at *technet.microsoft.com/en-us/library/ee748653.aspx.*

- **Excel Services**   With this service application, you can publish Excel 2013 workbooks to SharePoint 2013, which allows users to view and interact with the workbooks in their browser.

You can find more information about Excel Services in Chapter 14, "Planning for business intelligence and key performance indicators," and Chapter 15, "Implementing better business intelligence with Excel Services and SQL Server 2012."

- **PerformancePoint Services**   To use PerformancePoint Services, Enterprise CALs are required. PerformancePoint Services enable you to monitor and analyze business tools by providing tools to build dashboards, reports, scorecards, and key performance indicators (KPIs). All data used in PerformancePoint is classified as external data, including data stored in SharePoint lists or Excel files published to Excel Services. However, data stored within SharePoint can be used in PerformancePoint only in read-only mode. You can use PerformancePoint to connect to tabular data in SQL Server tables, Excel workbooks, and multidimensional (Analysis Services) data sources, and you can use a PowerPivot model built using the PowerPivot add-in for Excel as a data source.

You can find more information about PerformancePoint Services in Chapter 14 and Chapter 16, "Building powerful dashboards with PerformancePoint Services."

- **Visio Services**   Visio Services enables you to share and view Visio 2013 files in the browser without the Visio client application or the Visio viewer installed on your local computer. To view your own Visio files using the Visio Service application, Enterprise CALs are required. The Visio drawing can contain visuals that are linked to data from an external data source. Visio Services can fetch the data from these linked data sources and update the visuals of a Visio drawing.

You can find more information about using Visio Services in Chapter 17, "Working with Visio Services."

- **Microsoft InfoPath**   With InfoPath, you can create both forms and browser-based forms. Users entering data into forms require Microsoft InfoPath Filler 2013. For browser-based forms, users need only a browser and InfoPath Form Services. Form templates for both types of forms can be created using Microsoft InfoPath Designer 2013. Forms created using InfoPath can connect to data sources such as SharePoint lists or web services. Forms or browser-based forms can be saved in a SharePoint

Form library. The ASPX pages in external lists that allow you to create, read, update, and modify data from an external system can be replaced with InfoPath browser-based forms.

- **InfoPath Form Services (IFS)** This service application enables InfoPath browser-based forms to be rendered in SharePoint 2013. To use this service, Enterprise CALs are required. However, if you only have Standard CALs, you can still see InfoPath association and initiation forms that have been created with SharePoint 2010 workflows. IFS is not a SharePoint 2013 service application; it is configured at the farm level using the Central Administration website.

For more information about InfoPath, see Chapter 21.

- **SQL Server 2012 SP1 Reporting Services (SSRS)** There are two components that integrate SSRS with SharePoint:

  - **Reporting Services SharePoint mode** Also known as *integrated mode*, Reporting Services SharePoint mode is based on a completely new architecture, which is why you will see it in the SharePoint Central Administration website as a service application with a SharePoint Shared Service Application Pool. You configure it using the SharePoint Central Administration website or using Windows PowerShell commands. You no longer use the Reporting Services Configuration Manager, as you did in SharePoint 2010.

  - **Reporting Services add-in** This add-in enables you to run SSRS Report Server within SharePoint 2013, where the SSRS reports, items, and properties are stored in SharePoint. Users can browse to SharePoint libraries to find the reports.

You can find information on installing SSRS on SharePoint 2013 at *blogs.msdn.com/b/biblog/archive/2012/12/04/installing-and-configuring-sql-reporting-services-on-sharepoint-2013.aspx*.

- **Data Sources gallery using SharePoint Designer** Using Microsoft FrontPage 2003, and then later Microsoft SharePoint Designer 2007, you could connect, present, and modify data from several types of external data sources using the Data Source Library and Data Source Details task panes. This method is still available with SharePoint Designer 2013 by using the Data Sources gallery, which you can access through the Navigation pane. However, SharePoint Designer no longer has the Design or Split view; therefore, once you have added a Data Form Web Part (DFWP) using the ribbon, much of the subsequent customization needs to be completed using XSLT in Code view.

More information on SharePoint 2013 composites can be found in the updated SharePoint Composites Handbook at *msdn.microsoft.com/en-us/library/jj938032.aspx*.

Using BCS

BCS is implemented as a service application, known as the *Business Data Connectivity (BDC) service application,* which is named for the fact that it is the component that connects to the external system and passes the data to the presentation layer. You create external system definitions once, and not only share those definitions to many sites within the same site collection or SharePoint web application, but also share those definitions with more than one web application.

In addition, a SharePoint farm—a SharePoint installation that is installed on one or more servers that share the same SharePoint configuration database—can host more than one BCS; each one can be configured independently by different sets of administrators. By storing external system definitions stored in a BCS on one SharePoint farm, which can be referenced from other SharePoint farms, you can manage all your external system definitions centrally. Once the external system definitions are retrieved, each SharePoint farm will connect directly to the external systems. A BCS can also be partitioned in a multitenancy configuration, which is the term commonly used to describe the isolation of websites in a hosting environment, such as SharePoint Online.

Although multiple BDC service applications can exist, the browser and SharePoint Designer can use only the BDC service application that is labeled as the default BDC service application. If you associate a web application with multiple BDC service applications, you can use the nondefault BDC service applications only with custom code.

INSIDE OUT   Service applications

In Microsoft SharePoint Foundation, you can create only one type of service application. In SharePoint Server 2013, many service applications are provided, such as the Managed Metadata Service (MMS), Access Services, Visio Graphics Service, and Secure Store Service (SSS).

BCS may be divided into four areas:

- **External system** This is where the external content resides. It may be maintained by one of your organization's business critical applications, often known as line-of-business (LoB) applications. They may have a custom UI or a programmable interface, such as Open Data (OData), Microsoft Windows Communication Foundation (WCF) service, web 2.0 source, or as a database.

  The OData data source type is newly supported for BCS in SharePoint 2013, and is used by many systems, including SharePoint, SSRS, Windows Azure Table Storage,

Azure Data Marketplace, Facebook, Netflix, and others, such as those built using Open Government Data Initiative (OGDI), as well as the Microsoft .NET Framework. In fact, Windows Server 2012 includes a new feature that enables you to expose Windows PowerShell commands and scripts as OData Web service entities. Data is returned from the OData producers as JavaScript Object Notation (JSON), Atom, or plain XML data.

Before using BCS, you should explore the external system you wish to connect to (for example, evaluate the best method of connecting to the external system). Check with creators of the external system as to the methods available to access the content. If there is more than one method, ask which one is the best option to use.

- **Connectivity** Before SharePoint can access the content from an external system, the definition on how to connect to the system and the authentication method used must be created, which is the BDC model. The BDC model consists of declaration XML that describes the external system you want to access, as well as the operations you might like to use on this external content—for example, read a list of data, read one item (row) of data, or update one item (row) of data.

  The BDC model can be created on a development or test SharePoint installation, from where it can be downloaded and imported into the SharePoint production farm, where it is stored in the BDC metadata store, or it can be used by Office applications.

  The BDC model can be used in a SharePoint installation to create ECTs, which are also known as *entities*. However, in a SharePoint 2013 installation, before you can create or upload a BDC model, you must create the BDC service application. Office 2013 applications contain only the components that allow you to upload a BDC model; therefore, there is no management or configuration interface provided.

- **Presentation** This is the client-side consumer of the external content, such as an Office 2013 application, or if you are using SharePoint, it could be an external list created from the ECT. As with SharePoint 2010 and Office 2010, you can use external data with Office client applications such as Word, Access, InfoPath, Excel, and Outlook. New with Visio 2013, you can now link data from an external list to a diagram and its shapes. Word and Visio can use only data from external systems, whereas Access, InfoPath, Excel, and Outlook can create, read, update, and delete data in the external system if the ECT is configured to complete those operations and the user is allowed to complete those operations.

- **Tools** Microsoft provides two tools to create the BDC model to interact with the BCS program interfaces and manipulate the BDC objects. These are SharePoint Designer 2013 and Visual Studio 2012. There are other third-party tools that can help ECT designers, such as BCS Meta Man, which can be found at *lightningtools.com*. You could also use an XML editor, such as XML Notepad 2007 or Notepad, to create a BDC model.

Figure 22-2 shows the high-level interaction among these four areas. Notice the symmetry—the BCS architect is the same for Office 2013 applications as it is for a SharePoint installation. However, the Office 2013 applications do not have a BDC metadata store. In its place is a BDC client-side cache, so that when content in an external list is taken offline, the BDC model is taken from the BDC metadata store on the server and stored in the BDC client-side cache. The offline content from the external list is also stored in the client-side cache, which uses a SQL Compact Edition client database so that the offline external content and the BDC model are both persisted when the user's computer is shut down.

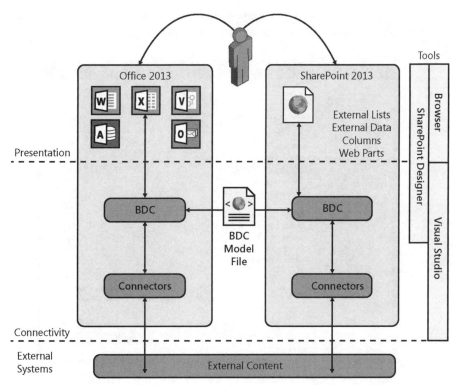

Figure 22-2 BCS is divided into four areas: presentation, connectivity, external systems, and tools.

Also note in Figure 22-2 that the Office 2013 applications have their own connectors; therefore, when a user switches to online mode, the Office application connects directly to the external content without connecting through SharePoint. Other Office 2013 applications, such as Access 2013, can import a client-side version of the BDC model. Thus, in this scenario, Access 2013 does not need to connect to SharePoint at all; it connects directly to the external system. This could potentially create challenges for users when accessing data hosted in SharePoint Online, as well as accessing on-premise data.

To use the Office 2013 applications, a user must have the application installed on Windows 7 or later and have the following three software components:

- SQL Server Compact 4.0

- .NET Framework 4

- WCF Data Services 5.0 for OData V3

If these three components are not installed when the user tries to connect to data within an Office application via BCS, the user will be prompted to download and install them. In addition, the Office client applications must be installed with the Business Connectivity Services Office Shared Feature, as shown in Figure 22-3.

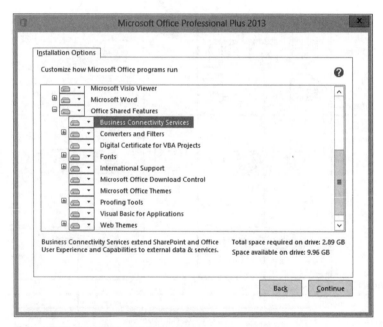

Figure 22-3 The BCS installation options.

The advantage of using BCS over using the Data Source gallery in SharePoint Designer is that you need to define the external system and ECT only once; you can then use that ECT on many sites across all web applications that are associated with the BDC service application. One disadvantage. For example, is that ECT designers must be given edit permissions to the metadata store, which requires a high level of security, whereas with the Data Source gallery, you only need to be a site owner. In addition, other BCS security settings are needed to allow users to access the external content that can only be set using the SharePoint 2013 Central Administration website or Windows PowerShell. This results in a level of collaboration between the ECT designers and the SharePoint farm administrators, which in large organizations are usually two different people.

To connect and retrieve data from an external system, complete the following tasks:

1. Create a BDC service application and set permissions on the BDC metadata store to allow for the creation of the BDC model, external system definitions, and ECTs.

2. Define the external system connection.

3. Define the operations to Create, Read, Update, and Delete (CRUD) content stored in that external system as appropriate to your business requirements.

4. Create an ECT based on an external system definition.

5. Configure the permissions on the ECT so that users can see content from the external system.

6. Use the ECT to present the data from the external data source as external lists, an external data column, web parts, or from within an Office application.

Presenting external content

Once an ECT is created, you can create solutions that use the external content. You can use the browser or SharePoint Designer to create these solutions. You can also create custom web parts or Windows form applications with Visual Studio that can access the data defined in the BDC metadata store.

Creating and managing external lists

External lists are the preferred method of displaying external content. These can be created using the browser, SharePoint Designer, or Windows PowerShell. Depending on the operations that you have defined on the ECT, you can create, read, update, and delete individual external content data, such as a specific customer, order, or employee from the external system. You can also add an XLV Web Part or a DFWP to a page that displays data from an external list.

Remember, the external content is not stored in SharePoint content databases; therefore, an external list cannot replicate all the same functionality as an internal SharePoint list. For example, you cannot use the Datasheet view, associate RSS feeds, or set item-level permissions; however, you can export the list data to Excel (a new feature with SharePoint 2013). In the Excel workbook, the data is linked to the external list, and therefore, when a user chooses to refresh the Excel workbook, the data is retrieved from the external system. As with internal SharePoint lists, this is a one-way synchronization process; that is, when a user modifies or deletes data in the Excel workbook, the data is not changed in the external system. And when a user synchronizes the workbook with the external system, all modifications in the Excel workbook are lost.

SharePoint does not have native control over the external content and does not know when data is in the external system; however, with the help of a developer, workflow can be triggered when data in the external system changes and alerts can be sent.

To create an external list using the browser, follow these steps:

1. Open the site where you want to create the external list. Click the Settings icon in the upper-right corner and then click Add An App.

2. On the Your App page, click External List to display the Adding External List dialog box.

   If you have a large number of list types, it is easier to find the External List option by typing **external** in the Find An App text box and pressing Enter.

3. On the Adding External List dialog box, enter the name and description for the external list.

   You will need to click Advanced Options to display the New page to add a description.

4. To the right of the External Content Type text box, click the Select External Content Type icon, as shown here.

   The External Content Type Picker dialog box appears, which displays the name of the external system and the display name of the ECT. It is important that your ECT designers have created a meaningful display name for the ECT so that your users can quickly identify the correct external content they wish to work with.

5. In the External Content Type Picker dialog box, select the ECT that defines the external content that you want to display in your external list, and then click OK.

The External Content Type Picker dialog box closes, and the ECT that you have chosen is specified in the External Content Type text box.

> ### Note
> If you choose the incorrect ECT, you cannot choose a different one once the external list is created. You will need to delete the list and re-create it, choosing the correct ECT. The external list acts as a virtual container displaying the contents from the external system; therefore, when you delete an external list or ECT, you are not deleting any content from the external system, just the virtual container and the definition of external content, as shown next.
>
>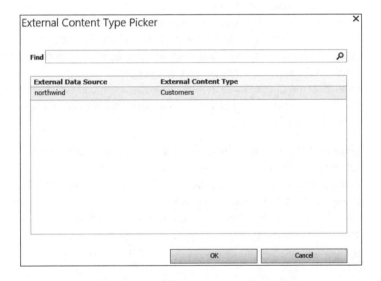

6. In the Adding External List dialog box, or if you clicked Advanced Options earlier, then on the New page, click Create.

The Site Contents page is displayed where the list you just created appears. When the external list is displayed, the default Read List operation is used as the default view and the content from the external system is displayed.

TROUBLESHOOTING

Once you have created an external list, you may find that no data from the external system is displayed. If the Read List view of the external list displays the error message, "Login failed for user 'NT AUTHORITY\ANONYMOUS LOGON'.", this could indicate the double hop issue, which is explained later in this chapter. The Login Failed message can occur if you are using the user's identity to authenticate with the external system, or if you do not have BDC permissions for the ECT or the external system or that your user ID does not have the correct access permissions in the external system.

Using external data columns

External data columns enable you to add external content to a standard SharePoint list or library. You create an external data column as you would any other column; that is, on the List or Library tab, click the Create Column command and then, on the Create Column page, enter a column name and then select External Data as the column type. In the Additional Column Settings section, to the right of the External Content Type text box are two icons: the Check ECT icon, which you use when you type the name of the ECT in the check box, and the Select ECT icon, that, when clicked, opens the External Content Type Picker dialog box.

Once an ECT is selected, the Additional Column Settings section contains a list of properties associated with the ECT, as shown in Figure 22-4. In the Select The Field To Be Shown On This Column drop-down list, select the column that your users will usually associate with the external data. If the external system is a CRM system, then this may be the company name or contact name. You can then choose to add one or more fields from the external content to become columns in the list or library, such as the customer's email address or phone number. You can then choose to add the fields to all content types, as well as adding it to the default view.

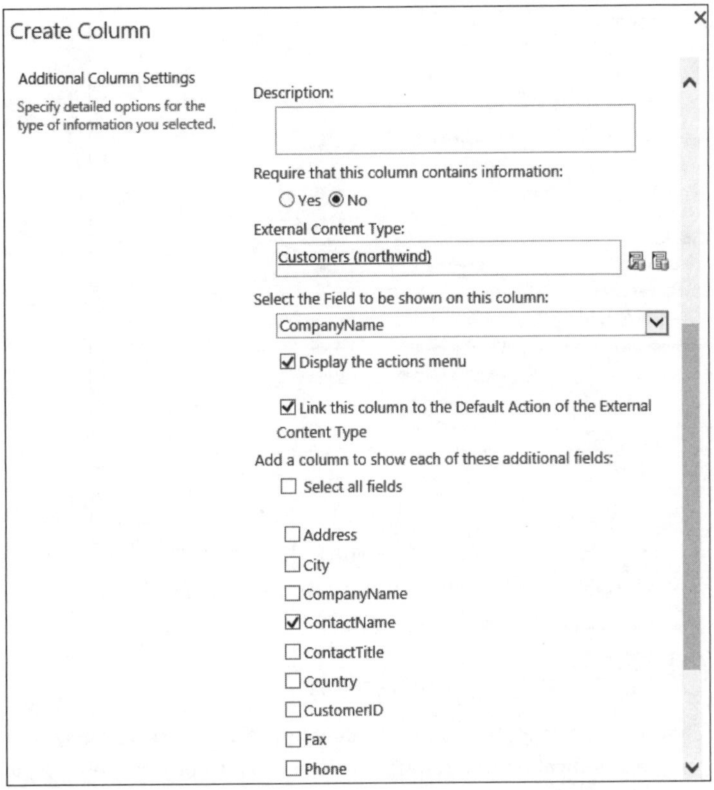

Chapter 22

Figure 22-4 The Additional Column Settings section contains a list of properties associated with the ECT.

It is only when you add a new list item and click the Select External Item(s) icon that the BDC server run time will connect to the external system to retrieve data to populate the Choose dialog box, as shown in Figure 22-5. The dialog box will only show those fields which had the external item picker check box selected when you configured the ECT operations. When the external item picker check box is not selected for any field, all fields are displayed in the Choose dialog box.

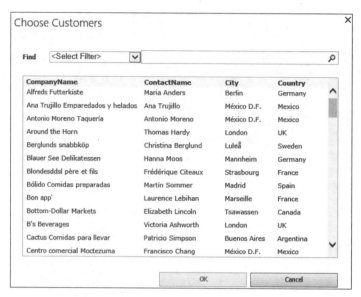

Figure 22-5 Choose an entity from the external system to populate a column in a list.

INSIDE OUT Global throttling limits

The Choose dialog box can show only 200 items at a time, so you may see a red error message indicating that results may have been truncated. This is a global BDC service application throttling limit, which can be modified by the SharePoint server administrator. When the external system has more than 200 items, it is best to create a filter on your read list operation when creating the ECT in SharePoint Designer. More information on changing throttling limits is given later in this chapter.

When the new list item is saved, the external content is stored in the list in the SharePoint SQL content database, unlike the external list, which only contains a link to the ECT definition. To update the data in the list, you can click the Refresh icon to the right of the external data column name, as shown in Figure 22-6. A webpage is displayed that warns you that this operation could take a long time. You can choose to sync this folder only or this folder and all subfolders. If you click OK, the BDC server run time connects to the external system to return the necessary data. By copying the external content in the list, it has inherited all list type operations, such as views, filters, and the ability to be used to trigger list workflows.

Figure 22-6 Refresh the external content stored in External Data columns.

To the right of the items in the external column is an icon and a down arrow; this is the External Data Action menu, as shown in Figure 22-7. The menu provides links to pages that display information relevant to the ECT item, such as displaying all the values for all the properties of the ECT item, known as the *profile page,* or by using the postal code property of the ECT item displaying a map of that location.

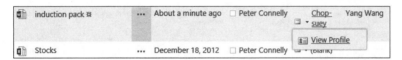

Figure 22-7 Use the External Data Action menu to view all the pages relevant to the ECT item.

Creating external data actions   External data actions can be created with the SharePoint Central Administration website by following these steps:

1. Navigate to the BDC Service where the ECT is defined, and then, on the Edit tab of the Service Application Information page, select External Content Types from the drop-down menu in the View group.

2. Click the ECT to display the External Content Type Information page, as shown next.

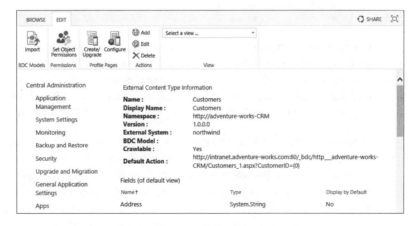

3. On the Edit tab, click Add in the Actions group.

4. On the Add Action page, type a name for the action, add the URL, specify whether to start the action in a new browser window or not (default), add parameters to the URL if required, and add the icon to display next to the action. You can choose from the Delete, Edit, or New icons, or you can choose your own image, as shown next.

Add Action

Name

Type a name for the action.

Action Name

| Customer Location |

URL

Type the URL to navigate to when you click on the action. If you want the URL to vary depending on the item to which it applies, add one or more parameters, then assign a property to each parameter below. Type a number in braces such as {0} where you want to insert a parameter in the URL.

Navigate To This URL

| http://www.bing.com/default.aspx?where1={0} |

Example: http://example.com/edit.aspx?id={0}

Launch the action in a new Web browser window (applies to External Data Web Parts only):

○ Yes ◉ No

URL Parameters

Assign a property to each parameter in the URL.

Parameter Property

0 | PostalCode ▾ | | Remove |

| Add Parameter |

Icon

Choose an icon to display next to the action.

◉ No icon
○ Standard icon | Delete ▾ | ✗
○ The image at this URL | |

Default action

Select the check box if you want this to be the default action.

☐ Default action

External lists created before adding an action will not list this action automatically. Only new external lists will display the action in the context menu.

Business data web parts   SharePoint 2013 ships with seven generic external data web parts, six of which are functionally the same as they were for the business data web parts in SharePoint Server 2007: Business Data Actions, Business Data Connectivity Filter, Business Data Item, Business Data Item Builder, Business Data List, and Business Data Related List. The seventh is the Chart Web Part, which was introduced in SharePoint 2010.

These web parts can be used to display any data using any ECT without writing any code. After they are configured, they will automatically be named after the entity data they are displaying. The web parts that display data from the external systems query the metadata cached on each web front-end server, and then the instance data is retrieved from the data source. To use the business data web parts on a site, you must activate the SharePoint Server Enterprise Site Collection features at the site-collection level.

Surfacing external data in Word   When an external data column is added to a library, the values in the external column can be made available in a .docx Word file by inserting a Quick Part onto a document, enabling you to embed BCS data. The first column to select would be the External Data column's display name (for example, Customer), as shown in Figure 22-8. You can only choose fields from the ECT that you choose to display in the library.

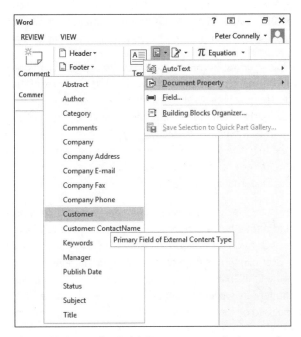

Figure 22-8 Use the Quick Parts menu on the Insert tab to embed BCS data into the Word document.

The document properties are inserted onto the page as controls, as shown in Figure 22-9, with two icons that allow you to select data from the external system.

Figure 22-9 Quick Parts are added as controls on the page.

Creating a BDC service application

Before you can create an ECT, you need to create a BDC service application, which can be created by using the SharePoint configuration wizard, the SharePoint Central Administration website, or Windows PowerShell. Using the SharePoint Central Administration website or Windows PowerShell allows you to specify the SQL Server database name or use a precon-figured database name. Although you can use the configuration wizard, which creates an automatically generated BDC database name, it is not recommended to use the configuration wizard in production because of the lack of control you have over what it creates.

When using the SharePoint Central Administration website or Windows PowerShell, first check that at least one BDC machine service instance is started on one of the servers in your SharePoint farm. The machine service instance, also known as the *SharePoint service*, uses the service binaries to manage components, such as any related timer jobs, to make the service application function correctly. If you have more than one server in your SharePoint farm, the machine instance can be started on one or more of your servers. SharePoint then provides its own round-robin load-balancing mechanism to distribute user requests for data from the external systems evenly.

Once a machine service instance is started, you can create the BDC service application. This allows you to manage and create the definitions for the external systems. When the BDC service machine instance is started and its associated service application is created, then an Internet Information Services (IIS) Virtual Application is created that runs in the context of an IIS application pool within the SharePoint Web Services IIS website. It exposes a WCF web service, also known as the service application endpoint, as shown in Figure 22-10. This is used by SharePoint and can be used by developers in your organization to develop new solutions. Such an endpoint is created by SharePoint on each server where the machine service instance is started.

Once the BDC service application is started, you will see in the Central Administration website on the Service Applications page, below the BDC service application, a BDC service application proxy, also known as the *service connection*, as shown in Figure 22-11. This provides the connection between the components, such as webpages that wish to access the data from the external systems and the BDC service application. The service application proxy also understands the load-balancing mechanism that SharePoint uses, and if you publish a BDC service application for use on other farms, the service application proxy will be used for managing those connections as well.

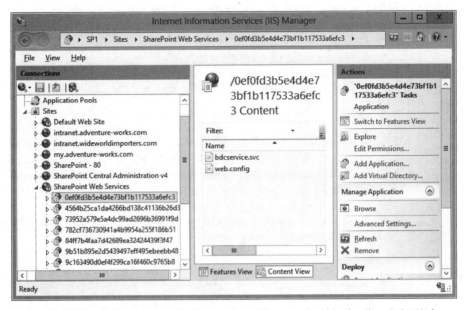

Figure 22-10 The BDC service application endpoint is created within the SharePoint Web Services IIS website.

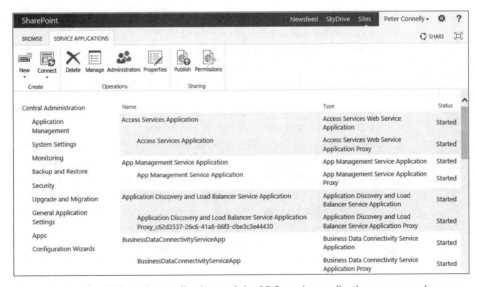

Figure 22-11 The BDC service application and the BDC service application proxy are shown on the Central Administration website.

Once you create the BDC service application, you will need to complete the following administrator tasks:

- Create BDC service application administrators.

- Import the BDC model that contains the metadata information.

- Set BDC Metadata Store permissions.

- If you are using SharePoint Server 2013 and have purchased Enterprise CALs, configure profile page creation (that is, the site where the profile pages are to be created). Ensure that the SharePoint Enterprise Site Collection features are activated on this site.

- If you are using SharePoint Server 2013, configure Single Store Service if you plan to import any BDC models into the metadata store then you should plan to use this authentication mechanism.

- Deploy any custom business data solutions, such as dashboards.

INSIDE OUT   Using profile pages

Profile pages display all the fields returned for a specific ECT instance. These pages can be created automatically using the SharePoint Central Administration website or SharePoint Designer. A profile page uses the business data web parts, which are only available with the Enterprise CAL for SharePoint Server 2013. You can create a profile page for an ECT manually by using an external list and BDC actions.

When using SharePoint Foundation, the ribbon on the Central Administration website is trimmed so that it does not display the Profile Page option; however, this is not the case within SharePoint Designer. If you click the Create Profile Page ribbon command, a SharePoint Designer dialog box opens, stating that the server could not complete your request, but it does not provide any details as to why the request could not be completed. Then a second dialog box opens, stating that the expected changes to the ECT could not happen and that you should create the profile page again! With SharePoint Foundation, ignore these messages.

Table 22-1 lists the metadata store permissions that you can use and the allowed actions of the user, group, or claim.

TABLE 22-1 BDC metadata store permissions

Permission	Description
Edit	Use to allow users to create and amend BDC models, external system definitions, and ECTs. Only allow highly trusted users to have this permission, especially in a production environment. Users with this permission can see external system definitions created by other users, and therefore this can be a security risk, where a malicious user can use the security information in the external system definition to access and corrupt external content, and adversely affect the running of the SharePoint installation. When you upload a BDC model from a development environment into a production environment with its security settings, remove the edit permissions from the BDC model for those users who created it in the development environment. If you do not have a development or prototype environment, you will need to give users who create external system definitions and ECTs using either SharePoint Designer or Visual Studio edit permission on the BDC model.
Execute Selectable In Clients	There is no execute or selectable in Clients permission on the metadata store; however, you can choose to propagate these settings to child objects in the BDC model, external systems, ECTs, methods, and method instances, and their child objects.
Set Permissions	Users with this permission can manage BCS permissions on the BDC metadata store, and by propagating a user's settings, the user can set permission on any object in the metadata store. This permission is usually only given to BCS service application administrators.

More information on BCS security can be found att.

Follow these steps to set permissions on the BDC metadata store:

1. Open the SharePoint Central Administration website in the browser. Under Application Management, click Manage Service Applications.

2. On the Service Applications page, click the name of the BDC service for which you want to manage permissions.

3. Click Set Metadata Store Permissions on the Edit tab of the Ribbon.

4. On the Set Metadata Store Permissions page, enter the appropriate users or groups and select the appropriate permissions, as shown in the following graphic.

Chapter 22

Set Metadata Store Permissions ✕

To add an account, or group, type or select it below and click 'Add'.

	Add

Peter Connelly
Everyone

To remove an account, or group, select it above and click 'Remove'. | Remove |

Permissions for Everyone:

Edit	☐
Execute	☑
Selectable In Clients	☑
Set Permissions	☐

☐ Propagate permissions to all BDC Models, External Systems and External Content Types in the BDC Metadata Store. Doing so will overwrite existing permissions.

| OK | Cancel |

Note

Do not select the Propagate Permissions To All check box as every External System, BDC Model, or ECT will inherit this configuration when added to the metadata store. This also prevents users from unnecessary access to any External System, BDC Model, or ECT that they should not have.

---

5. Click OK.

INSIDE OUT   BDC service application security

Farm administrators, SharePoint Windows PowerShell users, and application pool accounts have full permissions to a BDC service application. Farm administrators can then maintain or repair the BDC service if necessary and allow the deployment of solutions packages that use BCS. However, these accounts do not have execute permissions on any metadata store objects. Therefore, such accounts could create a BDC model with its associated external system definition and ECT, and could even create an external list from those ECTs. These accounts would not be able to execute any of the operations on the external content, and therefore, when the external list is displayed in the browser, an authentication error would be displayed.

Defining external systems connections

To create an external system definition, you need to know which protocol to use to connect to the external content, known as the *data source type,* and the authentication method to use, as well as the operations you want to use on the data. The following data source types can be used (these define the connector that the BDC server run time will use to connect to the external system):

- Databases, including SQL Server and SQL Azure

- Cloud-based services

- Windows Communication Foundation (WCF) endpoints

- Web services

- .NET assembly that gathers data from multiple sources

- All OData sources, including any SQL Server data source that is surfaced via OData

- Custom external systems that have a nonstatic interfaces that change dynamically

The authentication methods that the BDC server run time uses to retrieve, modify, and delete, if appropriate, the data from the external systems are:

- **User's identity (also known as PassThrough)** When a user requests a SharePoint page that displays data from an external system, SharePoint sends the user's credentials to the external system, which uses that identity to decide whether the user is allowed access or not. If you use Windows authentication and have a single server SharePoint farm and the external system is installed on that server, then using the user's identity works well. However, to use Windows authentication in any other configuration, the user's identity has to make one hop from the user's computer to the SharePoint server and another hop from the SharePoint server to the external system. This double hop requires the configuration of Kerberos in your environment.

  The other disadvantage of using the user's identity is that if the external system is a SQL database, it causes a new SQL connection pool to be created for each user who is using the ECT to access the external content, which can cause performance issues. Connection pooling can be disabled, which can also affect performance.

- **Impersonate Windows identity** Specific Windows identities are used to authenticate with the external system. This Windows identity could be the same for all users or there could be some mapping mechanism, so the user requesting the content from SharePoint is matched to a different Windows identity that is passed on to the external system. To use this and the next authentication method, an application that does this mapping is required. If you are using SharePoint Server 2013, you could use the SSS application, or if you are using SharePoint Foundation, you will have to write your own equivalent system.

For more information on SSS planning, see Chapter 14.

- **Impersonate custom identity** These could be credentials mapped in a database or could be claims-aware identities, which are sent to the external system.

- **BDC identity (also known as RevertToSelf)** SharePoint reverts to the web application's application pool identity to authenticate with the external system. This user name has a high level of privileges on a SharePoint installation. Any user who can create or edit a BDC Identity model can make themselves an administrator of SharePoint. Therefore, Microsoft does not recommend the use of this authentication mode and it is disabled by default. When a user tries to import or change the authentication mode to RevertToSelf, an error message displays. The error message that displays when using SharePoint Designer is shown in Figure 22-12.

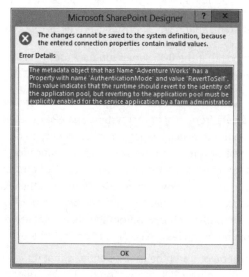

Figure 22-12 The BDC Identity (RevertToSelf) Import error dialog box.

INSIDE OUT   When to use RevertToSelf authentication mode

You should use the RevertToSelf authentication mode in a production environment only when all the following conditions are true:

- You are using SharePoint Foundation 2013.

- You do not have resources to create a custom SSS.

- You trust all the people who use SharePoint Designer as completely as if they were SharePoint administrators.

- The application pool account is locked down so that the attack surface exposed to a malicious user of SharePoint Designer is limited.

RevertToSelf can be turned on by code or by using Windows PowerShell, as shown in the following example, where the variable BCSName is the name of your BCS application:

```
$bcs = Get-SPServiceApplication | where {$_.displayname -eq $BCSname};
$bcs.RevertToSelfAllowed = $True;
```

Although the BDC server run time would use the application pool ID to retrieve data from the external system no matter which user wants to display the external content, remember that permission settings on the BDC service application can be used to restrict access to the external content.

Working with external content types

The easiest way of defining an external system is to use SharePoint Designer 2013 or Visual Studio 2012. The tooling to create a BDC model for an OData source type has been included within Visual Studio 2012 and not SharePoint Designer. The BCS tooling within SharePoint Designer 2013 remains as it was in SharePoint Designer 2010; that is, you can define ECTs that use the following data source types: SQL Server, .NET, and WCF Service. By including the new tooling within Visual Studio 2012, the BDC model can either be included in a SharePoint or Office app or imported into a BDC metadata store using the SharePoint Central Administration website, Windows PowerShell, or in a tenant environment, such as Office 365, using the tenant admin site.

Creating an external system using SharePoint Designer

Follow these steps to create a BDC model for an SQL Server database:

1. Open SharePoint Designer 2013 and then open a SharePoint site.

    You will not be storing anything in the site, so this can be any site in the web application that is associated with the BDC service application where you have edit permissions on the BDC metadata store.

2. In the Navigation pane, click External Content Types to open the External Content Types gallery that lists the ECTs to which you have permission.

    The gallery may be empty if no ECTs are created or you do not have permission to see any, as shown next.

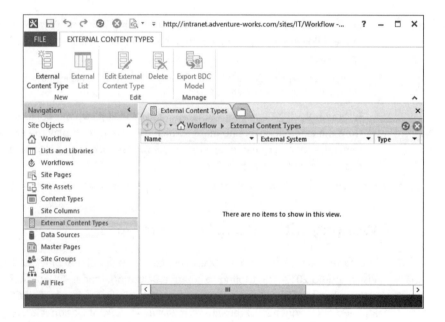

3. On the External Content Types tab, click External Content Type in the New group.

    The summary view of the ECT is displayed with an asterisk on the workspace label, indicating that the ECT has not been saved to the metadata store on the SharePoint server. You cannot save an ECT until you have given it a name and defined Read Item and Read List operations on an external system.

4. In the External Content Type Information area, to the right of Name, click New External Content, type the name of the ECT and enter a display name, which is the name displayed in the ECT picker dialog box.

The ECT name is usually a short, terse, but meaningful name that preferably does not contain spaces. You cannot save an ECT until it has a name. Once you have saved the ECT, you cannot change the ECT name in SharePoint Designer; however, you can change the ECT display name. You could export the ECT as part of a BDC model, alter the XML in the file (say in Visual Studio), and then reimport the BDC model into the BDC metadata store. This will create a new ECT. You could then remove the misspelled ECT, however, this will affect any external lists you have created from the misspelled ECT, as ECTs are based on the name of the ECT and the namespace.

The namespace of a SharePoint Designer–created ECT is the URL of the web application. The namespace is used to group ECTs, so you should change the namespace to reflect the business purpose for a group of ECTs. In the following example, *http://adventure-works-CRM* relates all the customer relationship records for your organization.

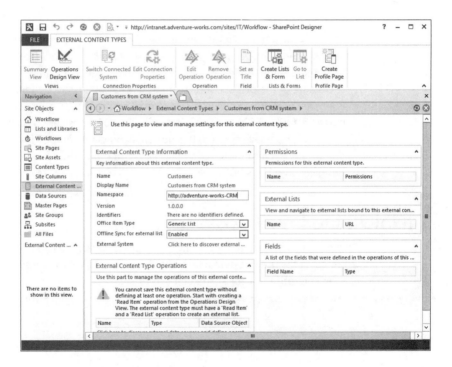

5. To the right of External System, click Click Here To Discover External Data Sources and Define Operations to display the Operations Design view of the ECT.

   You can toggle between the Summary view and the Operations Design view by using the two commands in the Views group on the External Content Types ribbon tab.

6. Click Add Connection.

Chapter 22

7. In the External Data Source Type Selection dialog box, select the appropriate data source type, such as SQL Server, and then click OK to display the source type connection dialog box.

8. Enter the connection details. For example, for a SQL Server source type, enter the database server name, the database name, and the authentication type: User's Identity, Impersonated Windows Identity, or Custom Identity.

For the two impersonated identities, you will need to use the SSS and provide the secure store application ID. The authentication details that you enter here will be used to authenticate with the external system as you use SharePoint Designer. You can specify different authentication methods for both SharePoint and Office applications that you wish to store in the BDC model, by clicking Edit Connection properties in the Connection Properties group.

9. Click OK.

The external system is registered in the BDC metadata store as an external system named SharePointDesigner-*<external system name>*-*<userid>*-*<guid>*, where *<external system name>* would be the name of the SQL database, *<userid>* is the user name of the person who created the external system definition, and *<guid>* is a generated number. One such example is SharePointDesigner-northwind-peter-581fd994-5891-49a5-8842-73b806483a04. These are placeholders to store the definitions you have created. It is not until you create an ECT for this external system that a valid external system definition is created that can be used by other ECT designers in other sites.

INSIDE OUT   Taking external data offline

On the Summary view, in the External Content Type area, the Offline Sync For External List refers to the use of external lists with Outlook 2013, which are available only if you have an Enterprise CAL for SharePoint Server 2013.

Creating external content types

Once the external system definition is defined, you can now create an ECT and specify the CRUD operations that you wish to execute on that external system. Many organizations use ECTs rather than the Data Sources gallery for security and logistic reasons. The ECT can be defined once and stored centrally in the BDC metadata store, but used many times for all sites and site collections depending on the permission settings of the ECT. The schema and authentication methods need only be explained to a small number of ECT designers. This is as opposed to the Data Sources gallery, where the data source definition would have to be created for each site where you want to use the external content.

Follow these steps to create an ECT using SharePoint Designer:

1. In the ECT Summary view, ensure that the ECT has a name, and if the external content is to be displayed in Outlook 2013, configure the Office item type as Appointment, Contact, Task, or Post. Switch to the Operations view of the ECT.

2. In the Data Source Explorer, expand the external system node by clicking the plus sign (+) to the right of the name.

    If the data source is a database, expand Tables, Views, or Routines.

3. Right-click the table you want to create a BDC model for and then click the operations you want to create.

    Depending on the operations exposed by the external system, you can add the operations create, read item, update, delete, and read list, as shown next.

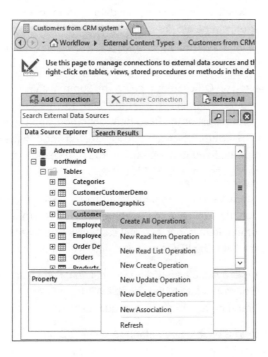

A three-page operations wizard opens, where each page contains a section that displays issues, warnings, and errors as you configure the operations. The three pages are:

- **Operation properties**   Use this page to set the operation name, operation display name, and operation type. For a database external system, you can create all operations. If you choose this option, then the operation properties are generated automatically and the operation names will be Create, Read Item, Update, Delete, and Read List.

  When you create an External List from an ECT, then a view is created for each Read List operation. You may consider modifying the automatically generated names for the Read List operations so that they are meaningful to users of the external list.

- **Parameters**   Use this page to select those fields, known as *elements,* you wish to use in your SharePoint solution. You can modify each data source element, including the identifier name, the field name, and the name of the field when it is displayed in the browser. By default, all fields will be shown in the external item picker when adding an external data column to a list or library. If the table, view, or routine returns a large number of fields, displaying them all in the external item picker may confuse users. Therefore, it is best to select a small set of elements that best describes an item.

  If you selected an Office item type on the Summary View, you will use this page to map the external content data fields to Office properties. The Office mapping form is part of the Read Item operation, and therefore, if you wish to modify these settings once an ECT is created, modify the return parameter properties of the Read Item operation. You also change the Office item type on the Summary page once an ECT is created.

- **Filter parameters**   Use this page to add your own throttling conditions to your solution; this will optimize the time taken to return the data from the external system. Remember, external content is not saved in the BCS database, but is retrieved by the BDC server run time when needed.

  The filter types available are Comparison, Limit, Page Number, Timestamp, and Wildcard. For string data types, use the Wildcard filter type because this will internally translate to a like clause in queries to get the data.

  BCS throttling is enabled by default to prevent Denial of Service (DoS) attacks. You are most likely to see the effect of this feature if no limit filter was created and when the BCS run time attempted to retrieve data from the external system it timed out due to the large amount of data it was trying to retrieve. For more information on BCS throttling, see the sidebar "Using external system throttling" later in this chapter.

4. Click Finish and then Save.

    This will create in the BDC metadata store an external system named <databasename> if this is the first ECT created for the external system, and an ECT with the name you typed in step 1.

INSIDE OUT   SharePoint 2013 performance improvements

BCS in SharePoint 2013 limits the data returned from the external system by processing the data source filters on the external system, as well as sending sort requests to the external system when a user sorts the data in an external list. This reduces the load on the SQL Server machines that are hosting the SharePoint databases.

Managing permissions on external content types

The ECT is just one of the BDC metadata store objects for which you can set permissions, as described in Table 22-2. These permissions affect the interface between the SharePoint server and the presentation layer; that is, they do not define the authentication and security settings between the SharePoint server and the external system—those security settings are defined in the external system definition. The other objects present in the BDC metadata store that have their own access control list (ACL) are the BDC model and external system definitions. These permissions can be set by using the SharePoint Central Administration website or Windows PowerShell.

TABLE 22-2 BDC model object permission settings

Permission	Applies to	Description
Edit	Access-controlled metadata objects	Users with this permission can perform the following actions: Update Delete Create a child object Add a property Remove a property Clear a property Add a localized display name Remove a localized display name Clear a localized display name Give edit rights to administrators and users who use SharePoint Designer.

Permission	Applies to	Description
Execute	ECT, Method Instance	Users with this permission can execute operations via various run-time API calls; that is, they can view the data of an ECT returned from a finder method. In most scenarios, you would assign this right to all users who have access to SharePoint.
Selectable In Clients	ECT	Users with this permission can use the external data picker to configure web parts and lists and create external lists. This permission should be available to administrators and users who design solutions using the browser or SharePoint Designer.
Set Permissions	Individually securable metadata objects	Users with this permission can manage BCS permissions on the object. This permission is usually given only to BCS service application administrators.

Using external system throttling

Each BDC application service can have a number of throttle configurations, and each configuration can be tuned by throttle type and/or scope. The throttle types are:

- **None**   No throttle type specified

- **Items**   The number of ECT items returned, such as the number of authors

- **Size**   The amount of data retrieved by the BDC server run time in bytes

- **Connections**   The number of open connections to a database, web service, or .NET assembly

- **Timeout**   The time until an open connection is terminated, in milliseconds

- **MetadataSize**   Used to restrict the size of the metadata returned by the external system

- **ModelSize**   Used to restrict the size of the BDC model that can be imported

- **MaxNumberOfModels**   Used to restrict the number of BDC models that can be imported into a tenancy

Throttle scopes refer to the external system connection type, which can be a specific connection type, such as Database or OData, or a Global scope that includes all connector types, except for custom connectors. When a BDC service application is first created, all combinations of throttle types and scopes do not exist. The throttling rules that exist are:

- Global Scope, Throttle Type Connections, ModelSize, and MaxNumberOfModels

- Database Scope, Throttle Type Items, and Timeout

- WebService Scope and Throttle Type Size

- WCF Scope, Throttle Type Size, Timeout, and MetadataSize

- OData Scope, Throttle Type Size, Timeout, and MetadataSize

You can retrieve and modify the throttling rules by using the BDC Windows PowerShell cmdlets. For example, obtain the BDC service application proxy in the variable BDCName and then display the throttling rules for a BDC service application:

```
$bdcproxy = Get-SPServiceApplicationProxy | where {$_.displayname -eq
$BDCname};
Get-SPBusinessDataCatalogThrottleConfig -ServiceApplication $bdcproxy '
   -Scope Global -ThrottleType Connections;
Scope        : Global
ThrottleType : Connections
Enforced     : True
Default      : 200
Max          : 500
```

The output displays five properties. The three properties that can be modified are:

- Enforced, which defines if the rule is enabled

- Default, which affects external lists and custom web parts, although custom web parts can override this value and therefore can present more data than external lists

- Max, which is the limit used when custom web parts override the value in the Default property

To disable a throttling rule, use the following command:

```
Get-SPBusinessDataCatalogThrottleConfig -ServiceApplication $bdcproxy '
   -Scope Global -ThrottleType Connections | Set-SPBusinessDataCatalogThrottle
Config '
   -Enforced:$False;
```

To modify a throttle rule, use the following command:

```
$dbrule = Get-SPBusinessDataCatalogThrottleConfig -ServiceApplication $bdcproxy
'
   -Scope Database -ThrottleType Items;
$dbrule | Set-SPBusinessDataCatalogThrottleConfig -Maximum 2000000 -Default
5000;
```

Exporting and importing BDC models and resource files

If you are fortunate to have a development environment, you may have created your external system definition and ECTs in that environment. If the testing was successful, you will now have to deploy these BDC definitions to the production farm by first exporting the appropriate BDC model from the BDC service application in the development environment and then importing the BDC model into the correct BDC service application in the production farm. You can use the SharePoint Central Administration website, a Windows PowerShell cmdlet, or SharePoint Designer to export the BDC model.

If you created the External System definition and ECT using SharePoint Designer then you should use that tool to export them. The BDC model, SharePointDesigner-*<databasename>*-*<userid>*-*<guid>*, created by SharePoint Designer, does not link to the ECTs that are created by SharePoint Designer. Therefore, you cannot use the SharePoint Central Administration website to export ECTs developed with SharePoint Designer.

If the BDC model is to be used by Office 2013 applications, then you can only export them in the correct format by using SharePoint Designer. The permissions you have configured on the BDC model, the external system, and ECT can also be included in the exported BDC model.

You can use the SharePoint Central Administration website or a Windows PowerShell cmdlet to import a BDC model. You cannot use SharePoint Designer to import BDC models.

When you export a BDC model, make changes and then import it into a BCS application; you should update the version number for the ECT. By default, the version number is set to 1.0.0.0. Changing the third or second number of the version number indicates a small change, such as adding a new method or changing connection information. Changing the first or second number of the version number signals a "breaking change" to BCS, such as adding a new field to the Read Item operation (Specific Finder method) or changing the identifier field. Breaking changes usually cause external lists that were defined using the previous version of the BDC model to fail. Therefore, before making an ECT widely available, ensure that your ECT meets all your business needs and is tested thoroughly.

More information on migrating the BDC model and ECT from a development environment to testing environments and production environments can be found at *msdn.microsoft.com/en-us/library/gg650431.aspx.*

Chapter 22

INSIDE OUT   Deploying BDC solutions with Visual Studio

With Visual Studio, you can create resource files and custom BCS web parts, as well as a BDC model. In this scenario, you would not use the export functionality but would commonly deploy the files as a solution package (.wsp). New to SharePoint 2013, you can also deploy your BDC solution as a SharePoint App, where the BDC model can be saved in a SharePoint App. This is known as an *app-scoped BDC model*. You can also include a BDC model in an Office App. More information on creating solution packages and SharePoint Apps can be found in Chapter 23, "Introduction to custom development."

To export a BDC model using SharePoint Designer, follow these steps:

1. Open SharePoint Designer 2013 and then open a SharePoint site in the web application that is associated with the BDC service application where you have created the external system definition and ECT.

2. In the Navigation pane, click External Content Types to open the External Content Types gallery.

3. Click the icon to the left of the ECT you wish to export, and then, on the External Content Types tab, click Export BDC Model in the Manage group.

4. In the Export BDC Model dialog box, type the BDC model name, and in the Settings list, select Default (as shown here) if the BDC model is to be imported into another SharePoint farm, or select Client if you are going to use the BDC model with Office 2013 applications.

5. Click OK and save the BDC model as an XML file.

   The file will have an extension of .bdcm. If you are importing the file into an Office 2013 application, change the extension to .xml.

To export a BDC model or the resource information in a separate file using the Central Administration website, follow these steps:

1. Under Application Management, click Manage Service Applications. On the Service Applications page, click the name of the BDC service application that contains the BDC model you wish to export.

2. In the View drop-down list, select BDC Models, if not already selected, and then, under Service Application Information, select the BDC model you wish to export.

3. On the Edit tab, click Export in the BDC Models group.

4. On the Export BDC Model page (shown here), select the Model or Resource file type option and the resource components you wish to export.

   If you select the resource file type option, then a separate resource XML file will be created, which usually has an extension of .bdcr. When you export a BDC model in SharePoint Designer, you cannot export the resources separately, nor can you choose which resources you wish to export. With SharePoint Designer, all resource information is exported.

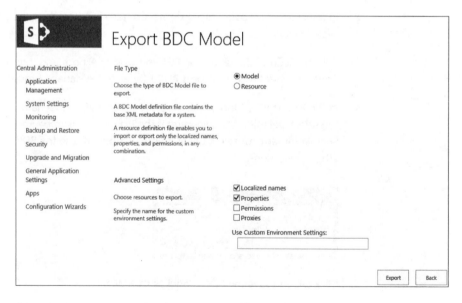

5. Click Export, and then save the file.

Information on the BDC model and resource files can be found at *msdn.microsoft.com/en-us/library/ee231601.aspx*.

To import a BDC model using the Central Administration website, follow these steps:

1. Under Application Management, click Manage Service Applications. On the Service Applications page, click the name of the BDC service application that contains the BDC model you wish to export.

2. On the Edit tab, click Import in the BDC Models group.

3. On the Import BDC Model page, in the BDC Model section, either use the Browse button to navigate to the Model file or type the location of the Model file into the text box.

4. In the Advanced Settings section, select the Resource option if you are importing a file that contains only localized names, properties, or permissions.

5. Click Import to display the Importing webpage.

> **Note**
>
> When you choose to import permissions that are defined in your BDC model and an entry for an ECT already exists in the ACL, its value is overwritten with the permission information from the imported file.

TROUBLESHOOTING

> The import process parses the file and validates it; however, you should not rely on the import process to identify all errors in the BDC model. If errors or warnings are found during the import process, the webpage will display additional information. Additional information can be found in the Windows event logs and in the SharePoint log file located at %ProgramFiles%\Common Files\Microsoft Shared\web server extensions\15\ LOGS, where the relevant messages will be in the Business Data category. The software development kit (SDK) contains more information on troubleshooting metadata exceptions and interpreting the log files.

Once the BDC model is imported, SharePoint 2013 separates the external system and the ECT information. You should review both these objects and set permissions according to your requirements. You should then check that an external list can be created from the ECT, and external content can be included in an external data column in a list or library.

You can also use the Delete command on the Edit tab to delete BCD models, external systems, or ECTs.

Using Visual Studio 2012 with BCS

BCS is all about bringing data that lives outside SharePoint into SharePoint. The BCS provides connectivity to your external LOB systems by using connectors. Earlier in this chapter, SharePoint Designer was used as a no-code method to define the BDC model and use ECT as external lists and external data columns. This method has some limitations:

- You can only create CRUD operations. BCS supports other operations that cannot be created using SharePoint Designer, such as the stream operation that allows you to access a file that is stored as a Binary Large Object (BLOB) in a SQL database.

- The declarative XML created in the BDC model can be amended only if you export the BDC model and then open the file created by the export activity in SharePoint Designer. You would then need to know the BCS model schema to amend the XML. SharePoint Designer does not provide any no-code assistance in editing the BDC model XML file.

- External lists cannot be used to represent any hierarchy or relationship between the content that is stored in the external systems. The data is presented as a flat, table-like structure; there is no inbuilt tree-like or folder structure that you can configure to match the relationship between the content.

- SharePoint Designer only allows the use of SQL Server, .NET assembly, and WCF connectors.

- SharePoint Designer does not allow you to create the VSTO add-ins that could provide extract functionality to work with the external content.

Visual Studio 2012 includes additional tooling for BCS—the SharePoint Customization Wizard—that was not included in Visual Studio 2010. You can use this wizard to create an OData BDC model and the BDC model operations that match the external system operations exposed via the OData endpoints. The Visual Studio wizard creates ECTs with fewer steps than it would take you to create ECTs in SharePoint Designer. Unfortunately, you cannot create or modify an OData ECT with SharePoint Designer.

To create a BDC model based on an OData producer using Visual Studio, complete the following steps:

1. In the Solution Explorer, right-click the project name, select Add, and then click Content Types for an External Data Source to display the SharePoint Customization Wizard page, as shown in the graphic on the following graphic.

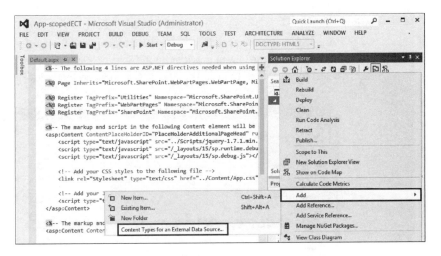

2. On the Specify OData source page of the SharePoint Customization Wizard (shown here), type the OData Service URL and the Data Source Name.

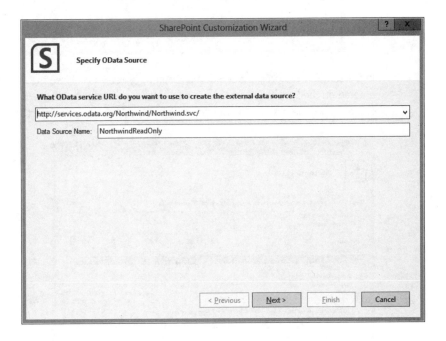

3. Click Next.

Visual Studio connects to the $metadata endpoint and then displays the data entities available from the OData provider on the Select The Data Entities page. Use this page to select those entities to include in the BDC model and then click Finish, as shown next.

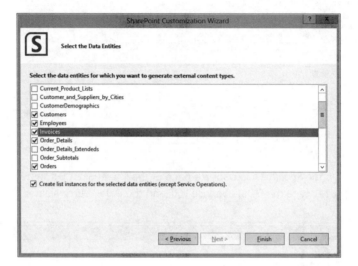

In the Solution Explorer, under External Content Types, you will see the data source that you entered on the Specify OData Source page. When the data source is expanded, as shown in Figure 22-13, there is an ECT for each data entity selected on the Select The Data Entities page.

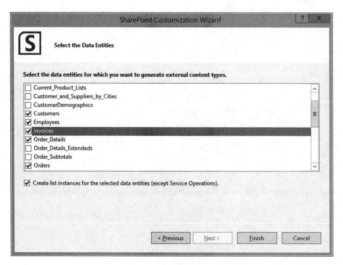

Figure 22-13 Use the Solution Explorer to display the ECT files and the external list definitions.

> **Note**
>
> Visual Studio automatically generates the OData ECTs to use *https,* and therefore, the ECTs need to be amended if your OData provider endpoints use *http.*

When the Create List Instances For The Selected Data Entities check box is selected on the Select The Data Entities page, an External List definition (Elements.xml) is created and shown in the Solution Explorer.

The ECT files can be opened to display their contents as XML, or if you double-click an ECT file, it will open in Designer view, as shown in Figure 22-14. The Designer view allows you to easily configure the columns for the ECT and to add filters that you can use to limit the data that is returned from the data source. A filter named Limit is generated automatically with a default value of 100.

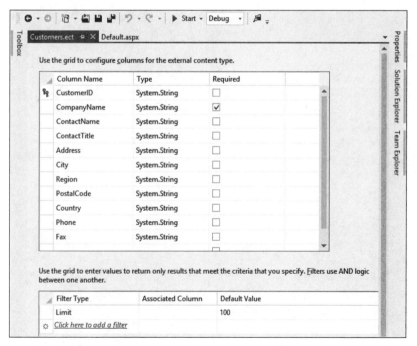

Figure 22-14 Use the Designer view to configure the ECT.

The Microsoft Business Connectivity Services resource center can be found at *technet.microsoft.com/en-us/sharepoint/ee518675.aspx.*

Summary

This chapter detailed how to incorporate external content by basic SharePoint no-code solutions with SharePoint Designer using BCS components: ECTs, external lists, and external data columns. More advanced solutions can be built using Visual Studio 2012.

BCS provides a method of providing access to external content without having to redefine how to connect the external systems for each site that needs to use that external content. However, as an ECT designer, you do need high permissions and will need to collaborate closely with the SharePoint administrator to implement BCS solutions. Also, as changes to BCS solutions can affect many sites over many web applications, a release management process should be implemented.

Introduction to custom development

AVE you reached the limits of what you can do with Microsoft SharePoint? Using custom code, you can extend SharePoint in many areas. You've seen examples of custom development in the chapters of this book on form development, web content management, and workflow. When you add custom development, solutions in all three of those areas of SharePoint can be improved in one way or another. But those are not the only areas of SharePoint that benefit.

Custom development is taking advantage of the application programming interface (API) provided with SharePoint. There are a number of categories of APIs for SharePoint provided out of the box. One thing they all have in common is the need to use a programming language or custom code. The most common approach in the past has been to use the Microsoft .NET platform and the C# language. However, JavaScript has also become a common language for custom development for the web. And in SharePoint 2013, more than ever, excellent capabilities are provided for JavaScript programmers to extend SharePoint as well.

The SharePoint App Store is another important custom development concept. Through the app store, SharePoint users can extend their implementation by taking advantage of custom code written by others. The app authors and publishers are taking advantage of an area of the SharePoint API called the *app model*.

SharePoint 2013 has an entirely new workflow engine enhanced by changes to the overall Microsoft platform. This new engine enables new capabilities for creating workflows beyond the tools of the standard information worker, such as SharePoint Designer. Workflow creation through Microsoft Visual Studio provides enhanced capability, reuse in custom solutions, and more solution maintenance tools.

Continue reading this chapter to learn why, when, and how to take advantage of code, probably written by others, to make your SharePoint experience better.

Exploring custom development

Is SharePoint an application or a platform? Many similar software products are one or the other, but SharePoint is really both. While the majority of this book focuses on the use of SharePoint as an application, it is also important to consider this other aspect of the product. When you make decisions about how and when to extend the application, consider the features of the platform described in this chapter.

Microsoft products have a rich history of providing tools for extending the products with code. Microsoft's first product was included a BASIC interpreter allowing any user to write programs right out of the box. SharePoint is no different. From the earliest version, Microsoft has provided libraries, often called APIs, for extending the product. SharePoint Portal Server 2001 provided only minimal opportunities to extend the product with custom development compared to the future versions of the product. And 11 years later, SharePoint 2013 offers the most opportunity yet for extending the product with the introduction of the app model.

Previous chapters in this book have already covered some solution types that are created through Visual Studio. Chapter 12, "Designing web content management sites," and Chapter 20, "Creating, managing, and designing sites," cover master pages and page layouts that can be deployed through features and solution packages. Chapter 19, "Creating a customized SharePoint 2013 search experience," covered building display templates to build better search results. Chapter 21, "Creating enterprise forms," covered two topics, HTML5 forms and form apps. There is so much coverage already because many SharePoint features live in a gray area between information worker and web developer. This chapter, however, focuses on how experienced developers can help information workers extend SharePoint.

As an advanced information user, you may often be in the position of helping determine how your SharePoint installation is extended with custom or third-party solutions. Whether the source of your addition to SharePoint is an independent software vendor, a custom development group, or your in-house programmers, the end product can come to you in various forms. Not only that, but some of the design decisions made in developing or applying the additional functionality can affect how and where you can use the new functionality.

As you become more familiar with the new app model and the more traditional solution packages, you will be able to determine when solutions built with either may apply to your SharePoint installation.

The app model

Figure 23-1 shows an example of an extension of SharePoint 2013 created with the new app model. With the introduction of the app model, the barrier to entry for enhancements through custom development is lower than ever. The App store makes selecting, purchasing, and installing apps easy for SharePoint 2013 users. The app model gives developers greater choice in deployment platform and a better way to distribute solutions.

Adding an app such as the one shown in Figure 23-1 is as simple as clicking the Add It button in the SharePoint App Store on any of the apps listed. Creating an app has fewer dependencies than the deployment model of previous versions of SharePoint. SharePoint development for previous versions required each developer to have a SharePoint server. For the app model, development can be done on the desktop. For these reasons, the introduction of this new model of custom development is one of the most important changes in SharePoint 2013.

Figure 23-1 A SharePoint app uses Bing Maps.

Server API solution packages

The traditional method of deploying custom solutions since SharePoint 2007, Server API solution packages, continues to be available in SharePoint 2013. In fact, some types of solutions still depend on this method of deployment.

There are two types of deployments for the traditional solution package: farm solutions and sandbox solutions. Both types combine the solution assets in one file with an extension of .wsp. This .wsp solution package is deployed to SharePoint directly from the server or by uploading to the Site Collection Solution gallery.

Farm solutions

Farm solutions must be installed from a physical SharePoint server and require a high level of trust. Farm solutions must be used to deploy certain types of solutions. For example, a common enhancement discussed earlier in Chapter 12 is branding. If you want to create consistent branding across an entire SharePoint farm, use a farm solution.

For more information on when to choose the Server API and farm solutions, go to *http://msdn.microsoft.com/en-us/library/jj164060(v=office.15).aspx.*

Sandbox solutions

Sandbox solutions are uploaded to a Site Collection Solution gallery through a link on the Site Collection Settings page. The Microsoft SharePoint Foundation Sandboxed Code Service must be running. Also, the user uploading the solution must have permissions to install sandbox solutions, typically through the Site Collection Administrator role.

> **Note**
>
> Sandbox solutions are deprecated in SharePoint 2013 in favor of developing apps in SharePoint.

For more detail on deprecation of sandbox solutions, read the Important Message section at *msdn.microsoft.com/en-us/library/jj163114.aspx.*

Understanding client-side APIs and web services

SharePoint 2013 allows for extensive improvements for accessing the product from beyond the server. The so-called client-side APIs provide programming language–specific hooks into SharePoint. The Representational State Transfer (REST) and Open Data (OData) endpoints provide more generic access to SharePoint through web services. Both provide access beyond what had been possible without developing code directly on a SharePoint server.

Neither method of access is entirely new, but there are many changes, including the depth of the access provided. In part, these changes were necessary to power the new app model deployment method. This access is not limited to app model enhancements, but their use in the app model is a great place to start.

INSIDE OUT   Client-side APIs or client-side object model (CSOM)?

If you've read much about extending SharePoint 2010, you may notice a change in terminology. Together, the JavaScript and .NET client-side APIs were commonly referred to as the *client-side object model,* or *CSOM,* in SharePoint 2010 references. In Microsoft documentation for SharePoint 2013, you will find the phrases *Client Object Model (Client OM)* or *client-side APIs* used more often. You can still find the occasional uses of the acronym *CSOM,* the phrase *Client Object Model,* and other variations. It's a small change in wording among a much larger change in SharePoint as a development platform. Whichever technical terms are used, remember that they are different ways of referring to the same thing.

All of the client access methods provide access to a large range of SharePoint functions. For example, here are the new areas of functionality that can be accessed through the client APIs and REST:

- User profiles
- Search
- Taxonomy
- Feeds
- Publishing
- Sharing
- Workflow
- eDiscovery
- IRM
- Analytics
- Business data

With all of the client APIs and REST providing such widespread access, the choice of method comes down to other considerations, which are listed in the next few sections.

.NET client API

Extending SharePoint from .NET code in C# or VB.Net will be familiar to experienced SharePoint developers. The Microsoft .NET Framework is a key part of Microsoft's overall platform, so it's not surprising that the latest enhancements to SharePoint include this API. Because of this history, it is likely to be the most popular method of accessing SharePoint when not using the .NET server API.

The .NET client API is accessed through a .NET assembly that must be available on the server the SharePoint Extension is deployed to. This will be common when deploying apps in a SharePoint Hosted mode.

JavaScript client API

The JavaScript client API provides custom development options for developers unfamiliar with .NET. JavaScript has become a common language for web development across many platforms. This API will introduce SharePoint development to a new range of capable web developers who have built their programming knowledge on other platforms.

The JavaScript client API is provided through a link to the SharePoint server. This makes it available directly in HTML webpages where the .NET API is not.

REST and OData endpoints

REST developers create, update, and delete SharePoint objects using calls following the OData protocol. The REST API is not bound to any particular language, which makes it open for use by developers on open-source platforms.

The REST services are accessed by HTTP addresses at your SharePoint site. For example, if you had a site at: *http://intranet.adventureworks.com,* the new REST endpoint addresses would start at *http://intranet.adventureworks.com/_api/.*

To read more about the implementation of REST services and the OData protocol in SharePoint 2013, read "Get started with the SharePoint 2013 REST service," at *msdn.microsoft.com/en-us/library/fp142380(v=office.15).aspx.*

Determining build vs. buy

When you'd like to extend SharePoint using any of the available methods, you have a choice of building the solution yourself, purchasing an off-the-shelf solution, or paying for a service organization's help. The decision is not always straightforward, but it's important to consider all your options. The most obvious solution may not always be the best fit, so it can be helpful to do a little research.

Discovering and evaluating third-party products

With the introduction of the app model in SharePoint Server 2013, the availability of third-party, off-the-shelf products is expected to grow. While you are still free to find solutions the old way, the apps for the SharePoint 2013 section of the public Office Store is already stocked with products from Microsoft and independent software vendors (ISVs). SharePoint Server 2013 also included the ability to provide a private app management area, which can be stocked by farm administrators.

Browse apps for SharePoint 2013 on the Microsoft Office Store at *office.microsoft.com/en-us/ store/apps-for-sharepoint-FX102804987.aspx.*

When adding an app after your selection from an app store, you will be prompted with permissions requests for the app configured by the publisher. Permissions for apps range from basic information, like the host site name and URL, to full access by the app to the host site. The process of choosing and adding an app with the request for permissions is illustrated in Figure 23-2.

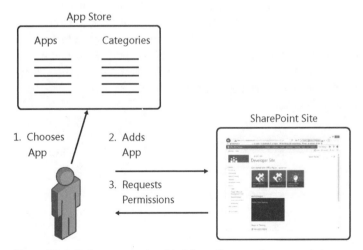

Figure 23-2 Before an app is added from the app store, permissions are requested.

Ratings and reviews by other purchasers is another benefit of the app store model. The traditional server-deployed SharePoint Solution model lacks a central list of out-of-the-box solutions. Websites created by the SharePoint community have attempted to fill the void, but none have achieved 100 percent participation by the vendors or purchasers. With the apps for SharePoint 2013 section of the public Office Store, Microsoft has created a marketplace that will attract third-party developers to advertise their products. This marketplace allows easy rating and reviews by purchasers, which will provide a new level of insight for you when making your selections.

Seeking expert help for custom solution development

A thriving Microsoft partner network exists for SharePoint custom solution development. When you can't find an out-of-the box product that solves your needs, engaging a Microsoft partner for custom development can be a helpful option. Careful evaluation of potential partners is necessary, and the best firms are in high demand. If you go this route, make sure that your organization has someone familiar with SharePoint custom solution options as part of the selection and application processes. As with the other methods, part of your end result should be either a SharePoint solution package or an app. Documentation, warranty support, and training are value-added services to watch out for. This option is likely when experienced and knowledgeable in-house development resources are not available or need to be augmented.

Extending SharePoint with Visual Studio

Visual Studio continues to be one of the top developer environments in the marketplace. The latest version, Visual Studio 2012, brings improvements tailored to web development, including increased support for HTML and JavaScript. Adding the freely downloadable Office Developer Tools for Visual Studio 2012 provides tools and templates specific to SharePoint solution package and app model development. Equipped with Visual Studio and the software development kits for client and server APIs for SharePoint, your in-house developers can create powerful extensions to SharePoint when you are unable to find them in the third-party market.

When undertaking a custom development project, don't forget the soft side. Great programmers can build great end products with the proper input and guidance on the business needs. However, SharePoint solution development is not immune to the general custom software development challenges of delivering great results on time and on budget.

App model development

For the first time in the product's history, SharePoint Server 2013 provides the opportunity to write custom solutions on a developer workstation without SharePoint installed. Traditional SharePoint solution package development continues to require a SharePoint server for each developer authoring SharePoint custom solutions. The new opportunity is for developers coding against the newly improved client APIs and REST in the app model. While app development requires a SharePoint server for deployment and testing, that server can be shared by many developers and even by users. Any workstation that meets the minimum requirements of Visual Studio 2012 can be used to write code for the .NET client API. Using JavaScript or REST, the possibilities open up even wider.

The effect of this change for development environments should not be underestimated. Installing and configuring Sharepoint is a significant task that many developers lack the time or resources to undertake. On top of that, the cost of hardware and software resources for a SharePoint server adds to the overall cost of traditional SharePoint solution package development. The move off the server alone reduces obstacles that have prevented many potential SharePoint developers from making the move to learn SharePoint. Add to that the effect of extending beyond the .NET platform to other programming models, and you add another large set of potential programmers for SharePoint extensions.

There are many great resources for SharePoint development, including other Microsoft Press titles. This section does not serve as a programmer's reference for programming against SharePoint. However, it does provide an introduction to developing with the app model—the easiest and quickest way to get started.

For an in-depth exploration of SharePoint 2013 app development, read *Microsoft SharePoint 2013 App Development* by Scott Hillier and Ted Pattison, published by Microsoft Press.

Configuring your development environment

To write an app for SharePoint from Visual Studio, you must have the following basic minimum requirements:

- Visual Studio 2012 Professional

- Office Developer Tools for Visual Studio 2012

> **Note**
>
> A download called the SharePoint 2013 Developer Tools Preview was available was available during the SharePoint 2013 preview period. If you see references to a tool with that name, it has now been replaced with the name Office Developer Tools for Visual Studio 2012.
>
> The free, Express edition of Visual Studio is not supported for SharePoint 2013 development, but the most basic paid version, Professional, is (as are the more premium editions).

That's it! With just those two tools on your Windows desktop, you are ready to get started developing for SharePoint. To deploy and test your new app, you will need a SharePoint Server 2013 standard development site.

SharePoint Foundation 2013 doesn't support app deployment, but both the Standard and Enterprise editions do. The target of your deployment is a site collection created with the Developer Site template. In addition, your server must be configured for app management with the required Domain Name System (DNS) configuration on your network. When an app is added to a site, a corresponding app web is created. This app web has a unique address, like app-123456789.apps.adventureworks.com. The creation of this app web at the unique address is what requires the DNS configuration by your network administrator.

For your network administrator's reference, please read "Configure an environment for apps for SharePoint," at *technet.microsoft.com/en-us/library/fp161236(v=office.15).aspx*.

INSIDE OUT   App head start with "Napa" Office 365 Development Tools

An interesting option for experimenting with the new app model is a beta tool called "Napa" Office 365 Development Tools. While Napa is lacking some tools for enterprise development, like versioning and source control, it provides a quick way to get your feet wet with the new custom development option. The following graphic shows a screenshot of a SharePoint Online Developer Site on Office 365 with the "Napa" Office 365 Development Tools installed.

When Napa is installed from the SharePoint App Store, clicking the "Napa" Office 365 Development Tools link takes you to an in-browser SharePoint Development Environment. The graphic that follows shows an example of the in-browser editor experience. As the name implies, Napa is only available on the Office 365 offering, not for on-premises deployments. When accessed in Office 365, Napa provides an editing experience with syntax highlighting, bracket matching, and code completion for JavaScript, CSS, and HTML. It also provides an option to build and deploy your solution to your SharePoint Online Developer Site hosted on Office 365 and an option to share your solution with others. For a more complete development experience, including modifications to advanced project settings, there is an option to export to Visual Studio.

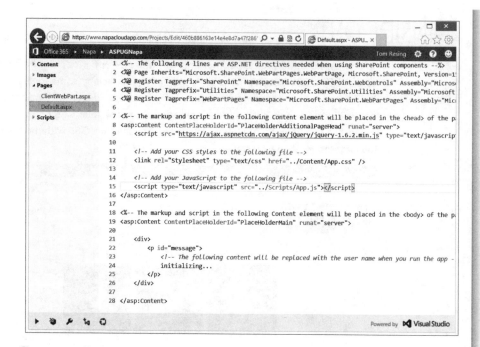

```
1   <%-- The following 4 lines are ASP.NET directives needed when using SharePoint components --%>
2   <%@ Page Inherits="Microsoft.SharePoint.WebPartPages.WebPartPage, Microsoft.SharePoint, Version=1!
3   <%@ Register Tagprefix="SharePoint" Namespace="Microsoft.SharePoint.WebControls" Assembly="Micros
4   <%@ Register Tagprefix="Utilities" Namespace="Microsoft.SharePoint.Utilities" Assembly="Microsoft
5   <%@ Register Tagprefix="WebPartPages" Namespace="Microsoft.SharePoint.WebPartPages" Assembly="Mic
6
7   <%-- The markup and script in the following Content element will be placed in the <head> of the p
8   <asp:Content ContentPlaceHolderId="PlaceHolderAdditionalPageHead" runat="server">
9       <script src="https://ajax.aspnetcdn.com/ajax/jQuery/jquery-1.6.2.min.js" type="text/javascrip
10
11      <!-- Add your CSS styles to the following file -->
12      <link rel="Stylesheet" type="text/css" href="../Content/App.css" />
13
14      <!-- Add your JavaScript to the following file -->
15      <script type="text/javascript" src="../Scripts/App.js"></script>
16  </asp:Content>
17
18  <%-- The markup and script in the following Content element will be placed in the <body> of the p
19  <asp:Content ContentPlaceHolderId="PlaceHolderMain" runat="server">
20
21      <div>
22          <p id="message">
23              <!-- The following content will be replaced with the user name when you run the app -
24              initializing...
25          </p>
26      </div>
27
28  </asp:Content>
```

Read more about using Office 365 for starting with SharePoint app development in the MSDN topic "Apps for Office and SharePoint," at *msdn.microsoft.com/en-us/library/ fp161507(v=office.15).aspx.*

Creating a map app

With the minimum requirements for SharePoint app development, you can get started developing useful extensions to your SharePoint site quickly. Figure 23-3 shows the New Project selection dialog box with the SharePoint App Project template selected. When you create a new project based on the SharePoint App Project template, you see that the items in Figure 23-4 have been created for you based on the name you gave the new project. The first property you must set is the site URL of the project properties. This property can be edited by selecting the project title in the Solution Explorer and scrolling through the properties in the lower-right Properties pane to select the site URL property. The site URL property should be set to the address of your developer site. This developer site can be on-premises or in the cloud, so long as you have permissions to access and deploy to it.

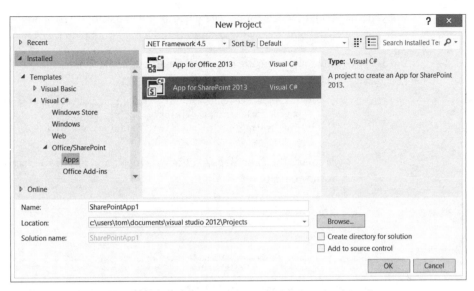

Figure 23-3 The SharePoint App Project template is selected in Visual Studio.

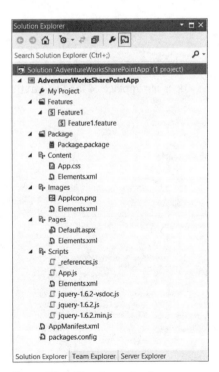

Figure 23-4 The elements of a new app are created automatically with a new project.

If you'd like to get the feel for how easy it is to add visual appeal to SharePoint 2013 with an app for SharePoint, follow these steps to add a map from Bing Maps:

1. Insert the following code into the Default.aspx content area, starting after the `<div>` tag and before the `</div>` tag:

```
<script type="text/javascript" src="http://dev.virtualearth.net/
    mapcontrol/mapcontrol.ashx?v=6.2"></script>
<div id='myMap' style="position: relative; width: 650px; height:
    400px;"></div>
```

This will source the Bing Maps API from Microsoft and provide a placeholder for the map, as shown next.

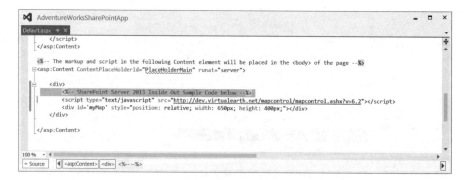

2. Insert the following code into the App.js file in place of the line `getUserName()`:

```
var map = null;
map = new VEMap('myMap');
map.LoadMap();
```

It will draw the map inside the placeholder.

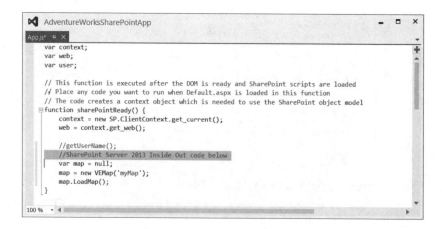

3. Right-click your project title in Solution Explorer and select Deploy.

   Watch the results in the output window for a successful deployment to your developer site.

4. Navigate to your developer site in your browser and click the new link for your deployed app. You should see a map on the new page.

Congratulations on creating your first app for SharePoint Server 2013. Figure 23-5 shows an example of the result.

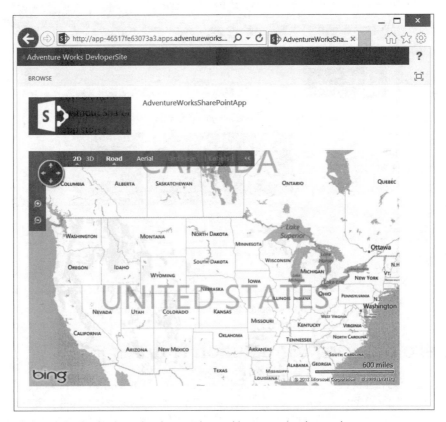

Figure 23-5 The final app has been enhanced by some visual appeal.

Using internal app stores

As you've seen, one place a completed app can be published is the public Office Store. There are stringent requirements and a review process to publish new app store apps, so sharing your app on the Office.Microsoft.com site is a serious undertaking. Also, the public

Office Store is meant only for SharePoint apps that can be downloaded and used by others. If the custom app being developed for your SharePoint site doesn't meet either of those requirements, you can use an internal app catalog to distribute your SharePoint app within your organization. While you should govern the apps that are distributed to a wide internal audience, your requirements will be different from the Microsoft store and you can use your own discretion. To set up your internal app catalog, your farm administrator must add one in the apps section of Central Administration. Figure 23-6 shows an example of an internal app catalog.

Figure 23-6 This is an example of an internal app catalog.

SharePoint Server API solution features

As mentioned earlier in this chapter, the app model is a powerful new addition to SharePoint, but the traditional Server API solution approach is likely to be used for some enhancements. Many developers are already familiar with this approach and will be more efficient developing Server API solutions until they learn the intricacies of the new app model. In addition, legacy code may need to be maintained that can be deployed across versions of the product. In this case, more code can be reused when using Server API solutions than the new app model.

Whatever the reason for writing a new enhancement with the Server API, the solution is likely to result in a new feature or features added to the SharePoint farm. Web parts, application pages, event receivers, workflows, web templates, and custom forms are all deployed in custom features in a solution package. Some other elements are provisioned through solution packages outside of features. Any enhancement deployed through a feature is subject to feature scope.

As in the "App model development" section earlier in this chapter, what follows is an overview of the most relevant SharePoint Server API development topics. There are plenty of great references on SharePoint development for 2010, and not much has changed in the Server API side of SharePoint development.

For an in-depth exploration of SharePoint Server API development, read *Inside Microsoft SharePoint 2010* by Ted Pattison, Andrew Connell, Scot Hillier, and David Mann, published by Microsoft Press.

Feature scope

Whether an enhancement is deployed by a farm solution or a sandbox solution, the solution package will generally install a new SharePoint feature or features on your farm. Features can be scoped at the farm, web-application, site-collection, or site level. The scope level will determine where you see the feature listed. Farm- and web-application-scoped features will be visible only through Central Administration or Windows PowerShell and must be deployed through a farm solution. Site-collection and site features can be deployed by either method and will be visible in Site Settings to users with permission.

Table 23-1 shows the location in the browser where features of different scopes can be activated and deactivated. A feature of any scope can be activated by an administrator through Windows PowerShell.

TABLE 23-1 **Location of activation page by feature scope**

Scope of feature	Location of feature activation page
Farm	Central Administration, Farm Features
Web application	Central Administration, Web Application Features
Site collection	Site Settings, Site Collection Features
Site	Site Settings, Site Features

Typically, users in the Site Collection Administrator role control activating and deactivating site-collection features. Site owners or site collection administrators can control activation of site features.

INSIDE OUT Is my farm customized?

Among the reasons for the introduction of the new app model is reducing infrastructure issues caused by enhancements. However, the app model has not entirely displaced the traditional deployment model.

In certain situations, like moving or upgrading your farm, it is important to determine if your farm has solutions deployed outside the app model. If your farm has custom SharePoint features deployed, it can be easy to determine. For example, the first graphic here shows a partial list of site-collection features on a SharePoint Server Standard 2013 team site. The second graphic shows the site-collection features of a team site with a custom feature.

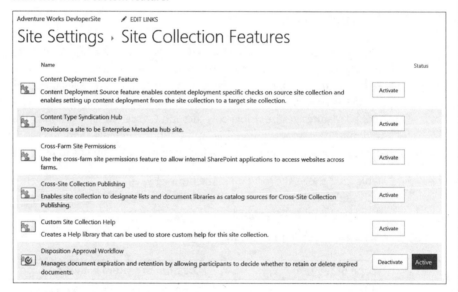

Other types of enhancements can also be revealed by exploration. The farm administrator can use Windows PowerShell or Central Administration to list all the solution packages that should contain features of all scopes. The ability to catalog installed enhancements is a benefit of the solution package model.

Sometimes, however, changes are made to SharePoint in other ways that are not recommended. Because of their impact on the infrastructure, these types of changes are important to detect.

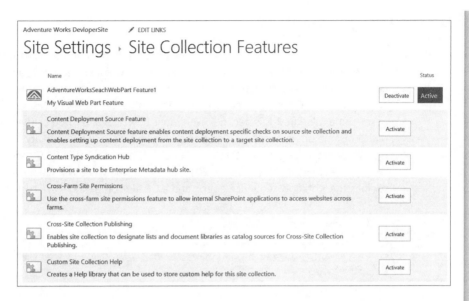

One example is when files in the SharePoint installation directories are directly changed, removed, or added outside the solution package model. These types of changes may not be as easy to detect through the user interface, but an experienced SharePoint administrator can report them to you through a file-by-file comparison. It might go without saying that this type of change is not recommended, but should be accounted for when moving or upgrading.

SharePoint site provisioning

One area of SharePoint enhancement that still falls primarily within the realm of SharePoint solution package deployment is the creation of site definitions and web templates. Both site definitions and web templates can be used to define a basis for new site creation, but the web template method is preferred because it doesn't affect infrastructure changes like upgrades or migrations to the extent that site definitions do.

A key component of a web template is an XML configuration file, called Onet.xml, deployed through a standard SharePoint solution package as a sandbox solution. The Onet.xml file defines the lists, pages, and events of a new site. When you have many sites that must be created with specific configuration items, web templates can be a great solution.

Customizing workflow

The SharePoint workflow engine has been redesigned for SharePoint 2013. The new engine relies on improvements to Windows Workflow Foundation (WF) and Windows Communication Foundation (WCF). The Windows Azure service bus protocol is used for communication. OAuth, an open standard for authorization, is another key piece of the new engine. Workflow has become even more powerful and more connected to Microsoft platforms and open standards. Creating a workflow or workflow activity in Visual Studio is as simple as adding a new item to a SharePoint project. Figure 23-7 shows SharePoint workflow features for Visual Studio 2012, including the workflow actions available in the toolbar, the workflow sequence editor, and a C# file containing a WF custom activity.

Figure 23-7 A Visual Studio custom workflow action project.

For more detail on changes in SharePoint 2013 workflow, visit SharePoint 2013 workflow fundamentals at *msdn.microsoft.com/en-us/library/jj163181(v=office.15).aspx*.

Why custom development?

Chapter 7, "Using and creating workflows," focused on explaining what can be done with workflow in SharePoint 2013 and how to use SharePoint Designer 2013 to create no-code workflows. In fact, reading Chapter 7 will give you a great introduction to the standard actions and capabilities of the new SharePoint 2013 workflow model. To go beyond those standard actions, experienced developers can create more highly customized workflows with Office Developer Tools for Visual Studio 2012. In addition, developers can write custom actions for workflow designers to use in SharePoint Designer 2013. The benefits of customization fall mainly in to three areas: enhanced capability, reusability in custom solutions, and solution maintenance.

Enhanced capability

There are four types of workflow solutions that can be built with Visual Studio. One type, the declarative workflow, can also be built outside Visual Studio. In Visual Studio, declarative workflow developers have the ability to edit the XML file directly in Code view. When limitations of the workflow model are encountered using the methods described in Chapter 7, look to Visual Studio to extend the reach of the model.

Reusability in custom solutions

Workflows created in Visual Studio are deployed by SharePoint solution packages and can be combined with other enhancements in the package. The combination can either be wrapped in an app package or deployed as a farm solution. The ability to deploy workflows in these two ways allows for reuse in ways that are not possible through information worker tools. When you want to create a workflow once and use it in combination with other code in a package or across many sites, consider using a Visual Studio workflow.

Solution maintenance

The tools available to the Visual Studio developer make long-term maintenance of workflows easier and more efficient. Visual Studio includes tools for editing workflows through a Design view, direct editing of workflow XML, or Extensible Object Markup Language (XOML), and additional custom code compiled into .NET assemblies. In addition, there are other tools that extend Visual Studio and support workflow solutions. For example, Team Foundation Server allows for storage and management of workflow versions over time. Together, these tools represent a mature platform for solution development and maintenance that goes beyond what is available to most information workers. When SharePoint workflows grow in complexity or require different maintenance tools, consider using a Visual Studio workflow.

Custom workflow enhancements

When you consider using Visual Studio to develop workflow solutions, there are four main types of enhancements to consider. Understanding the types will help you plan workflow solutions.

Declarative workflow

The term *declarative* isn't needed to distinguish workflow types outside Visual Studio because it is the only type that can be used to create solutions with standard information worker tools. A declarative workflow is defined by a file using a type of XML markup called XOML. Declarative workflows defined with XOML are different from the code-based workflows available to developers of SharePoint 2010 workflows because they are limited to XML code. .NET code is not available in the new SharePoint 2013 workflow outside of custom activities.

Custom action

A custom action can be used as a step in a Visual Studio or SharePoint Designer workflow. A custom action is also defined by an XOML file. However, a custom action can also wrap a custom WF activity written in .NET. Writing custom activities in .NET allows the SharePoint 2013 workflow model to use the full, rich foundation of the .NET Framework.

Workflow object model

The SharePoint 2013 workflow object model provides workflow instance management, deployment, interop, and messaging services. These services use .NET 4.0 WF enhancements over the .NET Framework 3.5 base of the SharePoint 2010 workflow. The workflow object model can be accessed both from code running on a server and code running on the client side.

2010 workflow interop

The SharePoint 2010 Workflow model is deprecated in SharePoint 2013. While it is still available to run workflows developed for SharePoint 2010, it is not recommended for new development because it may be removed in a future version of SharePoint. 2010 Workflow Interop allows SharePoint 2013 workflows to access and use older SharePoint workflows.

Summary

This chapter is the last chapter in this book, but it is also the start of a journey exploring custom development. You can choose from a custom look for SharePoint, better forms for data input, a workflow that matches your processes, or other enhancements of the out-of-the-box features for SharePoint. And now you understand the options to extend SharePoint. You can use code written by others through SharePoint app stores, buy third-party software outside the app stores, hire a software development company, or use in-house programmers to add custom solutions to your SharePoint implementation. Because you have an advanced understanding of SharePoint, you can take full advantage of the customization process. Enhance SharePoint through custom solutions when necessary in order to serve your business and technical requirements more effectively.

Chapter 23

Index

About the authors

Darvish ("D") Shadravan is a senior technical specialist employed by Microsoft, where he focuses on Microsoft SharePoint and related technologies. He has been with Microsoft for 16 years in various technical roles, working directly with enterprise customers. In addition to performing as lead author of this book, Darvish is also the coauthor of the Microsoft Press book *Using Microsoft InfoPath 2010 with Microsoft SharePoint 2010 Step by Step*. Darvish is a frequent speaker at SharePoint conferences worldwide. He can be reached via Twitter (@dshadravan) and LinkedIn.

Penelope Coventry is a multiyear recipient of Microsoft's Most Valuable Professional (MVP) for Microsoft SharePoint Server, and has obtained the following certifications: MCSE (SharePoint 2013), MCITP (SharePoint Administration 2010), and MCPD (SharePoint Developer 2010). Based in the United Kingdom, she is an author, independent consultant, and trainer with more than 30 years of industry experience. Penny has authored and coauthored more than 10 SharePoint-related books, including *Exploring Microsoft Share-Point 2013: New Features and Functions, Microsoft SharePoint 2013 Step by Step, Microsoft SharePoint Designer 2010 Step by Step*, and *Microsoft SharePoint 2010 Administrator's Companion*.

Penny has worked with SharePoint since 2001. When she is not writing, she works on large SharePoint deployments. In addition, Penny speaks about SharePoint at SharePoint events, including SharePoint conferences, TechEd North America, SharePoint Evolution conferences, Australia and New Zealand SharePoint conferences, SharePoint Best Practices conferences, the Swedish SharePoint and Exchange Forum, and the SharePoint Summit in Toronto, as well as user group meetings and SharePoint Saturdays.

Tom Resing is well versed in helping customers take advantage of the features of SharePoint. As a SharePoint consultant at Rackspace, he strives to find the right level of SharePoint customization for every business. His skills have earned him the Microsoft Certified Master certification in SharePoint 2007, and the Microsoft MVP award in 2012.

Tom shares his knowledge through a variety of mediums. He has coauthored books on SharePoint 2010 and SharePoint 2013, and has spoken at many SharePoint conferences on Business Connectivity Services (BCS).

Aside from his technology interests, Tom is an avid community supporter and entrepreneur. Along with his wife, he owns two learning and development centers for children in San Antonio. You can read Tom's latest thoughts on SharePoint on his blog (*http://tomresing.com*) and short messages on Twitter (@resing).

Christina Wheeler is an independent consultant and SharePoint trainer with over 15 years of experience in information technology, software, and web development. She is a goal-oriented, highly experienced Microsoft Certified Technology Specialist who is greatly respected and active in the SharePoint community. She has knowledge in graphic design, web development, custom development, and administration, with her work primarily targeted toward educational and financial institutions. As a trainer, Christina brings her real-world experience to the classroom and enjoys teaching others. Christina is the coauthor of the *SharePoint 2010 Field Guide* and the technical editor of the *SharePoint 2007 Developer's Guide to Business Data Catalog*. She speaks at SharePoint community events and conferences and enjoys sharing and learning with the community. Christina can be reached via Twitter (@cwheeler76) and LinkedIn.

About the contributors

Javier Barrera is a SharePoint engineer at Rackspace (San Antonio, TX), a premier service leader focusing on business class audiences. He is the senior lead engineer and an architect and administrator to hundreds of enterprise-level SharePoint farms. Javier has delivered over 30 presentations at SharePoint-focused events. In addition, he has written numerous blogs, articles, and book contributions. Javier, his beautiful wife, Roxanne, and three children live in San Antonio, Texas. He may be reached at *http://JavierBarrera.com*.

Sam Larko has been attracted to software development since he started teaching himself QBasic in grade school. After graduating with a degree in applied computer science, Sam spent a year as an ASP.NET and VB.NET developer. He was then introduced to the SharePoint platform, specifically SharePoint Server 2003, and hasn't looked back. He has now logged seven years with SharePoint, spanning the last four versions of the product. Most of this time, he has been a developer, but in recent years, he has involved himself in administration projects. Sam started speaking at local events such as SharePoint Saturday in San Antonio, Austin, and St. Louis, and regularly frequents Twitter under the guise of @SPSamL. He can also be found contributing to the Applied Information Sciences blog (*http://blog.appliedis.com/author/sam-larko*), as well as his personal blog (*http://sharepointtherapy.blogspot.com*).

How To Download Your eBook

To download your eBook, go to

http://aka.ms/PressEbook

and follow the instructions.

Please note: You will be asked to create a free online account and enter the access code below.

Your access code:

> # WTGHBDG

Microsoft® SharePoint® 2013 Inside Out

Your PDF eBook allows you to:

- Search the full text
- Print
- Copy and paste

Best yet, you will be notified about free updates to your eBook.

If you ever lose your eBook file, you can download it again just by logging in to your account.

Need help? Please contact:
msinput@microsoft.com

Now that you've read the book...

Tell us what you think!

Was it useful?
Did it teach you what you wanted to learn?
Was there room for improvement?

Let us know at http://aka.ms/tellpress

Your feedback goes directly to the staff at Microsoft Press,
and we read every one of your responses. Thanks in advance!

 Microsoft